# Fingerprinting the Iron Age

Approaches to Identity in the European Iron Age.
Integrating South-Eastern Europe into the Debate

Cătălin Nicolae Popa and Simon Stoddart

OXBOW BOOKS
Oxford & Philadelphia

Published in the United Kingdom in 2014 by
OXBOW BOOKS
10 Hythe Bridge Street, Oxford OX1 2EW

and in the United States by
OXBOW BOOKS
908 Darny Road, Havertown, PA 19083

© Oxbow Books and the individual authors 2014

Hardback   ISBN: 978-1-78297-675-2
Digital    ISBN: 978-1-78297-676-9

A CIP record for this book is available from the British Library

All rights reserved. No part of this book may be reproduced or transmitted in any form or by any means, electronic or mechanical including photocopying, recording or by any information storage and retrieval system, without permission from the publisher in writing.

Typeset by M.C. Bishop at The Armatura Press
Printed in England by Short Run Press, Exeter

For a complete list of Oxbow titles, please contact:

| UNITED KINGDOM | UNITED STATES OF AMERICA |
|---|---|
| Oxbow Books | Oxbow Books |
| Telephone (01865) 241249, Fax (01865) 794449 | Telephone (800) 7919354, Fax (610) 8539146 |
| Email: oxbow@oxbowbooks.com | Email: queries@casemateacademic.com |
| www.oxbowbooks.com | www.casemateacademic.com/oxbow |

Oxbow Books is part of the Casemate Group
Front Cover: Designed by Barbara Hausmair and Catalin Popa
Back Cover: Silver bracelet from Tekija hoard with axe-shaped pendant (Courtesy of National Museum, Belgrade).

The publication of this book was supported by

BREWIN DOLPHIN

# Contents

| | |
|---|---|
| Preface | vi |
| Contributors | vii |

1. Tribute to John Alexander  1
*Simon Stoddart*

2. Introduction: the Challenge of Iron Age Identity  3
*Simon Stoddart and Cătălin Nicolae Popa*

PERSPECTIVES FROM SOUTH EAST EUROPE

3. The Coexistence and Interference of the Late Iron Age Transylvanian Communities  11
*Sándor Berecki*

4. Identities of the Early Iron Age in North Eastern Slovenia  18
*Matija Črešnar and Dimitrij Mlekuž*

5. Royal Bodies, Invisible Victims: Gender in the Funerary Record of Late Iron Age and Early Hellenistic Thrace  33
*Bela Dimova*

6. Mediterranean Wine and Dacian Conviviality. Ancient and Modern Myths and Archaeological Evidence  48
*Mariana Egri*

7. Sarmizegetusa Regia – the Identity of a Royal Site?  63
*Gelu Florea*

8. The Ethnic Construction of Early Iron Age Burials in Transylvania. Scythians, Agathyrsi or Thracians?  76
*Alexandra Ghenghea*

9. Negotiating Identities at the Edge of the Roman Empire  89
*Marko A. Janković*

10. Tracing Ethnicity Backwards: the Case of the 'Central Balkan Tribes'  97
*Vladimir D. Mihajlović*

11. The Quest for Group Identity in Late Iron Age Romania. Statistical Reconstruction of Groups based on Funerary Evidence  108
*Cătălin Nicolae Popa*

12. Changing Identities of the Iron Age Communities of Southern Pannonia 123
*Hrvoje Potrebica and Marko Dizdar*

13. Indigenous and Colonist Communities in the Eastern Carpathian Basin at the Beginning of the Late Iron Age. The Genesis of an Eastern Celtic World 142
*Aurel Rustoiu*

14. Ancient Thrace between the East and the West 157
*Nikola Theodossiev*

15. 'Hellenisation' and Ethnicity in the Continental Balkan Iron Age 161
*Ivan Vranić*

PERSPECTIVES FROM THE WEST

16. Central Places and the Construction of Collective Identities in the Middle Rhine-Moselle Region 175
*Manuel Fernández-Götz*

17. Fingerprinting Iron Age Communities in South-West Germany and an Integrative Theory of Culture 187
*Oliver Nakoinz*

18. Iron Age Identities in Central Europe: Some Initial Approaches 200
*Peter C. Ramsl*

PERSPECTIVES FROM THE FAR WEST

19. Negotiating Identity on the Edge of Empire 211
*Louisa Campbell*

20. Personal Adornment in Iron Age Britain. The Case of the Missing Glass Beads 223
*Elizabeth Foulds*

PERSPECTIVES FROM THE SOUTH WEST

21. Spoiling for a Fight: Using Spear Typologies to Identify Aspects of Warrior Identity and Fighting Style in Iron Age South Italy 241
*Yvonne Inall*

22. Communal vs. Individual: the Role of Identity in the Burials of Peucetia 254
*Olivia Kelley*

23. A View from the South (West). Identity in Tyrrhenian Central Italy    266
*Simon Stoddart*

SYNTHESIS

24. Identity, Integration, Power Relations and the Study of the European
Iron Age: Implications from Serbia    283
*Staša Babić*

25. The Celts: More Myths and Inventions    291
*John Collis*

26 Material Culture and Identity. The Problem of Identifying Celts,
Germans and Romans in Late Iron Age Europe    306
*Peter Wells*

27. Fingerprinting the European Iron Age. Historical, Cultural and
Intellectual Perspectives on Identity and Ethnicity    323
*Cătălin Nicolae Popa and Simon Stoddart*

Bibliography    332
Index    415

# Preface

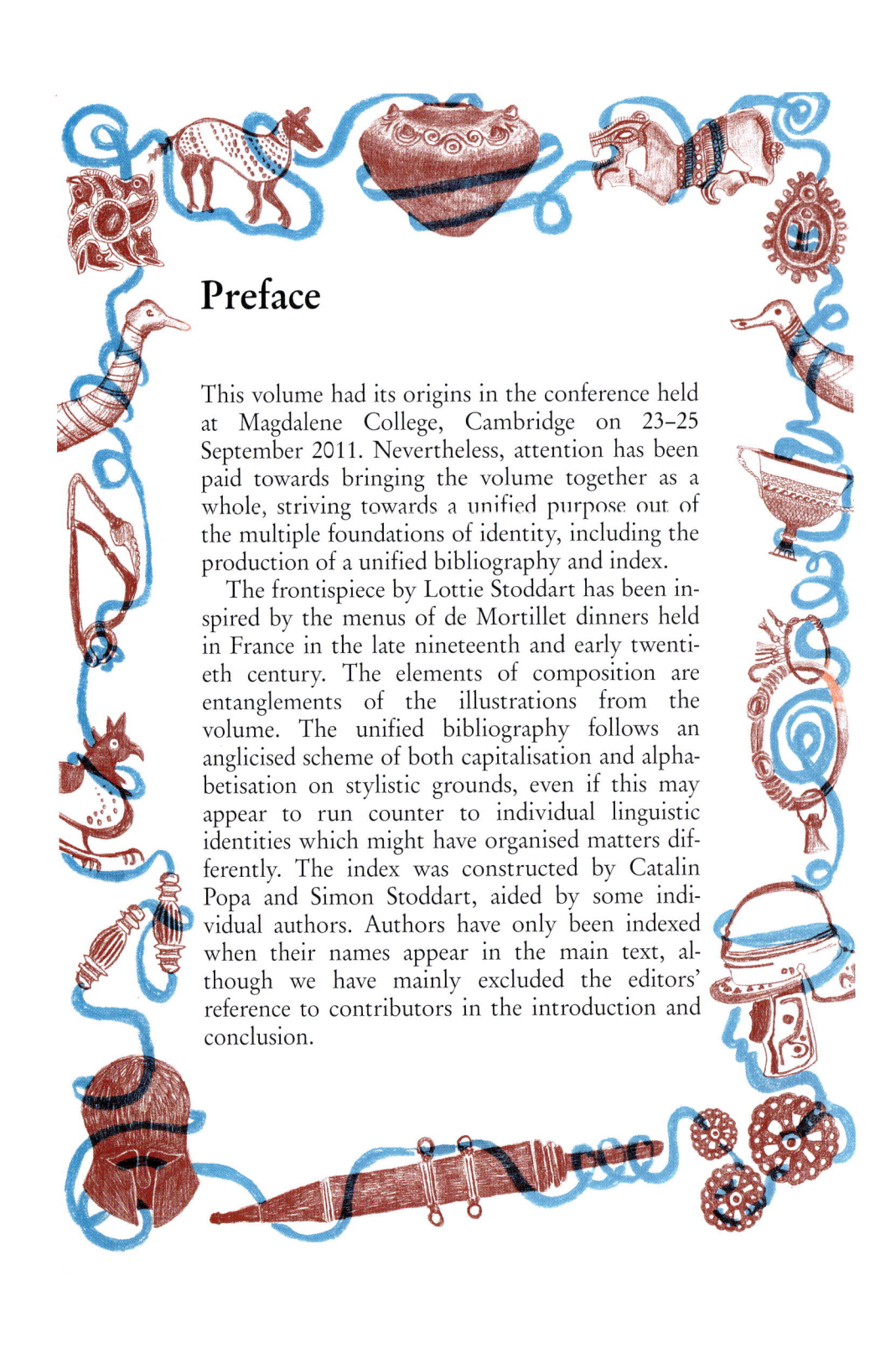

This volume had its origins in the conference held at Magdalene College, Cambridge on 23–25 September 2011. Nevertheless, attention has been paid towards bringing the volume together as a whole, striving towards a unified purpose out of the multiple foundations of identity, including the production of a unified bibliography and index.

The frontispiece by Lottie Stoddart has been inspired by the menus of de Mortillet dinners held in France in the late nineteenth and early twentieth century. The elements of composition are entanglements of the illustrations from the volume. The unified bibliography follows an anglicised scheme of both capitalisation and alphabetisation on stylistic grounds, even if this may appear to run counter to individual linguistic identities which might have organised matters differently. The index was constructed by Catalin Popa and Simon Stoddart, aided by some individual authors. Authors have only been indexed when their names appear in the main text, although we have mainly excluded the editors' reference to contributors in the introduction and conclusion.

# Contributors

(IN ALPHABETICAL ORDER)

**Staša Babić** (BA, MA, PhD, University of Belgrade) is an Associate Professor of Classical Archaeology, Department of Archaeology, Faculty of Philosophy, Belgrade. Her major publications include *Poglavarstvo i polis – Starije gvozdeno doba centralnog Balkana i grčki svet* (*Chiefdom and Polis – Early Iron Age of the Central Balkans and the Greek World*), Belgrade: Institiute for Balkan Studies, 2004; *Grci i Drugi – Antička percepcija i percepcija antike* (*Greeks and Others – Ancient Perceptions and Perceptions of Antiquity*), Belgrade: Klio, 2008; (co-authors M. Diaz-Andreu, S. J. Lucy and D. Edwards) *The Archaeology of Identity. Approaches to gender, age, status, ethnicity and religion*, London: Routledge, 2005.

**Sándor Berecki** is an archaeologist at the Mureş County Museum in Târgu Mureş, Romania. He studied Archaeology in Cluj Napoca and Alba Iulia, completing his doctorate on Transylvanian La Tène finds in 2009. He has written on various features – chronology, rites and ritual, material culture – of the Late Iron Age in the Carpathian Basin. He initiated the Târgu Mureş Colloquia in 2008 and edits their proceedings.

**Louisa Campbell** graduated with a PhD in Archaeology from the University of Glasgow in 2011 and is an Honorary Research Associate in Archaeology at the university. A Roman ceramic specialist, her main research interests are threefold: material culture, the Roman and Provincial interface with a particular focus on frontier contexts and theoretical approaches to the study of culture contact. She teaches at the University of Glasgow's Centre for Open studies and coordinates a programme of public engagement for the Strathern Environs Royal Forteviot project. She has recently taken up the position of Coordinator for the EAA Glasgow 2015, the 21st Annual Meeting of the European Association of Archaeologists.

**John Collis** is Professor emeritus of the University of Sheffield where he taught the European Iron Age and field methods. He studied Archaeology in Cambridge, completing his doctorate on Oppida in 1973; he also studied in Prague and Tübingen, and has excavated mainly in southern England and central France, but has also done fieldwork in central Spain and Italy. He has written extensively on various aspects of urbanisation in Iron Age Europe, on the Celts, coinage and excavation methods.

**Matija Črešnar** is research associate at the Department of Archaeology of the University of Ljubljana and archaeologist at the Centre for Preventive Archaeology of the Institute for the Protection of Cultural Heritage of Slovenia, where he is currently involved in different research projects. He studied archaeology at the University of Ljubljana, completing his doctorate on Bronze and Early Iron Age of Eastern Slovenia in 2009. His main interests are Bronze and Iron Age Europe, landscape archaeology and protection of archaeological heritage.

**Bela Dimova** read Archaeology and Anthropology at Cambridge, and obtained a Master's in Archaeology of the Eastern Mediterranean and Middle East from the Institute of Archaeology in London. Her ongoing PhD project at Cambridge deals with long-term social change and cultural encounters between Thrace and Greece through the Iron Age.

**Marko Dizdar** is a senior research fellow at the Institute of Archaeology. He graduated from the Zagreb Faculty of Humanities and Social Sciences, and earned his PhD degree at the same Faculty, having defended a dissertation on the Late Iron Age in the territory of central Croatia. He has led excavations of the Iron Age sites in northern Croatia, especially of the Middle La Tène cemetery in Zvonimirevo. His scientific research focuses on the identity of the Late Iron Age in the territory of southern Pannonia and its contacts with northern Italy and central Europe. Another topic of his interest is the process of Romanisation of the population of southern Pannonia. He is currently the director of the Institute of Archaeology in Zagreb.

**Mariana Egri** is lecturer in Archaeology at the Babeş-Bolyai University of Cluj Napoca, Romania; works primarily on the history and archaeology of the Late Iron Age and early Roman period on the middle and lower Danube area; main fields of interest – the interactions between the Mediterranean world and indigenous populations; the manipulation of material culture in various Roman provincial settings; the history of convivial practices; most recent publication: *The Celts from the Carpathian Basin between Continental Traditions and the Fascination of the Mediterranean* (2011), with A. Rustoiu.

**Manuel Fernández-Götz** is Chancellor Fellow at the School of History, Classics and Archaeology of the University of Edinburgh. Between 2008 and 2011 he completed his binational PhD at the Christian-Albrechts-Universität Kiel (Germany) and the Complutense University of Madrid (Spain) on the transformation of Iron Age societies in northeast Gaul (book published as: Identity and Power: The transformation of Iron Age societies in northeast Gaul, Amsterdam University Press, 2014). Before joining the University of Edinburgh, he worked as coordinator of the Heuneburg project in the State Office for Cultural Heritage Baden-Württemberg (2011–2013), gaining substantial experience in the scientific direction of fieldwork, financial planning and management of human resources. He has authored around 90 publications on Iron Age societies in central and western Europe, and the archaeology of identities from a theoretical perspective.

# Contributors

**Gelu A. Florea** is senior lecturer in the Ancient History and Archaeology Department of the Babes-Bolyai University in Cluj-Napoca, Romania. His works are dealing with Late Iron Age art and archaeology. Since 2009 he is the director of the excavations on the site of Sarmizegetusa Regia.

**Elizabeth Foulds** completed her PhD at Durham University with a thesis on the social context of glass beads. Her interests are in Iron Age Europe, specialising in material culture, dress and identity, and is interested in the history of later prehistoric studies.

**Alexandra Ghenghea** is currently a PhD student at the Institute of Archaeology 'Vasile Pârvan' Bucharest of the Romanian Academy. Her PhD thesis deals with the Late Hallstatt in Transylvania in seeking models that would explain the way life developed during this period of time. In order to accomplish this goal, it is important firstly to re-evaluate the archaeological and historical sources which proved so far to sustain an unacceptable view of Early Iron Age in Transylvania. She graduated from the University of Bucharest, Faculty of History with one final paper regarding the Picene civilisation. The MA dissertation debated theoretical points of view related to the anthropology of technology.

**Ms Yvonne Inall** completed her Master of Philosophy at the University of Sydney in 2009. In 2010 Ms Inall became a Research Affiliate of the Australian Archaeological Institute at Athens. In 2011 Ms Inall commenced her PhD candidacy at the University of Hull.

**Marko A. Janković** studied for his PhD at the Department of Archaeology at Belgrade University. He is dealing with late Iron Age and early Roman archaeology, specialising in archaeology of everyday life. Janković is the author of several articles on Roman leisure and everyday life published in distinguished national and international journals. He is employed in the Archaeology department as a research associate lecturing on Roman archaeology in the Faculty of Philosophy. Besides his engagement in the "Archaeological cultures and identities of Western Balkans" project, he is also working on the popularisation of archaeology through various public exhibitions and popular literature.

**Olivia Kelley** is currently undertaking a PhD at the University of Sydney. Her dissertation is entitled "Intersecting Identities. The burials of Peucetia (central Puglia) from the sixth to fourth centuries bc".

**Vladimir D. Mihajlović** graduated from the Department of Archaeology, Faculty of Philosophy (University of Belgrade), where he also received his MA degree and is currently a PhD candidate. The author's interests covers issues on interactions between local communities and the Roman Empire, social and cultural changes taking place in such a context, ethnicity in the Roman Empire, classical, funeral, and theoretical archaeologies in general. He works at Department of History,

Faculty of Philosophy (University of Novi Sad) where he is a teaching assistant with the courses in Archaeology.

**Dimitrij Mlekuž** is a research associate at the Department of Archaeology of University of Ljubljana and an archaeologist at the Centre for Preventive Archaeology of the Institute for the Protection of Cultural Heritage of Slovenia. He studied archaeology at the University of Ljubljana, completed a doctorate on Neolithic pastoralist landscapes of Eastern Adriatic and worked as a Marie Curie fellow at the University of Ghent, Belgium. His main interests are landscape archaeology, archaeological theory and the digital humanities.

**Oliver Nakoinz** studied prehistoric archaeology, physics and chemistry at the University of Kiel and earned his diploma in 1998. In 2004 he earned his PhD with a thesis about the geographical borders and inner structure of the ancient Hunsrück-Eifel-Kultur. The habilitation followed in 2010 with a work about settlement hierarchy and cultural space in the Early Iron Age. He worked in the DFG priority project 1171, the excellence cluster Topoi (Berlin) and the cultural heritage management. Currently he is Heisenberg-Fellow (DFG) at the University of Kiel. He is interested in the Iron Age, quantitative Archaeology, spatial analysis and GIS, theory of culture, theory of central places and under water archaeology.

**Cătălin Popa** completed his PhD at the University of Cambridge with an undergraduate degree from the Babeș-Boylai University in Cluj-Napoca and now has a post-doctoral position in Berlin. His main interest is in the European Iron Age, specialising on questions of identity and the use of statistical methods in archaeology. He has also written on issues of nationalism in archaeology.

**Hrvoje Potrebica** is an Associate Professor at the Department of Archaeology, University of Zagreb where he teaches the European and Croatian Bronze and Iron Age. He studied archaeology in Zagreb where he also earned his PhD degree with a dissertation on contacts between Pannonia and Aegea in the Early Iron Age. He worked briefly in Underwater Archaeology, but his main research interest is Early Iron Age archaeology. He is head of the excavation project at the Hallstatt centre in Kaptol as well as several other sites in Croatia. He has published several works on the Early Iron Age communication network between Central and South-eastern Europe. He is currently the president of the Croatian Archaeological Society.

**Peter C. Ramsl** was born in 1967 in Vienna, Austria and started his study in Prehistory, History and Ethnology in 1986. In 1995 he finished his Master (The Iron Age settlement of Inzersdorf-Walpersdorf), in 2001 his doctoral thesis (The Iron Age cemetery of Pottenbrunn). In the meantime, he was external lecturer at the Universities of Vienna, Brno and Nitra also supervising MA and PhD students. Recently he has devised and led three multi-year scientific projects

(Austrian Science Fund – FWF) and worked on many excavations. His main interests are La Tène Culture, La Tène art styles, Migration phenomena and Iron Age identities. Finally in 2010, he finished his habilitation (Phenomena of cultural expressions in La Tène age) and got the *venia* for "Prehistory". At present he is working as the head of the project "Celts at the Traisen valley" at the Austrian Academy of Science in Vienna.

**Auriel Rustiou** is a senior researcher at the Institute of Archaeology and History of Art of the Romanian Academy, Cluj-Napoca; works primarily on the history and archaeology of the Late Iron Age and early Roman period in the Carpathian Basin and northern Balkans; main fields of interest – ancient metallurgical technologies and manufactured goods; interactions between the Mediterranean world and the Carpathian Basin; the society of the Late Iron Age; most recent publications: *Warriors and Society in Celtic Transylvania. Studies on the Grave with Helmet from Ciumeşti* (2008), in Romanian; *The Celts from the Carpathian Basin between Continental Traditions and the Fascination of the Mediterranean* (2011), with M. Egri.

**Simon Stoddart** is a Reader in Prehistory at the University of Cambridge and a fellow of Magdalene College, Cambridge. He undertook post-graduate work at the British School at Rome (Rome Scholar) and the University of Michigan (MA Anthropology), before completing his PhD at Cambridge on Etruscan settlement organisation in 1987. He has held posts in Cambridge (Junior Research Fellow, Magdalene College; University Lecturer and University Senior Lecturer), Oxford (Charter Fellow, Wolfson College), Bristol (Lecturer and Senior Lecturer) and York (Lecturer) and was until 2002 editor of *Antiquity*. He has directed several fieldwork projects in Central Italy (Casentino, Grotte di Castro, Montelabate, Gubbio and Nepi) and has written/edited books on Etruscan Italy, the Mediterranean Bronze Age, Mediterranean ethnicity, Maltese mortuary customs, the Gubbio fieldwork, landscapes and the Celts.

**Dr. Nikola Theodossiev** teaches at Sofia University St. Kliment Ohridski. He participated in the foundation of the American Research Center in Sofia and served as its Associate Director. Dr. Theodossiev is Honorary Member of Associazione Internazionale di Archeologia Classica and Corresponding Member of the Archaeological Institute of America. He is on the Editorial Board of *Ancient West & East* and *Fasti Online*. Dr. Theodossiev was awarded fellowships at St. Peter's College and St. John's College in Oxford, American School of Classical Studies at Athens, American Academy in Rome, Institute for Advanced Studies in the Humanities at the University of Edinburgh, Netherlands Institute for Advanced Study in the Humanities and Social Sciences, Maison des Sciences de l'Homme, Center for Advanced Study in the Visual Arts at the National Gallery of Art. He was Samuel H. Kress Lecturer at the Archaeological Institute of America.

**Ivan Vranić** is Research Associate of the Institute of Archaeology Belgrade, Serbia. He studied archaeology in the Faculty of Philosophy, Department of Archaeology, University of Belgrade where he completed his doctorate on 'Hellenisation' and identity constructions in the Balkan Iron Age in 2012. He has written on ethnic and cultural identities in the Iron Age, Late Iron Age 'urbanisation' and economic aspects of interrelations between the Greek World and 'Pale-Balkan' groups. He is excavating in southeastern Serbia at the site of Kale Krševica.

**Peter S. Wells** is Professor of Anthropology at the University of Minnesota. His principal field of interest is the Iron Age in temperate Europe, with emphasis on interactions with Greek and Roman societies and expression of identity through material culture. Among his books are *The Barbarians Speak: How the Conquered Peoples Shaped Roman Europe* (Princeton 1999), *Beyond Celts, Germans and Scythians: Archaeology and Identity in Iron Age Europe* (Duckworth 2001), *Image and Response in Early Europe* (Duckworth 2008), and *How Ancient Europeans Saw the World: Vision, Patterns, and the Shaping of the Mind in Prehistoric Times* (Princeton 2012).

# 1. Tribute to John Alexander

*Simon Stoddart*

The editors of this volume would like to take the opportunity to remember, even if briefly, the contribution of the late Dr. John Alexander (27 January 1922 – 16 August 2010) to the Iron Age archaeology of the Balkans, and more broadly in Europe as a whole. He taught the Iron Age in Cambridge from 1974 until his retirement in 1984 and was the lecturer who introduced this editor to the subject, and was warmly generous in his support with his gifts of time, ideas, books and photographic slides. Nevertheless, although his role in local (Evans *et al.* 2008; Legge *et al.* 2011), national and African (particularly Sudanese) archaeology (e.g Renfrew 2004; Shinnie 2004; Wahida and Wahida 2004b) has been well recognised, the attempt to publish a conference held in Oxford (including Stoddart unpublished) on his contribution to the Iron Age never materialised. The Azania festschrift (Wahida and Wahida 2004a; 2004b; Shinnie 2004) draws attention to his contribution within the European Iron Age, but there has never, to our knowledge, been a specific reference to his contribution towards the first millennium bc in Europe. This short dedication meekly meets that requirement.

His central contribution to the study of the Balkans in the Iron Age was, appropriately for this volume, his book *Jugoslavia before the Roman conquest* in the Thames and Hudson People and Places Series (Alexander 1972b) and a significant earlier article for Antiquity on the Balkans' geopolitical position in the European Iron Age (Alexander 1962), as well as broader syntheses (Alexander 1980a). In many important respects, he was a figure who encouraged dialogue between South East European and British Archaeology by undertaking his doctoral dissertation on this region too little known in Britain at the time. The People and Places volume was reviewed by Alan McPherron (1973) as an important, albeit traditionally grounded, piece of scholarship that provided the best assessment of the Iron Age of the Balkans in English at the time. It is true that much of his work focused on the development of the leitmotifs of material culture, most notably the pin (Alexander 1964) and the fibula (Alexander 1965; 1973a; 1973b; Alexander & Hopkin 1982), but he did move purposefully on from these foundations to look at key themes. In this respect he was ahead of his time, or perhaps affected by the presence of David Clarke writing on similar themes (Clarke 1987), a transitional figure who was comfortable with the details of material culture, but also interested in new interpretative frameworks. For some themes, such as urbanism (Alexander 1972a), he contributed to the collective studies of others. In other themes, he very much benefited from forging the comparison between the African and European evidence, looking at the parallel pathways in Africa and Europe for themes as diverse as iron (Alexander 1980b; 1981; 1983), salt production (Alexander 1975; 1982; 1985), religion (Alexander 1979) and the dynamic frontier (Alexander 1977). Another prominent theme in his teaching was to re-assess the traditional categories of Hallstatt and La Tène in terms of their socio-political implications, and ultimately argue that such categories should be replaced by the understanding of cross-cutting processes articulated by absolute chronologies. On the other hand, it is perhaps indicative in terms of this present edited volume, that he is not cited outside this preface, because Balkan archaeologists have made so many strides in terms of data collection as well as interpretation over the last forty years, and although he laid some foundations in terms of material culture, identity was not a theme prominent in his vocabulary. As many authors point out in this volume, identity is more emphatically a rhetoric of this current age rather than of his, and the impact of these modern concerns is more readily seen in current studies of the first millennium BC.

# 2. Introduction: the Challenge of Iron Age Identity

*Simon Stoddart and Cătălin Nicolae Popa*

Issues of identity and ethnicity have gained much in popularity over the last two decades. A considerable number of studies have been dedicated to investigating how small and large scale solidarities were constructed and maintained and how they were reflected at the level of the individual. Archaeology has been dealing with identity, and especially with ethnicity issues, as far back as Kossinna's time, but modern approaches are radically different, emphasising dynamic and fluid construction.

The archaeology of the Iron Age strongly reflects such a situation. The appearance of written sources in this technological horizon has led researchers to associate the features they excavate with populations named by Greek or Latin writers. Under the influence of anthropological studies, a number of scholars coming from the Anglo-Saxon school have identified biases and dangers inherent in such an approach to the material record. This has led many scholars to write forcefully against Iron Age ethnic constructions, such as the Celts. At the other extreme, some archaeological traditions have had their entire structure built around notions of ethnicity, around the relationships existing between large groups of people conceived together as forming unitary ethnic units.

These approaches constantly need to be debated, and this volume, broadly based on the 2011 Cambridge conference, presents debates which have had greater problems penetrating a very fertile region for Iron Age studies, the geographical region of south east Europe. In this part of the continent, the mainstream view of ethnicity remained, until recently, that of a solid, clearly defined structure, easily identifiable in the archaeological record and dangerously played out in the present. The Iron Age of this region has, until late, been populated with numerous ethnic groups with which specific material culture forms have been associated, and which modern politicians and military leaders have exploited. The divorce between studies of south east Europe, at one limit of Europe, and Britain, at the other, has had a profoundly negative impact on Iron Age studies, particularly when it comes to how ethnicity is perceived and conceptualised, and has had, for at least the second time in the twentieth century, deleterious effects on modern politics. In the opinion of the editors, these radically different views (and their political consequences) emerged from a lack of dialogue as well as interrogation of the available data. This volume attempts to present the diversity of this dialogue, and its theoretical repercussions, undertaken initially in the harmonious precincts of Magdalene College, Cambridge, but now transferred, at least in part, into printed format.

The conference forms part of a wider series where a key theme in the "long" Iron Age is combined an appropriate region in a comparative European framework. The framework was conceived by one editor (Stoddart) and has already seen the full cycle from conference to publication in a theme related to the current volume of ethnicity bedded in Mediterranean landscape (Cifani *et al.* 2012). The current region and theme was selected by the second editor (Popa) who brought the fresh stimulus of the early career scholar, supported by his research focus on identity, drawn principally through burial in south east Europe.

The volume contains twenty four contributions which have been arranged alphabetically by first author within five sections. The first most populous section is devoted to the core geographical area (Fig. 2.1) of south east Europe. This has contributions from the modern countries of Bulgaria, Croatia, Romania, Serbia and Slovenia that also make reference to Albania and the Former Yugoslav Republic of Macedonia. The following three sections allow comparison with regions further to the west and the south west. A section where three papers investigate central and western Europe is followed by two papers in a smaller section on the British Isles. The regional theme is completed with a section including three papers on the Italian peninsula, although one links back into modern Croatia. The volume concludes with four papers which provide more synthetic statements that cut across geographical boundaries. The final of these contributions by the editors brings together some of the key themes of the volume.

The overall analysis of the lessons of the volume is deliberately left to the final chapter, but it is worth outlining some of the cross cutting approaches ahead of the papers themselves. In line with current trends of the study of identity, most of the approaches are substantially qualitative in their analysis. However, it is worth noting the prominence of quantitative analysis of material culture in six of the 24 papers (Dimova, Inall, Kelley, Nakoinz, Popa and Foulds) and this prominence necessarily raises one issue about the level to which identity can be measured explicitly, an issue that a number of the same papers deliberate. The remaining papers all focus on the more qualitative assessment of identity. For some, it is the heavy hand of the recent present that has all too readily defined the engagement with the past, a perspective that is strongly argued by Babic, Collis, Ghenghea, Mihajlovic, Popa, Stoddart, Vranic and Wells, amongst others. For other authors, there is a more confident identification of identity in material culture (Berecki and the Celts; Potrebica/Dizdar for various identities; Rustiou for mobile identities; Theodossiev through literary sources). For some, multiplicity, hybridity and ultimately fuzziness are dominant themes (Campbell, Cresnar/Mlekuž, Stoddart and Wells). Issues of biology are largely ignored, although this has proved impossible to ignore completely in the case of Etruria for reasons which lack the dangerous historicity of areas further north. Material culture is generally of the portable kind, but some papers do introduce issues of landscape (notably Cresnar/Mlekuž and Fernandez-Gotz), in common with other recent attempts in the same direction (Stoddart and Neil 2012). The wide array of approaches to identity reflects the continuing debate on how to integrate material culture, protohistoric evidence (largely classical authors looking in on first millennium BC societies) and the impact of recent nationalistic agendas. Fortunately, there is at least now relative agreement about the last of these, and one success of the conference was to bring together for harmonious debate scholars from countries who had so recently employed similar agendas in the prosecution of war and discord on European soil.

In more detail, in order of appearance within the volumes, this is succinctly what each article offers. The volume opens with a brief tribute to John Alexander who was one of the first scholars (together with Roy Hodson) to set up the engagement of Britain with the Iron Age of south east Europe. The thirteen papers from south east Europe demonstrate the diversity of approach. Sándor Berecki emphasises the multiplicity of elements within the characterisation of Celticity, and indeed considers multiplicity to be an underlying character of Celtic identity in Transylvania. Matija Črešnar and Dimitrij Mlekuž underline the importance of situating ambiguous identities in the landscape of Slovenia, and bring fresh archaeological evidence and methodologies in support of their case. Bela Dimova examines principally one dimension of identity, namely gender, engaging modern theory with the rich *Thracian* evidence at her disposal, whilst acknowledging multi-scalar relationships. Mariana Egri focuses on the widely acknowledged performance of identity in the act of drinking during the first millennium BC, successfully engaging with the tension provided by textual commentaries on non-Classical practice in the region of ancient Romania. Gelu Florea investigates the identity of *place*, by examining in detail one key politically orchestrated site in Transylvania, drawing together old and recent evidence. Alexandra Ghenghea takes a strongly historiographical approach, showing how forcefully bounded identities, tinged with Romanian nationalism, emerge from pre-contemporary scholarship. Some scholars suggest that ethnicity is more likely to occur in competitive political conditions, but Marko Janković questions the presence of ethnicity even in a context, the Roman province of Moesia Superior, where such conditions might be intimated to exist, and suggests that such a term should be replaced by the cross-cutting identity of status. Vladimir Mihajlović rightly criticises the retrojection of ethnic terms in the central Balkans back onto prehistory, running against the stream of time and political development. Catalin Popa processes apparently unpromising funerary data from Romania into a coherent understanding of identity that deconstructs the standard accounts of Dacians. Hrvoje Potrebica and Marko Dizdar combine their temporal specialisations to look at the long-term changes in identity over the full period of the Iron Age of the Southern Pannonian plain, working with concepts old and new. Aurel Rustoiu tackles the key issue of mobility of populations and retention of identity in the dynamic world of the late Iron Age of the Carpathians. Nikola Theodossiev synthesises the history of Thrace in the light of broader inter-regional trends. Finally, in this section, Ivan Vranić takes a post-colonial approach to Hellenisation, that overtly acknowledges the enduring impact of the political present, centred on differential interpretation of regions such as Macedonia.

The next five papers transport the reader west. The first by Manuel Fernández-Götz places ritual at the centre of imagined communities, taking as his evidence new data from the Titelberg and similar sites in north western Europe. Oliver Nakoinz's work concentrates on the mathematically modelled definition of identities in south west Germany, differentiating between different outcomes on quantitative grounds, whilst attempting to link this to qualitatively based theory. Peter Ramsl dissects some examples of graves from the peri-Alpine area which he proposes permit a dis-assembling of compounded identities. Louisa Campbell interprets the presence of *Roman* material culture beyond the political frontier of the Roman world in northern Britain in terms of locally negotiated identities. Elizabeth Foulds looks at how glass adornment can inform on the multiple identities of dress in Iron Age Britain.

The next small section moves into the Italian peninsula where, if the written sources are to be believed, firmly defined identities might have been expected to be present in the Iron Age. Yvonne Inall shows the fluidity of martial identity interpreted through a new typology of spearheads from southern Italy. Olivia Kelley illustrates the multiplicity of identities read from the burials of Peucetia in southern Italy. Simon Stoddart presents the contrast between the fluid, multi-scaled identities of the Etruscans and the unitary identity sought by ancient writers and early scholars, and seeks to stress the multivalency of Etruscan identity by looking at the discovery of multiple exotic examples of material culture as well as local hybridity in the Croatian site of Nesactium.

The volume closes with synthesis. Staša Babić shows how the interpretations of past identities have been historically deeply seated in the present within her own native Serbia. John Collis provides an update of his identity of Celticity contrasted with the identities of others, expressed in his own personal, inimitable style. Peter Wells investigates some of the key identities drawn from the ancient authors in terms of modern interpretation and illustrative examples from central Europe. Finally the editors draw together the key themes of the volume.

ACKNOWLEDGEMENTS

The original conference of 23–25, September 2011 was supported by the McDonald Institute for Archaeological Research, the ACE Foundation and the Ironmongers Livery Company. The record of the original conference has been archived on the internet: http://www3.arch.cam.ac.uk/iron_age_conference_2011/. The publication has been enabled by the kind support of Brewin Dolphin Investment Managers who characteristically invested with good judgement in emerging intellectual markets. David Redhouse supplied the map in this introductory chapter. The peer review was kindly undertaken by a range of scholars whose importance and investment of time will be acknowledged by sending them a copy of the finished product. The main editing was undertaken by Simon Stoddart, ably supported by Catalin Popa. The index was constructed by Catalin Popa and Simon Stoddart. The front cover was conceived by Barbara Hausmair. Formatting was undertaken by Mike Bishop and the Oxbow production was overseen by Clare Litt.

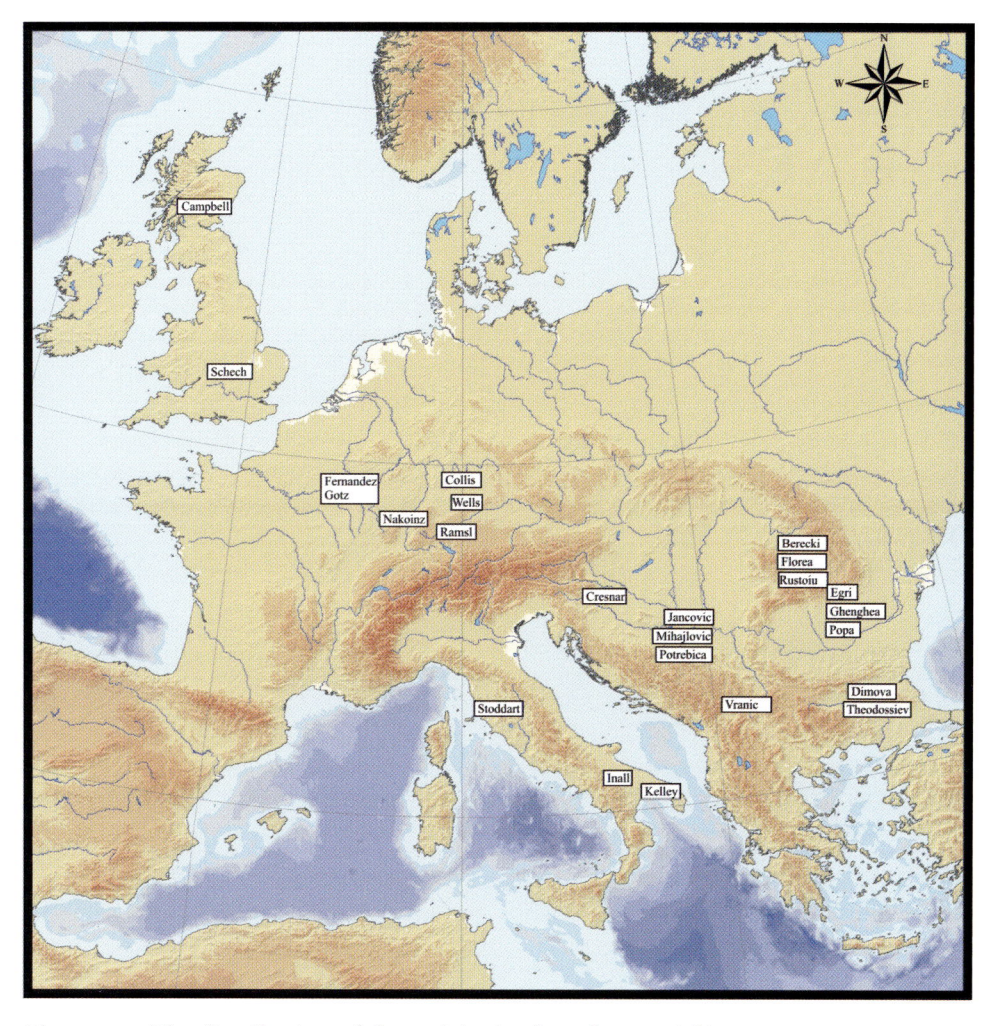

*Figure 2.1. The distribution of the articles in the volume within Europe.*

*Perspectives from South East Europe*

# 3. The Coexistence and Interference of the Late Iron Age Transylvanian Communities

*Sándor Berecki*

**Keywords:** Carpathian Basin, spiritual interferences, material culture, Late Iron Age

Every society is given a special character by its embedded 'foreign' elements. In its process of expansion and colonisation (Szabó 1994: 40), Celtic society proved to be widely receptive to the influences of the indigenous populations of conquered territories. Celtic communities had contact with several populations in a period starting in the last third of the fourth century BC (Berecki 2008a: 47–65), as they expanded towards the eastern part of the Carpathian Basin. These local groups directly or indirectly influenced the spiritual and material culture of the newcomers. On the other hand, the Celts promoted a material culture adopted by the communities of the region, coming to create the heterogeneity of the Transylvanian 'Celtic' Iron Age. This paper emphasises some features of the identity of these communities, which are interpreted as derived from the coexistence and interference of the Late Iron Age Transylvanian populations and their neighbours.

In the southern regions of the Carpathian Basin, reciprocal interferences of the fourth century BC resulted in the admixture of Illyrian, Pannonian, Thracian and Celtic elements, while in the Upper Tisa region, at the beginning of the 1980s, Borbála Maráz detected 129 Celtic discoveries with Scythian elements. The key data for these interpretations are contained in the cemeteries of Muhi, Kistokaj, Radostyán, Rozvány, and the settlements of Polgár and Sajópetri (Maráz 1981: 108, Pl. 6). Unfortunately, there is a lack of information about the inhabitants of the eastern part of the Carpathian Basin. The presence in Transylvania of Scythian populations in the fourth century BC, once presumed on the basis of some finds from Mugeni and the warrior grave from Aiud (Roska 1915: 41; 1944: 73; Nestor 1941: 159–82) has been repeatedly disproved (Crişan 1971a; Woźniak 1974: 36, 60; Zirra 1975a; Berecki 2008a: 52), even though the warrior grave contained an *akinakes*, a weapon sometimes considered the ethnic and social marker of the Scythian military elite. The Transylvanian discoveries dating from the beginning of the fourth century are scarce and equivocal. One of the most important finds of the pre-Celtic period is the warrior grave from Ocna Sibiului that contained a cheek guard from a Chalcidian helmet (Rustoiu & Berecki 2012). In spite of these finds, the ethnic character of the inhabitants of the region remains unclear.

For the period during which Transylvania was dominated by Celtic popula-

*Figure 3.1. Aerial photograph of Fântânele–Dealul Iușului (Z. Czajlik, June 2009), with the researched area and the further possible archaeological features (state of research in 2011).*

tions, more than 101 archaeological sites with traces of their material culture are known. Most of them were discovered in the last quarter of the twentieth century (Berecki 2004: 87; 2006: Fig. 1). The overwhelming number of these finds is without a clear archaeological context and are often chance discoveries. The number of properly researched sites is low and almost all of them are cemeteries or isolated graves. Even so, based on burial evidence and smaller number of settlements, the heterogeneous character of the Late Iron Age civilisation from Transylvania can be outlined.

The excavation undertaken in the last decade at the second cemetery from Fântânele (Bistrița-Năsăud County, Romania), at a topographical point called *Dealul Iușului* or *La Gâța* (Vaida 2003; 2009) has allowed scholars to stress the diversity shown by these communities in their funerary ritual and traceable foreign influences. Aerial photography, combined with geophysics, indicates that site is very much larger than the excavated area (Fig. 3.1). Even so, based on current results, some remarks regarding the rites and rituals of the Celts and the indigenous communities from this region are possible.

In 2011, 31 Late Iron Age graves were unearthed, 24 containing cremated bones, one inurned and six inhumation graves, of which three were crouched burials.[1] Accordingly, four different types of burial rite could be identified. Biritualism was common in the region during the Late Iron Age, where cremation

---

[1] For information about the current stage of the excavations we wish to thank Lucian Dan Vaida.

was the principal rite for Transylvania (Berecki 2006: Fig. 3), with a more balanced distribution in the north western Romanian cemetery of Pișcolt (Németi 1993: 117; Zirra 1997: 87).

The characteristic rite of the Celts from Central Europe was inhumation. Only in La Tène D did cremation become the main rite of cemeteries all over Europe, reflecting a major change in the mentality of the whole Celtic area. By contrast, the characteristic funerary rite for the Carpathian Basin was already cremation, but the assumption that the inhabitants of the eastern part of the Carpathian Basin were responsible for this major ideological and spiritual change is debateable. The practice of cremation in Transylvania was linked by Ion Horațiu Crișan and Vlad Zirra with the Dacians. This interpretation should also be re-examined and rebalanced, given the funerary discoveries in the Carpathian basin. Thus, the arrival of Celtic groups, themselves of diverse character in these eastern regions, with cremation, should be also taken into consideration, without excluding the possibility of the local influence.

The practice of inurned cremation in Transylvania in most of the cases is only presumed, since the records are equivocal. In the most representative cemetery from north western Romania, at Pișcolt, the inurned cremation burials are also rare, and they were connected to the communities of the Scythian Age Szentes–Vekerzug culture (Németi 1993: 122), as in all similar situations from the region, like Ciumești and Sanislău. Therefore, it is very probable that the same influence can also be recognised at Fântânele. It should be mentioned, however, that the rite of the Dacian communities from the very eastern periphery of the Carpathian Basin – a mountainous region of low population lacking Celtic discoveries – was also inurned or pit cremation. This is certainly the case with the fourth to third centuries BC cemetery of Olteni, Covasna County (Sîrbu *et al.* 2008a; b).

In the cemetery from Fântânele–*Dealul Iușului*, three burials were unearthed with crouched skeletons from the La Tène B2 period. In Transylvania, at Budești, as well as in the Great Hungarian Plain at Kesznyéten, Muhi or Sándorfalva, a few examples of crouched inhumations are known, dating from the end of the Early Iron Age, from the sixth and fifth centuries BC. In these cemeteries assigned to the Scythian population, the rite was considered derived from a pre-Scythian tradition (Hellebrandt 1988). At Fântânele, the grave goods from two of the graves, with brooches and wheel-thrown pottery clearly date the funerary features to the Late Iron Age. For this period, this type of rite is not found in Transylvania, while at Pișcolt the rare cases when this rite was practised were dated to the first phase of the cemetery (Németi 1993: 122), while similar patterns are known from the western parts of the Carpathian Basin. Therefore, the practice of inhumation in a crouched position from Fântânele might have its origin either in these distant regions or it could reflect a continuing local tradition of ritual.

A general survey of Celtic funerary rituals in Transylvania indicates that many features were not narrowly regulated by their communities. The plans of the cemeteries were without apparent order and the graves were not grouped according to any apparent rules. This contrasts with some other European cemeteries where linear developmental trends or circular arrangements were observed, suggesting: family groupings at Magyarszerdahely, Hungary (Horváth 1979: 64); gender at Münsingen-Rain, Switzerland (Kaenel & Müller 1991: 219); and social entities at Muhi, Hungary (Hellebrandt 1999: 233, Fig. 173) and Vác, Hungary (Hellebrandt 1999: 98–102); or chronological phasing of the cemetery at Pişcolt, north western Romania (Németi 1993: 128). At Fântânele–*Dealul Iuşului,* the variety of the shapes and depths of the pits, the position of the animal offerings or human bones inside the pits all indicate the flexibility of the funerary ritual. However, the rites and rituals were not so flexible in all respects: the grave goods had a relationship to differentiated social entities: aristocracy, military elite, maybe even ritual specialists. It is clear that they marked out the identity and self-image of the individuals, or reflected the perception by the community of the buried person. Even so, such communities easily accepted new influences coming from integrated or neighbouring populations.

This receptiveness explains the presence of the hand-made pottery amongst the grave goods of Celtic graves. Their shapes and manufacturing technique indicate a foreign origin, while other common features can be found in the Early Iron Age sites of the region. They were first analysed by Crişan and Zirra (Zirra 1967: 107–08; 1975b: 30–1; 1980: 73–4; Crişan 1971b: 42), who considered their appearance the influence or the presence of Dacian populations. Zirra also interpreted the patterns as representing the coexistence of Celts and Dacians, underlining the possibility of a subservient relationship, or one where Dacians benefitted from certain advantages under the rule of a Celtic military aristocracy (Zirra 1975b: 31). From the point of view of our present interpretation, one of the key questions regarding these graves, that represent about the 20 percent of the whole Early and Middle La Tène burials, is whether the choice of grave goods was meant to focus on their ethnicity, and, if so, were these buried persons Dacians or Celts?

The complexity of the question is also reflected in some of the graves from Apahida. For this purpose, one grave without inventory number, discovered on 2 March 1900 (Zirra 1976: 145, Fig. 12) is crucial. In this grave, two hand-made wares, defined as 'local' products, were found next to the six wheel-thrown, so called, 'Celtic' vessels, and a bronze hollow-cast hemispherical ankle-ring, typical of Celtic grave goods in the Carpathian Basin. What kind of self identity was intended for the buried person from Aţel? Two hand-made shallow bowls of Early Iron Age tradition and an imported Hellenistic vessel were placed in the grave (Fig. 3.2), in association with the so called 'Celtic' artefacts (three brooches, a horse-bit, a knife, a masked bead, a glass and a bronze bracelet). The other artefacts are not unusual in these communities, but how can we explain the hand-made pottery? Perhaps these poorly fired wares did not have any ethnic connotation, and that, whenever they appear, they do not represent an individual from the indigenous community, but the influence and interference of neighbouring or integrated populations and the mobility of individuals and groups.

*Figure 3.2. Grave goods from Aţel: a 'Celtic' glass bracelet, a 'local' shallow bowl and a Hellenistic lekythos.*

The main archaeological sources for the definition of Transylvanian Late Iron Age identities are the cemeteries, but what can settlements suggest in terms of the organisation of these entities and the mobility of groups and individuals? For Transylvania, there are only a few fourth and the second centuries BC settlements which have been studied. Moreşti from Mureş County is one of the most intensively researched settlements, which was excavated in the 1950s (Horedt 1979). The quantitative reanalysis of the forms of the La Tène pottery from this site permits further interpretation of the inter-cultural relations of this community with neighbouring communities at the beginning of the second century BC (Berecki 2008b).

Among the fine pottery from the settlement there are a few special wares (Fig. 3.3): deep bowls with faceted rims and pots with X-shaped handles (Horedt 1965: 65, Abb. 10/1–4; 1979: 47, Abb. 21/1–4; Berecki 2008b: 68–70). Such bowls and handles are frequent discoveries in the settlements of the Poieneşti–Lukaševka culture (Babeş 1985: 184; 1993) east of the Carpathians and date from the second and first centuries BC. Such finds have traditionally been assigned to the Bastarnae groups.

This raises the question of how these wares appeared in Transylvania? Kurt Horedt, who excavated the site, excludes commercial contact as an explanation, considering them the result of the physical presence of a community of the Poieneşti–Lukaševka culture. He also considered it possible that this Germanic population would have had a role in the disappearance of the Celts from Transylvania. However, such a historical implication would have involved the presence of considerable military forces in the region, which have not yet been documented archaeologically. The presence of some similar pottery at Şeuşa, Alba County in central Transylvania has led to the reopening of the discussion (Ferencz & Ciută 2005: 239–240; Ferencz 2011). However, the stratigraphic provenance of these finds is problematic. If these problems are discounted, the materials from Moreşti and Şeuşa have been considered evidence supportive of

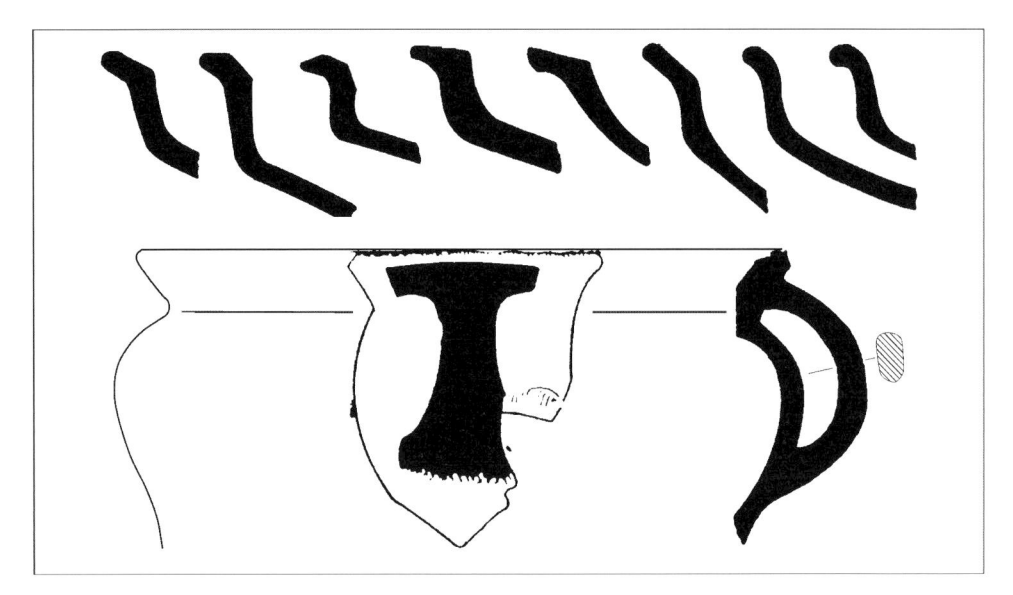

*Figure 3.3. Faceted rim and pot with X-shaped handle from Moreşti (after Horedt 1979).*

the itinerary through Transylvania of the military campaigns of the Bastarnae, undertaken in 184–2 BC by Philip the Fifth of Macedonia against the Dardanii. Considering the geographical conditions of the epoch, as well as the discoveries from Dobrudja, the stratigraphic position of the pottery and the conditions of both Transylvanian sites, it is more probable that the army advanced into the regions east of the Carpathian Arch (southern Moldova and Muntenia), heading towards the south (Berecki 2008b: 70).

At Moreşti, the grouping of the Bastarnic materials only in one particular zone, around some of the features, might suggest a Bastarnic family enclave. However, the rejection of possible commercial exchanges between the two neighbouring regions should be also reconsidered, since Late Iron Age wares from the Carpathian Basin (Babeş 1985: 193) and Hellenistic artefacts from the south (Teodor 1988: 36) also reached the eastern Bastarnic region. In his work on warriors and the society in Celtic Transylvania, Aurel Rustoiu emphasises the nature of the individual and group mobility from the Late Iron Age as well as the consequent cultural interferences (Rustoiu 2008). Commercial contacts are considered one of the main vectors in the diffusion of goods (Woolf 2003), but when artefacts appear regionally isolated, without the possibility of commercial contact, other alternatives should be also taken into account. The mobility of warriors, craftsmen and artisans, the social contracts and gifts of the elites mentioned in the contemporary ancient sources, or even matrimonial alliances are all generators of visible and invisible spiritual and material exchanges (Renfrew 1969). Therefore, the potential interpretations of the finds from Şeuşa and Moreşti should be widened in scope.

The heterogeneous character of the Celtic culture from these regions marks out its receptivity in phases of expansion/colonisation. There is clear evidence of close connections with central Europe; the expedition from the Balkans with a large participation of Celts from all over the Carpathian Basin is one of the historical data supporting these connections. By incorporating new influences, these communities took on a colourful flavour: the multiple cultural interferences in the region resulted in a pronounced and distinctive La Tène culture.

# 4. Identities of the Early Iron Age in North Eastern Slovenia

*Matija Črešnar and Dimitrij Mlekuž*

**KEYWORDS:** EARLY IRON AGE, NORTH EASTERN SLOVENIA, LANDSCAPE, REMOTE SENSING, IDENTITIES.

INTRODUCTION

The geomorphological and geographical position of north eastern Slovenia is in many ways distinctive. On the western side, it touches the Pohorje range of hills, i.e. the very south eastern edge of the Alps, whereas in the east it reaches the western part of the wide Pannonian plain. The area is more easily accessible and passable because of the presence of the Drava and Mura rivers and their flat plains, Podravje and Pomurje, which provide an eastern route around the Alps or bypass both parts of modern Carinthia to reach the heartland of the eastern Alps. However, the better explored Drava plain is, on the other hand, surrounded by hills, which make it more easily controllable, and can, because of that, (as already visible in the preceding Urnfield Period) develop a character of its own (e.g. Teržan 1990: 204–08; 1995a; Tomedi 2001; Gleirscher 2005).

The local Early Iron Age was deeply rooted in the Late Urnfield Period, but it can be additionally linked to broader regional changes (Teržan 1990: 21–5, 54–8, 204–08; 1995a; 2001; Metzner-Nebelsick 1992; Eibner 2001). The lowlands of the region were densely populated in the Urnfield Period, when the mainly undefended rural settlements and extensive urnfield cemeteries were prominent (Fig. 4.1a) (e.g. Črešnar 2010: 74–80). It was the late ninth and the beginning of the eighth century BC that introduced a change in the settlement pattern, marked by a decline of the majority of the lowland settlements and the foundation of new hillforts. There were already a defended lowland settlement (Ormož) and hillforts (Brinjeva gora, Ptujski grad and Gornja Radgona) in the Urnfield Period that continued into the Early Iron Age, even if two (Brinjeva gora and Gornja Radgona) were substantially remodelled (Teržan 2001: 133).

Beyond that, there were obvious changes in burial practice. Although cremation remained the dominant rite, the grave arrangement mainly changed from flat to barrow (Teržan 1990: 21–6, 118–21, 204–08; 2001: 133–4). Furthermore, hillforts and barrows most directly and most evidently constituted the Iron Age landscape and thus also played a very important role in the creation of the identity/-ies of Iron Age communities. That is also why, until recently, the Early Iron Age landscape of north eastern Slovenia was associated mainly with these monumental structures, which had been studied since the nineteenth century

(Teržan 1990: 13–20). By contrast, landscape study of the central lowlands was rather neglected because of a lack of finds.

In the last two decades, the discovery of new lowland sites, settlements and cemeteries, from the Early Iron Age (Fig. 4.1b), has underwritten a rather significant change in the understanding of the local Early Iron Age. The majority of the newly excavated lowland sites have not yet been fully studied, but a first overview can be given, as some case studies can already help us to sketch out the complexity of the period.

## THEORETICAL POSITION

The differences in the ritual, funerary structures and grave goods were related to distinct social groups, be they family relations, sex, gender, status, craft-orientation or other differentiated identities. Studies of different social structures have often been based principally on material culture (e.g. Teržan 1990; 1995b). The same material culture has also been employed to trace their connections, trade and exchange over wider areas (e.g. Scarre & Healey 1993; Hänsel 1995). In addition, landscape studies, based on remote sensing and GIS analysis, can add a further meaningful understanding.

'Identity' is an ambiguous term. It can refer both to individual or group identity, covering aspects such as status, sex and gender, personhood, kinship, age, community or culture. These are all interrelated in culturally specific ways, yet are often treated as distinct, yet equally interchangeable, categories. Identities are historical, fluid and subject to persistent change. Group affiliation entails constant active engagement with other members of the group and a shared material world (Díaz-Andreu & Lucy 2005). Identity is therefore not a fixed, static, property, but a continual process of identification and these narratives are often negotiated through material means. This is why archaeologies of material practice are suited to the study of identity. Without material expression, social relations have little substantive reality, as there is nothing through which these relations can be mediated. Materiality conveys meaning. Social relations can be fixed and stabilised by the use of durable material resources. Thus the material world provides the means by which social relations are durable enough to persist beyond face to face interactions. It is through materiality that we articulate meaning and thus it is the frame through which people communicate identities (Sofaer 2007).

Landscape, as a part of material world, is a key element of the experienced and engaged world. Landscapes are meaningfully constituted environments, where meaning is woven into the fabric of landscape through experience. As people create, modify and move through landscape, the mediation between spatial experience and perception creates, legitimates and reinforces social relations and ideas (Bourdieu 1977; Lefebvre 1991; Van Dyke 2007: 277). Memory is closely integrated with places and landscapes (De Certeau 1984; Casey 1987). Places, meaning and memory intertwine and create a 'sense of place'. Construction of memory is often a material practice, leaving traces – such as barrows. We can un-

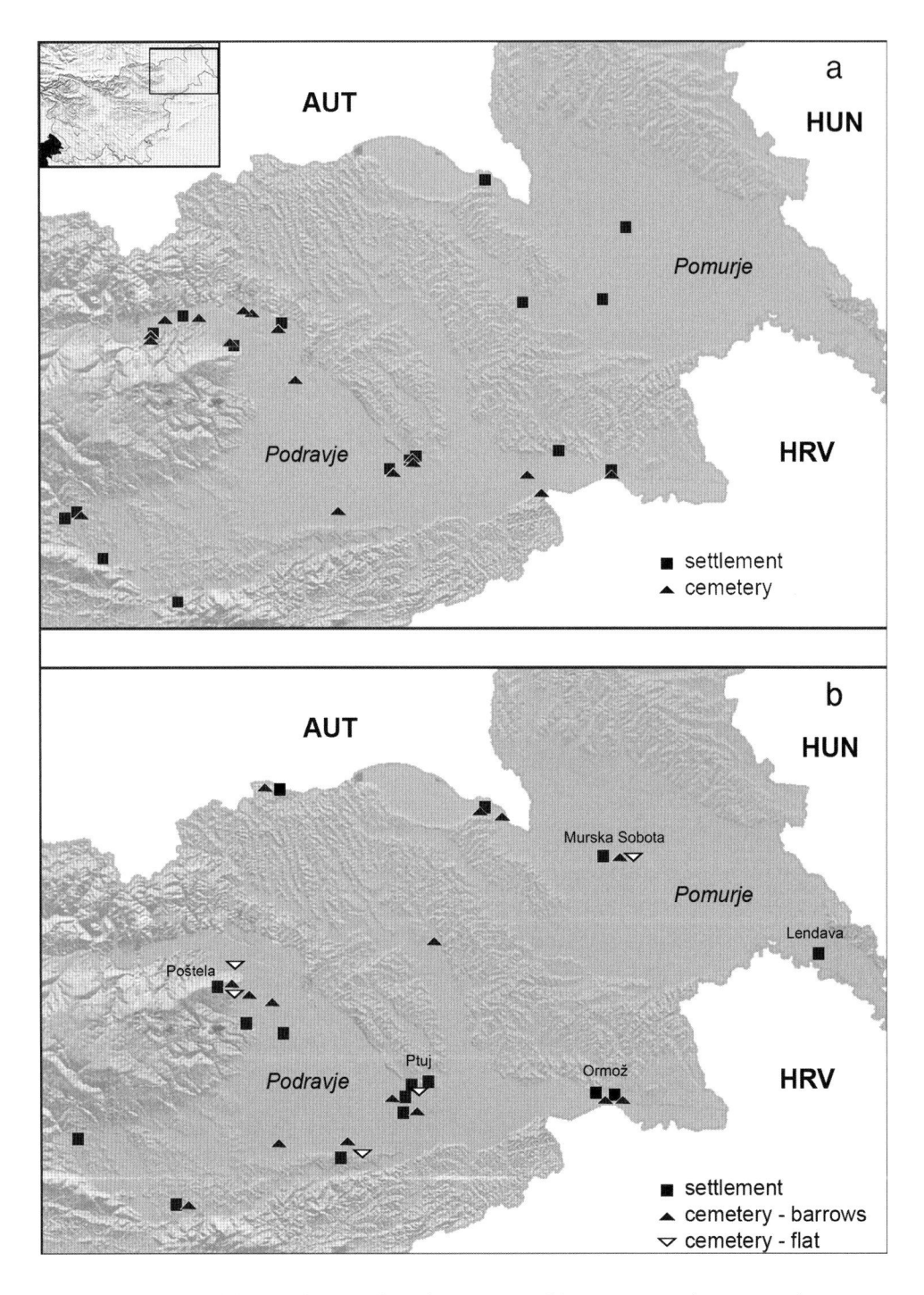

*Figure 4.1. Urnfield Period (a) and Early Iron Age (b) sites in north eastern Slovenia.*

derstand them as *lieux de memoire* (Nora 1989), places of memory and conscious built statements about what to remember.

Mortuary rituals are events where memorisation, as well as selective forgetting, take place. As the dead are mourned, memories and identities are created. Erection of barrows thus creates powerful visual remainders or material memory. Barrows link ancestors to the living and procreate places in the landscape with all that this connection involves. The material activities are thus creative acts, not just in the sense of creating material culture but in sense of making society and identities. And because they bring identities into being, objects, things, substances are powerful media for social action and shared public understandings (cf. Verger 2000; Izzet 2001; Milcent 2001; Tilley & Bennett 2001).

These places are part of the landscape, and thus linked to other places in different ways, through inter-visibility, connectedness or proximity. These spatial relations can express conceptual links between ideas and memories and weave them together in complex narratives. Geographical information systems (GIS) are increasingly being used in landscape archaeology. One of the basic tools in the GIS toolbox is 'viewshed' analysis, which shows which parts of the landscape are visible from a particular location (Wheatley 1995; Wheatley & Gillings 2000). Viewshed analysis is not without problems, as it treats landscape as a purely visual phenomenon. Landscapes are multisensual and engage all senses (cf. Mlekuž 2004), but communicate how identities and memories were expressed, enhanced and contested also through visual relations between places in the landscape.

## Pomurje

The first study area of Pomurje was, less than two decades ago, an almost empty region when it came to the Early Iron Age (Šavel 2001). The most interesting area after recent research lies south of Murska Sobota and is generally known for the abundance of archaeological remains from various periods. Here we can also observe a number of Early Iron Age sites, which concentrate mainly on a plateau between the Dobel stream to the south and another former stream bed to the north (Fig. 4.2).The Early Iron Age site Pri Muri, located at a higher altitude near Lendava, was excavated in the southern part of the Pomurje region. This lies on a gravel terrace of the Mura River and comprises a range of earth-cut structures. The two ring-ditches are probably barrow boundaries or grave plots, as we know them from the area around Murska Sobota as part of a cemetery. However, there are also postholes and other pits mainly without clear function. The exception is one pit, which appears to be a sunken-floor hut, most probably part of a settlement (Šavel & Sankovič 2011: 43–7).

The first key site is Kotare near Murska Sobota, where, on slightly elevated ground less susceptible to flooding, just above the Dobel stream, a settlement dated to the Early Iron Age has been excavated. The excavated remains show groups of buildings, some of them erected on vertical posts, with the probable use of wattle and daub, some earth dug structures of nearly rectangular shape, some probable sunken-floor huts and numerous pits without a clear function (Kerman 2011a: 28–40). Very nearby, at a distance from approximately 220 metres to 1400 metres, there are six locations of excavated graves or groups of graves dated to the Early Iron Age and four groups of ditch features with cemetery characteristics recovered by aerial photography.

Another contemporary site Rakičan – Pri Starem križu, unearthed in a trial trench excavation, is located a little further eastwards (Fig. 4.2). The smallest of the excavated cemeteries is Za Raščico located to the west of the settlement and the only site known to the south of the stream, with only one modest excavated grave, i.e. an urn in a simple round pit (Šavel & Sankovič 2010, 60–1). Other locations comprise isolated graves or groups of graves, some gathered in small pits and others set within circular or square ditches. Some of these appear to be the boundaries of grave plots or barrows, but not all contain a grave. Some variation may be a product of intensive agriculture, removing all but earth-cut features. Different authors have given different interpretations of these structures in other regions from Burgenland to southern Germany; Tiefengraber (2001: 86–9) proposes the term 'cultic complex', but many retain the barrow explanation. Evidence from Slovenia at Rogoza near Maribor retained the barrow overburden in spite of extensive damage (Fig. 4.4).

To the east, there are five groups of graves, which belong to two sites, Kotare – Krogi and Nova Tabla. In the most detailed preliminary publication of the site of Nova Tabla (Tiefengraber 2001) the cemetery groups are named after their location (Cemetery west, Cemetery Middle-west, Cemetery Middle, Cemetery East), but further sub-groups are likely to be defined in the future. Two groups are currently identified approximately 220–300 metres away from the settlement, whereas the other three groups are approximately 1100–1350 metres away (Fig. 4.2a–c). To the north and north west, there are four potential sites, where circular ditches have been documented by aerial photography. However, barrows and ditches of similar form and proportions were also erected in the Roman period and therefore the allocation of all the those structures to the Early Iron Age (and contemporary settlement) is only provisional (Kerman 2001: 57–8, Abb. 4, 10; 2011a: 6–9, sl. 6–7; 2011b: 6–7, sl. 4–5). At Kotare – Krogi, the group is formed of a structure consisting of four ring-ditches and what seems to be a flat urn grave to the south east (Fig. 4.2a) (Kerman 2011b: 28–31). At the Nova Tabla site, some 90 graves set within circular or square pits were documented in four groups varying in arrangement and the form of subsidiary structures (Fig. 4.2b–c). Those can be ring-ditches, rectangular ditches and even stone circles, which always include an 'entrance', i.e. a break in the ditch or stone setting. Some of them inter-cut or abut each other, whereas some appear to be adjunct structures. The publication of the cemetery Nova Tabla is not yet complete, preventing more detailed analysis (Tiefengraber 2001: 82). Some other remains in the form of a sunken-floor huts and other pits complete this complex spatial patterning.

The material remains found in Pomurje date to between the Early Hallstatt Period (Hallstatt B/C) and the beginning of the Late Hallstatt period (beginning

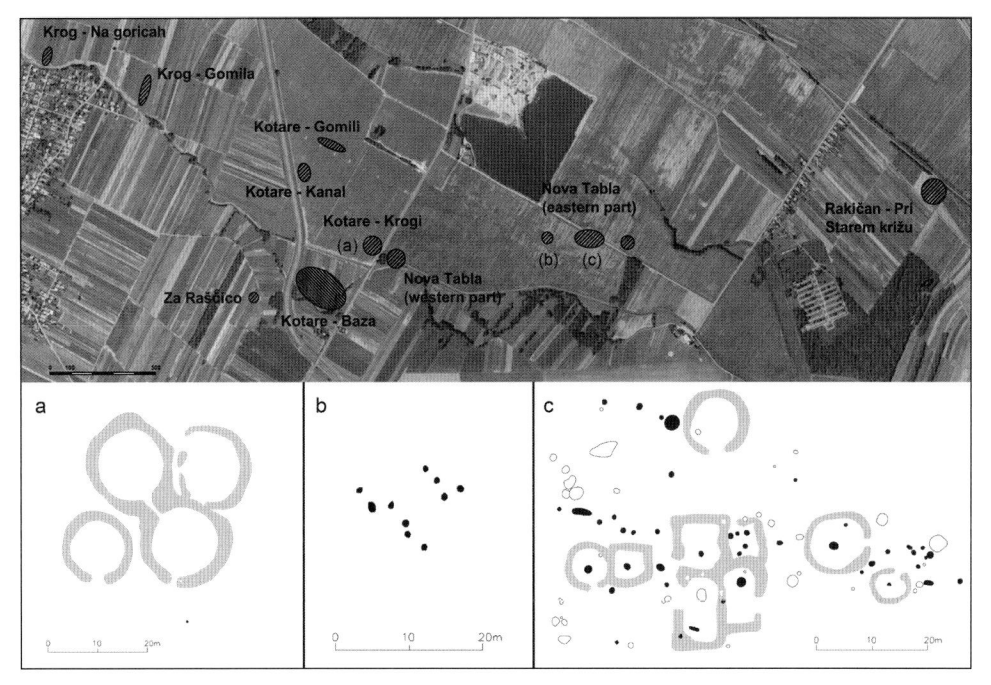

*Figure 4.2. Sites mentioned in the vicinity of Murska Sobota (after Guštin & Tiefengraber 2001: sl. 3 (c); Tiefengraber 2001: Abb. 3–7 (b); Kerman 2011a; Kerman 2011b: sl. 28 (a); Šavel & Sankovič 2010).*

of Hallstatt D1). They show similarities to those from: Ormož, Rabelčja vas and Poštela in Slovenian Štajerska (Styria); Kleinklein, Bergl near St. Martin in Austrian Steiermark (Styria); Bad Fishau in Lower Austria; and Kaptol near Slavonska Požega in Croatia. The overall pattern forms a trans-regional Early Iron Age stylistic group (Guštin & Tiefengraber 2001: 110–12; Tiefengraber 2001: 82–93; Guštin 2003: 65–6; Šavel and Sankovič 2011: 47).

## Podravje

Podravje to the south occupied one of the most prominent strategic positions, where the south eastern entrance was held by Ormož, a site already in place as a fortified lowland settlement on the banks of the Drava River in the Urnfield Period. This settlement had a rectangular ground plan, paved roads and substantial evidence for metallurgy (Lamut 1988–89; 2001; Teržan 1995b; 1999; Tomanič Jevremov 2001; Dular & Tomanič Jevremov 2010). The layout included cemeteries, an 'extra muros' settlement area, and, at least from the beginning of the Early Iron Age, an undefended (rural) settlement, at Hajndl, placed on the same high terrace above the Drava river, approximately 1300 metres to the west. An interesting difference between these two settlements is in house construction. Ormož employed the 'traditional' method of vertical posts (preserved archaeologically as postholes). Hajndl mainly employed foundation beams (preserved archaeologically as foundation trenches) in combination with vertical posts (Mele 2005a; 2005b; 2009). In the field-walking campaign prior to the construction of the Ptuj – Ormož motorway, numerous other archaeological sites were located on the Ormož bypass and in other selected locations around Ormož. Two of these Early Iron Age sites (Hajnd and Hardek) were also excavated (Tomanič Jevremov 2005).

Numerous other rescue excavations have taken place in Podravje in the last two decades. One important site is Srednjica near Ptuj, a lowland settlement and associated cemetery of densely grouped ring ditch graves (Lubšina Tušek 2008). Like Hajndl near Ormož, this has added important new data to the broader Ptuj settlement area, which already had a prominent role in the Late Urnfield Period that continued into the following Early Iron Age and later (Teržan 1990: 43–4, 346–8; Lubšina Tušek 2001).

To the north, the important site is Poštela hillfort, placed on a sloping plateau on the edges of Pohorje hills in a dominant position overlooking the whole eastern part of the Ptujsko-Dravsko polje (Drava-Ptuj plain), in the foothills of the Slovenske gorice hills and the Drava river floodplain. The associated cemetery can be divided into several groups, the first a concentration of flat urn graves and barrows just below the settlement on the Habakuk plateau. In this group, individual barrows cover the slopes facing the southern entrance into the plain at Razvanje, and are concentrated at Pivola (Fig. 4.3). This is the most important Early Iron Age complex in Podravje and is amongst the most significant sites in the area between the Eastern Alps and the Pannonian plain. The site has been investigated since the nineteenth century (Teržan 1990: 256–338), but recently remote sensing, including LiDAR, has shed new light onto the whole complex (Teržan 1990: 256–338; Strmčnik Gulič & Teržan 2004; Teržan et al. 2007). If we combine the spread of the barrows mapped on the LiDAR derived DTM with the geological map of the area, we can clearly see that all the barrows are located above the band of sandy clay, which was deposited from the slopes of the Pohorje hills onto the gravel-rich Pleistocene river terraces, and which even today form a very humid and scarcely habitable environment (Fig. 4.6).

The recent excavation of sites, particularly in the lowlands, has had a major impact on our understanding of settlement distribution. At least 12 ribbed bracelets have been identified at the site of Maribor – Tržaška cesta, located approximately 2300 metres from the Poštela rescue excavations. These bracelets are similar to those found in the richer female graves at the most prominent sites of the wider region (e.g. Poštela, Kleinklein (Austrian Styria) and Breg/Frög (Austrian Carinthia)). These probably cremated grave goods were found with a few burned bone fragments and charcoal placed on the natural geological surface just below the ploughsoil (Kavur 2008). A further 1500 metres to the east, at Rogoza, four partly destroyed barrows dating to the Early Iron Age were unearthed. They are contemporary and similar in form to the graves of Murska Sobota, Lendava and Srednjica (Fig. 4.4) (Črešnar 2011: 68–9, insert 2; Črešnar in press). It is difficult to assess whether they belong to Poštela or to some other farm/farmstead/ settlements located in the plain. Both sites are located on gravel

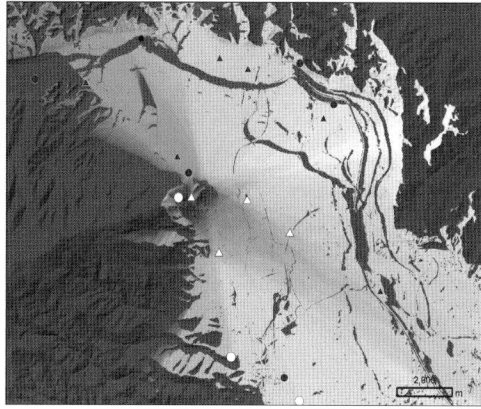

*Figure 4.3. The map of northern Podravje with sites from the late Urnfield Period (dark) and Early Iron age (light). Settlements are shown by circles and cemeteries by triangles (left). Cumulative viewsheds (Wheatley 1995) from Poštela ramparts. The density of the shading depends on the proportion of the rampart that is visible from particular location and range from dark (invisible) to light (fully visible) (right).*

terraces of the Drava, while a strip of sandy clay sediments separated them from the alluvial layers just at the foot of the hills on which all the other barrows were erected. The distance of the grave at Maribor – Tržaška cesta from Poštela is equal to the distance of the hillfort from the barrows at Pivola, whereas Rogoza is even further away.

The first example of one of these settlements in the immediate vicinity, Hotinja vas, has been recently excavated and is now being thoroughly studied. It is located to the south east, approx 7.5 kilometres from Poštela and has, even from preliminary reports, already provided a range of interesting new information. The buildings and other structures concentrate in two groups, in a pattern that holds true for Urnfield Period settlements in the region (Črešnar 2011), and are interpreted as farmsteads, collectively forming a wider community. A new building technique has been detected, perhaps a log-cabin type of building (Strmčnik Gulič *et al.* 2008) of sunken-floor huts, apparently accompanied by wooden floors and wooden substructures, with no vertical posts. This contrasts with the building technique of the lowlands (Črešnar 2007). The excavators do also mention a fireplace of bigger dimensions, which has a central position, and is therefore interpreted as a communal facility.

A further hillfort, Četa above Slivnica, is located on the fringes of Pohorje hills approximately five kilometres south of Poštela. This less well known site has been known for some time (Pahič 1974; Teržan 1990: 340–1, T.72:1–9).

This brief overview of the Early Iron Age sites of north eastern Slovenia, focusing on a selection of newly obtained data, not only fills some blank areas and broadens our knowledge of the interstices between the most obvious settlement locations, the hillforts, but, moreover, opens up an array of new questions. How can we understand the complex landscape organisation which has arisen from

*Figure 4.4. Rogoza. Remains of Early Iron Age barrows during excavation.*

this latest research? How should we analyse the cemeteries presumably attached to individual settlements (e.g. below Poštela hillfort and in the lowlands around Murska Sobota)? How did different parts of dispersed communities relate to each other (e.g near Ormož, Ptuj and also Poštela)?

Some of the questions can only be addressed once all the archaeological data and material are published. However, using the following case study of Poštela and its surroundings, we seek to deepen our insight into the complex Early Iron Age society as currently available from newly acquired LiDAR data and other publication.

### Landscape and identities of Poštela hillfort

The first issue relating to Poštela hillfort is the cemetery. It is not difficult to distinguish some individual barrows and at least three barrow groups, but there is also at least one area of flat cremation graves, which was located on the Habakuk plateau (Fig. 4.6). Another flat cremation cemetery was found in the lowlands north of Poštela at Radvanje, but dates mainly to the Late Urnfield Period, although there are some Early Iron Age finds, when Poštela was already inhabited (Teržan 1990: 59–60, Tab. 67–8).

The barrows on the Habakuk plateau can be separated into two groups on separate ridges, a northern and a southern western group with flat cremation graves. In spite of a poorly reported excavation in the early twentieth century, there are still some interesting data.

The excavation reports of the southern barrow group always mention pieces of brown iron ore, often associated with stone tools and iron fragments. This suggests male orientated craft production. In the northern group, only the iron fragments were regularly present, with a greater frequency of 'female' artefacts,

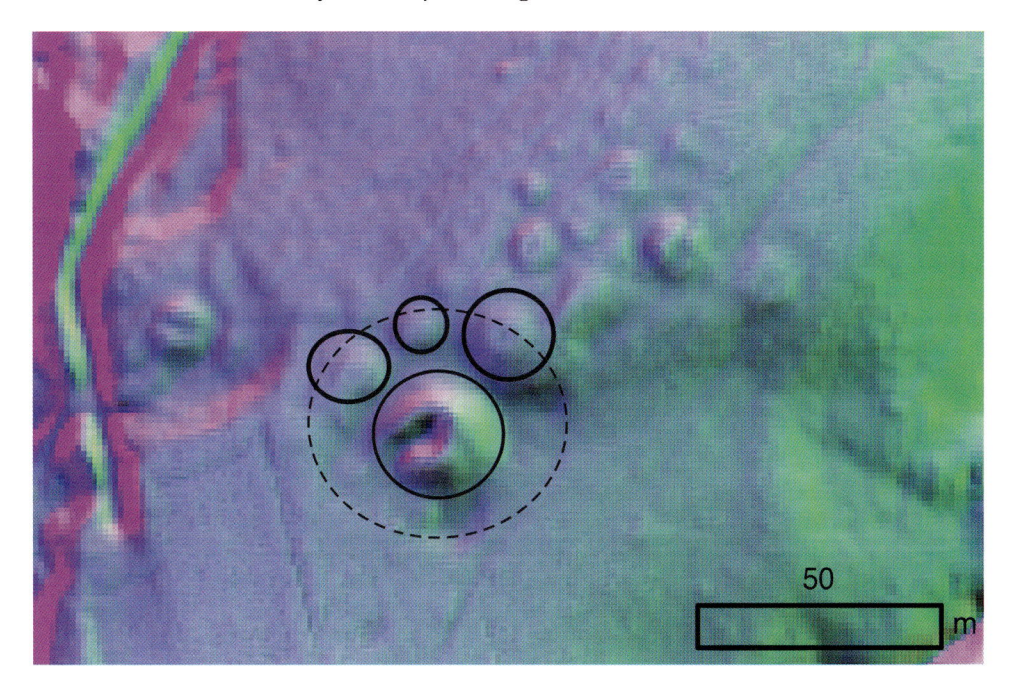

*Figure 4.5. Northern barrow group at Habakuk bellow Poštela. Barrow 28 with subsidiary barrows around it.*

such as loom-weights, spindle-whorls and bracelets, and only one axe and one spear. This suggests female craft production. The incompleteness of data prevents us from giving any final conclusions, but the distinctiveness of the finds is paralleled by their spatial separation.

The newly gathered precise LiDAR derived DTM gives us even more insight into the spatial arrangement of the barrow groups. The most important information is new information that ring-ditches surround every barrow. In addition, we can interpret the chronology and horizontal stratigraphy of the cemetery. Barrow 28, which was already partly excavated at the beginning of the twentieth century (Teržan 1990: 323, T.62: 15) appears to be the founding feature of the cemetery. It has a tumulus with a diameter of approximately twenty metres, surrounded by a nine metre wide ring-ditch, and its position as a prominent marker in the cemetery is underlined by the erection of at least three later barrows in its ditch or at its edge (Fig. 4.5).

The flat cemetery was also divided into two groups. Two excavation programmes, under different directors, took place in two separate locations: one rescue and the other sampling to establish the limits of the cemetery. Both excavations were, nevertheless, to a high standard, allowing Biba Teržan (1990) to build a useful synthesis. In the graves of the eastern group a single large urn generally held all the burnt human remains and the grave goods. In the western group, most of the cremation ashes were put directly into the pit, and only a small portion retained in varied types of small vessel. There were similar

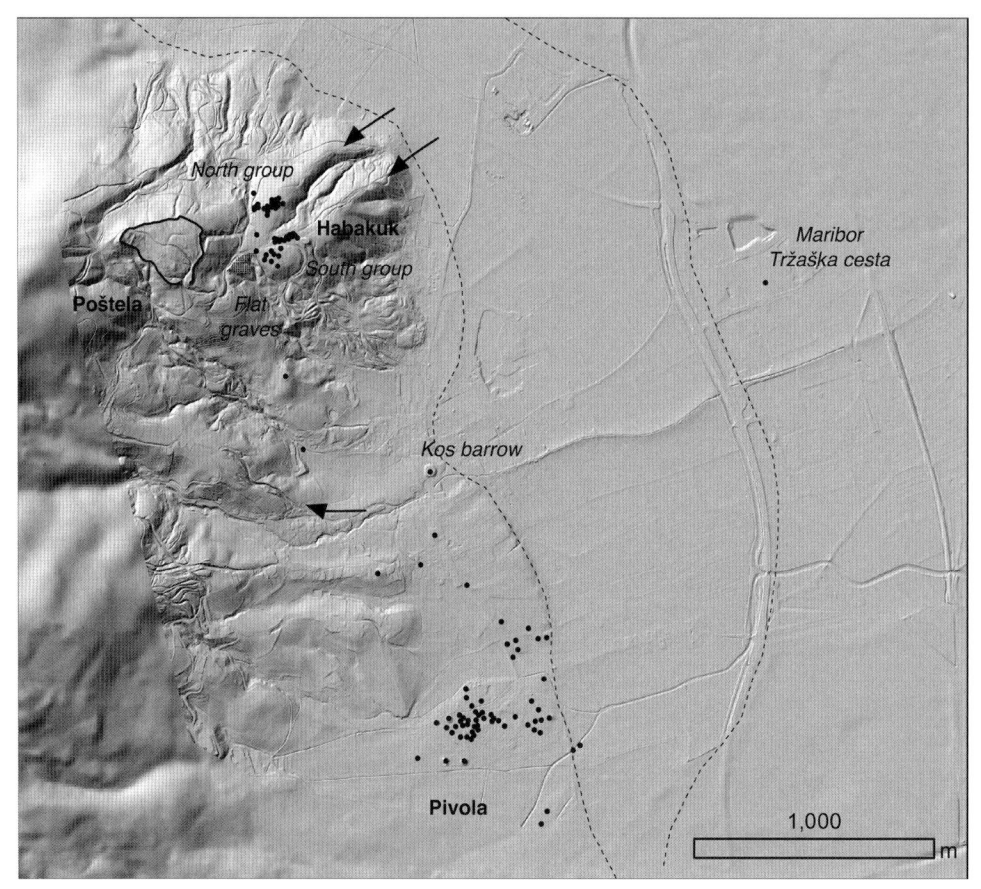

*Figure 4.6. The Poštela complex with showing geological zones in the plain (from left: colluvium, sandy clays, gravel terrace).*

contrasts in terms of grave goods. The eastern group had many more additional ceramic vessels. The western group had numerous pottery fragments. A further distinction related to female dress styles. The eastern group had pairs of bracelets. Members of the western group had only individual dress items such as a fibula or a bracelet, but also a glass bead and loom-weights (Teržan 1990: 60–1, T. 53–59).

The two groups of flat graves and the oldest barrows on the plateau and in the plain below the Pohorje hills and the first phase of the hillfort were all contemporary, that is dating to the end of ninth and the eighth century BC. (Teržan 1990: 61–70). The practice of flat burial seems not to have persisted into the next occupational phase of the settlement, although burial in the barrow cemetery continued. In the Razvanje – Pivola area, there are some much bigger barrows most notably on Habakuk, focused on the prominent Kos barrow (diameter of 57 metres, height of six metres and a ring-ditch width of 15 metres). The data quality was not good enough to undertake more detailed spatial analysis of material culture as undertaken at Breg/Frög and Kleinklein. The Kleinklein pattern is similar to that of Poštela in that the largest barrows tend to have prominent positions and to be among the more distant from the settlement (Teržan 1990: 124–42, 184–204).

As already stated, Poštela hillfort, with its monumental ramparts, visually dominated the whole Dravsko-Ptujsko polje. The position was obviously chosen to be visible and to control visually the approaches along and towards the River Drava, especially from south and south east. Poštela appeared prominently on the skyline to anyone traversing the northern part of the plain or approaching from along the south eastern slopes of Pohorje or along the Drava river from the south or south east. Moreover, most, if not all, settlements and cemeteries located in this part of the Dravsko-Ptujsko polje are placed within the viewshed of the Poštela hillfort. In this way, Poštela hillfort can be seen as a key, central settlement in the region, communicating ideas of power, control and domination.

When we look at the relationship between the hillfort and its barrows, the situation becomes more complicated. We have already mentioned that there are at least three barrow groups clearly connected to the Poštela hillfort. The viewsheds from these different barrow groups are mutually exclusive. The Pivola group is clearly visible from the slopes below the hillfort and especially well from its monumental entrance. It creates a compact visual envelope in the lowland, as it is situated in a shallow depression, bounded by low features such as a low ridge to the north. Some barrows of the southern Habakuk group, located on the ridge below Poštela are clearly visible in the skyline. However, the monumental Kos barrow, even though it was a prominent marker in the landscape, as it is visible almost throughout the northern Dravsko-Ptujsko polje, was not visible from the Pivola group since this viewshed was blocked by a gentle ridge. The southern Habakuk group, part of it also visually connected to the Kos barrow, is visible from the plain to the north, south east and south of the hillfort. On the other hand, the northern Habakuk group has a very small visible envelope and is only visible from the north and north east, where the Drava plain becomes much narrower and was densely populated in the preceding Urnfield Period and where the partly contemporary cemetery and maybe also a settlement at Radvanje were also located (Fig. 4.7). Furthermore the Habakuk group is spatially and visually connected to the southern group and the flat cemetery located on the same plateau, but had no visual contacts with any of the barrows positioned on the ridge in front of the main entrance or in the plain towards Pivola, where the southern group was focused (Fig. 4.7).

These relations between visual envelopes of barrows created an interesting spatial narrative for people moving along the natural corridors in the landscape. It is interesting that the barrows are located on the alluvial sediments abutting the strip of damp sandy-clays. It is most probable that this area was used also as a corridor for passing through this region.

For a person moving along the south eastern slope of Pohorje towards Drava, Poštela dominated the skyline. The barrows on the edge of the southern Habakuk group on the ridge below the hillfort were visible on the horizon most of the time. As one crossed the low ridge at Slivnica, the traveller entered the visual

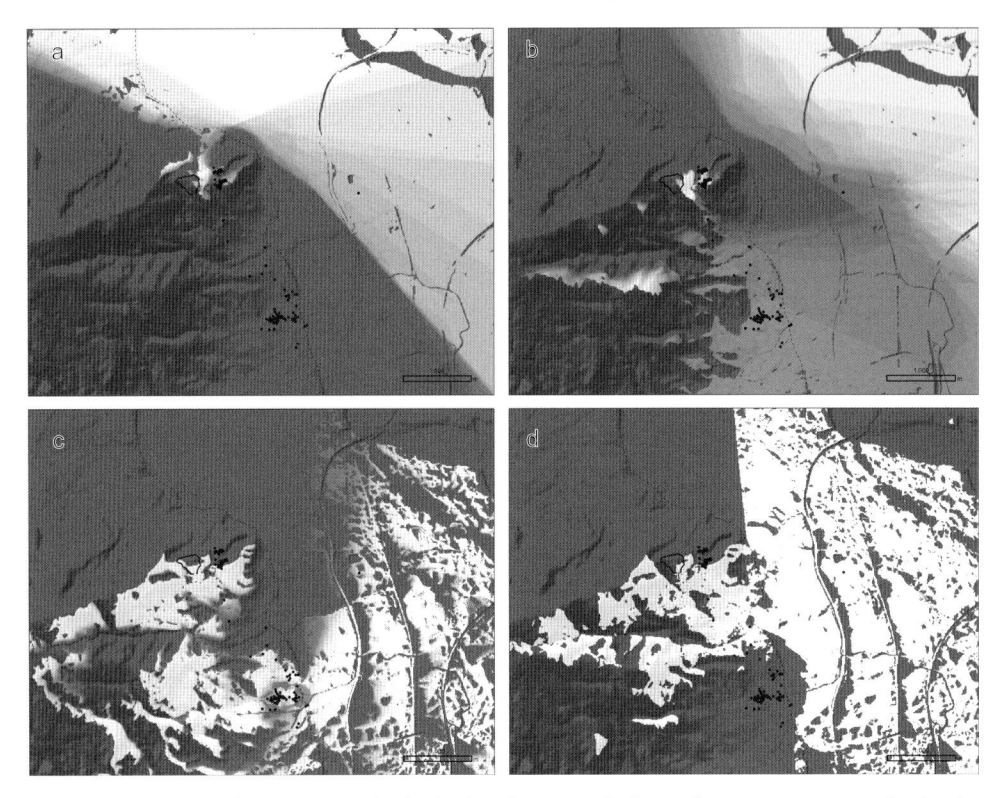

*Figure 4.7. Cumulative viewsheds (Wheatley 1995) from barrow groups. Shade depends on number of barrows that are visible from a particular location and range from dark (not visible) to light (visible from all barrows); a – northern Habakuk group; b – southern Habakuk group; c – Pivola group; d – Kos barrow.*

envelope of the first barrow group, moved along or through the barrows and passed over a gentle ridge at Razvanje. At that same place the largest Kos barrow appeared, located at the place where the strip of alluvial sediments comes to its narrowest and where a creek coming from the slopes below Poštela must be crossed. This is also an eventual crossroads, and a possible approach way to Poštela may be traceable in some partly degraded hollow ways on the nearby ridges. Barrows of the southern Habakuk group were still visible on the skyline. As one leaves the visual envelope of Kos barrow, Poštela and the barrows disappear, and appear again only when the traveller leaves the Pohorje edge and moves towards Drava, where iron finds from the river indicate the presence of Iron Age activity (Teržan 1990: 344).

If Poštela were to be approached from the eastern slopes of the Pohorje, where multiple parallel hollow-ways have been noted along ridges, Poštela and the northern and southern Habakuk barrow group appear dramatically only when one reaches them.

From this analysis we can conclude that the barrow locations were carefully selected, and that monuments were purposefully positioned in specific parts of the landscape, to afford views to the hillfort and other barrow groups (cf. Arnold 2002). The spatial relations between barrows and hillfort suggest that they all expressed the basic idea of enhancing a belonging to the Poštela community. However, their interrelation suggests a more nuanced story. The fact that the groups coexist and have very different visual envelopes, suggests that they simultaneously convey different identities within the Poštela community.

The Habakuk groups are spatially the most isolated. They are located close to the hillfort, but see only a small part of its rampart. The northern group is especially visible only to those from the north and east of Poštela, but it establishes relations of intervisibility and proximity to the southern group of barrows. On the other hand, the southern Habakuk group communicated with the northern group and the largest isolated (Kos) barrow below the hillfort, struggling to become part of the single visual envelope and acted as mediator between first group and the rest of the barrows. The Pivola group obviously connects to the monumental entrance to the hillfort; however, its compact visual envelope means that it does not communicate with the wider landscape. It is thereby stating a strong idea of belonging to the community or even equating the group with the community.

Each group communicates a distinct identity within the community, based either on lineage, rank or other criteria. Barrows were therefore powerful visual reminders, places of memory that reiterated ideas about the identity of community and distinct kinship or rank group identities within the community. Spatial and visual relations between barrow groups and relations to the hillfort not only reflect, but actively establish the community of Poštela and the different identities of its inhabitants. And because they bring identities into being, barrows and their relations are powerful media for social action and shared public understandings. Their pattern is thus a result of the internal identity politics and idea of belonging and identity of groups within the Poštela community. This process was never finished and completed. The landscape of memory around Poštela became a political landscape, an arena for expressing new ideas and messages. Respecting, relating to, or changing the existing spatial order was a powerful political message, which reproduced or subverted the existing political configurations.

## Conclusion

The north eastern Slovenia in the Early Iron Age presents itself as a very diverse region, formerly known mostly through hillforts and barrow cemeteries. However, the research conducted in the last two decades has changed that situation, but, by answering some existing questions, many new ones appeared. Different types of grave constructions and various building techniques and settlement types appear close one to another, but the reasons for the diversity can be appropriately addressed only after the excavated material is published.

On the other hand, new technical possibilities such as remote sensing and GIS analysis are also opening up new viewpoints in our studies and the results show themselves to be very useful and complementary to other archaeological data.

In Podravje, Poštela proved itself to be a central settlement, visually dominating the settlements at least in the northern Dravsko-Ptujsko polje. The spatial relations between barrow groups and the hillfort suggest that their position is not random. They form distinctive groups, which are purposefully positioned to afford views to the hillfort and other barrow groups. Their relations suggest different identities, based either on kinship, rank or other criteria. Barrows were places of memory that expressed ideas about the belonging to the community, but other group identities within the community as well.

The landscape of memory around Poštela suggests that we should not understand communities as monolithic units, but as composed of different groups, with their own sub-identities. The landscape around Poštela was used to express first of all an idea of group identity, but also of competing, fluid identities within the community. The landscape around it was a locus of identity politics and played an active role in its formation.

We are aware that having focused on the complex situation at Poštela we have not addressed any specific questions at other sites like Murska Sobota, Ormož and Ptuj. However, we are presenting a possible approach that is transferable to a better understanding of the region as a whole. Only after you understand a reasonable amount of sites can the broader picture become a reachable goal. However, even at Poštela our research is still in progress and other remote sensing methods (geophysical methods) will be applied and finally combined with ground-truthing, and targeted and limited excavations. In that way, a lot of new information can still be obtained and we can move bit by bit towards a less misty picture of the Early Iron Age in the region.

**Acknowledgements**

The research at Poštela was conducted in the framework of the project Continuity and Innovation in Prehistory – Case study between the Alps and the Pannonian Plain for the period 1300–600 BC (N6-0004) financed by the Slovenian Research Agency and directed by Prof. Dr. Ljubinka Teržan, whom we thank for the opportunity given to us. The study of Hotinja vas is by Teja Gerbec as a focus of her doctoral dissertation at the University of Ljubljana, Faculty of Arts, Department of Archaeology, and we thank her for the generous sharing of information ahead of publication (Gerbec in press).

# 5. Royal Bodies, Invisible Victims: Gender in the Funerary Record of Late Iron Age and Early Hellenistic Thrace

*Bela Dimova*

**Keywords:** gender, Thrace, burials, Bulgaria

This paper investigates gender in Late Iron Age Thrace through funerary evidence by presenting the key points of a more detailed study (Dimova 2011). Gender is a productive entry point to approach aspects of identity and social relations, which scholars assume are explained by the written sources, but which are in need of re-assessment. Here the terms Thrace and Thracian refer to the region and its inhabitants in the first millennium BC, without implying ethnic identity. The chronological framework encompasses the Late Iron Age, and more specifically the fifth to third century BC. The Late Iron Age in Thrace saw the formation of regional polities, and the rise of elites increasingly connected to the cultural and political dynamics of the Mediterranean, Asia Minor and central Europe (Archibald 1998; Theodossiev this volume). The defining processes of the Late Iron Age (state-formation, expanding trade, and elite interactions), are associated with rulers, warriors, and traders assumed to be men, leaving women virtually absent from the image of this crucial period.

This study makes a step towards remedying the situation by scrutinising the current perception of gender roles in mortuary practice. I do this by analysing the construction of gender roles in literary sources and archaeological writing. I highlight the current assumptions about gender roles, and then I examine them against the archaeological record. These steps are important, because if gender assumptions are not critically examined, they are inscribed in the past with harmful consequences and give historical permanence to certain stereotypes (Brumfiel 1992: 555). In the current image of ancient Thrace, men do war, trade, and politics; women (if ever mentioned) act as loyal self-sacrificing wives. I argue that the archaeological record does not support this. Contrary to popular opinion, there is no archaeological evidence for the custom of widow-slaying. Some female burials display high status, and some women probably even wielded political power. As for men, not all elite males were buried with a recognisable warrior identity.

Tumulus burials constitute the majority of available data for Late Iron Age Thrace. An up-to-date synthesis of the material is currently lacking, but existing overviews (cf. Archibald 1998; Theodossiev 2000) reveal an overwhelming amount of poorly published data. This study focuses on burials from two of the most intensively excavated areas of Thrace: south central and north east Bulgaria. I collated the data into a relational database

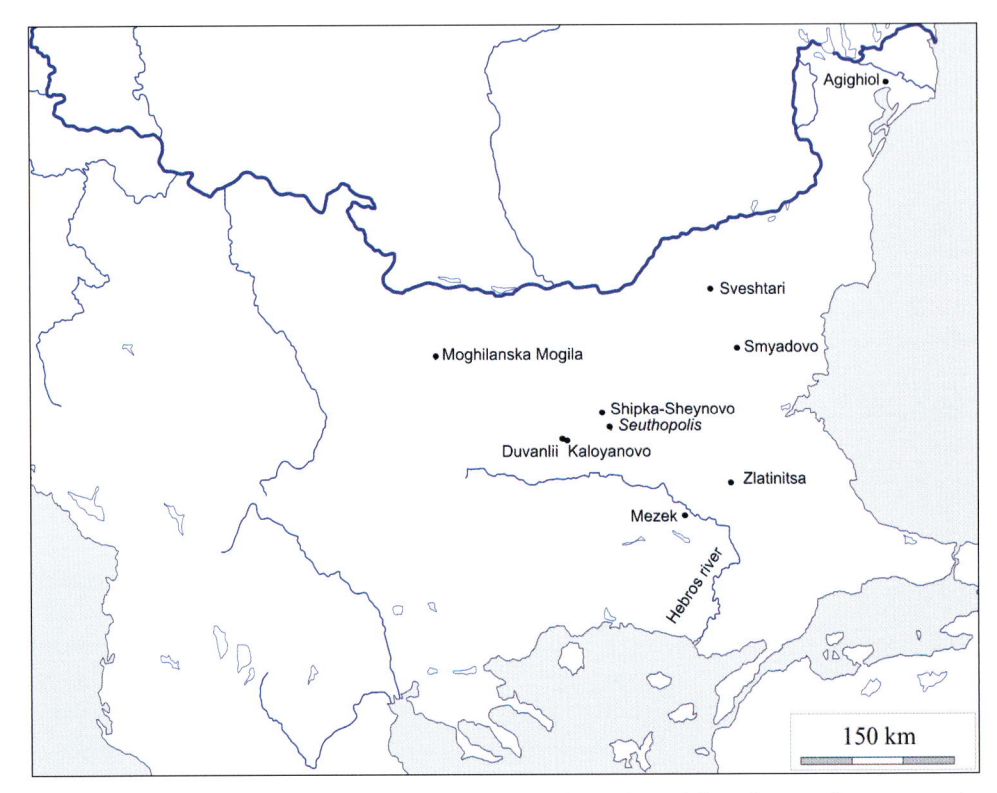

*Figure 5.1. Map of sites mentioned in the text. Template adapted from http://d-maps.com/.*

comprising 316 individuals (available online at http://bit.ly/ThraceDatabase). As Late Iron Age burial mounds cluster around centres of power, my dataset is biased towards 'rich' graves. The data quality is extremely variable, so the quantitative analysis is based on 116 well-preserved and published graves. The investigation of gender is further challenged by the scarcity of osteological studies. I collected all available anthropological reports, published and unpublished.

#### Feminism and funerals

A critical engagement with gender has helped to identify and re-evaluate many problematic assumptions about prehistory (Gilchrist 1999): 'when gender roles are not explicitly defined, they are implicitly assumed' (Brumfiel 1992: 555). Second-wave feminism postulates that if women and other 'marginalised' groups have no part in historical narratives, then they have fewer resources to claim their role in modern society. As archaeologists, we have a duty to consider the political consequences of our assumptions, and work to unsettle historicised gender stereotypes. To this end, some of this paper is dedicated to deconstructing archaeologists' current gender assumptions using Critical Discourse Analysis (Fairclough 1989) and reading 'against the grain' (following Mani 1998), and then testing if they have any grounding in the material record.

While politically important in the modern world, gender is not necessarily represented in the burials of past societies (e.g. Eisner 1991; Crass 2001), and its most common markers like clothing are not always archaeologically visible. The identities represented in death may reflect, contrive, or override the identities of the living person. Grave attributes such as objects, structures and burial rites mark personal and social relationships (Sørensen 2004). Grave goods can belong to the deceased, or be deposited in the grave as 'gifts' or 'wealth', and they can have complex biographies (Kopytoff 1986). The burial is also an event where political power, wealth and status are contested among the living (Parker Pearson 1999). In sum, the archaeological remains of the grave are the result of the interlocking agencies of the deceased, the living community which buried them, and a range of habits and traditions which are reproduced or rejected. Any analysis of funerary identity needs to be aware of these complications. My study therefore investigates *if* and *how* gender is visible in the material record of individual funerary performances.

Conventional identity archaeology has been criticised for describing static groups of people (e.g. social classes, ethnicities), looking top-down – an unsatisfactory approach, since societies are dynamic compositions, ridden with tensions and negotiations between groups and individuals (Brumfiel 1992: 558). To avoid this problem I alternate between individual- and group-scale analysis, following Meskell (2000). Methodologically this means combining a quantitative overview of patterns in the data with in-depth case studies.

The current consensus is that gender should be studied within a palimpsest of identities (Casella & Fowler 2004), including age, race, sexuality, etc. In order to capture the social dynamics, and to see how gender intersects with other identities, I investigate lines of tension visible in the Late Iron Age Thracian material including gender, status and regional identity. This is achieved by recording a wide range of grave attributes in the database, and identifying patterns between them using Microsoft Access queries and cross-tabulation tables.

Finally, archaeology has been late to acknowledge that sex and gender are not straightforward categories, but that their definition depends on the context of knowledge-production (Laqueur 1990 cited in Meskell 2000: 13–14). Both archaeological 'gendering' and osteological 'sexing' are constructions of their disciplinary context – there is no prediscursive biological sex (Butler 1990). The archaeological construction of sex can be equally contextual, as I go on to show. To avoid confusion, I use 'gender' to signify individuals designated male or female through grave goods, and 'sex' to signify osteologically determined male or female skeletons. The possibility of a non-binary gender structure exists, but is difficult to investigate without ethnographic data.

The theoretical positions adopted here regard graves as the material record of multiple agencies. This approach allows us to find multi-faceted and varied identities. The 'elite warrior grave' is a gender-laden idea which has been taken for granted and deserves discursive re-assessment, attempted in the next section.

## Thracian women, ancient authors, and modern archaeologists

Most commentaries on gender in Thrace (Mihaylov 1972: 99–105; Venedikov 1977; Kotova 1998; 2000a; b; 2002; 2004; Janakieva 2005) extract information from a small amount of ancient text (Aristotle Fragments 611; Atheneus 12.42; Euripides, *Andromachy* 215–218; Herodotos, *Histories* 5; Mela, *De situ orbis* 2.2; Solin 10.1–11; Strabo 7.3.4; Xenophon, *Anabasis* 7 2.38–3.27). Modern commentaries give little consideration to the layers of mediation and the texts' original context, which are crucial because the sources are cross-referential and produced within a politically charged Graeco-Roman environment. Most authors only offer tangential remarks, except a couple of oft-cited paragraphs by Herodotos and Mela.

Herodotos (5.5) depicts a funeral, during which the favourite wife of a polygamous warrior is slain to join him in death. Herodotos is primarily concerned with the religion and curious customs of foreigners – i.e. constructing the Other in the Greek imagination (Hartog 1988; Munson 2001). He introduces the passage on uxoricide as an exceptional custom of a particular tribe, rather than a common Thracian practice (Herodotos 5.3.2.). Written five centuries later, Mela's *De situ orbis* (2.2.) follows Herodotos' words so closely, it suggests that Mela copied from the *Histories*. Thracian women are bought according to their beauty and virtue, narrates Mela, and wives are passed along as inheritance. In Herodotos' text, women are secondary characters; in Mela's, they are objects of transaction between men.

Herodotos' narrative technique delivers a sensational effect, as he announces the wife's death (Munson 2001: 161). Later texts take up Herodotos' dramatic tone. In the same passage Mela writes that the widow to be slain is judged by her beauty (*decus ... apud judicaturos*) and is considered to win in a dispute (*in contenditur vincere*). The word Herodotos uses for the dispute is '*krisis*' – which translates as crisis, argument, judgment, or contest (as in the judgement of Paris). The Greek term is general, but in translation '*krisis*' becomes a contest of female virtue or beauty (Mela translated by Macaulay 1890), or a disorderly quarrel (Kitov *et al.* 1980: 12–14). Mela's reiteration of Herodotos objectifies women as men's wealth. Baudet's (1843) translation of Mela in turn produces a disembodied, sanitised account of what is meant to be a violent event of social negotiation in which one widow is killed, and the others are passed on to other men as inheritance. In academic reiterations, Kitov *et al.* (1980) and Yordanov (2000) emphasise the widow's loyalty and beauty, which augment the drama of her death. In their versions the story acquires a moralising and victim eroticising discourse – although such is not evident in the standard Bulgarian translations of Herodotos (Kacarov & Dechev 1949; Gocheva 1981). Each step of narration, translation or re-contextualisation re-invents the Thracians by generalising the custom to all tribes, and normalises violence against women.

No archaeologist takes Herodotos' words at face value, yet he retains authority as 'the father of history' and his account of uxoricide has been evoked to explain a series of graves (Dremsizova 1955: 80; 1962: 181; Nikolov 1967; Kitov *et al.* 1980: 11; Archibald 1998: 174). These authors refer to Herodotos and to each other's tentative interpretations as supporting evidence. No archaeologist cites the original text, nor a specific translation; rather, they reiterate a familiar scene along with the discourses which mediate it (sensationalism, moral judgment, objectification, and sanitisation), to the effect that the violence of the ritual is lost and Herodotos' narrative appears corroborated. The repetition ultimately shapes our image of Thracian women as virtuous victims.

In a number of cases, the excavators cited above have resorted to the narrative of widow-slaying to explain double or group burials. Anonymous piles of ashes or partial skeletons have been imagined as faithful widows who willingly ended their lives, following a violent custom. Finally, the tentative conclusions of Bulgarian archaeologists have become uncritically generalised in summary volumes on European prehistory: 'In Thrace, burial and literary evidence suggests a more subordinate position for women at all stages of life' (Taylor 2001: 398). The silent bones and ashes that archaeologists find can not convey whether the deceased was slain as a loyal widow, and they can not support the vivid literary narrative. Hence, the idea of women's self-sacrifice and subordination persists, based on a network of uncritical citations. Without attention to the sources' context and cross-references, archaeologists reproduce a series of assumptions about the identity, motivations, and religion of disembodied Thracian women.

## Constructing femaleness and maleness

The construction of gender has not been approached as an issue in its own right, but the image of women as self-sacrificial wives and men as warriors has a complex historiographical development in Thracian archaeology beyond the written sources. While excavating Duvanlii, Filov interpreted graves with earrings as female, and graves with weapons as male (1934: 190–1). He left several graves ungendered, (nos. 5, 8, 13, 15–17), but in later literature Filov's uncertainty was lost and they were also considered male (e.g. Archibald 1998: 160–5). This approach produces a gender bias: elite graves are assumed to be male, unless there is jewellery. This assumption persisted into the 1990s, when 'rich graves' were assigned to the (male) warrior aristocracy. The construction of gender has not been approached as an issue in its own right.

The existence of rich female tombs in Late Iron Age Thrace has only been accepted since the discovery of a tomb near Smyadovo, where a Greek inscription names the deceased: 'Gonimasedze, Seuthes' wife'. The excavators challenged Herodotos' narrative, arguing that monumental tombs were constructed for women too (Atanassov & Nedelchev 2002). The inscription implies Gonimasedze might be honoured in her capacity as Seuthes' wife (Tzochev pers. comm.), but an alternative explanation sees this as an inscription made by a loving husband (Nankov 2011: 15, n. 22). Georgieva's (2007) paper marks a significant departure from text-focused scholarship on Thracian women (cf. Mihaylov 1972: 99–105; Venedikov 1977; Kotova 1998; 2000a; 2002; 2004; Janakieva 2005). Georgieva scrutinises the archaeological evidence for female graves in the Early Iron Age and concludes that the funerary data do not support the hypothetical tradition of elite widow sacrifice, or any other particularity of female graves in Thrace. One unpublished paper compares several Thracian Late Iron Age graves to Phrygian female graves (Vassileva 2010). Sirbu and Stefan (2010) examine iconography, funerary representation, and epigraphic data as different discourses constituting gendered identities in northern Thrace, highlighting that warrior identity may have a limited role and multi-faceted meanings. Other authors (Archibald 1998: 258–9; Bouzek & Ondřejová 2004: 128) list several exceptional female graves, none of which are securely sexed or clearly published. These attempts to address gender face a common challenge: insufficient osteological studies and gender-biased excavation recording. Of the osteologically sexed skeletons in my database, 16 are female and 22 – male, but females are half as likely to be identified by grave goods (31:61).

For the most part, gender archaeology considers osteological sex an objective part of identity (cf. Arnold & Wicker 2001). However, bone analysis does not happen in a vacuum. Osteologists draw on and contribute to the overall construction of gender in Late Iron Age Thrace, founded upon the written sources. Nowhere is this clearer than at Mogilanska Mogila in Vratsa (Venedikov 1966; Nikolov 1967; Torbov 2005 – for a critical synthesis). Tomb II in this mound contained an alleged case of uxoricide: one of the bodies lay face-down in the antechamber, in a distorted position, surrounded by both jewellery and weapons. Only half of the skull was recovered, in extremely inclement excavation conditions. The anthropology report classified it as a female, aged 14–16, emphasising the poor preservation of the bones. Incited by the Vratsa museum director, the physical anthropologist then famously reconstructed the skull as a show-piece, thus consolidating the 'Thracian princess' as a gendered image in popular culture (Fig. 5.2). Beyond the cranial measurements, Yordanov's publication takes an erotic/fatalistic tone and betrays admiration for the girl's beauty, which is contrasted with her alleged fate: 'it can be assumed that she has followed her husband in his eternal immortality – a brave warrior and chief. She – the most beautiful, the youngest, the most lovable one' (Yordanov 2000: 127). Clearly the osteological publication draws heavily on the mood in Herodotos' passage, discussed above. Though 'the Thracian princess' is an extreme example, gender predilections permeate all levels of archaeological practice, and beyond – into popular visions of ancient Thrace.

Even routine archaeological descriptions betray the assumption that women were of secondary importance in Thracian society. Spectacular objects identify the buried men as kings or warriors with political networks, but objects from women's graves seldom merit such interpretation – e.g. the Persian amphora in a female grave at Duvanlii. Interpreting objects in female/male graves with a double standard is a common gender bias (Stalsberg *et al.* 2001). Similarly, stratigraphic descriptions locate women in the lexical field of second-rank: '[e]lite females were probably buried alongside men in chamber tombs. There were *subsidiary inhumations* in the Southern Tumulus at Rozovets and at Kazanlak and two *underfloor female cremations* at Mal tepe' (Archibald 1998: 258, emphasis added). Here stratigraphic and chronological relations are reiterated in downgrading gender terms. These are nuances of language and

*Figure 5.2. The Thracian princess reconstruction. Source: Torbov 2005: 40.*

terminology, or choice of subjects, which subtly shape our vision of Thracian women as subsidiary individuals. Gender is constructed in a binary model, in which women are a residual category, or virtuous victims, and men are 'warriors' or 'priests'. There can be no comprehensive criteria for identifying 'women's' graves in Late Iron Age Thrace, considering regional and chronological variability, and the anticipated diversity of female/feminine identities. My database recorded the basis on which each burial was 'gendered' in publications – this reveals assumptions and guidelines, which archaeologists share to a varying extent. Usually excavators identify female graves by the presence of jewellery, mirrors, and small clay figurines. Weaponry, drinking equipment, and horse burials are thought to mark out male graves. Fibulae and pottery are considered unisex attributes. Rings and pectorals are usually associated with males, and considered a sign of kingship, but they are also known to occur in female graves (see Fig. 5.3). Having outlined the construction of gender in the archaeological literature, I proceed to test the assumed correlations between gender and object categories in the database. The table in Figure 5.3 comprises 116 graves with good preservation, of which 66 were gendered in the literature; the discussion includes all graves in which the objects occur. I test the correlations by comparing the expected and the observed frequency of each object category (Fig. 5.3.). I expect that objects are evenly distributed between male and female graves. If a class of objects occurs in female or male graves more than statistically expected, it is a gender marker.

| Gender Attribute | N graves | F obs | (F sexed) | F exp | M obs | (M sexed) | M exp | N/A | Disp-uted | Assumed association |
|---|---|---|---|---|---|---|---|---|---|---|
| Earrings | 9 | 8 | (1) | 2 | 0 | (0) | 6 | 0 | 1 | F |
| Beads | 23 | 13 | (2) | 5 | 6 | (2) | 14 | 3 | 1 | F (M possible) |
| Mirror | 10 | 7 | (1) | 2 | 1 | (1) | 6 | 2 | 0 | F |
| Spear | 29 | 0 | (0) | 7 | 26 | (3) | 20 | 3 | 1 | M |
| Rings | 19 | 6 | (1) | 4 | 11 | (2) | 13 | 1 | 1 | M (F possible) |
| Wreath | 13 | 3 | (0) | 3 | 8 | (1) | 8 | 1 | 1 | M (F possible) |
| | | | | | | | | | | |
| Cremation | 55 | 10 | (2) | 7 | 21 | (3) | 24 | 23 | 1 | |
| Inhumation | 51 | 7 | (1) | 8 | 26 | (6) | 25 | 17 | 1 | |
| Other | 10 | 0 | (0) | | 3 | (0) | | 7 | 0 | |
| Total | 116 | 17 | (3) | | 50 | (9) | | 47 | 2 | |

*Figure 5.3. Observed and expected frequency of some objects assumed to be gender attributes in gendered graves. Observed values include osteologically sexed individuals (in brackets). Expected values are obtained by dividing the product of the row and column totals by the grand total for all objects (cf. papers in Arnold & Wicker 2001). Cremated remains are notoriously difficult to sex; the sexed cremations in Figure 5.3. were studied by Dr Slavi Cholakov (unpublished reports for Montina and Tonkova Mogila; Gergova and Valcheva 2005: 63–4 for Sboryanovo west cemetry Mound 35).*

### EARRINGS, NECKLACES, AND MIRRORS

13 graves contained 61 earrings between them. The finds confirm the assumption that earrings are associated with female graves (cf. expected and observed values in Figure 5.3.). There are a few exceptions: earrings are found in one male, and three disputed or non-gendered graves. The publications do not allow us to ascertain relations between earrings and male skeletons, except perhaps tomb 3 from the Mound II in Seuthopolis (Chichikova 1970: 17). Most earrings are made of gold, and styled in several established forms known from across the Mediterranean (Tonkova 2007).

31 graves contained a total of 565 beads. Beads occur in assumed female graves three times more often than in male graves (18:6). However, beads are almost equally common in osteologically sexed male and female graves (5:4). This goes against the assumption that necklaces are only women's jewellery.

14 mirrors were found in 16 graves (two double burials). 10 were found in female graves, two of which were securely sexed. At least one mirror is associated with a reportedly sexed male, at Malkata Mogila. These data support the assumed link between mirrors and female graves, but the connection is not exclusive.

### WEAPONRY AND HORSE GEAR

Weapons, protective gear and horse trappings occur in men's graves more frequently than statistically expected in a random distribution. Only knives are systematically found with both genders – but they can be classified as both tools and weapons. A few female graves have weapons other than knives, but the contextual relations and the sexing are unreliable (e.g. Mogilanska Mogila). Hence, weapons clearly mark men's graves, as assumed.

## Rings

25 rings were found in 20 graves, including three mid-fifth century graves at Duvanlii. Most often rings co-occur with imported ceramics, metal vessels, weapons, and necklaces, which makes them part of the 'richest' grave inventories. 17 rings come from well-preserved gendered graves, and their split between female/male graves (6:11) is close to the expected in a random sample (4:13), slightly in favour of female graves. This undermines the interpretation of graves where rings are the main argument for identifying 'a king or aristocrat' (Kitov et al. 2008; Dimitrova & Sirakov 2009). They are an attribute of high status, rather than gender, especially in south central Bulgaria.

Existing literature considers rings in ornamental and iconographic terms, as 'one of the most representative symbols of the Odrysai aristocracy' (Tonkova 1997: 19; Archibald 1998: 193). Their 'Greek' or 'native' provenance is another concern (Boardman 2001: 230, 425). It is accepted that Thracian elites commissioned the rings from local and Greek craftsmen. The images are personalised, sometimes with an added inscription. The iconography and their context make the rings part of the language of power in Thrace (compare the Zlatinitsa ring (Agre 2011: 39–44) and Sveshtari tomb mural).

One important aspect has been overlooked: how were the rings used? Signs of long wear on the rings from Arabadzhiiska (Duvanlii), Zlatinitsa and Malkata Mogila suggest they may have been heirlooms. At least 14 rings have intaglio images which can be used as seals for marking, identifying, closing, authorising, and certifying property or spaces. The fact that both men and women were buried with (often used) signet rings suggests that they both wielded these powers: a possibility which demands further investigation.

## Beyond gender

As stated at the beginning, gender is part of a person's palimpsestic identity, in which multiple layers interact. I now turn to social status and regional affiliation: two other archaeologically visible aspects of identity.

Few people in Late Iron Age Thrace could afford adornments of precious metal. Earrings are found in six per cent of all graves (nine per cent of the graves with good preservation). Necklaces are found in merely four per cent of all graves (eight per cent of the graves with good preservation). The distribution of earrings and beads is remarkably concentrated: three graves at Duvanlii contain 54 per cent of all the earrings; two necklaces – from Agighiol and Mezek – together comprise 41 per cent of all the beads. Hence, even within those few who were buried with jewellery, there was remarkable differentiation. Earrings and necklaces occur most commonly with each other, and with imported pottery. The skewed distribution of earrings and necklaces, and their relative rarity suggest that they were the adornments of an extremely wealthy part of society, which had access to luxuries and imports, and was further stratified internally.

Similarly, weaponry is not simply a gender-marker, but an attribute of only certain males. Almost half the male graves did not have any weapons at all. While the maximum number of weapons in a grave is 21, half of the graves with weapons (24) contained three items or fewer. Large items (swords, helmets, armour) are most often deposited with other weapons, imported ceramics and horse gear. The data suggest that weapons and horse gear expressed social status through the symbols of militarism. The nature of the objects strengthens this impression: armour and greaves were made to order, often decorated with gold and silver. At least one cuirass was handed down as an heirloom (Filov 1930; Taylor 1985). This testifies to the value and highly personalised nature of the weapons as markers of social status and personal wealth.

Social-status differentiation is also evident in the distribution of total object numbers in graves, and the distribution of imported pottery. The Kaloyanovo tomb near Sliven had over 40 items (Chichikova 1969) while at the other end of the spectrum, 28 per cent of all graves with good preservation contained no grave goods except local pottery. The 22 wreaths and 16 pectorals co-occur with male and female graves with the expected frequency in a random sample. But they are fairly rare objects – even in a dataset biased towards rich graves, wreaths only occur in nine per cent, and pectorals – in 12 per cent of the Late Iron Age graves with good preservation. Evidently beyond the minority of 'warrior' and 'elite' graves, there were many people whose funerary identities were manifested in more subtle ways, and whose significance has so far been ignored. One can only hope that further studies will produce the kind of data that can shed light on the lives and deaths of those people, and their role in wider historical processes.

The scope of this paper allows only a cursory consideration of regional identity by comparing overall trends in two broad areas. Roughly equal numbers of graves were considered from south central Bulgaria (114) and north east Bulgaria (111). Both areas practised biritualism, but cremation was more common in the north east, and inhumation in the south central area. Clearly cremations were carried out differently in each region (on a constructed pyre in situ in the south central area, and away from the grave in the north east). The funerary structures show a more pronounced division: all stone-slab graves are in the north east, except one, whereas ashlar-built graves, brick tombs, wooden coffins, platforms, and pyres occur in the south central area. The monumental tombs cluster around centres of power, as do high status objects (earrings, necklaces, rings, wreaths, precious metal weaponry), and the graves with largest numbers of objects. Despite the differences, elites in both regions set themselves apart using a similar repertoire of funerary architecture and grave goods.

Certain tombs and objects found in Thracian graves fit with supra-regional fashions and trends. As such, they construct and communicate elite identities across regional boundaries. For example, in the Hellenistic period the tombs with barrel vaults were popular across Macedonia and Thrace, with local variations (Stoyanova 2011: 345–7). The earrings were part of a recognisable Hellenistic repertoire, from which people chose according to local taste (Dimitrova 1989). Similarly, the funerary wreaths gained popularity in Thrace at the same time as the height of their fashion across the Greek world (Williams and Ogden 1994: 36).

Having reviewed patterns of group identity, I now move on to consider individual identity through case-studies, chosen for their good preservation and publication. The intriguing nature of the case-studies emphasises the characteristic uniqueness of Late Iron Age Thracian burials.

## Malkata Mogila and Duvanlii

Malkata Mogila lies in the Shipka-Sheynovo mound cemetery, in the southern foothills of Haemus. Despite its unassuming chamber made of unworked stones, Malkata Mogila contained one of the richest burials of the Late Iron Age (Kitov 1994a; 1994b; 2003; Kitov & Theodossiev 1995). A mature male individual (aged 50–55) was laid on the ground, orientated north–south. He was adorned lavishly with a gilded wreath and two golden necklaces with exquisite amphora-shaped pendants. His clothes were decorated with buttons and gilded rosettes, a pendant, and two silver chains attached to three fibulae. One fibula and the beaded necklace showed a striking similarity to the fibulae and beaded necklaces from Duvanlii dated to the late sixth century BC, decorated with granulation and filigree rosettes (Kitov 2003: 31).

To the left of the body, a small clay sphere was put on a bronze mirror. On the right side of the body lay two silver *phialae* in a bronze bowl, a table amphora, an *askos*, a bronze *situla* with a strainer for the grape pips from wine, and other vessels with unspecified positions (Kitov 1994a).

The excavator interprets the jewellery, mirror, clay figurines, two bone staffs, and the ring as the attributes of 'a Thracian priest-ruler' (Kitov 1994b; 2003: 31; Kitov & Theodossiev 1995: 322). He also mentions that the bones were sexed by an anthropologist, though no detailed measurements have been published.

However, elsewhere this assemblage of grave goods – jewellery, mirror, a small clay figurines – would be interpreted as a female grave. The objects from Malkata Mogila strongly resemble the grave goods from three Duvanlii mounds, Mushovitsa, Koukova and Arabadjiiska, assigned to females (Filov 1934). They all have gold pectorals, similar beaded necklaces, bronze mirrors, clay figurines, drinking and serving vessels, etc. Some elements differ: the Duvanlii graves are pits with wooden constructions or ashlar-built graves while Malkata is a rubble stone structure. The position of the fibulae and the buttons in Malkata suggests the deceased wore different clothes. Chronology accounts for some differences – Malkata is at least a century later than the Duvanlii graves – and yet the similarity is strong.

So what do we make of the contradicting gender indicators? While certain objects seem to constitute an elite female costume, other objects like necklaces, mirrors, and drinking sets, are more versatile with respect to gender. They mark other aspects of funerary representation which are worth examining. The grave goods are carefully selected and composed: in Malkata, the objects were propped up by pebbles, and at Duvanlii the grave goods and body were arranged in a consistent pattern. The resulting funerary representation at Malkata and Duvanlii has several key components: wine-drinking equipment and gold jewellery sets around the head/chest. Wine-drinking sets of precious metal vessels and imported pottery evoke wealth and conviviality, in both male and female graves. As established above, jewellery marks gender and status. Significantly, it also signals familiarity with foreign fashions, or allegiance to long-lived traditions in elite costume (Tonkova 2002).

Besides being imports, the Achaemenid-type silver *phiale* and a bronze *hydria* from Mushovitsa could be up to half a century older than the Attic pottery in the grave (Archibald 1998: 162). The jewellery from the three Duvanlii mounds also predates the ceramics (Tonkova 2002). In Malkata Mogila, Kitov sees the use-wear on the ring as evidence for its age (Kitov 2003: 31). The possible heirloom status of these objects adds to their value, although their precise dating is debateable. More visibly than gender or militarism, the grave goods here demonstrate social status, and connections to distant sources of luxury and possibly to the past. The reference to the past, especially through personal heirlooms worn on the body, emphasises connections through which power was transferred over time – such as lineage or kinship. This is perhaps also the case of the cuirass from Dalboki (see below).

## KALOYANOVO-CHERNOZEM TUMULUS 1

The Kaloyanovo-Chernozem mound cemetery lies 500 metres east of Duvanlii. One 'warrior' burial here offers useful contrast to the graves discussed above. Tumulus 1 covered the ashlar-built grave of a securely sexed male, aged 20–25, inhumed in the last quarter of the fifth century BC (Kissyov 2005: 16–60). The body was covered with red fabric. The deceased wore a golden pectoral and a signet-ring. The grave goods were arranged in three groups (Fig. 5.4). One set of arrows, a *lekythos* and two spearheads were laid to the left of the head. Two silver cups were laid to the right of the body, next to the upright cuirass and a quiver of arrows. The rest of the vessels and two silver spoons were arranged along the east wall, by the feet. Embers and ashes were spread around the grave.

The iconography of the grave goods evokes the themes of heroism, fighting, and monsters. The *gorgoneion* on the pectoral and the cuirass has apotropaic powers. The pectoral is further decorated with alternating lions and deer. Bellerophon, the slayer of monsters is depicted on the silver *kylix*. Finally, the signet-ring bears the image of a man with a spear and a shield.

The only object whose iconography deviates from the theme of animals and fighting is the red-figured *hydria*, depicting a *gynaikon*. It might indicate discord between the militaristic iconography and a women's scene, or it might be treated as an imported luxury vessel, its iconography irrelevant in a Thracian context.

Several contemporary graves from the same area share the characteristics of

5. Royal Bodies, Invisible Victims 45

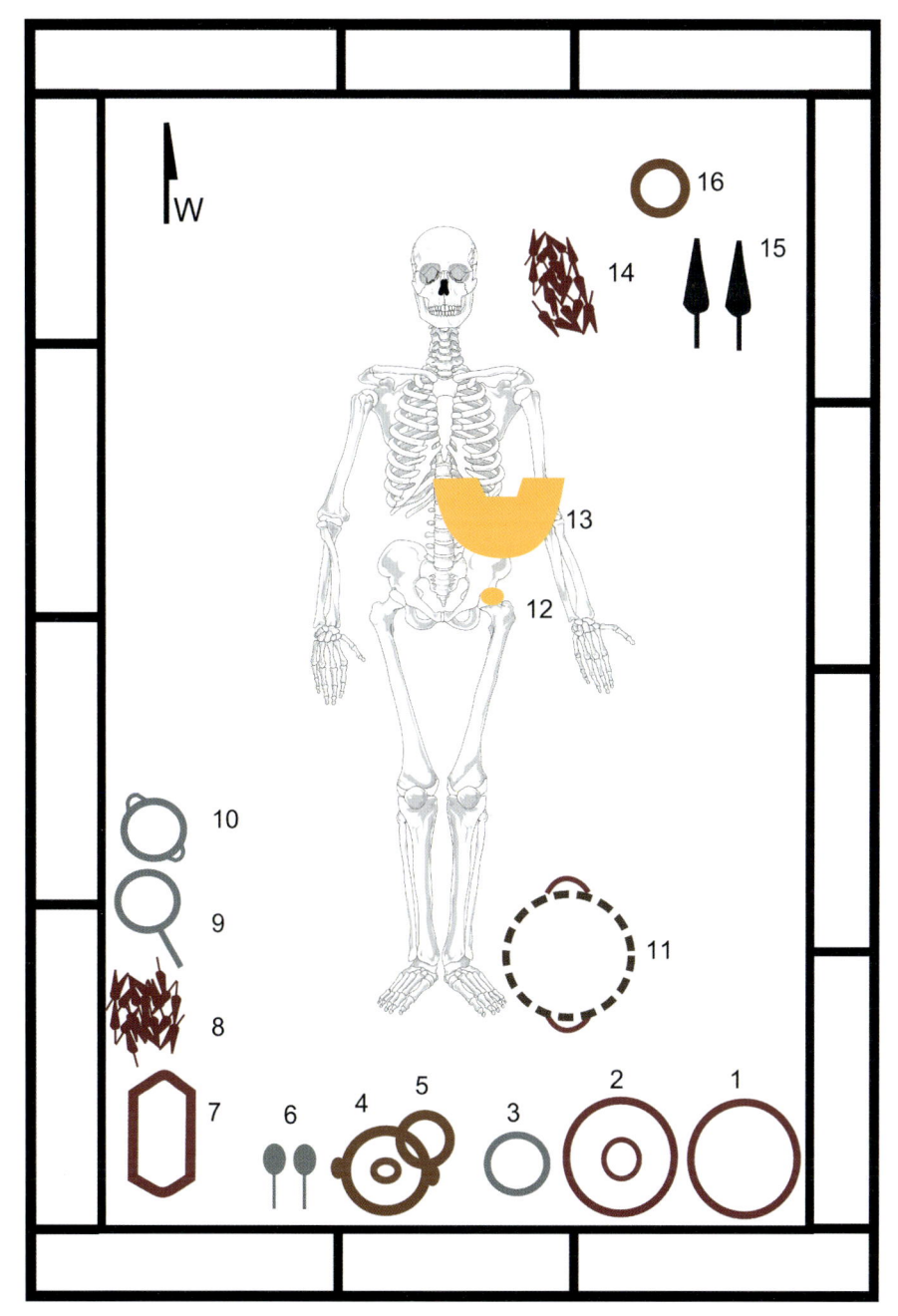

*Figure 5.4. Plan of Kaloyanovo-Chernozem Tumulus 1 – arrangement of grave goods: 1) bronze basin, 2) bronze hydria, 3) silver vessel, 4) red-figure hydria, 5) lekythos, 6) 2 silver spoons, 7) cuirass with remainders of leather belt for the quiver of arrows, 8) arrowheads, 9) silver kylix, 10) strainer, 11) wooden vessel with bronze handles, 12) gold ring with chalcedony scaraboid, 13) gold pectoral, 14) arrowheads, 15) spearheads, 16) lekythos.*

Tumulus 1 at Kaloyanovo-Chernozem. Dalboki, 150 kilometres to the east, Bashova and Golyamata Mogila at Duvanlii, all constitute ashlar-built graves, orientated east-west. Each contained the same loosely defined set of grave goods: a gold pectoral, a bronze cuirass, two spearheads, several imported drinking and serving vessels. The weaponry marks a military masculine identity. The painted decorations in Kaloyanovo-Chernozem (Kissyov 2004: Plates 19–20), and the imports from the other graves show connections with the Aegean.

Notwithstanding their similarities, these graves also had some strongly individualising elements. The architecture and many of the objects were made to order or personalised, for instance the armour, the gold pectorals with individualised designs visibly worn on the body, the artefacts with inscriptions. The rings, pectorals and grave decoration were commissioned on the basis of personal taste, and sense of group identity.

As the contrast between Malkata Mogila and Kaloyanovo-Chernozem demonstrates, there were different ways of performing masculinity in Late Iron Age Thrace, besides a military identity, and a common, but variable, language of power. We should expect that through more critical archaeological practice, future research will reveal also multiple ways of performing female and other identities.

## Conclusions

This paper presented a multi-scalar picture of gender identity, by combining a quantitative overview with case studies. This was inspired by Brumfiel's (1992) and Meskell's (2000) theoretical objections to an archaeology of identity that sidelines agents, and paints a top-down vision of society. The analysis outlined how patterns in group identity (social status, regional identity, lineage, gender among some) relate to performances of individual identity within them (e.g. through lavish ornamentation highlighting the individual body and face). With regard to gender, the review of previous research outlined the problems with perceiving different genders in the record, and hopefully laid the theoretical and methodological groundwork for more critical future research. Two core issues to address are intersectionality and inner pluralism of categories such as 'elite', 'Thracian', and 'woman'. Judging by the jewellery, weaponry, and imports, both men and women of certain wealth had access to luxury exchange networks, and were honoured with monumental tombs. However, the fact that women had prestigious burials does not entail that they had autonomy – social life often revolves around trade-offs – and we must turn to skeletal data to investigate well-being at every stage of life and across society (Brumfiel 2006: 33–4). After the deconstruction of the factors behind women's invisibility, it seems important to ask what other identities might not be visible, and why – and to take a step towards more holistic depictions of diverse communities, possibly with multiple hierarchies. Gender archaeology might be opening a new direction of inquiry into Iron Age societies so often dominated by deceptively familiar 'warrior kings'.

## Acknowledgements

This paper emerged out of my Master's dissertation completed in 2011 at the Institute of Archaeology in London, and I am grateful to Dr Corinna Riva for being an encouraging, critical and patient supervisor. Also, to Julij Emilov – for many helpful discussions. I am indebted to Dr Victoria Russeva and Dr Nelly Kondova who supplied me with Dr Slavi Cholakov's unpublished osteological studies and the permission to use them. Dr Maya Vassileva, Anastasia Cholakova, and Magdalena Stefan shared publications I did not have access to. Dr Chavdar Tzochev made useful remarks on an earlier draft. Finally, my thanks go to Dr Simon Stoddart and Dr Catalin Popa for the opportunity to participate in this stimulating conference. Any remaining errors and omissions are my own.

# 6. Mediterranean Wine and Dacian Conviviality. Ancient and Modern Myths and Archaeological Evidence

*Mariana Egri*

**Keywords:** Dacia, wine, convivial practices, identity, cultural interactions.

**The story**
It is well known that Barbarians' Bacchic excesses are a recurrent motif in ancient Greek or Roman texts, and were used in a variety of circumstances, including philosophical or political disputes. The Dacians, a conglomerate of various tribal entities inhabiting territories situated on both sides of the Carpathians and bordered by the lower Danube, the Tisza and the Prut rivers, did not escape that perspective. The Romans got in direct contact with them towards the end of the Republic, and almost instantly they were described as fierce enemies alongside other excess-driven Barbarians. However, the episode first mentioned by Strabo, in which a Dacian king named Burebista imposed a wine prohibition at the recommendation of the high priest Deceneus, brings an interesting twist to a quite common story. More precisely, Strabo (VII 3.11.C304 in Jones 1924) writes that Deceneus 'convinced the Dacians to destroy their vineyards and to abstain from wine drinking', supposedly to strengthen them morally.

King Burebista is a historical character, appearing in several ancient texts and on an inscription honouring Akornion, from Dionysopolis (Bulgaria) (Mihailov 1970: 13). He ruled roughly between 82 and 44 BC and managed to control several local tribes and a large territory between the middle and lower Danube, the north western Black Sea coast and the Carpathians. This region was incorporated into a kingdom that was perhaps of Hellenistic inspiration (Crişan 1977 is the sole comprehensive study of this period, albeit marred by ideological prejudices and exaggerations). Far less is known about the high priest Deceneus, who is only mentioned by Strabo and Jordanes, the latter writing centuries later and copying ample parts from the works of Strabo and other authors, whose texts were lost (see an analysis of all of the ancient texts in Petre 2004: 210–17). According to Strabo, Deceneus was the driving force behind most of the reforms imposed by the king.

**The interpretation**
The ways in which this short story has been interpreted over time are indisputably connected with the manner in which Dacian culture and society in general

and their religion in particular have been seen. The Dacians experienced an ever-changing fate in the history and archaeology of Romania, and politics frequently played an important role. Thus they were the corner-stone of national fabric whenever it was considered that Romanians needed their own outstanding and ethnically pure origin. On the other hand the Dacians were relegated to far less significant roles, outplayed by the Romans, when the main scope was to be seen as a cosmopolitan nation, an intrinsic part of civilised Europe. Burebista himself became a star of Romanian historiography in the 1980s, a time in which *protochronism* (the nationalist doctrine giving primacy to Romanian history) was rife. The king and his high priest were ideal characters, exceptional predecessors of the 'Great Leader' Ceaușescu. Their exploits were hyperbolised, despite the limited written or archaeological information. Still, the image of the noble and fearless Dacians has not been invented by the communist regime, but by the nationalist movement of the late 1920s and 1930s, eager to discover or create a truly Romanian myth of origin.

The Dacians' ideological avatar has been comprehensively discussed by D. Dana in his recent book about Dacian religion (Dana 2008: 293–415; see also Lockyear 2004: 34–6; Oltean 2007: 4–7). The story of the wine prohibition and of the other 'reforms' of Burebista, was part of a broader pattern. The interpretations provided by various specialists reflect their views about Dacian religion and society. Those who favoured the image of Burebista the great reformer considered the wine prohibition to be real and part of his plan to create a centralised state (Crişan 1986: 140). Others included this decision in a wider attempt to reform Dacian religion by forbidding excessive ritual wine consumption either within certain traditional institutions of the tribal aristocracy (Avram 1989: 11–13), or during the supposedly widespread communal orgiastic practices of a Bacchic nature (Oişteanu 1998: 52–8; Rustoiu 2002a: 136–7; Florea 2004: 518). On the other hand, the interpretation proposed by Zoe Petre places Strabo's story in the wider Roman historical narrative of Stoic origin, focusing on the decline of a society which would only be saved by a radical reformist action bringing moral renewal. Her analysis thus casts doubts upon its authenticity (Petre 2004: 178, 235). The question is what can archaeology bring to this debate.

## THE ARCHAEOLOGY

The evidence for imported wine consumption consists of amphorae and some related drinking implements made mostly of ceramic or metal. Their distribution and frequency, as well as the nature of the contexts in which such objects were discovered, may contribute to the identification of specific consumption patterns which characterised different communities and social groups from pre-Roman Dacia. Their inter- and intra-communal variability may suggest a differentiation of the convivial practices which were frequently used as a social and political means of constructing, reiterating, enforcing or challenging individual and group identities.

Unfortunately the dating of most contexts of discovery, structures or phases from different Dacian sites is generalised. Furthermore only a few published monographs provide consistent quantitative data regarding the finds (e.g. Ursachi 1995; Trohani 2006; in part Sîrbu 1996). In many cases the imported artefacts were taken out of their contexts of discovery, by inclusion in basic typologies or catalogues, and were mostly used to date certain phases and structures, or to illustrate the 'economic relationships' with other areas. In the case of amphorae, the unstamped examples or those fragments difficult to identify were often ignored. Some types of amphorae circulating in pre-Roman Dacia were not stamped at all, whereas others were only occasionally stamped (Garlan 1985: 240–2); the body fragments of some Pontic containers may resemble those of large jugs for less experienced archaeologists. These methodological problems may have contributed to the current presumption that the wine consumption significantly decreased between the second half of the first century BC and the Roman conquest (this hypothesis also ignores the variable capacity of different types of amphorae; see Egri 2007). The situation is slightly better in the case of relief-decorated hemispherical cups, as their presence is always highlighted in archaeological reports, articles and monographs. Thus all of the finds up to 1976 were collected and analysed in a specialist article (Vulpe & Gheorghiță 1976), that has recently been brought up to date by Irimia 30 years later (Irimia 2006). Nevertheless, these impediments detract from the absolute nature of the quantitative data included in the present article, and we must be content with a relative measure of the frequency of the main ceramic forms.

Greek colonists were the first who brought Mediterranean wine and related drinking vessels to pre-Roman Dacia, but the earliest examples are concentrated on sites from, or close to, the Black Sea coast and the mouth of the Prut and Siret rivers (Sîrbu 1983). The present analysis only considers the finds dated roughly to the last two centuries before the Roman conquest. During the late second century and the first century BC, Rhodes and south eastern Aegean were the main sources of wine, while smaller quantities came from producers from the Black Sea region. Roughly a century later, the assemblages were dominated by containers coming from the Black Sea region, followed by those from Kos and Rhodes. The changes in wine supply sources were very probably determined by the impact of the newly-established Roman military supply routes along the lower course of the Danube and in the Black Sea, and the incorporation of the Dobrogea region into the Empire (Egri 2008: 116–21). At the same time, the number of Italic Dressel 6A and Dressel 2–4 amphorae was reduced; the contexts in which they appeared were dated from the second half of the first century AD to the Roman conquest (Egri 2008: 110, fig. 6.4a). Their scarce presence in pre-Roman Dacia might be related to the increasing Roman military and commercial activities along the Sava and Drava rivers in southern Pannonia. Both types of amphorae are commonly found in civilian and military sites from this region (Egri 2007: 44–50, fig. 2, 3b, 4a; 2008: fig. 3.2, 4.4, 5.5) and occasionally they might have also reached western and south western Dacia alongside other goods (Egri 2008: 113 and 117; Rustoiu 2005: 75–81). Some merchants might have ventured eastward along the lower Sava valley, reaching the lower Danube and the Mureș River (the main waterway in Transylvania). Another hypothesis which

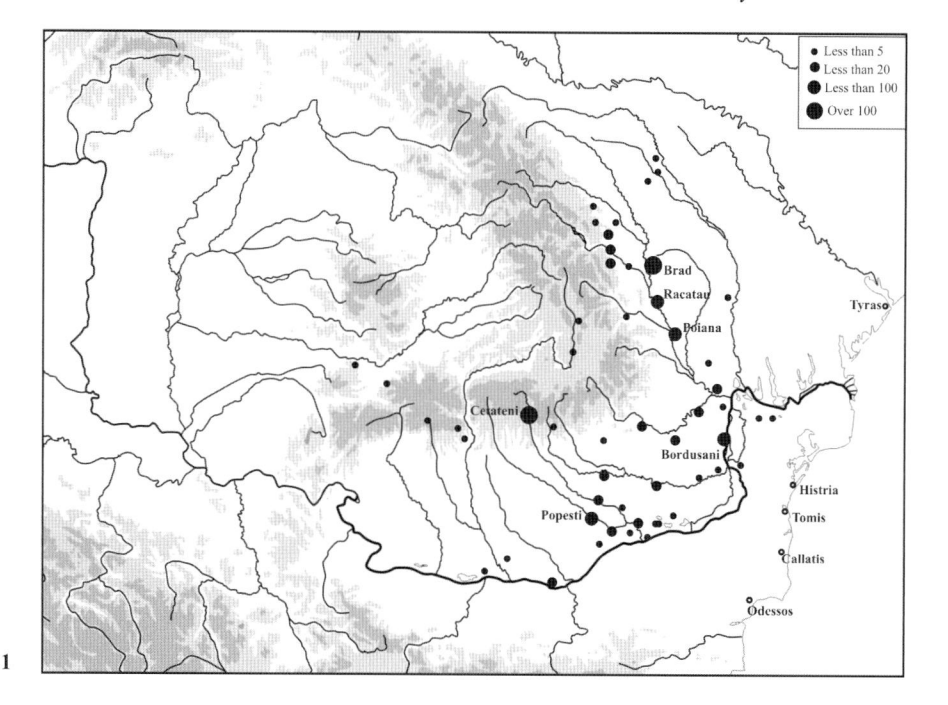

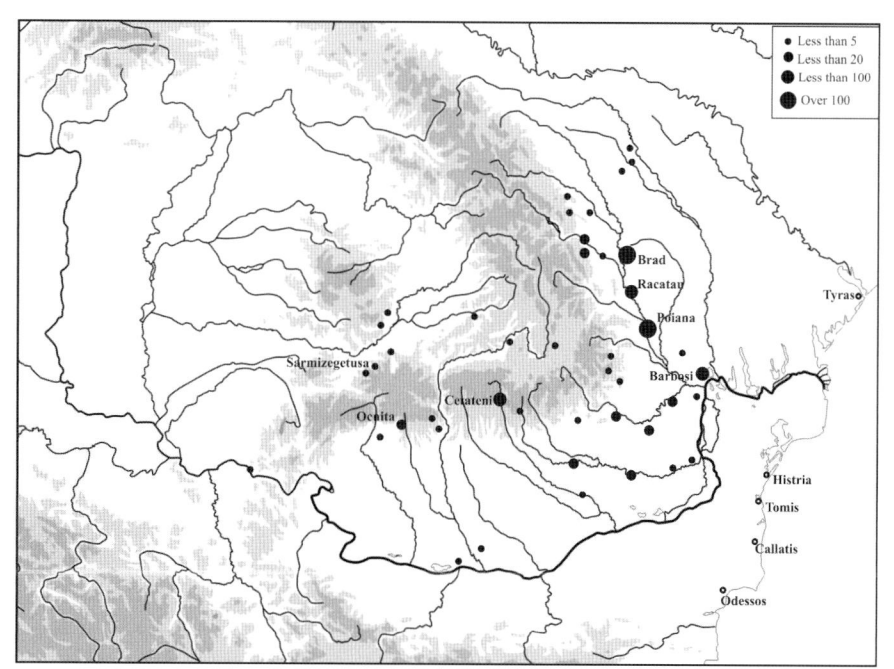

*Figure 6.1. 1. Distribution map of the amphorae dated from the late second century to the first century BC; 2. Distribution map of the amphorae dated from the first century to the beginning of the second century AD.*

needs further examination is that some of the local rulers might have received diplomatic gifts or stipends consisting of Italic wine and drinking-related implements, amongst other things, as part of their relationships with Roman power.

It is important to note that the distribution of imported amphorae is uneven, and that larger quantities were concentrated outside the Carpathians, on sites from southern Moldavia (mainly at Poiana, Brad and Răcătău) and eastern Muntenia (Bordușani, Cetățeni, Popești, Grădiștea-Brăila and Tinosu) (Fig. 6.1). It was not just the major centres of power that had political, military and commercial functions which received the material, since many smaller, even rural, settlements from the same regions provided at least a few wine containers. On the other hand, amphorae were rare in Transylvania, so it has been supposed that the wine was transferred into barrels or wineskins, in trading centres located close to the Carpathian passes (for example at Poiana or Cetățeni), and transported with carts or pack animals across the mountains. This hypothesis may be sustained by the presence of other artefacts produced outside the Carpathians, like fine tableware and jewellery, suggesting some regular exchanges between the communities living on both sides of the mountains (Andrițoiu & Rustoiu 1997: 126; Crișan 2000: 131; Rustoiu 2002a: 110–11). Still, the number of ceramic vessels imported from the Mediterranean area or produced by Dacian workshops outside the Carpathians, and related to wine drinking, is reduced in Transylvania, as it will be shown below.

The ceramic assemblages recovered from a variety of sites indicate that pitchers, cups and beakers were also imported during both periods. In the late second century and most of the first century BC, the relief-decorated hemispherical cup produced by various workshops from Greece, Asia Minor and the Black Sea region was probably the most popular drinking form (for production centres and dating see Rotroff 1982). Such vessels must have been brought over mainly by merchants from the Greek colonies on the Black Sea coast, in which large quantities of similar wares have been found (see for example the finds from Histria in Domăneanțu 2000). However, the number of imported cups is reduced in Dacian sites, which may suggest that the vessels either arrived as gifts together with other goods, or as occasional small secondary loads accompanying wine cargoes (Florea 2004: 519), rather than constituting independently traded goods in themselves.

On the contrary, indigenous imitations were found on almost every site outside the Carpathians (Fig. 6.2), including several rural settlements and some aristocratic tumulus graves (Vulpe 1976). Unfortunately, there are no fabric analyses or systematic studies of the characteristics and distribution area of any of the Dacian workshops (apart from an article by Vulpe & Gheorghiță from 1976 about the shape and decoration of the finds from Popești). Consequently, the vessels have only been identified through the presence of some moulds and wasters. The existence of some others has been presumed on the account of some specific decorative patterns (Irimia 2006: 74). Popești was most likely an important production centre, but moulds are also known from Crăsani, Poiana, Radovanu and Zimnicea (Casan-Franga 1967: fig. 5/1–5; Turcu 1976: pl. 12/1–2; Vulpe & Gheorghiță 1976: 177, pl. 11/1–6; Vulpe & Teodor 2003: 83, note 256).

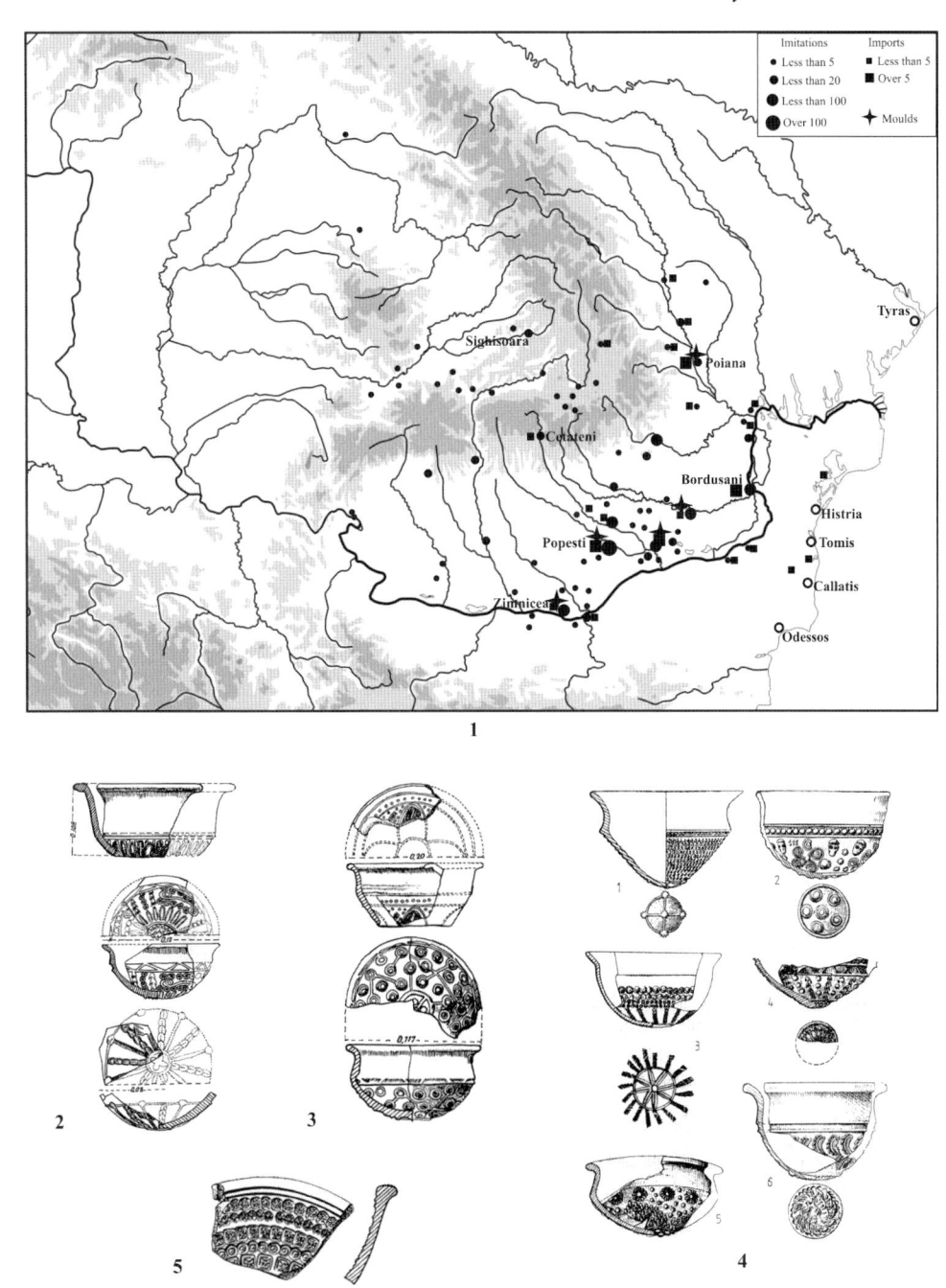

*Figure 6.2. 1. Distribution map of the relief-decorated hemispherical cups; 2–4. locally produced relief-decorated hemispherical cups (after Turcu 1976 and Preda 1986); 5. ceramic mould for relief-decorated hemispherical cups from Popeşti (after Turcu 1976).*

Several Dacian cups display a local decorative repertoire, including typical geometric, zoomorphic and anthropomorphic details, sometimes combined with vegetal elements of Mediterranean inspiration, and in certain cases entire narrative scenes are depicted (Vulpe & Gheorghiță 1976: 177–9; Conovici 1978: 175; Irimia 2006, 73; further comments about their symbolic meanings in Sîrbu & Florea 1997: 86–7, 97–8). These characteristics point to the use of certain adaptive mechanisms through which the late Hellenistic ceramic form was integrated into the local convivial practices. Some decorative motifs were also commonly used in pottery and decorative metal manufacture; a good example is the bronze punching tool discovered in the settlement at București-Cățelu Nou (Turcu 1979: 103, pl. XXXVI/2), showing a human head at its functional end, which is similar to the one depicted on a hemispherical cup from Crăsani (Conovici 1981: 574–6; for the function of the punching tool see Rustoiu 2002b: 35–6).

At the same time, imported relief-decorated hemispherical cups are missing from Transylvania (Fig. 6.2/1), whereas the number of indigenous imitations is very small, each site providing not more than one or two examples. The single exception is the fortified settlement at Sighișoara-Wietenberg, probably a transit centre on the route across the mountains from southern Moldavia, in which several cups were discovered. The existence of a local workshop, perhaps set up by potters coming from outside the Carpathians, can only be presumed because of a lack of direct archaeological evidence (Andrițoiu & Rustoiu 1997: 89). Unfortunately systematic fabric analyses have not been undertaken, but the decorative repertoire seems to be quite different from those characterising other local production sites (Irimia 2006: 74).

Other Mediterranean drinking-related forms of the same date, like pitchers, *skyphoi*, beakers and perhaps craters, also arrived in Dacia but the number of finds is reduced and they are mostly present in major trading centres from southern Moldavia and eastern Muntenia (Glodariu 1976: 17–25, table 2; Ursachi 1995: 211–23; Dupoi & Sîrbu 2001: 43; Vulpe & Teodor 2003: 89–91). The forms were sometimes copied by local potters, without achieving the popularity of relief-decorated hemispherical cups, and local products remained confined to the large fortified settlements and their surroundings (Crișan 1969: 193; Glodariu 1976: 179–96; Berciu 1981: pl. 70/5, 86/9; Morintz & Șerbănescu 1985: 27; Ursachi 1995: 188; Sîrbu *et al.* 2005: 57).

Towards the end of the first century BC, the relief-decorated hemispherical cups were replaced by other late Hellenistic drinking vessels, mainly *skyphoi* and *kantharoi* originating from Asia Minor or the Pontic region. According to a common opinion, this was a consequence of the cessation of such cup production in the eastern Mediterranean (Vulpe & Gheorghiță 1976: 182). However, the demand was covered mainly by local workshops during the first century BC, so the fate of Mediterranean workshops would have had a limited impact in Dacia. Most probably their replacement resulted from a change in local drinking habits, determined by the introduction of different vessels which accompanied the cargoes of imported wines coming mostly from the Pontic region and to a smaller extent from eastern Mediterranean. The political and economic changes of the

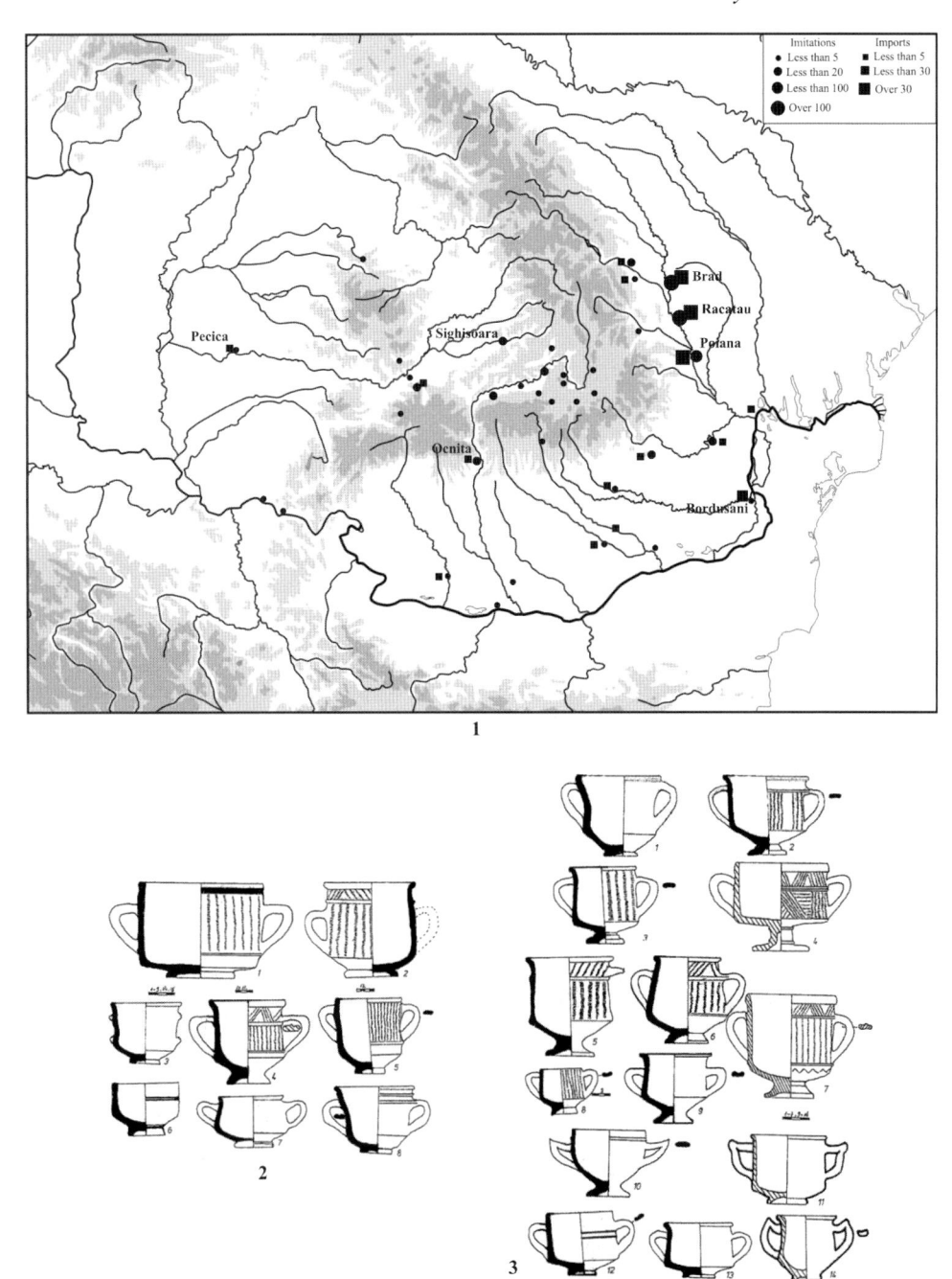

6. *Mediterranean Wine and Dacian Conviviality*　　　　55

*Figure 6.3. 1. Distribution map of the kantharoi and skyphoi; 2–3. locally produced kantharoi (after Ursachi 1995).*

early first century AD in the Eastern Mediterranean and the Black Sea further transformed the regional supply networks, leading to an increased commercial activity which also influenced the consumption patterns of the indigenous communities from outside the Carpathians (Egri 2008: 115–17, with further bibliography). Again the number of imported ceramic vessels is far larger in settlements outside the Carpathians (Fig. 6.3/1), especially in the major centres from southern Moldavia like Brad, Poiana and Răcătău. A recent study of the finds from Poiana, Răcătău and Popeşti indicates that, from a functional point of view, drinking-related forms predominated, where the *kantharoi* and *skyphoi* were the most popular and widely imitated (Popescu 2011: 11–13; see also Popescu 2006). On the other hand, only a handful of similar imported vessels are known from Transylvania, while the number of imitations is also quite reduced. Outside the Carpathians, the distribution pattern of locally produced *kantharoi*, *skyphoi* and pitchers reflected that of the imported ones, where larger settlements provided a wider range of forms and a larger number of vessels, while only a few examples come from each of the small, rural, settlements; some finds are also known from a few tumulus graves investigated at Răcătău (Căpitanu 1986: 119–20; Ursachi *et al.* 2003: fig. 3–4).

The *kantharoi* and *skyphoi* followed a broadly similar process of integration into the local ceramic repertoire of forms, using specific decorative techniques and motifs (Fig. 6.3/2–3). They were mostly painted with geometric motifs, while the original barbotine decoration was less popular, sometimes combined with painting or burnishing in a traditional manner (Florea 1998: 235–6; Popescu 2011: 12–13). More than that, the *kantharoi* were frequently integrated into local drinking sets alongside pitchers or tall beakers, where all the vessels carried a similar painted decoration, for example at Brad (Ursachi 1995: 202–04; Florea 1998: 106). Some major workshops were active in the large commercial centres in the lower Siret valley and it seems that their products circulated across wider areas, sometimes reaching settlements in southern and south eastern Transylvania (Florea 1998: 105–06; finds from Transylvania – Crişan & Ferenczi 1994: 386; Andriţoiu & Rustoiu 1997: 87; Crişan 2000: 131). On the other hand, Roman bowls, cups and small beakers were imitated by potters from the Dacian capital at *Sarmizegetusa Regia* (Grădiştea Muncelului) and these foreign forms also influenced the production of local fine tableware towards the end of the first century AD (Florea 1993: 99 and 108, fig. 1–3; Florea 1994: 55, fig. 3/1–5).

During the first century BC, in contrast to the scarcity of imported or locally made ceramic drinking-related vessels, many bronze and silver vessels are concentrated in Transylvania (Fig. 6.4/1), mostly in fortresses and fortified settlements, whereas the number of similar finds is smaller outside the Carpathians (Egri 2008: 108, fig. 6.3). Some of these vessels were recovered from hoards, while a single piece (*a situla*) is known from a funerary context, the second tumulus at Cugir. Aside from a small group of finds (some silver cups and perhaps the fragmentary crater from Costeşti) coming from eastern Mediterranean, many bronze vessels were most likely produced in workshops from the Italic Peninsula (Rustoiu 2005: 73–9). The *situla* is the most popular form, with 21 typologically identified

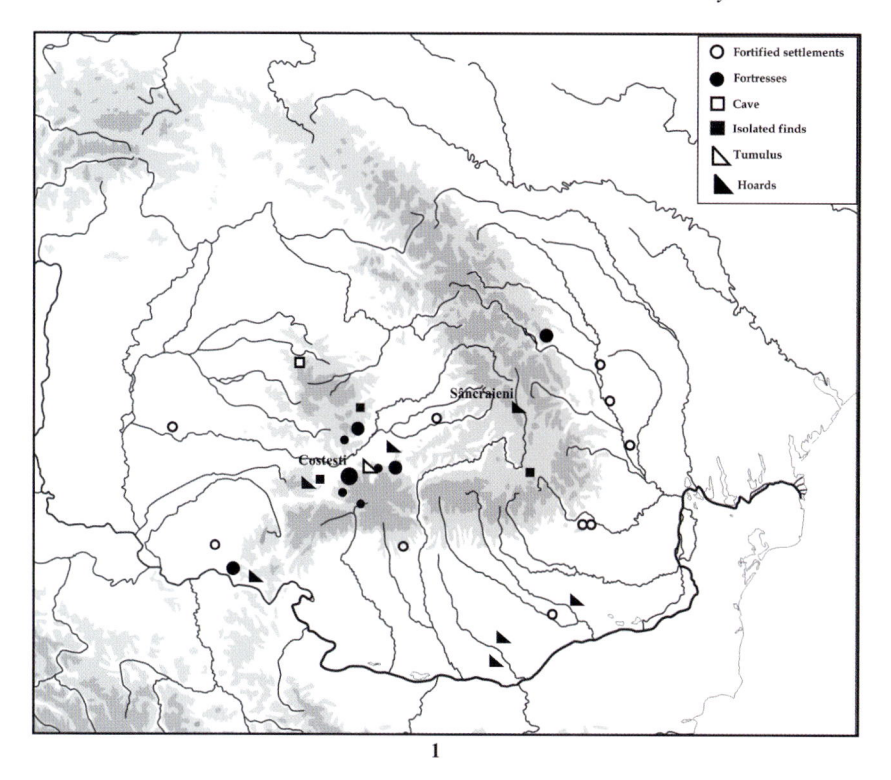

6. *Mediterranean Wine and Dacian Conviviality* 57

*Figure 6.4. 1. Distribution map of the metal vessels (after Rustoiu 2005 with updates); 2–4. some of the silver cups and kantharoi from Sâncrăieni (after Popescu 1958); 5. the hoard from Lupu (photo A. Rustoiu).*

examples, not to mention other poorly preserved fragments from different sites which cannot be ascribed to a precise type, followed by beakers and *simpula*. Eight silver *kantharoi* dated to the Late Republican or early Augustan period have been found in a hoard at Sâncrăieni, in eastern Transylvania, together with a group of seven silver conical or hemispherical cups and jewellery and coins (Popescu 1958; the hoard's dating is still debated, for the history of discovery see Crişan 2000: 69 and 142–3, pl. 119–22) (Fig. 6.4/2–4).

A key question is the way in which the imported metal vessels were integrated into Dacian conviviality, especially in Transylvania, and whether their adoption implied a regular consumption of wine. Although the most popular forms were similar to those commonly included in the so-called north Italic drinking set of the late Republican period (Piana Agostinetti & Priuli 1985; Bolla 1991: 147–9), not a single assemblage of this kind has been found in Dacia. The very small number of aristocratic graves from Transylvania may partially explain their absence (the total number of graves from the entire pre-Roman Dacia is also very small, see Babeş 1988), given that in northern Italy and the Scordiscian area metal drinking sets have been usually discovered in funerary contexts. The two, already-mentioned, distinct drinking sets, consisting of silver *kantharoi* and conical or hemispherical cups respectively, discovered at Sâncrăieni, are the only examples from pre-Roman Dacia. Previous analyses considered that they belonged to a chieftain from the nearby fortress at Jigodin (for the history of discovery see Crişan 2000: 69–71), but a very recent re-examination of the entire inventory and of its context of discovery has concluded that they are part of a commemorative ritual related to a priestess (Egri & Rustoiu forthcoming). On the other hand some pairs of vessels consisting of a beaker or a *situla* and a cup, recovered from a series of hoards (Bucureşti-Herăstrău, Lupu and Vedea), have been interpreted as simplified drinking sets derived from the north Italic examples of the Late Republican period (Spânu 2002: 115–20). However, in these cases, the metal vessels are always associated with silver jewellery sets belonging to a single person, most probably a priestess according to the iconography of certain accompanying *phalerae*, so these vessels might have had ritual functions (Rustoiu 2005: 72; Egri & Rustoiu forthcoming). These local sets combine an Italic form (a beaker or a *situla* made of bronze) with another vessel, usually made of silver, the hemispherical or conical cup frequently encountered in the Balkans and the territory between the Danube and the Carpathians (Glodariu & Moga 1994: 42–3).

## Discussion

Before discussing archaeological evidence, it has to be mentioned that alcoholic beverages in general, and wine in particular, played a particular role in a variety of activities (religious or lay, public or private) which aimed to maintain social cohesion at a familial, group or community level. At the same time a variety of drinking practices and related paraphernalia were carefully designed to construct, perform, transform or challenge real or imagined identities within these activities (see Dietler 2006: 235–7 for further comments). As a consequence there were a wide variety of convivial norms and habits related mainly to the ways in which local social structures and mechanisms were functioning, even if economic, geographic or climatic factors cannot be ignored.

Returning to the data already discussed, a series of observations can be made by summarising the patterns interpretable from the analysis of archaeological evidence. Several Dacian communities manifested an early and constant interest in Mediterranean wine and some drinking-related implements, but there were important differences between the consumption patterns in Transylvania and outside the Carpathians. Many communities from eastern and south eastern Dacia had the advantage of an early direct access to such goods because of their geographical proximity and the frequent contacts with Greek colonies on the north western Black Sea coast. Furthermore, some botanical remains and several specific tools suggest the existence of local viticulture (Suciu 2001: 171; Florea 2004: 519, note 20). The apparently widespread presence of the local imitations of early Rhodian and Koan amphorae outside the Carpathians was considered evidence for a significant local wine market, but it may also be an indicator of the higher appreciation of the imported wine. As a consequence the local producers might have tried to pass off their wine as foreign using a suggestive container (for the imitated forms see Glodariu 1976: 74–7 and 159–63, but some amphorae listed as locally-produced on the account of a coarse fabric may be imports; the author also does not consider the relatively frequent use of illegible or figurative stamps (pl. 18–19) as an attempt to pass local wines as Mediterranean; furthermore there are no potter's marks; consequently, this approach does not provide an alternative explanation).

The constant presence of imported amphorae indicates that the wine was regularly included in the exchanges between Greek colonies and Dacian communities, while drinking vessels were only occasionally imported, most probably as secondary loads. The widespread popularity of the local imitations of certain foreign drinking vessels may suggest that these ceramic forms were rapidly adopted outside the Carpathians. Furthermore, their integration into the indigenous convivial practices involved a process of appropriation using the traditional decorative repertoire and techniques. The frequent presence of amphorae, as well as the systematic imitation of Mediterranean drinking vessels, points to a regular wine consumption at both familial and community levels, and probably also during certain rituals (Florea 2004: 522; Egri 2008: 107–08). The fragments of imported amphorae, usually scattered over the few aristocratic tumulus graves from eastern Muntenia and southern Moldavia, amongst other remains of the funerary feast, underlines the fact that the wine itself was not considered a marker of status, but merely an element of the ritual, and perhaps only its conspicuous consumption was a matter of prestige and a field for social competition. At Conţeşti-Lacul lui Bârcă, in south eastern Dacia, archaeological evidence indicates that the imported wine was also used in some indigenous rituals that involved the communal consumption of large quantities of food and alcoholic beverages (Vulpe & Popescu 1976).

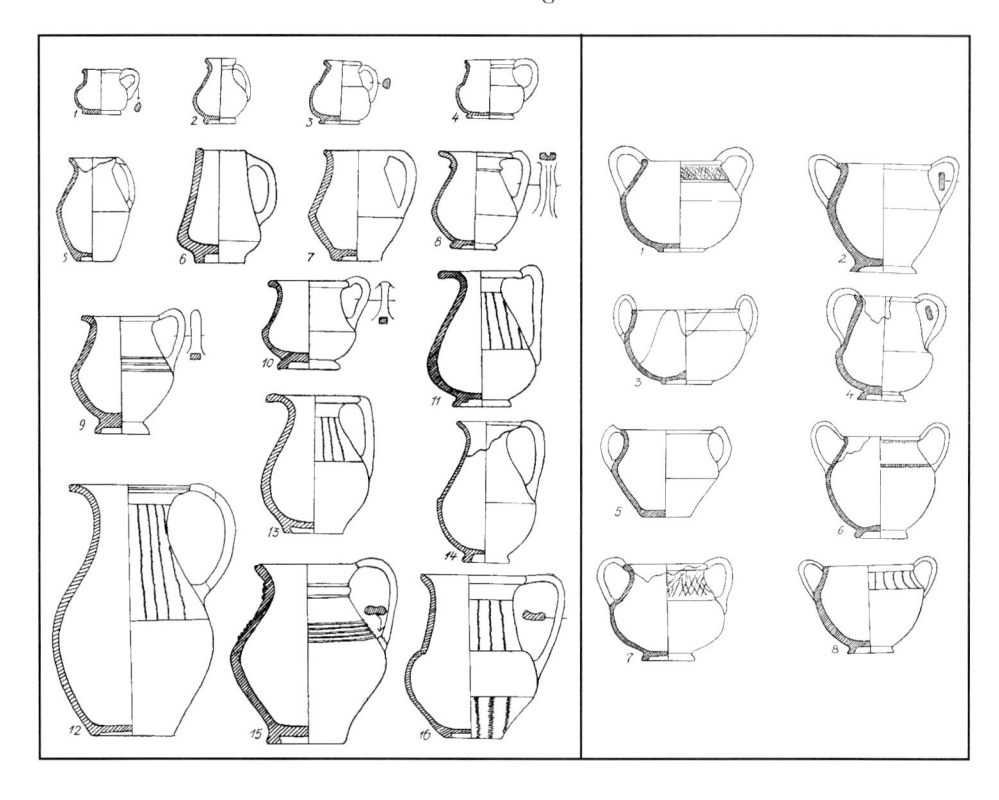

*Figure 6.5. Beakers with one or two handles discovered in different Transylvanian sites (after Crişan 1969).*

On the other hand, the range and distribution of imported amphorae and drinking-related vessels and of their imitations in Transylvania suggest different consumption patterns, although there is a similar preference for feasting-related goods. It is important to note that these communities lacked a direct access to Mediterranean sources, so the wine and other associated implements probably came mainly through some well-positioned centres across the Carpathians. At the same time, the distribution of late Republican bronze vessels points to two other different routes, one starting from the eastern Adriatic and crossing Dalmatia and the western Balkans before reaching the Sava and the lower Danube, and another along the Via Egnatia and the Morava valley. Octavian's Illyrian campaigns at the end of the first century BC opened another route, which connected Aquileia and the south eastern Alpine region with the lower Danube along the Sava valley (Rustoiu 2005: 75–81, fig. 18 and 21). As mentioned above, the opening of this route might have contributed to an increasing range of interactions and flow of goods between Transylvania and the Roman world.

The scarce presence of imported amphorae and the absence of any archaeological traces indicating local wine production, together with a predominance of different drinking vessels (mainly ovoid or bi-conical beakers with one or two handles, see Crişan 1969: 176–8, pl. LXVIII–LXXI) (Fig. 6.5), may suggest a limited interest in wine. The local beakers usually have a larger capacity, so perhaps most of the people were accustomed to other beverages that had a lower alcohol content, for example beer, mead or cider, for which the required raw materials were locally available (Florea 2004: 518–19; see also Suciu 2001: 162 and 172). The identified patterns may suggest that the wine consumption was limited and perhaps controlled, where the imported alcoholic beverage was only accessible to some groups and individuals within the communities from Transylvania.

A similar socially differentiated consumption of imported wine was identified in Early Iron Age Gaul, within the local communities without direct access to Mediterranean sources from the so-called Western Hallstatt region (the upper Rhône-Saône valley in Burgundy, southern Germany and Switzerland). They were characterised by a variable degree of political centralisation and a well-defined social hierarchy, so the convivial practices were used as powerful social and political instruments. The imported wine and other related goods were regarded as elite-only products, their use aiming to underline and enforce a differentiated status of the consumers, usually members of the warlike elites (Dietler 1990: 384–6; 1996: 112–15). Apart from that, a feasting hierarchy which seems to reflect the social hierarchy was identified in certain Late Iron Age communities from Gaul (Poux 2004: 222–6, fig. 124–25) and the Scordiscian area (Egri 2008: 87–8, fig. 5.4b; Egri & Rustoiu 2008: 84–5, fig. 3). In these cases, alcoholic beverages and food (mostly meat) were distributed by higher-status 'organisers' to the participants, and were consumed according to certain rules and using specific implements. These convivial practices were designed to contribute actively to the construction of particular individual and group identities, while supporting the social cohesion at different levels.

Within Dacian society from Transylvania of the first century BC, dominated by a warlike aristocracy that also had religious functions (Rustoiu 2002a: 21–33; Petre 2004: 253–7; Florea 2006: 6–7), the imported wine was probably consumed only during special feasts, or it was used in ritual practices. The imported amphorae and drinking vessels, as well as their imitations, have been found almost exclusively in fortresses, large trading centres and sanctuaries, suggesting an elite-oriented distribution, so the question is whether the access to such goods was under direct royal control. It seems that the consumers were almost exclusively members of the local warlike and religious elites, and perhaps the symbolic use of wine, a powerful psychoactive agent, was meant not only to differentiate this group socially, but also to enforce the personal bonds between the king and his close followers (Egri 2008: 119–20).

The distribution of imported bronze vessels is similar to that of the ceramic wine-related goods, albeit in smaller numbers than for the ceramic examples, so they might also have played an important role in these practices. An outstanding example is the already mentioned hoard from Sâncrăieni, consisting of 15 different silver drinking vessels, most likely used in a particular convivial ritual in which a deceased priestess (whose specific 'costume' was buried alongside the vessels) was commemorated by a number of participating individuals who had access to such goods and might have shared a particular social status or function (Egri & Rustoiu forthcoming). On the other hand a bronze *situla* was placed in the second tumulus at Cugir, belonging to a warrior, alongside an unusually large 'fruit-bowl' (broken on top of the grave) probably after being used in the funerary feast (Crişan 1980: 82). The special status-related role ascribed to the metal vessels may also explain the limited interest in imported ceramic ware and their Dacian imitations identified in Transylvania.

At the same time, the structure of the local drinking sets, frequently combining vessels of different origins or hybrid ware, as well as the marked preference for certain forms, underlines the existence of different local convivial practices in Transylvania and outside the Carpathians, with different meanings and scopes. The regular and systematic process of selection carried out by local consumers and the mechanisms of appropriation through which the foreign forms were integrated into the local ceramic repertoires indicate that these practices were also unrelated to the ones from eastern Mediterranean or northern Italy.

In this context what can be said about the episode described by Strabo? Perhaps Burebista also wanted to impose these restrictions outside the Carpathians, amongst other actions aimed at establishing a centrally controlled kingdom. It is difficult to say if he was successful, even for a short period, since the generalised dating of certain phases or contexts from sites outside the Carpathians and the lack of reliable quantitative data hamper the identification of fluctuations in the consumption of imported wine during his rule. Still, it is important to note that the distribution patterns remained differentiated in Transylvania and outside the Carpathians during the first century AD, and the communities from the latter area continued to consume significant quantities of imported wine. The political structure created by Burebista, mostly through the force of arms did not survive his assassination, since that same political structure was undermined by the centrifugal tendencies of the local chieftains. The core part of Transylvania remained a particular entity probably with distinct social-political and religious structures, whereas the territories outside the Carpathians experienced a different evolution, directly related to the ways in which the local political entities were organised. At least some of the latter gradually developed economic and even political relationships with the rising Roman power which reached the lower Danube in the same period (Egri 2008: 116–18).

This is precisely the time when Strabo wrote his accounts and the extraordinary military events which characterised the last decades before Christ were still vivid in the minds of the period. The sudden menace of a new rising Barbarian power close to the Roman borders might have had an impact, making the Dacians and their sometimes peculiar habits a fashionable subject for moral writings.

## Acknowledgements

Some of the documentation for this article was carried out during the tenure of Mellon Fellowship at the American School of Classical Studies at Athens (Greece) in January–April 2011, for which I would like to thank the Andrew W. Mellon Foundation. I am also thankful to Aurel Rustoiu and Gelu Florea for fruitful discussions of various themes tackled in this article.

# 7. Sarmizegetusa Regia – the Identity of a Royal Site?

*Gelu Florea*

**Keywords:** Sarmizegetusa Regia, Late Iron Age, identity, rituals, art.

## The argument

The site at Sarmizegetusa Regia (modern Grădiştea de Munte, Hunedoara County, Romania) displays some characteristics and urban functions unknown in other similar indigenous settlements from the region. In this respect it is comparable (albeit not identical) to those of some central – western European oppida (Florea 2011: 173–5). The substantial monumental size of the settlement in spite of an unwelcoming landscape, the focus on large-scale iron exploitation and manufacturing, the purchase of grain through an exchange network established with the productive, lowland, agricultural areas, as well as the importance of ritual activities, indicate a distinctive profile of the local community at the end of the Late Iron Age. Furthermore, current data suggest that the civilian settlement developed rapidly, mainly in the first century AD, without much preceding activity, focused on sacred areas.

Peter Wells notes that in the Iron Age, when large town-like communities emerged they tended to develop their own distinctive identity, which can be revealed through a comprehensive analysis of archaeological evidence. Sometimes these particular, assumed features seem to be a reaction against the tendencies of cultural uniformity, commonly encountered towards the end of the Iron Age (Wells 1998: 260–1). Sarmizegetusa was one such example of the construction of a distinctive identity, using bold, outstanding means, highly visible and relevant amongst the local centres of power. This community asserted and reiterated a prestigious status in a region in which the control of resources and the legitimacy of authority became important (Lockyear 2004: 70).

## The archaeology of the site

The site stands in the mountains, at over 1000 metres above sea level, at the margin of an area densely inhabited in the Late Iron Age, south of the Mures River, which crosses Transylvania from east to west. Its valley seems to have been the most important natural access into the region, since archaeological surveys and excavations have recovered a large number of finds from all periods.

Information about the ruins of a lost city, hidden in the woodlands up in the mountains go back to the beginning of the nineteenth century, and became more and more frequent, particularly once some hoards were found by the local people. A gold rush developed amongst the local peasantry to such an extent that the authorities had to take control of the situation and send in the military. The intention of the authorities was also to dig for gold, but at least they recorded most of their finds and some of their observations. More and more data accumulated gradually, about the monuments and artefacts found on the mountain, and in other locations within an approximately 20 kilometres radius. Most of them were identified as dating back to the Late Iron Age, and also as being related to the Dacian Kingdom of Decebalus, conquered in 106 AD by the Roman emperor Trajan, after two wars.

Systematic archaeological excavations, starting in the 1920s and carried out ever since, have revealed a complex and dense occupation of the area: hillforts with limestone block walls (using an architectural technique surprisingly similar to late Hellenistic masonry), villages, hamlets and scattered farmsteads perfectly adapted to the highland landscape. The results of the excavations and of extensive field survey coalesced to form a general opinion of the integration of most of these sites into part of a system of hierarchical occupation in the Late Iron Age. The interpretative perspective of Romanian archaeology was culture-historical, and so the finds were linked to the discussion in the written sources of a Dacian Kingdom, and its conflict with the Roman empire (Lockyear 2004: 35). From this perspective, the site of Grădiștea de Munte (Hunedoara county) was identified with Sarmizegetusa (*Basileion*, or in Latin transcription *Regia*), the central place of the realm of Decebalus, or/and with *Kogaionon* – 'the Sacred Mountain' of the Dacian religion, as mentioned by Strabo. (Daicoviciu *et al.* 1989: 230)

The site (referred to here as Sarmizegetusa), located at the foot of a mountain bordered by two streams, remains the largest known Late Iron Age settlement in Romania. The recently completed site survey, undertaken over a period of several years, has revealed its real dimensions: its main axis along the ridge extends to some 5.5 kilometres, and comprises more than 250 artificial terraces (covering altogether more than 400 hectares) which were presumably all once inhabited. It is clear that the eastern and principally the southern slopes of the mountain were preferentially occupied because of the harsh, cold, wet climate where snow can persist for several months.

Sarmizegetusa seems to be organised in three distinct functional parts. A fortress was built on the highest part of the landscape (at 1000 metres) from limestone blocks to enclose a defended area of one hectare that dominated the surrounding area. The 'sacred area' (i.e. a ceremonial centre) was placed close to the fortress and consists of several circular and rectangular temples, including a round andesite rock altar (seven metres in diameter). All these buildings (some of them multi-phase) were constructed on two large terraces, over a surface area of more than two and a half hectares, and supported by massive stone walls. The mapping of the site revealed that the undefended civilian settlement lay on terraces, of variable dimensions, scattered, or organised in clusters on the slopes of the mountain. Some of them were excavated and a number of timber or wattle-and-daub buildings (dwellings, workshops etc.) were uncovered.

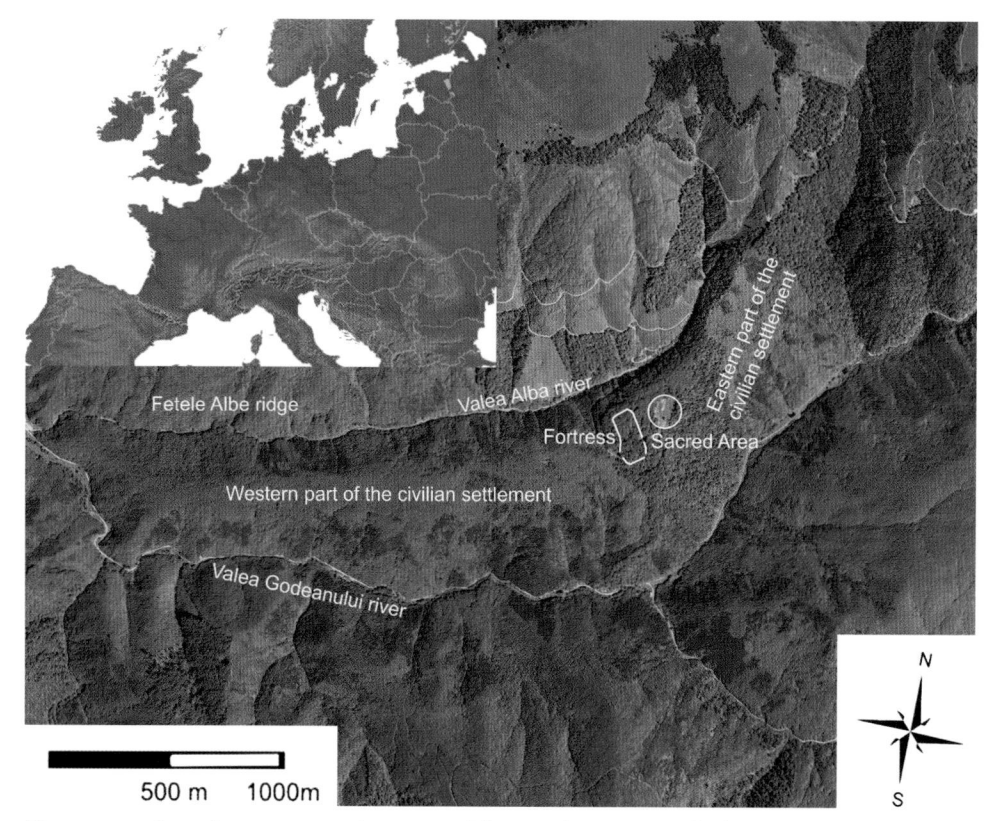

## 7. Sarmizegetusa Regia – the Identity of a Royal Site? 65

*Figure 7.1. Sarmizegetusa Regia. Map of the site (I. Rus, I. Glodariu, R. Mateescu).*

The three parts of the site continue without interruption, and seem to be connected by roads: previous excavations uncovered some sort of a 'main road' that followed the ridge of the mountain, passing through the civilian settlement. Some other secondary, smaller routeways (paved with local stones) were also found in different parts of the site (for instance on terrace VIII, situated just above the 'sacred area', and also near the so called 'western gate' of the Roman extension of the fortress).

We are far from knowing the detailed history of the beginnings of the settlement, since only between five and eight per cent of the entire site has been excavated. The long history of excavation since the 1920s has given rise to another problem: many records of the stratigraphy are missing or unreliable. The 'sacred area' has been particularly affected by this issue. Today, there are many new trial excavations, but the recovery of the earlier data is currently an almost impossible task. The general chronology of the site from the first century BC to 106 AD, followed by a short Roman occupation, probably until the beginning of Hadrian's reign, can, however, be confirmed, although plans to refine this chronology remain the major priority.

## WAS THERE A SITE IDENTITY?

A particular feature of this site derives from comparison with the similarly dated sites in the same region and further afield, along lines of size and internal organisation, as well as of the quantity and character of certain recovered artefacts. Most archaeologists who have analysed Sarmizegetusa have agreed that there is a notable difference between the character of the site and that of other contemporary sites from the same region. The recent fieldwork confirms the surprising dimensions of the settlement and introduces new arguments about its structure, which was organised in complementary functional parts. The settlement seems to be structured around a central zone, where the fortress and the sacred area were mainly located. The sacred area is notable for its considerable monumentality and complexity, making it a veritable ceremonial and religious centre.

Although fortresses and upland settlements are common in the region, the location of Sarmizegetusa, at some remove from communication routes, in quite a hostile environment, suggests that criteria other than the economic or strategic determined the selection of this place. It is highly probable that religious motives were taken into consideration when the location was selected, even if access to reasonably rich iron sources may have been a secondary consideration. It is almost certain that for this reason the 'sacred area' is the most important sector of the site. This is where the most complex stratigraphy has been found, and the monumental proportions of these elaborate buildings seem to have been the main concern of the building project which continued over the course of more than a century, starting sometime in the first century BC).

One of the oldest temples known in Sarmizegetusa, which was rebuilt at least three times, was identified in a layer some four and a half metres deep. The second reconstruction, the most elaborate one, was dated by a coin issued by Emperor Claudius. An earlier limestone temple was identified beneath the largest andesite stone temple in the 'sacred area' and this was apparently still unfinished in 106 AD. The dimensions and complexity of the area are unique and the successive rebuilding of some temples on the same locations demonstrates a continuation of ritual activities during the course of at least a century (Glodariu *et al.* 1996: 109–30).

The construction of the two large terraces of the religious centre, sustained by massive walls, and the sourcing of limestone and andesite stone required by these works from distant quarries point to an outstanding level of collective effort invested in the construction of some structures of important local and regional significance.

Although other contemporary centres also had sanctuaries, the 'sacred area' of Sarmizegetusa is the most complex display of power and prestige. Such a project was meant not only to demonstrate the authority and power, but also the external connections, of the elite. The location of these buildings, the layout of the entrances and the processional road leading to this 'sacred area' indicate an organisation of the ceremonial space as a theatre for public rituals. These architectural features created a unique appearance for Sarmizegetusa in the regional landscape.

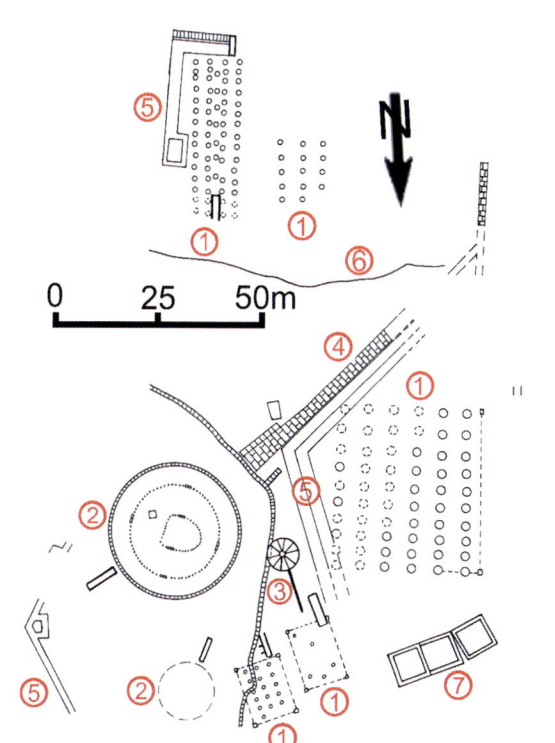

1. rectangular temples
2. round temples
3. the andesite altar
4. processional way
5. supporting walls
6. spring
7. other buildings

*Figure 7.2. Sarmizegetusa Regia. Map of the "sacred area" (after Glodariu et al. 1996, photo R. Mateescu).*

The whole effect is a perfect example of the blending of landscape and monumental architecture into a conscious and emphatic reinforcement of the elite's legitimacy and prominent position in society. Furthermore, none of the religious monuments escaped the attention of the Roman conquest. The destruction of the ceremonial and religious centre, representative as it was of the identity of the Dacian Kingdom's elites, was a deliberate, symbolic action which underlined the definitive termination of a particular ideology (Lockyear 2004: 70; Florea & Pupeza 2008: 290–5).

The civilian settlement was the largest sector of the site, and also the least excavated, because of its size. On current evidence, there was no occupation earlier than the first century AD, and in my opinion a politically orchestrated growth of the civilian settlement is more plausible than a natural (spontaneous) development, in what is a rather inhospitable environment. The presence of a 'sacred mountain' (suggested by the first temples in the 'sacred area') probably attracted the elites in their search for legitimacy. The monumental construction project, as well as the richness of the local iron ore deposits, might have additionally mobilised local population to settle there (Florea 2011: 119)

The domestic architecture, as much as it is currently understood after limited investigation, displays a number of specific features. Most of the earlier excavations focused on the inhabited terraces closer to the central area. More recently, another sector, 1.5 kilometres distant from the sacred area, has been investigated, to allow comparison of features and artefact assemblages from the two different areas of the site. Some early observations, after limited study, seem to suggest that the structures and pottery assemblages are very similar. For instance, the forms of pottery (storage jars and table ware) are almost identical to those found on terrace VII, which is close to the ceremonial centre. The same *graffiti,* using Greek letters or other signs of uncertain type, were identified on some of these wares, while the iron tools are also similar. In 2011, a terracotta water supply pipe, similar to those already known from the central area of the settlement, was found in the immediate vicinity of the remote terraces from the north-eastern side of the mountain. These observations suggest that there was little functional difference between the two areas and that living areas really covered the full area of the site.

The size and shape of the Late Iron Age houses found in Sarmizegetusa also differ from those at contemporary sites. Firstly, the lack of sunken featured buildings, which are quite frequent in other sites, even in other Alpine regions (in Eastern Transylvania, for instance), is notable. Most of the dwellings have either discontinuous stone foundations and timber walls, or wattle-and-daub walls, supported by posts. Their plan is either rectangular, with one or several rooms, or round or polygonal, with one or two concentric rooms. Most of them are unusually large (between 28 and 122 metres square), much larger than most known from other Late Iron Age sites. It is likely that some of the largest known civilian buildings might have had a public use, as might be case with a circular example where a unique vessel inscribed with the names DECEBALVS and SCORILO (possibly two Dacian royal names) was found (Suciu 2000: 41).

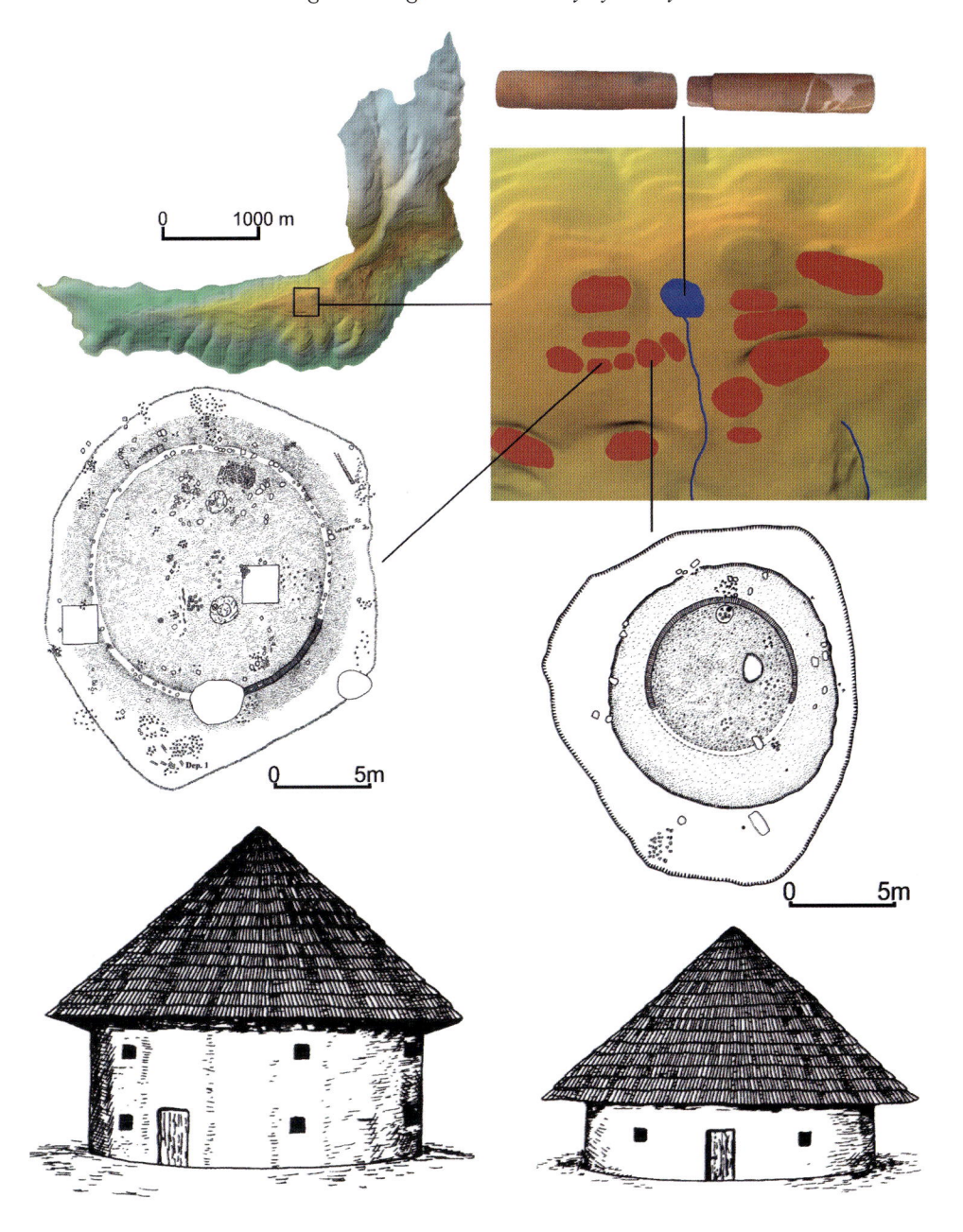

*Figure 7.3. Sarmizegetusa Regia. Map of a cluster of inhabited terraces in the central area of the site, and some finds: dwellings (plans and reconstructions) and terracotta water supply pipes (I. Rus, R. Mateescu).*

The round and polygonal house plans seem to be specific to Sarmizegetusa and its surrounding area, since only two or three examples are known from elsewhere. These might symbolise the individual status, or the social structure of individuals within this very distinctive community (Wason 1994: 136), but it might also be an expression of collective identity. Similarity can be the sign of collective identity, but similarity cannot be recognised without simultaneously evoking difference (Jenkins 2008: 102, 145). Even though only a small number of dwellings and annexes from the civilian settlement have been investigated relative to its surface area, the apparent structure and functional complexity are remarkable and suggest a rather sophisticated social structure. The material culture also points to a higher status and conspicuous consumption of the occupants.

### IDENTITY THROUGH WRITING

Several types of small inscriptions have been found in different contexts at Sarmizegetusa, showing an unexpected popularity of the use of written signs. Greek (or Latin) letters and some few other unidentified signs were carved on several dozens of limestone wall blocks especially from the 'sacred area'. Most of them have been interpreted as masonry or quarry signs, and as potential proof of the presence of Mediterranean architects and engineers who were somehow involved in the building project. These finds are not uncommon in other Late Iron Age fortresses of the region, within a 40 kilometre radius, but are more frequent at Sarmizegetusa (Glodariu 1997: 74–8). Pottery *graffiti* (with already more than 50 examples) also seem to have been very popular among the inhabitants of the settlement. These were found in various contexts all over the site (in dwellings, ironsmith workshops etc.) and scratched especially on table ware and on some storage jars. The forms include monograms, Greek letters and other signs that are hard to recognise or interpret. Although such finds occur every now and then in other Late Iron Age sites, they seem to be relatively common at Sarmizegetusa, showing the higher prevalence of members of the community with the habit of writing. The presence among the locals of at least one Roman, before the conquest, is indicated by his name (*tria nomina*) inscribed on the bottom of an indigenous coarseware bowl (Florea 2001: 183–5). This might be only a hint, among others, of a more open and cosmopolitan milieu than one would expect in a Late Iron Age settlement high up in the mountains of southern Transylvania.

The most spectacular find of this kind is still the huge ceramic vessel found in the largest polygonal building known in the civilian settlement. Unique in its shape, it was stamped four times around its rim, with two Dacian names: DECEBALVS/and/PER SCORILO. Most scholars interpreted this inscription as a reference to the last king of the Dacians, and, perhaps his descent from Scorilo, another royal name according to some ancient written sources (Glodariu 2001: 779).

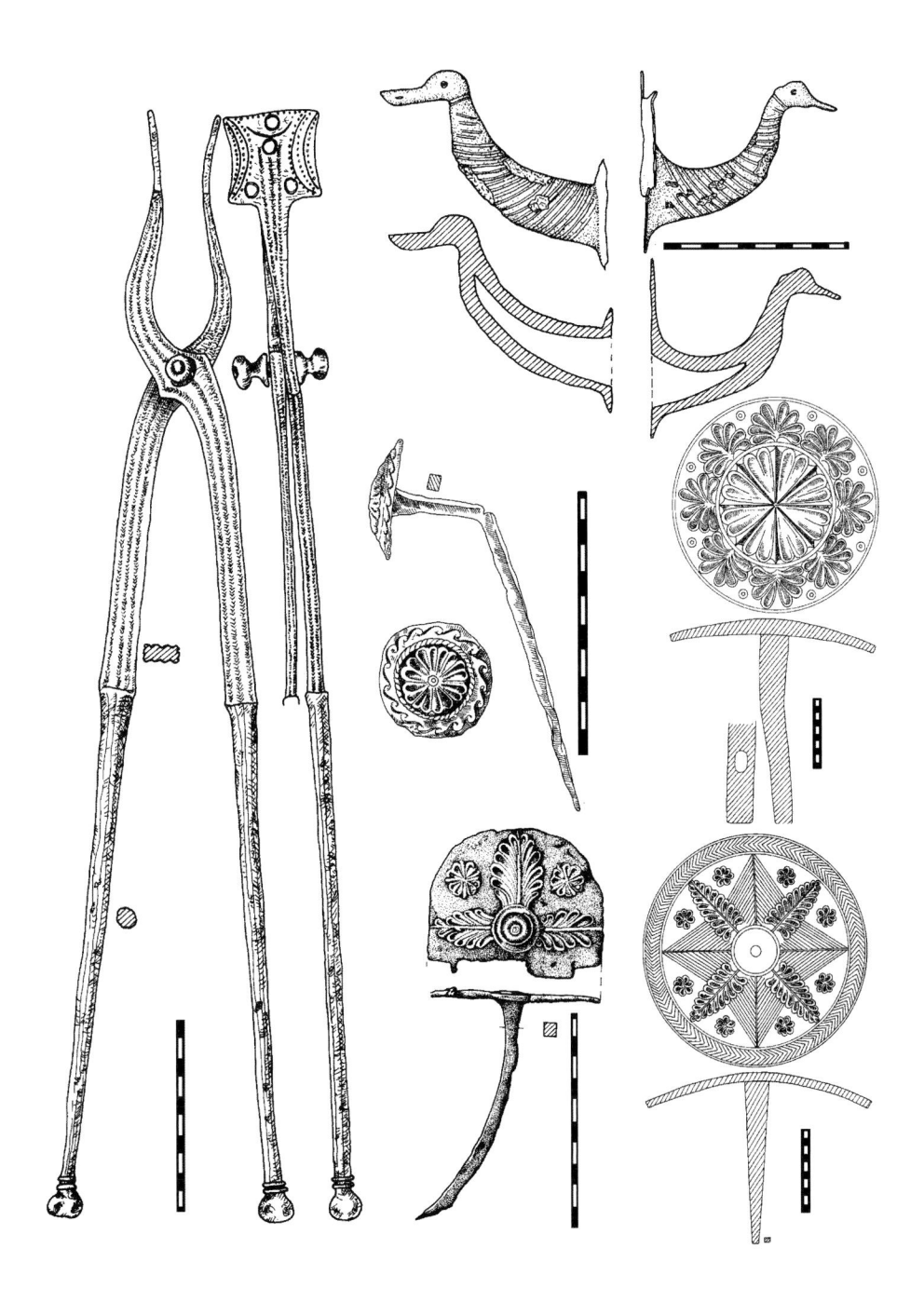

7. *Sarmizegetusa Regia – the Identity of a Royal Site?*   71

*Figure 7.4. Sarmizegetusa Regia. Decorated iron artefacts (after Glodariu & Iaroslavschi 1979).*

## ART AS AN EXPRESSION OF IDENTITY

One of the most important aspects of the site is the enormous quantity of iron artefacts found in different contexts (and at least two large forges excavated in two different parts of the site, accompanied by tool and bloom hoards spread all over the settlement etc.). Several huge iron anvils, which could also be direct proof of metal working, were retrieved by archaeologists after being discarded by treasure hunters in different spots within the civilian settlement, again showing the widespread distribution of iron processing.

The smith's craftsmanship sometimes turned into art. There are some examples of iron tools or other artefacts which can be properly defined as works of art: some richly decorated tongs were found in the forge excavated on terrace VIII (which is in the immediate vicinity of the 'sacred area'), and it might be inferred that these had a ritual use. There are also wrought iron ornaments, shaped as large nails. Some of them, with a diameter of 30 centimetres, were found in temples and apparently decorated the wooden parts of the buildings. The intricate decoration required great blacksmithing skill, inspiration and the knowledge of using a pair of compasses. Although these artefacts are also found in a few other sites, especially in the Late Iron Age hillforts of southern Transylvania, it seems that they (mainly the very large ones) were especially popular in Sarmizegetusa (Glodariu & Iaroslavschi 1979: 118–19).

Although the cooking pottery is rather similar to that found in other sites, the table ware is generally of a different quality and design. A recent typological study of the ceramics found in some contexts showed that the pottery is distinctive, since some of the vessels were inspired by (not copied from) Mediterranean table ware, even if in many cases it is difficult to identify the prototypes (Cristescu 2011: 129–30). The most eloquent example of local distinctiveness is provided by the painted pottery. In common with the central and western parts of temperate Europe in the Late Iron Age, painted pottery in Dacia represents a rather common type of artefact: it was found in at least 50 sites in the region of modern Romania, dating mainly from the first century BC to the first century AD. The settlement of Brad (located east of the Carpathians, in the valley of River Siret) was probably the most important centre of local painted pottery-production in Dacia, between the second half of the first century BC and the Roman conquest of 106 AD. More than 1100 fragments and vessels were found there (Ursachi 1995: 202–07). Significant, but less numerous finds also come from another important Late Iron Age site, Ocnita, in the southern part of Romania. Most of the local painted pottery is decorated with reddish stripes and rather simple geometrical motifs. The most common forms are the so called 'fruit bowls', two handled drinking cups and jugs (Florea 1998: 62–5).

Several hundred fragments were also found in Sarmizegetusa, especially during the early excavations, in more than 15 locations all over the site, stretching from the central zone to the far north-eastern side. Most of these came from dwellings or workshops, within the inhabited terraces of the settlement, whereas none was found in any of the temples from the 'sacred area'. The range of forms is different from that at any other site. Most of the fragments come from medium size

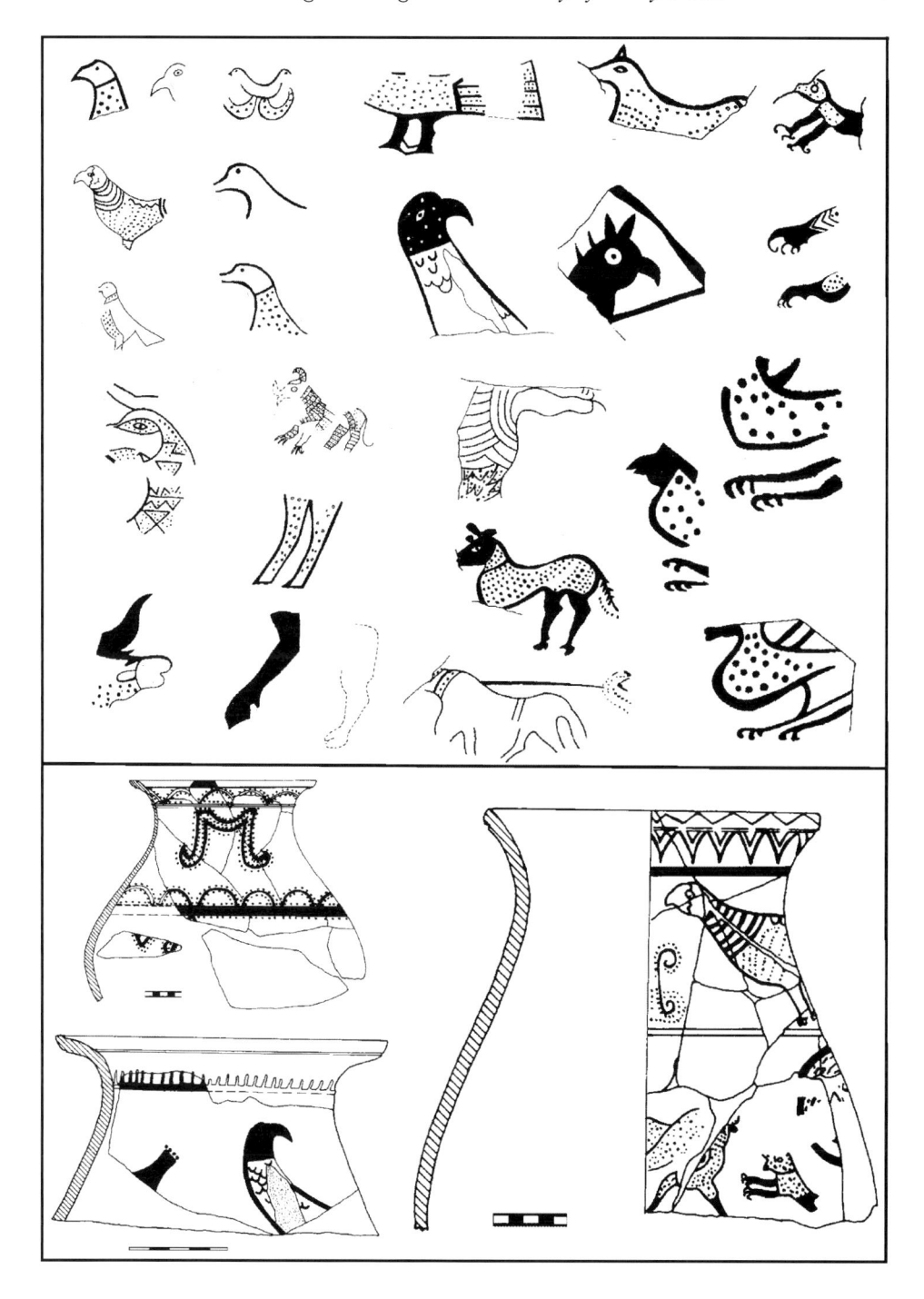

*Figure 7.5. Sarmizegetusa Regia. Painted pottery motifs and vessels (after G. Florea 1998).*

jars, specific types of bowls and very few examples of jugs or cups. Not a single 'fruit bowl' was found, although it is the most common type of painted ware everywhere else in other contemporary sites. The most surprising distinctive feature of these wares is the style of the painted pottery; the unique figurative ornaments depict animals, plants and intricate geometrical motifs. All of them were part of larger and complex compositions. Animal ornaments include real birds (ducks or geese, eagles or hawks), but also fantastic winged beasts with horns or ears and four-legged mammals, both real and fantastic (stags, bulls or felines with strong claws, dogs or wolves)

Some are hybrid forms which associate horns with claws and beaks. Larger compositions are completed by wavy lines, dots, triangles, circles etc. This expressive style has a spontaneous folk art characteristic perhaps taken from textile production. There is a remarkable diversity of motifs, where almost each one is unique, but, all in all, the general aspect of the decoration is very much homogeneous. Surprisingly no human representation is depicted on the painted wares, and that in itself might have some significance.

The frequent depiction of ferocious beasts (birds of prey, felines, etc.) may be related to the ideology of the warrior elites who also were supposed to reside in Sarmizegetusa, or to a specific mythological background (Florea 1998: 250–1). More generally, the exclusive presence of these painted vessels in Sarmizegetusa and a few other neighbouring sites, speaks to a certain artistic choice specific only to this political environment.

## WAS THERE INDEED A COLLECTIVE IDENTITY?

In many respects this site has an 'archaeological identity' of its own which is revealed especially by comparison with other contemporary sites. Although there are other mountain regions inhabited in the Late Iron Age Dacia, the area of Sarmizegetusa, and the site itself, stands out as having the most elaborate internal organisation. The landscape had to be significantly transformed in order to make it more habitable. The construction of all of the artificial terraces, the ceremonial centre, and the fortress involved significant collective effort and resources, undertaken on a large scale for several generations. There are other sites, some of them close to Sarmizegetusa, in which one or several temples were found, but none presents such a 'sacred area' showing a developed and organised plan fit for collective acts of worship or other public ceremonies with political and ideological meanings, celebrating prestige and power. Everything was planned on a monumental scale and the landscape was modified in order to emphasise monumentality in religious architecture. All these collective efforts to organise and rationalise the space can be also seen as the materialisation of a specific concept underwriting the territory of a community.

An important component of the collective identity seems to have been the artisan activity on the site, centred mainly on iron manufacture. The discovery of some workshops and of a large quantity of iron tools and objects in the dwellings suggests an intense activity of a number of specialised craftsmen, who sometimes transformed their trade into art. The unusual high frequency of deposits of iron products, or the decorated tongs might have been connected with ritual or ceremonial practices related to blacksmithing. As Brysbaert and Wetters noted, in respect to specific social identities connected to craftsmanship and production in the Aegean Bronze Age 'the construction of these identities, through material means (...) was probably enmeshed with ceremonial practices, public activities and rituals' (Brysbaert & Wetters 2010: 28).

Style in art – the way things are done – is perhaps the most elaborate expression of identity, because it is not directly linked to the economic purpose of the object. In this case, the figurative painted pottery, specific to Sarmizegetusa and a small area around it, represents a perfect example. The animals they chose to represent, the frequency of those motifs and the details of their forms may illustrate, metaphorically, a moral code and a system of values promoted by the community. The very existence of this style might be one of the strongest arguments for the existence of an identity taken on by the community.

The importance of this centre of power, in which religious and military elites resided, along with craftsmen, probably foreign merchants and other people, is also emphasised by other archaeological finds. For example, carbonised cereals (wheat and barley in large quantities) were brought in from the plains, a distance of some 40–45 kilometres. Other imports include glass and bronze vessels and even a medical kit, found during earlier excavations in the civilian settlement (Glodariu 1976: 13, 31, 39), even though the site is far away from the main trade routes of the time.

At the end of the two wars fought by Emperor Trajan against the Dacian kingdom, Sarmizegetusa ceased to exist. According to Cassius Dio, it seems that the region of the central place, and the 'royal site' itself, became a principal target during the military campaigns of the Romans. The Roman garrison that was left in place, after the victory, dismantled the temples and deported the survivors, and the place remained deserted until today (Florea & Pupeza 2008: 294–5). The capital city of the new province was built in the lowlands, but somehow symbolically assumed the memory (and the identity) of an important place, since the emperor's choice was to name it officially Colonia Ulpia Traiana Augusta Dacica *Sarmizegetusa* (for discussion of the foundation of the colony and the earliest known inscription bearing this name see Piso 2008: 320–1, notes 184–5, with further bibliography).

**ACKNOWLEDGEMENTS**

I am grateful to my colleagues, Professor. I. Rus, Dr. Mariana Egri, Dr. Razvan Mateescu and Catalin Cristescu for their generous help.

# 8. The Ethnic Construction of Early Iron Age Burials in Transylvania. Scythians, Agathyrsi or Thracians?

*Alexandra Ghenghea*

**KEYWORDS:** *SCYTHIAN* DEBATE, AGATHYRSI, HERODOTOS, ETHNOS, IDENTITY

'Each emergent nation-state had to construct its own national identity, which required the active forgetting or misremembering and the rediscovery or inventing of one's past. Myths of national origin had to be elaborated from a variety of sources, including, notably, the material remains found within the state's demarcated territorial borders.' (Kohl 1998: 228).

INTRODUCTION

The Late Hallstatt or Hallstatt D (approx. 650–450 BC) in Transylvania is defined, from an archaeological point of view, by the so-called Ciumbrud type discoveries. The Late Hallstatt covers the time between the second half of the seventh century BC and the second half of the fifth century BC and is considered by Vulpe to be the first part of the Late Iron Age (Vulpe 2010: 484), even though it was previously the last period of Early Iron Age. The term 'Hallstatt', derived from the famous cemetery in Upper Austria, designates two different concepts of relevance to the present discussion. Firstly, it denotes a cultural horizon previously defined by Kossak as *Westhallstattkreis* and *Osthallstattkreis* (Kossak 1959). Secondly, it has a conventional chronological meaning (Vulpe 2010). Mihály Párducz also introduced the term *Skythenzeit*, by linkage to the intrusion of north Pontic warrior groups in Transylvania and other regions located in eastern Carpathian Basin (Párducz 1973). This *Skythenzeit* covers mainly the period between the seventh century BC and the second half of the fourth century BC when these eastern infiltrations were interrupted by the intrusion of *Celtic* groups coming from the west (Rustoiu 2008: 69). The most ancient discoveries that were related to these eastern infiltrations are those from Mărişelu and Budeşti-Fânaţe and have been dated to the seventh century BC because of the Posmuş type daggers found in the graves (Marinescu 1984; Vulpe 1990), which are found from the beginning of the seventh century BC. The *Celtic* infiltration dates from the second half of the fourth century BC. Some cemeteries have been recently excavated (i.e. the cemetery from Pişcolt and the one from Fântânele-Dealu Popii- in north west Romania) that were related with the first *Celtic* infiltrations and dated to the beginning of the La Tène B2 and the even to the end of La Tène B1 in the case of Pişcolt (Rustoiu 2008).

These Late Hallstatt discoveries were also termed 'the Ciumbrud group' or

# 8. The Ethnic Construction of Early Iron Age Burials in Transylvania

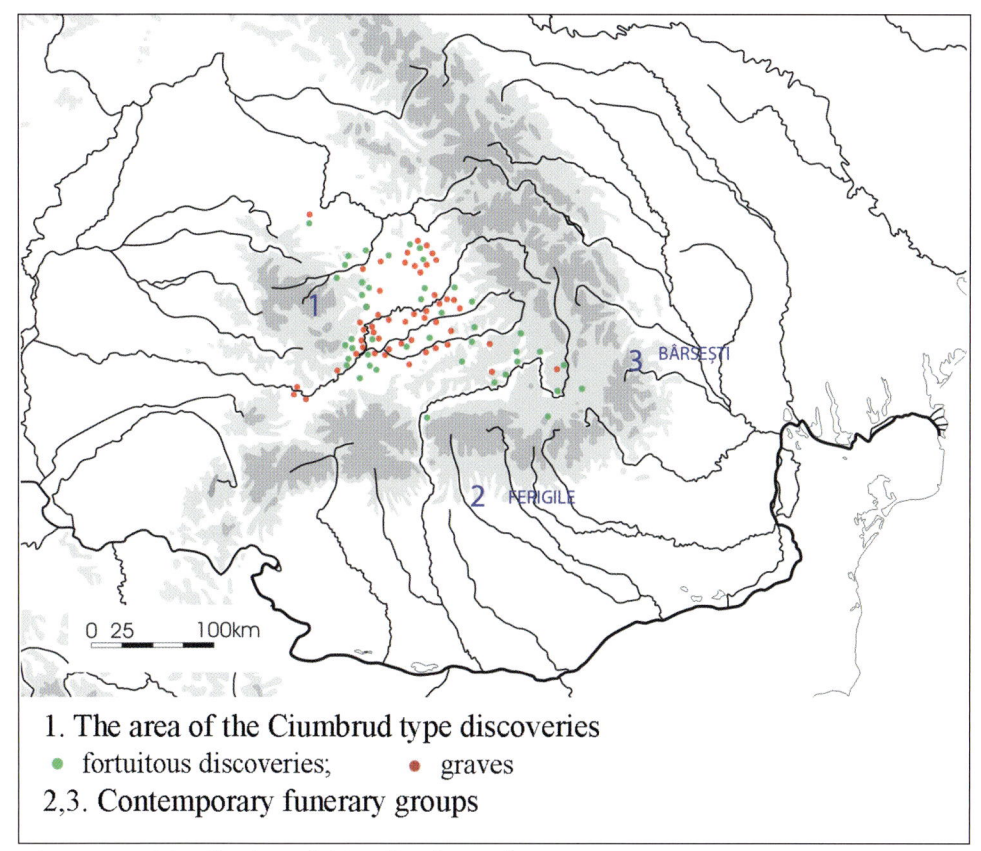

*Figure 8.1. Distribution of Ciumbrud type discoveries.*

1. The area of the Ciumbrud type discoveries
 • fortuitous discoveries; • graves
2,3. Contemporary funerary groups

the 'Ciumbrud type discoveries' (Vulpe 2010; Vulpe 2012), a name related to the first systematic examination of the cemetery from Ciumbrud by Ferenczi and published in five studies (Ferenczi 1965; 1966; 1967; 1969; 1971). During the nineteenth century, these finds were related to the '*Scythian* debate' and strongly rooted in the nationalistic thought of historians and archaeologists of the last two centuries. They were named *Scythian* discoveries/group, '*Skythische* Altertümer', *Agathyrs* group and even *Scythian-Agathyrs* group (Vasiliev 1980).

The last decade has witnessed the advent of new studies focused on ethnic identities and the relevance of the remote past in creating present identity structures (Brown 1994; Chapman 1994 and recently Rieckhoff & Sommer 2007). One relevant study is that of Sommer and Gramsch (2011) investigating the current trends of central European archaeology focusing on politics, nationalism and related archaeological theories. Many other studies have investigated our understanding of the way the past was adapted to serve the national interests during the nineteenth and twentieth centuries (i.e. Kohl & Fawcett 1995; Díaz-Andreu & Champion 1996; Kohl 1998; Meskell 2001; Jones 2007).

In Romania, archaeology was also a discipline serving the creation and preservation the national state, but there are relatively few studies of this subject

(Niculescu 2004–2005) and the so-called '*Scythian* debate' was only briefly tackled. An approach is required to show how nationalism used archaeology to justify its own ideals within the Romanian academic environment and what the effects of such attitude have been. It is unlikely that the historians of the nineteenth century deliberately lied, denying the archaeological records, but rather that they idealistically believed in their constructed model. During the nineteenth century, archaeological data were very few and therefore the theories were first advocated and then demonstrated and adapted as new archaeological data were unearthed. Archaeology produced the raw material for the shared 'identifications' that form 'modern large group identity', as Russell (2006) has put it.

My aim in this paper is to show, in this vein, how the Ciumbrud burial pattern was superimposed on the written sources within Romanian archaeology and how the Traditional View was constructed and sustained within a very cultural-historical perspective. I will also be pointing out the diversity of the philological interpretations of Herodotos, the main historical source for this subject. Therefore, I will challenge and dismantle the Traditional View, which still remains the most powerful view in Romanian archaeology and show which issues may be significant to understand the Ciumbrud burials.

### THE ARCHAEOLOGICAL REMAINS

Most discoveries were unearthed during the late nineteenth and twentieth centuries. These are mainly graves and stray finds of weapons and ornaments, providing a contrast with the Middle Hallstatt when most of the discoveries were settlements and hoards. For many of the Ciumbrud type archaeological records, the context of discovery remains unknown, masked by the confusion of agricultural and constructional activities. The cemeteries commonly contain less than 30 graves, but it is difficult, at present, to evaluate their real number. Some further cemeteries were better excavated after the sixties (i.e. Ciumbrud (Ferenczi 1965; 1966; 1967; 1969; 1971), Ozd (Vasiliev & Zrinyi 1974), Mărișelu (Marinescu 1984), Budești-Fânațe (Marinescu 1984), Băița (Vasiliev 1976)).

The total known data set reaches some 300 graves. They are generally flat supine inhumations, although there are also some bi-ritual cemeteries (e.g. Băița (Babeș & Mirițoiu 2011) and Uioara de Sus (Vasiliev 1999)), dated in the second half of the fifth century BC. Grave goods include three recurrent types of pottery containers (Crișan 1969), bronze, iron or bone arrowheads, iron, bronze or bi-metallic *akinakai* daggers, and a few brooches, gold pieces, and bronze mirrors. Grave goods also included *Cypraea moneta* shells, associated with bronze *saltaleoni* and animal meat. The presence of horse-gear pieces is very scarce. Only 12 of the Ciumbrud bodies (Necrasov 1982) and one skull (Crișan 1964) were studied anthropologically and these studies indicate a local origin, although some doubt can be placed on this interpretation.

## 8. The Ethnic Construction of Early Iron Age Burials in Transylvania

### THE TRADITIONAL VIEW OF THE EARLY IRON AGE IN TRANSYLVANIA

The second half of seventh century to the fifth century BC (Late Hallstatt) has been commonly known as the time of a *Scythian* or *Agathyrs* enclave, suggesting an eastern origin and ethnic differentiation from the local people located within the area of present Transylvania. There has been no agreement about the ethnic identity of the intrusive group (ranging from *Scythians* to the ambiguous category of the *Agathyrsi*-). The traditional view is that a nomadic group (there are very few settlements for this time and area) invaded Transylvania, at the beginning of the sixth century BC subduing the local people, represented by pottery found in the cemeteries of the intrusive nomadic groups. The burial ritual used by nomads was inhumation, whereas the local people, the *Thracians* were accustomed to cremate their human remains after death. During the fourth century BC, this intrusive nomadic group vanished and groups of *Celts* began to invade the territory. During the subsequent second century BC, the *Dacian* civilisation was taking shape. In this historical reconstruction, what happened to the intrusive nomadic group who came from the faraway east? The explanations were straightforward. Their culture was so simple and organic, that its identity has been changed by the more numerous local groups, becoming themselves *Thracians*. This view has been clearly expressed more recently:

> '... la présence d'un groupe scythique dans l'aire intracarpathique de la Roumanie, dans le Hallstatt Tardif, ne saurait être niée. Quoique peu nombreux, le groupe infiltré a produit initialement un choc, ressenti par la culture locale, circonstance qui est prouve pas la cessation des établissements fortifiées hallstattiens. Cependant, pas à pas, la culture autochtone revient à elle (tel que le démontre, par exemple, la nécropole à incinération d'Uioara de Sus) et influence à son tour l'évolution du groupe scythique, lequel disparaît (comme entité ethno-culturelle) vers ou après le milieu du Ve siècle av. J.Chr.' (Vasiliev 2004: 470)

This Traditional View is an artificial story created from a number of rather improbable events, shuffling facts from the Herodotean story with archaeological aspirations projected onto a remote past.

### THE UNDERLYING ARGUMENTS AND FOUNDATION OF THE TRADITIONAL VIEW

The data underlying this traditional View include a few fragments from the fourth book of Herodotos' writings which have sustained an animated and simplistic debate about the seventh to fifth centuries BC. One passage is the following:

> ἐκ δέ Ἀγαθύρσον Μάρις ποταμὸς Ῥέων. 'From the country of the Agathyrsi comes down another river, the Maris, which empties itself into the same...Ister' (IV. 49); Ἀγάθυρσοι δέ ἀβρατατοι ἀνδρῶν εἰσι καὶ χρυσοφόροι τὰ μάλιστα, ἐπίκοινον δέ τῶν γυναικῶν τὴν μῖξιν ποιεῦνται, ἵνα κασίγνητοί τε ἀλλήλων ἔωσι καὶ οἰκήιοι ἐόντες πάντες μέτε φθόνῳ μέτε ἔχθεϊ χρέωνται ἐς ἀλλήλους. τὰ δὲ ἄλλα νόμαια Θρήιξι προσκεχωρήκασι (ed. Macan 1895).

> 'The Agathyrsi are a race of men very luxurious, and very fond of wearing gold on their persons. They have wives in common, so that they may be all brothers, and, as members of one family, may neither envy nor hate one another. In other respects their customs resemble much those of the Thracians' (ed. Rawlinson 1933) (IV. 104).

There is also another passage regarding one possible origin of the *Scythians*: a tale told by the *Greeks* who dwell in the Pontus region about the serpent woman and the fact that Herakles had three sons:

> τῷ μὲν Ἀγάθυρσον αὐτῶν, τῷ δ᾽ ἑπομένῳ Γελωνόν, Σκύθην δὲ τῷ νεωτάτῳ (ed. Macan 1895).

> 'One she called Agathyrsus, one Gelonus, and the other, who was the youngest, Scythes' (ed. Rawlinson 1933) (IV. 10).

An entire research direction developed that tried to locate geographically and archaeologically the material culture of the Herodotean ethnonym known as *Agathyrsi*. Trying to locate 'the mythical country of the *Agathyrsi*' is a fruitless and ineffective endeavour. The written sources are very ambiguous: it is possible that Herodotos placed the *Agathyrsi* in the Mureş Valley, but later written sources state the *Agathyrsi* were to be found in the Eurasian territory:

> 'ab eis (Arimapsae) Essedones usque ad Maeotida, hujus flexum Buce amnis secat: Agathyrsi et Sauromatae ambiunt; quia pro sedibus plaustra habent, dicti Hamaxobiae.' (Pomponius Mela II, 1) (ed. Frick 1880).

> 'Au delà sont les Essédons, jusqu'au Méotide. Le contour de ce lac, où se jette le Bucès, est habité par les Agathyrses et les Sauromates, peuples qui vivent dans le chars, et qui reçoivent par cette raison le surnom d'Hamaxobiens' (ed. Nisard 1883)

*\*\**

> 'A Thapris per continentem introrsus tenent Aucheate apud quos Hypanis oritur, Neuroe apud quos Borysthenes, Geloni, Thyssagetae, Budini, Basilidae et caeruleo capillo Agathyrsi.' (Pliny, *Natural History* IV. 88)

> 'After Taphrae, the interior of the mainland is occupied by the Auchetai and the Neuroi, in whose territories respectively are the sources of the Bug and the Dnieper, the Geloni, Thyssagetae, Budini, Basilidae and Agathyrsi, the last a dark-haired people.' (ed. Rackham 1961)

*\*\**

'Gelonis Agathyrsi conlimitant, interstincti colore caeruleo corpora simul et crines, et humiles quidem minutis atque raris, nobiles vero latius fucati et densioribus notis.' (Ammianus Marcellinus XXXI, 2, 14) (ed. Sabath 1999)

'Next to the Geloni are the Agathyrsi, who dye both their bodies and their hair with a blue colour, the lower classes using spots few and small in number, whereas the nobles employ broad spots, close and thick, and of a deeper hue.' (ed. Yonge 1862)

It has been argued that these later authors renewed the ancient and unclear image of the immense territory that lay beneath the *oikoumene*, identified by Homer and Herodotos. The image of this space gradually moved towards the north and east accompanying the extension of the Roman Empire to south east Europe and a concomitant increase in geographical knowledge (Vulpe 2012).

We can conclude that there have been two historical stages in the conceptualisation of the *Agathyrs ethnos*. Firstly, during the nineteenth century, the early historians considered that *Agathyrsi* to be predecessors of *Dacians* or *Thracians*, working from the written sources. Niebuhr was one of the first historians who discussed the ethnos of Agathyrsi, considering them predecessors of Dacians (Niebuhr 1828). During the nineteenth century, Agathyrsi were regarded as Thracians (Tomaschek 1893). Even Lindner considered them Thracians but under Scythians rule (Lindner 1841). Kazarow thought they were a mixture of Thracians and Scythians (Kazarov 1916). Secondly, with the emergence of archaeological discoveries, the idea was advanced in the early twentieth century that the *Agathyrsi* were a *Scythian* group that settled during the seventh–fifth centuries BC in Transylvania (Vulpe 1989; 2004; 2012). This model became so powerful that it lasted even once much archaeological evidence became available and has endured to the present day.

The many archaeologically based arguments are inconclusive. The scarcity of settlements is interpreted as a nomadic type of life. The contrast between intrusive inhumation and local cremation is interpreted as ethnic. On this basis, a bi-ritual cemetery has been interpreted as an example of the 'Thracianisation' of the *Scythian* enclave (Vasiliev 1976). This was also employed as an argument for the *immanence* (a form of geopolitical teleology) of the native *Thraco-Dacian* culture, which had to assimilate the intrusive people. The archaeological reasoning is very naive because these so-called *Scythian* elements of material culture were present over a very large area, not exclusively in Transylvania and the north Pontic Region. However, some defining elements of the north Pontic Region such as tumuli or horse-gear artefacts were not present among Ciumbrud discoveries. Furthermore, there are very few finds in Transylvania associated with the local population. If they were later to assimilate the intrusive nomadic groups, why were they so little visible during Late Hallstatt?

## THE HISTORIANS OF THE NINETEENTH AND EARLY TWENTIETH CENTURY: BUILDING THE TRADITIONAL VIEW

Study of the work of influential historians (i.e. Tocilescu (1880), Xenopol (1888), Pârvan (1926), Iorga (1913)), who shaped the research during late nineteenth and early twentieth centuries outlines some key historiographical features of the *Scythian* debate.

1. An obsession with *ethnos* and ethnic elements, the search for origins, the formation of the Romanian people and the local continuity of the Romanian people in the same area. On this basis, the *Scythians* were a formative ingredient in the recipe of Romanian Ethnogenesis, dated to the seventh century AD;
2. A complete trust in the accounts of Herodotos;
3. The use of archaeological data as exemplification of the written sources. This approach served to historicise the material record and archaeology;
4. The prominence of three methodologies: the study of Greek and Latin authors, archaeological investigation and etymology.

Tocilescu was one of the first historians who tackled the *Agathyrs* problem, but his view differed from that of his contemporaries and successors. When he wrote '*Dacia înainte de romani*', there was a lack of archaeological evidence, so he employed the classical authors, ethnography and linguistics. His research methodology was different from that of later researchers. He eruditely considered all the historiographical hypotheses available at his time, presenting the arguments of each viewpoint and its critics, and pursuing the directions that were imposed by the written sources literature, pointing out his scientific reasoning. He agrees that:

> It is of main concern to analyse carefully all these opinions and to question the arguments on which they are based (Tocilescu 1880: 152).*

For example, in his discourse about the *Scythians*, he supports the pre-existing theory that the term 'Scythian' could have been a generic name common to all the populations 'of North and East' that shared the same nomadic type of life (Tocilescu 1880, 110).

Xenopol was another scholar of his time, known mainly as the author of a monumental historical synthesis. This mainly deals with medieval and modern history, and is striking for its fervent disproof of Rösler's theory which questioned the continuity of Romanian people in former Dacia (Vulpe 1972). Xenopol professes a discourse filled with nationalistic aspirations, where he was entirely devoted to his motherland and where he considered his work a necessary addition to the fulfilment of national union and development. For these reasons, he 'proferred' his work 'to his nation' (Xenopol 1888). He stated

---

\* The quotations from Romanian archaeological and historical studies have been translated by the author and corrected by the English editor.

## 8. The Ethnic Construction of Early Iron Age Burials in Transylvania

that the role of the historian was to seek the truth following the logic of facts and not from a priori statements. He considered his work as

> 'not being dictated by an a priori conception of historical facts, but as the obvious result of their course. We do not believe that there could be another view concerning the complex of all circumstances regarding our history, different from ours' (Xenopol 1888, 36).

A central tenet of his work was that he agreed with the idea of an uninterrupted continuity between the ethnicities of 513 BC and those of the present day. The first part of history was a period of the constitution of the Romanian people (emerging also from his choice of title: 'Istoria românilor'). The geographical information and Herodotos' statement that the *Agathyrsi* raised bees was considered to correspond to the present bee cultures from the Mehedinţi district. These facts were considered proof of the historical continuity of the Romanian people for more than two millennia (Xenopol 1888: 53). He was interested in proving the kinship of the *Thracians* (the local people) and the *Scythians*, and for this reason he drew on prehistoric discoveries, mainly those from the Neolithic. Thus a central theme of his work was the discovery of a connection between the people from the past and the later Romanians, underlining the local origin of the Romanians, who had continuously occupied one geographical area.

Pârvan (1926), perhaps one of the most influential historians and archaeologist of the early twentieth century, designated the Mureş Valley funerary group 'thracianised *Scythians*'. His archaeological evidence was based on less than 30 chance finds. Thus the core of his theory was a short passage of Herodotos stating that the customs of the *Agathyrsi* 'approach closely those of the *Thracians*' (IV. 104). Pârvan took this to mean, in the nationalistic spirit of his time, that the native people from 'Dacia' could not possibly have been assimilated into a foreign civilisation. Furthermore, the local people had to be the civilising force of foreign influences. This way of thinking was very typical of this period and of later communist Romania, in all matters dealing with the *Scythians*, *Celts* (in Transylvania), and *Illyrians* (in Oltenia). Most considered the *Scythians* assimilated into the local population, but also contributing to the creation of the *Thracian* culture. A variation on the theme was that of Andrieşescu, who considered the mountainous Transylvanian region inhabited by sedentary communities like Thracians, because it was unsuitable for nomadic life (Andrieşescu 1912: 117). All these powerful nationalistic interpretations of the early twentieth century had little or no factual support.

Iorga was another influential historian, but also an active politician of the interwar period. He was conversant with the scientific literature of his time on the *Cimmerians* and *Scythians*. He cast doubt on the *Scythian* invasion routes through Danube valley and Carpathian mountains advocated by Pârvan, but agreed that:

> the material found here and there could have reached there by commerce, in times of peace, but also by plundering in times of war (Iorga 1936: 139).

He also had doubts about the precision of the Herodotean geography:

> Herodotos had a confused geography which we are wrong to treat it as if it was an exact map of our times...(Iorga 1936: 149).

He saw history as being governed by a geopolitical teleology or *immanence*, and thus tried to find traces of the Scythians in present evidence. For example, he compared traditional Romanian clothing with the examples represented on the famous vessel from Voronej. According to this view, ethnic kinship was permanent and genetic, linking the remote past with present.

This obsession for finding the historical truth, the origin of the Romanian people and its permanence in the area of present Romania is connected to nationalism and the creation of the modern nineteenth-century state. The people from the past were merely a justification for the current political state, and the past was studied to legitimate the present in a search for *l'état de droit*.

A later scholar Radu Vulpe defines the Iron Age as follows:

> the Iron Age is above all the age of the Geto-Dacian substratum, from which, through Romanisation, the Romanian people has been born (Vulpe 1970: 9)

and this remains the most popular recipe for Romanian Ethnogenesis. He deliberately compared the activities of Pârvan and Tocilescu with the archaeology and its evolution of the Romanian state:

> 'Dacia înainte de romani' was an early work which reflected a triple youth: of an author of less than 30 years old, of a state that had barely obtained its political self, and of a science which was still looking for its way. 'Getica' is the work of a fully formed maturity: of an author who had outgrown his 40s and gathered a great experience, of a country which had reunified and consolidated its position in the world, of Romanian culture which had affirmed its position in many fields because of its exceptional values, of an archaeology which had completely developed, and had imposed itself in the first rank of historical sciences (Vulpe 1970: 17).

## ARCHAEOLOGICAL THOUGHT

Despite some minor differences of opinion, twentieth century archaeologists have trusted the same historical scenario. One of the most obvious features of archaeological thought during the twentieth century was the ethnicisation of archaeological findings and material. In different ways, this applied to many of the archaeologists of the twentieth century, such as Rostovtzev, Fettich, Roska, Popescu (mainly in his 1943 study, because he later regarded the Ciumbrud type discoveries as influenced by Scythian culture), Daicoviciu, Crișan, Ferenczi, Nestor, Vasiliev and Vulpe (in his early work, because he later changed his mind). Thus, the main interest of Romanian archaeology under the communist government and before was the construction of the Ethnogenesis. The *Agathyrs/*

## 8. The Ethnic Construction of Early Iron Age Burials in Transylvania

*Scythian* element had to be placed somewhere in the process of formation of the Romanian people. The concept of *ethnos* had an essentialist, permanent and deterministic character within archaeological thought. Modern Romanians were organically and timelessly connected with archaeologically defined cultures.

One of the more important archaeologies of the first half of the twentieth century dealing with this problem was the Cluj school of archaeology. Among them the name of Roska stands out. Fettich (1931), the author of the well-known addendum of the work of Rostovzev, *Skythien und der Bosporus* provides the formative background for this scholar by seeing many of the newly discovered grave goods as originating from the east. In this way, a model of an infiltrating nomad Scythian group in Transylvania took shape. In response, Roska (1937) named his well known work 'Der bestand der skythischen Altertümer Siebenbürgens', employing in the title an Ethnonym that mirrored his interpretation of the archaeological finds. His ideas moulded the archaeological research and had a major impact on other opinions. A different perspective was that of Kovács, who was the first to research the inhumation necropolis of Targu Mures that was later considered part of the Ciumbrud complex. He did not think that the eastern influences reached the cemetery (Kovács, 1915).

A further scholar Popescu sees the archaeological material as fundamental in 'elucidating the past'. It may confirm the written source and

> it has upon that the advantage of presenting to us a more or less understandable interpretation that is honest, pure, and with no intention of dissimulation or corruption (Popescu 1943: 5).

By these means, the political discourse is dominant and Popescu is interested in the pursuing the origin of *Scythians* to legitimate the political contacts with other modern states:

> We believe we may say from the beginning and without any hesitation that this discussion is about the so-called ethnic origin of the Scythians. We can ask if they are of Turanic or Ural-Altaic origin and if this is the case they could be claimed by Hungarians and consequently their invasion into our lands could be regarded as an avantgarde of the Hungarian invasion which only occurred a millennium and a half later. Or are they of an Iranian origin? (Popescu 1943: 18)

Daicoviciu, in 'Brève histoire de la Transylvanie' thought that a small number of '*Scythians / Agathyrsi*' had infiltrated into Transylvania

> ils finirent rapidement par se fondre dans la masse des autochtones (Daicoviciu 1965: 14).

Daicoviciu's thought was governed by the idea of a constant regional unity of Romania. Consequently, he advocated the idea that:

> Les contacts des Gèto-Daces de Transylvanie, au cours de cette époque, avec leurs frères de Moldavie, Dobroudja, Olténie et Munténie et, par leurs intermédiaire, avec le monde thrace du sud du Danube et les villes grecques des bords de la mer Noire, furent constants et féconds (Daicoviciu 1965: 15).

In reality, there is no support for the common kinship of the Late Hallstatt inhabitants from Transylvania and other regions which form modern Romania. However, this representation of the Iron Age once again reflects the ideals and aspirations of contemporary political models that express an enduring unity of Romania across the generations. 'The *Geto-Dacians* brothers' from Transylvania and the other regions are the Romanians from nineteenth century who, trusting that they were all shared the same blood, fought together to forge the same mother-kingdom. This achieved ideal infused the entire historiography of the twentieth century.

Following the same model as his predecessors, a further scholar Nestor also gave an ethnic explanation to the differences recorded in funeral ritual. Thus, the cremation graves were local groups and inhumation graves intrusive. He thought the local, *Thracian* population was located in the Tisza Region and the intrusive groups in the Transylvania. He also thought that the local population would have assimilated the intrusive infiltrations, because the 'foreign' elements in material culture disappeared over the course of time. When discussing the case of *Agathyrsi*, he agreed that the ceramics were local provenience, the other elements of material culture eastern (Nestor 1970).

The archaeological thought of the Late Hallstatt in Transylvania in the second half of the twentieth century was built on these ideas with the following variations. Ferenczi considered the inhumation cemeteries of Transylvania unprecedented during Early Iron Age, because there were different from the local material culture (Ferenczi 1971: 11). Nevertheless, archaeologists always regarded the ceramics from the graves as local. He agreed that the cemetery of Ciumbrud was of a Scythian origin, by making connections with groups from the Caucasus, and identified the Agathyrsi with the Ferigile discoveries. Vasiliev argued in the introduction of 'Sciţii agatirşi pe teritoriul României' which investigated 'the characteristics of first Iron Age in Transylvania' that the '*Scythian* group' originated from none of the discoveries or phases of Early Hallstatt or Middle Hallstatt (Vasiliev 1980: 25). Vulpe also trusted in the same invasion theory during his early work, but identified the Agathyrsi with the Ferigile and Bârseşti funerary groups, because of grave goods which shared eastern links and considered Ferigile and Bârseşti as reflecting a Thracian-Agathyrs cultural horizon (Vulpe 1967). He later changed his mind and took a more philological approach.

The way in which material culture has been used in illustrating models which were established *a priori* has been pointed out by Vulpe (1983). He showed how Dušek (1978) and Vasiliev (1980) used mostly the same archaeological records in supporting two antagonistically different ideas. Dušek was intent on a local, *Thracian* element, arguing against the eastern invasion, while Vasiliev regarded the material culture as being of a *Scythian* origin (Vulpe 1983).

Archaeology had the same obsession for origins, for the giving of dignity to kinship, as has been seen in the medieval search for a mythical ancestry deriving from Troy (Sommer & Gramsch 2011).

## THE PHILOLOGY OF HERODOTOS

All these approaches have recreated the meaning of Herodotos' text and, as Hartog has noticed, new books and articles commenting on the *History* are constantly being written. This entire literature that started in the nineteenth century regarded the Herodotean text with suspicion, although Hartog (1980), Fehling (1971), West (1985; 2002) and Armayor (1978) are not familiar with the *Scythian* debate in Romanian research.

Archaeologists were not the only scholars failing to use their data effectively. The classical philologists, trying to ascertain the veracity of Herodotos' text, have turned to archaeology. In a strongly worded critique, Pritchett (1993) tried to invalidate 'the Liar School of Herodotos' the school which entirely doubted the ancient author's writings. Pritchett considered the archaeological evidence proof of Herodotos' accounts. This mixture of methodologies is what Hachmann has described as 'die gemischte Argumentation' (Hachmann 1970: 11). However, there are only a few certainties that archaeology can provide (see Ivantchik 1999), such as the Greek imports of pottery in north Pontic contexts, but otherwise archaeological evidence is too general to establish the presence of Herodotean identities. The current search for a Herodotean geography is an endless road, and the locating of groups of people named by Herodotos on a modern map is an idealistic endeavour. There has been a fervent debate in the search for the many proposed models of Herodotean ethnic groups, and none has a certain outcome.

This is not to mean that Herodotos' account is an invention, it is merely a Greek translation of the meaning of a situation that he experienced, an *otherness* from a Greek perspective. Archaeology cannot tell us who the Agathyrsi were. The *Scythian* debate is a dichotomised methodology: some archaeologists consider Herodotos an authority able to solve a particular case and in pursuit of this point of view and have chosen to decorate their thesis with fragments from the Fourth book. On the other hand, some philologists consider archaeology an objective and clarifying discipline. What is clear from these contrasts is that there needs to be a more studied dialogue between archaeology and philology. A good illustration is the views of Pydyn:

> The Histories do(es) not reflect 'an objective reality' but instead represent a stage of Greek knowledge of the world from the middle of the fifth century BC,... Yet, one has to remember that all historical writing is about available knowledge and not about 'an objective reality', and Herodotos' knowledge and the quality of information decreased as the distance from Greece increased, or at least from Olbia' (Pydyn 1999: 44).

## Transylvania during the Late Hallstatt?

The preoccupation with the search for the ethnic element within archaeological data has obstructed the production of more plausible models to explain the Ciumbrud discoveries. The repeated search for *Agathyrsi*, *Scythians* or *Thracians* is an erroneous approach.

How should this period of the Iron Age be approached? It is still uncertain whether there really was a concrete group lying under the rubric 'Ciumbrud'. One possible line of research is attitudes to death. Some of the grave goods (e.g. *Cypraea moneta* shells, the mineral Realgar ($As_4S_4$) and animal meat) may be interesting lines of enquiry. Further work also needs to be undertaken to correct the lack of settlement evidence. In spite of the density of research in Transylvania, archaeologists have failed to explain how life really developed during the Late Hallstatt. New models still need to be advocated and different questions formulated.

# 9. Negotiating Identities at the Edge of the Roman Empire

*Marko A. Janković*

**Keywords:** Western Balkans, Iron Age, Romanisation, ethnicity, status

## Introduction

During the last two decades, the concept of identity has been extensively researched within archaeology (Jones 1997; Huskinson 2000; Casella & Fowler 2004; Díaz-Andreu *et al.* 2005; Hingley 2005). Nevertheless, this approach has been ignored in some archaeological communities, and one such community is the Serbian. Archaeological work on social change and cultural contacts is mostly burdened with the cultural-historical heritage of twentieth century, still trying to demarcate different communities and place well defined cartographic lines between prehistoric European societies (Johnson 1999; Babić 2010). Such a practice, as has been frequently argued, led to an interpretative sequence where archaeological evidence and classical texts were stretched to fit one another with the purpose of recognising, defining and definitively packaging all prehistoric cultural groups (Jones 1997; Meskell 2007). The equation 'one culture-one nation' has been used so many times in archaeological work that it is a real challenge today to undo the influence these interpretations have had on the Public. General terms of ethnicity, nation, people or even more specific terms like Celts, Romans and Greeks were so intensively used during the last century that this practice resulted in taking the 'facts' for granted without any reconsideration of the terms (Wells 2001). On the other hand, identity is a concept which does not have a fixed point in space or time. It is a very fluid, changing concept, which is constructed by the very researchers themselves. It is most likely that communities of the past did not perceive their surrounding world in terms of identity, in the same way as they lacked a concept of cultural groups. The researchers of identity should be aware that they are able to see only certain aspects of someone's identity. The fact that archaeologists only recover identity as static and frozen should not disguise the fact that this is not all that there has been in the past.

In simple terms, it is very difficult to know if our concept of identity is the same as one in the past. This is brought to a head by the collision of prehistoric populations with Roman culture. Just like the cultural groups, Roman culture used to be observed as a uniform, independent entity with luminous, civilising attributes that spread and pushed aside the pre-existing material culture that it encountered. The state of Being Roman was, as we know today, not a simple concept, and it was not the same in each moment and in every place (Curchin

2004; Hingley 2005; Revell 2009). Although it is often emphasised that the Roman Empire was the first grand multicultural society with myriads of people, religions and customs, Roman culture is still too often characterised as uniform.

The most frequent concept used for explaining the relations between Roman and non-Roman societies is traditionally known as Romanisation and such a concept implies that one, in all ways better, civilised and harmonic side was influencing the other, worse, savage and barbarian side. In such a scenario, the savage are always changed forever, simply because they recognise the benefits of Being Roman. During the last decade, different authors have challenged this concept, criticising it mainly because of the assumed unidirectional changes that disregard the impact of local cultures on the Romans themselves. Most of these authors have focused on regional discrepancies, showing that Roman culture is always considered a cause of stress, but that the results were not the same every time. The final outcome was not a bipolar contrast of Romans and non-Romans, but a unique hybrid culture (Madsen 2000; Revell 2009).

## Classical texts and ethnicity

Readings of classical authors were observed as definite and objective for a long period of the history of the archaeology and ancient history. All of those texts were accurately analysed in search for linguistic and chronological consistency in order to confirm authenticity and validity. Much more attention was paid to the form, at the expense of the content, of the texts and events described in them were usually taken for granted as true, objective and unquestionable. Many archaeologists accepted these observations and gave classical sources a privileged status in their interpretations of archaeological material. Such formal, unquestionable connections between classical texts and archaeological material were used as a means to recognise certain historical events described previously in actual archaeological material (Hingley 2005: 3). In their endeavours to classify archaeological material, usually in accordance with classical texts, archaeologists reached out for the classical texts which described past societies, without any regard to the possibility that ancient authors were also attempting to accomplish the same goal of describing past societies. Just as archaeologists and ancient historians today, classical authors were 'outsiders' who tried to describe neighbouring populations in their own terms and probably in order to present them to their own social groups (Wells 2001: 30). Instead of taking the Greek and Roman texts for granted, we must recognise them as cultural constructs, made for specific purposes and specific audiences. We can further assume that the purposes and audiences were not the same every time, and that classical sources could be one of a number of possible perspectives on an observed society (Wells 2001: 105). Unfortunately, many other aspects of life of past societies were never described, and all we have today are random sources, that are at best suggestive.

Nevertheless, those descriptions of past societies, together with 'precise' descriptions of their territories and cultures were used in most of the interpretations of archaeological material, often creating an inconsistency and incoherence among them. A similar situation occurs in Balkan archaeology, where classical descriptions of Iron Age populations are used to explain the material culture within the terms of ethnicity, with little regard to the social, political or any other consequences of the term's usage. One of the milestones of such reasoning was the publication of Fanula Papazoglu '*Srednjobalkanska plemena u predrimsko doba*' (Central Balkan tribes in pre-Roman times) issued in 1969 by the Balcanological Research Centre in Sarajevo (Papazoglu 1969). This publication was not only the first to put all of the classical texts covering Balkans in one place, but also the first to provide a map that showed the 'tribal' territories. This work has become a point of reference to explain all of the Iron Age material culture ever since and although minor corrections have been made over the last four decades, many publications still rely greatly on Papazoglu's work.

Usage of Greek and Roman texts as the source of interpretation has led to the situation where everyday material culture (pottery, jewellery, weaponry, etc.) is labeled ethnically and marked as Illyrian, Celtic, or Thracian. Such an interpretative sequence caused two major issues for those same archaeologists. First of all, archaeologists could not explain areas where different ethnically labeled material culture was emerging at the same time, and secondly, they could not explain the situations where such material culture was present in the same context, so they often tried to blur the problem using unsupported 'common sense' explanations such as imports, looting or even intermarriage (Mano-Zisi 1957: 48).

## ROMAN ARCHAEOLOGY AND IDENTITY

From the late nineteenth century, the main intellectual concerns of Roman archaeology were to study cultural change within the context of Roman Imperialism, and the main researchers were burdened with concepts of Empire and its civilising mission. Two of the most important fields of research were the incorporation of populations into the Roman Empire and the nature of the cultural transformation known also as Romanisation (Hingley 2005). Such concepts led to specific results in most of the twentieth century, implying that there were two different entities defined as Romans and Natives. Most of the problems of these concepts derived from three basic assumptions. First of all, most advocates of such an approach assumed that it is possible to determine two different groups using only material culture. The second assumption of this model is that the arrival of the *Romanitas* was fixed in time. The final problem was the assumption that Natives and Romans were placed at different points in social evolution, where Romans were much closer to civilisation (Revell 2009). Roman archaeology engaged in the debate on past identity mainly as a part of the study of Romanisation, that is the transformation caused through contacts of Romans and non-Roman populations. Some recent work has focused on making and maintaining local and individual identities, and on power relations in the imperial context (Curchin 2004; Hingley 2005; Oltean 2007; Revell 2009; Mattingly 2011). The different archaeological outcome in different Roman provinces has led to the belief that cultural change was more fluid than previously thought.

Some parts of Roman culture were effectively incorporated into local needs creating new hybrid cultures (Revell 2009). Becoming Roman allowed the coexistence within the imperial context of social changes and local incorporation of Roman culture in order to maintain power simultaneously at a local and imperial level. On the other hand, Roman administration had an interest in the acceptance by the local elite of Roman culture in order to achieve a stability of Empire (Woolf 1998; Hingley 2005: 47). Romanisation is perceived today as an integrative model of transculturation which stresses connections between Roman and non-Roman cultures and recognises a new hybrid (provincial) culture as a result of that transculturation.

## MATERIAL CULTURE AND IDENTITY

Interpretation becomes even more complicated in the early Roman period when new elements of material culture were introduced to the Balkans. Very soon, with an appearance of 'Roman' culture, Iron Age populations were stirred into a cauldron of Romanised people confronted with Romans who were once again recognised as an ethnically, socially and politically monolithic. Each and every piece of Roman material culture was often recognised as a Roman physical presence or sometimes as a Romanised native people (e.g. Zotović 2003). Although there is some awareness of the Romans as a mixture of people with different social, economic, religious and geographical backgrounds, such a realisation was abandoned when it came to the explanation of their relationship with local people, and Romans are still observed as one great civilising initiator of cultural changes, which naturally can only have one effect on a less civilised local people.

These traditional positions on Romanisation have been challenged during the past two decades and the bipolar contrast between Romans and non-Romans has been mainly abandoned. New ideas have focused on the routine of everyday practice (Revell 2009), and the making of new hybrid identities as the result of the collision of Romans and non-Roman population expressing the regional differences within Roman imperial culture (Hingley 2005). Within these new perspectives, many aspects of individual and collective identities were involved in the interpretation of different positions within the relations of non-Roman communities and Roman administration. By doing so, material culture is often used as a tool of expression of range of aspects of identity such as status, religious beliefs, sex or gender. One of the main differences between identity and the traditional 'archaeological cultures' is that identity changes according to the social circumstances within which it is perceived and maintained. Identity is fluid, ever changing and there is not a precise point which should be reached and maintained (Revell 2009: 8). Nevertheless, some authors are still trying to recognise ethnic attributes in various material cultures. Such a situation occurs in interpretations of the archaeology of the western Balkans during the late first century AD, where Roman archaeologists have tried to explain the situation in terms of the traditional framework of

*Figure 9.1. Roman silverware from Tekija hoard with axe-shaped pendant. (Courtesy of National Museum, Belgrade).*

Romanisation, greatly relying on ethnic attribution of material culture (Mano Zisi 1957; Popović & Borić-Brešković 1994).

## Archaeological evidence

Most of the first century AD in the Roman province of Moesia Superior is 'no man's land' in Serbian archaeology. Prehistorians stand back from this period because Roman culture is already present, even though there is plenty of material culture traditionally labeled as Iron Age. Roman archaeologists have never gathered enough evidence to reconstruct the events that took place or even to describe Roman culture.

This territory became of interest to the Romans from the end of first century BC, and after a period of conflict they established the province of Moesia in 15 AD (Mirković 1968). This period of the establishment and organisation of the Roman province is almost unknown to researchers. Most data were gathered from the rescue excavation of military camps on the Danube *limes* during the construction of the Đerdap power plant (Petrović & Vasić 1996). The legionary camps of Singidunum (Belgrade) and Viminacium (Kostolac) provided some more data over a longer period, but the evidence is very thin. The most significant other group of material culture from this period came from hoards discovered near military camps – Tekija, Bare and Boljetin (Mano-Zisi 1957; Jovanović 1990; Popović & Borić-Brešković 1994; Mihajlović 2010). The last of

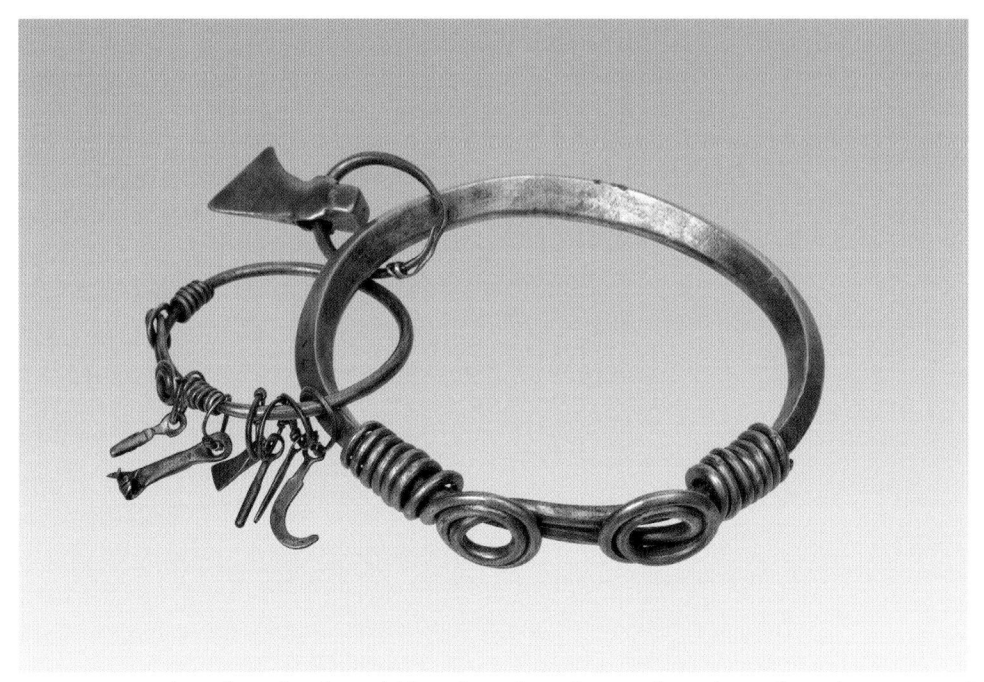

*Figure 9.2. Silver bracelet from Tekija hoard with axe- shaped pendant (Courtesy of National Museum, Belgrade).*

the three hoards (Boljetin) was only partially preserved, so the main evidence comes from the first two.

The hoard of Tekija (accidentally discovered in 1948) (Figs. 9.1–2), was preserved in a bronze vessel within a 'Roman' stone container. The precise location of the material with respect to the Roman fort of Tekija is still not known. Nevertheless, the hoard consisted of a wide range of silver and gold material: Roman coins, jewellery, military equipment and some votive plaques (Mano Zisi 1957). The hoard was originally explained as Roman military property, brought about by looting or intermarriage. Researchers were very interested in the precise date of the hoard to connect it with the exact date of the Domitian wars on the Danube. The material was considered as a whole but was divided into three 'cultural circles' – local, Roman and Hellenistic/Oriental. By doing so, researchers established two major premises in their interpretation which greatly influenced further explanations. First, they claimed that the hoard was Roman which gave a precise filter through which to observe the complete hoard, but yet none of the authors ever explained what 'Roman' actually implied, and secondly they emphasised the three groups of material culture, observed as mutually independent and with no impact on the hoard as a whole. Later the publication provided precise analogies from all over the Empire, with discussion of cultural influences and import routes, but no discussion of the owner of the hoard because he was by definition 'Roman'.

The Bare hoard was unearthed some twenty years later, and consisted of similar material to the hoard from Tekija: gold and silver jewelry, Roman silver coins and votive plaques, once again all from local, Roman and Hellenistic/Oriental cultural circles. Nevertheless, the interpretation of this find was somewhat different. The original researchers assumed that most of the objects were made locally (by Dacians) and concluded that the owner must have been Dacian himself. Roman objects, on the other hand, were explained by trade and looting, and the hoard was generally presented as the result of 'complicated relationship between Romans and local population' (Popović & Borić-Brešković 1994).

What was the nature of the finds that presented such a stumbling block for all these researchers? First of all, a great deal of silverware is recognised as early Roman imports from Italian workshops and, if so, such objects could probably have found their way to the Danube only through the Roman army or accompanying civilians. Another object, found at Tekija and often used as a clinching argument for marking a Roman soldier as the owner is a silver belt buckle with a Latin inscription of a name *G. Valerius Crescus* from the *Legio VII Claudia*. Yet, it is not clear why a Roman soldier would have placed his military belt in the ground during a military campaign. Votive plaques depicted with oriental deities are another issue, and they are commonly explained as material brought to the Danube by the Roman army, and which through various routes found their way to the local population. The handles of some of the *paterae* were perforated and decorated with a small axe-shaped pendant. The same pendants are familiar in other locally made material (bracelets) from both the Bare and Tekija hoards. Such alteration has not been confirmed in any other form of Roman material culture, so we must assume that it was a local practice. The rest of the material consisted mostly of locally made jewelry and Roman coins which were dated from the period between the late Republic and the rule of Domitian (Mano Zisi 1957; Jovanović 1990; Popović & Borić-Brešković 1994).

## Discussion

In the light of previous discussion of ethnicity and identity, it is important to try to put the first century hoards into a new and different explanatory framework. For a start, we need to debate the idea that material culture could be used as an indicator of ethnicity. Designating material culture as Roman, native, Greek or any other ethnic indicator may be a false lead towards the identity of the owner, and neither the heterogeneous material of the Tekija hoard any longer needs be identified as belonging to a Roman officer with a native wife (Mano Zisi 1957; Jovanović 1990), nor the Bare hoard perceived as a Dacian product affected by trade and plunder (Popović & Borić-Brešković 1994). The material culture could have been used to express some other facet of identity such as status. The fact that all the material was made out of precious metals (gold and silver) and that the hoards may present some kind of long-term accumulation of treasure and coinage (Popović & Borić-Brešković 1994) is supportive of that alternative interpretation of status identity. In this case, the various objects may have been collected more for their material value than for their ethnic attribution. The physical alteration of the Roman objects in a local fashion suggests a period of local ownership. New elements of everyday material culture (e.g. Roman silverware) were introduced into the local communities and these forms of Roman culture were most probably used as a means of maintaining status identity. With these objects, the owner of the hoard could easily regulate his/her position in the newly established relations of power in both Roman and local contexts. From that perspective, status is more appropriate than ethnicity.

## Conclusions

In more than one place, this paper has attempted to criticise the use of ethnicity in archaeological practice. The contemporary term of ethnicity cannot be transplanted into the past, for the simple reason that we cannot measure its importance in the past. It is more likely that various communities in the past employed different criteria to establish collective identities. The use of material culture as an indicator of someone's ethnicity is a false premise. As we know, the use of material culture to maintain different identities depends on the context more than anything else. We must observe material culture, as Peter Wells said, as a means of communication, rather than as a means of defining someone's exact position in time and place on the map of prehistoric Europe. The hoards of the Roman *limes* appear to have communicated new status in the newly formed political contexts brought into play by Roman power.

## Acknowledgments

This paper was written as part of the '*Archaeological Culture and Identity of Western Balkans* (no. 177008)' project, fully financed by the Ministry of Education and Science of Republic of Serbia.

# 10. Tracing Ethnicity Backwards: the Case of the 'Central Balkan Tribes'

*Vladimir D. Mihajlović*

**Keywords:** ethnicity, Iron Age, the Central Balkan tribes, written sources, archaeology

Iron Age studies in Serbia (and in the states of former Yugoslavia) are still dominated by a traditional approach which implies the use of concepts such as archaeological culture, tribe and ethnicity. Generally speaking, there is a tendency to link the names known from the written sources of the Greek and Roman authors to archaeological remains classified as different archaeological cultures, and even to trace their origins, using the prefixes such as 'proto-' and 'pre-', back to the Bronze Age, Eneolithic or Neolithic cultures (Vranić 2011). In this paper, I want to pay special attention to the 'backwards-methodology' used in such interpretations. By this term I mean the frequent utilisation of Roman evidence in defining the ethnic character of the pre-Roman/Iron Age, and even older collective identities, and their 'core territories' neglecting the changes that took place under direct Roman influence, as well as the malleable character of identity constructions in general. I'll try to focus on the so-called 'Central Balkan tribes' – a demarcation which was created and defined by the distinguished historian Fanula Papazoglu, and has provided ever since a kind of historical and theoretical frame of reference. Consequently, the basic problems this paper addresses concern the relations of archaeology and ancient history, the use of written sources as accurate narratives, the use of modern understandings of collective/ethnic identities, and relying on traditional concepts of culture-historical archaeology. Let us begin by reviewing some of the dominant concepts relevant to the issues of ethnicity in the studies of the Iron Age central Balkans.

## Concepts of ethnicity, tribes, and archaeological cultures in Serbian/Yugoslavian studies of prehistory

Clear articulation of the theoretical standpoints have not been and still are not very common practice in Serbian/ex-Yugoslavian archaeology. The archaeologists in the region have rarely defined their theoretical positions, embracing instead the commonsense analytical approach built on rudimentary social evolution theory, various sorts of comparisons to modern societies (usually rural or 'primitive' ones), migrations and cultural diffusions. This kind of archaeological interpretation adheres to the traditional culture-historical school of thought, derived from the wider European archaeological tradition (Johnson 1999: 1–22;

Babić 2002a; 2006; Trigger 2006: 166–312; Novaković 2011: 396–400, 443). A very important feature of interpretation in the Serbian/Yugoslavian archaeological practice has been the concept of continuity which was/is frequently used by the authors to explain different phenomena spanning from the Neolithic to the Middle Ages and beyond (Palavestra 2011). The question of continuity also represents one of the rare examples of theoretically discussed and developed archaeological issues, for which the meanings and possibilities of use were defined by Milutin Garašanin, one of the most important Serbian/Yugoslavian archaeologists of the twentieth century. He separated two kinds of continuity in archaeological studies of the past: cultural and ethnic. As he pointed out, cultural continuity, which means 'continued life of certain cultural elements, above all material, in a defined limited or broader region' (Garašanin 1964: 10, 42–3), does not have to correspond to the ethnic continuity, or vice versa. Also, Garašanin calls for caution and the use of precisely defined criteria in claiming ethnic continuity by means of material culture (Garašanin 1964: 11–31, 43; Palavestra 2011: 587–88; Babić this volume). Additionally, he emphasises that it is possible to talk about ethnicity in the broadest sense, since archaeology mainly deals with periods when the nation ('the spiritual community of humans that differ from within only in some narrower cultural elements'), was not yet formed (Garašanin 1964: 10). What is nevertheless interesting in his theoretical speculations is a comprehension that written sources have greater importance for the investigation of ethnic rather than cultural continuity, and that the combination of written and archaeological evidence could produce reliable notions of ethnic continuity (Garašanin 1964: 31–6, 44–5).

At about the same time, Alojz Benac (1964), another prominent figure in the field, tried to explain the ethno-genesis of the Illyrians using archaeological data. He proposed a gradual evolution of the ethnic group through several stages corresponding to the established general timeframe of prehistory of the region. For the first phase, which occurred during the Eneolithic, when the great Indo-European migration took groups from the East to the Balkans, Benac presumes the creation of a substratum, which had a decisive influence on further ethnic development. The population of this stage is regarded as 'pre-Illyrians' (*Prediliri*) because there were numerous different groups that could not yet be seen as the Illyrians. The next stage, that of 'proto-Illyrians', is characterised by internal, autochthonous and continuous development and social progress, taking place during the Bronze Age. In this period, the process of differentiation was still operating (since a broader cultural unity could not be seen by archaeologists), and this was the time when certain larger or smaller groups were formed, later to become tribal communities. The phase of the 'Early-Illyrian' community, occurring at the end of the Bronze and early Iron Age, is a period when the process of differentiation was completed, and a process of assimilation had began, and when some groups were already formed as more solid tribal communities. The real Illyrian epoch coincided with the Iron Age, when economic contacts and military activities contributed to strong assimilation, and the emergence of great tribes that incorporated smaller tribal groups in single, separate, communities (Benac 1964).

## 10. Tracing Ethnicity Backwards: the Case of the 'Central Balkan Tribes'

More than twenty years later, Benac (1987) addressed the problem of prehistoric collectivities again, this time on a more general level, in a publication that compiled the results of the Iron Age studies in Yugoslavia. Drawing on Garašanin and his own earlier conclusions, he offers the overall framework inside the chapter: *On the ethnic communities of the early Iron Age in Yugoslavia* (Benac 1987). According to his view at this time, the term *ethnos* is better suited for prehistory than the term *nation* or *people*, because it offers a more flexible approach for prehistoric studies. As he saw the problem, many cultural groups show greater inherent compactness and lifestyle habits, uniformity of material and spiritual culture, so they could be regarded as ethnic communities in the elementary sense of the term (Benac 1987: 737–9). Nevertheless, Benac warns that the names such as Illyrians, Thracians and Pannonians could not be treated as signifiers for specific, defined, peoples or compact ethnic communities, but as insufficiently coherent groupings without firm socio-political connections and strictly defined territories. These large groupings also lacked uniformity of material culture, and generally could be understood as similar to the cultural complexes of early prehistory, but with the possibility of a more accurate understanding thanks to the interest of the more advanced southern neighbours (i.e. Greeks). Hence, although the populations mentioned above had been labelled as firm ethnicities by ancient authors, they actually were a multitude of small and large tribes and tribal communities – a fact known from the written narratives (Benac 1987: 740). However, the caution of ascribing ethnicity to the populations of the Iron Age decreases when it comes to the concept of tribe and tribal community. First, Benac emphasised that it is beyond doubt that the Iron Age populations of the Balkans were based on lineage structure, and that the *gens* (a brotherhood or small community originating from the same ancestor) was a fundamental building block of this kind of social organisation. Accordingly, a number of lineages (*gentes*) constituted a clan, and a number of these created a tribe – the highest form of lineage structure. The tribe as a social formation took care of the common territory and interests of all its members, especially those interests concerned with interaction with other tribes. Furthermore, several kin tribes formed a tribal community/alliance (for example: the Dardanians, Histri, Liburnians, etc.), and only these were grouped into larger incoherent groupings mentioned in the historical records (Illyrians, Thracians etc.) (Benac 1987: 740–3). The consolidation of tribal divisions happened in the early and middle Iron Age, when some of the tribes united clan-, and smaller tribe-groups into larger units. During this process, such tribal communities defined the limits of their territories and established separate political units, which afterwards faced the Roman invasion and continued to live under the Roman rule. Only this type of tribal community can be considered as separate peoples/nations in the prehistoric sense of the term. On the other hand, there were also tribal alliances without fixed territorial limits and with a changeable inner structure, and these were unstable 'ethnic' communities that could not be fully compared with the kind represented by Thracians and Illyrians (Benac 1987: 743–4). Another important speculation of Benac pursues the notion of continuity, and implies that if there was an unbroken cultural link between the older prehistoric periods and the Iron Age, one has to consider an internally derived ethno-genesis without migratory influences. On this premise, a number of tribal communities, each with their own specific features, were founded on the enduring tradition of large Eneolithic and Bronze Age cultural complexes (Benac 1987: 749–50, 800).

These general theoretical premises were implemented twice by Garašanin, who described the process of ethno-genesis firstly for the Illyrians (1988), and then for the 'Palaeo-Balkan' tribes in general (1991). According to his view, which combines the older notions of continuity and Benac's conceptions of ethnicity, ethnic groups imply the existence of populations who shared a common material and spiritual culture, language, origin, and a sense of collectivity. Ethnogenesis is a long and complex process of cultural, social, and economic development during which various differentiations, regroupings, disintegrations and reintegration of different former communities lead to the formation of a broader community over a wider area. The creation of ethnic groups in the Balkans was gradual and evolutionary: in the initial phase, set in the Eneolithic and early Bronze Age, the Indo-European substratum was created; the phase of stabilisation, marked by the existence of a number of regional groups in the territories of later ethnic units, came in the Bronze Age; the final phase of ethno-genesis happened at the end of Bronze and the beginning of Iron Age, and resulted in the emergence of the ethnicities that one can find in the ancient written traditions. Because of uncertainties over the strength of collective identity, and frequent clashes between populations in the Iron Age Balkans, Garašanin thought that the term ethnic group (or ethno-cultural group, as defined by Benac) was better suited than the terms nation or people. He also pointed out that the process of ethno-genesis could be studied via the continuity of certain categories of material culture such as 'every-day' ceramic vessels, or via social practices such as funeral customs which could be specific to particular ethnicities (Garašanin 1988; 1991).

The interpretations mentioned here were by no means unique, but represent the most elaborate examples of their kind. They have been chosen because they offer the clearest synthesis of their type of explanation. Many other authors utilised all or some of these assumptions, often with far less caution and detail (see below). Although this kinds of theoretical position is not unusual in European archaeology of the second half of the twentieth century, the main problem in Serbia was the general lack of change in approach towards Iron Age studies. Several very important breakthroughs in the implementation of different perspectives (for example Palavestra 1984; 1993; Babić 2002b; 2004; 2007; Vranić 2009; 2011) were regrettably not sufficient to overturn the mainstream interpretative framework.

The salient problem of the prevailing paradigm is a strong reliance on written narratives to understand the meaning of the collective names of the inland Balkan populations in the Iron Age (for general overview of written sources see Babić 1994; Grant 1995; Potter 1999; Jones 1999). As we have seen above, the ethnicities in the Iron Age are understood as more solidly constructed precisely because there is written evidence. In practice, this means that we are allowed to suppose the existence of ethnic affiliations because of the survival of some group names, which in turn justifies the attempt to ascribe to them precise material remains and territories. If, for some reason, the ancient authors had not written about *Others* and left no collective names, the tendency to presuppose the existence of an ethnically structured Iron Age probably would not have been the dominant model. With the exception of the ancient authors' perception of the Iron Age communities, there is, in fact, no other independent evidence for ethnic-type collectivities in the Central Balkans. This brings us to the second main problem of the traditional perspective: the general assumption that material culture could underwrite ethnicity (generally on the problem: Jones 1997; 2007; Lucy 2005). These two premises impinge on interpretations of the so called 'Central Balkan tribes'.

## THE 'CENTRAL BALKAN TRIBES' IN HISTORY AND ARCHAEOLOGY

Although there were several earlier works on populations whose names were preserved in accounts of the ancient authors, the turning point, with far-reaching consequences for study of the inland Balkan populations in the Iron Age, happened in 1969. In this year, the prominent historian Fanula Papazoglu (1969) published the results of her elaborate study of all the available historical and archaeological evidence on the inhabitants of 'the protohistoric Balkans'. This work gained the status of the most influential study about the Iron Age tribes and became the unavoidable point of reference in all the subsequent studies of the issue. Her book was also published in English (Papazoglu 1978) and, to my best knowledge, has remained the only publication on the issue in a foreign language to this day. Professor Papazoglu not only synthesised all the existent data and results, but also offered some new interpretations and the general reconstruction of the separate histories of the peoples mentioned in the texts (the Triballi, the Autariatae, the Dardanians, the Scordisci, and the Moesinas) (Fig. 10.1). She described the political history of every 'tribe', and discussed their social organisation and structure, economy, and cultural practices in general. Her methodology involved the (re)constructions of the sequences of events known from surviving written material, and bridged the remaining gaps with hypotheses that fitted established linear historical narratives in the most plausible way. The implementation of cultural evolutionary theory and the employment of detailed analysis enabled this work to become widely applicable in archaeological research. In other words, archaeologists were provided with the historical framework, which could then be filled with details and referred to in speculations on the Iron Age. Let us see now how this works by reviewing the interpretations of four out of the five 'Central Balkan tribes'.

## THE DARDANIANS

According to the written sources, the majority of which originated from the second half of the first century BC onwards, the Dardanians were the population

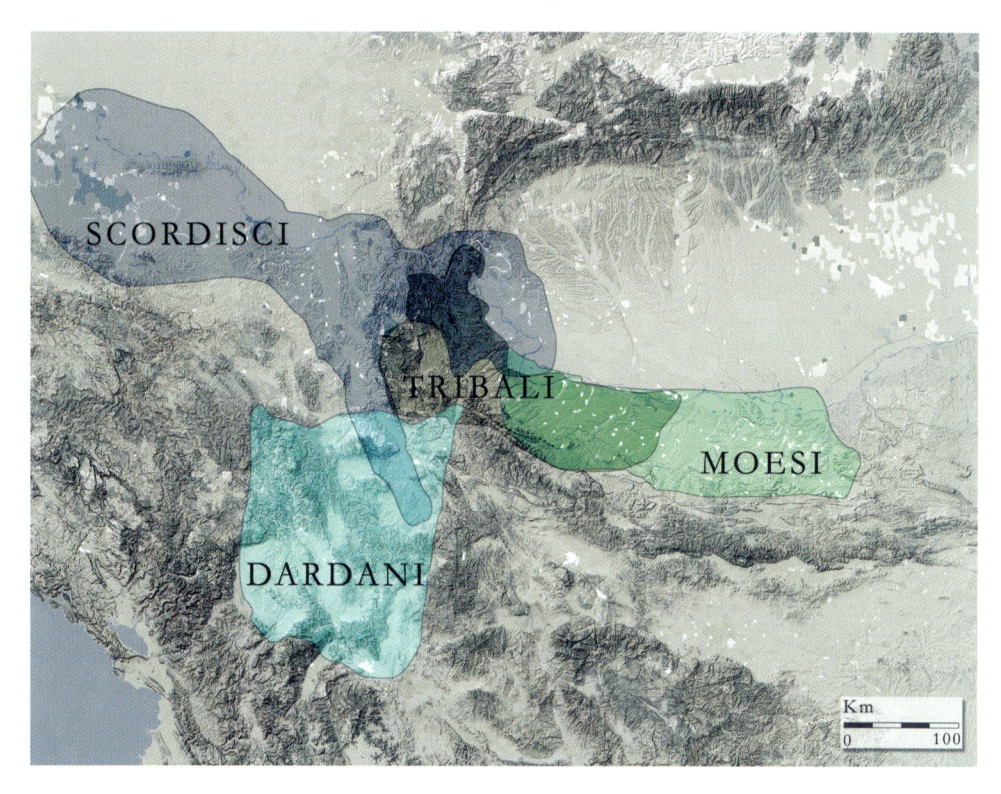

*Figure 10.1. The position of the Central Balkan tribes according to Papazoglu 1978.*

that gave considerable trouble first to the Macedonians and then to the Romans. The climax of their power supposedly took place between the middle of the third to the middle of the second century BC. The written sources describe them as the constant threat to, and fearsome enemies of, the Macedonians who fought them until their subjugation by the Romans. Afterwards, the Dardanians were mentioned as threat for the Roman province of Macedonia as well, which resulted in several separate Roman military actions and pacification in about 75 BC (Papazoglu 1978: 131–87). Except for the scarce mention of four leaders of uncertain title and status, the supposed compositional character of supra-tribal organisation, and military units of 8000 men phalanges (Papazoglu 1978: 442–5, 456–7), there is no other circumstantial evidence about the Dardanian political organisation. Even if we accept that the Dardanians were at the peak of their strength under the rule of one family, which is far from certain, the problem remains that we do not know what was actually meant by this collective name. The notion of a stable collective identity is assumed on the grounds that ethnic affiliations are a natural mode of social gathering that persisted through time. Accordingly, the mention of a couple of the Dardanian leaders hinted that an established ethnic proto-state existed which widened its boundaries at the expense of the neighbouring tribes. As there is no emic information that can help in determining what was meant by this affiliation, the combination of the Greek and

## 10. Tracing Ethnicity Backwards: the Case of the 'Central Balkan Tribes'

Roman with modern views resulted in what seems at first glance a sound interpretation. In fact, this is not necessarily the case, because there are no data that suggest a central organisation of the Dardanians, and we lack any evidence on their social organisation or the meaning of the name. The term could refer to a group of regionally based identities, acting separately or collectively through time. It could equally have meant some sort of confederation fleetingly united. It could point to a particular ethnic stereotype that grouped together the fuzzy notion of the border populations, that in the eyes of the Macedonians and Romans shared some common features. It could have represented some vague geographical location with no specific social implications at all. In sum, the only certain feature of the term *Dardanians* is that it represents an ancient construct that served its purpose in the historical narratives adapted to the social and cultural habits of the ancient audience (compare Wells 1999: 111, 116–18; Mattingly 2000: 32; Dzino 2008; 2010: 38, 143).

The problem becomes even more evident when we come to the question of the Dardanian territory. In the Hellenistic period, the only clues exist for the southern borders of the phenomenon called the Dardanians, since the rest of their central and extended area is defined with the help of the Roman Imperial sources. Thus, all kinds of available evidence are put together in order to determine the area of Dardania within the province of Upper Moesia, and by extension define the preceding Iron Age territory of the Dardanian tribe (Papazoglu 1978: 187–209). The implications of this method are clear: it creates the impression of a demarcated space constantly linked with the name of one population, even though we do not know what the term actually meant in social, political, linguistic or other terms, or even if its meaning changed through time and, if so, under what constraints. The problem is complicated further by the fact that the Roman imperial authorities had a tendency to manipulate conquered territories and populations by creating administrative units that followed their own perceptions and interests (Mattern 1999: 209; Dzino 2010: 18–19, 22, 116). This meant that one administrative unit could have been demarcated and linked with one group of people and one name that became the signifier of the all the territory and population. In this process, no pre-Roman relations needed to be respected, and depending on various conditions, the old structures could have been mostly or completely changed. Additionally, the Roman labelling could have created its own sense of a wide social cohesion among the designated people, which correspondingly could have created new collective identities with ethnic prerogatives (Orejas 1994: 276; Orejas & Sastre 1999: 171, 175–176; Wells 1999: 33, 57; Laurence 2001; Orejas & Sánchez-Palencia 2002: 590; Curchin 2004: 26, 53–6; Roymans 2004: 4, 205, 209; Dzino 2009; 2010: 161, 163–7, 181–2; Derks & Roymans 2009; Whittaker 2009: 196). In the case of Dardania, events could easily have adhered to this scenario, especially given that the organisation of mining may have had a major impact after incorporation in the Roman world. If the presumptions about the administrative structure of the mining activities are accurate, the whole southern part of Moesia was organised as a complex of imperial estates under the name *metalli Dardanici* (Dušanić 1977a; 2003), as shown by the coins with this legend (Dušanić 1971; Hirt 2010: 64–7). In other words, the Dardanian imperial domain might simply have been created in order to exploit mineral wealth as efficiently as possible, and the definition of the territory with this name, and the appearance of affiliations attached to it, could point to the process of identity creation only during the Roman times. Even the assessment of the Dardanian mining estate is exaggerated, there is a good chance that in the imperial period the Dardanians and their territory represent the outcome of identity construction in the context of new social settings, that possibly had nothing or very little to do with the pre-Roman situation. In other words, the Dardanians from the period of the Macedonian kingdom, the Dardanians from the period of the Roman Republic, and finally the people with the same name in the Roman Empire did not have to represent the same political, territorial or ethnic construct.

Difficulties in the interpretation of Dardanian ethnicity are enlarged by the lack of extensive archaeological research of the Iron Age sites within their assumed territory. Archaeological surveys and small scale excavations of some sites have furthermore been framed by the automatic designation of this ethnic affiliation (Tasić 1998: 163–89). The resistance of the traditional view has been recently demonstrated by an archaeological study that, drawing on the traditional reconstruction of the Dardanian territory, traces the ethno-genesis of the Dardanians back to the beginning of the Iron Age, linking changes in the material culture in the area to the newcomers identified as the Dardanians who, according to some ancient authors, migrated from Asia Minor to the Balkans (Lazić 2009). Interestingly, this interpretation was meant to challenge the older one identifying even earlier archaeological cultures as belonging to the Dardanian ethnic substratum (for example: Srejović 1973; 1979; Vasić 1987: 685–9; 1990: 122–3; Mirdita 1991; Tasić 1998: 157–63; Kapuran 2009: 154–5).

## THE SCORDISCI

The other Central Balkan tribe with a somewhat different 'historical/archaeological destiny' is the Scordisci. They are believed to be the remnants of the Celts that invaded Delphi, and after their defeat settled at the confluence of the Sava and the Danube, where they, mingling with the natives, created a powerful entity which terrorised the Balkans for a very long time. Military efficiency in their frequent clashes with the Romans at the end of the second and first quarter of the first centuries BC, earned them credit in modern times as a tribe at the upper scale of the pre-state development. Additionally, the written sources placing them along the Danube and in the border of Macedonia and Thrace, in combination with the La Tene material culture found in the areas of Slavonia and Srem/Syrmia, and the Danube and Great Morava Valleys, gave birth to the notion that they dominated very large territories and had their power base in area of the confluence of the Sava and Danube rivers, permitting them to cross very long distances and ravage Macedonian territory (Papazoglu 1978: 271–345). Although there was some discussion over the status of the Scordisci as one tribe or

## 10. Tracing Ethnicity Backwards: the Case of the 'Central Balkan Tribes'

a loose confederation that, according to the Celtic custom, only occasionally assembled to wage war (Papazoglu 1978: 446–7), there is general agreement on the extent of their territory defined by the La Tene finds (Papazoglu 1978: 354–89; Popović 1992; 1994; 2006: 532–6; Jovanović 1987; 1992). In this way, the existence of the Celtic Scordisci, settled in the flood plains of these major rivers, became an unquestioned historical and archaeological fact. Here again we have a problem in identifying the meaning behind the name, since we do not know what criteria are used to ascribe this term. As Danijel Džino warned, the Celts in the Balkans could have been a pseudo ethnical construct caused by a stereotyped understanding of a people who belonged to a wide cultural koine that had features understood by the Greeks and Romans as typical of the Celtic world (2007; 2008). Instead of treating the Scordisci as a defined ethnic and territorial phenomenon, I am inclined to believe that a better approach would be to see this name as a signifier of people who lived 'beyond' the borders of Macedonia and, as Dzino pointed out, shared cultural features perceived by the Romans as decisive for the designation of society and ethnicity. This might explain why they are frequently mentioned at the borders of Macedonia and associated with the populations from Thrace. In other words, both communities at the border, and those further north, were defined as the Scordisci, although they did not represent a single ethnic or political creation. Another problem rises from the fact that the linkage of the core territory of the Scordisci to the Danube and Sava was mentioned by the writers from the Imperial Roman period (Papazoglu 1978: 354–67; Popović 1994: 13), when a supposedly small local community under this name existed precisely on the right bank of the Danube in eastern Srem (Mócsy 1957; Dušanić 1967: 68, 70; Mirković 1971: 13–15). This allows for the possibility that the narrative about the core of the Scordiscian land largely emerged under the influence of a contemporary state of affairs that the authors of the imperial Roman period projected back onto the past and modern scholars subsequently took for granted.

The events after the incorporation of the area into the Roman Empire militate against the traditional reconstruction. Many groups appear with their own names, along with the supposedly small *civitas Scordiscorum* (Mócsy 1974: 53–5, 66; Papazoglu 1978: 344–5; Dautova-Ruševljan & Vujović 2006: 5–7). This is explained away in the modern reconstruction by suggesting that the newly appeared groups were parts of a previously integrated political group, the Scordisci (for example Mirković 1968: 19, 160–1; Papazoglu 1978: 378; Popović 1992: 51). However, since it is very probable that the term *Scordisci* was loosely constructed, signifying separate, regionally based, smaller communities, a more productive approach may be to see the new collective names as a creation of the Roman rule resulting from a more detailed acquaintance with the area's relations and the implementation of imperial interests. In other words, the imprecise Roman understanding of northern barbarian borders, originally given one name, might have given way to more precisely defined administrative units after incorporation in the Roman jurisdiction (that may or may not reflect older relationships). This is exactly the reason why these other names cannot be employed in speculation about the pre-roman Scordisci or seen as its constitutive elements.

The volatile character of Roman understanding and their manipulation of collective identities can be recognised in the different accounts of the population in Moesia in Pliny's and Ptolemy's reports. Pliny states that in the province of Moesia there are the *Dardanians*, *Celegeri*, *Triballi*, *Tmachi* and *Moesi*, of which the *Celegeri* would have been located in the north of the province. This is believed to represent the situation at the moment of the establishment of the province (14 AD) and several decades afterwards. On the other hand, Ptolemy's account, describing the situation in the early second century AD, mentions the *Tricrornenses*, *Pincenses* and *Moesi* in the area of northern Moesia which is seen as Scordiscian in the pre-Roman times (Mócsy 1974: 66–8; Papazoglu 1978: 344–5, 431). This discrepancy indicates that an administrative change happened in the second half of the first century AD which, again, might have something to do with mineral exploitation. The administrative unit of Pincenses, like the Dardanian one, is attested in a coin legend *(mettala) Aeliana Pincensia* (Dušanić 1971; Hirt 2010: 65, 73), and there are chances that the abbreviations on some lead ingots could be read as *(metalla) Tricornensia* (Dušanić 1977b). Anyway, we should be aware that these collective attributes could be a consequence of the new social structuring that developed under Roman rule. Therefore, we should probably choose another theoretical approach which does not have as a basic premise the ethnic continuities and genetic links with the pre-Roman populations, because neither the written sources nor the archaeological material give us that kind of static ethnic picture.

## THE TRIBALLI AND THE MOESI

The last two examples have a somewhat different interpretation since both ethnic and geographical connotations are presumed for the name *Triballi* (Papazoglu 1978: 61, 63), whereas only a geographical connotation is presumed for the term *Moesi* (Papazoglu 1978: 404, 414). Nevertheless, the Triballi have a strong ethnic association in the contemporary interpretations, as is clear from the attempts to define their territory in a strict sense and attach some types of material culture to their name. But, as in the cases already discussed, we do not possess precise information on what exactly this collective name meant and if it referred to a specific or rather more vague definition of territory. In Claudian Roman times, the communities of Triballi and Moesi were under the supervision of one Roman official, and, according to Ptolemy, the Triballi were located in the area of the Roman *Oescus* in the western part of the province of Lower Moesia. Ptolemy's entry is seen as conclusive proof for the eastern boundary of the Triballi, whereas the western boundary was reconstructed from the interpretation of the Angros and Brongos rivers (names provided by Herodotos) as Great and Southern Morava (Papazoglu 1978: 58–67). This view has had a profound influence in archaeology since data from fifth and fourth century BC (and even earlier) are commonly interpreted as Triballian on the basis of the reconstruction of their territory (Stojić 1986: 102–03, 121; 1990; 2009; Srejović 1991; Jevtić 2007; Jevtić & Peković 2008). Additionally, the notion of the existence of the Triballi in the imperial period motivated speculations about the presence of their ethnic substratum in the provinces of Upper and Lower Moesia. Accordingly, the *Timachi*, a population unknown before the Imperial times, is seen as some kind of a remnant of the Triballi, on the grounds that it was located in the previous Triballian territory. Since it was presumed that the name of the Moesi represents a whole range of populations between the Danube and the Balkan mountains, the Timachi is also seen as a part of the Moesian tribes (Papazoglu 1978: 436; Petrović 1995: 31). Once again, the persistent search for a clear ethnic picture omitted the fact that the Timachi were a Roman administrative creation, and possibly a newly constructed form of collective identity, and thus do not have to be understood as genetically linked with the historically and archaeologically imagined communities of the Triballi or Moesi.

\*\*\*

In conclusion, I must emphasise that it has not been my intention to deny the possibility of grand-scale collective identity constructions among the Iron Age populations in the Balkans. However, the problem remains that we have only a one-sided and inevitably biased set of evidence which, instead of being subjected to careful scrutiny, has been largely embraced wholesale and linked to the contemporary understandings of ethnic and national structures. Moreover, the course of interpretation moved in a reversed direction: instead of gathering archaeological data, and drawing hypotheses from these data about the possible construction of the Iron Age identities, the pre-set framework was developed first, into which the data have been squeezed to fit at any price. Thus, it is not at all surprising why the written accounts and material culture will not peacefully co-exist with our presuppositions, and why our static picture cannot provide the answers to the most basic questions. In other words, it is irrelevant whether we should locate some collective name more to the right or more to the left on the map or in space, because we do not possess the elementary notion about what that term actually signified. Now that we have reached the point where ethnic affiliations have gained the status of a dominant narrative in Iron Age studies, the best solution is to put the problem of ethnicity aside until, at some point, more accurate archaeological data can be placed alongside the written sources. Even when this eventually happens, we must be aware of the indirect character of our evidence, as well as the fact that social relations in the past were dynamic and prone to various changes, including the creation of new collective identities of all kinds.

The paper is a result of the research project *The region of Vojvodina in the context of European history* (OI177002), funded by the Ministry of Education, Science and Technological Development of the Republic of Serbia.

# 11. The Quest for Group Identity in Late Iron Age Romania. Statistical Reconstruction of Groups based on Funerary Evidence

*Cătălin Nicolae Popa*

**Keywords:** identity, burials, statistics, Late La Tène, Romania

Late La Tène Romania (second century BC–first century AD) has received very few studies that deal with identity in a broader sense, and most of these are quite recent (Florea 2006; Egri 2008; Rustoiu 2008; C. N. Popa 2010). The current situation has been determined to a large extent by the belief, shared by numerous south east European academics, that identity, especially ethnicity, has at its core a very real cultural and linguistic component (cf. Jones & Graves-Brown 1996: 7–8). For this reason, it was relatively straightforward to force such a belief onto the past and populate it with clearly bounded ethnic units. The group thought to have occupied Romania in the final part of the Late Iron Age, the Late La Tène, was given the name 'Dacians' (Daicoviciu 1981; Gostar & Lica 1984; Pescaru & Ferencz 2004; Popa 2008). The Dacians were brought by archaeology and politics to the status of ancestors, and for this reason much archaeology relating to them had, and for some still has, nationalist connotations (O'Riagáin and Popa 2012; C. N. Popa in press).

The funerary evidence from this period has been the target of a considerable number of studies (e.g. Alexandrescu 1980; Crişan 1980; Babeş 1988; Rustoiu *et al.* 1993; Sîrbu 2003). However, these works only dealt with cremation graves, since the inhumations were not seen as the outcome of regular burial practices, but associated with deviant behaviour. The few volumes that did consider the entire array of mortuary practices together were usually catalogues (Protase 1971; Sîrbu 1993). Generally, the graves are given interpretations relating to social status or occupation, such as warrior, craftsmen, priest etc. (Sîrbu *et al.* 2007). Interpretations of identity only go as far as determining whether the deceased were Dacians or something else, usually Celts or Romans (Vulpe 1976; Bondoc 2008; C. I. Popa 2008).

This paper will draw on previous research, but also point to a new direction by proposing different questions to ask of the data and different ways of approaching them. Firstly, the *a priori* assumption of ethnicity reflected in the material record is abandoned; as a corollary, all ethnic names are also put aside. This will allow the formulation of new questions about the various types of identity present in burials. Secondly, all funerary data coming from Late La Tène Romania, and which are available to me, will be considered. This refers to all features containing human remains that can be considered burials. Burials are defined as the outcome of an intentional act of depositing a partial or complete human body, embedded within a mortuary ritual, which serves to separate the dead from the living (Robben 2004: 2). Therefore, isolated finds of single or a small number of body parts are not considered, as these may be the result of taphonomic processes or the outcome of practices not related to mortuary rituals and body disposal (see for example Hill 1995: 105–08). On the other hand, the so called 'not ordinary burials' (Sîrbu 2008: 86) containing complete and partial skeletons in anatomic or non-anatomic positions and placed in features that can resemble rubbish pits, will be considered. A burial that is not ordinary remains, however, a burial. It has been proposed that some of these individuals were sacrificial victims, but in no case was there evidence of a violent death, leading to speculations about drowning, strangulation or poisoning (Babeș 1988: 13–16; Sîrbu 2008: 86–7). The same is true for cenotaphs, although in this case the presence of the body is symbolic (Parker Pearson 1999: 55–6).

## IDENTITY AND MATERIAL CULTURE

Identity is generally understood as the essence of an individual or a group in relation to a larger social context; it defines what is unique about that individual or group (Wells 1998: 242). It can draw on different elements since it is based on qualities that people see themselves as sharing with members of the same community, as well as criteria they perceive as distinguishing themselves from others (Jenkins 1997: 6; Canuto & Yaeger 2000: 2). Thus there are multiple types of identities that an individual can hold: family, religious, class, state etc. Additionally, following on the point of Jovanović (2005: 77) and O'Shea (1981: 49–52), there is a vertical hierarchy of identities according to their level of generality and which function concomitantly (e.g. local, regional, ethnic, national).

Identity exists only within social relations, since it is through them that people become aware of what makes them similar or different from the other participants (Bourdieu 1994: 24). Each person, the primary actor (*sensu* Latour 2005), is thus engaged in a network of relations that defines them. The relations between primary actors are often mediated through material culture, which is also part of the network of relations and constitutes secondary actors. Hence material culture represents the materialisation (*sensu* DeMarrais *et al.* 1996) of the relationships between people and thus of their identities.

Still, there is no one-to-one link between material culture and identity. Objects do indeed participate in mediating the relationships between people, but their role can change with every relationship where they are involved depending on the primary and secondary actors engaged in that contexts (Hakenbeck 2004). For example, a T-shirt with the US flag can participate in various relationships and thus identities, depending on who is wearing it, who is observing it and the cultural context: when worn in the US, it can express a strong national identity; when worn in some European countries, it can contribute to a relationships of otherness and antipathy, especially if the wearer is a young person and the observer is middle-aged or older; when worn in Afghanistan, it can trigger strong violent reactions as it creates an enemy identity. Therefore, material culture clearly participates in identity construction through the relationships that it mediates, but it does not carry an *intrinsic* identity. For this reason, objects cannot be attributed ethnic attributes; there are no Dacian cups or Celtic swords.

There is no doubt, however, that the material record can serve to infer past identities. By observing object associations, the context in which items appear, the activities that artefacts are connected with, one can access the relationships, and thus the identities, in which they are involved. Nonetheless, it is rarely possible to obtain a detailed identity characterisation, but rather only loose signs of these identities. In the case of the Late La Tène of the Carpathian basin, for instance, Egri (2008; this volume) observed that item sets associated with wine drinking commonly appeared outside of the Carpathian arch, while inside it, in Transylvania, that rarely happened. While some of those items were found also in Transylvania, they did not form similar sets and evidence for wine drinking in general was scarce. Consequently, the same items were involved in different drinking habits, possibly suggesting some kind of separate group identity.

## GROUP IDENTITY IN LATE LA TÈNE ROMANIA

For the purpose of my investigation into identity, the funerary record was chosen. This is because the funerary context is generally one where the sameness-otherness principle of identity seems to be especially present. Since the death of a community member is a traumatic event in which the group's integrity is thrown off balance (Malinowski 2004), group identity is often prominent as a means of reaffirming its cohesion and re-establishing its equilibrium. During the funerary ritual, the relationship between the deceased and the community members gets materialised, along with that between different groups (Fowler 2004: 97). It is through these relationships that personal identity and the community identity, as a whole, are formed and maintained.

The large majority of the burials available for Late La Tène Romania are poorly recorded. This means that many of the details of the mortuary ritual, as well as those relating to at least some of the grave goods, were very loosely noted down, if at all. Therefore, it would be an impossible task to attempt to extract detailed identity characterisations. Consequently I have opted to approach the data with the general concept of group identity and to strip it down to its very core: the concept of same-other which is fundamental to every identity construction.

### The Data

The number of individual graves used for this analysis is 210. This small number is a product of the phenomenon that affects the Carpathian Basin, and other parts of Europe, from the second century BC until the Roman conquest, which led to a dramatic decrease in the number of burials that left archaeological traces (Spânu 2002: 103). While 210 burials are indeed not many, the number is high enough to give statistically relevant results.

## Methodology. Statistical Analysis

The analysis of the burials was done through statistical modelling methods, by practically transposing the same-other principle into statistical terms (for a detailed description of the statistical method see C. N. Popa 2014). In the first instance, a specially developed algorithm calculates the similarity between each of the graves by spotting similarities and differences at various levels of manifestation, especially in the case of grave goods. Each artefact is described according to four hierarchical categories, defined in both functional and typological terms. Additional information about material, decoration and other elements is considered as well. Data about the mortuary ritual itself, such as the use of inhumation or cremation, flat or tumulus graves, single or multiple burials etc were also added to the equation. Biological information and geographical position were not considered in the statistical analysis at this point to avoid groupings based on these factors. Chronological data could not be used since most burials have a very wide or uncertain dating, making it impossible to break down the time sequence further.

The results of the similarity algorithm were employed in order to run a series of clustering procedures. Three different clustering algorithms were run, as well as an advanced multidimensional scaling procedure. Each of the algorithms determined the most likely way in which the burials could be grouped. By internally validating every result, as well as by cross-validating them through comparison, a final grouping solution was proposed (see Annex for more details).

The clustering outcome, together with the initial data, was subjected to further exploratory statistical techniques which allowed for a close characterisation of each of the burial groups. The biological and geographical information, left out of the initial analysis, were added at this stage so that specific types of group identities, such as gender or regional, might be singled out. Moreover, smaller subgroups or variants, not identified through clustering, might become obvious at this stage.

Finally, with the help of satellite imagery, each of the clusters, as well as other information, was geographically mapped. The differences and similarities between the statistical and geographical distribution of the burials, or burial elements, could help to recognise the existence of identity barriers as well as trace the dynamic interaction between the clusters.

## The Results

Following the statistical analysis, two large groups were identified within the sample, each containing further subgroups as well as several variants (Table 11.1).

Group 1 was made up of 110 individuals (Fig. 11.1). The main elements characterising it were the exclusive use of inhumation as well as the relative scarcity of grave goods. Its components were further subdivided into two subgroups.

Subgroup 1.1 was the most numerous of all the subgroups obtained, containing 58 individuals, 56 of which came from flat burials. An important factor

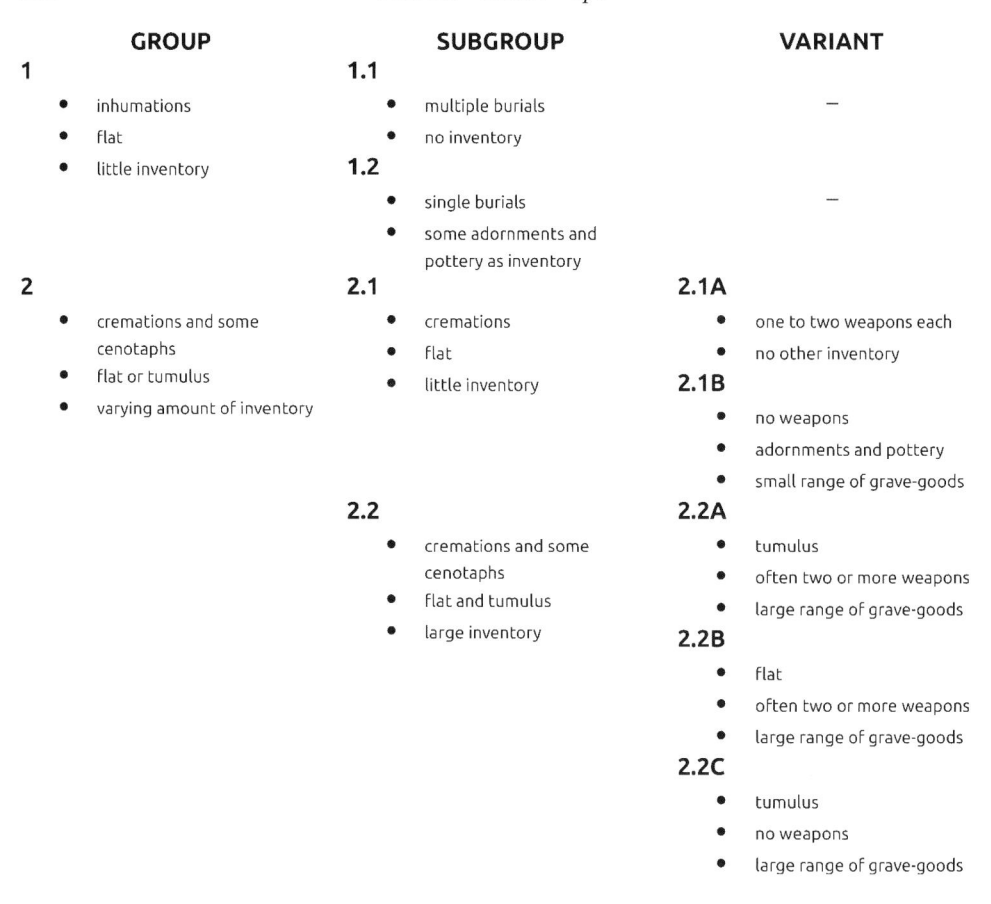

| GROUP | SUBGROUP | VARIANT |
|---|---|---|
| **1**<br>• inhumations<br>• flat<br>• little inventory | **1.1**<br>• multiple burials<br>• no inventory<br>**1.2**<br>• single burials<br>• some adornments and pottery as inventory | —<br><br><br>— |
| **2**<br>• cremations and some cenotaphs<br>• flat or tumulus<br>• varying amount of inventory | **2.1**<br>• cremations<br>• flat<br>• little inventory | **2.1A**<br>• one to two weapons each<br>• no other inventory<br>**2.1B**<br>• no weapons<br>• adornments and pottery<br>• small range of grave-goods |
| | **2.2**<br>• cremations and some cenotaphs<br>• flat and tumulus<br>• large inventory | **2.2A**<br>• tumulus<br>• often two or more weapons<br>• large range of grave-goods<br>**2.2B**<br>• flat<br>• often two or more weapons<br>• large range of grave-goods<br>**2.2C**<br>• tumulus<br>• no weapons<br>• large range of grave-goods |

*Table 11.1. Summary of groups, subgroups and variants with main characteristics.*

seemed to be that more than two thirds of these individuals came from multiple burials, meaning that at least two bodies dating to the Late La Tène period were present in the grave. Additionally, all the burials were situated either within the perceivable limits or close to a contemporary settlement. Of the 46 individuals that were given approximate age estimation, most were identified as being either newborn babies or children and only 11 of them were adults. Just 11 skeletons were sexed; the male:female ratio determined was five to six. Only three of the graves had grave goods, every time only one object, none of which was identifiable. Geographically, the burials of this subgroup appeared to be distributed across the entire area under study, despite the fact that all the burials came from only 10 sites. Most sites were located to the South of the Carpathians, especially in Muntenia. Nonetheless one third of the individuals came from south west Transylvania. Only four of the burials came from Moldova, to the East of the Carpathians. The large geographical spread of this subgroup highly contrasts with its statistical spread, since this was the tightest of all the subgroups,

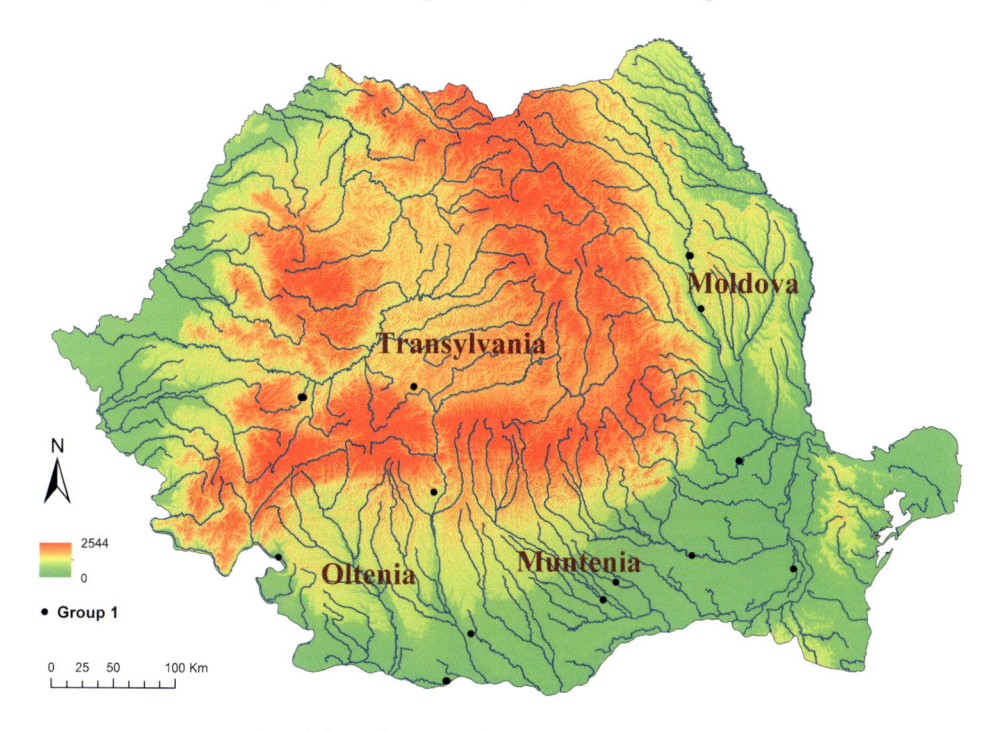

*Figure 11.1. Geographical distribution of Group 1.*

meaning that its individuals were extremely similar to one another. The ideal for the individuals from this subgroup seems to be the use of inhumation, in a flat grave, preferably multiple burials and without grave goods.

Subgroup 1.2 consisted of 52 burials of which 49 were flat and only three from tumuli. Half of the skeletons came from single burials, while the others occurred in multiple burials. As in the case of the first subgroup, all individuals were found either close to, or within, a contemporary settlement. Of the individuals that had their age determined, just seven were adults, while the rest were younger. Most burials could not be sexed, but the few skeletons that had their sex determined reveal an approximately equal male to female ratio. All burials had grave goods, although generally only one to two objects were present. More than 70 per cent of the grave goods were adornments or clothing accessories and were found together with 46 individuals. Of the adornments, especially common seem to be the bead and pendant necklaces, particularly the so-called bucket-pendants. The bucket-pendants probably functioned as protective amulets and contained organic materials, such as seeds, flowers, animal hair or bones etc. (Egri and Rustoiu personal comment). Fibulae were less numerous, but also significant. As with the last subgroup, the individuals seem to be distributed across the entire study area, although, proportionally, most graves were located in south west Transylvania. This concentration is probably a statistical bias, since the site of Hunedoara-Grădina Castelului from Transylvania is one of the few where a large number of inhumations have been systematically excavated. The

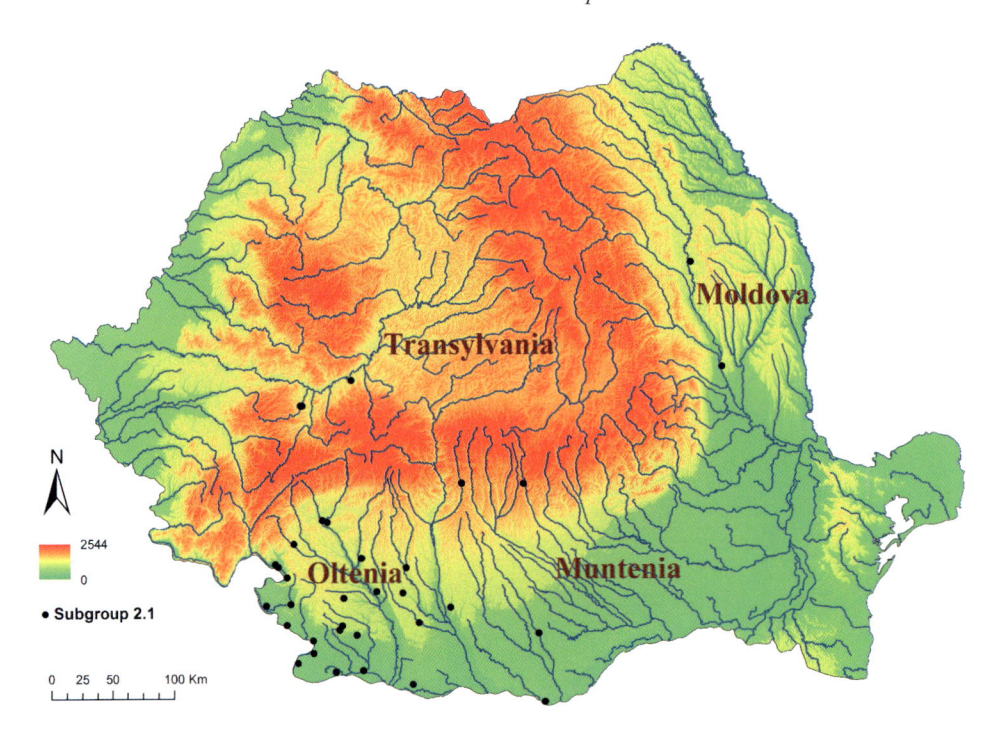

*Figure 11.2. Geographical distribution of Subgroup 2.1.*

geographical spread of the burials contrasts in this case as well with their high statistical similarity. The ideal for the individuals from this subgroup appears to be the use of inhumation, in a flat grave, single or multiple burials, with one to two personal objects as grave goods, usually adornments.

Group 2 contained 100 individuals. Its main features were the use of cremation, although a small number of cenotaphs were also included, and the presence of weapons in a substantial number of graves. Its components were further subdivided in two subgroups.

Subgroup 2.1 was made of 52 burials, nearly all of which were flat cremations (Fig. 11.2). Almost all of the deceased came from single burials. The position relative to a settlement was only determined in about half of the cases; with this proviso, the graves were generally situated close to a contemporary settlement, but never actually within its limits. No sex or age information was usually available. Only three burials contained no grave goods. The rest had approximately 108 objects of which 48 were weapons, 90 per cent of them offensive (*i.e.* swords, spears or battle knives). These weapons were found in 28 of the graves, half of which had two or more pieces of weaponry. Less numerous, but also significant in number, were ceramic vessels and adornments or clothing accessories. It is possible to observe that there is an inverse correlation between adornments or clothing accessories and weapons in this subgroup. Generally if one appeared the other did not. The same point holds true for pottery and weapons. In the case of

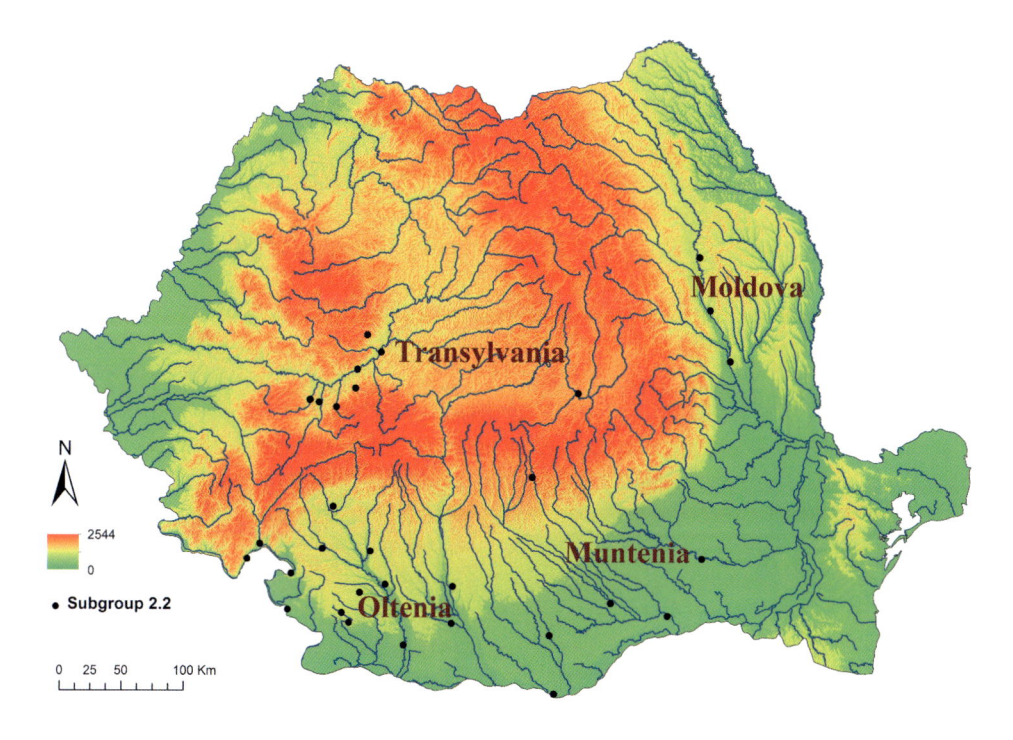

*Figure 11.3. Geographical distribution of Subgroup 2.2.*

pottery, problems of recording can be invoked. Many of these burials were chance finds and often pottery fragments were not gathered or mentioned. These two observations suggest the existence of two subgroup variants, one with weapons (2.1A) and the other without (2.1B). The geographical distribution of the burials shows far less dispersal than in the previous cases. Approximately 70 per cent of the graves were located in the western part of the region south of the Carpathians (Oltenia), very frequently on the banks of the Danube. With the exception of three burials, all the graves containing weapons were placed in Oltenia, whereas the others appeared in Muntenia and south west Transylvania. The weapon-less burials were placed either in Muntenia or Oltenia; two of them were outliers, as they appeared in Moldova and were very likely misplaced by the clustering algorithms. The ideal for the individuals from this subgroup was apparently flat cremations with or without weapons. The graves with weapons contained no other grave goods, where the model appears to have been simplicity. The burials without weapons had either pottery or adornments and contained a small number and range type of artefacts.

Subgroup 2.2 was the smallest of the four, containing 48 individuals; at the same time, it was the most widespread geographically and had the largest internal variation (Fig. 11.3). The subgroup contained 40 cremations and seven cenotaphs, plus one burial of unknown ritual, probably a cremation. It was made up of an almost equal amount of flat and tumulus graves and the bodies came almost exclusively from single burials. The large majority of the graves were located near a contemporary settlement. Age and sex were mostly not established. 46 of the burials had grave goods and generally contained a significant number of finds, as this subgroup incorporated more than 65 per cent of all material culture from the database. 115 of these grave goods were weapons, from 37 individuals. Three possible correlations can be observed based on the grave goods. Firstly, 12 out of 13 burials that contained horse gear elements also had weapons, most of them offensive. Secondly, in nine out of the 14 cases where a defensive weapon appeared (i.e. shield, helmet, chainmail) an offensive weapon was also present. Thirdly, there seemed to be a significant correlation between weapons, adornments or clothing accessories (generally no necklaces but fibulae instead, especially in the flat graves) and pottery, as the three have the tendency to appear together in the same burial. Spatially, this subgroup appears to have the largest and the most uniform spread, with an almost equal number of burials coming from south west Transylvania, the East of the Carpathians (Moldova) as well as the area south of the Carpathians, Muntenia and Oltenia. However, one should note that there were practically no weapons found to the East of the Carpathians. Therefore, the ideal for the individuals of this subgroup seems to correspond to a model of flat or tumulus cremations, generally with weapons as grave goods. Almost all the flat graves had weapons, usually more than one, and always contained other items associated with them, especially horse gear, adornments or clothing accessories and ceramic vessels. As for the tumulus burials, they also seem to correspond to the model of having weapons and several other associated items. However, there is also a smaller group of tumulus burials without weapons, half of them cenotaphs and almost all situated to the East of the Carpathians. All this suggests the existence of three variants: 2.2A, tumulus with weapons, in Muntenia and south western Transylvania; 2.2B, flat with weapons, in Oltenia and south western Transylvania; 2.2C, tumulus without weapons, in Moldova.

## Discussion

The two large groups that were identified appear to have coexisted together: there is an almost perfect spatial and chronological overlap. In some cases, burials from the two groups even appeared within the same site. However, there is little similarity between the two, in the case of both the mortuary ritual and the grave goods. Beside the different choice in dealing with the body, inhumation in one case, cremation in the other, there is a fundamental contrast in the placement of the burials: the graves from group 1 were often found within the perceivable limits of a Late La Tène settlement; those from group 2 almost never occurred within settlements. Moreover, two thirds of the individuals form group 1 came from multiple burials, while nearly all from group 2 were found in single graves. Furthermore, the burials of group 1 usually came from sites where three or more individuals were found, while in the case of group 2 the overwhelming majority of the graves were isolated. Only some of the tumulus burials were gathered in groups of four to five or more. In most such cases merely a sample of the tumulus cemeteries was excavated, but the existence of more burials is often indicated. Such is the case at Brad (Ursachi 1995), Răcătău (Căpitanu 1986), Poiana (Vulpe & Teodor 2003) or Popeşti (Vulpe 1976). The grave goods also suggest essential differences between the two large groups. First of all, there is a radical distinction in the sheer quantity of artefacts found in the burials: close to 85 per cent of all the items came from the graves of group 2. The type of objects deposited with individuals from the two groups also shows an important contrast. In group 1 the large majority of the grave goods were adornments or clothing accessories, usually necklaces and fibulae, but also a small number of earrings and belts; the few other items were coarse pottery and some tools. In group 2 there was a much wider diversity of items. The most numerous were weapons, followed by ceramic vessels and adornments; an important number of horse gear elements and some tools were also found. Therefore it would appear that the items of the individuals from group 1 were very personal objects, probably related strictly to the deceased; nearly all of them would have been in direct contact with the body. The large majority of the objects from group 2 probably had a less personal relationship to the deceased; many could have been linked to status. Even in the few instances where there is some overlap between the two groups, in the case of adornments or clothing accessories, significant differences are immediately noticeable. Most of the adornments of group 1 were necklaces, both made of beads and having a bucket-pendant; fibulae occupied the second place. The majority of the adornments of group 2, however, were fibulae. The few necklaces from group 2, less than half the number of those from group 1, were mostly bead necklaces; only four of them had a bucket-pendant. Additionally, the few fibulae from group 1 were, with the exception of one, of a different type from those of group 2. The only type that appears in both groups, although in only one instance, is the type 17 as defined by Rustoiu (1997), the so-called Jezerine fibula. However, it should be noted that the Jezerine fibula from the burial of group 2, found at Piatra Craivii, presented important local variations: it was made of iron rather than bronze and it was much larger than the standard type. This suggests that it was not part of the normal costume in which a Jezerine fibula was usually included (Rustoiu & Gheorghiu 2009; 2010).

All these differences indicate that we are dealing with two separate group identities. Nevertheless, because there was total overlap in space and time between them, the groups were not conflicting, one with another, but were rather complementary in society, functioning in a sort of symbiosis, although always keeping completely separate mortuary rituals. Since evidence suggests that gender was not a factor that influenced group membership (though this conclusion may be determined by a data bias, given the small numbered of sexed individuals), the most likely theory would be that it was determined by a difference in social status. This hypothesis fits well with the discrepancies in richness (that is quantity and assumed value) and in the care given to the graves. The burials of group 2 contained far more items and many of the graves, especially those of subgroup 2.2, were obviously set up with a lot of attention and sometimes effort. In group 1, however, we occasionally find that there was almost negligence in burying the individuals: some of them were encountered in features that resembled rubbish pits. Additionally, it sometimes seemed as if the bodies were just thrown in the grave pit rather than laid in carefully. Often multiple skeletons appeared to be disposed of in the same pit. There are nonetheless cases where at least some care was taken in preparing the grave pit and in placing the bodies: for example the inhumations at Hunedoara-Grădina Castelului (Sîrbu *et al.* 2007) or some of those from Grădiştea (Sîrbu 1986). Consequently, it would seem that the burials of group 2 belonged to a high status part of the population (i.e. the elite), while those of group 1 were comparatively less prominent people.

On the other hand, the latter graves also indicate a different conception of the body, which may have to do with the special position occupied by these particular individuals in society. It is unlikely that the inhumations belonged to ordinary community members since only 110 were found; hence the majority received a funeral that did not leave any archaeological trace. Moreover, only 18 of the 95 skeletons that had their age determined were adults, as the rest were younger, mostly newborns and young children. The percentage of adults is extremely low not just on the level of the whole group, but also when reducing the analysis to individual sites. This proportion of children to adults is abnormal considering the estimated child mortality for prehistoric times of approximately 50 per cent (Chamberlain 1997: 249; 2000: 208–09) and even more unusual in comparison to what is generally found in the archaeological record, which is always much lower (Lucy 1994; Chamberlain 2000; Röder 2002). Therefore, the individuals of group 1, besides belonging to a part of the population that did not enjoy a high status, were perceived as sharing a property which was most commonly associated with children. Yet, only the children that had this particular social status were perceived as having this property, since there are at least two cases when children were cremated and buried with weapons (Rustoiu & Comşa 2004). Consequently, it is possible that the deceased of group 1 were regarded as not being a full social person (*sensu* La Fontaine 1985); the children because of their age, the rest because of some other factor. A rather similar case was found at the Iron Age hillfort of Danebury, although in that case most of the skeletons belonged to adults. Nonetheless Walker (1984) reaches a similar conclusion about the deceased being social outsiders.

It is hard to understand what the two divisions of this group, 1.1 and 1.2, stood for and what the relationship between them was. Both of them were equally spread spatially and frequently appeared on the same site. Little variation could be seen between the different geographical regions. Therefore, considering also the high statistical similarity of the subgroup elements, it looks like we are dealing with a large and unitary phenomenon. The two subgroups related to very close identities, whose very subtle differences cannot be grasped at this point. Unfortunately the current data does not allow for any further conclusions to be reached.

The picture presented by the subgroups and variants of group 2 is much more complex. It seems that two independent subgroups existed with little admixture, one in Muntenia and one in Oltenia. The one in Muntenia, 2.2A, was a tumulus

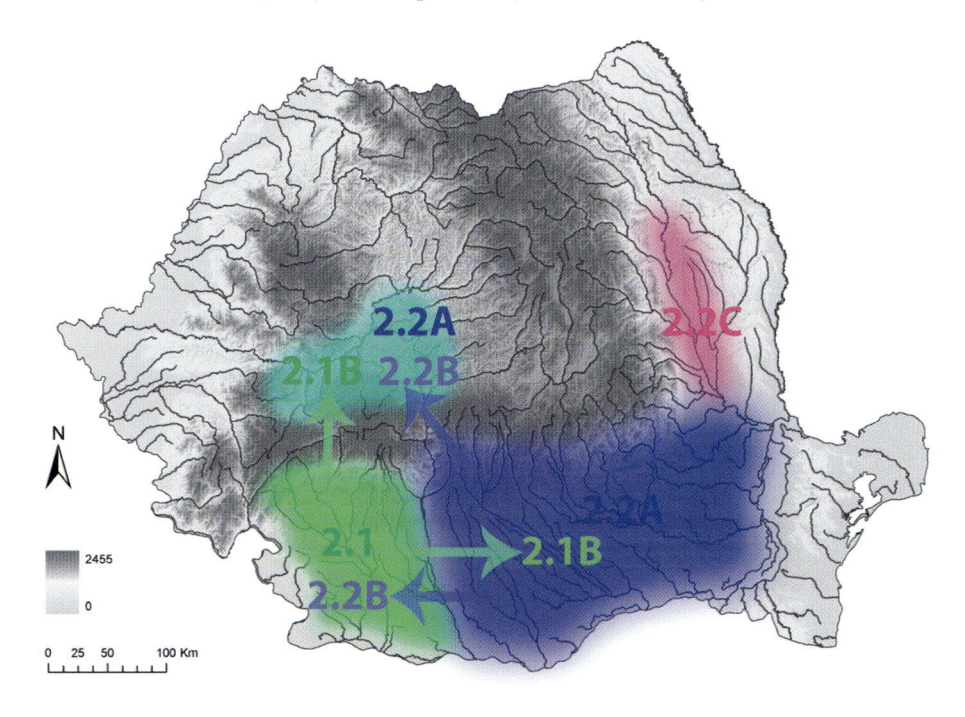

*Figure 11.4. Subgroup interaction within Group 2.*

burial, generally with a number of weapons but also other items. This subgroup extended also into south west Transylvania, maybe at a later date or maybe at the same time, and in Moldova, where the dating was certainly later, and where it got a local variation, 2.2C, without weapons. When extending into Oltenia, the type of burials change from tumulus to flat (2.2B), probably due to contact with subgroup 2.1, but retained the rest of the elements of 2.2A, especially the presence of weapons which seems to be actually increased, probably again due to contact with subgroup 2.1. In Oltenia, the dominant subgroup was 2.1, consisting of flat cremations, with or without weapons. It extended also into Muntenia but, with the exception of two graves, strictly with the weapon-less variant, 2.1B. The same is true for south west Transylvania, although there it extended in smaller numbers. This last region, south west Transylvania appears thus to be a melting pot, where numerous traditions coexisted. This is where, maybe on a 2.2A background, 2.2B and 2.1B penetrated from Muntenia and Oltenia, although this directionality cannot be confirmed because of a lack of chronological understanding. These results, although they do not fully confirm Rustoiu's theory about the migration, at least of elites, from Muntenia and Oltenia to Transylvania (Rustoiu 2002: 33–40), do not contradict it either. A good chronological sequence of the mortuary finds would allow for a better investigation into this theory. On the other hand, Moldova was the opposite of Transylvania, since only one model ever functioned there, 2.2C (Fig. 11.4).

These observations suggest the existence of several identity groups that related with each other in different ways. A possible interpretation would be that we are dealing with two, probably warrior elite, identity models in Oltenia and Muntenia, 2.1A and 2.2A. These models did not coexist within the same community. Two likely scenarios come to mind. It could be that we are dealing with an antagonistic, maybe even hostile relationship between the two warrior groups. Alternatively, it may be that these variants are representative of a wider shared warrior elite tradition, having homologous roles in communities to which they related in a different manner. Regardless of the explanation, it resulted in an identity boundary being maintained between the two, probably running along the Olt River, which separates the two regions. However, this boundary was not rigid, since it was crossed by the 2.1B and 2.2B variants. These last variants could be adaptations of the original ones, born through constant interaction. In south west Transylvania, however, any such boundaries were dissipated, as the three variants coexisted.

A separate, single identity model, 2.2C, functioned in Moldova. The total lack of weapons from the elite burials of this region indicates an identity that never had or had lost its martial characteristics, although most of the other elements present in the well-furnished graves from Muntenia were maintained. This absence of elements linked to conflict is also supported by the finds from the three settlements associated with the burials from Moldova. The only thing that can be linked to military activity was the existence of a fortification system in all three settlements, Poiana (Vulpe & Teodor 2003: 40–1), Brad (Ursachi 1995: 99–102) and Răcătău (Căpitanu 1992), for a very short period of time: approximately from the middle of the first century BC to the end of the same century or start of the next (Florea 2011: 76–7). Afterwards, despite the lack of a destruction layer, the fortifications are abandoned and in some cases built over by domestic structures. Commercial rather than military factors seem to have prevailed at these sites (Florea 2011: 75–87). Consequently, the local elites developed an identity that corresponded with the main activities from their communities.

## Conclusion

The ideas put forward in this paper argue for a complex group identity dynamic functioning in Late La Tène Romania. By employing a statistical method which is based on a critical approach to identity through the material record, it has been shown that the funerary data hold exciting information regarding the Late Iron Age communities. The existence of two large groups has been determined, most likely reflecting their status and social perception. They were defined by a different funerary ritual and the use of almost exclusively different grave goods. The first group, probably of individuals that did not enjoy a high status, contained inhumations with no grave goods or just very personal items such as necklaces. It can be divided into two further subgroups, although it is unsure what each stood for. The subgroups had a large and relatively equal geographical spread that contrasted with their high statistical similarity; this is suggestive of a very unitary funerary phenomenon which linked into a basic identity shared throughout the entire territory. The second group, probably that of the elites, was characterised mostly by cremations. Based on the mortuary ritual and the grave goods, in which an important place was played by weapons, two subgroups and several subgroup variants were identified. The statistical similarities and geographical distribution of these subgroups and variants sketched a picture with identity boundaries of variable intensity. In some regions, identity borders were totally non-existent, with different models coexisting without any sign of divergence (south west Transylvania). In other parts, identity barriers were present, but these barriers were strongly permeated by other models. Nonetheless, when multiple models functioned in parallel, at least one of them underwent a local development which allowed for cohabitation with the other identity types, as it is the case with Oltenia and Muntenia. The eastern region (Moldova) illustrates, however, the case where a model became highly localised and strongly rooted. It dominated the area as the single model, suggesting the active maintenance of an identity barrier.

## Acknowledgements

I would like to thank my PhD supervisors, Simon Stoddart and Gelu Florea, for the help and support they have given me throughout my research. My thanks also go to Mariana Egri and Aurel Rustoiu for the considerable advice and encouragement received. Last but not least, I am grateful to Barbara Hausmair for the countless discussions relating to archaeological theory, identity and mortuary practices.

## Annex

The similarity algorithm has three basic steps. During the first step, graves are compared amongst each other based on a series of variables linked to mortuary ritual and position of the graves. For this study the variables are: grave ritual (inhumation/cremation), grave type (flat/tumulus), multiple burial (yes/no), settlement proximity (far/near/inside), river proximity (far/near/banks), grave goods (yes/no). All variables have a specific weight associated with them which fixes how much they contribute to the similarity calculation. The sum of all weights is used to divide the similarity result in order to standardise it to a value between 0 and 1.

In the second step, graves are again compared with one another but this time based on their grave good items. Every item, just like the graves in step one, is defined according to a series of weighted variables: four hierarchically-related categorical variables that describe the function and shape of the artefact (e.g. weapon/offensive/sword/sword type 1), one variable containing information about the main material that it was made from (e.g. iron, bronze), another variable containing information about the state of the item (whether it was burned or folded) and a final variable recording the presence or absence of decoration. Using them, each item from a grave is compared with every other item from another grave. With the help of a simplified version of the so-called Hungarian algorithm (Kuhn 1955), the grave goods comparisons that give the maximum similarity for each two graves are selected and summed. The result, just like in step one, is standardised using the sum of all variable weights, producing a value between 0 and 1.

The third and final step of the similarity algorithm consists of combining the values obtained in the previous two steps. This is done through a weighted mean that varies the emphasis placed on the mortuary ritual comparison or on the grave goods based on the number of items found in each grave.

The results of the similarity algorithm are used to run three separate clustering procedures: Hierarchical Clustering, Partitioning Around Medoids and Fuzzy Clustering (Kaufman & Rousseeuw 2005). Their outcome is internally validated using the Dunn index (Dunn 1974) and especially through silhouette calculations (Rousseeuw 1987). Additionally, the clustering results are manually validated using exploratory procedures. A valid solution is considered to be reached when all three, or at least two of the clustering procedures, produce valid results which resemble each other to a large degree. In order to infer how similar the clustering results are to one another the adjusted Rand index is used as well as simple crosstabulation observations (Hubert & Arabie 1985; Miligan & Cooper 1986; Everitt *et al.* 2011: 264–5).

# 12. Changing Identities of the Iron Age Communities of Southern Pannonia

*Hrvoje Potrebica and Marko Dizdar*

KEYWORDS: IRON AGE, HALLSTATT, LA TÈNE, IDENTITY, PANNONIA

The region of northern Croatia covers a part of the southern Pannonian plain, stretching between the eastern Alps and the Danube valley, while the Drava valley roughly marks its northern border. It lies on the crossroads of the most important communication routes between central and south east Europe. A branch of the very important Amber Road also passed through it, linking northern Europe with the eastern Adriatic coast and the eastern Mediterranean region. These facts exerted a major influence on the dynamic development of Iron Age communities in the territory of northern Croatia.

The first significant Iron Age sites with prominent finds were discovered in the late nineteenth century, predominantly in the Danube area (Batina, Dalj, Sotin etc.), and gave rise to the first syntheses (Hoffiller 1938; Vinski & Vinski-Gasparini 1962). Unfortunately, the most recent synthesis of the Iron Age of this region was published more than 30 years ago (Vinski-Gasparini 1987). It was based on the assumption that many significant changes in the material culture of this region can be explained by migrations of various communities from the lower Danube region (in the Early Iron Age), from the Balkans (at the turn of the Early to the Late Hallstatt period) and from Central Europe (at the beginning of the Late Iron Age). The Roman conquest at the end of the first millennium BC marked the end of the autochthonous development of individual Southern Pannonian communities, and, according to some authors (Majnarić-Pandžić 1970), once again deeply changed the region in question.

The perception of the Iron Age has been significantly modified in the past ten years. The simple picture of uniform development present in earlier works on this area was the result of the low level of research of the Iron Age sites in Croatia, and also of the differing level of knowledge about the period in the neighbouring regions. For this reason, Southern Pannonia, with its intense and complex cultural dynamics in the period between the Late Bronze Age and the historical times of the Roman conquest, provides an excellent arena for study of all kinds of identity issues relating to various communities and their interactions.

In the last decade, excavation of several sites, mostly cemeteries, has brought to light new evidence that has significantly altered our perspective on the creation and development of the Iron Age communities of Southern Pannonia. In addition, knowledge of the period in the neighbouring regions has been reassessed, especially on the subject of cultural phenomena that can be compared

*Figure 12.1. Batina – grave 12 (photo: Tomislav Hršak).*

with the sites and finds discovered in northern Croatia (Teržan 1990; Gavranović 2011). All of this has posed important questions about the chronological framework, which needs to be synchronised with the relevant Central European chronologies of the Early Iron Age (Teržan 1990; Metzner-Nebelsick 2002; Trachsel 2004) and of the Late Iron Age (Krämer 1985; Gebhard 1989; Rieckhoff 1995).

The results presented in this paper are based on previously published finds, and on the results of excavations made in the past ten years, at the Early Iron Age cemeteries in Budinjak, Kaptol, Dolina, Batina and Sotin, and at several Late Iron Age sites, such as Zvonimirevo, Mali Bilač, Osijek and Sotin. What is still lacking for a full understanding of this complex period is excavation of some larger areas of the settlements, and this will be one of the most important tasks of future research.

The first important period is the transition from the Late Bronze to the Early Iron Age, which in this area, in most cases, means the transition from the Urnfield Culture to the Hallstatt Culture. During the Late Bronze Age, the region of northern Croatia belonged to the Urnfield Culture, which is divided into two main phases, with several distinct cultural groups in each (Vinski-Gasparini 1973; 1983; Karavanić 2009). The relevant cultural groups for the transition period leading to the Early Iron Age are those of the late phase of the Urnfield Culture (Dalj, Donja Dolina, Ruše, Velika Gorica-Dobova). Although the beginning of all of these groups is dated to the eleventh century BC, and they all went through the main development phases, the last phases of individual groups are

## 12. Changing Identities of the Iron Age Communities of Southern Pannonia 125

*Figure 12.2a. Sotin – grave 69 (photo: Daria Ložnjak).*

*Figure 12.2b. Sotin – grave 69 – loom weights (photo: M. Dizdar).*

*Figure 12.3. Budinjak – tumulus 139 – grave 6 (photo: Municipal museum Zagreb).*

marked by significant variations. There are two basic concepts used to describe this change. Advocates of *'Hallstattisation'* describe it as a transformational process, while others see the introduction of the Hallstatt Culture as a consequence of the collapse of the Old (Bronze Age) World, caused or followed by the emergence of the New (Iron Age) World (Stegmann-Rajtar 1992; Nebelsick 1994; Kemenczei 2000). This New World was based on new and introduced cultural elements, with the use of some reconstructed cultural features and traditions from the Old. At this moment, we can describe the common cultural features of the Late Urnfield Culture in northern Croatia, as well as the general features of the Hallstatt Culture, but what happened in between remains clouded to a large extent.

The latest research indicates that the transition process differed significantly among the various territories of northern Croatia. The situation was most complex in the eastern part of northern Croatia, in the Danube region, where two cultural groups of different origins coexisted, and their development paths were also different.

In the sites in the Danube region, such as Dalj, Vukovar, Sotin, Šarengrad and Ilok, there were some characteristic of the Dalj Group, among the Early Iron Age finds discovered, as well as others characteristic of the Bosut Group. The Dalj Group was present in the territory of eastern Slavonia, south west Bačka and Baranja, and it marked the south east border of the distribution area of the Late Urnfield Culture. The group continued its uninterrupted development throughout the Early Iron Age, with certain novelties among the finds (such as the use of iron objects, burials under tumuli etc.), but some characteristic features, such as the burial ritual (cremation in flat graves), remained unchanged

(Vinski & Vinski-Gasparini 1962; Vinski-Gasparini 1973; Metzner-Nebelsick 2002). One important novelty that marked the beginning of the Early Iron Age is the burial of prominent individuals under tumuli, as was the case in Batina (Metzner-Nebelsick 2002; Bojčić et al. 2009; 2011). Such graves were furnished with rich grave goods: for example, with offensive and defensive weapons, jewellery and characteristic vessels belonging to banquet sets. Therefore, the transition from the Late Bronze Age to the Early Iron Age was very slow, and it was not reflected in any major changes, which can also be observed in the results of the analysis of pottery shapes and decorative motifs. The transition occurred in the late ninth century BC, at a time when this community, which controlled the important communication route along the Danube, was participating in the transfer of new ideas and technologies, probably supervised by the local elite.

At the same time, the Bosut Group, which was part of the eastern Carpathian complex of fluted pottery was present in Syrmia, southern Bačka and Banat, and northern Serbia, (Tasić 1971; 1980; Vasić 1973; 1977; 1987; Medović 1978; 1988). The Bosut Group is synonymous with the Early Iron Age of this region, with its earliest phase (Kalakača) dated to the end of the second and the beginning of the first millennium BC (Medović 1988), concomitantly with the inception of the Dalj Group of the Late Urnfield Culture. In sites such as Dalj, Vukovar and Sotin, the same facilities and graves, dated to the period between the eleventh and the eighth century BC, have yielded finds that can be attributed to both groups; but the finds of the Dalj Group originate from the Late Bronze Age, while those of the Bosut Group originate from the Early Iron Age (Vinski-Gasparini 1973; Šimić 1984; Ložnjak Dizdar 2004). Particularly important are the nine inhumation graves characteristic of the Bosut Group, discovered in an cremation cemetery of the Dalj Group at Lijeva Bara in Vukovar (Vinski & Vinski-Gasparini 1961; Vinski-Gasparini 1973). They indicate that the region of eastern Slavonia and western Syrmia was the contact area of different cultural influences. At the beginning of the Iron Age, in this area, influences from the lower Danube region came across those from Central Europe. Such influences left profound marks on local communities, which in turn spread them to other regions.

In view of the current level of research, the main problem is posed by the chronological framework mentioned above. Each of the groups has its relative chronology, although a number of similar features can be observed, especially among the shapes of metal objects, which allow for a synchronisation of individual development phases. The results of some recent excavations (Sotin, Batina), and analysis of already familiar finds (Dalj, Vukovar), support the hypothesis of their dissimilar origins. Although the idea of the uninterrupted development of the Bosut Group until the beginning of the Late Iron Age still exists (Medović & Medović 2011), in the second half of the seventh century BC certain changes can be observed in both groups, suggesting the emergence of a transitional phase at the beginning of the Late Hallstatt Period. At that time, the Danube region was already involved in intensive contacts with the Balkans (Vasić 1987). In parallel, in the neighbouring region, the development of the Dalj Group ceased, and some finds of Balkan origin appeared. In the Late Hallstatt period, both cultural groups were replaced by a single cultural phenomenon, but the exposure of the region to various influences continued, especially from the south east Alps and the lower Danube region.

One of the most important sites with finds from the transition phase between the Late Urnfield Culture and the Early Iron Age is Dolina, in the central part of the Sava valley. It is located just across the river from Donja Dolina, an extremely important Iron Age communication centre, situated in present-day Bosnia (Marić 1964; Čović 1987). The oldest finds from the settlement in Dolina can be dated to the Late Urnfield Culture, but the most abundant finds originate from the beginning of the Early Iron Age. The settlement was located on a low elevation on the northern bank of the River Sava, with a cemetery in its immediate vicinity. At the beginning of the Early Iron Age, tumuli with cremation burials appeared, reflecting a continuation of the funerary practices of the previous period. Finds discovered in graves, such as elements of male and female dress and pottery vessels, provide an interesting insight into the beginning of the Early Iron Age and document strong ties with the south east Alps to the west, and northern Bosnia to the south (Ložnjak Dizdar *et al.* 2010; 2011). The Dolina settlement, together with the well-known site in Donja Dolina, was an important stronghold on the communication route along the Sava valley, which linked central and south east Europe. On the other hand, the settlements in Dolina and Donja Dolina were transfer points for goods and ideas from the south. The very large tumuli discovered in Dolina suggest that there was an upper class that controlled the trade and exchange network. The same has been confirmed by the latest excavations in Kaptol, near Požega. In Donja Dolina, skeletal burials became predominant in the Late Hallstatt Period, probably due to the influence of the intensive contacts with the area of the Glasinac Group (Čović 1987).

A similar model at the transition between the Late Urnfield Culture and the Early Iron Age can also be recognised in the Budinjak Group, which developed in the west as a modification of the well-known features of the Lower Carniola Hallstatt Group. As can be observed in Batina and Dolina, cremation graves under tumuli appeared at the beginning of the Early Iron Age. Although some elements of the grave goods, such as pottery, continue from the previous period, it would appear that new elements prevailed, and they are especially prominent in the male and female dress. Some male graves are particularly rich in grave goods such as weaponry and horse gear (Škoberne 1999), demonstrating that the concept of warrior-horseman was closely related to perception of ruling elite of that period. Soon after the beginning of the Early Iron Age, the burial ritual changed from cremation to inhumation, which is one of the main differences between this group and the Kaptol and Dalj groups, in which cremation remained the predominant form of burial throughout.

Cremation graves under tumuli are characteristic of the Kaptol Group, which belongs to the eastern Hallstatt group (Vinski-Gasparini 1961; 1987). In the Drava region, in which this group was also present, little is known about the preceding Late Urnfield Culture, and thus we cannot offer any precise model of transition to the Early Iron Age. The small necropolis in Dvorišće suggests an

## 12. Changing Identities of the Iron Age Communities of Southern Pannonia 129

*Figure 12.4. Kaptol – Čemernica – tumulus 10 – partial inventory (photo: Archaeological museum Zagreb).*

*Figure 12.5. Kaptol – Čemernica – tumulus 3 – grave chamber with (photo: H. Potrebica).*

early beginning of this group, which can be dated to the eighth century BC. The largest necropolis belonging to this group which has been explored – but unfortunately not published – is located in the immediate vicinity, in Goričan, and, as far as chronology is concerned, it suggests uninterrupted development from the Hallstatt C2 period to the end of the Hallstatt D1 period, when tumuli disappeared (Vidović 1990; 2003). Still, in contrast to these cemeteries, consisting of up to twenty smaller tumuli (Goričan), there are also cemeteries with a smaller number of monumental tumuli, such as Martijanec and Jalžabet, the location of the largest tumulus in Croatia, which, given its size (75 metres in diameter and eight metres in height) is amongst the largest burial mounds in Central Europe. A small tumulus in its immediate vicinity enclosed a monumental central chamber consisting of a wooden structure covered with stone, with an adjacent *dromos*. The finds suggest a date of the Hallstatt D1 period, that is to the early sixth century BC, and the analysis of the cremated bones has shown that there were no human but rather equine remains, opening up the possibility of various interpretations (Šimek 1998; 2001). The only settlement in this region that has been excavated more extensively is Sv. Petar Ludbreški. There, the most significant finds are undoubtedly the remains of a kiln and a pit containing moulds for casting bronze objects, some of which belong to the last phase of the Urnfield Culture (for example, laurel-shaped spearheads and shafted knives), while other moulds were used for casting objects with Pontic-Caucasian features: for example, pendants for horse gear and socketed axes with two loops (Šimek 2004). By the same token, this is the best Early Iron Age metal-production context in the territory of Croatia. Between these sites in the Drava region and those in the Požega valley, dominated by Kaptol, there is a noticeable void, which is probably a result of the poor level of exploration of this region. The same conclusion is suggested by the most recent discovery of large tumuli to the west of Psunj.

What can be said about the transition between the Late Urnfield Culture and the Early Iron Age in northern Croatia? The earlier known finds and the recent excavations provide only a general picture of the process, thus calling for further exploration of those sites that can contribute to the understanding of this very dynamic period. In northern Croatia, the Late Urnfield Culture was marked by various groups sharing many common features, such as a cremation burial rite and a larger number of metal items placed in graves than in the preceding period. The differences among them are reflected in pottery shapes and ornamentation and bronze objects appearing on female and male clothing. Those could be considered to be differentiating factors among regional communities of the late ninth century BC, which were exposed to new ideas from the lower Danube region in the east, the Balkans in the south and the south east Alps in the west. These new ideas, such as introduction of iron metallurgy or using new types of the horse gear, had a significant impact on the beginning of the Early Iron Age and the emergence of new social and economic concepts.

Perhaps we should leave our understanding of the transition between the Late Urnfield and the Early Iron Age as transformation of a single cultural package. However, separation of that package into individual elements, allows us to see the process of transition in each community as a unique combination of some or all the general features. The process starts in the rather compact Urnfield cultural complex. From that point, each cultural group followed its own dynamics of change and developed a unique model of cultural transformation which again resulted in the more or less compact Hallstatt cultural complex. This is why communities in transition demonstrate the highest level of differentiation, while, before and after that process, they shared a more common cultural framework.

The beginning of the Iron Age in this region poses another problem, and that is how to define, from an archaeological point of view, cultural groups or entities which included several communities and inhabited an area larger than that physically controlled by each of the communities. The application of any of the usual criteria quickly runs into obstacles and limitations. Here are some examples:

**Material culture:** Some communities may share pottery ornamentation styles while having completely different clothing and body ornaments or types of weapons.

**Immaterial ('spiritual') culture:** While sharing one or more elements of material culture, communities may significantly differ in their burial customs or perhaps language (we know very little about the linguistics of the Early Iron Age).

**Social and political organisation:** Inclusion in some sort of higher-level organisational structure (political or otherwise) can be based on many features. It can also be a simple spatial organisation, reinforced by shared cultural features. On the other hand, fierce competition resulting from similar, if not identical, economic patterns, as well as perception of landscape, can result in conflict and act as a divisive, rather than a cohesive force.

What we are missing is the dynamics of the cultural change in particular societies as well as in their interaction with other groups.

After the dynamic transitional phase, the following period was marked by the development of various cultural groups that are synonymous with the beginning of the Early Iron Age in this region. One of the most important among them, in the area of northern Croatia, was the Kaptol Group. In the past decade, the excavation of elite burials under tumuli in Kaptol has established this liminal group of the eastern Hallstatt cultural complex as one of the most important links for the transfer of culture between Central Europe, on the one side, and the Balkans and the Mediterranean, on the other. The same group was also significantly influenced by the uninterrupted east–west communication along the Sava valley (Vinski-Gasparini 1987; Potrebica 2002).

In Kaptol, these cultural processes were reflected in the emergence of an elite identity, resulting, at a material level, in the transformation of the landscape (construction of burial mounds and hillforts), and in rich burials of warriors and female members of the society. Monumental structures with wooden burial chambers, stone walls and *dromoi* have been found here too, very similar in type to those discovered in Jalžabet, Kleinklein and Süttő, but the finds are very different. Rich grave goods in elite burials include rich sets of weapons that are not just prestigious goods, but also exotic goods imported from distant areas: from the south as well as from Italy and Alpine areas. The southern influences are demonstrated by a Graeco-Illyrian and Corinthian helmet and a pair of bronze greaves (Potrebica 2008), a bronze breast-plate is probably of Italian origin, and a bowl helmet is distinctively Alpine product. While defensive arms are strongly southern, probably because they acted more as status symbols than functional weapons, the offensive arms, such as axes and spears, are much more frequent and, with two exceptions, belong to the Hallstatt world. The first exception is a bimetallic axe probably of Italian origin and the other is a bronze sword of the Kostel type which probably comes from the area of western Bosnia and inland Adriatic Croatia. This piece is probably significantly older (more than a century) than the grave in which it was discovered together with the bowl helmet and an undecorated bronze *situla* (Potrebica 2012). It belongs to a distinctive category of objects that demonstrate the social power of the Kaptol elite and their connections to the South. Moreover, it is possible to distinguish between at least two categories of such goods: one that is a product of long-distance exchange (e.g. sets of defensive weapons) and another consisting of items produced locally (e.g. decorated whetstones/sceptres and specific types of pins) (Potrebica 2008). These categories probably reflect different levels of communication. It seems that the general exchange network was superimposed over a patchwork of regional exchange networks, which were both operated by local elites.

In all the Hallstatt graves in the area discussed here there is not a single piece of amber! In the same period, amber is abundant in the territory of the Japodi Group in Croatia (which is not part of the Hallstatt cultural complex) and the Lower Carniola Group in Slovenia (Palavestra 1993; Bakarić *et al.* 2006). Although the Kaptol Group demonstrates close connections with the Lower Carniola Group in the Alpine area as well as with the Donja Dolina Group and the Glasinac Group in the South, this communication network is marked by prestigious goods such as arms (primarily helmets) and specific elements of dress (e.g. multi-headed pins). If we exclude a recently discovered single bead from the Middle Bronze Age, the first amber in this area appears in the grave in Velika with early La Tène fibulae and glass beads (Dizdar & Potrebica 2003). It probably does not indicate the degree of involvement of these communities in wider exchange networks, but reflects more the choice of material which demonstrates the social power of the elite controlling communication with other communities. However, the explanation could be much simpler since the dominant burial ritual in the Early Iron Age of this area is cremation and the first inhumation burials were discovered in rare Late Hallstatt or Early La Tène graves such as the grave from Velika.

Furthermore, it appears that individual Iron Age centres within this network did not act merely as passive distributors of goods, but rather played a more active role in filtering the content of this exchange and thus modifying its conceptual meaning. As a consequence of its transit position, Kaptol was the ultimate point of distribution for many specific types of pottery, weapons and other items, but it was probably even more important as a place of cultural transfer between major cultural zones in Early Iron Age Europe. If it operated as an active agent in modifying and filtering the conceptual content of cultural

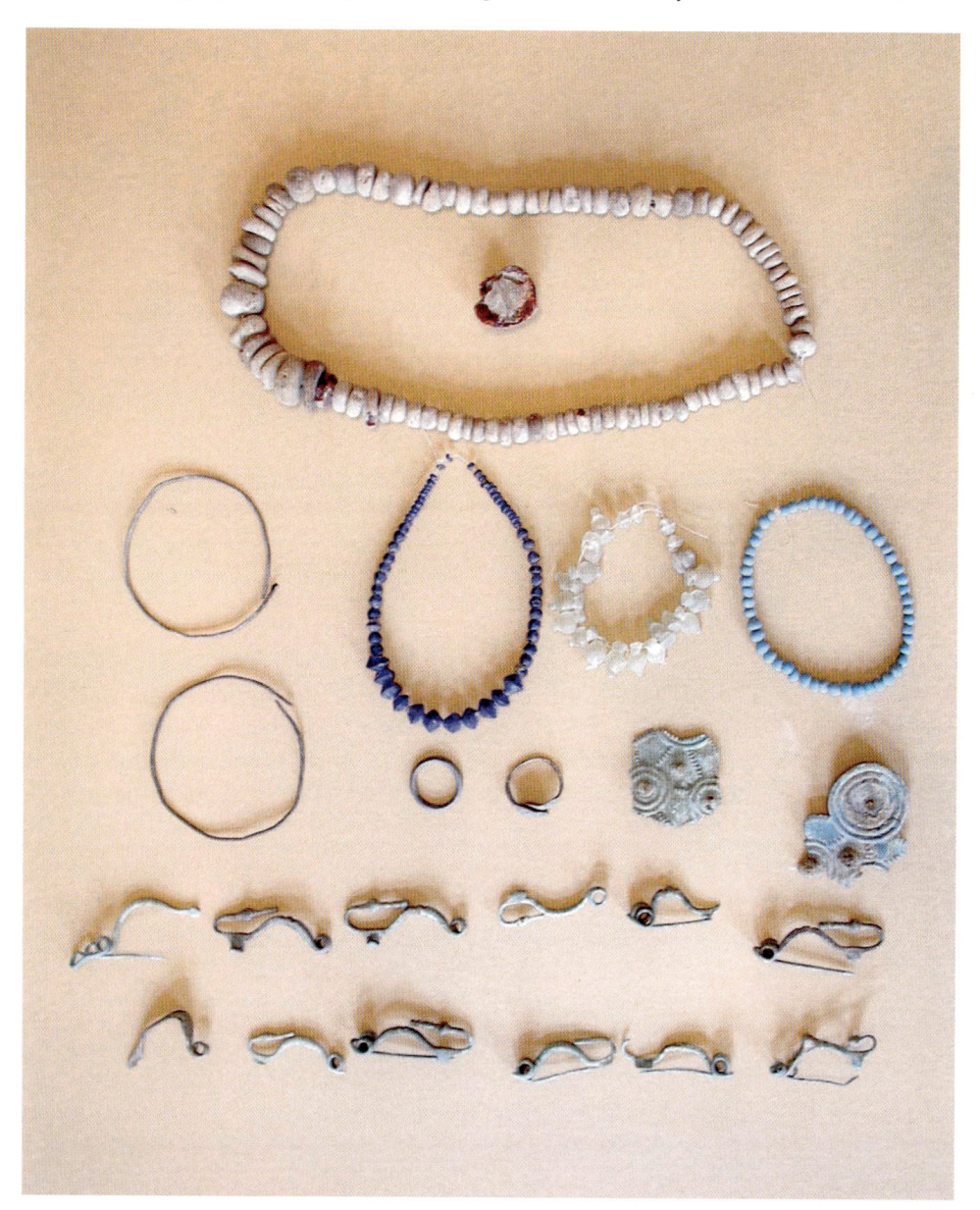

## 12. Changing Identities of the Iron Age Communities of Southern Pannonia 133

*Figure 12.6. Velika – partial grave inventory (photo: Municipal museum Požega).*

transfers, it had a direct influence on the cultural dynamics of the entire eastern Hallstatt area, and perhaps even beyond. Paradoxically, if that is the case, cultural innovation would start at the 'periphery', which could mean that there is no conceptual, but merely a spatial periphery (Potrebica 2012).

However, as early as the seventh century BC, this region underwent a fundamental change that later affected the area of the eastern Hallstatt circle by the

*Figure 12.7. Zvonimirovo – grave 45 (photo: M. Dizdar).*

mid sixth century BC. Tumulus burials disappeared, giving place to the elusive cultural features of the Late Hallstatt period. Tumulus 2 in Jalžabet is one of the most important discoveries from the transitional period between the Early and Late Hallstatt periods in northern Croatia. The rich grave inventory included warrior equipment (plate armour and spearheads) and horse gear, with analogies in the eastern part of the Carpathian valley (Šimek 1998; 2001; Teržan 1998). In other areas of northern Croatia, finds dating from the Late Hallstatt period are very rare. The only exception is the zone of eastern Slavonia and western Syrmia, but most finds originating from that territory were discovered in the late nineteenth and early twentieth century (Brunšmid 1909). Those finds have been linked to the southern Pannonian group, which covered the territory between Lake Balaton and the River Sava, characterised by flat graves with almost exclusively inhumation burials (Teržan 1977; Vasić 1982; Majnarić-Pandžić 2003). The material culture of the group includes frequent equine burials and horse gear, and Greek and Italic imports (Guštin & Teržan 1976; Teržan 1990). This group, which accepted various influences and transformed them into its own recognisable heritage, has been dated to the period between the sixth century BC and the first half of the fourth century BC, although the relations between the beginning of this group and the end of the Dalj and Bosut groups still remains unclear. The largest number of finds came from female graves, such as can be found in the wide area from the south east Alps to Glasinac and the Danube region (Teržan 1977; Jerem 1981). Items made of precious metals are explained by influence from the Balkans, where the frequency of gold and silver finds rises steeply from the sixth century BC onwards, at the same date as the appearance of princely graves (Vasić 1995; 2001). Still, some local workshops could also have existed in Syrmia (Vasić 2001; 2005). The equine burial discovered in Vinkovci, containing horse gear sets probably originating from Central Europe and the lower Danube region, can be dated to the end of the fifth and the beginning of the fourth century BC (Majnarić-Pandžić 2003), while later graves of this group include Early La Tène fibulae, which can be dated to the first half of the fourth century BC (Jerem 1968; Majnarić-Pandžić 1995; Popović 1996). This horizon is best represented by a female grave in Velika, in which the deceased woman was dressed in line with Early La Tène fashion, including some characteristic local shapes (Majnarić-Pandžić 1995; Dizdar & Potrebica 2003). The grave shows the emergence of Early La Tène influences in southern Pannonia and contacts with the already *Latenised* territory in the northern Carpathian valley. This process had begun as early as the first half of the fourth century BC. The female graves from the period also contain some local jewellery forms, such as bracelets, made of twisted silver wire, and earrings. In any case, the final phase of this group is characterised by dress that combined Late Hallstatt features and a growing number of Early La Tène elements. It is difficult to say whether the changes were caused by cultural influence or movement of people, but what most probably happened was a combination of both models. All this shows the beginning of the process of *Latenisation*, soon to be followed by *Celticisation*, that is, by the appearance of a new population. Grave inventories from the beginning of the last quarter of the fourth century BC are dominated by new shapes, and the burial ritual also changed at that time, dominated by flat grave cremation. The changes were much more intensive in the vicinity of important communication routes, usually along river valleys. Although in the fourth century BC both the burial rituals were in use for some time, by the end of the fourth century BC the transition was complete.

The indigenous Pannonian population, which was exposed to the intense changes, still kept some of its traditional shapes in the newly created material culture: mostly the shapes of its pottery vessels, especially *kantharoi*. This points to the continuity of the indigenous population, which took over the technological and cultural achievements of the La Tène Culture, but maintained elements of its own recognisable material heritage. The heterogeneous nature of the newly-emerged communities of the Late Iron Age can be explained precisely through diverse cultural and/or ethnic substrates having their origin in the Late Hallstatt period.

In addition, with the advent of written history in this region, two new concepts entered the arena – ethnicity and language. Research relating to 'protohistoric', that is, the continental European Iron Age, communities always raises the question: *Who* (in terms of names = ethnicity) *were these people, and what was their relation to well-known historical populations* (such as Greeks and Romans) *and/or events?* Given that, in this part of the world, the Celts have never been a part of national identity and political mythology, they have remained a historical category. This implies that they belong to the world of the past, to the old world, and that Celtic 'reality' is perceived almost exclusively through references in historical sources (Roman and Greek). Historical sources often (but not always) named La Tène communities as Celts thus implying that this name describes some sort of compact ethnic category. This has often resulted in perception of 'Celts' as population that spreads from some imagined 'core' invading the 'periphery'. For a long time La Tène archaeology tried to document the relation between the 'invading Celts' and the 'local population'. However, in many cases there has been no archaeological evidence of invaders identifiable as a significantly different group from the contemporary local population. In older scholarship, this was often explained by the relatively small size of the invading group, which eventually imposed itself on the local society as a small ruling class. Closer examination has revealed that the fundamental structural change of the Hallstatt communities in this region took place before any of the La Tène features reached this part of the world. In this region, the difference between the processes of *Latenisation* and *Celticisation* is clearly visible, but what remains unclear is how the indigenous populations perceived the newcomers. Did they see the new arrivals as Celts? And what was their understanding of who the Celts were, if any, given that these communities were already *Latenised* to some extent? The issue of the Celtic identity in this region has been discussed in detail elsewhere, so here we will only briefly outline the main problem: can we apply the same criteria used to define the identity of 'others' to the perception of a community's own identity? Given that there is no evidence that any (prehistoric) community defined itself as 'Celts', it would appear that the Celts were always 'the others'!

The Late Iron Age of northern Croatia is dominated by communities of presumed Celtic origin living on the south east frontier of the Celtic world.

Through the process of Celticisation, newcomers developed new identities in contact with the indigenous population – the Scordisci in the Danube region and the Taurisci in the south east Alpine region and south west Pannonia. Although both the Scordisci and Taurisci are described by ancient historians as Celtic communities, they demonstrated significantly different identities, documented mostly through their material culture. We presume that the central area between them, which in the Early Iron Age belonged to the Kaptol Group, was inhabited by indigenous Pannonian communities about which we know very little. The material legacy of these groups includes a number of La Tène shapes, but marked with a dominant local component, suggesting the possible uninterrupted development of these communities from the Late Hallstatt period.

The new identities emerging in southern Pannonia at the beginning of the Late Iron Age were accompanied by the development of a dominant La Tène material culture. Technological advances were reflected in new forms of weapons, tools and jewellery, present across a wide area. At the same time, some indigenous traditions can also be observed, marking out these local groups within the Central European La Tène culture. The features of material culture are best demonstrated by the shapes and decorative motifs of pottery vessels, and certain elements of clothing and jewellery. The best illustration is provided by the only systematically excavated La Tène Culture cemetery in northern Croatia, at Zvonimirevo in the central Drava region. The site yielded numerous warrior graves and richly fitted female graves. On the basis of the analyses of female clothing, this Middle La Tène cemetery has been attributed to the Mokronog Group, linked to the tribal alliance of the Taurisci. That said, some finds, mostly from female graves, also reflect intense links with the neighbouring Scordisci, who lived in the territory of eastern Slavonia and Syrmia (Tomičić & Dizdar 2005; Dizdar 2011). The indigenous legacy can be seen in hand-made pottery vessels, which have direct analogies in shapes and motifs characteristic of the southern Pannonian group of the Late Hallstatt (Dizdar 2010).

The uninterrupted development continued into the Late La Tène period, with some changes to the social structure and organisation of communities in the region. In addition to fortified settlements, the emergence of a warrior elite is particularly important for this period. It can be observed in richly fitted graves containing weapons, such as those at Mali Bilač and Sotin (Majnarić-Pandžić 1972–1973; Dizdar & Potrebica 2003). The grave goods included weapons and warrior equipment, presenting the warriors as horsemen, and thus emphasising their prominent social status, further confirmed by their possession of prestigious goods, such as imported bronze vessels (Dizdar & Radman-Livaja 2004). Bronze vessels from northern Italian workshops were used, together with pottery vessels of local origin (*kantharoi*), for wine preparation and consumption during banquets. The discovery of such vessels in the graves of rich Scordisci warriors proves that their position within the social structure was linked to the control exercised over the trade in goods (Egri & Rustoiu 2008).

The Late La Tène warrior elite played an important role in social and economic changes occurring in the first half of the second century BC. In addition

*Figure 12.8. Nova Gradiška – river Sava – helmet (photo: Archaeological museum Zagreb).*

to the grave goods, the existence of such a warrior elite has been confirmed by finds of luxury weapons in river beds, explained as sacrifices made to gods. Such finds include helmets of the Novo Mesto type discovered in the River Sava near Sesvete and Nova Gradiška (Sokol 2001; Mihaljević & Dizdar 2007). The recent discovery of a Scordisci sanctuary fits into the same picture. It contained trophies, probably dedicated to gods of war, to secure success in battle. Many elements of horse gear discovered in the sanctuary suggest that the horse-riding aristocracy held a prominent position within the Scordisci social structure. At the same time, fortified settlements appeared, and these have been well explored in the Danube region, in the territory that was inhabited by the Scordisci (Jovanović & Jovanović 1988; Dizdar 2001). In the territory of the Taurisci, similar fortified settlements can be found in prominent hillfort locations (Gabrovec 1994). Fortified settlements developed into centres of trade and exchange, as part of communication networks that covered some very distant regions, and they achieved the status of political, administrative, military and religious centres of their respective regions (Dizdar 2001).

The identity of the Scordisci and Taurisci could be defined as a symbiosis of the newly arrived 'Celts' and various indigenous communities, united by the warrior aristocracy. This particularly relates to the elites, who took over some of the external signs of the identities of those communities in which they acquired a prestigious status (Rustoiu 2005; 2008).

We need to adjust our analysis to the fact that large scale theoretical models are insufficient and must be balanced by the study of smaller groups of actual people. In this respect, knowledge of the social and economic development of communities populating the territory of southern Pannonia is of key importance for understanding the processes that occurred in this region during the Roman conquest. Until recently, archaeological texts always emphasised the active role of the Romans, while indigenous communities were mostly seen as passive recipients of new forms of organisation amd and material culture. The latest research has shown that the elite classes of indigenous communities, especially the Taurisci and Scordisci, also played an important role in the process (Dizdar 2012).

The final shift of identity in this region came with the Roman conquest, when *'indigenous'* become *'Roman',* but in that process the concept of what is *'Roman'* was inevitably altered, as illustrated by burials of local Scordisci aristocracy at the cemetery in Ilok. Items discovered in the graves included weapons, jewellery, cosmetic kits and dishes. A large number of pottery vessels, and bronze and glass objects found in the graves, could have arrived in the region to satisfy the demand of the local military aristocracy and the higher social classes of pre-Roman communities (Dizdar *et al.* 2003; Dizdar 2010a). On the other hand, these items reflect ethnic and economic influences of the early Romanisation period in southern Pannonia. An important role in that process was played by the Scordisci aristocracy, who were Roman allies at the time. They maintained their old burial ritual, in which weapons held a prominent place, but in addition to pottery shapes of local origin, there were also many imported goods.

As with some other contemporary finds in the territory of the south east Alps, the graves of members of the warrior elite in Ilok confirm the important role played by local communities at the time of the Roman conquest. The Scordisci acted as Roman allies in operations against Pannonian populations, but they were also instrumental in the consolidation of the newly-conquered territory, which secured them a better position in the new political and administrative structure. Local elites also participated in recruitment for allied troops and auxiliary units, thus facilitating the Roman control over these communities, as well as border protection. The fact that Roman cultural features and ideology were implemented through the ruling social class, meant that the warrior elite of these communities could retain their previously acquired status. On the other hand, because of their resistance to the Romans, the Pannonian communities had a very different destiny. Members of the highest social classes were sold into slavery, while able-bodied men were recruited into auxiliary units and sent to

Figure 12.9. a. Ilok – grave 5; b. Ilok – grave 5 – sword; c. Ilok – grave 5 – pottery (photos: M. Dizdar).

distant parts of the Empire. Nonetheless, although general features of Roman culture such as language, ideas and social values, spread quickly through the area, the differences between individual communities could still be observed. Indigenous communities adapted previous forms of economic and social organisation into a new social and political framework (Dizdar 2012). Despite the relatively modest amount of research, this hypothesis seems to be supported by finds from early Roman contexts. These local differences could be explained by the different scope and intensity of exposure to Roman influences, but we must keep in mind that up to a certain level the construction of their local identities was matter of choice and combination of local traditions and Roman influences and ideology. For example, while populations of larger centres that evolved from Late La Tène settlements were exposed to an intense Romanisation, resulting from the settling of Italian population and veterans, rural communities maintained their material culture for a long time, acquiring only certain selected elements of the newly-established Roman provincial culture. In brief, the indigenous heritage played an active role in the process of social change that resulted in the ethnic structure of the new province of Pannonia.

The Iron Age draws attention to the problem of diverse definitions (or, even more importantly, diverse perceptions or concepts) of archaeological culture, consciously or subconsciously used when attempting to describe the cultural scene in a region. Over the years, European Iron Age studies have demonstrated that there are significant and fundamental differences in understanding, and in spatial and conceptual definitions of, different cultural entities: for example, cultural complexes, cultural groups, ethnic groups, and communities. This creates major confusion in the creation of a general picture of Iron Age cultural dynamics, and seriously affects all attempts to study the character, content and meaning of various interactions between specific groups of people.

The relations between such entities are mostly based on sets of individual inclusive or exclusive criteria, resulting inevitably in a two-dimensional ('flat') picture. For this reason, we cannot help wondering if **Fingerprinting the Iron Age** is, at least to some extent, also fingerprinting our own cultural identity, or our own personal understanding of the world.

# 13. Indigenous and Colonist Communities in the Eastern Carpathian Basin at the Beginning of the Late Iron Age. The Genesis of an Eastern Celtic World

*Aurel Rustoiu*

**Keywords:** Carpathian Basin, Celts, indigenous populations, colonisation, identity

## Introduction

At the beginning of the Empire, when Romans sought to re-construct their history and myths of origin from a new ideological perspective, Titus Livius mentioned an old tradition about the Celts (Roberts 1912: 5.34.2–5):

> Ambigatus was king at that time, a man eminent for his own personal courage and prosperity as much as for those of his dominions. During his sway the harvests were so abundant and the population increased so rapidly in Gaul that the government of such vast numbers seemed almost impossible. [3] He was now an old man, and anxious to relieve his realm from the burden of over-population. With this view he signified his intention of sending his sister's sons Bellovesus and Segovesus, both enterprising young men, to settle in whatever locality the gods should by augury assign to them. [4] They were to invite as many as wished to accompany them, sufficient to prevent any nation from repelling their approach. When the auspices were taken, the Hercynian forest was assigned to Segovesus; to Bellovesus the gods gave the far pleasanter way into Italy. [5] He invited the surplus population of six tribes – the Bituriges, the Averni, the Senones, the Aedui, the Ambarri, the Carnutes, and the Aulerci.

The Roman historian used this story to indicate the directions of Celtic migrations (eastward and southward), as well as the perceived causes, motivations and mechanisms which might have determined these movements. From this moment onwards, his writings influenced both the ancient views and the modern interpretations of this complicated phenomenon. Today specialists are still trying to correlate the written accounts with archaeological evidence which may reveal such population movements. In some cases, the analysis of archaeological data has lead to some hypotheses that suggest the migration of some groups of people from western Europe towards the east (or of others in the opposite direction) in areas which remained outside the sphere of interest of the ancient authors (see Kruta 1985). The theories about Celtic migrations witnessed a long evolution from the nineteenth century until the present day, influenced by the ways in which written and archaeological information were interpreted, or by the methodological advance in the processing of archaeological finds etc (for a synthesis of these theories see Kaenel 2007).

Before starting the discussion, the meaning of several important terms has to be clarified. The term 'colonisation', as it is used here, is different from 'mobility' and 'migration'. 'Mobility' defines the movement of an individual or of a group, with different intentions, at variable distances from the area of origin, where the travellers usually returned to their community of origin (although not always) (Ramsl 2003). The movements of Celtic mercenaries are a good example (see the case of the chieftain from Ciumești in Rustoiu 2006). On the other hand 'migration', albeit sometimes defined as the definitive movement of an individual or a group from one area to another, was where the intention was to settle at the destination (Ramsl 2003). Migration is, furthermore, an umbrella term covering a larger range of population movements, frequently designating the displacement of larger groups ('nations', populations or tribes). The specialists who focus on 'colonial archaeology' noted that the term 'colonisation' had different meanings according to the historical situation in which it was used. For example, it was frequently correlated with the term 'colony', which in turn had a double meaning: 'that is, either a settlement of foreigners established in the territory of others or a subject province ruled by an alien power' (Dietler 2005: 53–4; see also Stein 2005: 8–9). Gosden also underlined the importance of the relationship between material culture and 'colonialism', defined as 'a particular grip that material culture gets on the bodies and minds of people, moving them across space and attaching them to new values' (Gosden 2004: 3; see also Carstens 2006: 122–3).

In this article the term 'colonisation' describes the movement of part of a community, or of some groups consisting of people coming from different communities, organised around elites (or around some principles, ideas etc), where the intention was to occupy permanently a new territory outside the 'ancestral' space. The colonist movements had various causes and were influenced by specific conditions: over-population, challenging economic, social, political or religious situations, climatic changes etc. Some recent studies point to the fact that a single 'theory of colonialism' or 'model of colonisation' cannot be devised (Dietler 2005: 54–5). Such models and their effects are different according to the historical, cultural or social frameworks in which the respective communities evolved (see for example the three main types of encounters proposed in Gosden 2004). At the same time, 'colonisation' cannot be regarded as a simple movement from a territory to another, as it presumes a diverse range of interactions between the 'colonists', having their own personal and group identities and agendas, seeking to impose their own norms, habits and ideology, and the 'colonised' who also have specific identities and are either exerting various forms of resistance, or are expressing a degree of openness towards integration within the newly built communal structures (Given 2004). These diverse interactions contribute to the transformation of individual and group identities, leading to the creation of some new identities through 'creolisation' or cultural 'hybridisation' and even through the re-invention of some traditions etc.

The analyses of strontium isotopes from human remains taken from some representative cemeteries have allowed the identification of the geographical origin of some individuals involved in long distance movements (Hauschild 2010). Still, even in these cases, the results offer different interpretations. For example, the analyses made on skeletons coming from a small La Tène cemetery at Dornach, in Bavaria, revealed that some of the deceased came from Bohemia or Moravia, supported by the fact that their graves also contained some grave goods specific to these regions (weaponry, garment accessories etc). On the other hand, some of these 'foreign' objects were also adopted by other local members of this community, illustrating the variable nature of the interactions between the colonists and the indigenous people (Eggl 2003). For Transylvania and the Great Hungarian Plain such analyses, made on remains coming from representative cemeteries, are under way and will be soon be published (information from M. Hauschild and M. Scheeres, Mainz). Nevertheless, the analysis of archaeological evidence from funerary contexts allows the identification of some of the social practices through which individual and group identities were constructed, displayed and manipulated. The information has to be assembled with other data about the ways in which the respective community organised its daily life and habitat, in order to identify other relevant local social practices.

Starting from this theoretical background, the present article investigates the cultural impact of the migration of Celtic groups from the east, more precisely to the regions eastward of the middle Danube (Great Hungarian Plain and Transylvania). Thus the main scope is to identify the ways in which Celtic colonists who arrived in the eastern part of the Carpathian Basin interacted with local communities and if archaeological evidence may reveal the creation of some new communal identities. The analysis takes into consideration the finds coming from several representative cemeteries and some settlements.

Another aim is to identify the manner in which some indigenous communities from the same area, which were unaffected by Celtic movements, expressed their own communal identity. Amongst them are included the fortified settlements from Maramureș and some settlements and cemeteries from eastern Transylvania. The comparison between the patterns from areas which remained under indigenous control and those coming from regions dominated by the newcomers may allow the identification of different manners of expressing the communal identity in relation with others.

Some details about the mechanisms by which these groups of colonists established themselves are important. The total number of individuals in a group was quite small, as suggested by the relatively low percentage of early burials in any given cemetery. The early colonists were probably recruited from different communities, thus contributing to the appearance of some new mixed communities. In Transdanubia or south western Slovakia, both regions of origin for a large number of colonists, the cemeteries continued in use, so a mass migration of entire communities can be excluded.

The warlike elites played a major role in the organisation of these groups of colonists and as leaders of the movements (Strobel 1996: 154–5). In general, the warriors were one of the most mobile segments of the society. Their movements facilitated the distribution over large areas of various goods associated with them. The swords that had scabbards decorated with face-to-face dragons, or the so-called Hatvan-Boldog-Silivaş swords, are some of the best examples (Stöllner 1998: 162–70, Maps 2–3).

The colonist groups also included other frequently mobile members, like the craftsmen and some of the women. The mobility of the women explains the occurrence of some specific feminine costume sets far from their regions of origin. The most commonly mentioned example (Kruta 2000: 249; Kaenel 2007: 395; Hauschild 2010: 174 etc) is that of the rigid necklaces decorated with discs inlayed with coral or enamel (the so-called 'Oberrheinischer Scheibenhalsring') known in the upper Rhine region, but also encountered on the middle Danube and the Great Hungarian Plain in burials dated to the end of the fourth century or the beginning of the third century BC (Müller 1989). At the same time the technological transfers and the introduction of some new manufacturing techniques, tools and artefacts (some ceramic types, garments accessories, weaponry etc) are a consequence of the mobility of the artisans which accompanied these colonist groups (Rustoiu 2008: 116–26; 2009).

The role played by the social networks established between neighbouring communities or with more distant communities is also important for understanding the mechanisms through which such groups were constituted. More precisely these networks allowed a form of 'selection' of the individuals destined to leave the original communities to participate in the construction of a new one (Ramsl 2003: 104). Lastly the movements towards new territories required the establishing of some new contacts and social networks in which the indigenous communities, or at least their elites, had to be involved. Sometimes such new social contacts were established with more distant communities through matrimonial alliances (Arnold 2005), for example those between the newcomers from Transylvania and some communities from northern Balkans (Rustoiu 2004–2005; 2008: 126–32; 2011: 166–8).

An important element in the interpretation of the colonisation process in the Carpathian Basin is the rural character of both the incoming and indigenous communities. For that reason the most probable aim of Celtic colonisation was the acquisition of agricultural and pastoral resources. In addition, the control of some important mineral resources, such as salt, may have been another target. Salt was abundant in Transylvania, but relatively rare on the Great Hungarian Plain and in Transdanubia (Medeleţ 1995).

## THE CULTURAL CONFIGURATION OF THE EASTERN CARPATHIAN BASIN AT THE END OF THE EARLY IRON AGE

The cultural layout at the end of the Early Iron Age in the Great Hungarian Plain and Transylvania (Fig. 13.1/1) before Celtic colonisation can be analysed as follows. Several decades ago Mihály Párducz noted areas with different cultural patterns, dominated by features from the northern Pontic region. For this reason

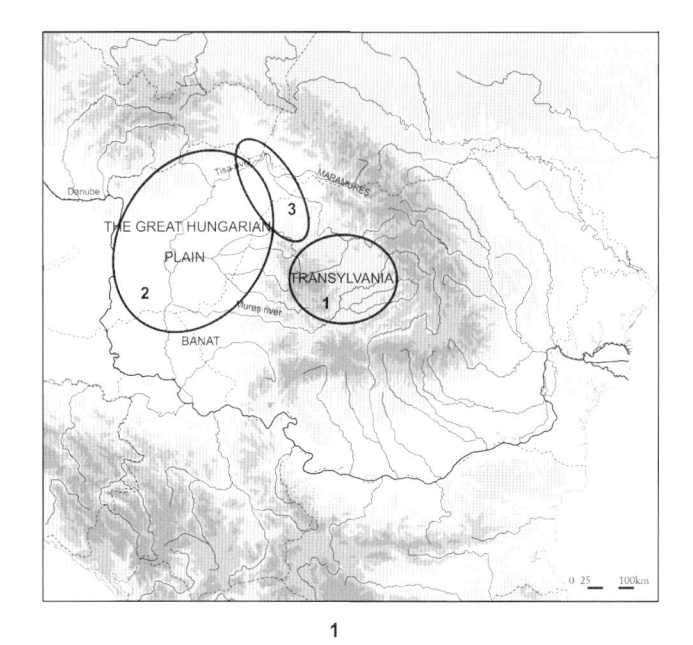

*Figure 13.1. 1. Map showing the main geographical entities mentioned in the text and the cultural groups of the end of the Early Iron Age in the eastern Carpathian Basin: Ciumbrud group (1), Vekerzug culture (2) and Sanislău-Nir group (3). 2. Map of the cemeteries beginning in the La Tène B1/B2 period (circles) or in the La Tène B2 period (black dots); the direction of the advancing colonist groups towards the eastern Carpathian Basin; the indigenous fortified settlements on the Tisza River (triangles) and the settlement and cemetery from Olteni (square).*

he defined the entire period as the 'Scythian Age' (Skythenzeit) (Párducz 1973).

The Transylvanian group, sometimes known as the Ciumbrud group (Vulpe 1988: 104–5), or as the Agathyrsi group (Vasiliev 1980), is characterised by flat grave warrior inhumations. More recently it has been noted that cremation in rectangular pits became the most common rite towards the middle of the fifth century BC, for example in the cemeteries at Băiţa (Vasiliev 1976) and Uioara de Sus (Vasiliev 1999). Cremation and inhumation burials, sometimes containing horses or carts, were identified on the Great Hungarian Plain and as far as southern and south western Slovakia, in an area occupied by Vekerzug communities (Párducz 1973: 40; Chochorowski 1985). Finally, on the upper Tisza, cremation burials predominate, where the burnt remains were placed in simple pits or in urns. Some recent investigations have shown that from the middle of the fifth century until the fourth century BC flat in-urned cremation cemeteries were almost the sole funerary rite in the communities from the Nyrség region, and eastern artefacts were very rare. These distinctive features led Ioan Németi to define the Sanislău-Nir group, on the edge of the Vekerzug culture area (Németi 1982).

The so-called 'Skythenzeit' is in fact culturally diverse, caused by the amalgamation of local communities with some warlike groups which arrived in the region in the sixth century BC from various areas of the northern Pontic region. The evolution of these mixed groups, which developed cultural connections mainly to the east or/and the northern Balkans, was interrupted after the middle of the fourth century BC by the arrival of Celtic communities from the west.

## Celtic colonisation. The colonists, the colonised and new communal identities

The first Celtic groups advanced westwards from Transdanubia, in the northern area of the Great Hungarian Plain and up to the upper Tisza. From these areas, they moved southwards along the western Carpathians and later also settled in Transylvania (Fig. 13.1/2). This advance is documented by a series of cemeteries located along the route. Some of them began at the end of the La Tène B1 and the beginning of the La Tène B2 sub-phase. Other cemeteries were established only in the La Tène B2, suggesting that the advance was slow, in successive steps, during the second half of the fourth century BC and up to the beginning of the next century (Rustoiu 2008: 69–70, Fig. 27).

The advance of the Celts eastward of the middle Danube basin changed the cultural layout of these regions. At the same time, the newly formed communities, which brought together elements of both populations, created new and varied forms of expression of communal identities. The interactions between the colonists and the indigenous populations differed from one place to another, and this variation can be identified through an analysis of the funerary practices from each cemetery.

In the cemetery at Muhi – Kocsmadomb, in Hungary, the locals and the newcomers were buried in the same consecrated area. Magdolna Hellebrandt noted that in general 'Scythian' and 'Celtic' graves were grouped around some

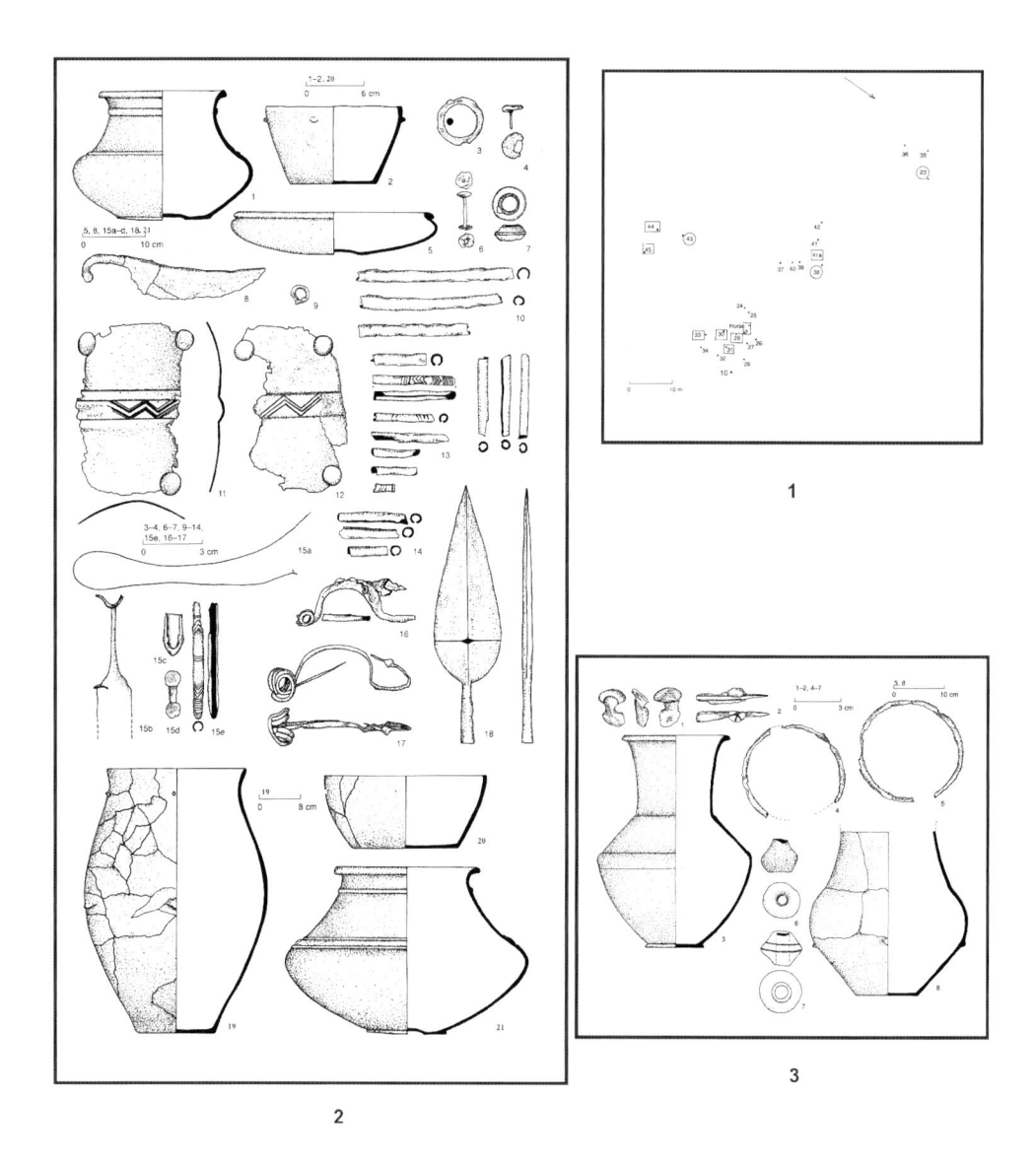

*Figure 13.2. 1. Plan of the Muhi – Kocsmadomb cemetery. 'Celtic' graves with weapons (circles) and indigenous graves (squares). 2. The grave-goods of 'Celtic' grave no. 43. 3. The grave-goods of the indigenous graves 44 (1–3) and 45 (4–8) (after Hellebrandt 1999).*

burials containing weaponry and having typical La Tène features (Fig. 13.2/1). The Hungarian researcher underlined the existence of a similar situation in the cemetery at Vác – Gravel pit, which may suggest the organisation of these burials in groups belonging to specific families or clans, in which warriors had a

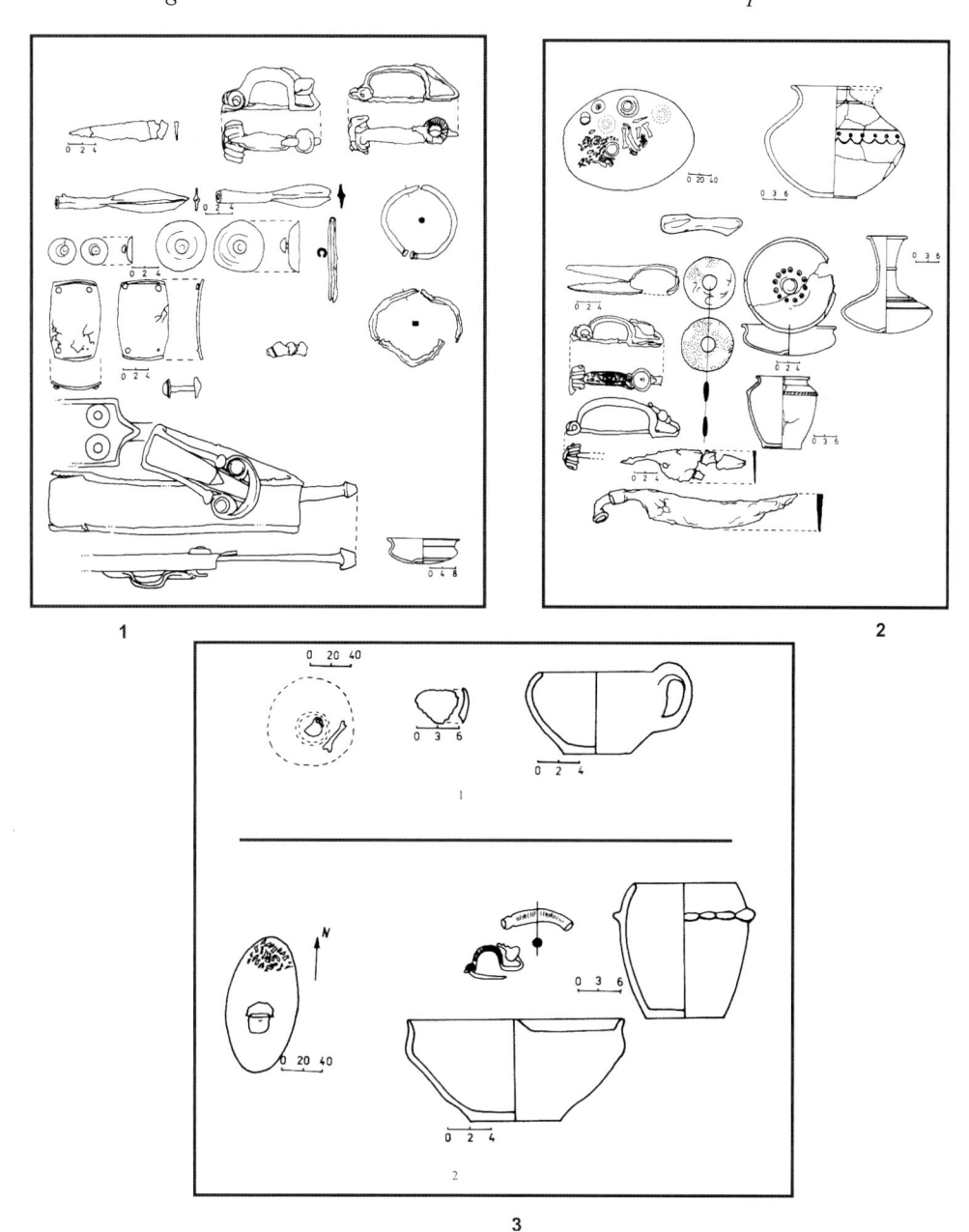

*Figure 13.3. Pișcolt, graves belonging to the first phase of the cemetery. 1. The grave-goods of the La Tène grave 36 with weapons. 2. The grave-goods of the La Tène grave 180 without weapons. 3. The grave-goods of the indigenous graves 198 (1) and 203 (2) (after Németi 1988).*

dominant role (Hellebrandt 1999: 233–6; Almássy 2010: 12). The evidence from Muhi–Kocsmadomb indicates that the indigenous people were integrated into the new community formed after the arrival of the 'colonists', but also that a series of local traditions were preserved (see for comparison Fig. 13.2/2 – a 'Celtic' grave and Fig. 13.2/3 – indigenous graves). These traditions are illustrated by the preservation of specific funerary rituals and the presence of older ceramic forms. These vessels suggest that some indigenous craftsmen continued to produce pottery specific to the Vekerzug communities, and also that specific culinary practices, more precisely particular ways of cooking and eating, were still used (about the role of dining practices and of other related activities in expressing specific identities see Dietler 2006).

The cemetery at Pișcolt (Satu Mare County), in north western Romania, provides another specific situation (Németi 1988; 1989). The burials began at the end of the La Tène B1 and the beginning of the La Tène B2, documenting the arrival of one of the first Celtic groups eastwards of the middle Danube in the second half of the fourth century BC. The funerary rite and most of the rituals, as well as the grave goods, are typical of Central European Celtic communities (Fig. 13.3/1–2). Apart from the characteristic La Tène ceramic forms, several vessels typical of the Sanislău-Nir group that preceded colonisation also appear. Furthermore, a few burials display ritual features that have similarities in the cemetery at Sanislău, only a few kilometres away from Pișcolt, dated to the end of the Early Iron Age (Németi 1982). For example, the in-urned cremation graves 198 and 203 from Pișcolt (Németi 1988: 61, Fig. 9, 11) have funerary features and ceramic grave goods specific to the Sanislău-Nir group, for this reason probably belonging to some indigenous people (Fig. 13.3/3). It seems that, like at Muhi-Kocsmadomb, several locals continued to be buried in the Celtic cemetery of Pișcolt, albeit preserving their own funerary traditions. However, the total number of burials which may be considered as belonging to the local population is limited, suggesting that they were rather rapidly affected by the Celtic community which settled in the region. On the other hand, it is possible that some of the La Tène graves usually described as 'Celtic', belonged to members of the local community integrated, in one way or another, into the newly arrived group.

In Transylvania, the situation is different from the Great Hungarian Plain. One of the most significant La Tène cemeteries has been uncovered at Fântânele – Dealul Popii (Bistrița-Năsăud County), in north western Transylvania (still largely unpublished, see Rustoiu & Megaw 2011, 217–18). The burial plot includes about 100 graves and was used from the beginning of the La Tène B2 to the end of the La Tène C1. The majority of the graves are pit cremations, whereas inhumations (around 12 per cent) are mostly dated to the latest phases of the cemetery. The funerary rite and other rituals are specific to the Central European area, but a series of artefacts illustrates the mixed cultural patterns of the newly arrived people and local communities. It is significant that around 80 per cent of the graves are dated to the early phases of the cemetery (La Tène B2a and La Tène B2b) contain typical La Tène artefacts (wheel-made pottery, jewellery, weaponry etc) combined with ceramic vessels of local origin. In two situations, the ceramic grave goods only include local vessels. The grave 10/1969, an oval pit cremation, is a good example (Fig. 13.4). The burnt bones, together

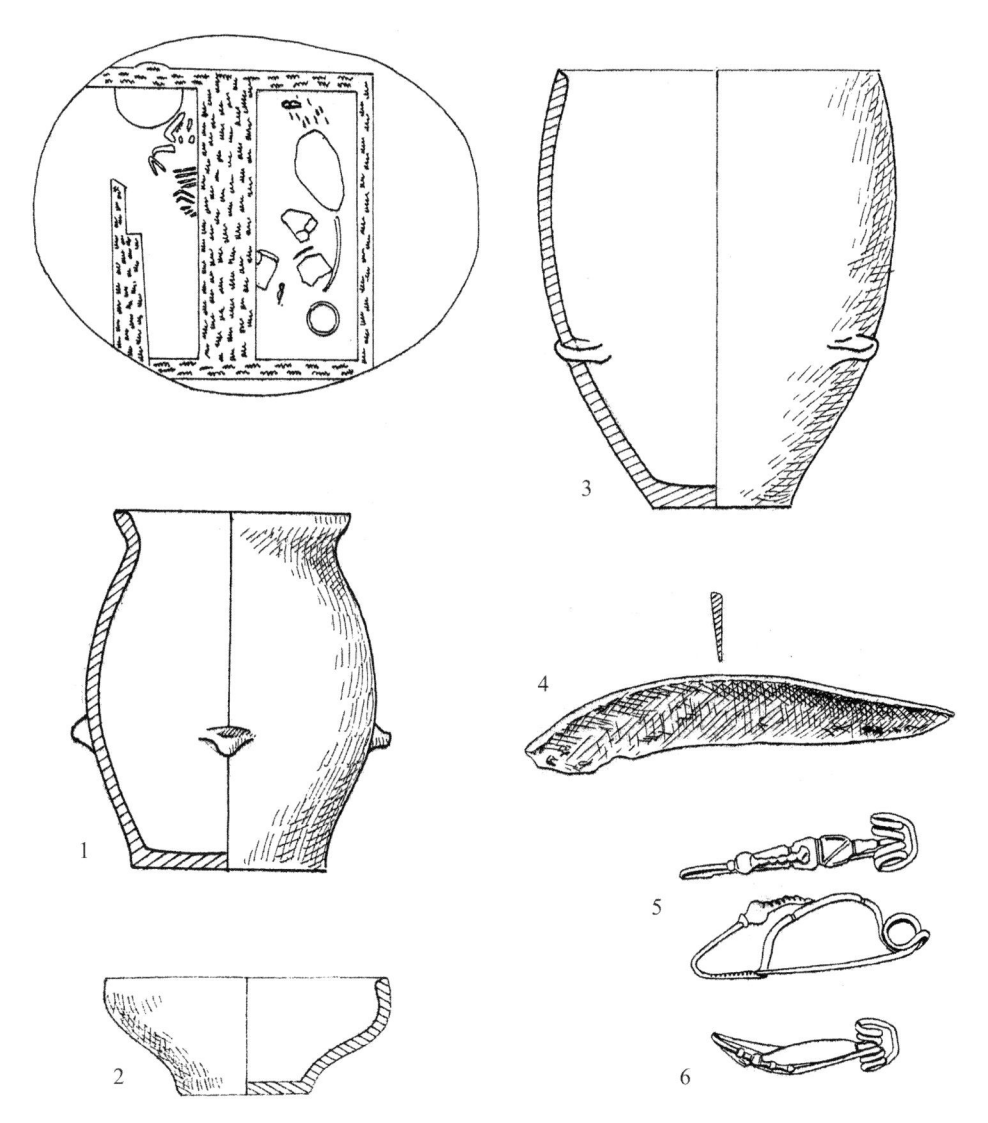

*Figure 13.4. Fântânele-Dealul Popii. Grave 10/1969. Not to scale (after Rustoiu 2008).*

with two handmade vessels (a bell-shaped one and a jar, both with flattened lugs placed on the narrow part of the vessel) and two bronze brooches of early La Tène type, were placed on the north western side of the pit. A hand-made bowl with an inverted rim and an offering of meat (pig and fowl) were placed on the opposite side of the pit. The curved blade of an iron knife was found amongst the animal bones. A 'box' made of boards was placed inside the pit, separating the space in two compartments in which the burnt remains and the grave goods were laid (Rustoiu 2008: 77–8). All of these elements, including the wooden structures inside some graves, are known from other La Tène cemeteries in the middle Danube region. The handmade vessels from the Fântânele cemetery have general similarities to 'Thracian' environment to the south and east of the Carpathians. Nevertheless, the general structure of the cemetery resembles typical Central European La Tène context. The mixture of indigenous and Celtic artefacts and practices from Fântânele indicates that the local population was relatively rapidly integrated within the newly arrived communities. Just as at Muhi-Kocsmadomb and Pişcolt, it can be presumed that the local potters continued to make typical indigenous forms for a while, but also that the amalgamation of these two communities lead to the appearance of some hybrid culinary or dining practices, as suggested by the funerary assemblages containing local and La Tène vessels. The appearance of a mixed cuisine was frequently encountered in the contact areas between populations with different traditions, in many different geographical situations, even in Transylvania up to the present day.

The three archaeological situations described above point to the fact that the arrival of Celtic groups to the east of the middle Danube, on the Great Hungarian Plain and in Transylvania, determined the cultural reconfiguration of these regions. Nevertheless, several features of the interactions between the colonists and the indigenous populations differ significantly from one community to another.

In some situations, local populations maintained their traditional funerary rite and other rituals, at least during the initial period of coexistence with the newcomers. Thus it can be said that they deliberately preserved and publicly expressed a specific identity, for example in funerary ceremonies. However the absence of weaponry from graves displaying local funerary features indicates that the indigenous people were not integrated into the warlike elites of the newcomers. The pattern identified in the Muhi – Kocsmadomb cemetery, discussed above, is relevant for this interpretation: the indigenous graves and those of the colonists are grouped around some burials containing weaponry, which always belong to newly arrived individuals.

In other situations local populations were quite rapidly integrated into the new communal structures, as the adoption of the funerary rite and ritual of the newcomers suggests, although they continued to influence some aspects of the material culture during the following few generations. The persistence of traditional pottery is perhaps the most visible example of this point.

Furthermore, analysis of some cemeteries also allows identification of the manner in which the new communities were organised. As previously mentioned, at Vác – Gravel pit and Muhi – Kocsmadomb, the graves are grouped around the burials containing weaponry. An almost similar situation has been observed in other cemeteries. For example at Fântânele – Dealul Popii in Transylvania and at Chotin in south western Slovakia (Ratimorská 1981: 18, Fig. 2 – map of the cemetery), the graves belonging to the earlier phases are concentrated in groups around the oldest burials (albeit not all of them contain weaponry; at Fântânele the oldest burials contain female grave goods). These features suggest that the communities were organised in large families or clans, where each had its own funerary space within the cemetery, and the interments were made around the burials belonging to the first 'colonists' (perhaps regarded as the 'founders' of the families settled in the new territories, and sometimes the women played this important role). These families or clans belonged to a larger community that owned the cemetery. In all these cases the situation changed several generations later, towards the middle or in the second half of the third century BC (in the La Tène C1), when the total number of burials increased significantly and the familial interment rules were no longer followed.

The integration of local populations into the new communities that emerged from the Celtic colonisation is also visible in some settlements. As in the case of the cemeteries, contemporary settlements have not been discovered with exclusively local or foreign material culture. Amongst the best examples are the fully investigated settlements from Ciumești (Satu Mare County), in north western Romania (Zirra 1980), and Morești (Mureș County), in central Transylvania (Horedt 1979: 35–52; Berecki 2008), where the ceramic forms belong to both groups of population.

Moreover, despite regional differences, the cultural patterns of the communities situated eastward of the middle Danube, on the Great Hungarian Plain and in Transylvania, were substantially modified after the arrival of the La Tène groups. The process of colonisation lead to the creation of new communities, with different modes of expression of individual and group identities, according to the new sets of norms that emerged from the amalgamation of these populations.

INDIGENOUS COMMUNITIES ON THE MARGINS

On the other hand, the colonists did not settle in the entire Carpathian Basin. For example, in the Maramureș depression (in the upper Tisza basin) and in the mountainous depressions from eastern Transylvania, local communities had an evolution that was different from the one noted in most of Transylvania, in which Celtic communities settled.

In Maramureș, archaeological investigations of the last decade have lead to the identification of some fortified settlements dated to the fourth to third centuries BC, when Celtic groups arrived in the eastern part of the Carpathian Basin. Such settlements have been identified at Bila Cerkva (Biserica Albă in Romanian) (Rustoiu 2002a: 57–9; 2005: 13–14) and Solotvino (Slatina in Romanian) (Rustoiu 2002a: 59–61; 2002b: 46–56; 2005: 11–13), on the right bank of the Tisza, in Transcarpathian Ukraine (Fig. 13.5/1–2). The first settlement is located on a promontory above the Tisza, while the second is located a few kilometres downstream, on the river bank. Both sites were fortified with earthen ramparts and ditches, with elaborate palisades made of timber and wattle and daub. The living area consists of above ground buildings and storage pits. The ceramic finds include handmade vessels which continued the Early Iron Age tradition (Fig. 13.5/3): large bi-truncated vessels, bell-shaped pots, several types of jars with flattened lugs and relief-impressed stripes, bowls with inverted rims, some imitating Greek forms, beakers etc. In general, the fortification and living area features, as well as the ceramic finds, have similarities to those of 'Thracian' settlements east of the Carpathians (see for example the settlements from Stâncești and Cotu-Copălău, Botoșani County etc: Florescu & Florescu 2005; Șovan & Ignat 2005).

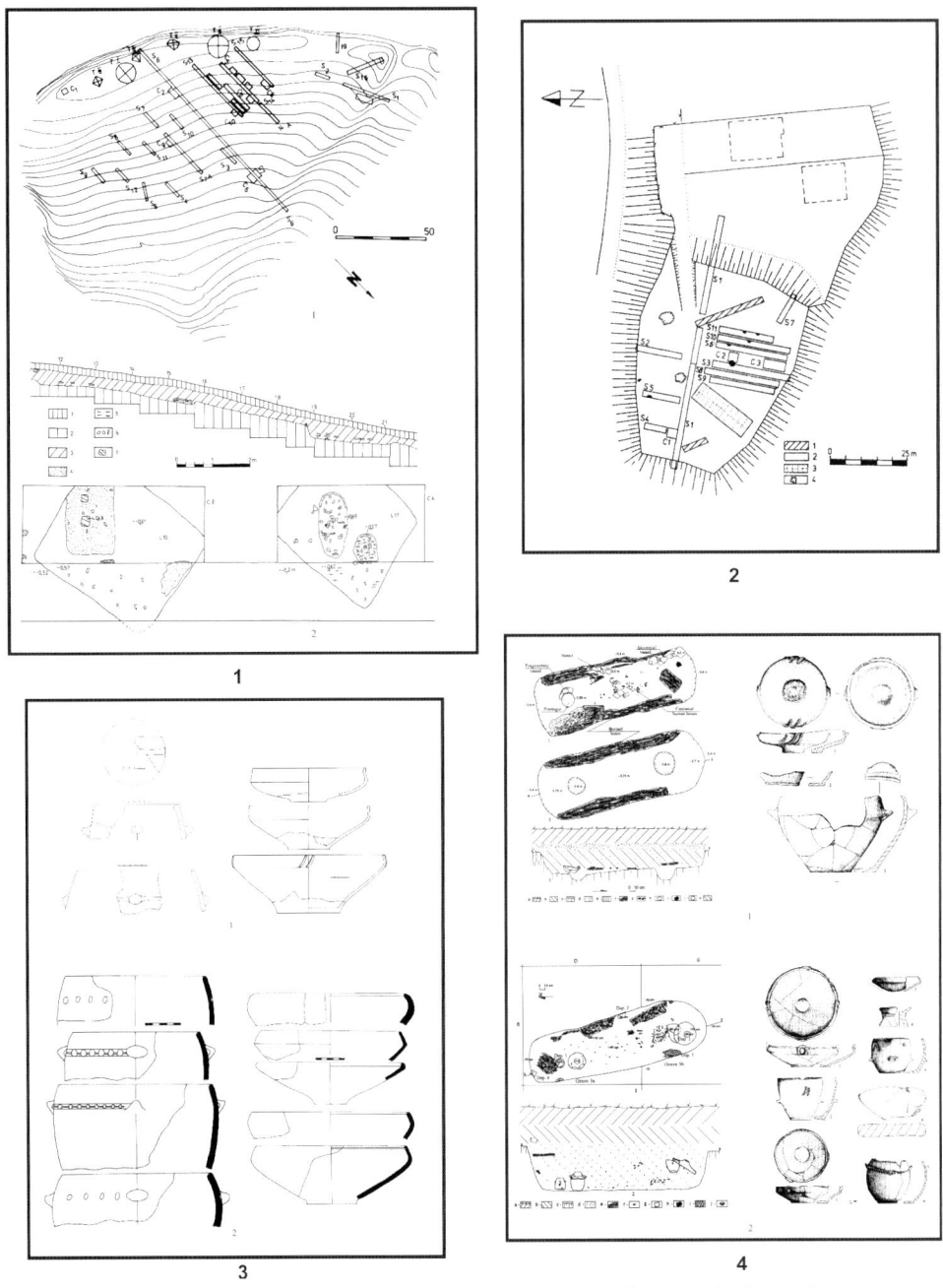

*Figure 13.5.* 1. Plan of the settlement from Bila Cerkva including the excavated trenches and surfaces (1) and the dwellings 10 and 11 (after Rustoiu 2002a). 2. Solotvino. Plan of the excavations with the contexts belonging to the phase dated to the fourth to third centuries BC (after Rustoiu 2002b). 3. Handmade ceramic vessels from Bila Cerkva (1) and Solotvino (2) (after Rustoiu 2008). 4. Graves no. 1 (1) and 3a–b (2), together with their ceramic grave-goods, from the Olteni cemetery (after Sîrbu et al. 2006).

The settlements from Bila Cerkva and Solotvino illustrate the typical evolution of local communities from Maramureș from the Early to the Late Iron Age, unchanged by the arrival of foreign groups, and different from what happened in Transylvania during the period of Celtic colonisation. The character of the settlements from Maramureș indicates that the local populations very probably had an internal organisation similar to that of the communities living to the east and south of the Carpathians (groups of people ruled by warlike elites, concentrated around a number of large fortified settlements) and different from the pattern which characterised the La Tène rural communities from Transylvania. These sites belong to a peripheral area of settlement organisation, usually defined as 'Thracian'. This peripheral location substantially hampered the development of regular trading connections with the Greek Pontic or eastern Scythian area. Contrary to the settlements in Maramureș, the finds from the sites located east of the Carpathians contained numerous imported Greek vessels, as well as a pooling of prestige objects or symbols of power. The finest and most eloquent examples were the hoards of gold and silver artefacts, from both settlements and graves (e.g the 'Thracian' treasures see Kull 1997; for Greek imports see Teleagă 2008).

Recent investigations within the depressions from eastern Transylvania also document a specific development of the local communities. For example, a cremation cemetery dated to the fourth and third centuries BC has been discovered at Olteni (Covasna County) (Fig. 13.5/4), together with a contemporary rural settlement (Cavruc & Buzea 2005; Sîrbu et al. 2006; 2008). The funerary rite and other rituals, as well as the ceramic grave goods, have similarities to those in the eastern Carpathian area, for example in the cemetery at Slobozia, Bacău County (Buzdugan 1968). On the other hand, La Tène artefacts were not identified, although both the cemetery and the settlement are of the same date as early Celtic horizons in Transylvania. In the same way as in the Maramureș depression, the community from Olteni seems to remain untouched by Celtic cultural influences. Its features also reflect, as in Maramureș, the evolution of a local population from the Early to the Late Iron Age, uninfluenced by the arrival of Celtic groups in Transylvania. Furthermore, this development again resembles the model of social organisation typical of the communities situated east of the Carpathians.

In conclusion, it seems that the local communities from Maramureș and the eastern Transylvanian depressions followed their own paths of development, given that their evolution was not disturbed by the arrival of foreign groups, as happened in most of the Carpathian Basin. These examples are useful for the interpretation of the evolution of local communities from Transylvania and of the impact of Celtic colonisation. Celtic colonisation determined the dissolution of some traditional community relationships and contributed to the creation of some new communities with different social structures, through integration with the indigenous populations. If Celtic groups had not affected these regions perhaps the local communities would have experienced a development that was much the same as that of the northern Balkans communities (which was mainly orientated towards Mediterranean and Pontic models), even if at the periphery of this cultural area.

## Conclusions

Towards the end of the Early Iron Age, the eastern part of the Carpathian Basin was characterised by a variety of cultural entities illustrating a specific evolution of the local communities. The indigenous populations were mixed with groups who arrived in successive stages from different areas of the northern Pontic region and introduced new elements of material culture, for example wheel-made pottery, and new symbols and ideologies, suggested by specific elements of the funerary rite and other rituals, as well as the objects decorated in the 'animal art' style. These communities apparently did not develop regular contacts with Central Europe, or at least such contacts left no visible traces in the local material culture.

Their evolution was interrupted in the second half of the fourth century BC by the arrival from the west of groups who colonised the northern and eastern part of the Great Hungarian Plain and Transylvania. The interactions between the colonists and the indigenous people can be identified by analysing the funerary rites and rituals from a series of representative cemeteries. The newcomers usually imposed their own way of life and norms, as well as several features of their material culture. For their part, the locals expressed different degrees of 'resistance' against various aspects of the foreign culture. For example, in some cases the indigenous communities preserved their own funerary practices, whereas others were quite rapidly integrated into the newly imposed structures. Since these situations are different from one community to another, a single model of interaction characterising the entire region cannot be constructed, but a general phenomenon of 'hybridisation' of the material culture is clearly visible. The communities which emerged from the interactions between colonising groups and local populations developed new modalities of expressing individual and group identities. These are different from the practices identified in the areas of origin of the colonists, but also from those which characterised the indigenous communities of the end of the Early Iron Age. Therefore it can be affirmed that their appearance contributed to the genesis of an eastern 'Celtic' world.

On the other hand the indigenous communities from northern and eastern Transylvania were not affected by colonisation and continued to evolve according to the specific cultural and communal models of the end of the Early Iron Age, which were similar to those encountered outside the Carpathians. The fortified settlements and the funerary contexts from the latter regions point to the existence of some social structures dominated by military elites who could have been able to block the advance of the colonist groups. On the other hand the mountainous depressions from eastern Transylvania might have been unsuitable geographically or economically for the incoming communities, who sought to establish particular types of settlements.

# 14. Ancient Thrace Between the East and the West

*Nikola Theodossiev*

**Keywords:** Thracians, Greeks, Persians, Macedonians, Celts

Ancient Thrace was an extensive region that occupied part of south eastern Europe during the first millennium BC, before it was incorporated into the Roman Empire in the period from the late first century BC to the early second century AD (Casson 1926; Kacarov 1930; Danov 1976; Fol & Marazov 1977; Fol & Spiridonov 1983; Hoddinott 1981; Oppermann 1984; Archibald 1998; Bouzek 2004; Theodossiev 2011). Its frontiers were relatively fluid and dynamic and its area spread from the western Black Sea coast to the Morava River and Struma/Vardar river valleys, and from the Transylvanian Alps, the Moldavian Carpathians and the lower Dniester River to the Bosporus, the northern coast of the Sea of Marmara and the northern Aegean coast, including the islands of Samothrace and Thasos. In addition, some historical records give information on Thracian tribes that inhabited some areas in central Greece, north western Asia Minor and several Aegean islands.

Ancient Thrace was not an ethnically and culturally homogeneous region and in fact, throughout the first millennium BC, some of its areas were under the domination and control of the Greek colonies, the Achaemenid Empire, the Macedonian Kingdom and the Celtic Kingdom of Thrace (Kacarov 1919; 1930; Danov 1976; Papazoglu 1978; Hoddinott 1981; Isaac 1986; Balcer 1988; Loukopoulou 1989; Zahrnt 1997; Theodossiev 2000a; Bouzek 2004; Boteva 2010). Moreover, ancient Thracians never did form a single nation and a unified state, although during the second half of the fifth and the first half of the fourth centuries BC, the Odrysian Kingdom emerged as a regional power that controlled the main part of the Thracian territory (Archibald 1998). In fact, 'Thracian' was a general and collective ethnic name, which included a number of local tribes, and was used by the Greek and Roman authors when they were describing various events and indigenous people living in the region. Although the modern scholars are heavily restricted by the lack of local historical records and any Thracian literature, numerous Thracian tribal names are well known in the ancient Greek and Roman historical sources and the Thracian tribes that inhabited the region during the first millennium BC numbered at least 80 (Fol & Spiridonov 1983). Very often these tribes shared a common material culture, mortuary practices and settlement patterns, and presumably spoke similar dialects, although sometimes the tribes were very different, especially when they were living long distances apart, or were exposed to different foreign cultural and political influences, particularly in the interaction zones inhabited by mixed populations consisting of indigenous Thracians and foreign ethnic groups.

A number of Greek and Roman historical records and some archaeological data allow us to identify clearly the ethnic groups who penetrated and settled in ancient Thrace and often mingled with the indigenous tribes. The historical and archaeological evidence also allow us to specify the complex interaction processes between Thracians and other ethnic groups who occupied the neighbouring areas of south eastern Europe. Thus, during the first millennium BC, the western periphery of Thrace was an interaction zone between Illyrian and Thracian tribes (Papazoglu 1978; Theodossiev 2000a). The ethnic affiliation of certain tribes in the area remains highly uncertain, because of the limited ancient written sources and the mixed cultural features, detectable in the archaeological data, but it is clear that the Paeonians who occupied the region along the Vardar River emerged as a separate ethnic group displaying some features typical of both Thracians and Illyrians (Theodossiev 2000b). At the same time, from the eighth–seventh centuries BC onwards, the local Thracians interacted actively with the Scythians in the north eastern areas of Thrace and on some occasions both ethnic groups mingled (Fol 1975; Melyukova 1979; Yordanov 1990; Bouzek 2004). The bilateral Thraco-Scythian interaction is easily detected in the metalwork, particularly the production of appliqués for horse-trappings, and also, in certain features of the mortuary practices related to the lavish burials of aristocrats and kings. In addition, the historical sources provide sufficient information on various political relations, intermarriage, military conflicts and conquest, while during the Hellenistic period several Scythian kings were dominant in a number of regions of north eastern Thrace.

The most significant historical event that produced a strong impact on the Thracian tribes was the Greek colonisation of the northern Aegean and western Black Sea coastline that began in the middle of the eighth century BC and lasted throughout several following centuries, although some archaeological material indicates active pre-colonial contacts between Greeks and Thracians (Danov 1976; Boardman 1980; Isaac 1986; Loukopoulou 1989; Archibald 1998; Tsetskhladze 1998; Oppermann 2004). The Greek colonisation in Thrace stimulated numerous ethnic and cultural interrelations and interactions and the ancient Greeks often mingled with Thracians in the newly established colonies. As a result, certain tribes who inhabited neighbouring regions gradually adopted many elements of Classical Civilisation and, from the sixth to fourth centuries BC, the Thracian tribal elite became partially Hellenised, while Greek became the official language of diplomacy and administration. Although the Thracians never created a literature of their own, in the course of various contacts and interactions, they adopted the Greek alphabet and, in certain cases, the script was used in ritual practice and political relations, while several inscriptions with Greek letters but in the Thracian language have been recovered. Some literary and epigraphic records provide information on other features of the dynamic bilateral relations and show that, during the Classical period, the Greeks travelled and settled in the inland part of Thrace, established emporia and became politically engaged with Thracian kings (Stronk 1995; Archibald 1998).

Another important historical event, at the time of the Graeco-Persian Wars, was the Persian occupation of Aegean Thrace during the late sixth and the first several decades of the fifth centuries BC, when this region became part of the Achaemenid Empire (Balcer 1988; Zahrnt 1997; Yordanov 2003). The Persian presence in and domination of Aegean Thrace not only influenced Thracian gold- and silverwork, but stimulated the process of state formation among the local Thracians and the powerful Odrysian Kingdom emerged immediately after the withdrawal of the Persians, thus displaying a dynamic process of political emancipation (Archibald 1998; Marazov 1998).

At the same time, in the course of the Argead (Macedonian) political and military expansion northward and eastward from the late sixth century BC onwards, a significant part of south western Thrace was gradually annexed by the Macedonian Kingdom (Casson 1926; Kacarov 1930; Danov 1976; Hoddinott 1981; Hatzopoulos & Loukopoulou 1992; 1996; Archibald 1998; Theodossiev 2000a; 2000b; Bouzek 2004). Later, during the reign of Philip of Macedon and Alexander the Great, almost all of Thrace was subdued and became part of the Macedonian Kingdom, while numerous Thracian aristocrats and warriors participated in the eastern military campaigns of Alexander the Great. In the time of the Diadochi, Lysimachus continued the Macedonian control over a significant part of the Thracian territory and declared himself King of Thrace. In fact, the Macedonian political domination and settlement in Thrace further reinforced the process of Hellenisation of the indigenous tribes who occupied the Thracian interior, especially during the Late Classical and Early Hellenistic periods.

During the early third century BC, the Celts invaded ancient Thrace and many of them settled in the region (Kacarov 1919; Theodossiev 2000a; Bouzek 2004; Boteva 2010; Emilov 2010). They established a Celtic Kingdom in south eastern Thrace that existed until the end of the third century BC when it was liquidated by the Thracians, although some Celtic tribes continued to live in Thrace. Simultaneously, Thracian culture adopted many Celtic elements in their weaponry and jewellery, especially in the northern areas. The dynamic complexity of the ethnic interrelations and interactions in this period is well illustrated in some historical sources of the last two centuries of the first millennium BC, which inform us of intermingled Thracians, Celts, Illyrians and Scythians, coexisting in certain regions of Hellenistic Thrace.

The geographical location of ancient Thrace between the East and the West, the dynamic historical events, the different political and cultural influences, and the various ethnic groups that inhabited the region and often mingled with each other, predetermined the specific features of the entire area and its inhabitants. On the one hand, ancient Thrace was exposed to the powerful influence of the Classical Civilisation of ancient Greece and other major Anatolian civilisations, particularly the Persians. As already mentioned, this resulted in the state formation and the partial Hellenisation of some tribes, especially those that inhabited southern Thrace and the areas alongside the western Black Sea coast. Many aspects of Classical Civilisation were adopted by the Thracians and reshaped according to their own mentality and taste, in the course of interaction with the ancient Greeks. Many of these achievements were transmitted further north and west to other central and eastern European regions that had never been in direct contact with the Hellenic and the Anatolian world. At the same time, in many aspects of its historical and cultural development, ancient Thrace remained part of temperate 'Barbarian' Europe. This duality of ancient Thrace and its inhabitants was further reinforced during the Hellenistic period with the penetration and settlement of the Celts from Central Europe when the local Thracians experienced strong new influences. In fact, three different interacting worlds coexisted in ancient Thrace: the world of the Classical Civilisation in the Greek colonies along the Thracian littorals, the world of 'Barbarian' Iron Age Europe in the deep inland of Thrace, and the intermediate world of multilateral interaction, interrelation and intermarriage, where the Classical Civilisation met Iron Age Europe and in the middle ground both shaped a new dynamic reality of duality and transformation, of centre and periphery, of East and West.

# 15. 'Hellenisation' and Ethnicity in the Continental Balkan Iron Age

*Ivan Vranić*

KEYWORDS: 'HELLENISATION', ETHNICITY, FORTIFIED LATE IRON AGE SETTLEMENTS, THE BALKANS, MODERNITY

'HELLENISED' SETTLEMENTS AND CULTURE-HISTORY, AN INTRODUCTION
Proximity to the Mediterranean and Greek world had a profound impact on development of archaeology in the Balkans. Ever since the culture-historical paradigm of the late nineteenth and first half of the twentieth century has recognised south eastern Europe (starting from the Neolithic onwards) as the key region in the 'spread' of Middle Eastern 'influences' (e.g. Childe 1929; 1957), the same theoretical perspective – favouring distant 'role models' for any changes in local material culture, has persisted in traditional epistemology. The concept of 'Hellenisation' is among the numerous consequences of this diffusionist standpoint. Loosely defined as unilateral acceptance of Greek culture by local Iron Age communities, narratives about 'Hellenisation' stand behind most interpretations of social and cultural changes in Balkan protohistory (e.g. Vasić 1973; 1987b; Benac 1987b).

The essentialist and primordial perspective on ethnicity is the second, and maybe even more influential, theoretical aspect of culture-history (Jenkins 1994; Hall 1997; Jones 1997). The pursuit of stable and monolithic group identities in the past has had a severe influence on the discipline, especially in the case of the Iron Age studies (Dietler 1994; Dzino 2007; 2008a; 2008b). Traditional researchers in the Balkans, following similar theoretical paths, established the Greek and Roman literary sources as historical 'data' that could provide an opportunity of relating the 'Palaeobalkan peoples' – known from the written sources (Papazoglu 1978; Šašel-Kos 2005), with specific archaeological cultures. This epistemology led to flawed and, up until recently, unchallenged conclusions about ethnic continuity that could be 'traced backwards' to the Late Bronze Age or even further into the prehistory, eventually, reaching their 'Indo-European' origins (e.g. Tasić 1995). This approach is still a very common trait of the national schools of archaeology in the Balkans (Novaković 2011; Vranić 2011).

This paper scrutinises *ethnicity* and *'Hellenisation'* – two paradigmatic and intertwined narratives that are most prominent features in the construction of traditional knowledge about 'spread' of the Greek 'civilisation' among strictly defined and stable local Iron Age communities: 'Palaeobalkan peoples' or 'tribes'. The case study is the different culture-historical interpretations of

162                                    Ivan Vranić

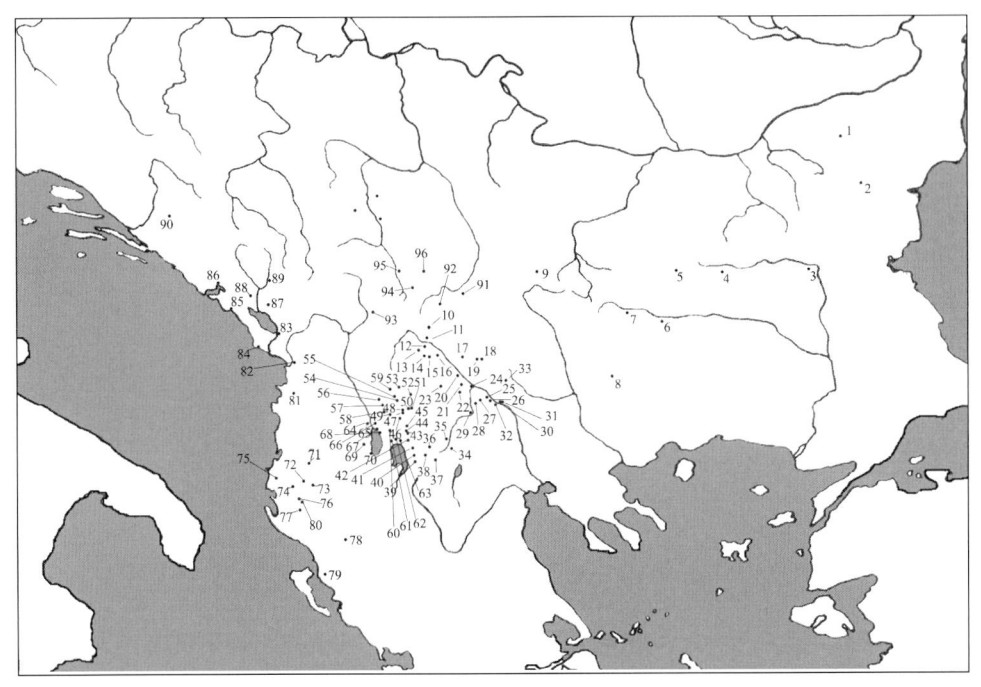

*Figure 15.1. Late Iron Age 'Hellenised' settlements in the Central Balkans.*

'Hellenised Iron Age settlements' (Fig. 15.1.). These Late Iron Age fortified settlements are located throughout the continental parts of Bulgaria (Popov 2002; Archibald 2000: 212–33; 2004: 885–99; Hansen 2006: 20–3; Cohen 1995: 79–88), Former Yugoslav Republic of Macedonia (Sokolovska 1986; Mikulčik 1999), Albania (Wilkes 1992; Ceka 2005) and, to a much smaller degree, Serbia (Popović 2005; 2006; 2007) and Kosovo (Shukriu 1996). Their features of architecture and artefacts that resemble Greek material culture, are an excellent case study for the deconstruction of the traditional inferences about ethnicity, cultural change and the role of modernity in the development of the discipline of archaeology in the Balkans.

Archaeologists in the region saw these sites (dated mostly from fifth to third century BC) as the final stage of 'ethnogenesis' of Thracian, Paionian, Illyrian, Dardanian, etc., ethnicities, moulding their interpretations into the well-known framework of evolution of cultures/peoples in Balkan prehistory. The quest for different 'peoples' remained of paramount importance leading into challenging and argumentative disputes about ethnicities in the later Iron Age, even though they acknowledged some similarities in material culture: the appearance of ashlar masonry and mudbricks (Fig. 15.2), attributed to Greek masons under contract (Tsetskhladze 1998b; Bitrakova-Grozdanova 2006; Nankov 2008); local 'grey' wheel made pottery that shows curious similarities with late Classical and early Hellenistic Greek (mostly Athenian) plain wares (Sokolovska 1992; Domaradski 2002; Bouzek & Domaradska 2009); loom-weights (Bouzek 1996; Dimitrova 2002; Popović & Vranić 2008); Attic red-figure, St. Valentin and early Hellenistic

*Figure 15.2. Ashlar architecture from Kale-Krsevica (south eastern Serbia).*

vases (e.g. Bitrakova-Grozdanova 1987; Archibald 2002; Krstić 2005); numerous stamped and unstamped northern Aegean amphorae (Titz 2002; Bouzek *et al.* 2007; Tzozhev 2009); and Greek and local coinage (e.g. Popović 1987), etc.

Traditional archaeology attributed the similarities in material culture, which all confirm some form of interrelations with Greece, to the process of 'Hellenisation'. At the same time, the strict ethnic division of archaeological cultures remained completely unchallenged (see Čangova 1981; Dimitrov & Ivanov 1984; Sokolovska 1986; Bouzek *et al.* 1996; 2002; Mikulčik 1999; Bozkova & Delev 2002; Ceka 2005). Scrutinising the literature on the subject, it becomes obvious that territories of supposed Iron Age ethnicities strikingly coincide with modern national borders. I argue here that reasons for this interpretative disparity are modern and political. The reflexive relation between past and present – in this case stable and recognisable Iron Age *ethnicity* constructed from different nationalistic narratives of modern Balkan countries, and *'Hellenisation'* interpreted following colonial arguments as 'civilisation' and acceptance of 'better' and 'more European' culture – remains intact.

## ETHNICITY

Numerous current theories of collective identity meticulously challenge all deterministic conclusions about stable and recognisable 'ethno-cultural' entities in prehistory – a distinguishing characteristic of the culture-historical approach (Graves-Brown *et al.* 1996; Días-Andreu *et al.* 2005; Insoll 2007). Recent constructivist and instrumentalist theories emphasis fluidity, contact with other groups and situational response as critical aspects in the conscious maintenance and constant rebuilding of a sense of community, eventually leading to the conclusion that ethnicity and culture are different forms of identity (Barth 1969a; Shennan 1989; Jenkins 1994; Banks 1996; Hall 1997; Jones 1997; 2007; Meskell 2002; Lucy 2005; Babić 2008a; Derks & Roymans 2009). This theoretical change led to the abandonment of the quest for continuity and 'ethnogenesis' – so typical of the Balkan culture-historical approach (Kaiser 1995; Kotsakis 1998: 50), and to a new focus on political aspects of modernity in the construction of the past ethnicities as stable categories.

The emergence of nation states is, probably, the most important socio-political feature of modernity (Gellner 1983; Anderson 1991), and a prolific context for nineteenth-century archaeology (Thomas 2004; Díaz-Andreu 2007). Since the chase for 'our' past has been an essential political necessity in the construction of national identity, it can be inferred that the establishment of the humanities as distinctive and recognised disciplines played an important role in nation building. Most authors today agree that deterministic theories of culture as an ethnic category surfaced when modern European identities of nation-state were, uncritically, implemented and built into the constructions of past group identities as 'our' mythic ancestors (Trigger 1995; Jones 1997; 2007; Meskell 2002; Lucy 2005).

The search for the modern political roles of archaeology in different countries today is a very prominent research interest (e.g. Kohl & Fawcett 1995; Meskell 1998; Galaty & Watkinson 2004; Silverman 2011), while the situation in the Balkans is exceptionally significant because of the political turmoil, the recent creation of new nations (a process that is still in progress) and the prominent role of archaeology in the public conscience. The tendencies of different national archaeologies to label similar material culture with diverse ethnicities are a very common situation in culture-historical research (cf. Dietler 1994; Rowlands 1994; 2007; Trigger 1996; Kohl 1998). The focus of Late Iron Age 'Hellenised' settlements in Bulgaria is on Thracian ethnicity; in the former Yugoslav Republic of Macedonia on Paionian, or more recently on Macedonian; in Kosovo on Dardanian; and in Albania on Illyrian ethnicity. Similarities in material culture and vigorous arguments within different Balkan archaeologies make it an interesting ground for a postprocessual deconstruction of the political role of past ethnicities, tradition and heritage in the construction of modern nationalism.

### 'HELLENISATION', A POST-COLONIAL VIEW

Ethnic determinism is just one example of an ethnocentric and reflexive position of the discipline (Jones 1997; Gosden 1999; 2007; Thomas 2004). The Culture-historical concept of 'Hellenisation' is equally problematic and thoroughly criticised within post-colonial studies (Hodos 2006). In a similar way to 'Romanisation' (Hingley 1999; 2005), the traditional perspective of 'Hellenisation' focuses on the 'spread' of Greek culture and 'civilisation' among local communities – viewed as 'normal', 'expected', and 'progressive', following the diffusionist methodology and modern politics of European domination as a role model (Dietler 1997: 296). The concept of 'Hellenisation' was established, in a broader sense, as the universal explanation for all cultural changes related to contact with Greek world, and was perceived as the supreme human achievement, reaching its climax after the death of Alexander III (356–323 BC) with Hellenism (e.g. Momigliano 1971). The concept, is though, a Eurocentric perspective that focuses on 'civilising' barbarian groups. The Iron Age Balkan context is interesting because of the numerous contacts with the Mediterranean world and the subsequent Macedonian conquest of parts of Thrace and Paeonia in the fourth century BC (Archibald 1998; 2000; 2010; Theodossiev 2011).

Fanula Papazoglu, the most prominent researcher of 'Hellenisation' and 'Romanisation' in socialist Yugoslavia, applied modern colonial and national models in her interpretation of cultural changes in the first millennium BC (e.g. 1978; 1988). Papzoglu also presented the only considered theoretical thesis (from a culture-historical and even unilinear evolutionary perspective) stating that 'Hellenisation' was, above all, a matter of linguistic change within barbarian elites who started speaking Greek and established their 'courts' imitating the practice of Hellenistic monarchies (1980). Papazoglu believed that this change constituted the beginning of 'civilisation' in the Balkans, which was introduced from the Greek world.

It is obvious that the concept of ethnicity remained unchallenged because, as Papazoglu believed, 'Hellenisation' influenced only the social elites, which were mimicking political institutions in the Hellenistic socio-political sphere. Later, this style of interpretation considered the fourth century BC socio-political entities of the inner Balkans to be 'archaic states' or even 'Barbarian Hellenistic monarchies' populated by Paionian, Odrisian or Illyrian 'nations'. Even from recent evolutionary perspectives, it is tendentious to consider these polities as Hellenistic monarchies and fully developed complex society (cf. Tainter 1988; Trigger 2003; Yoffee 2004). On the other hand, the concept of Illyrian or Thracian 'nations' in the fourth century BC is an obvious anachronism. Socio-political entities in the Late Iron Age must have been much smaller, consisting probably of numerous polities in constant struggle (cf. Renfrew & Cherry 1996; Wells 1998: 260–1), encompassing probably only a few neighbouring settlements.

Post-colonial criticism and reinterpretation of traditional understanding of Classical and Hellenistic Greece (Hall 2002; Gosden 2004; 2007; Dietler 2005; Goff 2005; Hurst & Owen 2005), or late prehistoric communities in the Balkans, can shed some light on the political and social reasons leading archaeologists toward different ethnic determinations of similar material culture, and even more importantly on the causes of the unilateral acceptance of Classical and Hellenistic culture. Concepts of hybridisation, fluidity and material culture agency in the meaningful creation of new identities during periods of contact have been missing from the Balkan archaeologies dealing with 'Hellenised settlements'. This paper argues that Western narratives of nationalism and colonialism found their way into Balkan archaeologies and remained almost completely unchallenged. Prominence of ethnic determinism roughly coincides with Trigger's nationalistic archaeology, a practice that usually emerges in countries where national issues were crucial in the moment when the discipline was formed (Trigger 1984; 1995; 1996).

**THE ROMANTIC AND THE MYTHICAL: BULGARIAN AND ALBANIAN ARCHAEOLOGY**
The deconstruction of the archaeological epistemology and interpretation of the region usually starts with the work of Maria Todorova (2009) on the Balkans as 'bridge or crossroad' between the West and the Orient. Presented in the Western colonial narrative as romantic, ambiguous and engulfed in long mythical tradition, the image of the Balkans was constructed in accordance with an already established picture of the Orient as 'exotic and different'. This modern social context influenced archaeology in the region. Bailey (1998), for instance, argues that Western scholars perceived Bulgarian archaeology as an 'exotic other' – discipline that could impress by large quantities of golden and silver artefacts, but usually without a substantial up-to-date research agenda or a theoretical approach.

The Bulgarian discipline and its traditional discourse about the 'Thracian past' is equally responsible for this image, because it has been constantly reproducing that same Western picture of the Balkans into the past. The basic principle is the glorification of a mystical Thracian heritage and fascination by art and culture of this exotic 'people', who have been constructed as the mythic ancestors of modern Bulgarians. Bailey (1998: 90) refers to this context of self-presentation as auto-exoticism, claiming that it became appropriate and even highly prized to present local history as exotic and engulfed with mystical traditions. This demand stems from the Romantic Movement of the nineteenth century and the creation of the Bulgarian nation state, the later political context of the communist reign and the difficulties of economic change during the nineties, but also as a response to the Western Colonial perspective. These socio-political contexts are fertile ground for a romantic perspective of the past, nationalism and subsequent culture-historical theory.

Following this epistemology, most Late Iron Age sites in Bulgaria have been interpreted as 'Thracian cities' (Popov 2002). The most prominent example is *Seuthopolis*, a fortified fourth-century B.C. settlement with blocks of *pastats* and *prostas* type houses, which architecturally resembles Greek cities planned on a grid. Excavated during the construction of the Gergi Dimitrov dam, the first major project in communist Bulgaria, this site has been interpreted as the capital of the 'Odrysian kingdom' (Dimitrov & Ivanov 1984; Popov 2002: 122–34), and the only urban centre in Thrace that had not been constructed by Greek political initiative (Webber 2001: 1). Even though it stands for the most 'Urbanised' and 'Hellenised' site in the Balkan hinterland, Greek agency is very much neglected. Interpreted as the capital of the Odrysian kingdom, it has been presented to the public as the highlight of Thracian politics and power, with no room for the Mediterranean world except in as much that Greek workers were employed by the Thracian elite.

Interpretation of Seuthopolis stands out as the best case of nationalism, romanticism and glorification of a 'Thracian past' in Bulgarian archaeology. On the other hand, a very similar Late Iron Age site at Adzijska Vodenica, located near the modern town of Vetren on the left bank of upper course of the Maritza river and excavated during the nineties within an international archaeological project, has been interpreted as the Greek trading colony of *emporion Pistiros* (Bouzek *et al.* 1996; 2002; 2007).

An attempt to deconstruct disparate ethnic interpretations presented in different political circumstances is a very interesting approach. Bulgaria during the Cold War was an isolated country under Soviet influence, a context in which it was necessary to point out some form of national pride. Consequently, Bulgarian scholars constructed the narrative of 'mighty Thracians' as a symbol of previous 'national' glory (cf. Kaiser 1995; Bailey 1998). Interpretation of Seuthopolis as the capital of the Odrysian Kingdom stands out as the most prominent example of this narrative. Following Trigger's classification, Bulgarian colleagues worked in the socio-political context of military or political turmoil – the conditions that favoured development of nationalistic archaeology (Trigger 1984; 1995; 1996). Ironically, the narrative that labelled the Bulgarian Iron Age heritage as 'the oldest' or the 'first', additionally fuelled the Western colonial image of Balkan archaeology, which was understood as a mythical and exotic discipline.

Archaeological interpretations of one very similar settlement – *Pistiros*, presented after the Cold War in circumstances that were more liberal, show a very different agenda and course of research. The more recent hypothesis is that ethnic Greeks founded a settlement, *emporion Pistiros*, by negotiation with the local rulers during the fifth century BC (Bouzek *et al.* 1996; 2002). This approach that faced some strong opposition (Tsetskhladze 2000: 233–46; Hansen 2006: 20–3) surfaced during a completely different political environment where Bulgaria was trying to become a recognised part of the Western world with all the social and cultural implications that follow from this political standpoint. The assertion of Greek superiority inherent in the dubious interpretations of Pistiros as a Greek inland colony stands for a total abandonment of Thracian history in the quest for proposing Classics as more 'valuable' past. The positing of Greek domination is a result of the unusual strain of colonial archaeology currently appearing in the Balkans that contrasts with the more logical interpretation of hybrid identities. All these debates are similar to Western traditions recognising Greek and Roman culture as evolutionarily more advanced and possessing a more valuable heritage. This trend surfaced in Bulgaria following the political changes since the late eighties and early nineties. Postcolonial studies have shown numerous cases of a causal link between modern European nationalism and imperial politics and the construction of Classical antiquity (Hingley 1999; 2005; Dietler 2005; Goff 2005; Hurst & Owen 2005; Gosden 2007). Moreover, it is not difficult to recognise similar cultural politics in modern day Bulgaria.

*Albania* developed a similar culture-historical practice in comparable circumstances of isolation and romanticism. The hypothesis that the modern Albanians were direct descendants from ancient Illyrians emerged, for the first time, during the nineteenth-century Austro-Hungarian excavations of Iron Age sites in modern day Albania (Gilkes 2004: 40). After gaining independence, and especially during the Enver Hoxha's communist regime, when the discipline of archaeology was widely promoted, this narrative became an integrated part of Albanian national identity (Galaty & Watkinson 2004; Gilkes 2004). Consequently, numerous Late Iron Age 'Hellenised' settlements (e.g.

Byllis, Amantia, Antigoneia) were recognised as 'urban' or part of the 'final phase' of Illyrian 'ethnogenesis' (e.g. Ceka 2005).

This nationalistic practice stands out as the most prominent case of the primordial approach to ethnicity in Europe. Recent deconstructions have pointed out that isolation and xenophobic foreign politics as the main 'culprits' for the development of concept of Illyrian/Albanian continuity and the construction of the ancient Illyrians as a 'people' who successfully defended their freedom against 'foreign enemies' like Greece and Rome, in their capacity as Albanian antecedents and mythic ancestors (Galaty *et al.* 1999; Galaty & Watkinson 2004; Galaty 2011).

A similar narrative is also very prominent in modern day Kosovo where the Albanian people regard the ancient Dardanians as their mythic ancestors. Local researchers constructed the image of Iron Age Dardanians as slightly different, but still of Illyrian ethnicity (e.g. Shukriu 1996; Mirdita 2009), a position which is in accordance with the modern socio-political context of the Albanian people living simultaneously in Kosovo and Albania. Political parties, banks and many other institutions labelled 'Dardanian' (*Democratic league of Dardania, Dardania University, Dardania Bank, Radio Dardania,* etc.) in Kosovo and Albania present a first-hand case of the nationalistic role of archaeology in modern politics.

### THE FORMER YUGOSLAVIA AND ITS NATIONALISMS

Outside the coastal zones of the Adriatic and the related issue of Greek maritime colonisation in the Balkans (see Wilkes & Fischer-Hansen 2004; Dzino 2010: 44–60), 'Hellenised settlements' in continental parts of former Yugoslavia are numerous only in Macedonia (Sokolovska 1986; Mikulčik 1999). There are, also, some rare cases in south eastern Serbia (Popović 2005; 2006; 2007) and Kosovo (Shukriu 1996). The key questions relevant to this region are different from those of Mediterranean hybridisation and contacts starting in the period of Archaic colonisation (Hall 2002; Gosden 2004). Instead, the focus is on continental interrelations between local communities and the northern Aegean and ancient Macedonia, intensifying from the fifth and reaching its climax in fourth and third century BC (Lund 1992; Archibald 1998; 2000; 2010; Theodossiev 2011).

The changing archaeological narratives about 'Hellenisation' and ethnicity in the Former Yugoslav Republic of Macedonia, during the time of the former Yugoslavia and afterwards, is an excellent example of the linkage between modernity and archaeological interpretations. The major difference in the Yugoslav form of nationalistic archaeology, contrary to the Bulgarian or Albanian versions, derives from the socio-political context. It seems that in this country, which had been more open and accessible, the question of an 'exotic past', and the urge to demonstrate to the world 'the oldest' heritage, had a much smaller importance. On the other hand, the dominant modern declaration of ethnic heterogeneity influenced the development of a different form of nationalistic archaeology (Kaiser 1995). Most member states and autonomous regions in socialist Yugoslavia took special care, especially during the seventies and eighties, to research and document different Iron Age ethnicities that, usually, coincided

## 15. 'Hellenisation' and Ethnicity in the Continental Balkan Iron Age

with modern political borders or later territorial ambitions. Throughout the years of crises and political turmoil, republics and autonomous regions within Yugoslavia managed to construct their own separate Iron Age 'ancestors' who are today the mythic ancestors of separate nations. The leading research goal in the Former Yugoslav Republic of Macedonia, during the time of Yugoslavia, was the search for Iron Age Paionian ethnicity.

Contrary to the romantic interest in the Illyrians in the nineteenth and early twentieth century (Wilkes 1992: 5), archaeologists in eastern parts of Yugoslavia (Serbia and Macedonia) subsequently developed an enduring interest in 'Daco-Moesian' identity (Garašanin 1979; 1988b). Before that change, researchers had considered most Iron Age ethnicities to be Illyrian in descent (e.g. Daradanians, Paionians). This earlier perspective is related to the tradition of *Illyrian movement*, fading Yugoslav nationalism and to the role of centralised government in the first decades after World War II. The emerging narrative of 'Daco-Moesians' in the seventies and eighties developed as a response to the foreign pressures of Bulgarian and Albanian scholars and even more profoundly to the internal changes and tensions developed by growing local nationalisms inside Yugoslavia. Subsequently, 'Daco-Moesian' groups living in eastern parts of former Yugoslavia were established as different and distinctive 'ethno-cultural' communities. This context favoured an interest in *Triballi*, the 'people' of the Morava valley (Serbia) that was different from the Thracian identities favoured by Bulgarian colleagues (Stojić 1986; *contra* Fol *et al.* 1986), *Dardanianas*, non-Illyrians in Kosovo (Srejović 1973; Srejović 1979; Papazoglu 1988; Tasić 1998; *contra* Shukriu 1996; Ceka 2005: 175–90; Mirdita 2009) and *Paionians*, the supposed inhabitants of major parts of the territory of Yugoslav Macedonia (where most 'Hellenisation' occurred). At the same time, this central region of the peninsula has been recognised as major communication artery linking Central Europe and Greece, making 'Daco-Moesian' communities a promising research interest that could answer major culture-historical questions of 'influences' and 'migrations' in later prehistory and determine the promising role of central Balkan in a broader European prehistory.

Paionian identity played an important role in Former Yugoslav Republic of Macedonia's Iron Age archaeology inside Yugoslavia showing that this territory was an equally important part of the multiethnic Iron Age context in the Balkans (Sokolovska 1986; Petrova 1991). The narrative of Paionian identity was constructed to show that Macedonian soil was 'neither Illyrian nor Thracian', providing a response to the neighbouring Bulgarian and Albanian interpretations that favoured a strict division of the Balkans between the Illyrian West and the Thracian East (e.g. Popov 2002; Ceka 2005). Recently, however, the focus has changed from 'independent Paionians' to a 'Paionian-Macedonian symbiosis' (Mitrevski 1997) or more straightforwardly to the question of 'Macedonian identity' in the Iron Age (Kuzman 2006; Školjev-Dončo *et al.* 2010). This change happened during the turbulent period of the nineties when modern Macedonian people were confronted with numerous problems following the newly gained independence. Identity issues with neighbours who consider the Macedonian language, religion or name to be 'stolen' applied strong pressure on the newly recognised nation. This change of interest in Iron Age archaeology (from Paionian to Macedonian identity) was an expected response to a different political context. Only after independence, following all these political and economic difficulties, Macedonian scholars reached out to the legacy of Philip II and Alexander III as the means of constructing a modern nation state (Jones & Graves-Brown 1996: 3; Brown 1998). Eventually, numerous Late Iron Age 'Hellenised settlements' became the most prominent case that 'proves' the symbiosis of Macedonian and Paionian identity, a material record of 'direct continuity' of the Iron Age communities with Philip II and Alexander III (e.g. Kuzman 2006; Školjev-Dončo et al. 2010).

The seriousness of the new politics sponsoring national identity, heritage and importance of ancient Macedonia, was materialised in the project *Skopje 2014* (http://www.skyscrapercity.com/showthread.php?t=1213587). Skopje, the capital of Macedonia and the biggest city in the country, is currently being reconstructed according to this project. When Skopje was destroyed in the earthquake of 1963, the city was rebuilt employing the architectural trends of socialist Yugoslavia leaving the now independent country with very few old buildings and potential tourist attractions in the city itself (which could not be said of the rest of the country). Beside numerous new statues, fountains and bridges, city officials decided to invest €200 million in the project that should also renew and create fresh city landmarks, including several official buildings (the Houses of Parliament, the Post Office, the Archaeological Museum, etc.) – designed in compliance with the postulates of classical architecture. The most prominent feature of the project is a large monument of Alexander III sitting on the rearing Bucephalus (Fig. 15.3.) in the central square – officially named *Warrior on the Horse* because of Greek protests (although Alexander the Great is also the official name of Skopje's International Airport). Besides Alexander, there are numerous monuments including Philip II (the largest football stadium also bears his name), Justin I and Emperor Samuilo.

The role of archaeology in the public scene is summarised in a passage of Pasko Kuzman, one of the leading Macedonian archaeologies and political figures.

'Since its name, sovereignty and statehood make it the only legitimate representative of the historic mission of the term Macedonia, we considered it appropriate to present humankind all over the world with our archaeological treasures that proceed from our own existence and the existence of all other past civilisations on this part of the Macedonian soil, which are an integral part of both our own and the world's cultural and historical heritage.' (Kuzman 2009).

## Conclusion

A more appropriate perspective on ethnicity and 'Hellenisation' in the Balkan hinterland than these deterministic models should be the search for new hybrid forms of social and cultural identities emerging from the middle of the fifth cen-

## 15. 'Hellenisation' and Ethnicity in the Continental Balkan Iron Age 171

*Figure 15.3. Warrior on the Horse, new monument in Skopje, Macedonia.*

tury BC onwards when more intensive contacts with the Greek world had begun. In the changing context created by Philip's conquests in the middle of fourth century BC, hybridisation of numerous local identities entered a new phase. Parts of the Former Yugoslav Republic of Macedonia and Bulgaria were, beyond any doubt, incorporated into ancient Macedonia in the mid fourth century (Roisman & Worthington 2010: Map. 3), and some Late Iron Age 'Hellenised settlements' could be garrisons of the Macedonian army (Archibald 1994: 470; Popov 2002: 138–41; Lilčik 2009). On the other hand, we do not really know what this short-term political change brought to the local communities. Following recent theories of collective identity, the settlements should be hybrid forms, sometimes even with a real possibility of a Greek presence. The conquest of vast territories in the hinterland (including Thrace and parts of Paionia), followed by recruitment of mercenaries and their return from the East, the period of the Heirs to Alexander and the Kingdom of Lisimachus, etc., created a very complex socio-political context of alignments and confrontations of numerous polities in the interior (see Lund 1992; Archibald 1998; 2000; 2004; 2010).

Heritage, on the other hand, is a discursive practice constructed in concurrence with modern identities and for modern consumption (Rowlands 2002a; 2002b; Russell 2006; Silverman 2011). Bearing that in mind, researchers have been concerned with the modern use and roles of constructed images of ancient identity that can be invested in different forms of politics, just as they are trying to grasp fluid identities in the past. Most authors today agree that literary sources considering 'barbarian ethnicities' do not necessarily present direct testimony of the social structures in the Mediterranean hinterland, but rather Greek and Roman ethnocentric pictures of the 'others' (Cartledge 2002; Harrison 2002; Hingley 2005: 1–13; Dzino 2007; 2008a; Babić 2008b). By favouring strict ethnic boundaries and divisions, based on the deep-rooted culture-historical tradition of Vere Gordon Childe–Gustav Kossina and flawed hypothesis about literary sources, traditional researchers in the Balkans, following the footsteps of their Western colleagues, continue to construct images of stable Iron Age ethnicities in accordance with the needs of modern politics. The consequence of this approach is an ethnocentric projection of national and nationalistic narratives into the past and a focus on ethnicity that might not even be the most prominent form of identity. At the same time, by implementing a Western colonial narrative, culture-historical archaeology in the Balkans recognised the appearance of 'Greek' material culture as the 'spread of civilisation', making the heritage even more politically valuable. These practices represent numerous and often conflicted political roles of the discipline in the different Balkan countries, just as was the case with Western archaeological traditions where the dangers of the modern roles of the discipline have already been recognised.

**ACKNOWLEDGMENTS**

This paper is a result of the project *Serbian Archaeology: Cultural identity, integration factors, technological processes and the role of Central Balkans in the development of European Prehistory* (OI177020), financed by the Ministry of Education and Science of the Republic of Serbia.

*Perspectives from the West*

# 16. Central Places and the Construction of Collective Identities in the Middle Rhine-Moselle Region

*Manuel Fernández-Götz*

**Keywords:** identity, sanctuaries, assemblies, oppida, Treveri.

## 1. Sanctuaries, oppida and identities

> Men came together by cities and by tribes, because they naturally tend to hold things in common, and at the same time because of their need of one another; and they met at the sacred places that were common to them for the same reasons, holding festivals and general assemblies; for everything of this kind tends to friendship, beginning with eating at the same table, drinking libations together, and lodging under the same roof (Strabo IX, 3, 5).

Identity has become a hot topic in archaeological research (Díaz-Andreu *et al.* 2005). Although definitions are always complicated, for the British sociologist Richard Jenkins (2008) identity could be described as the human capacity to know 'who's who' and hence 'what's what', which involves a multi-dimensional classification or mapping of the human world and our places in it, as individuals and as members of collectivities. Moreover, it should be understood as a process – *identification* –, not as a 'thing': it is not something that one can *have*, it is something that one *does*. If we had to choose two key points, they could be as follows: 1) identity is inextricably linked to the sense of belonging; 2) identity is not a static thing, but a continual process (Díaz-Andreu *et al.* 2005).

How should we approach the study of past identities? There is no single answer for this question, as they are many different types of social identity (ethnicity, gender, age, class, religion, etc; see Díaz-Andreu *et al.* 2005, Fernández-Götz 2014: Chapter 2 and Insoll 2007a for a recent review) and several layers that appear in a superimposed and co-integrated fashion. Ethnic identity, for example, can be defined as 'the temporary resultant of a process of developing collective self-images, attitudes and conduct that takes place in a context of interaction between those directly involved and outsiders' (Roymans 2004: 2). Furthermore, every archaeological analysis has necessarily to take into account the nature of the available sources, which means that there can be multiple approaches depending on the specific case-study and the focus of the research project.

Nevertheless, when dealing with Iron Age societies one of the best possibilities for gaining access to ethnic constructs of the past at different scales of social organisation is offered by the great sanctuaries of civic religion, as well as the meeting places of inter-group cult communities (Derks & Roymans 2009). As several historical and ethnographic studies clearly show, the regional and supra-regional cult centres must have played a key role in the formation of groups with a shared ethnic identity (Gerritsen & Roymans 2006). In this sense, a good example of interrelationship between ethnicity, politics and religion is provided by the Treveri (Fernández-Götz 2014), one of the main Late Iron Age Gaulish polities (Fichtl 2004; Collis 2007). Recent work on the *oppida* of this area has offered extensive information about public spaces and sanctuaries within these sites, which are dated between the end of the second and the first century BC (Metzler 1991, 1995; Krauße 2006; Metzler *et al.* 2006; Fernández-Götz 2011b). Starting with the best known case, Titelberg, this paper will analyse the evidence of political and religious activities in the central places of the Middle Rhine-Moselle region. Following Gerritsen and Roymans (2006), by central place I understand any kind of place with central functions for a supra-local community. Finally, a renewed approach to the genesis of *oppida* in temperate Europe is proposed.

## 2. Late Iron Age oppida and public spaces in the Middle Rhine-Moselle region

The most extensively researched settlement in the territory of the Treveri is the Titelberg *oppidum* in Luxembourg, which covers an area of 43 hectares (Metzler 1995). The fact that more than 5000 'Celtic' coins have been recovered, as well as the presence of several imports from the Mediterranean area, show that it enjoyed considerable prosperity. There is also strong evidence of different activities involving artisan crafts on a scale that went beyond supplying local needs, notably iron and bronze working and the minting of coins.

However, the most outstanding feature of Titelberg is without doubt the so-called public space or *area sacra* where assemblies, fairs and religious ceremonies were held (Metzler 2006; Metzler *et al.* 2006). This was a large area covering 10 hectares to the east of the *oppidum*, bounded by a ditch and an adobe wall (Fig. 16.1). The 500 metre long, four metre wide and 2.5 metre deep ditch was excavated in the rock. Its infill contained abundant animal bones, around a hundred *fibulae*, and numerous spearheads, miniature weapons, coins and fragments of human skulls. These finds demonstrate that cult practices were carried out indicating that the boundary marked by the ditch was not only physical but also to a large extent symbolic, as it separated the sacred space from the profane. Excavations have determined that the ditch was established around 100 BC at the same time the *murus gallicus* was built, which indicates that a rigorous large-scale planning of the *oppidum* took place around that time.

Most of the public space remained open and free of any structures during the Late La Tène period, which meant it could hold a great number of people who gathered for large public meetings, like the Treveran assembly described by Caesar (*De Bello Gallico* V, 56). However, excavations in the southern section have made it possible to identify a succession of structures in the area situated at the highest point of the *oppidum* that has come to be called the 'monumental

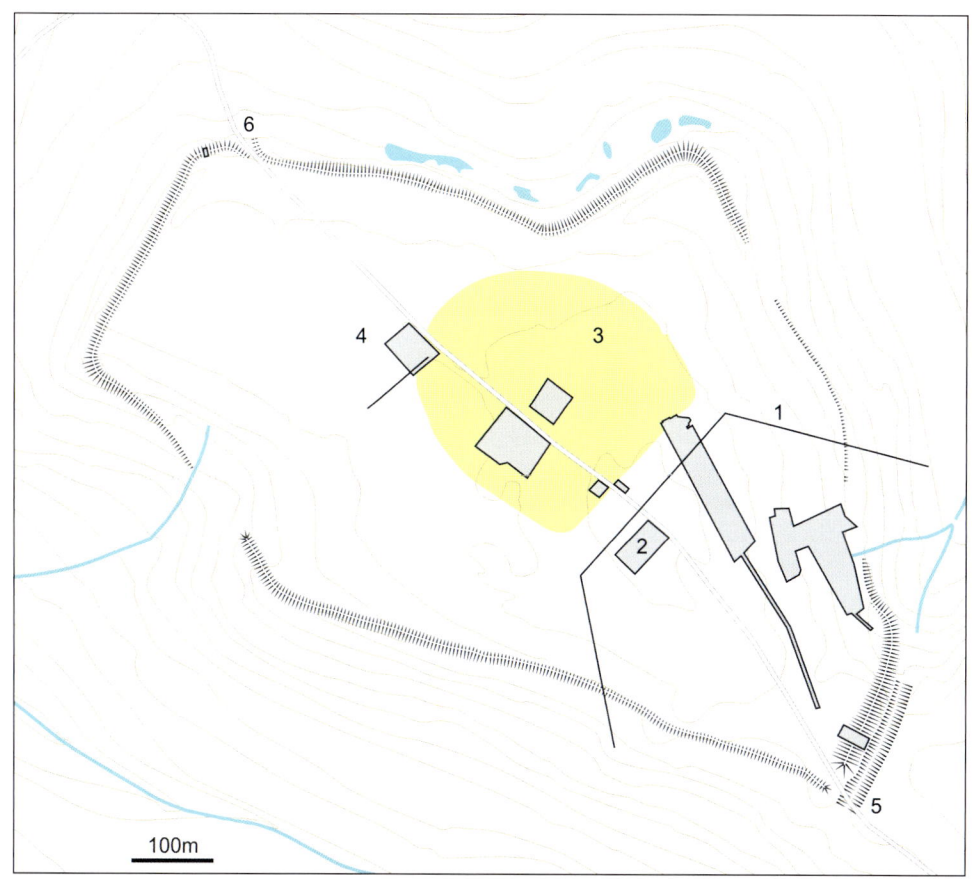

*Figure 16.1. Plan of the Titelberg-oppidum (Luxembourg): 1) cult ditch; 2) 'monumental centre' (after Metzler et al. 2006 with modifications).*

centre'. During most of the first half of the first century BC, a series of parallel movable palisades were built marking out a series of corridors about four metres wide and at least 60 metres long that were arranged perpendicular to the main road through the *oppidum*. These structures, which according to the stratigraphic studies were erected and taken down many times, have been interpreted as voting installations similar to the *saepta* of Italian cities like *Paestum, Fregellae* or Rome. Finds very similar to the one in Titelberg have also been discovered in the *oppidum* of Gournay-sur-Aronde in Picardy (Brunaux *et al.* 1985; Fichtl 2010).

Even before the middle of the first century BC a huge 15 × 14 metre three-aisle building was erected on the traces of these voting corridors on the highest point of the *oppidum*. In the square located in front of this building, there was a stone altar surrounded by large pits and bonfires. During the second last decade BC, these monumental constructions were taken down and the large cultic ditch was filled in. This was probably due to the foundation at the same time of the new capital of the *civitas*, *Augusta Treverorum*, which replaced Titelberg as the political and religious centre of the Treveri (Metzler 2008). A new open building, this time in stone, was built in the time of Tiberius, again on the highest point of the *oppidum*. Finally, in the second century AD a large Gallo-Roman *fanum* was erected on the same place, remaining until its destruction during the 'Germanic' invasions of the third century AD.

The succession of structures on the highest part of the *oppidum* over the generations, their location within the large public space, and the fact that the monumental programme culminated in the construction of a huge Gallo-roman temple leaves us in no doubt as to the sacred nature of the site. At the same time, the detailed study of the over 100,000 documented animal bones related to the public space provide evidence that animal slaughter was carried out on an almost industrial scale (Méniel 2008). This, together with traces of occasional work in leather and bone, suggests that fairs and markets were held throughout most of the first century BC, probably linked to religious festivals. We can think of general assemblies that would have been very similar to the *óenacha* of Ancient Ireland or the Thing of the Scandinavian world (Mac Niocaill 1972; Wenskus 1984). People whose daily lives were lived dispersed through the rural hinterland, had the opportunity to meet each other, exchange goods and information, establish closer social ties, arrange marriages, attend religious ceremonies, etc. It was a way of reaffirming the social order, power relations and the sense of belonging to a wider community.

After Titelberg, the most important centre seems to have been the *oppidum* of Martberg, which covers a total of 70 hectares on two plateaus. Its fame goes back to the nineteenth-century discovery of a votive inscription dedicated to *Lenus Mars*. The sanctuary is situated on the highest part of the *oppidum* and is highly complex, as it comprises 12 phases that date from the beginning of the first century BC to the end of the fourth century AD (Thoma 2000; Nickel *et al.* 2008). The profusion of finds is exceptional, with more than 7000 coins and hundreds of brooches that have been documented in the area of the sanctuary alone. Different materials such as Nauheim brooches and coins make it possible to date the beginnings of cult activity in La Tène D1.

Since the first half of the first century BC, there was a public space of approximately 50 × 60 metres at the highest point of the *oppidum*, enclosed by a palisade. It was in this area that the sanctuary was developed in different stages up to Late Antiquity. At the beginning, the interior remained free of any buildings, but in the centre there was an enclosure of 10 × 12 metres surrounded by a ditch. This would be the heart of the sanctuary during the next centuries. Later, in the final decades of the first century BC, an area measuring 100 × 103 metres was established with a V-shaped ditch round it. It was of a temporary nature, since before the end of the Augustan period this ditch had been filled in and the enclosure of the previous public space had reappeared, which would continue to undergo various transformations in the course of time. The first stone temples were built at the end of the first century AD and beginning of the second, forming part of a complex that would be remodelled several times. Despite the differences with Titelberg, we can keep in mind that at Martberg there was also a public space of sacred nature on the highest part of the *oppidum* at least since the beginning of the first century BC.

It was the scene of collective gatherings and cult practices, becoming monumentalised in the Gallo-Roman period and lasting till Late Antiquity.

In general terms, this model is also repeated in Wallendorf, which covers 41 hectares (Kraußé 2006). Of particular significance for the macro-regional comparison is the fact that there was a public space of approximately 60 × 30 metres on the highest point of the *oppidum* (Kraußé & Nübold 2007). Despite the development of a settlement both in the Early and in the Late La Tène period, this area remained free of any construction throughout the whole Iron Age. Different traces found nearby indicate that cult activities were already practised there before the Roman conquest. No later than the final decades of the first century BC, a small wooden temple was built on the highest point of the *oppidum*. This building, along with the discovery of some votive offerings, suggests that the sacred nature of the public space dated back to pre-Roman times. The subsequent history of the place underscores this interpretation, as a Gallo-Roman sanctuary consisting of two temples was developed on the same site during the first centuries AD.

More spectacular because of its colossal wall is the *oppidum* of Otzenhausen, with a Late La Tène settlement area of only 10 hectares (Hornung 2012). Although no evidence of a Gallo-Roman settlement has been found inside the fortified space, it should be noted that a small temple dating from the second to third centuries AD was built on the highest point, possibly dedicated to the goddess Diana. The great number of spearheads found nearby and the general abundance of La Tène finds discovered in the area, with some exceptional deposits such as a bronze pendant or a gold ring, suggests a pre-Roman origin for the cult tradition. Furthermore, Metzler (1991) believes to have identified the remains of a ditch that would delimit a public space of several hectares at the top of the fortified area, drawing attention to the fact that the Gallo-Roman temple was located exactly in the centre of the resulting area.

The largest fortified centre in the area under study is the impressive Donnersberg, which covers 240 hectares (Zeeb-Lanz 2008). In addition to the size of its fortifications, the most outstanding feature is the presence of a 98 × 66 metre rectangular enclosure, which has traditionally been included in the category of the *Viereckschanzen* (Wieland 1999). However, this has always raised a number of questions, because it would be the only known example of this type found inside an *oppidum*. Although we are far from being able to establish a precise date for this large enclosure, on the basis of pottery found there it is quite possible that it was constructed before the development of the *oppidum*. Considering its location at the top of the mountain, I believe that identifying it as a *Viereckschanze* creates unnecessary confusion. Both the structure and location make it more appropriate to classify this enclosure of Donnersberg in the same group as the assembly places of Martberg and 'La Terrasse' at Bibracte.

Until recently, two Treveran *oppida* had not yielded evidence of cult spaces within them: Kastel-Staadt and Bleidenberg. This situation has now changed: thanks to ongoing fieldwork, an important Gallo-Roman sanctuary has just been discovered at the highest point of the *oppidum* of Kastel-Staadt (Nortmann

2009). Different finds such as gold coins or parts of a sword show that the origins of this cult place go back to the pre-Roman period. But even more interesting, the sanctuary was accompanied by an important theatre with capacity for over 3000 people, much more than the number of persons that lived at Kastel-Staadt and its immediate surroundings at that time. As different scholars have pointed out, in northern Gaul rural theatres functioned as places where political assemblies where held (Derks 1998; Trunk 2007). All in all, these data suggest that Kastel-Staadt retained its role as a symbolic focus for the rural populations of a large area long after the *oppidum* itself was abandoned.

Finally, the problem of Bleidenberg still remains. To date, no public space or sanctuary has been found on the site (Brücken 2008). But this could be due to the fact that this *oppidum* was discovered only a few years ago and archaeological work on it is still scarce. Whatever the case, it is significant that on the highest point of the *oppidum* there is a church of Romanesque origin that has been a place of pilgrimage since medieval times, a situation that is reminiscent of the one observed in the *oppidum* of Bibracte (Fleischer & Rieckhoff 2002).

## 3. FROM TERRITORIAL ORGANISATION TO SOCIO-POLITICAL LEVELS

As might be expected, our knowledge of the different Treveran *oppida* is very uneven. Nevertheless, by undertaking a closer analysis, we can draw different general conclusions:

1) All Treveran *oppida* show a previous phase of occupation during the Late Hallstatt and/or Early La Tène period, followed by a more or less pronounced hiatus during the Middle La Tène period and a reoccupation in the Late La Tène period (Metzler *et al.* 2006; Fernández-Götz 2014).
2) The application of the Thiessen Polygon Method shows a nearly regular spatial distribution of the *oppida*, with the territory of the Treveri subdivided into six or seven entities, each one with an *oppidum* acting as a centre (Fig. 16.2). This type of territorial structure is to a large extent comparable with the situation found in other Gaulish areas, such as that of the Mediomatrici or the Bellovaci (Fichtl 2004). The average distance between the Treveran *oppida* is 53 kilometres (Fernández-Götz 2014), which reveals theoretical areas of influence that were much more extensive than those of the small hillforts of only a few hectares known in German as *Burgen* (Nortmann 2008–09).
3) Spaces for religious practices and assemblies have been identified in six of the seven Treveran *oppida*, in five cases at the highest point of the respective *oppidum*: Titelberg, Martberg, Wallendorf, Otzenhausen and Kastel-Staadt.

Taken as a whole, the data reflect an organisation of the territory of the Treveri around the *oppida*, which acted as elements of social and territorial aggregation (Fernández-Götz 2011b). These settlements would have served as centres of different entities that can be identified as the *pagi* known from written sources (Metzler *et al.* 2006). In fact, Late Iron Age Gaulish societies were organised in an ascending order in three main socio-political levels: local groups comprising several households, *pagi* (sub-ethnic communities) and *civitates* (ethnic

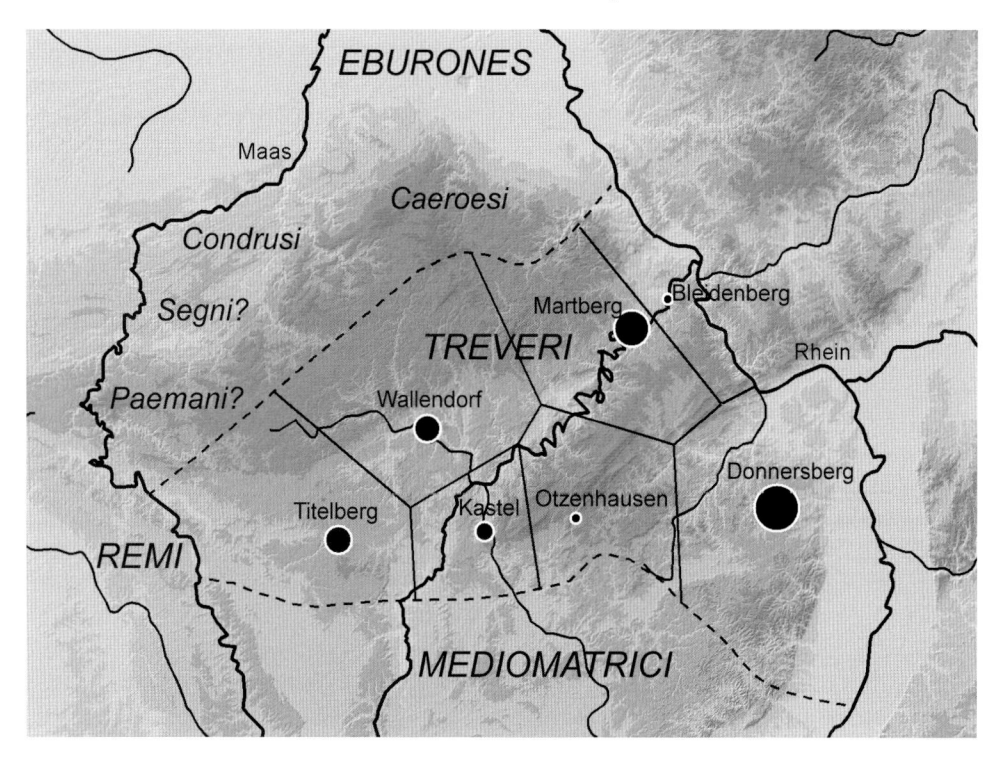

16. Central Places and the Construction of Collective Identities  181

*Figure 16.2. Application of the Thiessen Polygon Method to the Treveran territory, showing a nearly regular spatial distribution of the oppida (after Metzler 2006, modified).*

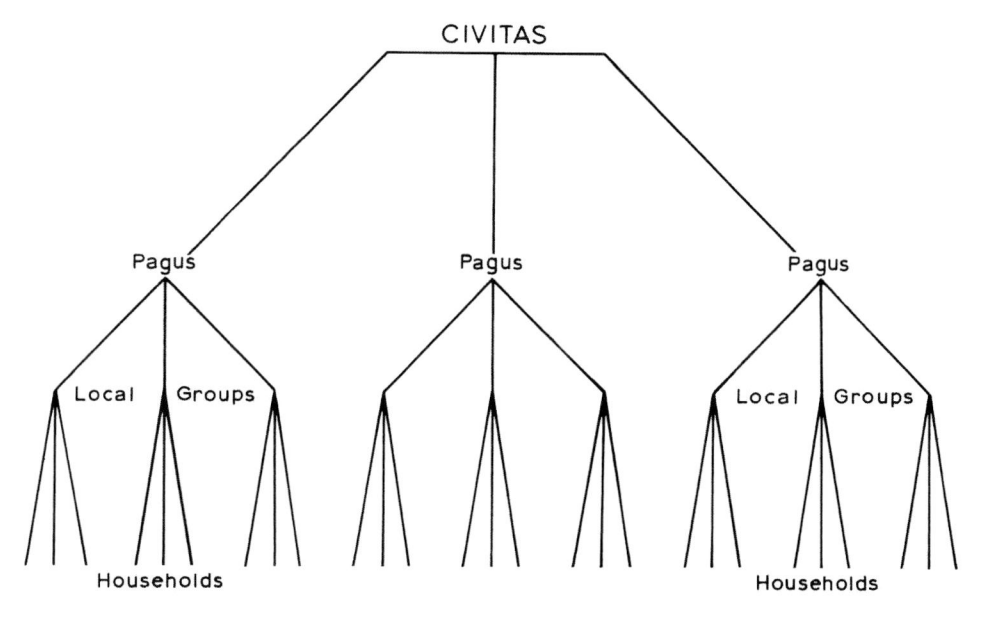

*Figure 16.3. Simplified schema of the main socio-political levels of pre-Roman Gaul (after Roymans 1990).*

communities) (Roymans 1990; Fichtl 2004; Verger 2009; Fernández-Götz 2011a; 2014) (Fig. 16.3). The best definition of pre-Roman *pagi* and *civitates* in the Gaulish context is given by Gerritsen and Roymans (2006), for whom they were politicised ethnic identities, i.e. ethnic groupings functioning as political communities. According to Caesar, in the middle of the first century BC the *civitas* of the Helvetii was subdivided into four *pagi* (*De Bello Gallico* I, 12, 4-6), and in the case of the Treveri, epigraphy testifies to a minimum of five *pagi* in the Gallo-Roman period (Trunk 2007).

The role of the Treveran *oppida* as political and religious centres is not only confirmed by their regular distribution in space and by the presence of public spaces and sanctuaries inside the walled perimeter, but also by the fact that at least four of them also acted as minting centres (Kaczynski 2009). Although many questions remain, in the case of the Treveri we find a perfect example of the interrelationship between political, religious and economic power. The territory of this group was integrated by different entities, each one with an *oppidum* equipped with a sanctuary as a core. These huge fortified centres were places for assemblies (→ political role), collective rituals (→ religious role), fairs and coin minting (→ economic role). The Treveri of the Late La Tène period constituted therefore a polycentric state, formed by the aggregation of various communities that would each have had their own territory, identity and a certain degree of independence, while also recognising another identity common to all of them and ceding part of their sovereignty to the supracommunity.

In this context, it should be noted that the best known example of a Gaulish popular assembly is precisely the Treveran gathering convened by Indutiomarus (*De Bello Gallico* V, 56):

> he proclaims an armed council (this according to the custom of the Gauls in the commencement of war) at which, by a common law, all the youth were wont to assemble in arms, whoever of them comes last is killed in the sight of the whole assembly after being racked with every torture. In that council he declares Cingetorix, the leader of the other faction [...] an enemy and confiscates his property.

## 4. Performances and the construction of collective identities

Identities are constructed through practice (Bourdieu 1972; Giddens 1984). Integral to them are memories: they are shaped through practical experience, and at the same time it is from these memories that identities are constituted (Jones 2003; Bommas 2011). In this sense, the rituals and celebrations held at sites such as Manching (Sievers 2003), Titelberg (Metzler 2006), Villeneuve-Saint-Germain (Peyre 2000), Bibracte (Fleischer & Rieckhoff 2002) or Corent (Poux 2006; 2011) would have been key elements in the fostering of social cohesion, self-awareness and shared identity (Fig. 16.4). As Derks and Roymans (2009: 8) say, great sanctuaries and gathering places were 'the concrete anchoring points in the landscape where the polity's core values –as exemplified in its tradition of origin– were transmitted to the wider community through recitals, dramatic performances

16. *Central Places and the Construction of Collective Identities* 183

*Figure 16.4. Idealised reconstruction of the sanctuary of Corent, Auvergne (after Poux 2006).*

and collective rituals'. In other words, these would be the places were the 'creation of tradition' could take place, a fundamental aspect of ethnogenetic processes (Wenskus 1961; Roymans 2004). They would therefore be sites in which politics, religion and the building of collective identities would go hand in hand, fulfilling a fundamental role in establishing, maintaining and strengthening ethnic ties (Gerritsen & Roymans 2006). The number of people that might have lived permanently inside the *oppida* would have been less important than the function of these centres as objects of identification for larger groups, generating collective identities and serving as nuclei of aggregation and points of reference in a world that was basically rural. In some way, we could say that it was around these centres that communities were 'constructed'. In fact, in recent years different authors have pointed out the close link that might have existed between the appearance of large cult centres like Gournay-sur-Aronde, Ribemont-sur-Ancre and Mirebeau, and the emergence of Gaulish entities such as *pagi* and *civitates* (Fichtl 2004: 2007; Wells 2006), in a similar way as François de Polignac (1995) has shown for the origins of the Greek *poleis*.

Communities are ultimately symbolic constructs (Cohen 1985). Given the fact that public cult places often functioned as *lieux de mémoire* where foundation myths were reproduced through rituals, cult celebrations, etc., we can conclude that these sites played a vital role in the symbolic construction of ethnic communities in Antiquity and in the creation of boundaries with outside groups (Roymans 2004; Gerritsen & Roymans 2006). At appointed times of the year people would gather in large numbers to affirm themselves as a cult community. This role of public sanctuaries as key locations for the creation of collective group identities is graphically illustrated in Tacitus' account of the Germanic Suebi and their central cult place:

> 'They describe the Semnones as the most ancient and best-born of the Suebi. This credibility of their antiquity is confirmed by religion. At fixed seasons all tribes of the same name and blood gather through their delegations at a certain forest [...]. And after publicly offering up a human life, they celebrate the grim initiation of their barbarous worship' (Tacitus, *Germania* 39).

Another example that can be relevant in this context is the celebration of the common ancestry myth of the Latins. Following Cornell (1997: 9): 'there can be little doubt about the antiquity of a Latin myth of common ancestry, and of its central element, the cult of Jupiter on the Alban Mount. The annual celebration of this cult, known as the *Latiar* or *Feriae Latinae*, was an assembly of the representatives of all the Latin communities [...]. The ceremony was an expression of ethnic solidarity, and constituted an annual renewal of the ties of kinship that the Latins believed they shared. Participation in the cult was a definition of membership; the Latins were those peoples who received meat at the annual festival of the *Latiar*'.

Although it has to remain hypothetical, the huge amount of animal bones documented in the public space of Titelberg could perhaps be related to ceremonies similar to the one described for the Latins, where membership was defined by the consumption of meat. In any case, ritual feasting at the public cult places was surely an important means of social interaction. Collective food and drink rituals sustained powerful networks, constituting a major mechanism of defining membership (Dietler & Hayden 2001; Roymans 2004).

## 5. A new model for the origin of the oppida?

The Late La Tène *oppida* of the Treveri seem to have been mainly politico-religious focal points for the rural population from the surrounding areas, acting as centres for cult-related functions, gatherings, markets, artisan activities and perhaps sometimes also defence. However, the only nuclei that acquired characteristics that could be described as 'urban' were Titelberg and Martberg, and both only in the course of the first century BC. In contrast, six of these seven *oppida* show evidence that they contained public spaces and sanctuaries. Moreover, the fact that the highest points of sites like Wallendorf remained free of any living structure in both the Early and Late La Tène period can only be ascribed to conscious choice, suggesting that its sacred significance could eventually go back to the fifth or fourth centuries BC. This leads us to consider a more global hypothesis: many Late La Tène *oppida* may have had their origin in spaces for ritual gatherings, and not the other way round (Fichtl *et al.* 2000; Fernández-Götz 2014). In other words, they were constituted on particular sites precisely because those places had a sacred significance and had already been frequented on a more or less regular basis since before the second and first centuries

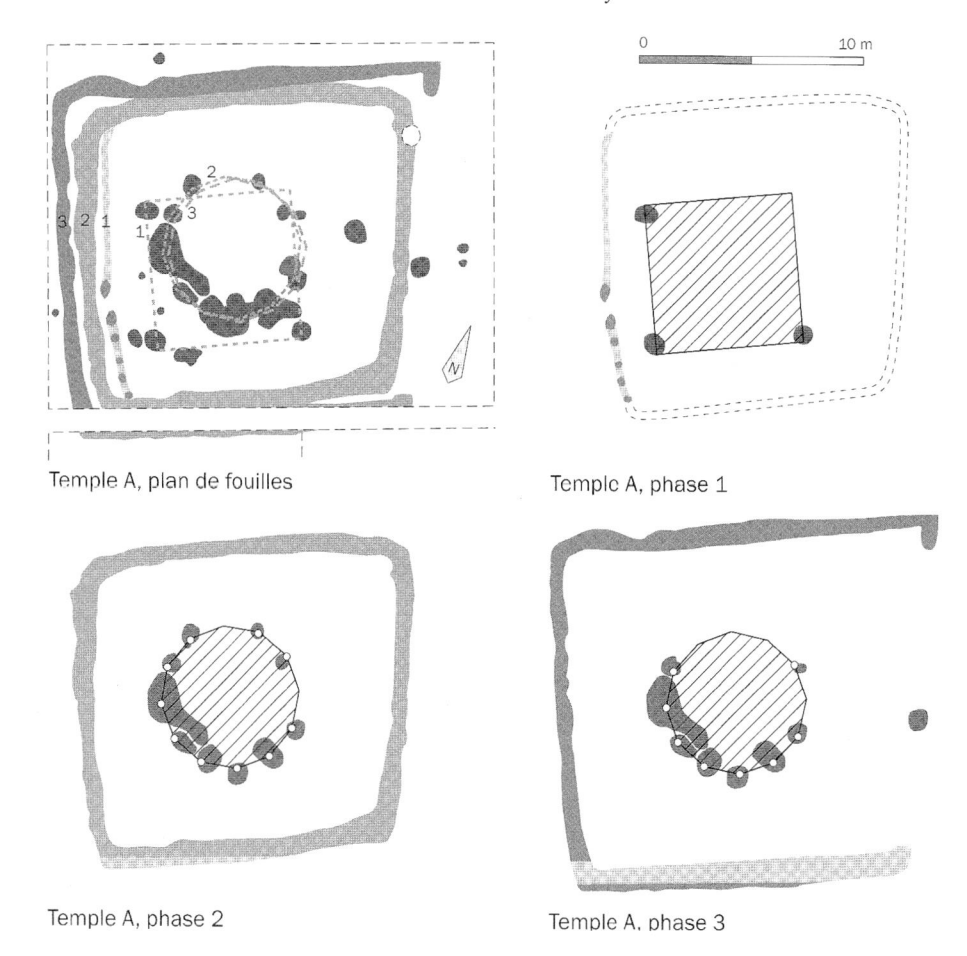

16. *Central Places and the Construction of Collective Identities* 185

Temple A, plan de fouilles

Temple A, phase 1

Temple A, phase 2

Temple A, phase 3

*Figure 16.5. Different phases of Manching tempel A (after Fichtl 2005).*

BC. The north-Italic inscription of Verceil (Peyre 2000), which mentions a *campus com(m)unis deis et hominibus*, provides us with some interesting clues for a better understanding of many Iron Age central places.

In temperate Europe there are various examples where it has been proved that a place for cult activities and/or assemblies preceded the concentration of a significant number of people or even the fortification of the area, a phenomenon that is particularly evident in Manching (Sievers 2003). At the centre of this *oppidum* was temple A, the first phase of which dates back to the end of the fourth century BC (Fig. 16.5). Nearby was a paved space covering 50 × 80 metres that may have been used as a meeting place, and several votive deposits of materials dating from between the fourth and second centuries BC. Gournay-sur-Aronde is also very revealing in this respect because, although the existence the famous sanctuary has its roots in the fourth century BC, the constitution of the *oppidum* did not take place until well into the first century BC (Brunaux *et al.* 1985). With respect to Bibracte, radiocarbon and dendrochronological dating indicate that the public space known as 'La Terrasse', measuring 110 × 92 metres, could have had its origins in the third century BC (Fleischer & Rieckhoff 2002). Although this last date has to be taken with caution, if true it would imply that the place was used and visited for meetings and religious purposes well before the establishment of the *oppidum* at the end of the second century BC. Recent research at the *oppidum* of Corent, capital of the Arverni, is also very important, since it reveals that the sanctuary there was founded before the settlement developed (Poux 2011). In short, these and other examples, such as that of Titelberg, show that twenty years after the famous article by Greg Woolf (1993), the task of 'rethinking the *oppida*' continues to be just as relevant today.

At the same time, the structuring of Treveri communities from sanctuaries allows us to propose a new model of collective identity construction in the Iron Age of the Middle Rhine-Moselle region. One that, far away from normative views of culture and traditional culture-historical approaches, is based on the integration of households and local groups into wider levels of socio-political organisation, in a process that can be described as 'bottom up' (Fernández-Götz 2014).

# 17. Fingerprinting Iron Age Communities in South-West Germany and an Integrative Theory of Culture

*Oliver Nakoinz*

KEYWORDS: IRON AGE, THEORY OF CULTURE, CULTURAL METRIC, INTERACTION, SPATIAL ANALYSIS

TRADITIONAL ARCHAEOLOGICAL CULTURE

Our starting point is the traditional concept of archaeological culture. This traditional concept of culture was a very respectable archaeological tool for more than a century. An archaeological culture was conceived as a geographical unit with a specific material culture. The advantage for archaeology was that we could identify a culture using archaeological finds and make linkages. For example the La Tène culture is defined by objects decorated in La Tène-style, the La Tène fibula and some other characteristics. Sometimes the La Tène culture is linked to the Early Celts (Spindler 1991). The impetuous critique of this identification by Collis (2010) makes clear that assigning cultures to other entities is very problematic. These assignments can be described as using an 'equation of culture'.

We should have a short look at some selected variations of the 'equation of culture'. First we have to mention Herder (1990 [1774], discussed by Taylor 2011), who was the first to equate culture with a particular certain ethnic unit. This was a step away from the normative concept of culture suggested by Kant (1964 [1803]) towards a total approach suggested by Tylor (2010 [1871]). Herder's ideas are based on empirical observations. He states that the difference between cultures is based on different environments and mental conditions ('Volksseelen'). The next step is to include material culture in the equation. This was a very modern concept in the decades before and after 1900 AD. The names we have to mention are Tylor (2010 [1871]), Frobenius (1898) and Graebner (1911) in ethnology, and Kossinna (1911; 1912; 1926) and Childe (1925; 1929; Veit 1984) in archaeology. Demoule (1999) analysed the unreflexive applications in France that have taken place up to the present day, implementing an assessment that also applies to other countries.

At the end of nineteenth century, the old term of race was becoming a key-term and was added to the equation of culture. This was caused by Darwin's (1859) theory which had at the time the aura of modern science (Galton 1869; 1904). From 1912 onwards, race was added to the equation of culture by Kossinna (1912; Grünert 2002, 240–248). This concept, which denies the Aristotelian concept of scholarship, also laid the foundations of National Socialist ideology. Concepts which do not equate culture with ethnic units but assume fuzzy relations between the two became current from the middle of the twentieth century. Wahle (1941) was one to promote this idea. Later the relation between material culture and archaeological culture was also interpreted as a fuzzy (Brather 2004).

A simple version of the equation of culture is the interpretation of archaeological culture as an archaeological classification of material. It was Clarke (1968) who worked out the theoretical basis of this concept, which was later used by other archaeologists. Some have tried only to avoid the problems of connecting culture to ethnic units and therefore used a rudimentary equation rather than one based on theory. Another approach is chronological. Thomsen (1836), Hildebrand (1876) and Lüning (1972), for example, envisaged cultures primarily as chronological units. In 2005, the present author proposed a version of the equation of culture based on systems theory that assumes interaction between material culture, culture and ethnic units. The author's current concept will be discussed later.

After this short history of research, we see that the concept of Kossinna (1911; 1912; 1926) continues to have its impact today in spite of many critics and the availability of much more advanced concepts. We will mention the most problematic aspects of this theory to avoid the same problems in a new theory. Kossinna sees prehistory as a 'Hervorragend nationale Wissenschaft'. He aims to reconstruct ethnic units as a tool to legitimate national units. This reminds us of Hobsbawn and Ranger's (1983) concept of the invented tradition and is not compatible with the Aristotelian concept of scholarship. We should not misuse archaeology for political ends. This also applies to Kossinna's extended equation of culture which includes valued races. Furthermore, he sees culture and ethnic units as actors. Cultures are treated as persons. This personification has a long tradition and it very powerfully harks back to Hegel (1997 [1830–1831]). Frobenius (1898; 1904; 1923) developed this idea in his 'Kulturkreislehre', developing the concept of culture as an organism. In practice, Kossinna made use of this powerful narrative technique which lacks the logic of historic processes. This leads to a strongly embedded bias since cultures cannot act – it is only people who act. For Kossinna, cultures are crisp spatial units which were indicated by diagnostic types. These restrictions exclude many aspects of culture. Working from an approach implicitly based on the idea of evolution which seems to indicate a continuous development, Kossinna tried to extrapolate knowledge back to older times. As a premise for this work of extrapolation, we should not suppose but have to prove a continuous development. Finally Kossinna offers a very limited spectrum of interpretations for cultural change. He only thinks of migrations. Besides these drawbacks, it was positive that Kossinna focussed archaeological research on geographical subjects. Knowing what to avoid, we can now try to find better concepts of culture.

## An Integrative Theory of Culture

First of all, we have to define culture. We use the definition from Hansen (2003: 39) who suggests that 'culture covers standardisations which are valid in collectives' that is: 'Kultur umfasst Standardisierungen, die in Kollektiven gelten'.

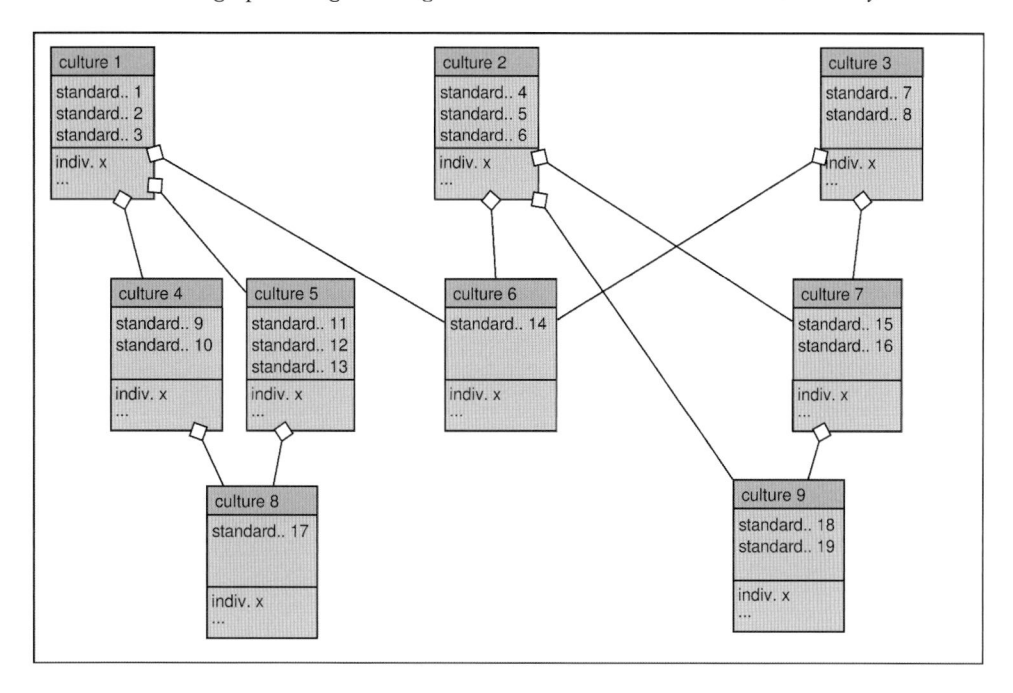

## 17. Fingerprinting Iron Age Communities in South-West Germany

*Figure 17.1. Model of culture as classes with associated standardisations and individuals.*

Standardisations are something held in common and a collective is a set of individuals. This definition brings together both an abstraction of the content of culture and the people who are sharing a culture. This definition does not contain information about the content of culture itself. It is a formal definition which is able to cover most other definitions which are based on commonality (Kroeber & Kluckhohn 1952). This simple definition has some essential implications. Each person belongs to many cultures which form a complex system. The number of cultures is extremely high but only a small part of them is significant. We can organise cultures in poly-hierarchical structures (Fig. 17.1). This arrangement can be based on standardisations or on individuals, so that as the number of standardisations increases, the number of individuals decreases. Hansen's (2003; 2009) definition thus leads to a wider variety and a much more complex system of culture than the traditional archaeological concepts of culture. At the same time, Hansen's concept gives us the opportunity to simplify this complex system of culture and use it in archaeology.

For Hansen, standardisations are established by communication. We prefer the more comprehensive term of interaction, so that interactions become a key term in the context of culture. Interaction is what makes standardisations possible. Interaction often leads to commonality and interaction maintains standardisations. Hence we can interpret culture as a response to the impact of interaction. Culture describes what is caused by interaction. It is a neutral term which does not depend on the conscious understanding of the content of culture. Another dimension of interaction (Fig. 17.2) is the realisation of interaction.

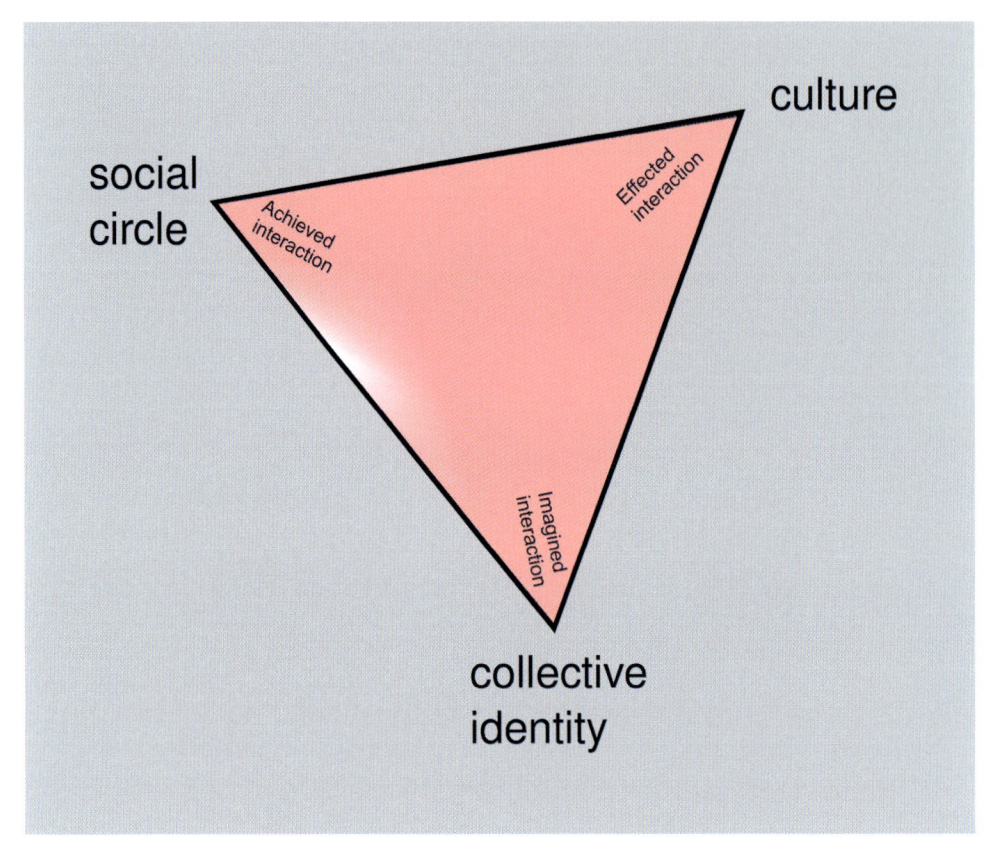

*Figure 17.2. Dimensions of interaction.*

This realisation can be connected to the concept of the social circle from Simmel (1890). The final concept that needs to be linked to interaction is that of collective identities. Today identities are frequently misused in archaeology. In psychology and sociology, identities are the equilibrium between totality and fragmentation which is expressed by the sum of differences to other units (Straub 1998). These differences define the line between the collective within which interaction is desired and the individuals we wish to exclude from interaction. Hence we can interpret identities as *intended* interactions. It is not necessary to achieve the interaction, but to *believe* that one belongs to an interacting group of people. This connection of culture and identities with interaction makes clear why there is no fixed link between culture and identities but only a slight connection. This is the explanation for many problems with the definition of culture.

We now turn to the point at which the benefit of our definition of culture is evident. The definition has the advantage to be formal and not to contain information about the content of culture. We can define humanities as disciplines which deal with the interpretation of predefined meaning. Analogical natural sciences are disciplines which do formal analysis on objects without predefined meaning and construct a frame of explanation. Snow (1960) stated that there are two incompatible cultures of scholarship. Ironically the term of culture bridges the gap between humanities and science. Culture is an object which contains meaning and allows formal analysis at the same time. We need not be conscious about the meaning of standardisations to do formal analysis. Most archaeological finds were not delivered with meaning, so we are lucky to be able to do formal analysis. Hansen's definition of culture is thus very useful. However a definition is not a theory of culture. There are many things which were not covered by this definition. This same statement applies to most other theories. Each theory is focussed on a special point. Questions dealing with these focal points allow us to subdivide theories of culture into several facets. This implies, that most theories were not rivals, but complement each other. Using the guiding questions, we can easily construct a system, an integrating theory, which contains a wide range of theories which have slightly different focal points and hence can be combined.

The question 'what is culture?' is settled for example by Hansen (2003) and Tylor (2010 [1871]). While Hansen gives an abstract definition, Tylor sees culture as acquired knowledge, beliefs, art and further more. Malinowski (1931) answers the question 'why do we use culture?' with the argument that culture is a tool to fulfil our needs. For Schweitzer (2007 [1923]) culture is a tool to perfect social and political conditions. The functionality of culture which answers the question 'how does culture operate?' is discussed by Kroeber and Parsons (1958) who interpret culture as symbolically meaningful systems which control behaviour. Dawkins (1976) deals with another facet of functionality since he is focussed on transmission. He sees an evolution of memes which were cultural atoms. Steger (2004) explores the question 'how are cultures related?' He sees the main mechanism of cultural interlacing in decontextualisation, transfer and recontextualisation.

The temporal development is touched on by the question 'how does culture change in time?'. Spengler (1918/1922) describes a periodic development while Redfield, Linton and Herskovits (1936) find acculturation to be an important mechanism of change.

Finally, we turn to the question 'what are the components of culture?' Huxley (1956) notes artefacts, mentifacts and sociofacts to be the components of culture. All of these components are represented by standardisations and all these components are interrelated. Especially for archaeology the interrelation between material culture, that is artefacts, with mentifacts and sociofacts is important. We can try to identify cultures using only artefacts. This is very important for our application of the theory of culture.

The integrative theory of culture which organises several particular theories around the definition of culture provides us with a tool to deal with different facets of culture and to answer a huge range of questions. In this sketch of an integrative theory, only a small part of the particular theory is described. Most theories can fit into this concept and are not concurrent. We only have to find the focal point of theory and the range and conditions of application. This also rebuts the critique of a particular theory since a lack of agreement with our point of view leads not to a criticism of the theory but to the choice of a particular theory with the right focal point. We expect this systematisation to be more useful than the model of permanently changing paradigms.

Before we tackle the issue of methodology we have to fit the traditional concept of culture into this integrative theory. An archaeological culture is a spatial unit with similar material culture. Archaeological cultures are restricted to spatial units with crisp borders and they may exist but can not be assumed. Spatial cultures which are bounded to a specific area with smooth and overlapping borders may also exist. Remembering Clarke's concept, overlapping spatial cultures seem to be the normal case. From this point of view archaeological cultures are a special case which is highly significant for the spatial organisation of cultural space. The significance is based on the perception of the crisp border. The border had a social meaning in the past which was known by most or all people. Thus if we use the concept of archaeological culture as an analytical tool, we have to make sure that these cultures in fact have crisp borders which could not have been overlooked. In general, culture is a tool to describe the behaviour of people with a minimal knowledge of what people think. All standardisations have a special meaning, some standardisations and corresponding collectives may be conscious whereas others may not. The reconstruction of meaning without written sources is in most cases impossible. Archaeological cultures do not solve these problems but they give us a hint about whether people have a collective approach in mind or not. If they have, it is more likely to identify the culture with a corresponding collective identity. This revitalisation of the old concept of archaeological culture is based on a slightly, but significantly, different definition of culture and archaeological culture. The interpretation is similar to the old ones: archaeological cultures are spatial units which had a special meaning for contemporary people. But in no case can we go so far as to assume the existence of archaeological cultures everywhere or that cultures can act instead of people.

Defining archaeological culture as a part of culture in general means that there is a kind of culture which is not archaeological culture. According to our definition this part of culture contains entities with smooth spatial borders and entities which are not spatially bounded. Of course these cultures are very important for archaeology as well as archaeological cultures. Examples are the cultures that apply to elites, handicraft and gender. The term of archaeological culture belongs to a special sphere of geographical questions while other types of culture have a wider range of applications. The term of archaeological culture as defined above lacks a social component which is essential for a general term of culture. In the next part of this paper we mainly focus on archaeological culture and geographical questions.

## A METHODOLOGICAL FRAMEWORK OF FINGERPRINTING CULTURES

The main methodological task is the Fingerprinting, namely the identification of cultures (Nakoinz 2005; 2009; 2010a; 2010b). At this point, we are not interested in the content of culture but we are interested in whether two entities have the same culture or not. As we discussed above, some standardisations are represented by artefacts. It is not easy to gain the meaning of these standardisations, but we can identify some standardisations using artefacts. Hence we can use the material culture represented by '*Typenspektren*' (spectrum of types) as a cultural fingerprint. A *Typenspektrum* gives us no clue to the meaning of standardisations but allows us to compare the culture of two entities. These *Typenspektren* contain the relative share of each type in all finds.

For comparing two *Typenspektren* it is necessary to have a measurement or metric. A metric defines distances between objects. Without a metric the geometrical relation of objects in a space is not defined. Examples of metrics are the Minkowski distance with all its special cases: the Euclidean distance and the Manhattan distance, the Mahalanobis distance, the Jaccard distance and the Levenshtein distance. The choice of metric depends on data and theory. *Typenspektren* consist of ratio scaled values (Stevens 1946). Since each type represents at least one standardisation we do not expect latent variables. The space of types is similar to the geometric space. This means that we should use the Euclidean distance and do no data preparation with principal component analysis. Metrics other than the Euclidean metric would not fit either the data or the theoretical assumptions. Hence we use the Euclidean distance of *Typenspektren* as a cultural metric.

At this point we turn to archaeological cultures which means we are looking at geographical units. The cultural distance between two *Typenspektren* can be used to verify identity and to perform a more developed analysis. For instance we can plot the cultural distances on geographical distances or draw contour lines of cultural distances on maps. In the case studies, we will see some cluster analysis which groups areas of similar culture.

We have developed the usage of *Typenspektren* from our particular theoretical perspective. At this point, we should compare the traditional usage of diagnostic types to *Typenspektren*. We can name some disadvantages of diagnostic types. Using diagnostic types carries the risk of circular reasoning. Before the analysis, we have no knowledge of the significance of types. We presume some types to be significant and therefore it is most likely to find those types in an analysis restricted to the types that are significant. Another problem is that the simple usage of diagnostic types does not allow us to differentiate overlapping areas of distribution. Even if the *Typenspektren* are reduced to diagnostic types we may be able to distinguish different parts of domination in the overlapping area. The impossibility of measuring cultural distances is also a disadvantage of the simple usage of diagnostic types. We do need quantitative information like those in *Typenspektren* to calculate distances. On the basis of cultural distances we are able to define the degree of membership of cultural groups which is not possible with diagnostic types. Equally, spatial hierarchies of cultural areas can only be reconstructed if we use *Typenspektren*. It seems perfectly clear that we must use *Typenspektren* whenever possible.

After discussing metrics and *Typenspektren* we can continue by grouping areas with similar *Typenspektren* using Cluster analysis. The spatial units for which we have sampled *Typenspektren*, they can have either crisp or fuzzy borders, can be delimited by natural or arbitrary borders and can focus on local or regional units. Of great importance is the theory based choice of the right clustering algorithm. We are searching for cultural units which are hierarchically structured. These cultures are defined by a certain set of standardisations and can merge into larger units with more members but fewer standardisations. A characteristic for cultures which emerge as a fusion of atomic or already merged cultures is not the presence of specific standardisations of types but the relative share of these standardisations. Among all types there are only a few which have specific relative shares of the type. The values for these types are nearly constant within the area of the corresponding culture. The comparison of this unit's culture with other cultures of the same level of fusion is based on the all materials from within the different areas. We do not compare the *Typenspektren* of subgroups of the cultures but the *Typenspektren* of the cultures we are interested in at this phase of analysis. These considerations have important implications for the method. First we have to use an agglomerative and hierarchical clustering algorithm which is able to map the expected hierarchy. Secondly the fact that each culture has its own *Typenspektren* leads to choosing a centroid method of clustering. All other algorithms (Everitt *et al.* 2001) like single linkage, average linkage or Ward's method, are not supported by our theory.

The cluster analysis results in groups of *Typenspektren* associated with spatial units. At this point two questions arise. 1. Are the spatial borders of the clusters crisp borders, so that we have archaeological cultures? 2. Are the detected clusters valid? The first question is answered by a comparison of different cluster analyses using different parts of the material. If we find the same border in most or all the analyses, we can speak of a crisp border and an archaeological culture. The second question is answered with several validation methods (Halkidi *et al.* 2001; Handl *et al.* 2005). A first criterion of validation is by comparison. The same borders are unlikely to occur in different analyses using different data if the results are not valid but arbitrary. We should keep in mind that not seeing the same borders does not mean that the results are not valid. Another external criterion of validation is the spatial closeness of the cluster results. A spatial clustering is unlikely if the cluster results are not valid. Since spatial information is not included in the cluster analysis, spatially dispersed cluster results do not mean invalid results. In this case, we may have a culture but not an archaeological culture as defined above. In addition to these external criteria several internal validation criteria should be used. Finally we should compare the results with a map of the density of finds to avoid clusters which are based on only a few finds. Only if a cluster has passed all the tests, can we be sure that we have detected an archaeological culture with all its implications for interpretation.

Another line of investigation is to analyse the dependence of cultural distances on spatial distances. This focuses on the examination of interaction models. Especially if we do not have crisp cultural borders and we see a continuous cultural space, we can try to understand the spatial organisation by using interaction models. Furthermore, analysis of cultural distance as an indicator of interaction can be used to verify cultural borders (Kimes *et al.* 1982).

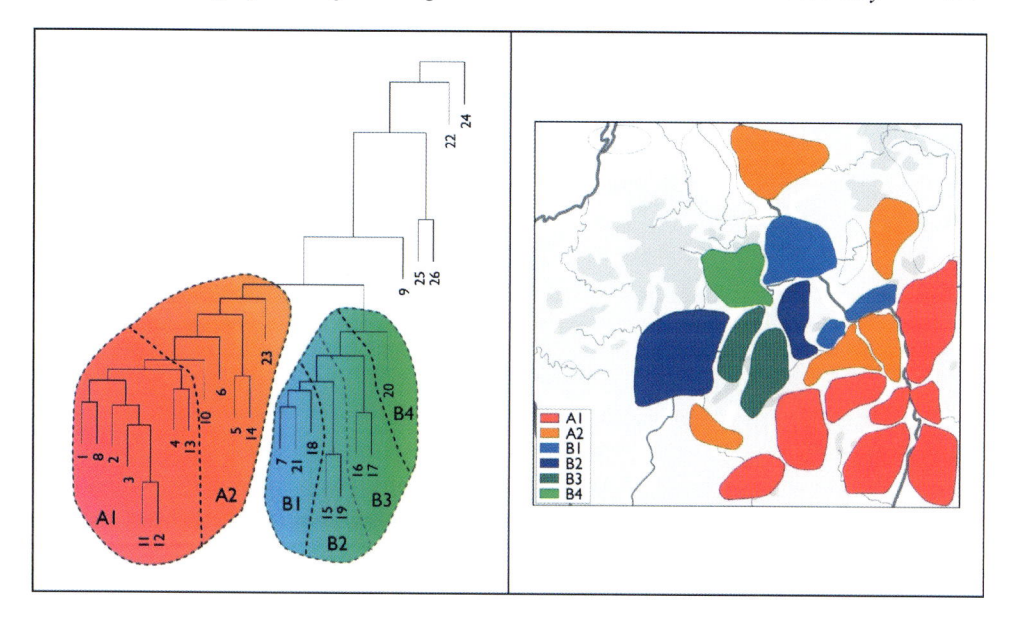

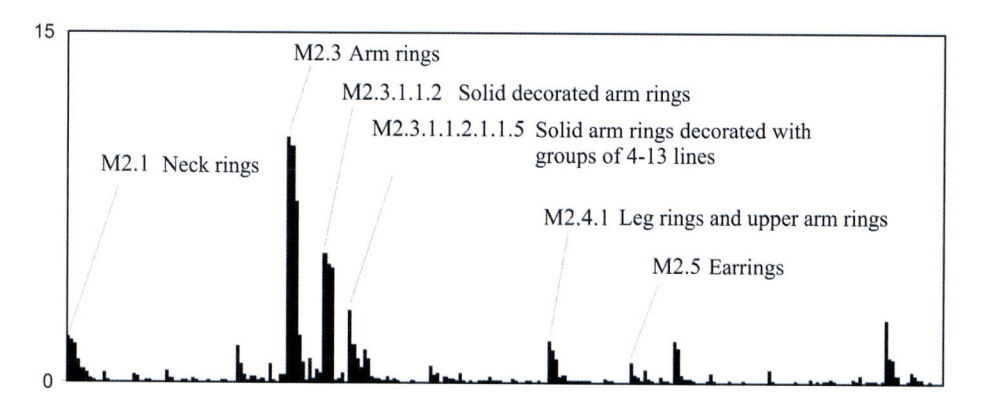

*17. Fingerprinting Iron Age Communities in South-West Germany* 195

*Figure 17.3. Example Early Hunsrück-Eifel-Kultur (Nakoinz 2005). Dendrogram, cluster map and synoptic Typenspektrum for the jewellery category.*

## CASE STUDIES

How can these ideas be applied in practice? The first example (Fig. 17.3) is the Hallstatt phase of the Hunsrück-Eifel-Kultur (HEK I) situated at the Middle-Rhine (Nakoinz 2005). Sometimes it is presumed that the Hunsrück-Eifel-Kultur is not an archaeological culture as defined above, but a transition zone between the Hallstatt culture and the Jastorf culture (Knopf 2002). We did the cluster analysis as described using certain parts of the material for different cluster analysis. About 12,000 finds were included in the analysis. If the borders of the cultural clusters were similar for all analyses, we would have an archaeological culture.

Nearly all parts of society have the same areas of interaction and hence the same border. In this case we have an archaeological culture with crisp borders. The material culture of the Hunsrück-Eifel-Kultur thus indicated a community which is a collective identity. We can suppose that the inhabitants were conscious of being a distinctive community between the diffuse cultural units of the Hallstatt culture in the South and the Jastorf culture in the North. The identity of this community is an equilibrium between communication with the surrounding cultures and delimitation of themselves from these other cultures. These processes of interaction remain a very important target of further research.

In south west Germany, we tried a similar analysis for the Early Iron Age (Nakoinz 2010a; 2010b). This study was performed in the project 'Siedlungshierarchien und kulturelle Räume' as part of the DFG priority project 1171 'Frühe Zentralisierungs- und Urbanisierungsprozesse' between 2004 and 2010 (Krauße 2004). The key question was whether the princely seats (e.g. Heuneburg) had an associated cultural area. Traditionally the princely seats were supposed to be administrative centres in big territories (Kimmig 1969; Härke 1979). In this project, more than 80,000 finds were included in the analysis. This quantity of data allows us to use many choices of material. In this analysis information about finds and some information about structures were also employed. The choice of material was drawn from several time slices and types of sources as well as from different categories of finds. Source filters were analysed using basic forms and materials, and both functional and social types were used to analyse regional groups of certain parts of the community. Altogether analysis of 225 different, although not disparate choices of material have been implemented. We undertook cluster analysis of the *Typenspektren* from regularly spaced geographical sample points. At the sample points we took the density of finds for each type. The vector of these values forms the *Typenspektren*, divided by the sum of densities at each point. When the hierarchical cluster analysis was performed, as described above, thousands of resulting maps have been validated using the density of finds, internal and external criteria and structural significance to exclude arbitrary results.

In this case, the result is that we do not have a border of an archaeological culture within the area of interest since most borders do not correspond. Instead of the expected mono-hierarchy of cultural areas we find a poly-hierarchy. Each segment of the social communities developed its own area of interaction. Each geographical cultural unit belonged to more than one higher-ranking unit. In this case, we cannot define an archaeological culture since we have an highly interconnected and complex society. However, an absence of archaeological cultures does not mean an absence of dominant cultural areas. In a secondary analysis we can compute dominant cultural areas (Fig. 17.4). We find examples in the north, middle and in the south that we can designate zones. This spatial organisation is superimposed by an East–West subdivision which corresponds with the main communication routes. All six cultural areas can be recorded in all the time-slices and many choices of material but not exactly with the same border. These dominant cultural areas are latent and do not have crisp borders.

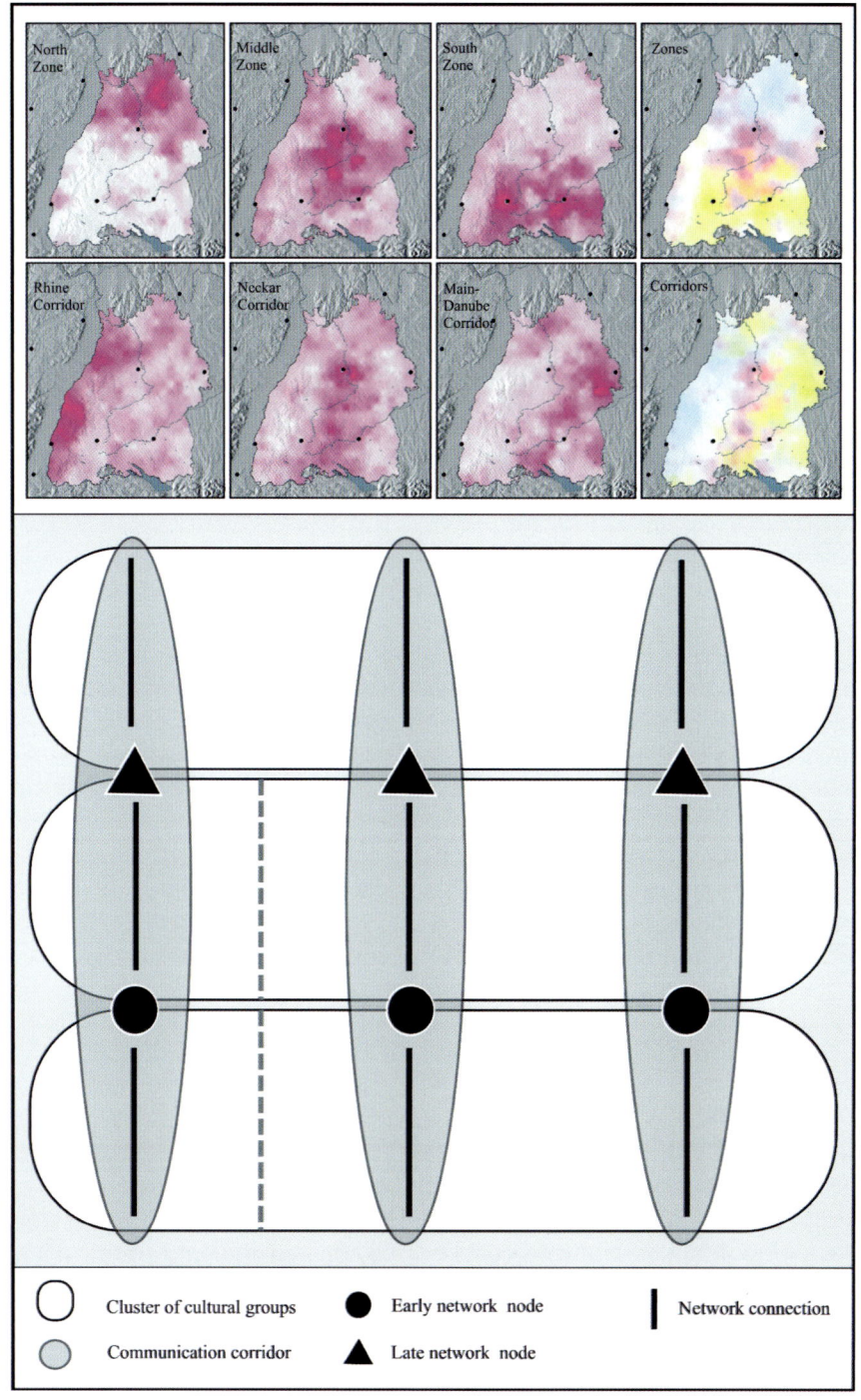

*Figure 17.4. The example of Early Iron Age Baden-Württemberg and the princely seats. (Nakoinz 2010b). Upper diagram: Dominant cultural areas as princely seats. Lower diagram: the gateway model of princely seats.*

The observed organisation of cultural space has an important impact on the interpretation of princely seats ('Fürstensitze'; Kimmig 1969) of the early Iron Age in the area of interest. The princely seats do not correspond either with the dominant cultural areas or with other cultural areas. Therefore the princely seats do not have a large or medium size territory which is strong, stable and long living enough to be visible as cultural area. We have not only to reject the idea of rulers of large territories but also the interpretation of the princely seats as central places in the sense of Christaller (1933; Haggett 1965; Gringmuth-Dallmer 1996). Christaller defines central places as places which supply more central functions for their surroundings than predicted by the population of the place. He suggests a model with minimised costs of transportation where the central places are located in the centre of the territory. Network models have been discussed for some time (Meijers 2007; Sindbæk 2007; Müller 2009; Nakoinz 2012). In these models, central places do not supply a certain area with central functions but have a structurally favourable position in an exchange network. One kind of these networks of central places is the gateway (Burghardt 1971; Hirth 1978) which controls exchange because of their border location. This model fits very well with the results of cultural areas in the case of princely seats. We can speak of a 'gateway model of princely seats' (Fig. 17.4). The status of the elites from princely seats is based on the mediation between two areas with a supposed different organisation. With the assimilation of the two areas connected by the gateway the zone of contact is running northwards in discrete steps (Brun 1993; 2002; Krauße 2008).

Coming back in this final example to geographical distances, we can analyse the interdependence of cultural distances and geographical distances. Gravity models for example do map this relationship (Haynes & Fotheringham 1984). In a simplified way, we can say the higher the geographical distance the higher the cultural distance. Certain parameters of this relationship can be compared for different regions and times. The borders of archaeological cultures appear at an angle (e.g. Kimes *et al.*1982) while the organisation of trade with relay stations leads to an undulated curve. This method allows us to study interaction on a small geographical scale. Hence this method complements the analysis of imported finds.

These two briefly described case studies gave us examples of the application of the definition of culture from Hansen and our definition of archaeological culture, as well as examples of the application of methods derived from theory. The most important methodological tool is the usage of Typenspektren which form a kind of cultural fingerprint and can be used for calculating cultural distances. This concept of a cultural metric transfers cultural analysis into the sphere of quantitative analysis in archaeology. Hence we have expressive examples for bridging the gap between humanities and sciences in archaeology.

From an archaeological point of view the case studies are likewise instructive. The first case study shows that the Hunsrück-Eifel-Kultur is an archaeological culture with crisp spatial borders. The second case study makes clear that we do not always have cultures of this type in archaeology. Here we see a highly interconnected society without crisp borders, but with latent cultural units. The location of princely seats along communication axes and at the border of these latent cultural units led us to reject the theory of princely seats as Christaller-central-places from which big territories were ruled and to accept the concept of gateways at which a control of communication was conducted. In this new model, the role of princely seats in the settlement structure is quite different from its role in the territorial models.

**ACKNOWLEDGEMENTS**

Since a considerable part of the ideas presented in this paper was developed in the DFG priority project 1171 I wish to thank, Dirk Krauße, Johannes Müller and Ulrich Müller for their support. I am also grateful for the support during the final preparation this paper by the excellence cluster Topoi (Berlin). Finally I wish to thank many colleagues for discussing the work on theory of culture and fingerprinting Iron Age communities.

# 18. Iron Age Identities in Central Europe: Some Initial Approaches

*Peter C. Ramsl*

KEYWORDS: IRON AGE, CENTRAL EUROPE, EASTERN AUSTRIA, IDENTITIES, SOCIAL IDENTITIES

INTRODUCTION: WHY IS IDENTITY A KEY QUESTION FOR ARCHAEOLOGY?
In the first chapter of the volume 'Soziale Gruppen – kulturelle Grenzen', Niels Müller-Scheeßel wrote, ' ...scheint das Thema Identität ein Problem der modernen westlichen Industriegesellschaften zu sein...', '...der Verlust sozialer Bezugssysteme und die damit einhergehende Identitätsdiffusion...' ['...identity is a problem of the modern western industrial society...' because of '...the loss of social reference systems and the dilution of identity...'] (Burmeister & Müller-Scheeßl 2006: 10). This topic has become fundamental for archaeology after decades of discussing ethnicity. Identity can be located at the interface between human beings and society, providing a permanent process of becoming for the construction of social membership (Fig. 18.1a). Identity is the current state of self-identification of an individual, and thus is never stable but permanently in a state of flux (Davidovic 2006: 44).

One valuable current approach to identity is that of Pierre Bourdieu. '*Da im Habitus soziale Strukturen eingeprägt sind, tendiert er zur Reproduktion dieser Strukturen, insbesondere wenn die Bedingungen zum Zeitpunkt der Anwendung noch mit den Entstehungsbedingungen identisch sind.*' (Rehbein 2006: 92–93) – ['Because social structures are imprinted in the 'habitus', there is an inclination to reproduce these structures, especially if the conditions at the point of action are identical with those of origin.'] From this we should also be aware, that '*Die Geschichte des Individuums [ist] nie etwas anderes als eine gewisse Spezifizierung des kollektiven Geschichte einer Gruppe*' (Bourdieu 1976: 189) – ['the History of an individual never is other than a specific path of the collective history of a group.']

If we look at archaeological evidence, we can detect the pattern of behaviour and action, based on a set of group-specific standards, where the *'habitus'* is creating the material culture related to the group. Burials combine evidence of the individual and social group. In this paper, I want to look for some evidence of the interaction of these two scales of identity in the Iron Age of eastern Austria: the shared identities of single persons.

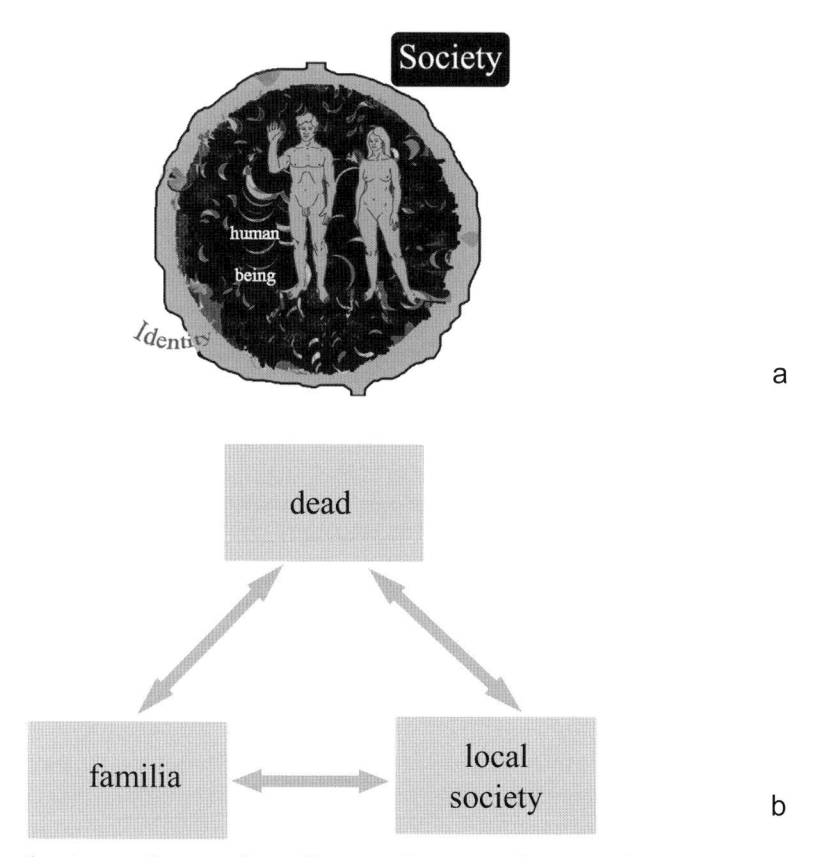

*Figure 18.1. a: Identity as the interface of human beings and society; b: The relationship between the dead, the family and the local society.*

EVIDENCE FROM THE FUNERARY MATERIAL CULTURE

Death rites achieve a processual character – with the occurrence of death – that involves not only the dead but also the whole community in an often long-lasting process of transition (Veit 2008: 26). The dead corpse is only the lifeless image of the living person, so the grave goods are mere indications of the former practical function that they performed (Veit 2008: 26). Nevertheless the grave goods are closely related with the dead (or rather the former living), and thus intrinsically involved in embedded ideas and discussions of the deceased. These discussions are mediated by the practice of the next of kin who by definition have a close relationship to the deceased. More specifically, the grave goods belong to the worldly property of the dead and are identified – in the imagination of the burying community – with the deceased person (as they have died with him). The grave goods are specially chosen, for their characteristic relationship to his/her personality and his/her social roles. The grave goods may be traces of the burial rites, participating in its conspicuous qualities or documenting its identity (Jung 2008: 274).

Broadly, there are three participants in the burial rite: the dead, the family and the local society (Brather 2008: 153). The dead individual may be characterised

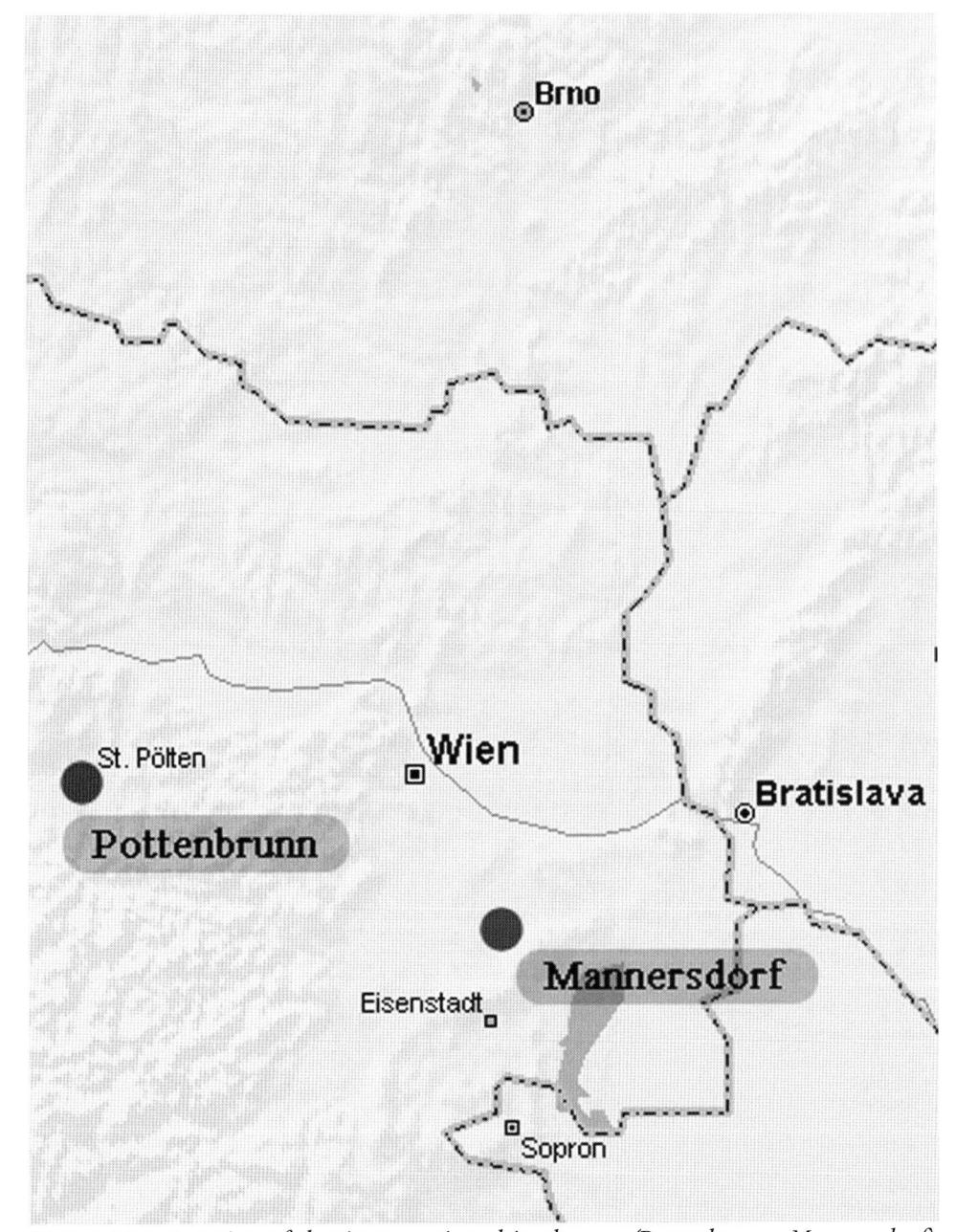

*Figure 18.2. Location of the sites mentioned in the text (Pottenbrunn, Mannersdorf); (graphics: P.C. Ramsl, basics: Encarta).*

by his status and prestige. The family is very interested to stress the social rank and prestige of the dead through the adequacy of ritual, and thus reflect on itself. The local society – of which the family is a participant – requires the expectations of public ceremony (Fig. 18.1b). In Roman law, 'familia' is (among others) the entirety of all people in a household (from the slaves up to the head) (Leonhard 1909 [1980–1982]). Similar structures are supposed to have existed in non-roman societies (Karl 2007: Abb. 4).The excavated image is often an idealised view, which does not reflect social reality, but a retrospective view of the identity of the dead. So it can be seen as the result of a transition process, which starts with the demise of a person and ends with final closing of the grave at the finalisation of all burial rites (which can often take a long time).

## EXAMPLES

In this paper I want to have a look at examples of different kind of evidence in the La Tène phase of eastern Austria, attempting to uncover identities or part/shared identities.

Geographically the precise region of eastern Austria is located near the cities of Vienna, Bratislava and Sopron (Fig. 18.2) and the selected sites are the cemeteries of Pottenbrunn (Ramsl 2002a) in the Traisen valley and Mannersdorf in the Leitha hills (Ramsl 2011).

These two areas are zones of geographical transition (or *cultural turntables*) between the different cardinal directions, albeit not always with the same emphasis, since the focus changes in different periods of the Iron Age: between the west (looking towards the Alpine area, the foothills of the Alps and further west to Bavaria and Switzerland), the east (towards the Carpathian basin (Ramsl 2002b)), the north (towards Moravia and south Poland) and the south (towards the Balkans and northern Italy).

### Pottenbrunn cemetery

This cemetery of about forty-five burials in the Traisen valley (similar to other sites like Franzhausen or Ossarn) was excavated in 1930 by Josef Bayer (Bayer 1930) and later especially in 1981/82 by J.-W. Neugebauer (Neugebauer 1992: 48).

My first example is grave 562. This burial of a 20–30 year old man was accompanied by an iron lance, shield rim fragments, and, for the period, a very large sword, strikingly similar to a Hungarian example from Kosd on the bend of the Danube. This sword clearly had an interesting biography, highlighted by the scabbard decoration and its embedded history. The decoration comprised an engraving of a distinctive dragon pair (Fig. 18.3a), overlaid by two discs of inlaid organic material (perhaps coral or ivory) and a third layer of openwork iron ornament on a foundation of gold foil. Thus at least three steps of ornamentation of this scabbard can be detected. In the interpretation of André Rapin, this reflects the expression of military ranking derived from war expeditions, and the symbolic recognition of military leagues in the pair of dragons or griffons (Rapin – pers comm; Kruta & Lička 2004: 85; Ginoux 2007: 118). The dating of the burial to La Tène B2/C1 (*c*.250 BC) (Ramsl 2002a: 144–5) might make the owner of this sword a participant in one of the historically recorded military expeditions (although it would be too precise to cite a particular event such as the sack

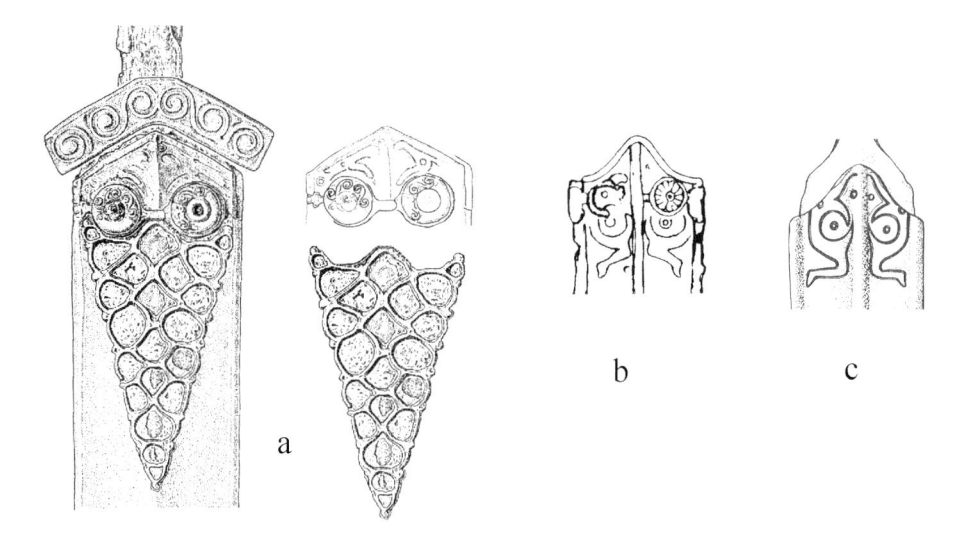

*Figure 18.3. a: Scabbard in grave 562 (Pottenbrunn); (graphics: M. Imam, P.C. Ramsl); b: Scabbard from Villeperrot (after Ginoux 2007: Pl. 62/1); c: Scabbard of unknown provenance (after Szabó & Petres 1992: Pl. 77).*

of Delphi). Whatever the precise historical specificity of the particular expedition, these events would have been a striking part of the life of this man, and thus part of his biographical identity, embedded in redolent material culture. The scabbard of Villeperrot in France (Ginoux 2007: Pl. 62/1), shows that this occurrence may not have been unique (Fig. 18.3b), and there are other examples such as a scabbard of unknown provenance (Fig. 18.3c) which had been recycled and used at least twice, with the same biographical implications.

A possibly even more developed example of multiple identities is represented by burial 520 from Pottenbrunn. The biological data suggest that this male died in his late forties or early fifties, an advanced age for the period. The high degree of inflammation of the palate can be interpreted as the product of preferential access to sugar (for which read honey). The attrition of the frontal teeth points to use of these as a third hand. The wear on some of his vertebrae and fingers suggest a specific combat related activity. His body was inhumed, stretched on his back, with the head orientated to the south south east, conforming to the local group practice. The man was armed with a typical Latène sword on the customary right hand side. Some probable shield fragments were found at his feet and a high quality spearhead or 'standard' to the left of his head. These items give him a specific position amongst the warrior elite. More distinctively, parts of the leg of a red deer, some domestic fowl bones and some arrowheads (to his right) were found with his body. This combination of the leisure of elite hunting with the prized plumage of the domestic fowl is a marker of substantial status. Furthermore, he is accompanied by an instrument that combines the function of saw and blade, placed together with three different small knives, a whetstone, another (mortar-like?) stone and a propeller shaped bone tool. These tools are

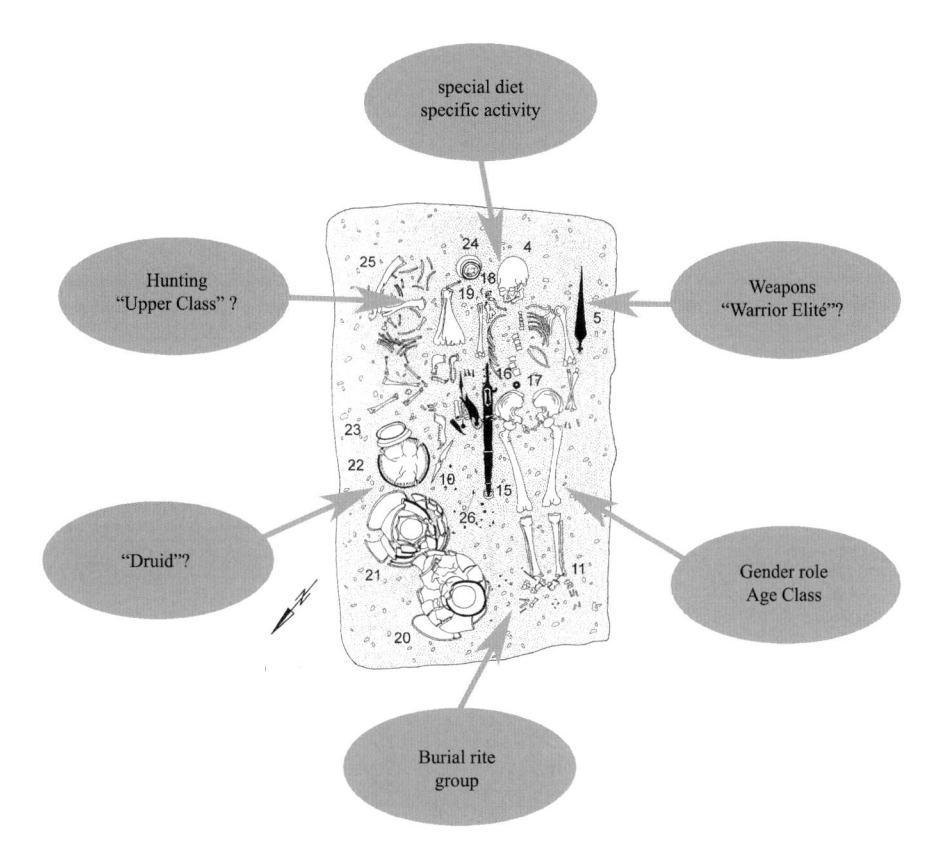

*Figure 18.4. The compartmentalized identities of grave 520 from Pottenbrunn (graphics: P.C. Ramsl; basics: A. Gattringer).*

suggestive of medical and pharmacological functions, involved in cutting, grinding, pulverising and applying of poultices.

In summary, we can define a series of overlapping multiple identities (Fig. 18.4) through these exceptional redolent survivals of distinctive material culture: Senior male; military prestige; dietary privilege; specialist activity related to the teeth; special burial rite; access to hunting; and medical knowledge

My final example of *Mannersdorf* is a site placed on the western border of the Leitha hills near the Neusiedler See/Fertö. This contains 96 burials and was occupied between 400 and 200 BC (Fig. 18.5). My chosen example is Grave 114, the burial place of a woman of unknown age. Her identity is given by several distinctive elements of material culture seen elsewhere in the cemetery: a group wearing looped bracelets; another individual in Grave 86 with a Champagne style s-shaped bracelet; another individual in grave 112 with Inner Alpine style pottery; a group of women with Swiss style double anklets like at Münsingen and Saint Sulpice (Fig. 18.6). The cemetery of Münsingen (near Bern) consists of 220 to 230 burials of the Early and Middle La Tène Period (Hodson 1968),

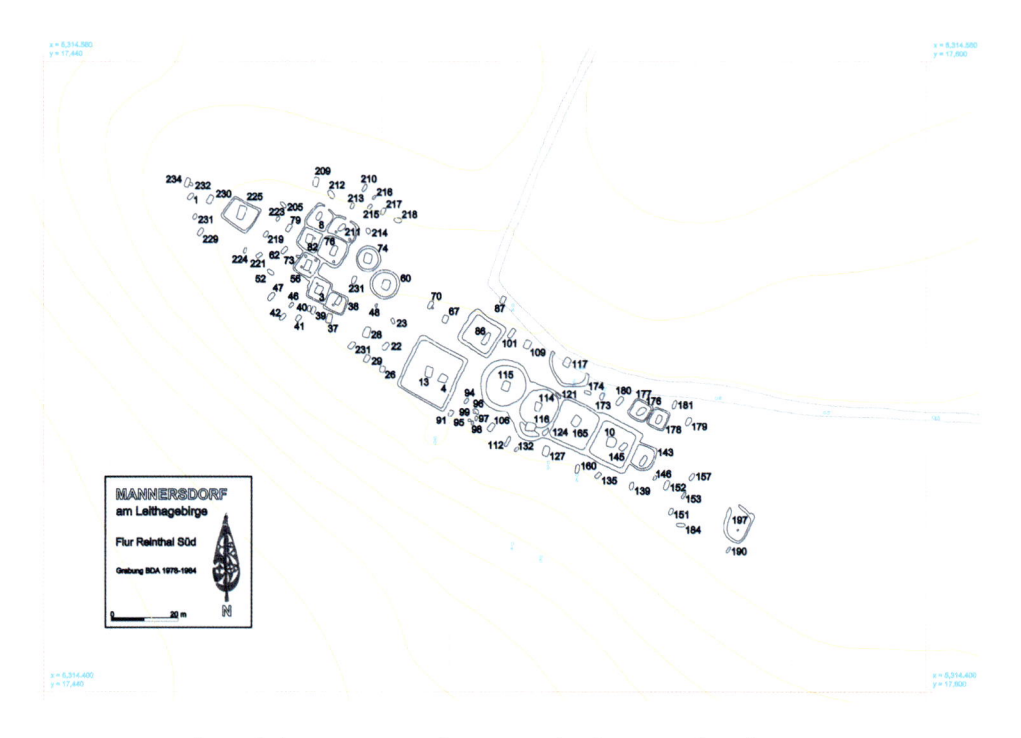

*Figure 18.5. Plan of the cemetery of Mannersdorf am Leithagebirge, Lower Austria (graphics: P.C. Ramsl).*

structured in groups of three to seven burials, which were interpreted at the outcome of endogamous marriage policy within the local community (Alt *et al.* 2005: 201). On the other hand, Saint Sulpice, placed on the shore of the Lake Geneva is represented by 87 graves, which were excavated from 1912–1914 (Kaenel 1990). The identity represented here is not that of wealth, but of connectivity (Fig. 18.7) to other members of local society.

The mobility of men and women were of a different kind (see also Arnold 2005). On the one hand, armed men would have been quite busy as mercenaries over longer distances in the Mediterranean (Tomaschitz 2002) – sometimes also accompanied by their women and children. On the other hand, women were probably more systematically mobile, but over shorter distances. That said, Caesar describes the marriage of the sister of the king of Noricum with Ariovist over a very substantial distance. The matter is not entirely simple (Arnold 2005). In our case, 'costume' is the translation of german 'Tracht'. In archaeological terms where most organic materials like textile and leather do not survive, we can only deal with the proxy elements like bracelets, anklets, necklaces and fibulae. Some of these elements, which can be interpreted as 'Ring–costumes' show the social role of the person (age, rank, status...) within society. Others provide a signal to the world outside. Once again consideration of 'dress' in the available literature is not simple (e.g. Entwistle 2000).

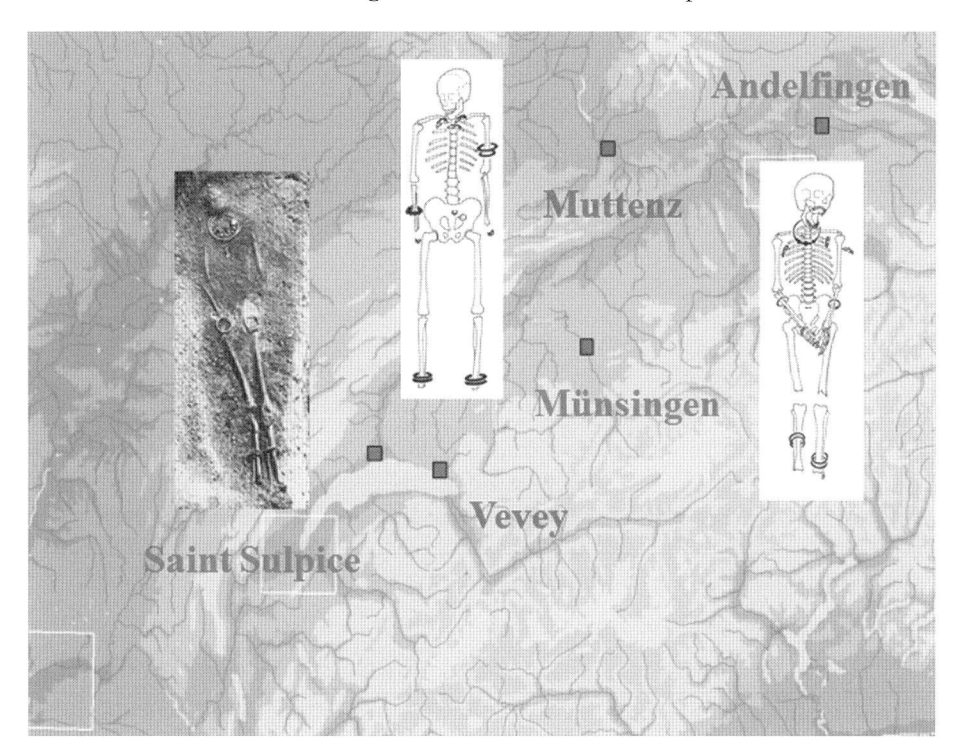

*Figure 18.6. Comparable La Tène cemeteries in Switzerland (basics: Encarta, pictures: Hodson 1968 ; Kaenel 1990; Viollier 1912).*

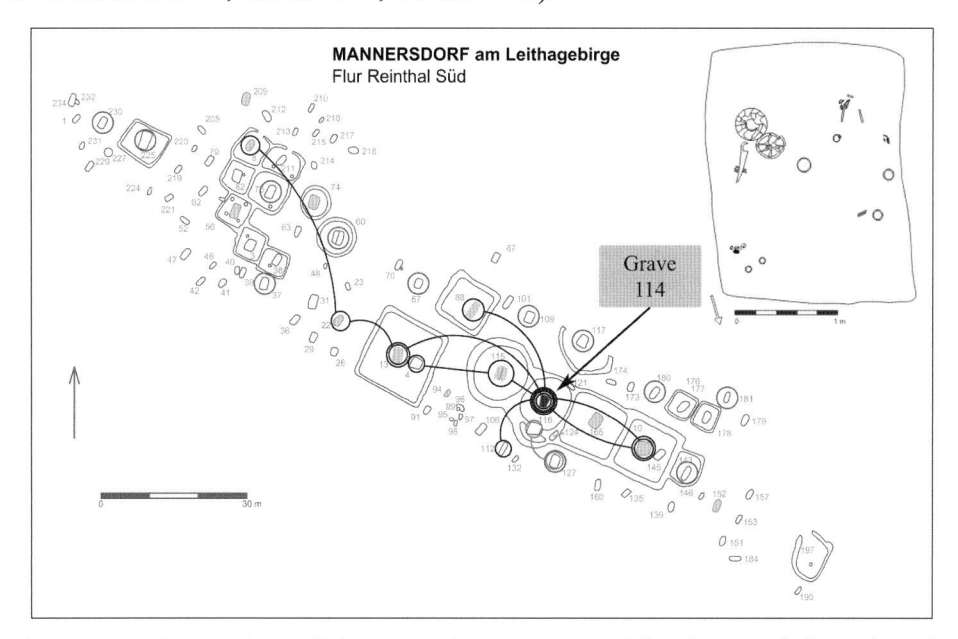

*Figure 18.7. Connections of the person in grave 114 with other people buried in this cemetery (graphics: P.C. Ramsl).*

In the area of the Traisen valley, we have some indication that we may postulate different local groups. On the one hand, we can see buried persons with different kinds of panoply, which may lead us to suppose different groups of 'weapon units'. On the other hand, it is possible to see conservative and innovative groups, as in the case of the costumes of the women. Further work will be needed to tease apart the degree to which chronology or contemporary spatial patterning contributes to these patterns. All these examples show that when we have rich and distinctive arrays of material culture it is possible to dissect the evidence to understand the complexity of competing identities at different scales between the individual and the wider community.

## Conclusion

This paper has dissected the burial evidence to show that rich material culture can be forensically examined to detect layers of identity, that range from special roles in life, to networks in death. Biographies of material culture can give powerful information on the layers of biographical identity in life.

## Acknowledgements

The research was funded by the Austrian Science Fund (FWF): P23517-G19, P12531-SPR and P15977-G02. I would like to thank Kerstin Kowarik, Micheline Welte and Simon Stoddart for checking the text and all colleagues at Cambridge for discussing my paper and giving me input into the topic.

*Perspectives from the Far West*

# 19. Negotiating Identity on the Edge of Empire

*Louisa Campbell*

KEYWORDS: IRON AGE, ROMAN, THEORY, IDENTITIES, MATERIAL CULTURE

INTRODUCTION

Northern Britain occupied a unique position beyond the edge of the Roman Empire's north western frontier during the early centuries AD. This paper is fundamentally theoretical in its approach and proposes that recent theoretical constructs offer an effective interpretive framework to explore complex negotiating strategies employed by Iron Age occupants of the region during sporadic and short-lived periods of Roman campaigns and occupation. This approach incorporates a detailed reappraisal of local manipulation of Roman material culture, specifically depositional practices, to assess the potential affect which Roman occupation may, or may not, have had upon the expression and reinforcement of identities within northern communities occupying the region.

While the construction of explicit theoretical models to address issues of contact between Romans and provincial societies has unquestionably been beneficial to the field of Roman archaeology, previously widely accepted models of Romanisation (Millett 1990), acculturation (Schortman & Urban 1998) and assimilation (Hanson 1994: 150) are generally based upon the underlying assumption of one society's dominance over a submissive other. They fail adequately to consider the perspectives of societies interacting with Rome or take account of local agency, inter and intra-regional variation, resistance, and the persistence of cultural identities (Campbell in preparation) within 'submissive' societies, which are often deemed to have become impoverished and fragmentary (Schortman & Urban 1998: 106). Hanson (1994: 150) has attempted to redefine the acculturation paradigm as a more neutral term denoting reciprocal processes of interaction between cultural groups resulting in changes to all participants. His proposed model has, regrettably, not been developed within Roman studies and the term has come to lose its intended focus on reciprocal interfacing practices.

Recent research, however, propose that frontier contexts offer a unique opportunity to explore the Roman and provincial interface because Roman cultural values and material culture were not so deeply entrenched into local conditions as in southern Britain or other parts of the Empire (Webster 2001: 217; Campbell 2011; in preparation). Thus, patterns of selective adoption (Jiménez 2008), hybrid practices (Jiménez 2011; van Dommelen and Rowlands 2011) or cultural transformations (Mattingly 2004; Stein 2005) may be more visible in the archaeological record than for other regions and a reassessment of Roman material culture from non-Roman contexts set within the framework of current theoretical constructs should facilitate a more nuanced interpretation of the evidence.

It is helpful, at the outset, to define what is meant here by the term 'identity' and explain how archaeologists might attempt to explore such a concept in the context of ancient societies existing on Imperial boundaries before outlining the practical application of such constructs.

## HYBRID IDENTITIES AND THE ROMANO-BRITISH PARADIGM

Identity is central to any discussion of people, past or present. Discourse on identity has more recently focussed upon differences, including the concept that people 'associate and live within multiple categories in the course of their life trajectory and further connect to others by various practices of identity' (Meskell & Preucel 2004: 124). Thus, identity is a social construct and agents possess a number of roles which they variously adopt and adapt according to different social issues, including class, gender, age, ethnicity or sexual orientation. Indeed, a person's self-identification may differ markedly from the way others identify them. Issues such as language, terminologies, political stances, embodiment, subjectivity and agency are central to any discussion of identity as well as an understanding that identity is fluid and changeable throughout the life cycle (Meskell & Preucel 2004: 125). People are, therefore, required to adopt an appropriate role for the various social situations in which they engage.

Central to identity is cultural identity and, although Childe's (1927; 1929; 1935) characterisation of culture as specific and repetitive ritual practices or associated artefacts has been described as minimalistic (Jones 1997: 17), his was the first attempt at the construction and application of implicit theoretical models to recognise an archaeological culture. This culture-historical epoch defined culture as a set of shared beliefs continually reinforced across successive generations by repeated socialisation within bounded, homogenous groups (Childe 1956: 8). The diffusionist model developed from this theoretical framework. This stance defines sudden large-scale cultural change as necessarily resulting from contact with other, more creative, dominant groups (Jones 1997: 135), a concept which closely parallels the previously widely accepted Romanisation paradigm.

More recent approaches recognise that social organisation is much more complex and nuanced than agents within cultural groups necessarily competing for dominance over others (*contra* Binford 1962; Clarke 1968). For instance, rather than signifying external competition or a method by which people can join new socio-economic groups, some forms of objectification can signify the maintenance of kinship within communities (Shankar 2006). By discussing objectified objects belonging to immediate family members, people actively create connections between themselves, the object and its owner thereby establishing and reinforcing a sense of identity and group identities. The ascription of issues such as gender, ethnicity, social class or the complex and multifaceted layers of identity adopted by people for various social situations may be illuminated through a detailed study of the small finds (Collins 2008: 48).

The traditional concept of Romanisation has now been challenged as it is recognised as being based upon the unsustainable assumption of linear progression from simple to complex societies through contact with Rome (Hingley 1996: 44; 2005: 118). It also implies a one-sided and unidirectional dominance of one culture over another (Barrett 1994) and reduces Iron Age communities to passive recipients of Romanising influences which they inevitably welcome (Thomas 1991; Woolf 1998) and imposes social structures which may not be appropriate for Iron Age communities coming into contact with Rome. It also fails to recognise the role of local religion or ideology in the processes (Freeman 1993: 441), overt or covert resistance to the processes (van Dommelen 1998: 44; 2007: 61; Herring 2007: 23), or the complex ethnic mix already inherent within the incoming Roman army (Hanson 1994: 152). These men were very often derived from far-flung corners of the Empire and would have undoubtedly retained certain elements of their own ethnic and cultural identities and social practices alongside more Romanised behaviours (Swan 1992; 1999; 2008). Therefore, the new culture to which the communities of newly acquired provinces were exposed would rarely have had its roots exclusively in Rome. But rather it was a cultural milieu, a mosaic of culturally diverse elements derived from numerous locations across the Empire and the concept of 'Roman' may be better understood as essentially hybrid (Millett *et al.* 1995), differing in meaning, character and context across the Empire (Hingley 1996: 42). The creation of new hybrid identities, such as Gallo-Roman or Romano-British, then, constitutes the fusion of these variable influences. However, 'Roman' has been predominantly perceived as the over-riding and dominant constituent part, highlighting a potential flaw in the traditionally accepted concept of Romanisation (Jones 1997; Webster 2001).

**IDENTIFYING IDENTITY – THE MULTIPLICITIES OF THE 'SELF'**

It is necessary, therefore, to propose an alternative, more nuanced, theoretical framework which might usefully be employed to investigate the construction and negotiation of identities as they relate to ancient societies variably engaged in contact with the Roman Empire, particularly in frontier contexts.

Within the realms of psychology, there is a recognised distinction between group-based identities (social identity theory) and role-based identities (identity theory). More negotiation and interaction is thought to be required from persons involved in role-based identity as one performs a role within reciprocal relationships, thus creating micro social networks within the group (Stets & Burke 2000: 227). Whereas, there is limited requirement for participants within group-based identities to interact because the group acts as a collective of similar people who hold the same perceptions and reinforces these perceptions, resulting in group formation and the depersonalisation of individuals (Turner *et al.* 1987). Both of these aspects are interconnected and 'being and doing are central features to one's identity' (Stets and Burke 2000: 234).

Central to the maintenance of group identities is trust and commitment to others within the group, which enables self-verification and enhances positive self perception, creating and reinforcing attachments to others (Burke & Stets 1999: 362). However, as a consequence, individual agency may be constrained within the group, as the cost of holding a sense of belonging potentially restricts a person's ability to operate in the singular (Stets & Burke 2000: 227) and conflict will inevitably affect group dynamics on various levels. Therefore, social restrictions may have dictated who was permitted to adopt incoming Roman objects and how these objects functioned within the recipient Iron Age communities of northern Britain.

Following on from Bourdieu's (1977) *habitus* concept, Butler (1990: 46) postulates that identity is socially constructed by the repeated performance of activities or ideological rituals so that behaviours and idealised characteristics and roles are learned from an early age. These notions of normality and values are then reinforced and maintained through objects and discursive, especially ritualised, and non-discursive practices (Sorensen 2000: 54). Consequently, artefacts are part of material conditions embedded in the cultural systems within which they are produced and used, their meanings are both constructed by and, in turn, construct social structures (Lucas 2002: 54). It is, therefore, crucial that we understand the contexts in which material culture is produced, used, reused, adapted and discarded and that, as these contexts change, so does the meaning of objects (Barrett 1994: 88). A similar approach can be adopted for the local selective adoption, reuse, manipulation and ultimate deposition of Roman material culture in non-Roman contexts in northern Britain.

Ethnicity is an integral aspect of identity and cannot be reduced to a pure, unchanging cultural entity. Ethnographic studies discuss ethnicity as complex, multi-dimensional concepts related to the self-definition of ethnic groups. Thus:

> 'ethnic groups are culturally ascribed identity groups, which are based on the expression of a real or assumed shared culture and common descent (usually through objectification of cultural, linguistic, religious, historical and/or physical characteristics)' (Jones 1997: 86, original italics).

Like gender, class or kinship then, ethnicity is a culturally constructed form of social grouping. However, unlike these aspects, which have been described as divisive differentiations between elements within society, such as men and women or elite and non-elite, ethnicity involves the reproduction of systematic and enduring differences through the interactive social lives of people who perceive themselves as *'culturally distinct'* (Jones 1997: 87, original italics). Fenton (2003: 2) has questioned the validity of a concept of ethnicity and proposes the issue cannot be separated from aspects of class, race or nationality. However, this oversimplifies a complex and multifarious strand of self or group definition which cannot be reduced to binary opposition.

Recent anthropological studies seek to define 'identities' and 'culture' as two distinct notions of being (Grimson 2010). Following on from Evans-Pritchard (1940), such studies define *symbolic spatiality* as a critical component of a person's being. Thus, connections are forged and maintained, potentially over very long distances, between members of social groups or families. People may feel a need to have a sense of belonging in whatever social setting they find themselves, thus 'a culture is a configuration that is made up of countless diverse elements that are complementarily, oppositionally and hierarchically interrelated' (Grimson 2010: 75), while 'an identity associated with a particular category is a key element in a culture' (Grimson 2010: 75). The relationship between culture and identity is, therefore, necessarily complex and interconnected as well as variable and situational. This variability is central to people's capacity to make appropriate choices for action and belonging within a social group.

Evidence of provincial emulation of Roman cultural values and material culture has previously been taken as evidence for the Romanisation of these societies. However, such examples might equally be explained as the multi-directional elements of acculturation (Kottak 2006) or appropriation (Thomas 1991: 1992), where foreign influences were being adopted and used in a culturally specific and relevant manner (Kopytoff 1986). As such, evidence of some Romanising influences being embraced by some provincials need not preclude their simultaneous and persistent participation in culturally acquired behaviours which reinforce the distinctiveness of their traditional cultural or ethnic identities. Ethnic groups self-consciously define themselves by comparison to other groups and the expression of ethnic identity can be manifest in everyday utilitarian objects or highly decorative objects alike (Hodder 1982b: 55), or by selectively appropriating foreign objects into existing cultural conditions, thereby altering their inherent meaning. In this way, such objects become hybrid entities, neither one thing nor another. But rather, they constitute the fusion of various connective elements to form an entirely new thing which requires the reformulation, development and manipulation of a whole new set of negotiating strategies.

Objects should be interpreted through symbolic meanings appropriate to, and generated by, the agents and groups producing and using them in a manner perceived by them as culturally relevant. The appropriation of Roman material culture by provincials need not, therefore, be a manifestation of Romanisation within bounded, homogenous societies, but could instead be linked to heterogeneous and culturally relevant expressions of ethnicity (Jones 1997: 135), or other aspects of identity. For example, the evident rejection of coinage in north east England throughout the Roman Iron Age could denote a communal and conscious decision to maintain decentralised political organisation (Willis 1999: 102) and continuity of cultural traditions and beliefs. The same could be said for regions further north, where some communities selectively adopted certain elements of Roman material and rejected others. For instance, a comprehensive review of Roman ceramics from non-Roman contexts in northern Britain has confirmed a preference for samian from Roman sources where these vessel types are numerically more restricted than coarsewares (Campbell 2011: 188).

One method of transmitting identity could have been through the medium of ritual practices and religious ideology. This research proposes that a detailed study of depositional practices is critical to understanding ideological belief systems and offers considerable potential for the practical application of the theoretical constructs outlined above. The following discussion will, therefore, explore the deposition of Roman objects from potentially ideologically significant Iron Age contexts in northern Britain to propose that this material culture was being culturally, conceptually and symbolically redefined in new cultural contexts to reinforce cultural identities, perhaps as a means of resisting the imposition of Roman cultural values.

**DEPOSITIONAL PRACTICES – NEGOTIATING THE ROMAN AND PROVINCIAL INTERFACE**
Religion (cf. Freeman 1993; Millett 1995), ideology (cf. Roymans 1996) and ritual practices (Wellington 2002) are here considered to be interconnected elements of cultural identity, social practices, lifestyles and concepts as a whole (Roymans 1990; Brück 1999). Material culture is proposed as a principal means by which people understand and interface with their world and artefacts adopt a symbolic role in these interactions (Hodder 1982b; Gosselain 1999). A cultural response to potentially dominant impositions may have been to invoke cultural memory (Garcia Sanjuan et al. 2008: 2) or material culture (Herring 2007: 23) as a means of ideological or cultural resistance to Rome and an upsurge in votive deposition in northern Britain (Willis 1999: 102) may have enabled communities who felt under threat to reinforce their cultural identity (Harding 2004: 81). This current research proposes that a study of contexts of structured votive deposition (Roymans 1990), taking account of changes before, during and after the period of Roman occupation (Owen 2005), can illuminate our understanding of these issues.

As I have discussed elsewhere (Campbell 2011; 2012), detailed analyses of material biographies (Hoskins 1998; 2006; Marshall & Gosden 1999; Meskell 1999; 2004; Gardner 2002; Gilchrist 2004; Stahl 2010) offer the most effective means of determining how foreign objects were being redefined and put to use in new cultural settings. One critical phase in the lifecycle of objects is their ultimate deposition. Of course, it is possible that the presence of Roman material culture in some non-Roman contexts could be residual in character (Wallace 2006) and such material can provide a wealth of information through archaeological survey (Haselgrove et al. 1985), particularly as it relates to discard (Schiffer 1972; 1975; Rathje 1974) and recycling practices (Keller 2005; Pena 2007) or the deliberate deposition of Roman artefacts in medieval and later contexts (e.g. Eckardt & Williams 2003). However, the concept of residuality cannot be applied uncritically to explain the presence of Roman objects in all Iron Age contexts. The over-reliance upon a vague concept of residuality as a meta-narrative denies any potential for symbolism ascribed to material (Hodder 1982b; Campbell 2012) or the structured votive deposition (Roymans 1990; Hill 1995; Millett 1995; Weekes 2008) of foreign objects perceived by the recipients as being intrinsically and culturally significant.

An important point of note here is recognition that Roman objects need not have been deposited contemporaneously with their date of manufacture or initial period of use. There has, in the past, been a tendency to use tightly dated classes of Roman material culture as chronological evidence for phases of activity on non-Roman sites (e.g. Hill 1982a; 1982b; Armit 1999; Alexander 2005: 92). Some Roman objects, however, have had lengthy lifecycles which could suggest the careful curation of highly prized artefacts (Keppie 1989: 68; Price 1997) or objects that were treated differently to others (Evans 1988; Willis 1997). That Roman artefacts have been specifically chosen for ritual reuse, such as samian bowls which have been in circulation for over a century then reused in Cumbrian cemeteries in cremations of predominantly older men (Cool 2004: 451–2), or samian sherds and glass bracelet fragments from Anglo-Saxon graves (Sherlock and Welch 1992: 152; Eckardt & Williams 2003), is proposed here as being a deeply significant practice.

## ROMAN OBJECTS IN FUNERARY CONTEXTS

Burial evidence is elusive for Iron Age Scotland. Much of the radiocarbon evidence from cremations (Cook 1999) and crouched (Brady *et al.* 2007) or flexed inhumations (e.g. Dunwell 2007) is restricted to the second to third Centuries AD. I propose that Northern Britain occupies a unique position beyond the edge of Empire because different parts of the region came intermittently within and without imperial boundaries. Therefore the extent of contact with Rome was variable, complex and inconsistent over a very short period – unlike, for example, northern England where the army was a consistent feature. Therefore, I suggest that this creates a unique context for contact and the potential for uptake of Roman influences. I do not propose here that flexed inhumations are confined to the second–third Centuries AD, but that much of the radiocarbon evidence from the burial traditions outlined dates to that period. Though this might signify the spread of Roman burial influences in northern Britain (Pearce *et al.* 2000) recent work refutes this stance (Maldonado 2011). Excluding cremation deposits close to Roman forts, e.g. Cramond (Macdonald 1897), Inveresk (Gallagher & Clarke 1993) and Camelon (Breeze *et al.* 1976), which are most likely to belong to associated fort or *vicus* occupants and therefore not relevant to this study, several northern burials contain Roman material culture (Fig. 19.1). The following discussion assesses the evidence from northern burials containing Roman material culture to determine whether structured votive deposition practices are discernable.

A total of 18 instances of northern funerary contexts have been found to contain Roman material culture. Three of these, at Stoneyfield in Inverness, Hallow Hill cemetery in Fife and High Torrs in Dumfries and Galloway, include Roman ceramics and other material. The remainder contain a range of objects, such as *paterae*, melon beads, a Romano-British glass bracelet fragments, an intaglio, brooches and glass cups.

Some interesting patterns have emerged with the placement of Roman pottery sherds in burial contexts. For instance, at High Torrs unburnt samian fragments had been placed into a cremated burial deposit (Mann 1933) signifying an additional layer of ritual practice after the cremation. While at Forteviot in Perth and Kinross, the University of Glasgow's Archaeological field school has recently recovered a rim sherd of an Argonne colour-coated bag-shaped beaker

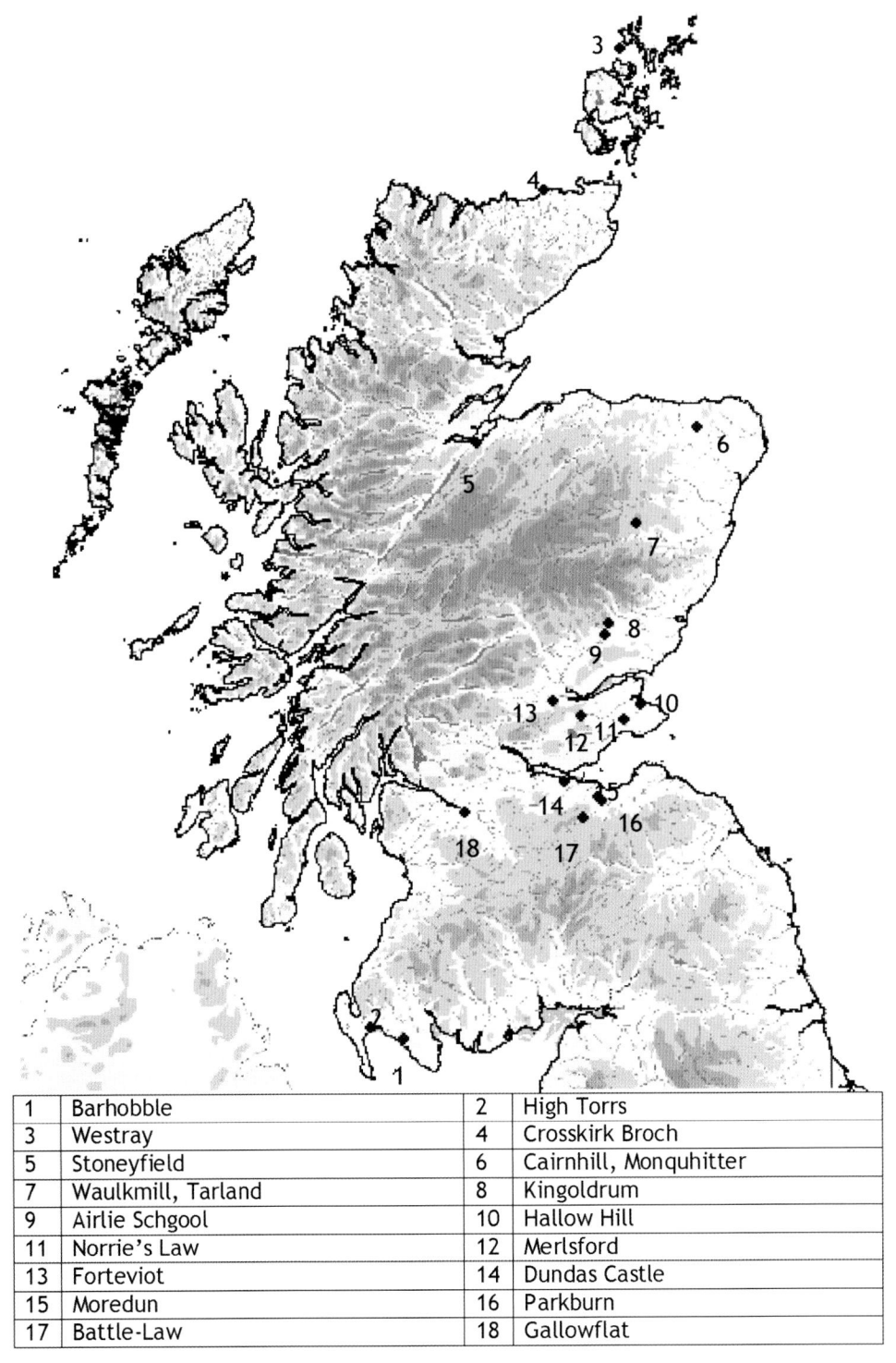

| 1 | Barhobble | 2 | High Torrs |
|---|---|---|---|
| 3 | Westray | 4 | Crosskirk Broch |
| 5 | Stoneyfield | 6 | Cairnhill, Monquhitter |
| 7 | Waulkmill, Tarland | 8 | Kingoldrum |
| 9 | Airlie Schgool | 10 | Hallow Hill |
| 11 | Norrie's Law | 12 | Merlsford |
| 13 | Forteviot | 14 | Dundas Castle |
| 15 | Moredun | 16 | Parkburn |
| 17 | Battle-Law | 18 | Gallowflat |

*Figure 19.1. Roman objects from funerary contexts in Scotland.*

from a silt deposit directly overlying cremated remains marked by a possible standing stone inside a henge, as well as a rim of Upchurch Ware associated with a Pictish cemetery (Ewan Campbell, pers. comm.).

Other sites, such as the Clava-cairn at Stoneyburn (Simpson, 1969: 74), a cist at Airlie School in Angus (Davidson 1886) and a burial cairn at Cairnhill in Aberdeenshire (Curle 1932: 295) constitute the deliberate placement of Roman material within ancient burial structures dating to the Neolithic period or Bronze Age. While other burials containing Roman objects are associated with the end of the lifecycle of brochs at Dun Mor Vaul on Tiree (Klein *et al.* 1982) and Crosskirk in Caithness (Fairhurst 1984: 115–16) or early medieval burials at Hallow Hill in Fife (Proudfoot 1996) and Whithorn Monastic town (Hill 1997: 292–97), confirming the inclusion of Roman objects within later burial contexts.

These very different practices serve as a reminder that the manipulation and deposition of Roman objects was complex as well as situationally and temporally variable. Given that the former artefacts cannot have been contemporaneously placed within ancient burial monuments, it is plausible to suggest that these were later placements above the interments. There are several potential interpretations of this practice. One might be that Iron Age people who were embracing Roman cultural values were posthumously appropriating the remains of the dead into these cultural values. Another could be that Iron Age peoples were using the material culture of Empire as talismans and the small dimensions of proportionalised inalienable Roman objects (Campbell 2011: 232–7) may have facilitated transportation of their meanings and cultural interpretations to different social contexts and locations. Thus, these objects could have been ascribed magical meanings and the transportation of such magical objects could constitute the commoditisation of occult things imbued with powerful medicinal properties for the protection of people and places (Sanders 2001: 174), thereby offering a culturally and ideologically effective means of active resistance to Rome and the reinforcement of traditional cultural identities.

Yet another interpretation could be that these Roman objects were used as an element of early Christian sanctifying practices, perhaps as a means of early pilgrims, spreading Christian religious practices and consecrating the remains of people known to have been previously buried in a non-Christian manner. This may have been a method of Christianising the deceased or providing them with posthumous Last Rites to enable their souls to progress to Heaven according to Christian beliefs, in the same way that St Columba and other saints sanctified places they perceived as poisonous but worshipped 'as a divinity [by] heathen people [Picts]' (Adomnán 625–704 [1875: 73–4]).

## Ritually deposited Roman objects

The interpretation of bronze vessels recovered during peat cutting or draining as being the result of either locals or Roman invaders dumping objects while taking flight, or as casual losses (Wilson 1851: 277), has long been abandoned along with the proposal that such activities are distinctly Roman as opposed to Iron

Age practices (Manning 1981). Recognition that such objects could, instead, constitute indigenous hoarding (Hunter 1996: 117) of culturally and ideologically important material has gained momentum (Bradley 1990) and a number of studies have revealed the potential of such material deposition for investigating social issues (Hedeager 1992: 122).

Hunter (1997) has assessed the hoarding of high-quality metalwork during the Iron Age across Scotland and Northern England. The study identified distinctive regionality in hoarding and votive practices as well as the type of material incorporated. For instance, Atlantic Scotland is almost devoid of hoards, while a reasonable spread exists across north east and southern Scotland as well as northern England. Yet further intra-regional distinctions are distinguishable with personal ornaments common in the north east of Scotland, while a considerable diversity in material is evident in the southern hoards which incorporate personal ornaments and horse equipment as well as tools and 'exotica' from other Iron Age communities in southern England (Hunter 1997: 111), such as Lamberton Moor (Curle 1932: 363; Robertson 1970), Blackburn Mill (Wilson 1854; Curle 1932: 362) and Ruberslaw (Curle 1905: 227) in the Scottish Borders, amongst others.

The types of objects selected for votive deposition are equally diverse, including glass bracelet fragments at Moss Raploch (Condry & Ansell 1978), an intricate and unique open gold crossbow brooch at Erickstanebrae (Curle 1932), a bronze Medusa head ewer handle from Cairnholly (Curle 1905: 230), a bronze statuette of Mercury from Stelloch (Maclagan 1876: 123), all Dumfries and Galloway, and another bronze statuette of Mercury from Mains of Throsk, Stirlingshire (Curle 1932: 385).

The structured votive deposition of selected objects constitutes elements of ideological practices (Roymans 1990; Hill 1995; Millett 1995; Weekes 2008) central to the construction and reinforcement of cultural identities. A deeper consideration of the small finds from sanctuaries in north eastern France has confirmed significant areas of continuity in centralised ritual activity from 200 BC to 100 AD (Wellington 2002). The material remains from some votive sites in northern Britain, including Bronze Age buckets and cauldrons from moss (Coles 1960: 88), Iron Age sites at Dowalton Loch (Hunter 1994) and the River Tay (Hunter 1996: 117), as well as Late Roman and 'Pictish' silver hoards such as at Norries' Law (Anderson 1884; Graham-Campbell 1991), demonstrate similar continuities. Meanwhile many others constitute single depositional episodes, such as examples of single *paterae* in peat as at Deskford near the findspot of a Carnyx (Hunter 1995: 29–30).

A total of sixty nine instances of Roman objects incorporated into recognised hoards or votive deposits have been identified across northern Britain. Only six of these contain Roman ceramics, while jewellery made from reused Roman glass is present in only four instances and no glass vessels are present. The remaining objects are predominantly metalwork, with twenty two instances of other material (Campbell 2011: 269–83). Where dates are discernable, second century objects predominate.

*Figure 19.2. Querns used in the construction of stone-built houses at Broxmouth (© W. Hanson, used with permission).*

The metalwork is dominated by bronze *paterae* and other vessels which occur in 30 contexts; bronze jewellery, mainly brooches, are present in 11; and other bronze objects, including statues or parts thereof, in a further 11. Although bronze brooches could constitute votive offerings, contextual data is absent for the vast majority which have, therefore, been excluded from this analysis. However, excavation is not necessarily the most effective means of recovering single votive objects. While 'stray finds' recovered through metal detecting could serve as indicators of previously unknown Roman military sites (Keppie 1990), they could equally have a significant role to play in the future discovery of single votive offerings (Johns 1996: 6).

Traditionally, attention has been firmly focussed upon metalwork in the context of votive deposition. However, this research suggests that this is an overly-simplistic and reductionist approach to the structured deposition of material. A more detailed study of depositional contexts has thrown up some intriguing patterns which could well be associated with votive or ritual deposition of specific non-metal objects, potentially at critical stages in the lifecycles of structures or people (Campbell 2011). For instance, the inclusion of rotary querns during the construction of buildings could have connections with the agricultural cycle (Hingley 1992: 32). The significance of querns is potentially best illustrated by the incorporation of eighty into stone-built houses at Broxmouth hillfort (Hill 1982a) in East Lothian (Fig. 19.2), Aitnock dun in North Ayrshire (Smith 1919) and Dalladies souterrain, Aberdeenshire (Watkins 1980: 157), which could signify people attempting actively to domesticate nature along the lines of Hodder's (1990) *domus* and *agrios* concept.

The incorporation of Roman objects into hoards containing other objects perceived as 'traditional' may have been accompanied by a votive prayer or oral story appropriating or 'taming' (Thomas 1992) the objects and, by implication, the invading army, into established cultural conditions. It is quite possible that certain people may have stood out as 'translators' and played an integral role in these transactions and they need not have been 'Romanised', as has been previously presumed.

## Conclusion

For Bourdieu (1977), identity and social practice are constructed by the repetition of actions performed within specific cultural settings from a young age, i.e. *habitus*. The concept of objectification, the non-verbal means by which people embody and manipulate material to create, idealise, negotiate, transform and reinforce social concepts (Tilley 2006), helps us to identify objectified objects which have become or are regarded as socially meaningful (Shankar 2006: 298). Having been culturally, physically and metaphysically reconstituted (Campbell 2012), Roman material culture reused in traditional activities, particularly ritualistic activities, may have come to be perceived by Iron Age recipients as culturally meaningful. These reconstituted Roman objects may then have enabled people to join ancestral memories with new experiences within the Roman world (Jiménez, 2008: 26), perhaps even manipulated to construct alternative foundation myths to form new hybrid identities. A certain amount of discourse may have been deliberate and silent forms of resistance (van Dommelen 2007) and some aspects of non-adoption could be interpreted as unconscious evasion (Hingley 2005: 70) to Roman influences. The selective adoption and votive deposition of foreign objects provide tantalising glimpses into practices that may have enabled the Iron Age occupants of northern Britain to negotiate changing socio-politico-economic conditions by altering culturally acquired behaviours which reinforce the distinctiveness of their traditional cultural or ethnic identities.

Current theoretical constructs have provided a helpful conceptual framework to explore the potential social and ritualistic significance ascribed to Roman material culture in non-Roman contexts. Objects absorb meanings through use and this research confirms that newly acquired foreign objects which were perceived as culturally relevant were being redefined and embedded into new cultural practices (Bourdieu 1977).

# 20. Personal Adornment in Iron Age Britain. The Case of the Missing Glass Beads

*Elizabeth Foulds*

**Keywords:** Iron Age, Britain, bodily adornment, identity, glass beads

## Introduction

Approaches to the study of bodily adornment in Iron Age Britain tend to be restricted in scope. They focus on studies of typology and distribution of artefacts (Fowler 1953; 1960; Boon & Dekówna 1966; Hattatt 1985; 1989; Hull & Hawkes 1987). In addition, emphasis is placed on metalwork, for example brooches and bracelets (Jope 2000), as well as items which are traditionally considered to be status indicators, such as the torc (Childe 1940: 222; MacGregor 1976: 93). Recent approaches to Iron Age artefacts have begun to break away from this approach and are beginning to interpret these objects as having much more than just passive presence in the past (Hutcheson 2004; Carr 2006; Garrow 2008; Giles 2008; Joy 2007). However, studies of identity in archaeology divide the subject into categories of analysis such as gender, status or ethnicity (Jones 1997; Díaz-Andreu *et al.* 2005). The danger of this approach is that aspects of identity are studied in isolation rather than taking a more holistic perspective. Although this usually is not the problem for Iron Age Britain because of the lack of burial evidence (Whimster 1981: 190), identity is often discussed in connection to issues of regionality, settlement, or methods for treatment of the dead (Armit 1997; 2007; Carr 2007; Giles 2007; Hunter 2007a).

This paper formulates a different approach, focusing specifically on glass beads in Iron Age Britain. Although it is recognised that a typological approach continues to be useful for discussing groups of similar objects, it is not the ultimate terminus for a research model. Instead, glass beads are considered as an object that can be used to actively portray or build identity within the social context. This paper accomplishes this by first exploring current approaches to understanding aspects of dress and objects of dress and the relation between dress and identity. It will also explore how glass beads have been approached in the past and the extent to which recent research can change our understanding of these objects. Finally, the question of how glass beads might have been utilised to construct identities through the use of colour and decorative motif will be investigated.

## FASHIONING IDENTITY

Recently, archaeology has seen a dramatic increase in research related to identity (Shennan 1994; Graves *et al.* 1996; Thomas 1996; Orser 2001; Wells 2001; Díaz-Andreu *et al.* 2005; Insoll 2007a). Some approaches explored specific categories of identity (Jones 1997; Hays-Gilpin & Whitley 1998; Sørensen 2000; Gardner 2007), while others investigate identity in terms of settlements and artefacts (Hutcheson 2004; Henderson 2007; Hunter 2007a). Thus, defining the term 'identity' when used as a research question becomes of utmost importance as the specific meaning or interpretation of the word, not to mention the method of research, can vary dramatically. Complicating matters, as Insoll points out, the definition of identity and words connected to this concept, such as gender and ethnicity, have changed over time (2007: 2). Díaz-Andreu and Lucy (2005: 1) have provided a cogent working definition for identity in archaeology: '[individual] identification with broader groups on the basis of differences socially sanctioned as significant'. Group identities are recognised as being constructed by individuals (Díaz-Andreu & Lucy 2005: 2) but can also be ascribed by others (Insoll 2007b: 4). This characterisation of identity will be used as the working definition for this paper.

In archaeology, the study of identity is often broken into elements, such as gender, ethnicity, age and religion (Jones 1997; Hays-Gilpin & Whitley 1998; Sørensen 2000; Orser 2001; Díaz-Andreu *et al.* 2005; Insoll 2007b). While it is recognised that identity itself is a fluid and dynamic process that is always changing and constructed of many complex layers (Díaz-Andreu & Lucy 2005: 2), approaches to the study of identity that categorise topics such as ethnicity and gender create static pictures of the past that often do not allow for the agency of the individual, or the group for that matter, to be considered as important aspects of everyday life in the past. This creates a dichotomy in the literature on identity. On the one hand the multiplicity of identity is often a part of its definition, while on the other it tends to be studied using types and categories.

Studies of past and current dress have followed similar approaches when considering the relationship between physical appearance and the identity of the wearer. As with studies of identity, these have tended to look at dress in terms of ethnicity (Eicher 1995), age (Roach-Higgins *et al.* 1995), and gender (Barnes & Eicher 1997). This often results in attempts to 'read' or 'de-code' the meaning of dress through a semiotic approach (Miller 2010: 12) referred to as 'reading dress'. In these studies, it is believed that simply viewing a person's dress reveals important information about their identity (Entwistle 2000: 119). However, we should recognise a common theme in Western thought that clothing is nothing more than a superficial mask covering the body and that the 'true' self is really found within (Entwistle 2000: 121; Miller 2010: 13), the process of reading dress as a form of analysis does not fit in with the way in which people perceive their own dress.

Recently there has been a reaction against simply reading dress and the categorisation of identity. Due to the fact that these studies tend to break these identity packages and aim to transform our understanding in different ways, it is difficult to describe without providing examples. Miller (2010: 13–23) has illustrated how dress is utilised differently. For example, he shows how dress embodies the identity of women in Trinidad and that their personality is actively portrayed through their choices. A different take on the post-semiotic approach to dress looks at the Indian sari. Miller (2010: 23–31) describes how the *pallau* becomes an extension of the physical body as it shades a sleeping child or protects the hands when moving hot cookware off a stove. Other studies have looked at contemporary modern Western culture, for example Woodward's (2005) study where the author shows how dress can fail to present identity if executed incorrectly in different social occasions and environments. What these studies create, through ethnographic research and by avoiding generalisation through identity categories, is a more fluid and realistic concept of how dress can be utilised to create and re-create identity, demonstrating how clothing is actively used to manipulate both a person's own feelings about their identity, as well as how others perceive them without resorting to categories.

One of the problems with the study of dress is applying these approaches to the archaeological record. All of the previously mentioned examples discuss recent historical and modern case studies, rather than prehistoric periods. These studies have the benefit of informants, not to mention a 'full assemblage' of objects to study. In contrast, archaeologists do not have informants who speak quite so readily and, in many cases, we are missing aspects of the material record due to both preservation and deposition factors. For those who study the British Iron Age, the artefacts we do have that relate to dress are those made of metal (brooches, torcs, bracelets/bangles/arm-rings/anklets, finger-rings), stone (beads, bangles and finger-rings), and glass (beads and bangles). In addition, in a British Iron Age context we can only speculate that garments were created from both hides and cloth as suggested by textile production artefacts and direct evidence from fragments and impressions (DeRoche 2012), and that piercing, or any other body modification occurred. There is of course, ample evidence for permanent or temporary tattooing as described by Carr (2005). Although sometimes connected with ideas about ritual, other artefacts suggest a concern for outward appearance, such as mirrors, razors, tweezers and cosmetic grinders. Most of these types of objects are found as early as the Later Bronze Age in Britain, such as at Potterne, Wiltshire (Gingell & Lawson 1985), but are also found especially, and sometimes in increased quantities, by the Later Iron Age (Hill 1997; Jundi & Hill 1997; Eckardt 2005; 2008; Eckardt & Crummy 2006; 2008).

Specifically in the case of glass beads, there are also considerable regional variances in glass bead deposition, but also in the methods used to discover them. For example, in south west England, many are found in settlement contexts, while in east Yorkshire they tend to be found in large numbers primarily in inhumations. In both of these regional examples, the glass beads have been found predominantly through excavation, through both old and new techniques. To contrast this, despite the large numbers of beads from north east Scotland, most are old stray finds. It is only from a limited number of recent excavations in this region that we have been able to confidently attribute Guido's Class 8 and 13 beads to Iron Age contexts. Of course, throughout Britain, differing antiquarian, amateur, and professional archaeologist's focus on different key interest areas, leaving some areas under-researched and possibly exaggerating regional differences. With these issues in mind, rather than seeing the shortcomings of the archaeological record as an impenetrable hurdle that prevents the ease of addressing topics such as gender and age, it would be more fruitful if different questions were asked and a methodology developed to suit the available data.

In order to do this, again it is worthwhile to consider the terminology in use. As Roach-Higgins and Eicher (1995: 9–10) point out, there are a number of different terms utilised to discuss non-biological changes or adaptations of the body, such as clothing, garments, and fashion. These terms risk ethnocentrism and exclusion of other modifications to the body. They propose that the term 'dress' should be used when discussing '[the] assemblage of modifications of the body and/or supplements to the body' (1995: 7). This term is preferred because it encompasses everything from tattoos and piercings to objects made from cloth or hide, as well as many other objects worn on the body.

At the risk of introducing value judgements into the discussion of dress, as cautioned against by Roach-Higgins and Eicher (1995: 9–10), this paper chooses to refer to the assemblage of evidence for dress that is archaeologically visible as 'bodily adornment'. Perhaps a more appropriate term would be 'objects for the body', as the term 'bodily adornment' suggests that such objects are worn to make the body more beautiful or attractive. However, this is problematic for archaeologists, as we do not know if these objects were used in this manner (cf. MacGregor 1976: 93). If we think of 'bodily adornment' less in terms of aesthetics and more in terms of a functional accoutrement then we can redefine the term for archaeological purposes. On its own, bodily adornment suggests that objects worn on the body were implemented in a passive way and are only used for their embellishment effect and serve no other purpose. However, Entwistle (2000: 138) stresses that dress is actively used to portray identity and Roach-Higgins and Eicher (1995: 9) emphasise that dress is a powerful visual and non-verbal form of communication. Thus, for this paper, it is important to consider bodily adornment (as only one part of the full dress assemblage) in terms of how objects actively participated within Iron Age society and influenced the actions of both the wearer and the viewer (Gosden 2005) in helping to create an identity or sense of place within society. The following sections will begin to explore how this can be achieved.

## Glass Beads in Iron Age Britain
### Past approaches
Past research on glass beads have centred on typological studies (Guido 1978) and scientific analysis by looking at chemical composition (for example: Henderson & Warren 1981; Henderson 1982; 1987; 1995). Although neither of these methods explicitly considered glass beads in conjunction with identity, it did form part of the basis of their approach. For example, Guido (1978) divided beads into

types based on their physical characteristics. However, the manner in which she grouped her types not only relates to the chronology of bead use, but to their original location of manufacture.

The typology was created with the aim of assigning date ranges to glass beads that could then in turn be used to date archaeological contexts. This is comparable to how brooches are used; however, whereas a development of brooch types over time can be demonstrated during the Iron Age (Haselgrove 1997), this does not seem to be the case for glass beads. The typology distinguished fourteen Iron Age classes and a number of Roman glass bead types, though this latter typology is not especially clear. In addition, she also encountered beads that presented a number of problems. These beads were placed into eight 'groups', including ones for both undecorated annular and globular glass beads.

While the typology distinguishes some major trends found within the physical traits of Iron Age beads, Guido only had a very vague understanding about glass working from Van der Sleen (1973). The typology may have taken a different shape if she had had a better understanding of glass working in general. In addition, although a typological approach is useful for making sense of object variation and distribution, it does imply certain assumptions about the manufacture of artefacts and the level of industry. For example, Guido (1978: 32–7) and Henderson (1989) often refer to manufacture locations based primarily on the density of glass bead finds in Britain. However, the archaeological evidence for glass bead manufacture in the Iron Age is very limited. In addition, when different types of bead are found in a given geographical area, it is generally assumed that the 'local types' are manufactured locally (for example Class 10) and that 'continental types' are the product of trade or migration (for example: Classes 1–7) (Guido 1978: 26). Although not explicit, this interpretation had implications for the perceived implicit identity inherent within each type, but also that glass beads in Britain generally did not move far from where they were manufactured or where they were imported.

Guido's approaches to glass beads produced a static understanding of objects within Iron Age and Roman period Britain. Many of the conclusions she made about glass beads can be reconsidered in light of current approaches to Iron Age Britain, especially in regards to the dates applied to each bead type. Instead, it is essential that we begin to build a new understanding based on recent research and new theoretical approaches. This demands that scholars begin to think of objects as active participants within the community of which they were a part (Gosden 2005). For instance, the chronological and cultural distinctions between the types of beads used in the Iron Age and into the post-Roman conquest period as suggested by Guido presents an interesting question for us to consider in light of recent theoretical developments. How were glass beads connected to identity? This question will be explored in the following sections.

## Towards a new understanding
Although we might criticise Guido's theoretical background and conclusions,

she nonetheless provided future researchers with a substantial amount of data with which to continue and develop the study of prehistoric glass beads. For example, her catalogue provides a near complete account of glass beads discovered in Britain up to about 1975. However, this catalogue is now more than 30 years old and, and there have been a substantial number of recent significant finds that have the potential to drastically alter our understanding.

This paper stems from a larger research project aimed at evaluating not only the evidence for dating and classifying glass beads but also looking at how they were utilised within the Iron Age period. It also explores physical attributes of the beads and how they might relate to concepts of identity. The data-set used has been obtained through a rigorous and systematic review of published excavation reports and incorporates data from unpublished excavations funded by commercial bodies and carried out by contract archaeology units collated from Historic Environment Records. Obtaining data from both research and commercially funded excavations has created a rich dataset that explores a wide range of sites and locations. In addition to this literature review, a number of museum visits were undertaken in order to view artefacts and take measurements and photographs for later comparison. This has proven extremely useful as excavation reports are often vague and tend to be unsystematic. Finally, as the increasingly effective role of the Portable Antiquities Scheme (PAS) in broadening our understanding of Iron Age objects is becoming apparent (Worrell 2007), it was necessary to consult the online database in order to include a growing number of recorded possible prehistoric and Roman period glass beads.

The data obtained were organised through the use of a relational database. It has two main tables that are related, one for information about the site, and another for information about individual glass beads. This allows the user to create a query of both the sites and objects with a specific question in mind, for example: by context and site type. One of the benefits of using a relational database to organise the data, is that it is now possible to evaluate beads by individual characteristics such as by size, shape and decorative motif. This makes assessing specific attributes such as colour or even the combination of colour and decorative motif possible. But again, as with typology, the ultimate aim here is not to create a typology or elaborate searchable catalogue, but to enable specific questions to be asked of the archaeology. In the context of this paper, these questions relate to the use of colour and decorative motif and how they were used to create identities.

## Creating an Identity

Understanding identity through a post-semiotic approach to glass beads thus becomes a novel method for understanding Iron Age society in Britain. Here this will be accomplished by comparing glass beads from two regions: south west Britain (mainly the modern counties of Gloucestershire, Somerset, Dorset and Wiltshire) and north east Scotland (mainly Aberdeenshire, Morayshire, and the eastern part of the Highlands). These areas were chosen for investigation due to

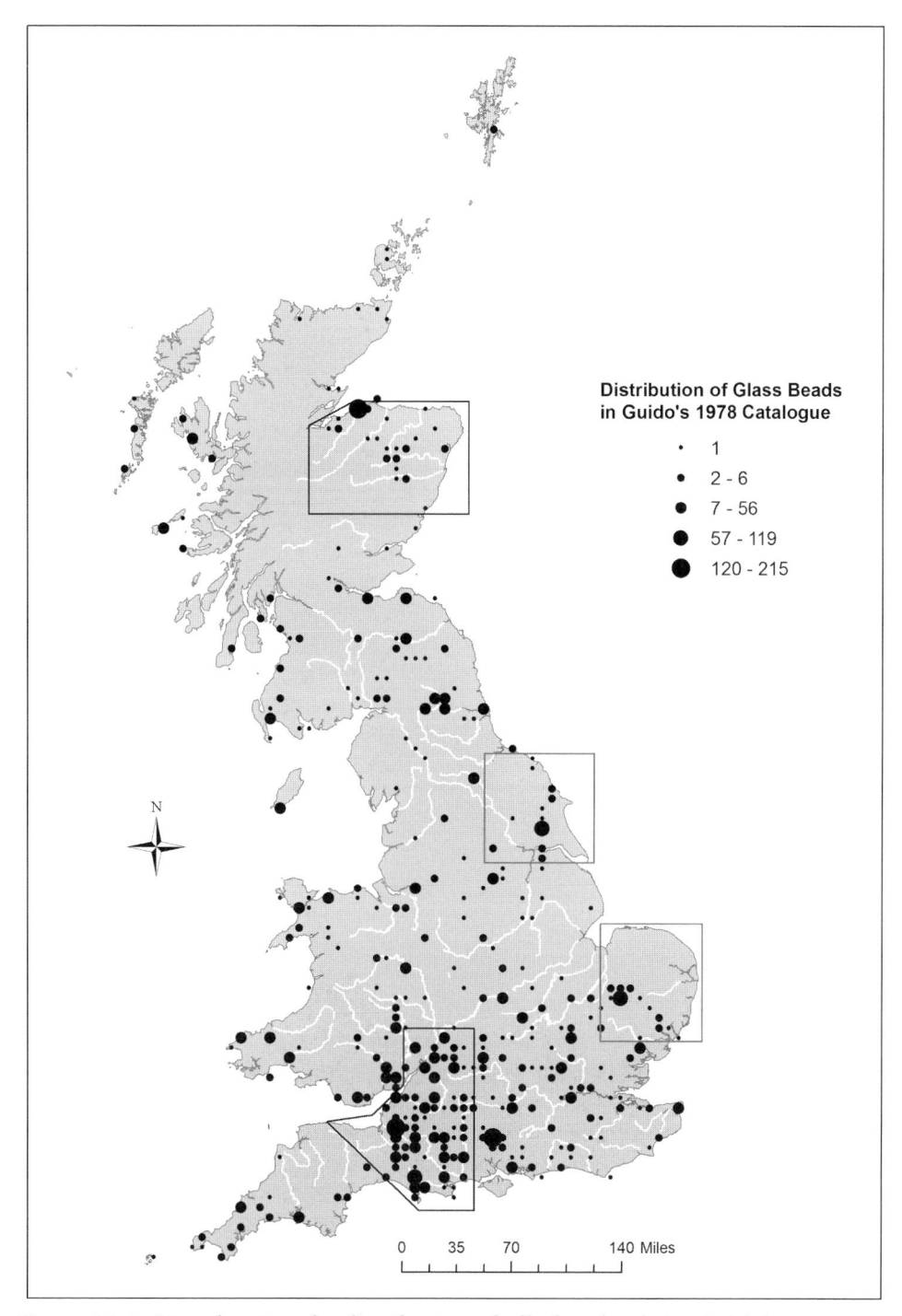

*Figure 20.1: Map showing the distribution of all glass beads in Guido's 1978 catalogue. © Crown copyright 2012. Contains Ordnance Survey data, an Ordnance Survey/EDINA supplied service.*

| Class | Description | Colours | Decorative Motif |
|---|---|---|---|
| Class 1 | Subdivided into two subtypes, but both are annular or cylindrical with 9 or 12 'eyes' | Translucent blue, opaque white | Simple eyes formed from two layers of glass |
| Class 2 | Large globular beads with 'eyes' | Translucent blue, opaque white | Complex eyes made from four layers of glass |
| Class 3 | Large annular bead with 3 eyes | Usually dark translucent blue and opaque white although some have an additional colour | Simple eyes formed from two layers of glass |
| Class 4 | Annular bead with 'eyes' that are placed in pairs around the bead | Opaque yellow, blue and white | Complex eyes made from four layers of glass |
| Class 5 | Large annular colourless beads with opaque yellow along the inside of the perforation and sometimes visible around the perforation | Colourless glass, opaque yellow | The colourless glass creates an effect that makes the bead glow |
| Class 6 | Large annular beads with small spirals, sometimes placed on protrusions, some variations noted | Translucent blue, opaque white | Spirals, sometimes placed on protrusions |
| Class 7 | Large annular beads, each is unique, subdivision based on colour | Variable | Rays or whirls, sometimes with circumferential lines |
| Class 8 | Small annular plain beads without decoration | Opaque yellow | None |
| Class 9 | Large annular beads with two-tone twisted cable meandering across the bead, subdivision based on colour | Variable | Meandering cable |
| Class 10 | Generally globular bead with three spirals that cover the surface | Colourless, opaque yellow | Spirals |
| Class 11 | Variations of Class 10 beads, subdivision based on motifs | Colourless, opaque yellow | Variable: chevrons, criss-cross, circumferential line, wave |
| Class 12 | 'Stud bead' because of its odd shape. Only two examples. | One is opaque yellow the other is colourless with opaque yellow | One has zigzags |
| Class 13 | Variable, often triangular with spirals placed on each protrusion | Variable, but almost all have an opaque yellow spiral | Spiral |
| Class 14 | Large annular beads, each is unique | Variable, but most incorporate opaque yellow | Variable but some are whirled and some have a two-tone cable |

*Table 20.1. Descriptions of each of Guido's classes (after Guido 1978).*

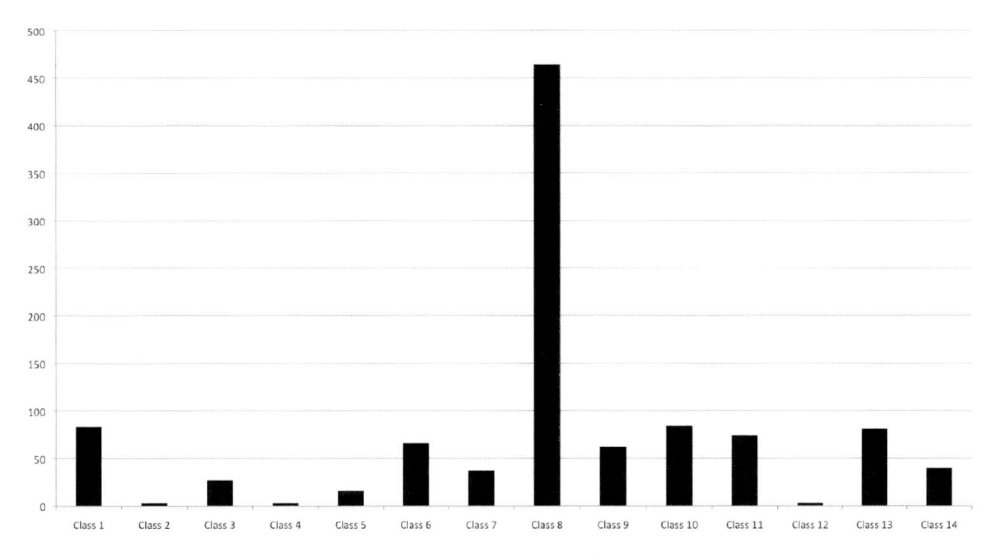

*Figure 20.2: Graph showing the frequency of each of Guido's classes.*

the large number of glass beads recorded in Guido's catalogue (Fig. 20.1). In addition, sites within both of these regions have been suggested to be areas of possible bead manufacture due to the large numbers of finds when compared to the rest of the country. Sites that display possible evidence for glass working include Culbin Sands, Morayshire, and Meare Lake Village in Somerset. However, direct evidence for bead production at both sites is unclear and such activity is debatable (cf. Henderson 1989). A review of recent archaeological evidence also suggests that bead production may have occurred at Culduthel Farm near Inverness in Scotland (Murray 2007: 26).

Before proceeding to the results, it should be noted here that Guido considered beads from these two regions to be dated to very different periods. Iron Age beads in the south west were generally considered to date prior to the Roman invasions and these beads were heavily reliant on the dating of Meare Lake Village and Glastonbury Lake Village. In north east Scotland, on the other hand, the majority of the region's characteristic beads (Classes 8, 13 and 14) were thought to have been made locally from recycled Roman glass within the first few centuries AD (Guido 1978: 34–5). However there is very little in the way of archaeological or contextual evidence to support this idea (Hunter 2007b: 37). Putting the issues of dating aside for the moment, this section will compare the use of colour and decorative motifs within these regions.

For the purposes of this paper, the following analysis will continue to use the typology set out by Guido and will be limited to her Classes 1–14 (Table 20.1). Ongoing research is working to re-evaluate the typology and the dates associated with each type. However, as Guido's typology is already established, for now it will provide a framework of analysis. Guido's catalogue has approximately 1281 entries, which represent approximately 2634 individual Iron Age and Roman period beads. Of these 790 were included in 14 classes, which can be reasonably assumed to date to the Iron Age. It should be pointed out that the majority of these beads belong to Guido's Class 8 (small opaque yellow annular beads (Fig. 20.2)). These beads have been found in large quantities in both Somerset and north east Scotland. They are also the only class of bead that uses only one colour. Other classes, such as Class 2 and 12, are made up of less than five examples each, so placing them within the Iron Age is problematic. However, most of the other classes are made up of between 50 and 100+ examples, although the definitions of each of these classes will be the subject of later debate.

## Colour

Unlike other objects of adornment in the Iron Age, glass beads are produced using bright colours. Most natural glass will be a pale translucent green due to iron oxide found naturally in the silica source (Henderson 2000: 27). Any other colour of glass is usually the result of manipulating the glass while in a molten state through the addition of oxides. These additions and a control of the level of oxygen and other factors will change the colour and opacity (Henderson 2000: 29–30). While some glass beads are made up of single colours, decorated beads will usually have a primary colour from which the main bead is formed and a secondary colour that is used in the motif.

The study presented here uses basic colour descriptors as the method for describing colour. Munsell charts were deemed impractical for describing colour in this case and their use has been criticised as being inappropriate for understanding the meaning of colour in the past (Saunders & Van Brakel 1988; Sivik 1997; Chapman 2002). By making a frequency chart of the occurrences of colour within glass bead classes, one immediately notices that yellow occurs much more frequently than any other colour (Fig. 20.3a). This is due to the large quantities of Class 8 beads. However, even if we remove these beads from the analysis (Fig. 20.3b) we see that opaque yellow still features to a high degree within the beads studied. Other colours, such as blue, white and colourless also play a large role, while green, brown or orange, black, purple and red are used much more rarely. However, each of these colours is used differently. Some colours are often used for the main body of the bead, while others are for decorative motifs. In some instances some colours are also used for both of these elements.

Through the use of the database, it is possible to look at how colour was used on each bead; either for the body or decorative motif. By excluding the Class 8 beads, we can see differences in how colour has been applied by comparing the study regions (Fig. 20.3c–d). For example, in south west England, colourless glass is used extensively for the body of beads, while blue, green, brown/orange, purple and red are used minimally. Decorative elements of the beads are often created through the use of yellow, but blue and white glasses also occur frequently. In contrast, the body colour of the north east Scotland beads are made up almost equally of blue, colourless, black, green and orange/brown glass, although yellow is used primarily for decorative elements.

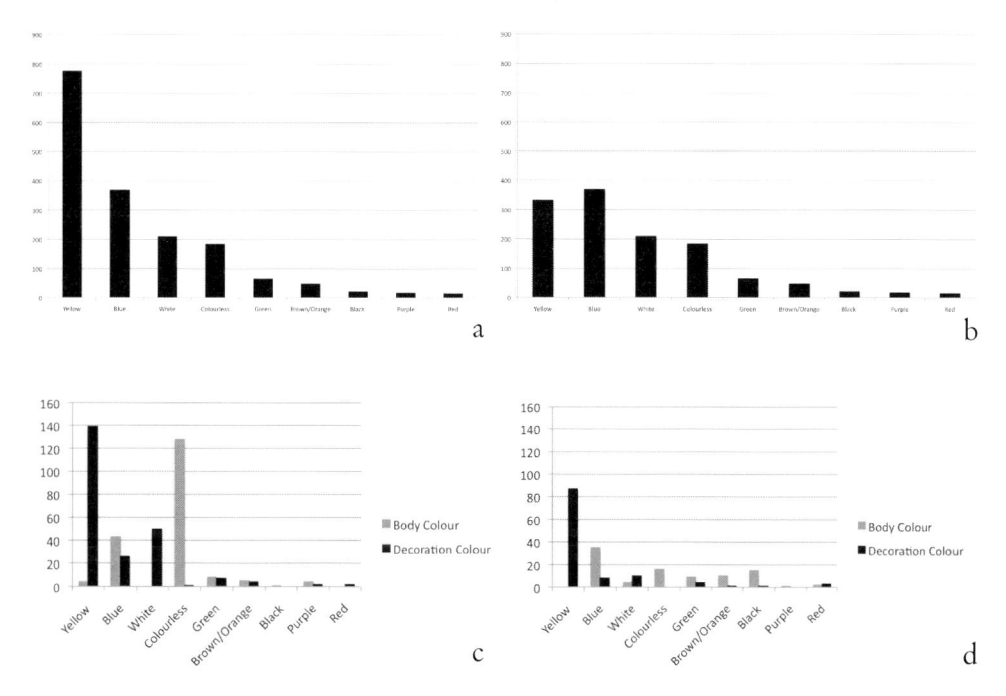

*Figure 20.3: Graph showing (a) the frequency of each colour in Guido's classes, (b) the frequency of each colour in Guido's classes excluding Class 8 opaque yellow annular beads, (c) a comparison for the use of colour in south west England, and (d) a comparison for the use of colour in north east Scotland.*

## Decorative Motif

For this paper 'decorative motif' is used to refer to those designs that are created through the application of different colours of glass to the body of the bead. Whilst other physical aspects of glass beads such as shape contribute to the overall effect of the bead, this has been excluded from the present study and will be presented in future publications. Motifs found on Iron Age glass beads can be broadly categorised into three main groups: dots, trailed designs, and wrapped designs. Dots are formed when molten glass is simply dabbed onto the bead. If left, it will form a bump on the surface, but if re-heated, the bump will melt and become flush with the surface of the bead. Many of the 'eyes' found on Classes 1 through 4 were probably made in this way, except here, layered of dots are created and then melted into the surface. Some are more complex than others, such as Class 2 beads, where eyes are made from four layers of glass. Trailed designs are created by taking 'stringer', a very fine filament of glass, and laying it on the surface of the bead while rotating the mandrel in order to produce the design. It allows the production of circumferential lines, waves, criss-crosses, lattices, and possibly the trailed cable designs seen on Class 9 beads. It may also be the method used to create the spirals on Class 6, 10, and 13 beads. The evidence of seams on wrapped beads suggests that these were possibly created by producing very large rods of coloured glass and wrapping them around a mandrel (pers. comm.

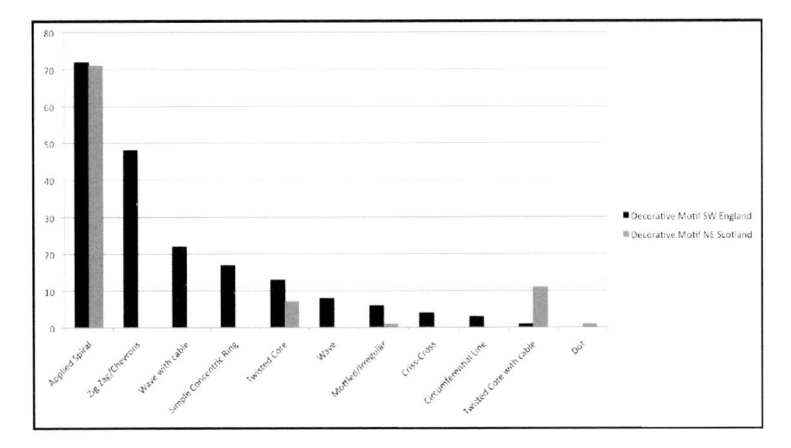

*Figure 20.4: Graph showing the frequency of decorative motif for south west England and north east Scotland.*

Nina Bertini). In addition, in several cases the rod appears to have been twisted prior to wrapping it around the mandrel, creating a wrapped whirl motif. This might be how some beads from both Class 7 and 14 were created.

A comparison of the motifs used in south west England and north east Scotland indicates some similarities between regions, but also highlights some notable differences (Fig. 20.4). The use of the applied spiral motif in both regions is immediately apparent, as Class 10 spiral beads are found almost exclusively in the south west, while Class 13 spiral beads are found predominately in the north east (Fig. 20.5). Guido (1978: 85–86) had suggested that the Class 13 beads found primarily in Scotland were inferior copies of the colourless Class 10 beads found especially in Somerset. What is interesting, however, is that three of Guido's classes of beads utilise a spiral motif: Class 6, Class 10 and Class 13 and the significance of this will be discussed in the following section.

## Discussion
### Colour

Unfortunately, the study of colour in archaeology is a relatively new discipline and is only just beginning to come to the fore of archaeological research (e.g. Jones & MacGregor 2002a). Part of this delay may stem from the Western concept that colour, as seen with clothing or fashion, is considered to be superficial when compared with other characteristics pertaining to object studies (Young 2006: 174). However, as Jones and MacGregor outline, one of the aims of 'an archaeology of colour' is '[to] move beyond...the abstract nature of colour perception and symbolism...' (Jones & MacGregor 2002b: 3). Therefore the application of colour studies to both dress and identity would allow new methodologies to be developed that explore this relationship in greater detail.

But how does colour relate to identity? Of course, the choice of colour may relate to technology and the difficulty or ease of making glass beads and the level

20. *Personal Adornment in Iron Age Britain* 235

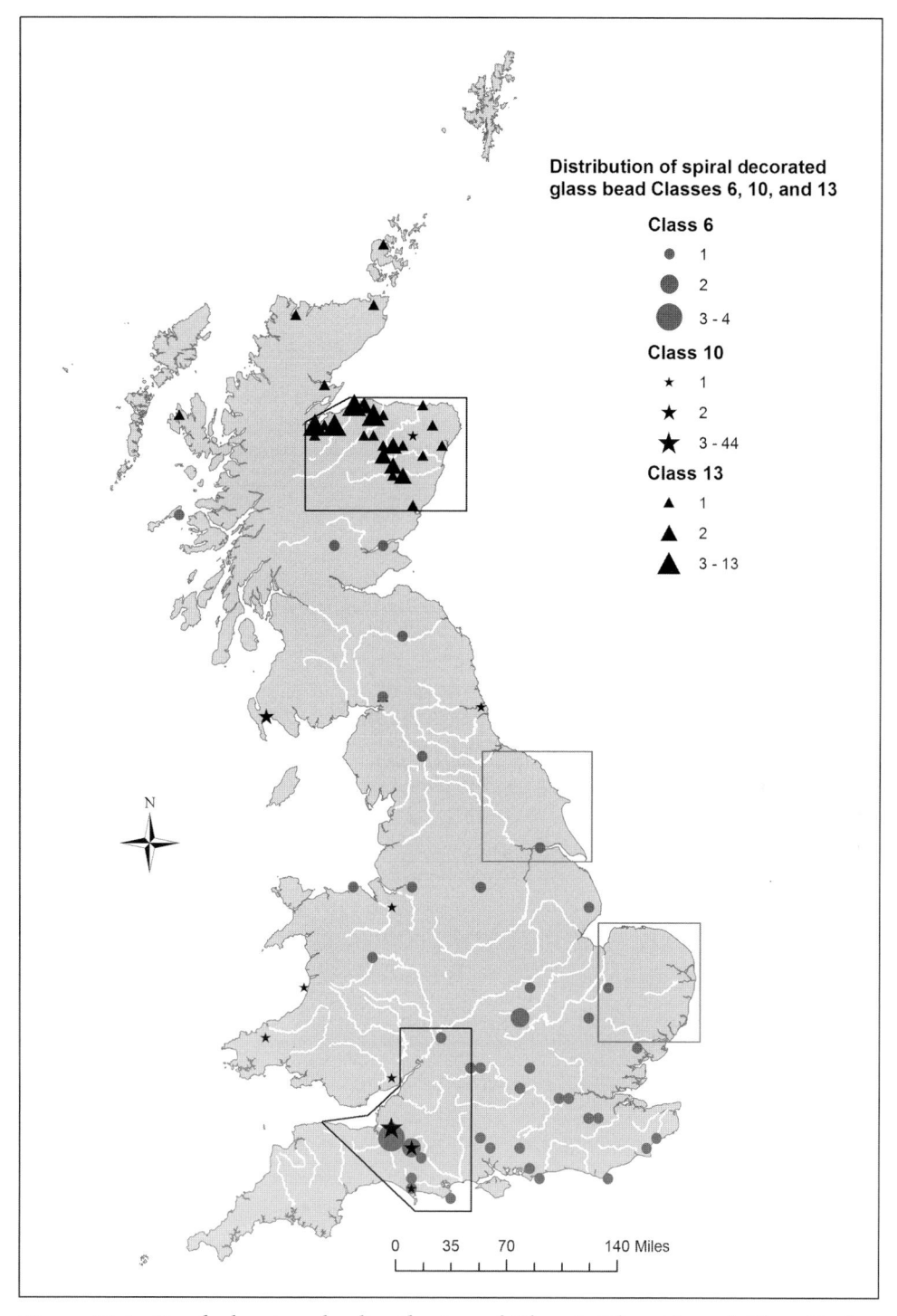

*Figure 20.5: Graph showing the distribution of Class 6, Class 10, and Class 13 glass beads.*

of their complexity. Yet, there does seem to be an emphasis on the use of yellow and, to a lesser extent, blue and white. It would be easy to draw a parallel between the yellow of the beads and metallic colour of gold and suggest that perhaps one represents the other, but this proposes a clear symbolic relationship between two materials with different finishes or textures. However, the bead colour data and preliminary discussions on the use of colour on metalwork (Davis & Gwilt 2008; Giles 2008) highlights the need for a wider systematic study on the materiality of colour in the Iron Age.

It seems significant that yellow plays a major role in decorating glass beads in both study regions. These are also two regions where Class 8 opaque yellow annular beads are found in large quantities. However, yellow is used on a number of very different styles of beads. In south west England, it is always found on Class 10 and 11 beads, where the main body of the bead is formed out of colourless glass and the decoration is created using opaque yellow. This creates a very lightly coloured bead. In contrast, most beads in north east Scotland with yellow are either Class 13 spiral beads or Class 14 decorated annular beads. Both of these types are very dark, but in both regions the opaque yellow provides a striking contrast to the background colour. This suggests that it is possibly either the colour of the decoration, or the decorative motif, that was really important during manufacture, rather than the base colour of the bead. In fact, one example from Class 14 (FJ 17 at the National Museum of Scotland) is different because the opaque yellow seems to have been applied after the creation of the bead, whereas most examples appear to have been created during one manufacture event. Again, this suggests that the application of opaque yellow was important and perhaps especially so to the person who would wear the bead.

**Decorative motif**
The distribution of beads with spiral motifs throughout Britain suggests that Classes 6, 10, and 13 were used in three regions. Class 10 is found mainly in Somerset, but a few isolated finds have been found along the western coast of England and some examples found in Scotland. Class 6 beads are usually found in southern central Britain, again with a few examples in Scotland. While Class 13 beads are concentrated in north east Scotland, with some examples found just to the north and one just on the border of England and Scotland. While Class 6 beads have been suggested as imports (Guido 1978: 53–7), Class 10 and 13 beads were potentially produced in Britain due to their high concentrations (Guido 1978: 79–81, 85–7). It may be that the distribution of beads represents real patterns of glass bead use and, thus, a potential source of regional identity (especially in the case of Class 10 and 13). But why are Class 6 beads so widely distributed when others are found in very tight groups? We could follow the traditional argument that suggests Class 6 beads were imports and Class 10 and 13 beads were locally made, but clearly some beads could be moved long distances while others did not. This suggests that although the beads exhibited similar motifs, it may be that they were utilised differently in order to convey identities.

However, other than the spiral motif, each region uses very different decorative motifs. In the south west, there are a greater variety of motifs: zig-zags or chevrons, cable waves, concentric rings ('eyes'), criss-cross, and so forth. In north east Scotland, motifs are much more restricted. In addition to the spiral motif, one also sees twisted core beads and the more complex twisted core bead with cable. Other motifs are rarely ever seen in this region. Traditional explanations for this may refer to Scotland as more insular in the Iron Age, suggesting this region saw less interaction with continental Europe and the Romans (Piggott 1966: 2). However, this perspective is demonstrably false in light of recent research on the interactions between the inhabitants of Iron Age Scotland and the Romans (Hunter 2001; 2007a; 2007c; Ingemark 2003). Other explanations are entirely possible when one takes ideas concerning dress and identity into consideration. For instance, it is possible that there were other ways to express identity in north east Scotland, considering that this is a region with a distinct 'massive metalwork' tradition (MacGregor 1976). This assemblage of artefacts is populated by very large armlets and some finger-rings. If glass beads were also being manufactured in north east Scotland, it is unlikely that technological difficulties impeded the choice of design, as most examples of Class 13 and 14 beads are very complex. Therefore, it is possible that people were selecting motifs with specific motives in mind. What is clear is that, by studying Guido's classes according to decorative motif, we see similar designs occurring over large areas. This suggests that it may not have been the motif itself that relates to identity, but the execution of the motif in different combinations of colours, the overall form of the bead, and the way in which the beads themselves were utilised in Iron Age Britain.

## Conclusion

Although the present study is ongoing, this paper has demonstrated how the study of artefacts related to dress can be approached in order to understand myriad identities in Iron Age Britain. Whilst this method could be utilised with any artefact of dress, this paper was specifically interested in glass beads as a way to highlight the diverse materiality of Iron Age Britain. Even though studies of dress are typically applied to modern or recent historical examples, it nonetheless provides an essential framework for the application of understanding dress and identity in prehistory. This, however, runs the risk of narrow interpretations of identity through the use of categories, but this paper has demonstrated that these approaches are beginning to change.

By looking specifically at the use of colour and decorative motif on glass beads, this paper was interested in exploring how identity may have been constructed within two study regions in Britain. It has demonstrated that the colour yellow and spiral motif may have played a central role in the creation of identity in both areas. However, as in the case of spirals, this motif was employed in differing manners suggesting that it was not just the motif itself that was important, but the way in which it was used on the bead. We can speculate that this can be extended to differences in how spirals beads were used on the body and the identity it communicated. Thus this paper demonstrates that by approaching glass beads from the perspective of dress and identity, it becomes possible to conceive of objects of bodily adornment as active participants within Iron Age society in Britain. However, glass beads need not be worn in isolation of other artefacts, and rather that there was a full-assemblage of objects that were utilised at any one time, but this will be a topic of later papers.

### Acknowledgements

Thanks to my supervisors Dr Tom Moore and Prof Richard Hingley for their guidance. Thanks also to Freddie Foulds, Jo Zalea Matias, and Sarah Schech for looking over my drafts. I am very grateful to the Rosemary Cramp Fund, the Prehistoric Society and the Association for the History of Glass for their financial support which allowed visits to the Historic Environment Record offices and museums. I must also thank the following Historic Environment Record offices: Somerset, Gloucestershire, Bristol City, Norfolk, Suffolk, North Yorkshire Moor National Park, York, North Yorkshire and Humber; and the following museums: the British Museum, Norwich Castle Museum, Stroud Museum, Gloucester Museum, Cirencester Museum, Bristol City Museum and Art Gallery, Museum of Somerset, Dorchester Museum, Gillingham Museum, Red House Museum, Wiltshire Heritage Museum, National Museum of Scotland, Yorkshire Museum, Hull and East Riding Museum, Marischall Museum, Inverness Museum and Art Gallery, Hunterian Museum, Elgin Museum and the Falconer Museum.

*Perspectives from the South West*

# 21. Spoiling for a Fight: Using Spear Typologies to Identify Aspects of Warrior Identity and Fighting Style in Iron Age South Italy

*Yvonne Inall*

**Keywords:** typology, warfare, warrior identity, south Italy, Mediterranean

## Introduction

The communication of elite male 'warrior' identities was of clear importance to the Oscan speaking peoples of Iron Age south Italy. During the period from the late ninth century BC to the late fourth century BC, ostensibly from the end of the Bronze Age to the Roman conquest of south Italy, the tombs of elite, adult males frequently included items associated with perceived warrior status, thereby demonstrating the martial prowess of the deceased. Weapons were often included in elite, adult male tombs (and very occasionally in the tombs of women and children). Spears were the most frequently represented class of weapon and in most cases the only class of weapon amongst the grave goods. Along with weapons, the wealthiest tombs included armour and horse equipment. In addition to these personal markers of warrior identity fifth and fourth century BC tombs further enhanced this construct through the inclusion of ceramics depicting a range of martial scenes. At the Lucanian city of Paestum, frescoed tombs portray victorious warriors returning from campaigns and engaging in what appear to be martial contests, in which spears feature prominently (Cipriani and Longo 1996; Pontrandolfo Greco 2004).

The funerary and votive contexts from which spearheads were recovered were clearly ritualised, expressing complex social statements about status and identity, not only at an individual level, but also conveying broader familial, community and ethnic levels of identity construction. Yet the interpretation of spears tends to be restricted to a one-dimensional symbol of social status (e.g. Bianco Peroni 1970; Bottini 1982), with little consideration of variations in the form, function and distribution of this class of weapon, aspects which remain poorly understood (Stary 1981; Small 2000). Most spearheads appear to have been functional objects, presenting an opportunity to look beyond ritual articulations to their function as tools created for the practices of warfare and hunting and to explore how they may have impacted on the construction of warrior identities in Iron Age south Italy.

Throughout this paper the term 'spearhead' is used as a general term to indicate weapon points of any long-arm form (excluding counterpoints such as the

*Figure 21.1. Map of south Italy showing sites assessed in this study.*

*sauroter*). The use of the term 'javelin' is avoided due to its quite specific functional connotations.

BACKGROUND

The spear is the most commonly depicted weapon in the pictorial evidence, and funerary assemblages from this region have yielded significantly greater numbers of spearheads than any other class of weapon: of the 475 tombs assessed for this

## 21. Spoiling for a Fight

| Type | Description | Sites Represented | |
|---|---|---|---|
| 1 Fig. 3.1 | Mould-cast bronze spearheads with broad, leaf shaped blade profile, lenticular blade section, circular/ovoid socket section with prominent midrib. | Daunia | Lavello; Ordona |
| | | Basilicata/Lucania | Incoronata |
| | | Campania | Pontecagnano; Sala Consilina |
| 2 Fig. 3.2 | Mould-cast bronze spearheads with narrow blade profile, lenticular blade section, circular/ovoid socket section with prominent midrib. | Daunia | Ordona: 1 |
| | | Basilicata/Lucania | Incoronata |
| | | Campania | Pontecagano; Sala Consilina |
| 3 Fig. 3.3 | Mould-cast bronze spearheads with a broad, leaf shaped blade profile, polygonal socket section, and polygonal midrib. | Daunia | None |
| | | Basilicata/Lucania | Incoronata |
| | | Campania | Pontecagnano; Sala Consilina |
| 4 Fig. 3.4 | Mould-cast bronze spearheads with a narrow blade profile, polygonal socket section and polygonal midrib. | Daunia | None |
| | | Basilicata/Lucania | None |
| | | Campania | Pontecagnano; Sala Consilina |
| 5 Fig. 3.5 | Broad-bladed iron spearhead, with lenticular blade sections, conical socket and no discernible midrib. | Daunia | Arpi; Lavello |
| | | Basilicata/Lucania | Oppido Lucano; Vaglio; Chiaromonte |
| | | Campania | Pontecagnano; Sala Consilina; Paestum |
| 6 Fig. 3.6 | Narrow-bladed iron spearhead, with lenticular blade sections, conical socket and no discernible midrib. | Daunia | Minervino Murge; Ordona; Lavello |
| | | Basilicata/Lucania | Oppido Lucano; Vaglio; Satrianum; Incoronata; Chiaromonte |
| | | Campania | Pontecagnano; Sala Consilina |
| 7 Fig. 3.7 | Broad-bladed iron spearhead with a prominent midrib rhomboidal, circular/conical socket half the length of the blade or less. | Daunia | Ordona; Ascoli Satriano; Lavello |
| | | Basilicata/Lucania | Vaglio; Satrianum; Incoronata |
| | | Campania | Pontecagnano; Sala Consilina |
| 8 Fig. 3.8 | Narrow-blade iron spearheads with rhomboidal blade section and distinct midrib | Daunia | Minervino Murge; Arpi; Lavello; Canosa |
| | | Basilicata/Lucania | Oppido Lucano; Vaglio; Satrianum; Incoronata; Chiaromonte |
| | | Campania | Pontecagnano; Sala Consilina; Paestum |
| 9 Fig. 3.9 and Fig. 4 | Iron spearheads distinguished by their very long sockets and small or non-existent blades. Best suited to being thrown and appear designed for this purpose. Sub-types are identified on the basis of blade profile, or in the absence of a blade, the section of the socket. The sub-types 9.1, 9.2, 9.3 and 9.4 all feature small, narrow blades with sockets which exceed the length of the blade. Sub-types 9.5 and 9.6 feature no apparent blade. Type 9.5 features a square section, while Type 9.6 has a round section. | Daunia | Minervino Murge; Ordona; Arpi; Ascoli Satriano; Lavello; Canosa |
| | | Basilicata/Lucania | Oppido Lucano; Vaglio; Satrianum |
| | | Campania | Pontecagnano; Sala Consilina; Paestum |
| 10 Fig. 3.10 | Short, broad-bladed spearheads which are small in their overall dimensions. Sub-types are identified on the basis of the presence or absence of a midrib. | Daunia | Ordona; Lavello; Canosa |
| | | Basilicata/Lucania | Incoronata |
| | | Campania | None |

*Table 21.1. Provenances of spear types. See Figure 21.3*

paper 443 (93 per cent) included at least one spearhead, while only 70 (15 per cent) included one or more swords. Thus, the spear was ostensibly the principal weapon used by the elite warriors of south Italy during the Iron Age and an essential item in the construction of 'warrior' identities. Unfortunately, spears are an understudied class of artefact and as a consequence their forms and associated martial functions are poorly understood. While a number of spearhead typologies have been published over the past century (Kilian 1970; Bottini 1988; d'Agostino & Gastaldi 1988; Russo Tagliente & Berlingò 1992; Chiartano 1994; Ruby 1995; Small 2000), these have generally been incomplete and do not focus on spear *function*. Typologies are site-specific, created to present an overview of multiple artefacts in the limited space of excavation reports, and rarely draw in material from other sites. No single typology has emerged as authoritative, and approaches to the material have varied enormously, with very little overlap in the criteria that each excavator considered type-determinant. Consequently, it is not possible to apply any existing typology to multiple sites. This paper presents a new typology of Iron Age spearheads, which forms a solid basis to map changes in technology and fighting styles, and by extension individual identity, throughout south Italy. It is anticipated that a typological approach to this element of the material culture inventory will facilitate a clearer understanding of how spears were used, not only in combat, but in communicating regional and ethnic warrior identities, and allow us to identify how the conception of these identities may have changed over time.

## A NEW TYPOLOGY

This new typology, presented in Figure 21.3 and Table 21.1 addresses some of the problems of past typologies by assessing a significantly larger sample than any previous spear typology drawing on more than 550 published spearheads from 475 tombs dated between the late ninth century and the end of the fourth century BC. The typology integrates material from 17 sites throughout the south Italian regions of Daunia, Basilicata and Campania (Fig. 21.1) overcoming issues associated with previous, site-specific typologies. The typology focuses on the relationship between form and function, facilitating the recognition of several distinct patterns in the distribution of specific spearhead forms.

The distribution and temporal span of the dataset, i.e. cutting across the regions of Daunia, Basilicata and Campania over about four centuries, encompasses important events between the late ninth century BC and the end of the fourth century BC: firstly, the technological transition from bronze to iron for the manufacture of weaponry in south Italy (Hartmann 1982; Chiartano 1994; Giardino 1998); secondly, cultural shifts, including the establishment of the settlements of Sala Consilina and Pontecagnano, the advent of Greek colonisation (between the eighth and fifth centuries BC) and the 'Lucanianisation' of parts of Basilicata and southern Campania in the fifth and fourth centuries BC (Pontrandolfo Greco 1982; Isayev, 2007). The fifth and fourth centuries were also times of recorded conflict between Greek colonies, colonists and indigenous peoples and between indigenous groups (Diodorus Siculus, Library, 11.52; Herodotos, Histories, 7.170; Pausanius. X 10.6; Frederiksen 1984). The typology illuminates the exchanges between the indigenous populations of south Italy and central Italian and Greek colonists to the region through the spear assemblage. The analysis allows us to explore questions

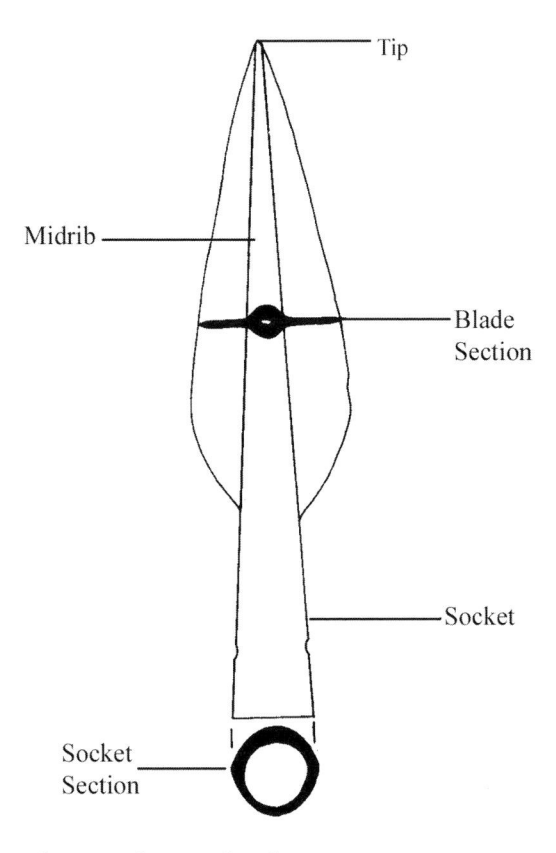

*Figure 21.2. Functional traits of a spearhead.*

about manufacture as well as the fighting styles that were employed and how these may have changed over time.

## Type determinate traits

Figure 21.2 shows the individual parts of a spearhead – identifying the fundamental traits whose variation would impact on function.

**Blade Profile and Section:** whether a blade is broad or narrow and the presence or absence of a midrib, would impact on the weight, strength, durability and aerodynamics of a spearhead, indicating differential function. Broad blades are better suited to the delivery of thrusting blows, while narrow blades, particularly without strengthening midribs indicate versatility, facilitating throwing actions.

**Socket Length:** A group of spearheads featured very long sockets, greater in length than the blade itself. This trait impacted significantly on blade durability, a longer socket both facilitating the transfer of impact stress along the socket to the haft and stabilising flight when thrown (Snodgrass 1964: 137–8). Long sockets, in conjunction with small, narrow blades are indicative of spearheads designed to be thrown.

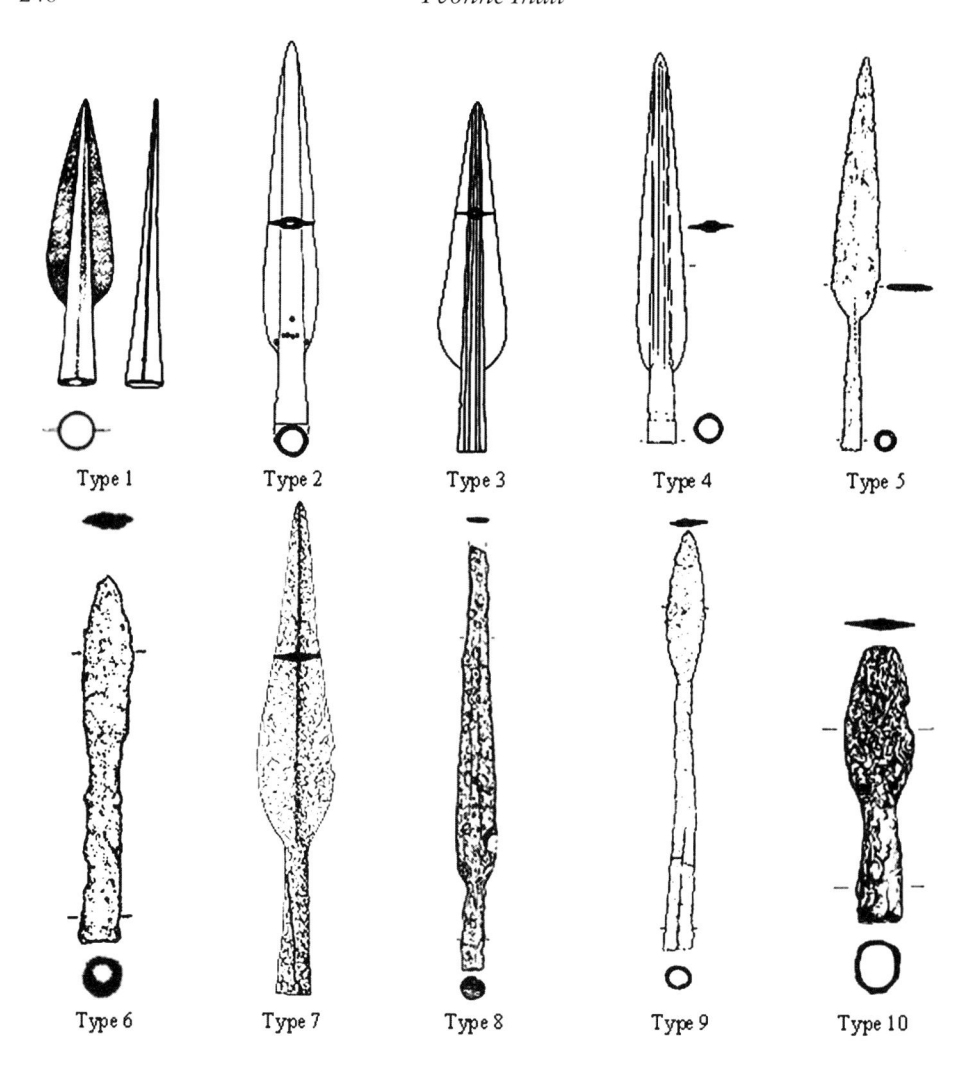

*Figure 21.3. The Basic Spear Type Groups, types 1–4 bronze; types 5–10 iron (not to scale).*

**Material of Manufacture:** Iron points had to be individually forged, in contrast to bronze's facility for casting (Hartman 1985: 96). The greater density of bronze meant an iron point of equivalent size would be significantly lighter than its bronze counterpart (Giardino 1998: 17 and 201–06). The lighter metal would have affected weight distribution and may have led to changes in form. The typology incorporates spearheads of both bronze and iron.

### Secondary traits
**Length:** While length is likely to have impacted on both form and function, data on length have not been published for a number of examples, resulting in an incomplete dataset. When examining material from multiple sites, Ruby (1995:

98–100) demonstrated that conclusions about length are of limited value.

The analysis of these traits has facilitated the construction of a system of 10 broad types, including four types of bronze spearhead, and six of iron spearhead (Fig. 21.3, Table 21.1). The bronze types can be divided into distinctive central Italian spear forms, identifiable by their polygonal blade and socket sections, and other forms with round or ovoid sockets which enjoyed a broad distribution throughout Italy, the Mediterranean and central Europe throughout the Bronze Age and the Early Iron Age (Stary 1981; Snodgrass 1964). Each of these two 'cultural' groups featured a broad-bladed type and a narrow-bladed type of spearhead.

Iron Spearhead Types 5–10 begin to appear in south Italy during the eighth century BC revealing a greater variety of forms than was evident in the bronze spearheads. The earliest examples tend to feature narrower blades than their contemporary bronze counterparts. Bronze spearheads continued to be manufactured and deposited in tombs and votive contexts during the Early Iron Age in south Italy, often in association with iron fibulae and, occasionally, iron swords. By the end of the eighth century BC, iron completely replaced bronze as the material for the manufacture of spearheads: though miniature bronze weapons continued to be used as votive dedications (Russo Tagliente 1995: 70–1). The iron spearhead forms were long-lived. While there is some variation in the dates of introduction for specific types in different regions, once introduced to a site the types continued throughout the period from eighth century BC to the fourth century BC and beyond.

## Discussion

Through the application of typological analysis we can move beyond the simple association between weapons and 'warrior' status to observe more nuanced layers of identity construction. Changes in the distribution of spearhead forms over time demonstrate that warrior identities were not static and that the accoutrements of warrior status were reflective of martial and social changes. As Isayev (2007) observed, there was no over-arching regional identity: individuals and communities constructed their own localised identities. It is apparent that, throughout the Iron Age in south Italy, spearheads were predominantly local productions and that there was no adoption of Greek or Phoenician spearhead forms (Snodgrass 1964; Anglim et al. 2002) so local cultural identities were clearly being asserted through the Italic weapons assemblage. The functional typology of spearheads presented here has identified three specific functional spear forms: broad-bladed thrusting spears (types 1, 3, 5 7 and 10) which were ill-suited to throwing, very narrow-bladed throwing spears (type 9) which were equally ill-suited to the delivery of thrusting blows and a range of versatile narrow-bladed spearhead forms (types 2, 4, 6 and 8) which could be effectively deployed in the delivery of thrusting or throwing actions. Differential distribution of these forms highlights changing preferences from site to site over time and may provide 'important insights into the nature, scale and practice of warfare' as

Armit suggests (2011: 507). For example, Paestan tomb paintings depicting warriors in action suggest that flexible fighting techniques were practised, showing fighters engaging in action using spears with clearly depicted throwing loops, the execution of thrusting actions and a phalanx formation clearly derived from Greek hoplite tactics (Pontrandolfo Greco *et al.* 2004). Versatile type 8 spearheads and type 9 throwing spears are strongly represented at Paestum, consistent with the action depicted in Paestan tomb paintings. More broadly, spears capable of use for both thrusting and throwing would have been ideal for south Italian Iron Age fighting strategies, facilitating expression of both individual and group identities.

Throughout the ninth and eighth centuries BC there was a distinct preference for broad-bladed bronze spearheads at all of the sites examined. At Pontecagnano and Sala Consilina 71 per cent and 68 per cent of spearheads respectively belong to the broad-bladed Types 1 and 3, while at Incoronata examples of Types 1 and 3 account for 97 per cent of all bronze spearheads. Signs of wear are evident on several bronze spearheads, indicating prolonged use, and presumably suggesting a personal preference for this particular weapon type. Unfortunately, the high levels of corrosion common in later iron spearheads renders evidence of wear in those examples largely undetectable, though metallurgical analysis that might reveal wear on iron spearheads has been conducted in the south Italian context (Giardino 1998: 217). Many of the weapons recovered from tombs were functional and were probably, in most cases, weapons used by the deceased in life and as such, formed part of their individual and community identity constructs.

The use of spears to communicate identity appears to be more complex than the mere martial function of these weapons suggests. Armit (2011: 508) has argued for the importance of projecting an ability to defend oneself and dependents was of widespread import during the Iron Age, especially amongst the social elite. Robb *et al.* (2001) demonstrated an inverse relationship between indicators of physical trauma and the inclusion of weapons in the elite tombs of Pontecagnano. Yet, it must be noted that, even if the deceased individual played no active martial role, decisions were made about what *type* of spear or sword should be placed in the grave, and these decisions reflect subtle nuances of identity construction which may be better understood through typological analysis of spears.

The typological analysis suggests that the cultural influence of the settlements of Pontecagnano and Sala Consilina on spearhead forms in southern Italy did not spread widely beyond these sites. As we move away from settlements with direct ties to Etruscan centres, the proportion of locally derived spear types increases significantly. At Pontecagnano, a settlement with close ties to Veii, Vulci and Tarquinia (d'Agostino & Gastaldi 1988; Bonghi Jovino 2000), central Italian spearhead forms dominated the spearhead assemblage in the ninth and eighth centuries BC, accounting for 67 per cent of bronze spearheads. At Sala Consilina, which also had close ties to Etruscan centres, but believed to have integrated with the local indigenous culture, locally produced forms dominate the bronze spearhead assemblage, whilst central Italian type 3 and type 4 spearheads make up just 38 per cent. Thus it seems that Sala Consilina's much-discussed cultural integration with the local population extended to the spearhead assemblage itself (Bonghi Jovino 2000). At Incoronata, a contemporary indigenous site in Basilicata, local spearhead forms dominate during the ninth and eighth centuries BC, making up 79 per cent of bronze spearheads. By contrast, central Italian spearhead forms accounted for only 18 per cent of bronze spearheads of identifiable type. The remaining 3 per cent is accounted for by a spearhead form, with a polygonal socket section, that appears to be a central European type with a parallel in Albania (Prendi 1982: Fig. 12).

The expression of childhood identities in death varied from region to region in Iron Age south Italy, extending to the way in which spears were included in the tombs of children. A number of child and adolescent tombs in Daunia and Campania included functional weapons (Bottini 1988: 115–16; Serritella 1995: 67). The inclusion of spearheads in the tombs of (presumed) male children reveals the importance of spearheads in the construction of aspirational or hereditary status associated with an elite martial role in society (Parker Pearson 1999: 102–04). At Pontecagnano, the construction of child burial deposits did not differ from those of adult males. In Daunia, though the burial assemblage of children differed from adult burials in other ways, the spear types were consistent with those included in the tombs of elite adult males. Adolescent males in Daunia appear to have been assigned paternal rights of accession due to their familial ties, though they may also have been accepted members of the adult community (Bottini 1991: 48). Several children's tombs at Lavello were recorded as including miniature spearheads (Bottini 1988: 24). However, when these spearheads were assessed using the new typology, the form and size of these weapons was consistent with functional examples. Consequently, the identification of these weapons as miniatures should be reconsidered. In clear contrast, spearheads and other weapons were excluded from the burial assemblages of children in Iron Age Basilicata, indicating spears were not associated with expressions of childhood identity in death in that region.

Women too were occasionally buried with spearheads. Two fourth century BC tombs from Lavello (Bottini 1988: 60 and 130) included spearheads in clear association with loom-weights, an artefact class excluded from male tombs throughout the Iron Age in south Italy. The weapons, which are types common at Lavello, could have been functional and may again indicate familial power or the social class of these women in life, as has been demonstrated in Etruria where elite women were buried with high-status vehicles (Emiliozzi 1999). These examples highlight the complexity of identity construction in Iron Age south Italy, and emphasises the challenges embedded in disentangling the expression of multiple social identities through ritualised articulation in death.

Following the introduction of iron spearhead forms in the eighth century BC, the preference for broad-blade spear types rapidly changed, with longer, narrow-bladed spearheads increasing in frequency throughout the period. By the beginning of the sixth century BC, narrow-bladed type 6 and type 8 spearheads dominated the spearhead assemblages of most south Italian sites. The increased frequency of narrow-bladed spear types may be a direct result of the transition to working in iron, a lighter metal than bronze and more labour intensive to work without heat. However, we must also consider that this shift represents a change in fighting style with warriors seeking weapons that provided greater versatility of function. The inclusion of narrow-bladed spearheads in tombs may also represent an expression of such a change in martial practice, highlighting the new roles being played in warfare and with these shifts also being articulated through new identity constructs.

Broad-bladed spear forms, type 5 and type 7, do continue throughout the period from the eighth to fourth centuries BC (approximately 12 per cent of the sample) and are particularly well represented in the most elite tombs of Campania and Basilicata, such as Tomb 101 at Braida di Vaglio, in Basilicata, dated to the late sixth or early fifth century BC. At this location, suites of weapons are presented, including members of all three classes of spear, thrusting, throwing and versatile forms. Large, broad-bladed spears, like the example included in Braida di Vaglio Tomb 101 (Bottini & Setari 2003: plate 35 No.42), were singled out by Xenophon as particularly suitable for the boar hunt (*On Hunting*, 10.3). While Xenophon was describing Greek practice, the practicalities which predicated his recommendation of spear type would also have been faced, and likely resolved in a similar manner, in south Italy. The boar hunt is an activity that is known to have been practised throughout Basilicata during the Iron Age, with depictions on Apulian and Campanian vase paintings. This was an elite pastime that required significant resources and analysis of faunal remains from the Biferno Valley reveal hunted species, including wild boar, account for less than 10 per cent of faunal remains, indicating hunts of this nature were occasional and limited to a small number of individuals (Barker 1995). The small number of tombs to include members of types 5 and 7, just 40 of the 475 examined tombs may reflect the exclusivity of the boar hunt. Success in the boar hunt was presumably demonstrable proof of a warrior's skill and bravery closely tied to perceptions of warrior/hunter identity. Possession of type 5 and type 7 spear forms were salient expressions of the dual role of protector and provider associated with warrior identities. The distribution of meat from elite hunting practices also appears to have been a significant marker of elite identity with spits and firedogs appearing in Iron Age tombs in Basilicata, Puglia and Campania (Emiliozzi 1999: 29–30).

One type of spearhead, type 9, stands out as a group distinct from other types due to their very long sockets and small or non-existent blades, an apparent design feature that would seem to have implications as to their function (Fig. 21.4). Type 9 spearheads are best suited to being thrown and appear to have been designed for this purpose: the long socket distributing the weight of the point more evenly, creating a more balanced weapon (Snodgrass 1964: 137). Type 9 Throwing spears are the most common form in Daunia, where they comprise 54 per cent of iron spearheads. They appear in Daunian tombs by the beginning of the seventh century BC. These frequencies suggest that the throwing of spears was widely practised, and was perhaps a 'specialty' of the region. The apparent preference for throwing spears was never as great in Basilicata or southern

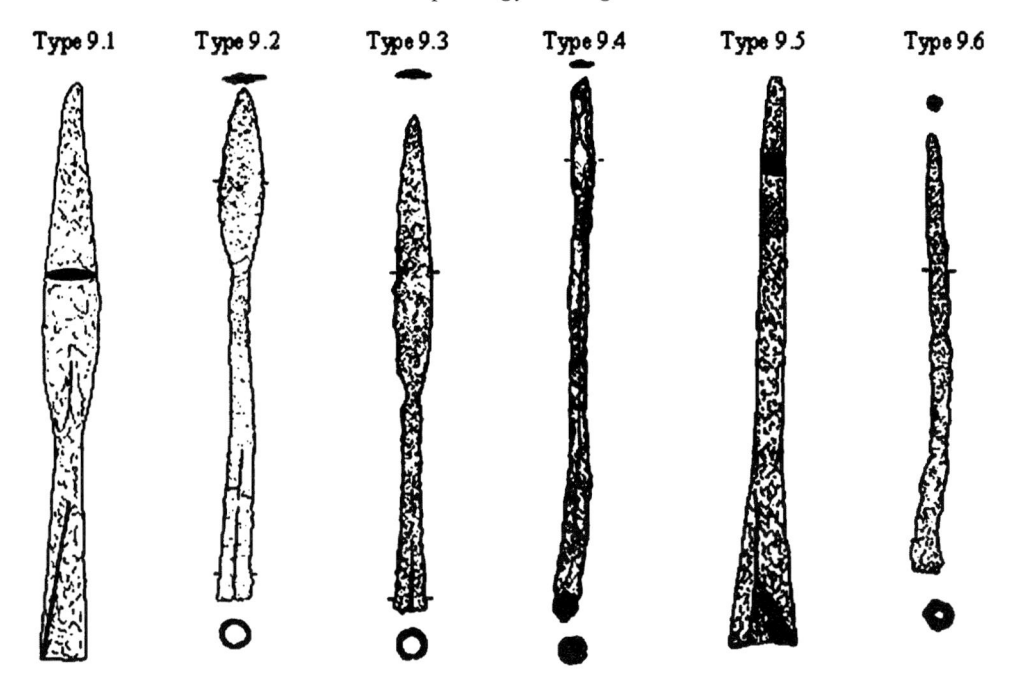

*Figure 21.4. Type 9 Spearhead sub-types.*

Campania as it was in Daunia, indicative that community or ethnic identity manifested itself in distinctive regional fighting styles.

An increase in the proportion of throwing spears in Basilicata and southern Campania was observed during the fifth and fourth centuries BC (increasing from 19 per cent to 42 per cent and from 13 per cent to 38 per cent respectively). The increasing popularity of this spear type during the fifth and fourth centuries BC implies a change in fighting techniques, with an increasing role for spear-throwing. It coincides with the rise of cavalry forces in these regions (Diodorus Siculus, *Library*, 11.52; Herodotos, *Histories*, 7.170; Pausanius, X 10.6; Frederiksen 1984). Deploying spears from horseback would have been preferable to engaging in close cavalry action with the sword. In the absence of a standing army, mounted warriors with throwing spears would have been highly effective in battle and would have required little training. Depictions of swords are conspicuously absent from the returning horse-borne warriors of Paestan tomb paintings. However, they were consistently represented as bearing one or more spears, revealing that the embodiment of the warrior identity was manifested in the spear.

Two sub-types, type 9.5 and 9.6 (Fig. 21.4, far right) have no distinct blade, consisting solely of a socket which tapers to a point. The absence of a blade raises the possibility that these examples may have functioned as *sauroteres* (a counter-point or butt-spike at the other end of the spear-shaft, in itself a useful weapon in instances when a warrior's spearhead had broken off). When other types of spearhead are found in association with examples of these forms, excav-

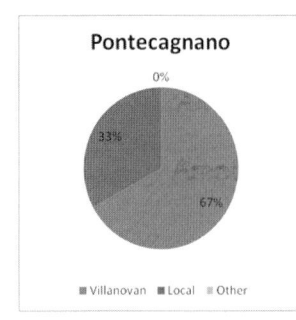

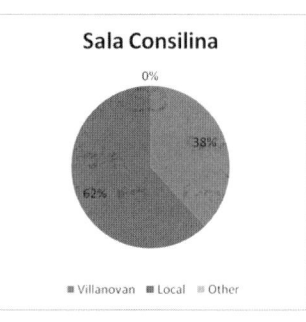

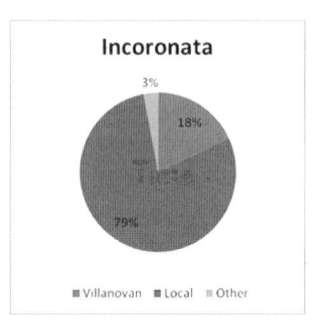

*Figure 21.5. Comparative proportion of Villanovan to locally produced spear types in eight century BC sites.*

ators frequently interpret them as *sauroteres* (de Juliis 1973: 337–40; Rossi 1983: 26–39; Bottini 1988). However, the distinction between point and counterpoint is elusive and in tombs where a type 9.5 or 9.6 point is the sole weapon an interpretation of *sauroter* becomes questionable.

It must be remembered that the spearhead is only one part of the composite weapon, and that the shaft was also important. Excavation reports occasionally mention partially preserved spear shafts; however details of overall spear length remain speculative. Artistic representations on Campanian vase paintings suggest that the total length of a spear was generally at least equal to the height of a man, though several Paestan tomb paintings depict shorter spears. The external socket diameter of most spearheads is between 2cm and 3cm indicating an optimum shaft diameter that was consistent across spear types between the ninth and fourth centuries BC. A number of spearheads throughout south Italy are reported to retain traces of wood in their sockets, though the author is not aware of any studies undertaken to determine wood species. The choice of wood for the shaft would clearly impact on flexibility and durability. It would be interesting to assess whether material analysis could reveal any associations between spear type and the wood species used for the shaft and recent advances present new possibilities in this area (Haneca *et al.* 2012).

## Conclusion

In summary, this research presents a comprehensive spearhead typology that classifies these weapons according to function. A typological approach (Fig. 21.5) to the material can inform our understanding of fighting styles, and provide direct insights into how warrior identities were constructed and communicated throughout the Iron Age in south Italy. All indications from the weapons assemblages analysed suggest that south Italian warriors of the Iron Age favoured a loose fighting style in which personal preference and versatility were valued. The functional nature of this new spear typology forms an effective tool for mapping functional differences, preferences and changes over time. The distribution of central Italian spearhead forms illuminates the level of cultural interaction and integration with neighbouring indigenous settlements. It is clear from the longevity of most spear types that effective functional forms were not readily discarded despite the introduction of new spear types. Such progressive adoption of new forms, particularly throughout Basilicata and Campania, clearly demonstrates that fighting styles and warrior identities were not static between the ninth to fourth centuries BC but that they underwent constant evolution, expressing new ideas and articulations of how warriors should act and be perceived. For example, the correlation between the increase in throwing spears and the rise of south Italian cavalry units, and the accompanying changes to identity constructs is intriguing and warrants further examination. Funerary assemblages often include multiple spearheads of different types presenting us with suites of weapons clearly designed to perform different functions, and also to express the diversity and prowess of the 'warriors' who were buried with them. Ultimately, a broader application of this spear typology would facilitate further investigation of the chronological and geographic evolution of indigenous warrior identities in the south Italian Iron Age.

## Acknowledgements

I would like to acknowledge the comments and support of Dr Edward G.D. Robinson who supervised my Masters thesis, Dr Peter Halkon and Dr Malcolm Lillie for their comments on a draft of this paper, though any errors or omissions are entirely my own. I would also like to acknowledge my research affiliation with the Australian Archaeological Institute at Athens at the University of Sydney.

# 22. Communal vs. Individual: the Role of Identity in the Burials of Peucetia

*Olivia Kelley*

Keywords: identity, Iron Age Italy, burial archaeology, material culture.

Introduction

Within sociological and psychological scholarship it has long been acknowledged that identity is formed through a combination of an individual's internal ego dimensions and an inner solidarity with a group or communities' ideals (Sokefeld 1999; Schwartz 2001; Schwartz & Montgomery 2002; Insoll 2007b). This definition of identity stresses the person-in-context and seeks to view identity as a constant negotiation between the social context and the needs and ideals of the specific individual. The construction of any identity is then, a dialogue between the different communal and individual elements. Yet very few archaeological interpretations stress this dynamic interplay between the different facets of communal and individual identities. Instead, most archaeological approaches to 'identity' have used the term as a general conceptual catch-all, what James Côté calls a conceptual 'rubber sheet' (Côté 2006: 6). The term identity has thus been applied independently to a multitude of different archaeological analyses for example, biological sex, gender, age, social status, class, individual self perception and specific group membership. These analyses typically view these individual identity facets in isolation, privileging one aspect (for instance ethnicity or gender) over another. Such frameworks, whilst undoubtedly important, deny the inherent complexity and duality of identity construction. Interpretative strategies are needed that allow for more pluralistic modes of understanding identity and its construction in past contexts, interpretations that examine how the different aspects of identity interact and coalesce in the formation of both individual and group identities.

The burials of the region of Peucetia in southern Italy (in the sixth to fourth centuries BC) perfectly illustrate the dynamic interplay between a multitude of different identity factors at both a communal and individual level. Through an analysis of the competing elements of the funerary ritual it is possible to challenge long held assumptions about gender identity, 'hellenisation', social status, and the hierarchical social organisation of the region. What this study illuminates is the role of the funerary ritual in the articulation of a number of communal and individual identities. These identities existed simultaneously and must be treated as facets of a larger whole. It is only through adopting a more integrated and multifaceted approach that questions of identity can be interrogated with greater sensitivity.

## THE ARCHAEOLOGY OF PEUCETIA AND ITS BURIAL ASSEMBLAGES

The term Peucetian traditionally refers to a group of indigenous Italic people who, in the pre-Roman era, occupied an area of modern day central Puglia on the Adriatic coast of Italy (De Juliis 2010: 151–5). Together with the Daunians to the north and the Messapians to the south, they formed a collective group known, according to the later Greek and Roman sources, as the Iapygians (Greiner 2003: 15–24). The pattern of settlement in Peucetia displayed a gradual movement towards greater urbanisation from the ninth century BC onwards. By the fourth century BC many of the large settlements were ringed by fortified walls and in some cases contained central public spaces and large public buildings (De Juliis 2010: 157–9). This trend toward urbanisation was seen to go hand in hand with increased social stratification and the emergence of an aristocratic warrior-led elite whose political power was expressed, in death, through elaborate burial treatment (De Juliis 1988: 99; Herring *et al.* 2000: 250–1; Lomas 2000: 82–3; Ciancio 2001: 20–3; Ciancio *et al.* 2009: 307–08).

The main source of evidence for the social and cultural organisation of Peucetia is the funerary material. From the sixth BC onwards, new and more elaborate burial types were introduced and an increasing plethora of different grave goods have been found. The burials are typically interpreted as static reflections of growing elite power structures with the increasing emphasis on burial display cited as evidence for the presence of nascent elite groups (Herring 2000: 68–9).

It is thought that the selection of tomb type reflected this growing emphasis on social stratification (Riccardi 1989: 69–89). The more elaborate burial types (the monolithic limestone sarcophagi, the so-called *'cassa'* tombs – cist burials constructed out of small overlapping stone blocks – and large rock cut chamber or *semicamera* tombs) are often interpreted as denoting high or elite status. The vast majority of the tombs are simple *fossa* inhumations cut into the bedrock or soil and it is thought that these reflect a lower level of investment in the funerary ritual (De Juliis 2010: 159). *Enchytrimoi* burials of infants and neonates in large ceramic pithoi have also been found, typically within domestic contexts. Despite the assertion that tomb type demonstrates social status, all burial types illustrate a pattern of increased investment in burial equipment with many tombs in the fourth century BC containing over 40 or 50 objects in their funeral *corredo* (tomb group).

Single burial is the norm across all these tomb types and the inhumed remains of the individual were invariably placed on their side in the *rannichiata* (crouched) position (Donvito 1992: 38). The positioning of the body in this way is often cited as characteristic of the native Italic population. Whilst other areas were quick to adopt the supine burial (notably the Messapians to the south), the peoples of Peucetia clung to this custom, almost exclusively, well into the period of Romanisation (De Juliis 2010: 159).

The typical Peucetian burial in the sixth century BC contained one large vessel for the serving of wine, several drinking cups, a cooking vessel, fibulae and occasionally an oil vessel. This repertoire was expanded and duplicated over the course of the subsequent centuries as new and varied object types were added (Riccardi 1989: 75–84). The grave goods can be divided into several main functional groups. The most prevalent are objects related to the drinking and service of wine. These vessels include large vessels such as craters and the locally made *olle* as well as both indigenous and imported drinking cups and pouring vessels. Other objects found within the tombs include: metal and ceramic objects for feasting, weapons and armour, cosmetic and unguent vessels in stone, glass, and ceramic, items of jewellery and ornamentation – including elaborately carved amber, and glass beads, and pendants – and items of so-called votive or ritual function including terracotta figurines, libation vessels and loom-weights.

## Community definition

The traditional interpretive paradigm applied to these burials has emphasised the presence of elite individuals and typically sees elaborate Greek objects as indicative of the passive 'hellenisation' of the Italic peoples (Riccardi 2003: 49–50; De Juliis 2010: 159–60). Such interpretations highlight the high status objects, typically couching analysis in terms of elite emulation and competition. The simple correlation between socio-economic status and burial wealth overlooks the inherent complexity of these tombs. Analysis of the functional role of objects within the funerary ritual, one that looks beyond their perceived 'elite' status or lack thereof, illustrates the way in which many object classes, for instance drinking or dining vessels were used to articulate locally-based communal identities, rather than merely being reflections of elite competition.

One of the key features of Peucetian burials in this period is the overwhelming presence of objects associated with drinking and feasting. In the sixth to fourth centuries BC, drinking vessels and vessels for the service of wine constituted over 40 per cent of all objects found within the burials of the entire region. At the site of Rutigliano (De Juliis 2007), for example, 91 of the 92 tombs recently published in detail, contained at least one drinking vessel and some of the richest tombs contained upwards of 25 drinking cups. 66 of these 92 tombs (71 per cent) also contained a large vessel of some kind for the service of wine. In the sixth century BC, these large vessels were mainly large Geometric Matt-painted *olla* or crater shapes whilst in the fifth century BC the introduction of first Attic and then Apulian red-figure saw a proliferation of Greek shapes alongside the more traditional matt-painted and banded ware vessels. These large wine vessels are found in equal numbers across all the three known tomb types found at the site (*fossa, cassa* and sarcophagus), despite the assertion that at Rutigliano tomb type was an indicator of social status or wealth. Only 34 of the tombs could be sexed anthropologically; of these 16 males and 13 females were found with a large vessel for the serving of wine, and a further six burials (mostly dated to the fourth century BC) contained children or infants who had been equipped with a similar large vessel (Tombs 4 and 7 from the Didonna necropolis and tombs 17, 35, 61 and 74 from the Purgatorio necropolis).

In other areas of south Italy, specifically Messapia, the use of large craters for the serving of wine in a funerary context was restricted, with only some members of the community receiving the vessel in their funerary kit (Giannotta forthcoming). In this instance, it is thought that access to such vessels was limited to the male members of the community specifically the leaders or chieftains of each generation. Maria Teresa Giannotta (forthcoming) has recently interpreted this selective use of large craters, specifically red-figure examples, as evidence of male members of the community controlling access to the symposium and its associated symbolic value system. This is, however, not the case in Peucetia where, as we have seen at Rutigliano, men, women and even small children were often equipped with large vessels for the service of wine.

The development of certain types of drinking vessels further demonstrates this selective manipulation of the drinking ritual to suit local ends. In the sixth century BC the favoured drinking cup shape is the so-called *olletta*-kantharoid vessel, made in the locally produced geometric matt-painted fabric. The work of Fabio Colivicchi illustrates the gradual development of this indigenous drinking shape in Peucetia and the parallel development in colonial centres of imitations of this shape in Greek and colonial Greek red-figure and black gloss fabrics (2004: 23–68). The copying of this local shape by Greek or colonial potters demonstrates the influence and impact the local population had on the construction of ritual practice, specifically in this case of drinking practice. The longevity of drinking practices in the region and selective appropriation of some (but not all) symposium equipment illustrates the manner in which the indigenous population were using drinking practices for the promulgation and continuation of their own social and political ideologies.

The consumption of wine and the accoutrements of drinking were clearly pivotal aspects of the burial ritual in Peucetia. The ubiquity with which vessels for the drinking and serving of wine have been found in tombs of all types and all social classes throughout the region indicates that acts of communal drinking must have had broad social significance and were perhaps linked to aspects of group membership. These communal signifiers are not, however, limited to drinking but can also be seen in objects associated with funerary feasting. One of the key differences between the communal drinking witnessed within the Greek world and that of the indigenous population of Peucetia is the consistent deposition of cooking ware vessels into tombs, alongside the more ubiquitous drinking vessels; a practice that seems to be specific to Peucetia and notably absent from the Greek colonies of Metaponto and Taranto. Whilst some cookingware *lopades* have been found at Taranto the *chytra* is conspicuous by its absence (Lippolis & Boschung 1994). At Metaponto cooking ware vessels are found in 11 out of total of 324 tombs in the Pantanello necropolis and the excavators note that it was not a common practice. All known examples from Metaponto date to the either the very late fifth or fourth centuries BC. (cf. Tombs 9, 12, 14, 111, 125, 136, 192, 193, 194 and 316 (Carter 1998)).

These cooking vessels, specifically small rounded bottom, single handled *chytrai*, often called a *pentolino rituale*, were present in Peucetian tombs from the start of the sixth century BC onwards. They are often referred to as the key constant elements of the funerary ritual and are found at sites all over the region (Scarfi 1961: 333; Labate 1987: 122; Labellarte 1988: 337; Ciancio 2001: 131). Despite this, these rather modest vessels are all too often overlooked in favour of the larger and more easily datable vessels in matt-painted or red-figure wares. From the fifth century BC onwards, the repertoire of cooking and food preparation vessels found in burials increased to include lidded *lopades*, large double handled cooking vessels (*chytrai*) – that were modelled on bronze prototypes, large spouted mortars (in cooking ware and plain-ware fabrics) and in some cases small curved pestles. This increase in these food related vessels was paralleled by an upswing in vessels for the serving of food, including shallow dishes, plates and bowls, all of which gained in popularity over the course of the fifth and fourth centuries BC (Riccardi 1989: 78–9).

Unlike weapons or bronze vessels, these cooking and food preparation objects have no clear-cut elite connotations. They have been found in equal numbers in the tombs of males and females and have even been found in some child burials. Their presence has not been limited to certain tomb types and they have, even in later periods, been found in the monumental chamber tombs, the supposed domain of elite families. At the site of Rutigliano, cooking or food preparation vessels of some kind have been found in 63 of the recently published 92 tombs. In total such vessels have been found in 63.1 per cent of *fossa* tombs, 73.9 per cent of sarcophagus tombs and 85 per cent of *cassa* burials at that site (Fig. 22.1). Despite the higher proportion of cooking vessels in both sarcophagus and *cassa* tombs this distribution cannot be seen as statistically significant. A chi-squared test performed comparing tomb type and the presence of a cooking or food preparation vessel indicates a lack of association between the two variables.[1]

Such analysis suggests that the choice of tomb type at the site of Rutigliano did not have an impact on the use of cooking or food preparation objects. As has been previously noted, it has been assumed that the division between tomb types was indicative of elite or non-elite status (De Juliis 2010: 159). Yet the presence of cooking and food preparation objects appears to suggest that some practices were common to all levels of society.

The *chytra*, for instance, was found in 58 of the tombs from the site, and of these 30 are found in *cassa* or sarcophagus burials, the supposed domain of the elite. *Cassa* tomb number 12 for instance contained two *chytrai* and three other cooking or food preparation vessels and has been interpreted as the tomb of an elite individual (De Juliis 2007: 43). The use of multiple examples of cooking types can be seen as an elaboration or duplication of ritual practice that was

---

[1] $\chi^2 = 3.172$, degree of freedom = 3, p = 0.205, sample size = 87 (4 tombs were enchytrismoi and a single burial was of an unknown type). The p value of this sample indicates a 20 per cent chance of these numbers being reached by chance, which is well above the commonly accepted level of five per cent (Drennan 1996: 187-91).

**Percentage of tombs by tomb type at Rutigliano which contained cooking or food preparation vessels**

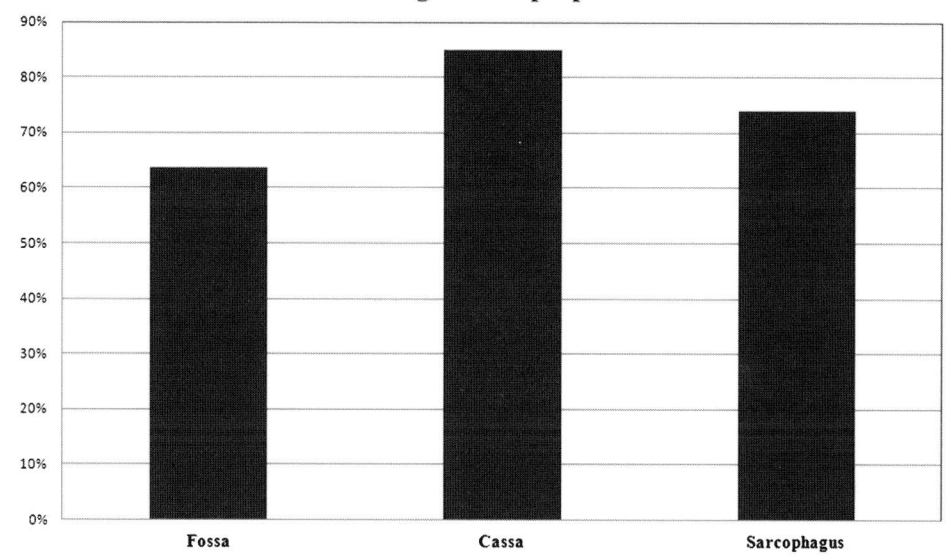

*Figure 22.1. Percentage of tombs which contained cooking or food preparation vessels, sorted by tomb type at the site of Rutigliano.*

specific to high status tombs. This use of multiple cooking objects by elite individuals both conforms to the common ritual practice (namely cooking vessels in tombs) and serves to highlight their status based identity. The elaboration of the ritual in this way thus demonstrates the complexity of factors that affected the choice of funerary equipment and illustrates how different scales of identity can be associated with single object types depending on the context of their use.

Whilst examples of the elaboration of the feasting ritual may be tied to displays of wealth and social status, the ubiquity with which cooking and food preparation vessels have been found across all tomb types, suggests that feasting was not only an arena for displays of elite competition but was open to all members of the community. It has long been acknowledged that feasts formed pivotal arenas in which social and political relations were constructed and negotiated (Dietler 1999: 490; 2001: 66–75; Bray 2003: 1–5; Adams 2004: 56; DeFrance 2009: 37). Feasts can, according to Dietler, act in a diacritical or associative manner (Dietler 1990: 377). That is to differentiate groups or individuals symbolically within a society (diacritical), or to unite and define a social group (associative). Diacritical feasts can be manipulated by individuals or groups in the creation of socio-cultural power. Associative practices, on the other hand, often serve as acts of communal bonding through which individuals can re-affirm their membership of a community or group (Dietler 2001: 68–9). Associative commensal acts such as feasts serve to reify the identity of both the individual and the group. In these instances, feasts serve to bind the community together and to strengthen group ties.

I would argue that the pervasiveness of both drinking vessels and modest cooking vessels in all tomb types in Peucetia indicates a level of communal investment in feasting. This feasting is not limited to the elites but rather is more inclusive and illustrates the presence of large scale communal identities that cross social and political boundaries. The communal nature of feasting and drinking and its apparent ubiquity across all the burials studied points to layers of identity construction that are focused on group membership rather than on the establishment of individual identities.

## Individual definition

The burials of Peucetia are, however, not merely static reflections of a group identity. These larger communal identities were complemented and cross-cut by other individual or sub-group identifiers. But what do we mean by the term individual? Some scholars believe that the individual is, in itself, a construct of modern Western ideology (Fowler 2004: 17; Knapp & van Dommelen 2008: 16) and anthropological data indicates that not all cultures and societies share the idea of the individual as the primary unit of social functioning (Strathern 1988: 13; Sokefeld 1999: 418–19; Leve 2010: 513–15). However, what is also apparent through anthropological investigation is the construction of the individual within its specific social context. According to such interpretive paradigms the individual is a socially constructed designation, built through an intricate network of interactions and social relations and predicated on the role and place of that person within their wider social or cultural framework. In archaeological terms it is therefore theoretically possible to recreate, not an actual living individual, but an idealised amalgam of the social relationships that they experienced (Gillespie 2001: 77–8).

In the burials of Peucetia it is thus possible to witness the impact and effect of a number of different aspects of that relational construct. Analysis of the presence and development of individual artefact types within burials, for instance weapons, strigils, or loom-weights, reveals much about the impact of different individual factors like gender, occupation, and social status. Through a detailed contextual understanding of the role of different objects in the funerary ritual it is possible to recreate some of the individual identities that were occurring in the burials of late Iron Age Peucetia.

Traditional interpretations of the Peucetian burial evidence have highlighted the impact of elite individuals only and seen the tombs as evidence for the tribal and kinship-based social organisation in which a warrior/chieftain paradigm is fundamental (Riccardi 2003: 89–96). As we have seen the presence of 'high status' Greek and Greek style objects have been understood solely as products of the Peucetians putative 'hellenisation'. The increasing number and variety of grave goods have been thought to reflect the presence of a nascent elite group whose power and status was demonstrated through elaborate funerary ritual (De Juliis 2010: 160–1). Pivotal to this understanding of the emergence of the aristocrat-led social system is the development of the warrior ideal, in which male members of the community used weapons and armour as diacritical indicators of their role and position within the community.

In the sixth century BC, this warrior identity is expressed through the presence of spearheads, the apparent standard weapon of the Italic warrior (Small 2000: 231). The association of these weapons with an elite male identity is so prevalent that most tombs in the region have been sexed on the basis of the presence of a spearhead alone and have sadly not been subjected to further anthropological analysis.

By the start of the fifth century BC, there was a general proliferation of objects associated with warriors and warfare, including new defensive armour types, helmets, greaves and occasionally horse armour. It is thought that these new types were introduced by the colonial Greek populations on the Ionian coast. A series of burials found within the Peucetian region contained these new object types and have been interpreted as a full panoply of so-called 'hoplite' armour and weapons (Chieco Bianchi Martini 1964: 148–64). These burials contain not only the usual spearhead but also bronze helmets, breast-plate and greaves, and in some cases iron or bronze strigils. These rich and elaborate burials are thought to represent the highest level of financial investment in a hellenising warrior ideal. Investment in this ideal is thought to reflect patterns of elite competition and display. More often, however, combinations of these objects are found and it has been suggested by Small that this might reflect the preferences, needs, status or financial ability of the individual warrior (Small 2000: 223–5). If this is the case then the presence of arms and armour in the tombs of Peucetia illustrates the impact of the needs and conditions of the individual. The articulation of a warrior identity is not a static association but rather is dependent on the social status, familial ties, wealth, and personal tastes of the individual. Such burials thus illustrate the complexity of the construction of individual identities and the impact that other factors, be they communal, familial or personal, had in the construction of the individual.

The impact of both individual preferences and the local cultural ideology is seen in the incorporation of objects into the burial ritual that fall outside the traditional remit of the 'hellenising' warrior (Herring *et al.* 2000: 252–5). The presence of strigils in burials has often been seen as a static reflection of a male gender. Their association with the gymnasium and athletic prowess has shaped our understanding and interpretation of their presence in the burials of indigenous Italy. In colonial Greek contexts, the association between strigils and the gymnasium is well attested, however in the burials of Peucetia they are more commonly found together with weapons or defensive armour (Carter 1998: 797). At the Greek colonial site of Metaponto on the Ionian coast, strigils have been found in 31 tombs and of these none can be associated with weapons of any kind. In Peucetia, strigils have been found at 13 sites in the region but only in a small handful of tombs – 45 in number (only those with secure context have been catalogued). Of these 45 tombs, 26 (57 per cent) also contained an iron spearhead – the apparent weapon of choice for the indigenous warrior – and 35 (77 per cent) of the 45 tombs contain either a weapon of some kind, a piece of armour or a bronze belt, that is 77 per cent of the tombs with strigils can also be associated with objects that have been linked to the articulation of an indigenous warrior identity. In this context, a strigil is not indicative of athletics or Greek heroism but has been actively associated with a warrior ideal, a concept that is seemingly at odds with the original object itself. This manipulation of the symbolic association of a Greek object is an excellent example of the impact of the Peucetian population on the way in which hellenising objects were used.

The associations of a male gendered identity with a warrior ideal, as expressed through weapons and armour is complicated by the presence of six tombs at the site of Rutigliano that contained the remains of female individuals who were buried with bronze belts, iron spearheads and in some cases bronze or iron strigils (Tombs 15, 33, 54, 84, 85 and 87 – De Juliis 2007). The inclusion of such objects within female burials should indicate to us that it is not enough assume a simplistic dichotomy between male and female in the grave assemblages of Peucetia. It cannot be assumed that a warrior identity is either limited to males or the only possible reason for the presence of weapons within a tomb. The construction of a gendered identity is clearly more complex than this. It is a distinct possibility that, in some instances, gender was not the prime motivating factor in the construction and choice of burial equipment. Despite this, it is clear that individual identities focused on warfare or weapons were crucial aspects of the burial ritual in Peucetia. The active manipulation of the traditional symbols of a Greek warrior that we see in the inclusion of strigils in these warrior tombs illustrates the impact of local cultural systems in the creation and articulation of the Peucetian identities.

Analysis of objects that have been conventionally associated with a female gendered identity illustrate the same level of complexity and plurality that we witnessed in the male warrior tombs. At the site of Rutigliano of the 92 tombs mentioned earlier, 34 have been positively sexed anthropologically. Of these 18 were male, 15 female and one burial contained a double deposition of a male and female buried together. Despite the relatively small size of this sample, these burials do allow for some exploration of the role of sex amongst the distribution of grave goods. Figure 22.2 illustrates the division of some key object classes on the basis of the sex of the deceased. Some objects have a clear association with a specific sex, for example the vast majority of fibulae were found in female burials but only nine can be associated with male tombs. *Phialae* also appear to be associated with females, seven examples of this ritual vessel were found in female burials however none were associated with men. On the other hand craters are found more frequently in male tombs but only by a small margin. If this is further broken down it is possible to see that certain crater shapes were associated with specific genders, the column-crater for instance is associated with male burials in six instances but found in only one female tomb, whilst the bell crater is found in seven female and five male tombs.

Many objects, for instance loom-weights and spindle whorls, have commonly been associated with a female gender. The association between women and weaving in South Italy is well established and the presence of loom-weights in female

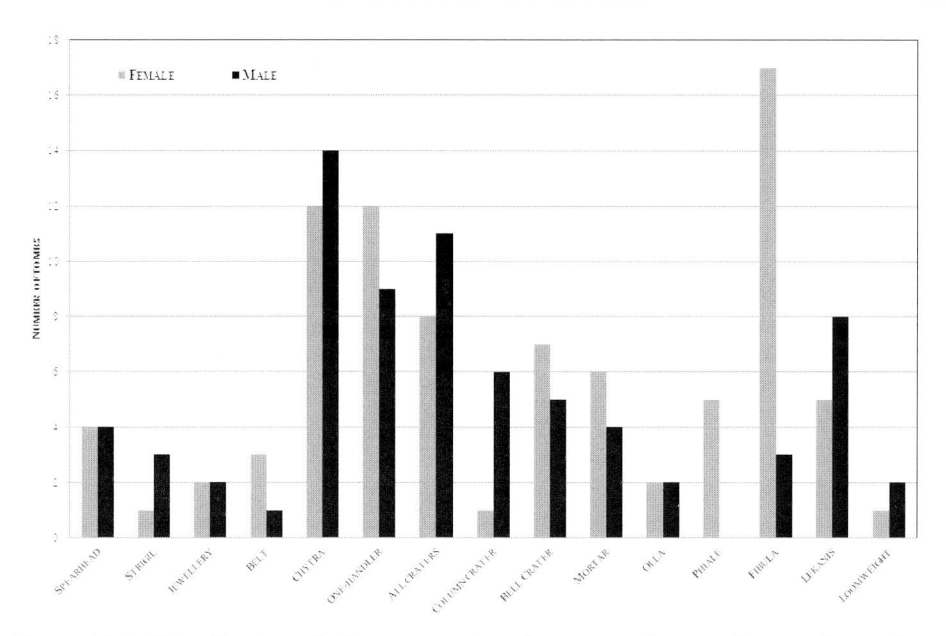

*Figure 22.2. Distribution of select categories of grave goods according to the anthropologically determined sex of the deceased at Rutigliano.*

tombs from the period is thought to reflect their role in the production of textiles (Riccardi 2003: 102–03; Gleba 2008: 173). In the burials of Peucetia, however, loom-weights are not all that common. Only 26 tombs with secure contexts have been published that contain one or more loom-weights and a further eight contain spindle-whorls. Only six of these have been positively sexed anthropologically (Rutigliano tombs 2, 5 (Didonna) and 38, Bitonto tomb 1 (1982) and tomb 2 (1983) and Bigetti tomb 1 (1990)). Of these, three have been gendered as female while the other three are males. Three of these tombs were from Rutigliano and, at this site, only one female burial contained a loom-weight whilst two male burials were found with them.

This lack of a clear gender distinction for loom-weights and their relative scarcity in the material record might indicate that they were specific to an identity that was based on an activity rather than a perceived gender differentiation. Weavers were undoubtedly pivotal members of society whose textile output was important for the economic and social life of a community. It is theorised that textile production was as vitally important for the Apulian economy in the late Iron Age as it was in the Roman period (Herring 1991: 123–4). Control over such a crucial economic activity would have facilitated the involvement of the local population in a wider Mediterranean network of trade, exchange and interaction (Purcell 2005: 125). If this is the case, then a loom-weight might have served as a powerful symbol of the role of the individual in a larger pan Mediterranean economy. The presence of loom-weights in such contexts may then be indicative of the deceased's membership of or association with a group of specialised craftspeople rather than merely a static reflection of their sex.

The idea of an identity which is aligned with a particular type of employment or economic production is further seen at the site of Bitonto where three tombs have been found that contain sickles and other agricultural tools. All three tombs ((Tombs 8 (1981), 2 (1982) and 2 (2002)) contained sickles together with a spearhead, ceramic vessels for drinking and dining and in one instance a bronze belt (Riccardi 2003: 61–9). Tomb 2 (1982) was particularly rich and contained a pair of pliers and a sickle as well as weapons, bronze feasting equipment and over 30 ceramic vessels (Riccardi 2003: 69). The presence of these agricultural tools, notably the sickles, has been interpreted by Ciancio as indicative of a wider group of individuals who were engaged in agricultural activity (Ciancio 2010: 235). The combination of sickles and spearheads would appear to suggest that the deceased in these tombs were associated with aspects of the warrior ideal as well as with agricultural labour and productivity. In the neighbouring region of Basilicata, the presence of iron sickles in the tombs of elite women in the same period has been interpreted as symbolic of land ownership (Markantonatos 1998: 189). If this is the case then these agricultural tools are indicative of an individual identity that was rooted in social status, and displays of wealth and property. The presence of tools together with weapons further illustrates the complexity of identity construction in Peucetia and the layered and multifaceted nature of the burial record in the region.

## Conclusion

The late Iron Age was, in Peucetia, a time of great social and political upheaval and, just as the people of Peucetia were responding to different economic, political and social stimuli, so too their burials reflect this process of negotiation between the different aspects that made up their social and personal identities. The impact of 'hellenisation' is, as we have seen from the evidence of strigils and drinking accoutrements, indelibly linked to local choice and activity. The people of Peucetia were actively manipulating aspects of Greek material culture and incorporating and changing their use and symbolism in order to employ them within their own social and cultural practices. The burials of the region indicate the ways in which Greek objects were used by the locals to express identities specific to them, rather than as generic symbols of the influence of the Greek colonies. These burials are an excellent example of the plurality of identity construction in the ancient world and serve as a reminder of the nuanced and complex nature of identity as a concept.

The construction of identity through the mortuary practice in Peucetia has illustrated the presence of a multitude of individual identities for instance, warriors, weavers and agricultural workers or land owners. Yet the objects designating these small personally based identities were also found with objects associated with community wide social activities, in this case drinking and dining objects. This combination of objects demonstrates the presence of different scales of identity, all of which were occurring simultaneously and were concurrently shaping the expression of Peucetian funerary practice. The burials of

Peucetia are demonstrably not merely indicative of the articulation of individual identities, but are simultaneously associated with larger community-wide social groupings. No one identity factor exists in isolation and this study has shown that the use of various objects as markers of identity is contingent on context, with single objects being used to express different facets of social, cultural or personal identity. These burials thus demonstrate the complex relationship between different levels of communal and individual identities and serve to emphasise the plurality of possible factors that impacted not only the life but the death of the individual.

**ACKNOWLEDGEMENTS**

I wish to thank Dr E.D.G Robinson and Prof. M. Miller for reading early versions of this paper. I would also like to thank the editors and the reviewers for their insightful comments and guidance.

# 23. A View from the South (West). Identity in Tyrrhenian Central Italy

*Simon Stoddart*

Keywords: community, descent group, entanglement, Etruria, Nesactium. temporality, regionality, scaling.

Introduction

The majority of papers in this volume are centred on the Balkan region. This contribution seeks to provide a contrasting construction of the variations of identity from the centre of the Italian peninsula, focusing on the Etruscans. However, the paper ends, by stretching out towards the identities of the Balkans with a consideration of a meeting point of identities in the Croatian site of Nesactium, where many elements of exotic material culture were brought together with local materialisations of identity to forge a distinctly alternative construction.

One of the key issues (returned to below) is the definition of what is meant by Etruscan identity. An aim of this paper is to break down the certainties supplied by traditional scholarship and the ancient authors, so it is best to the characterise the data under discussion as primarily relating to central Italy south and west of the Apennines and north of the River Tiber, between 700 and 10 BC. The link to Nesactium on Balkan soil is partly for the purposes of illustration, but also emphasises how the biographical identity of objects was entangled with the biographical identity of individuals, and specifically how distinctive objects such as, in this case, Etruscan fans were integrated with local identities. The short paper excludes from consideration the Po Valley and Campania, as well as a detailed study of the developmental sequence during which identities metamorphosed and crystallised over time. Nevertheless the term Etruscan will be employed as a generic category, in the much the same way as employed by Izzet (2007).

Theoretical statement

As already investigated in greater detail elsewhere (Stoddart and Neil 2012), identity and ethnicity are not the solid reified entities in the popular imagination. Indeed, some categories which are strong in the written sources of Ancient Italy, such as the Umbrians may be categorised as a fuzzy residual category (Stoddart and Redhouse 2014) that is simply *not* Etruscan, Picene or Latin, and thus lost, according to a reinterpretation of Pliny (Pliny Natural History III, 112), in the shadows of time. As succinctly expressed by Popa (this volume), the primary actor in the sense of Latour (2005) was engaged in a network of relations, that, furthermore, additionally changed through different scales of time, even contextually during a single day, but most notably throughout the course of life. Material culture was an active ingredient in this fluidity, that can be most effectively detected in the biography of objects, even if they substantially freeze the episodes of this fluidity, and give a level of reification.

The traditional temptation has been to see the Etruscans as characterised by some form of unitary identity, a perspective reinforced by the reading of ancient authors, a route followed by many more recent scholars and reawakened by early genetic studies. Many of the early studies of 'Etruscan' genetics propose an origin combining culture and biology in a way that makes little sense from a social anthropological perspective. It is no accident that identity is a term that has only very recently entered the vocabulary of Etruscan scholars. Vedia Izzet's (2007) book was one of the first, and this has been followed by others (Stoddart 2009; Swaddling and Perkins 2009). The employment of the term identity brings the realisation that culture and biology do not map coherently one onto another. Identity is based on what individuals, descent groups and communities consider to be their shifting allegiances and origins, in any given context, which may or may not be equivalent to biological linkages. Supra-community identity, that is Etruscan identity, was equally fluid and permeable, and cannot be considered uniform, except from a politically constructed external perspective. The much discussed Etruscan Language could have been adopted (and lost) as a product of emulation of political power, and does not, in itself indicate the common origin of populations whatever *origin* is defined as meaning in practice.

Many of these unitary explanations followed the political fashion of the time, seeking Germanic (Stenger 1994), Phoenician (Nicolucci 1869) and Eastern (Briquel 1991) solutions. Historically, studies of the identity of the Etruscans have equated identity with the origins of a unified people, as defined by the political continuity of settlement and culture, a pattern most notably followed by Pallottino (1947; 1961; 1978) and more recently by other scholars (Haynes 2000). The unitary approach persists in some recent treatments of the biological issues of identity as reported by Perkins: 'They were, potentially, a people different from their neighbours, they spoke a different language, they came from elsewhere. Therefore it should be possible to identify a genetic heritage that both characterises the Etruscans and differentiates them from their neighbours and to analyse their genetic inheritance and heritage.' (Perkins 2009: 98). This is a situation that modern archaeologists critique: 'most Etruscologists would question the premise that Etruscans might be either a biological population or just a people who shared a culture but not ancestry. Etruscan culture was diverse and geographically variable, and the notion that Etruscans shared "a culture" is an imprecise generalization.' (Perkins 2009: 99). Ultimately this biological investigation is of modern interest, rather than contributing directly or uncontrovertibly to the construction of the Etruscans' own conception of identity. This is for the simple reason that, in conditions of restricted literacy, distant blood linkages in space and time were not concretely recorded, and thus the constructed conceptions of identity were largely social memories implemented in the present, without the genetic knowledge that can now be brought into play.

In addition, the current biological definition of the Etruscans suffers so far from an essential defect, that it does not yet properly sample the diversity and regionality of the Etruscan region of central Italy. Biological studies have tended to concentrate on northern Etruria, both because of the political inheritance of the Dukes of Tuscany that this was the *real* Etruria, and because the absence of volcanism and the presence of limestone, leading to less acidic soils, permits a more detailed study of skeletal remains (and their potential DNA if present). One substantial complication is that this region had a substantially different demographic profile (broadly low density and dispersed) compared with South Etruria (high density and concentrated, but also with a larger rural population). This demographic history emerged and diverged from a low density Neolithic landscape, into increasingly profound differentiation in the Final Bronze Age. The consequences for genetic pools and founder effects would have been very substantial. In order to make a valid contribution to the mosaic of identity in its different facets, biological sampling (of both modern and ancient populations) needs to take place within a stratified framework, established on grounds of archaeologically established demography. This next stage is a natural progression in the same way as the study of other scientific techniques such as radiocarbon have matured through time: in this case, the implementation of a viable biological framework. However, this has not yet been achieved and the most recently studied genetic material simply adds to the complexity of the chronological patterns of mitochondrial DNA, placing the chronology of the 'arrival' of distinctive traits from the 'Near East' probably as much within the Roman as in the Etruscan period (Brisighelli *et al.* 2009).

## THE CHARACTERISTICS OF CENTRAL ITALY

Three important further matters need to be considered in the understanding of Etruscan identity: temporality, regionality and scaling. All these factors interconnect, and are additionally affected by a fundamental fluidity, albeit not as marked as in other case studies in this volume. The interconnections of temporality, regionality and scaling can be illustrated briefly. The temporal development of what came to considered Etruscan led to the appearance of a regionality which differentiated the identity of the Etruscans, so much so that their coherent ethnicity should be challenged. At a microscale, the temporal development of an individual's identity changed through the life course and profoundly affected the *dividuality*, the social context of that individual in respect to others. At the larger scale, the community identity locked into the patterns of regionality providing another framework of differentiation.

One of the great debates which will not be resolved here is the temporal dimension, that is when Etruscan identity emerged as a concept recognised from both within and without the population. The best model for that emergence is linked to the process of state formation (Wilkins 1990; 1991), and the construction of a network of distinct, but interlinked, communities centred on *place*. Higher order identity, that may or may not coincide with ethnicity, was often in response to external emulation and competition, in the case of Etruria generated by an approximation to peer polity interaction between the Etruscan communities. Scholars have argued extensively and inconclusively about the precise date when this occurred. The answer is largely related to the differentiation of the question (Stoddart 2010), by separating the foundation of the community (with an earlier chronology based on nucleation) from the construction of an urban community (with a middling chronology based on material forms of both the living and the dead) from the implementation of a higher scale of identity (where a later chronology was based on external relations at a supra community level). Scholars of different traditions perceive the formation of identity according to which of these measures they consider most important.

The multiple characteristics of central Italy, furthermore, reveal an essential regionality (Banti 1969; Redhouse and Stoddart 2011) that also has its outcome in the construction of identity. In the southern and coastal parts of Etruria, urban processes led to more powerful centralised places, more rapid infilling of the political landscape with rural settlement, and greater formalisation of boundaries between political entities. In northern and inland Etruria, the urban places were less centralised, permitting a greater devolution of political power into the countryside, although not always accompanied by rural settlement, and the construction of fuzzier boundaries between places of political power, including unallocated territory. The distinction between these two areas, north and south, cannot be absolutely characterised since there was considerable variation in its implementation according to particular regional trajectories at a much more local level. In the same way, the identity of the populations across these landscapes was correspondingly fluid in its formation, permitting slippage between contexts, particularly amongst the potentially more mobile elite. Other contemporary Iron Age identities in northern Europe (Carr and Stoddart 2002; and many papers in this volume) were even more fluid in the construction of identity, but whereas the relative stability of Etruscan identity does form an absolute contrast, it also reveals internally different levels of crystallisation and formality, that should not be seen in the unitary terms sometimes imposed by ancient authors. At close quarters, an author such as Livy realised the importance of the lower order identities since he gave equal attention to relations between Rome and individual Etruscan cities, and sometimes even to descent groups.

Scale, beyond the issue of regionality, is the other great consideration of identity. The richness of the archaeological data in Etruria permits the identification of a series of scales of the operation of identity that can be defined minimally as: the individual, the descent group, the community and the supra community (which can to a certain extent be equated with ethnicity). Across these spatial scales, the elite had a greater visibility, and indeed a greater motivation to be conspicuous, and perhaps also a greater ability to create, and slip between, different categories. Furthermore, allocation to a particular identity was context specific, a context determined by other scales of time and space, following the standard

## THE INDIVIDUAL

The separate categorisation of the Etruscan individual is convincingly demonstrated by the presence of inscriptions and iconography, often formally linked one to another. Indeed one of the major surviving uses of early literacy was related to granting identity to prominent elite individuals. A classic example of this is the sixth century BC funerary statue of Avile Tite from Volterra who is associated not only with his name but with attributes of sword and spear, other fundamental elements of his identity. This is a strongly defined male elite identity, but recent work has shown how some of the apparently clear-cut genderised tropes of identity were broken down. Wheeled vehicles were not exclusively found with men (Emiliozzi 1999) and mirrors not exclusively found with women (Izzet 2007; 45ff). As an extension of this, there is also forceful evidence that the identities of individuals were strongly interlinked through the biographies of objects. The essence of this was realised at a very early stage by Cristofani in his study of gift exchange (1975) which elegantly demonstrated how gifts linked individuals to identities outside their own local world, and, when writ large, new hybrid identities could be constructed out of the linkage of the local and the exotic. Riva (2010) does not explicitly employ the term identity, but the entanglement of the local and the exotic is an underlying thread of her analysis of the construction of individual as well as community authority. There is strong evidence that, nevertheless, a filter was applied along lines of age and sex. Women were much more prominent in the Etruscan world than in other contemporary societies (Stoddart 2007–8 (2009)), but there is clear evidence that this prominence was only relative, never, even in the late Etruscan period overtaking that of men, and according to Izzet (2007) varying over the course of time. This is illustrated most simply by the statistical representation of inscriptions by gender, where men are generally more prominent, only achieving equality in the one late Etruscan community of Tuscania (Rallo 1989). The study of the life course amongst the Etruscans is more limited, but there is some evidence that Etruscan individual identity was not properly formed until 5.5 years of age (Becker 2011), when individuals were first accorded access to formal burial. The complexity of the issue is shown by the discovery of late examples of *elogia* (praise genealogies or biographies) which are evidence that the descent group chose to give conspicuous illustration of both individual and collective ancestors, better to ground authority within the political present.

## THE DESCENT GROUP

The descent group was substantially a social construct, for 'genealogy is at once ideology and history' (Krader 1963: 157). Inscriptional evidence has proved to be a very powerful tool in reconstructing the strongly focused identity of the descent group (Marchesini 2007), where, although the female lines of descent are recorded as culturally significant, it is the burying group of the male line that is fundamental. Inscriptions provide a clear social persona of components of the network of social links between those buried together and pointers towards the nuances and emphases that these incorporate.

The network of the descent group is best represented materially by the feast. The feast was constantly depicted in the funerary context and there is some evidence (Riva 2010) that this moved from a more individualising focus and became increasingly vested within the identity of descent group. The biography of objects could also in this context bind together the generations, as the material culture of the feast moved with the descent group through its episodes of social and biological reproduction. The longevity of biographies can only be established if it was decided to place, and thus use, an object in a tomb some time after its original production, as was the case with a bronze vase with handles placed in the Regolini Galassi tomb at Cerveteri (Pareti 1947: 321, n325).

One important issue is that access to conspicuous display of the descent group was restricted, in much the same way as literacy. The elite themselves constructed a distinct identity that contrasted themselves with the vast majority of the population, and it can be estimated that access to distinctly visible identity was as restricted as was access to literacy, potentially in the order of a few per cent. This raises intense questions about the level to which that identity was widely shared, and although, as already remarked, conspicuous identity was an arena of the elite, the less ostentatious identities of the invisible Etruscans should be not be neglected. The lack of research on such communities makes assessment difficult, although some new research is moving in that direction (Malone *et al.* 2014). From current evidence, this exuberant expression of identity was concentrated at specific phases of political development. This was most powerfully expressed in the so-called Orientalising phase, broadly dated from the mid eighth to the late seventh century BC when accumulation of wealth and its display became an accepted operative mechanism of identity. It was employed to mark newly established political changes in a pattern of *novi homines* that is not unique to the world of Central Italy. The distinctiveness of this emerging political authority was reinforced by perfect representation of the body, and integration once again of powerfully biographical objects, ideally of an exotic origin.

Many of these processes have to be inferred from non-textual material culture in the earlier Etruscan period, but in the later Etruscan period, genealogies can be read directly from the tombs themselves since the habit of the inscriptional identification of individuals became commonplace. The examples of descent group genealogies illustrated here (Tarχna, Tute and Spurinna) show the variation in the implementation of identity towards the end of the Etruscan period, with fluctuating attention to the individual and the descent group in the construction of identity.

In the first example, the emphasis of identity seems to be pre-eminently on the deep history of the descent group (Fig. 23.1). This is the very well docu-

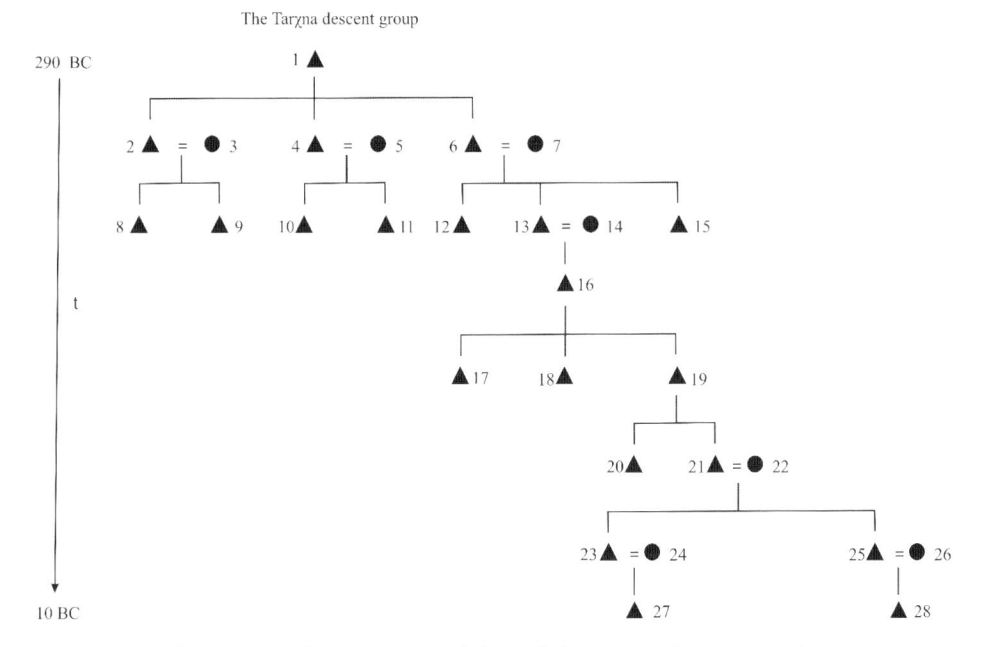

*Figure 23.1. The Tarχna descent group (adapted from Marchesini 2007)*

mented Tarχna descent group which can be traced through eight generations from about 290 BC to about 10 BC in the Tomb of Inscriptions of Cerveteri (Cristofani 1965; Marchesini 2007: 510–27). The principal founder of the decent group was Larθ Tarχnas. He had three sons – Avle, Laris and Marce – whose spouses and descent groups are all recorded. This genealogy can be broadly reconstructed over nearly three hundred years down to the names of their descendants who employed Latin nomenclature, such as Tarquitius Gallus. There is less emphasis in this descent group on individual achievement. The absence of explicit achievement of this descent group in Cerveteri may reflect reality (although the material evidence of their tomb makes this unlikely), but may more plausibly be a deliberate statement on the collective construction of identity bedded in the past.

Another well documented descent group is that of the Tute from the tomb of the Sarcophagi at Vulci (Marchesini 2007: 553–60), but, by contrast, here the emphasis on individual achievement is much more marked (Fig. 23.2). The recorded time depth of this descent group is modest in that it can be placed principally within the third century BC. It could be argued that this was a deliberate strategy to allow more focus on individuals. The founder of the descent group can be identified as Larθ, whose immediate descendant, Tute Arnθ, is the first occupant of the tomb and married to Haθli Ravnθu. Their first son who died at a recorded age of 72 or 82, surfaces from his descent group identity as an individual of considerable political authority, both in the material culture of his *nenfro* sarcophagus showing the procession of a magistrate, but also in the inscriptions that record his tenure of the office of zilaθ at least seven times. One of his sons Tutes Seθre is given a similar

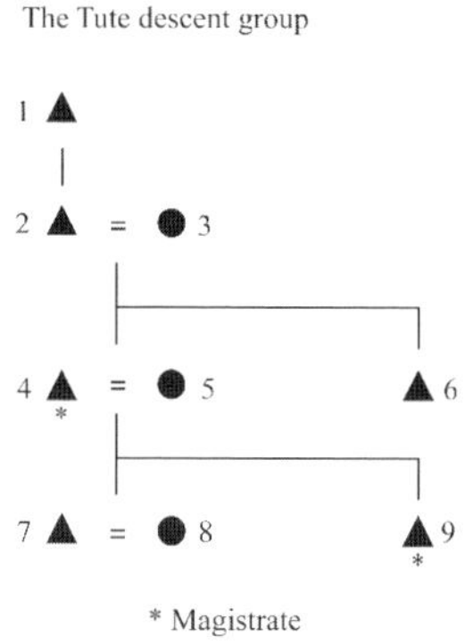

*Figure 23.2. The Tute descent group (adapted from Marchesini 2007)*

emphasis of identity vested in political office, even though (or perhaps because) he died young (25 years) during the tenure of his office. It can be argued that these political offices bolster the identity of the descent group, but they also display a substantially different specification of individual identity.

The interplay between individual identity and the glorification of the identity of the descent group can be shown no better than by the Spurinna descent group from Tarquinia. This descent group is widely known from tombs in Tarquinia and the probably dependent centres of Blera and Tuscania, expanding into north Etruria. However, they are most particularly remembered for an act of glorification in the dying moments of their political influence when they erected a series of marble slabs near the temple of Ara della Regina in the first century AD (Torelli 1975). On these slabs, T. Vestricius Spurinna, now fully latinised, recalled the titles of praetor amongst his ancestors.

This is not to deny the importance of biological relationships between the occupants of a tomb and thus of an Etruscan descent group, as has been shown by limited genetic studies of Etruscan tomb groups (Cappellini *et al.* 2003; Cappellini *et al.* 2004). A detailed contextual study of the four bodies buried in tomb 5859 of the Monterozzi cemetery of Tarquinia reconstructed the family group by DNA analysis (Fig. 23.3). The sex was convincingly attributed in each of four cases, as two males and two females overcoming any potential problems over artefactual and morphological ambiguities. Furthermore, the female line was demonstrated by the sharing of mitochondrial DNA, leaving the central male as the probable father.

Whereas social identity is unlikely to have had a purely biological counterpart, social issues may have been very important in governing the development of that other major issue, language. Perkins (2009) quite rightly emphasises that the tight biological differentiation of an elite was more probably (by implication) the product of complex historical empires such as the Norman or Indian. One might add that actual *biological* gene flow may have been less effectively controlled than represented in the *socially constructed* textual genealogies of the tombs. The presence of a tight endogamous elite may be one potential explanation of the rapid demise of the Etruscan language, but its rapid disappearance can be equally well attributed to emulation of new elite power, where the newly

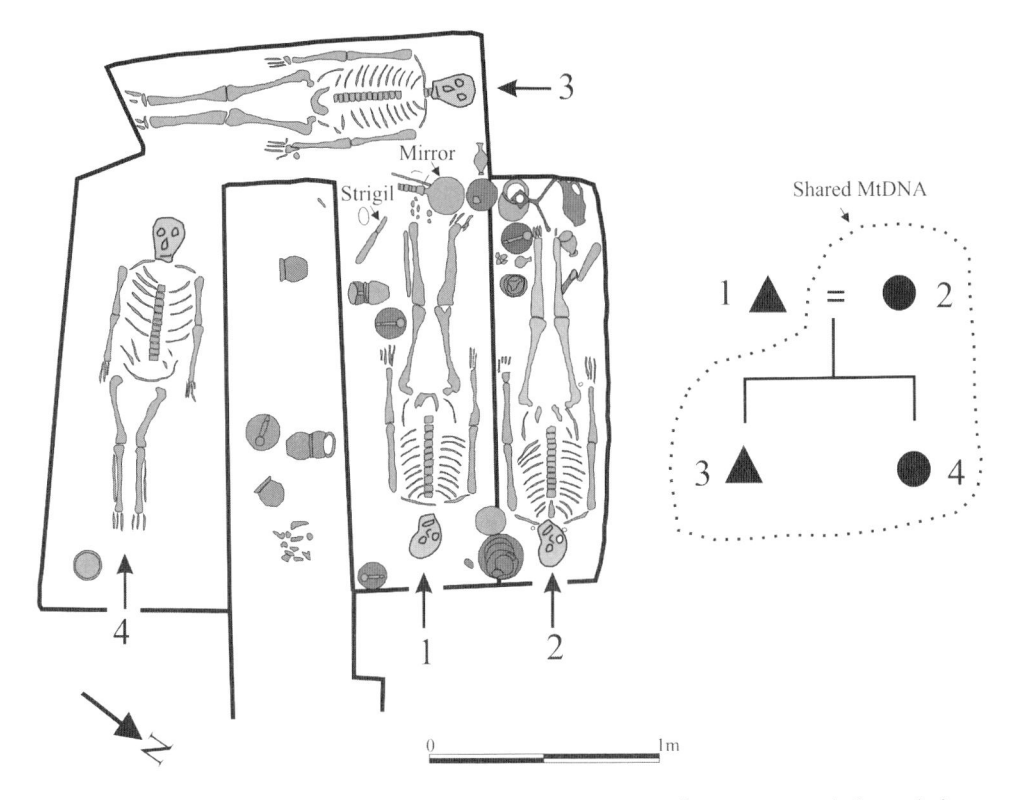

*Figure 23.3. Tomb 5859 of the Monterozzi cemetery of Tarquinia. (adapted from Cappellini et al. 2003; Cappellini et al. 2004).*

arrived Latin language offered more obvious opportunities than the ancestral Etruscan for the identity of the social elite.

Another scenario for the Etruscan elite is that their elite status enabled a great level of mobility. An extreme version of this is the Hapsburg family of historical times who combined a rather tightly contained marriage network with geographical mobility for dynastic purposes (Weiss-Krejci 2001; 2004). The Hapsburg outcome, detectable without resort to modern genetics in their portraiture, might have posed an interesting problem to scientific archaeologists without the aid of the historical context. In the Etruscan case, networking for marriage purposes might have been greater for the more highly mobile elite, but almost certainly undertaken on a more graded basis than the tightly knit endogamous dynasties of early modern Europe. Once again it is the social construction of identity that is fundamental, rather than the tight biological differentiation of populations.

One way in which the elite descent group demonstrated their separate identity was by access to power and knowledge. Literacy was one powerful example. Selected material culture was another, as already illustrated by means of the biography of objects. However, this selective access to exotic knowledge may also have extended to the biological, namely animals. This can be seen in the concept of augury, where particular animals may have had a special ritual power.

Another powerful animal was the horse since a clear social case can be made for their role in elite identity construction. In this sense, they form another class of potentially exotic material culture, even if the initial evidence for eastern imports of horse (Azzaroli 1972) has recently been challenged (De Grossi Mazzorin, et al. 1998). More recently, a more convoluted case has been made for modern bovine breeds such as the Chiana having an Etruscan inheritance and, on genetic grounds, an Eastern origin (Pellecchia *et al.* 2007). This linkage of argument is altogether too tenuous to form an argument for the origins of the Etruscans either in terms of the movement of a biological people or in terms of the construction of exotically powerful identity of prestigious animals associated with an elite.

## The community

There is a strong case that the second major locus of Etruscan identity was vested in the community, generally urban in nature. However, the collective was often challenged by the primary identity of the descent group, suggesting that the allocation of identity slipped between scales according to the living practice of the moment. The Etruscan community was typically defined by encircling cemeteries and walls, and contained communal ritual monuments and some communities in the later period struck coinage. The concretisation of this community identity, however, varied very considerably according to the principles of regionality already outlined. In the south, the identity of the frontier could be relatively ritualised and formalised (Riva and Stoddart 1996). In the north, the definition was much less formalised and even formless (Stoddart *et al.* 2012). In some phases of political development, places such as Murlo and Acquarossa fleetingly developed identities that were not, in the long term, tolerated by ultimately stronger political neighbours. The level of identity construction of the community thus morphed greatly according to its position in this varied archaeological landscape. A city such as Cerveteri in the south had very well defined topography, urban monuments and funerary architecture (Riva 2010). A frontier city such as Perugia, was placed at the interstices of different formulations of identity between the well defined styles of Chiusi in its less centralised landscape and the fuzzier identities of the Umbrian world (Stoddart and Redhouse 2014). However, the uncertainties of the frontier world of north east Etruria meant that no community appears to have been smaller than a small village, whereas, in South Etruria, small farmsteads were probably included under the umbrella of the identity of the larger centres. The community was very differently constituted in different parts of what is generically considered to be Etruria.

## The supra community

A number of different routes have been taken to imply a strong supra-community identity of the Etruscans: historical opinion, genetics, language and material culture. Recent genetic research at a theoretical level has confirmed that imagined ancestry is not always synonymous with the biological community (Chaix *et al.* 2004); there is no reason why this should not be the same for Etruscan ancestry. Genetic research that has taken place (Vernesi *et al.* 2004) shows that among the samples taken from the seventh to the third century BC, from Capua in the south to Adria in the north there was a comparable genetic range to modern populations, although limited biologically defined genealogical continuity with modern Tuscans.

Perkins, in an otherwise invaluable recent analysis of the issue of the DNA and the Etruscans, has claimed that the ethnic status of the Etruscans is incontrovertible (Perkins 2009: 106). However, this bold claim, whilst commonly accepted, can be challenged on the basis of context. Ethnicity needs to be situated in time and space, and even when accompanied by the fluctuations of spatial and chronological variation, attended by considerable nuancing of what was meant by ethnicity. There is a strong case to be made that the perceived concreteness of Etruscan identity is a response to later written sources, most forcefully applying to later political periods when a trend towards common identity may have been a response to external pressures and external characterisation. Even in this later period, nuances come from a full examination of the regional and descent based focus of identity that undermined the auto-identification of the communities that we define today as Etruscan.

In summary, the construction of the supra-community identity or ethnicity of the Etruscans was most probably the product of the force of political circumstance. As Rome advanced from the south, a supra community identity most probably strengthened, bringing together the building blocks of community and its constituent descent groups into temporary alliances of political control that in some contexts took on a character that approximated to what we might in anthropological terms characterise as Etruscan ethnicity. A balanced survey of the evidence suggests that the identity of the "Etruscans" was principally centred on the descent group and the community.

## The prominent theme of entangled contextuality

The search for a unitary identity of the Etruscans which has dominated most studies must now be put to one side in favour of multiple layers of entanglement. These operated at many levels, the individual, the descent group, the community, at the interstices between powerful places, and at a supra-community level. The cultural patterns detected by recent scholarship from multiple intellectual affinities (Zipf 2004; Iaia 2005; Riva and Vella 2006) have all detected networks of relations that can be interpreted in terms of mutual entanglement, contacts that had multiple receptions in different directions. The main economic and political momentum of the Etruscans was locally bedded, but the context was entangled within the connectivity of a wider political world of multiple identities. At least at the level of the elite this permitted the incorporation of those from outside (Magness 2001) who both contributed and

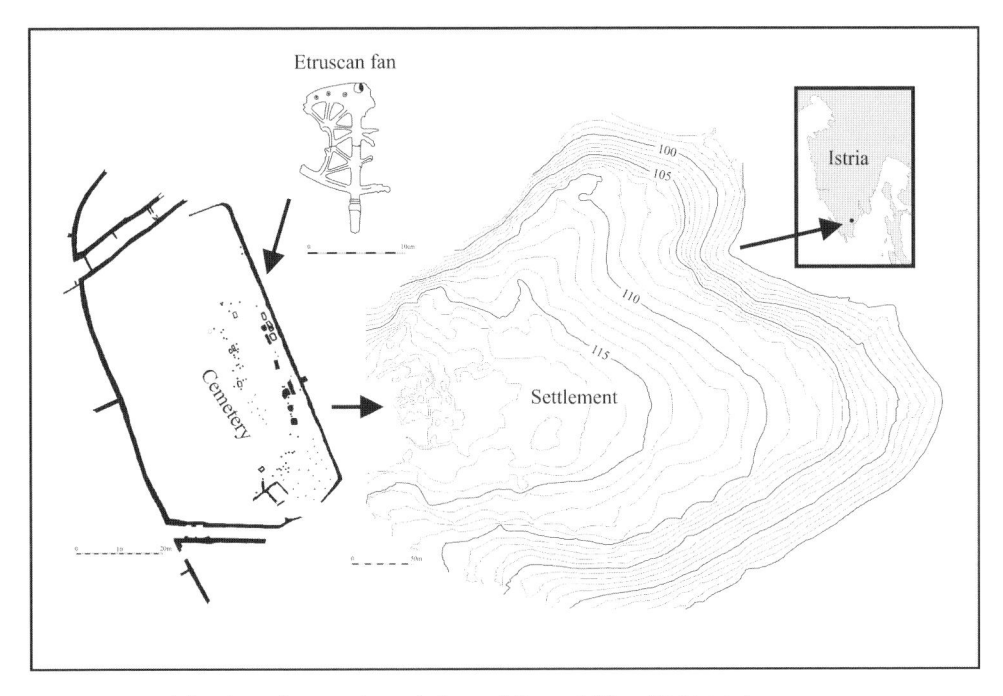

*Figure 23.4. The site of Vesactium (adapted from Mihovilić 2001)*

received from this engagement of multiple identities.

The community of Nesactium (Mihovilić 2001) located within the main study area (modern Croatia) of this volume provides a specific outlying context of this entangled contextuality, drawing on Etruscan and other worlds (Fig. 23.4). In the burial ground of this community, the power of exotic objects from the Etruscan and Daunian world combined to forge new identities. The ancient site of Nesactium is located on the Istrian coast at the head of the Adriatic, or more precisely in the bay and valley of Budava east of Pula, on a locally elevated plateau (123 metres asl). The identity of place was well defined by a defensive wall erected perhaps in the fourth to third century BC, and by a series of subsidiary hillforts that guarded access to, and communication with, the sea. A distinctive feature of the site was that, in common with contemporary sites in south eastern Italy, the cemetery area in part overlapped with the settlement, although the main funerary remains were in a distinct demarcated area to the west. The pottery evidence shows a gradual coalescence of the identity of place into more restricted locations on the site from at least the Neolithic through the Bronze Age into the Iron Age. The stylistic forms exhibit a common identity with styles on both sides of the head of the Adriatic (Caldarelli 1983) for much of the course of the Bronze Age and early Iron Age, both in settlement and cemetery evidence. In the course of eighth century, objects of distinct and crystallised identity such as Daunian craters (and one South Etruscan) began to appear in the graves (Mihovilić 2001: 68–82), transforming a common network of local identity in the second millennium BC into a new entanglement of objects of distant power in the early first millennium. Regionally distinct ceramic forms (and to a certain extent metalwork) were being made and, more crucially, imported. This pattern continued into the later phases of the cemetery (Mihovilić 2001: 83–105), with further imports of Daunian (*krater/oinochoe*) and Etruscan material (bronze fan handles), as well as the more widely shared ideology of situla art (although Nesactium is the only Istrian site to have such art, and Mihovilić suggests the production centre is Este). Furthermore, the construction of the local identity was given a local focus by the use of *machairai* (distinctive swords, apparently traded back across the Adriatic) and the carving of sixth century BC monumental sculpture of hybrid form, drawing on themes from the rest of the Mediterranean, but providing something clearly distinctive of this one place. These sculptural forms include naked horse riders, a woman giving birth and decorated altars (Mihovilić 2001: 99, 117–30), accompanied by evidence of ritual largesse in the form of offering plates and burning. Lastly, in the fifth century BC there were also Greek imports (Mihovilić 2001: 102–5).

The site of Nesactium demonstrates, in this way, how multiple biographies of objects could be drawn upon, to construct a distinct hybrid identity, that combined local and exotic features. In this particular case, it is the distinctiveness of the community, in its well defined place that appears to be the fundamental focus of identity. This sense of place was provided by the culturally transformed topography, associated with an increasingly well-defined cemetery. Its distinctiveness was provided by the inclusion of well-travelled material culture in combination with local sculptural forms of special ritual practice that marked out Nesactium from surrounding sites. However, the supra community level of identity appears to have been missing. Clearly defined ethnicity was not a feature of local practice. Individuals adhering to a community identity do appear to have been important, enabled by the employment of distinctive identities in areas as far away as Daunia, Este and Etruria, which themselves appeared from outside, at least to many modern scholars and ancient authors alike, to have had a supra community identity.

CONCLUSIONS

The interlocking of the two worlds of Nesactium and Etruria provides some lessons in the variations of the construction of identity in the first millennium BC. The identity of the community of Nesactium was constructed out of a powerful definition of place – walls, cemetery and topography – bolstered by the power of exotic objects drawn from distinct, at least archaeologically recognisable, identities from across the Adriatic. Against the pattern in maritime Croatia we can compare the situation in Etruria. Of these two identities, the Etruscan was the most complexly crafted in material terms, even if challenged by some of the sculptural forms of Nesactium, and the distinctive value of Etruria clearly extended beyond one place to characterise part of a peninsula and most probably had some significance beyond, not least from the evidence of languages found in differently defined communities such as Lattes in southern France (Landes 2003).

The individual from Etruria was powerfully represented as a building block of identity, as demonstrated by the personal inscription. However it was the descent group from Etruria in competition with the community from Etruria that formed the two principal pillars of identity drawn out over the full political development of the first millennium BC. The grouping of these communities together in Etruria was seen externally (that is in written sources) as a different expression of identity that might be characterised as Etruscan ethnicity. However, it remains an open question (in spite of the recent discoveries of a supposed federal sanctuary at Campo della Fiera near Orvieto (Stopponi 2011)) whether these communities saw their primary identity as Etruscan, except under the constraints of strong external pressure from Rome at a late phase in the sequence.

*Synthesis*

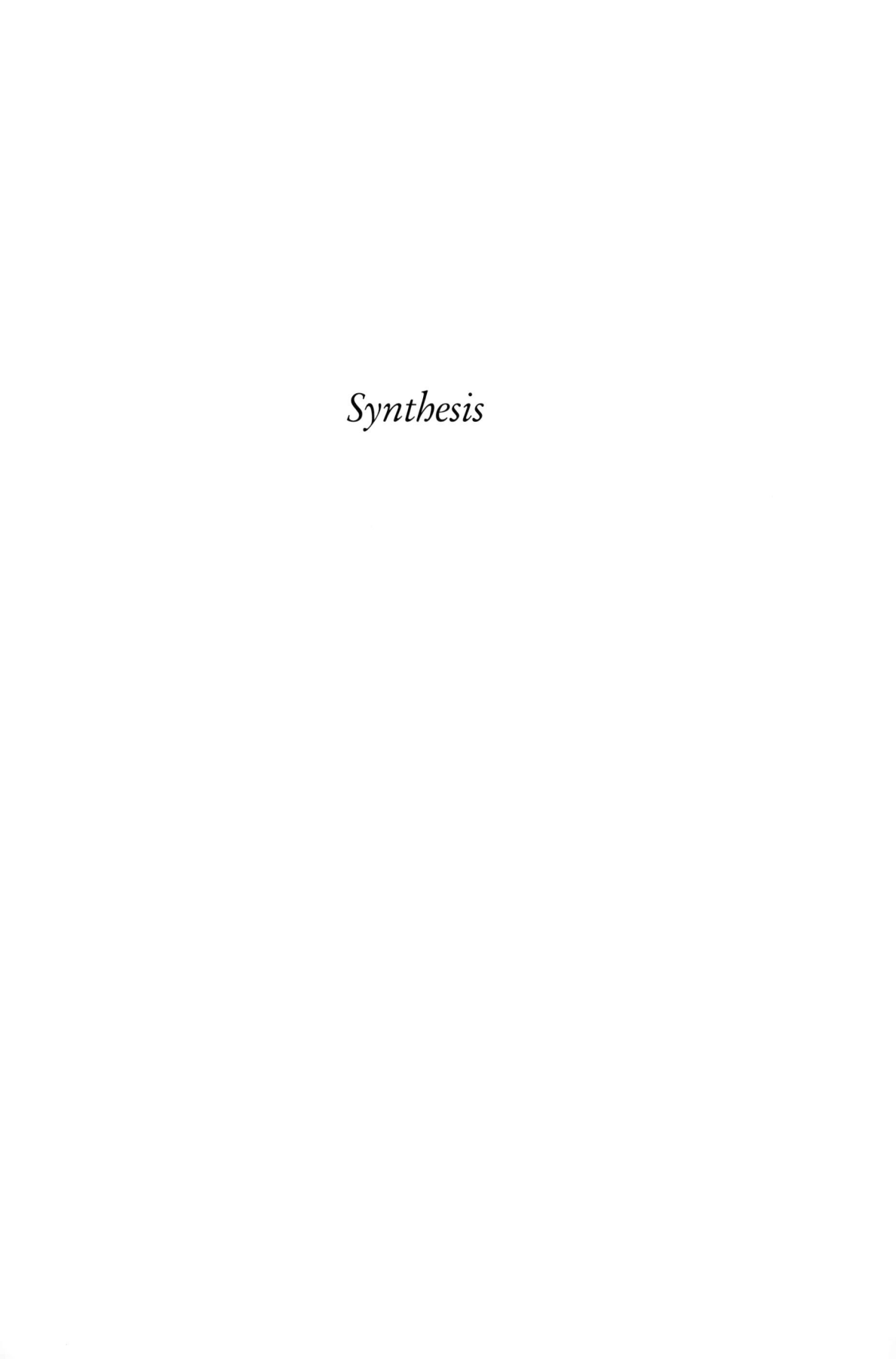

# 24. Identity, Integration, Power Relations and the Study of the European Iron Age: Implications from Serbia

*Staša Babić*

**Keywords:** social context and history of archaeology, global/local practices

One of the main aims of the project that engendered this volume has been 'to encourage the dialogue on a general level between South East European and British archaeology' – to *integrate* South Eastern Europe into the debate, as emphasised in the very title. In this way, two discrete geographical entities are implied and thus geographical denominators are equated with theoretical 'stages' or, at the very least, 'strands' of archaeological investigation. Bearing in mind the doubtless differences in archaeological practices around the globe, my aim here is to investigate briefly this state of *disintegration* among various archaeological academic communities in Europe, hoping that the exercise may contribute to more profound understanding inside the discipline.

The consensus reached during the second half of the twentieth century among the researchers in the field of humanities – that individual and group identities are constructed in constant processes of negotiation among social actors, has penetrated archaeology over the past couple of decades (Graves-Brown *et al.* 1996; Jones 1997; Hingley 1999; 2009; Casella & Fowler 2004; Díaz-Andreu *et al.* 2005; Hamilakis 2007; Insoll 2007a; Dzino 2010; among others). The results of this transfer of ideas are certainly of benefit to the discipline. Our interpretations of the past, informed by the concept of identity, have opened up new and challenging insights and brought us back into the lively arena of discussions among scholars of various disciplinary backgrounds. At the same time, the introduction of the constructivist concept of identity has enabled the archaeologists to reconsider introspectively the role of the discipline and its specialists in society. We have become increasingly concerned with the vivid interplay between the conditions we work and live in and our interpretations of the past, taking into account that *'narratives (including our own historical ones) are necessarily "interested", conditioned by power equations and varied expectations, bound by different kinds of narrative conventions, productive of different kinds of truth-effects'* (Pandey 2000: 286, see also Bond & Gilliam 1994). The challenge of introspection has been met with more vigour and has produced more substantial results in some parts of Europe, notably Great Britain. This is certainly one of the aspects of *disintegration* – significant differences in the practices of archaeology across Europe. In order to *integrate* these practices, it may be productive to investigate some of the possible reasons for different responses to the theoretical challenges posed before us all.

It has been plausibly argued that archaeology as an academic discipline – investigation of the material traces of human actions in the past, based upon a set of premises, positioned in respect to other fields of inquiry, '*bound by narrative conventions*' – is the product of *modernity*, the social, political, cultural condition of the Western European societies that emerged during the seventeenth century (Thomas 2004; Morley 2009). The legacy of the *age of reason* is profound and pervasive in all intellectual endeavours ever since (Latour 1997), still permeating our thinking about nature, culture, human affairs, science, research. In the process of institutionalisation of the academic disciplines during the eighteenth and nineteenth centuries, the outlook of contemporary society was built into their foundations and has endured up to the present day (Babić 2010b). Consequently, in spite of the efforts of many authors over the past decades, some of the premises of the formative period of archaeology are still lingering in our inferences. It is therefore still worth our efforts to investigate some of the building blocks of the discipline. The inquiry into the history of archaeology, just like into the history of any other human effort, may further our understanding of the present state of affairs in the field. At the same time, the constraints of the trade of history-writing equally apply (Jenkins 1995; Pandey 2000; Gaddis 2002), and the narratives about the past of archaeology are also the products of particular *narrative conventions*.

Let us take a cursory glance at one of the first academic texts on the beginnings of the discipline, the one written by the middle of the twentieth century by Glyn Daniel (1950). In the words of the author himself, it is '*no more than a discussion of some of the significant discoveries and developments of the last hundred years*', since '*the detailed history of prehistoric scholarship is yet to come*' (Daniel 1950: 10). Stating that '*archaeology was the creation of the Victorians*', Daniel (1950: 10) scrutinises the gradual formation of the ideas about the prehistory of man from its antiquarian beginnings. The main part of the book is a detailed account of the fieldwork campaigns of such famous researchers as Heinrich Schliemann, General Pitt Rivers and Flinders Petrie, and of the discovery of great sites in the Aegean, Egypt and the Near East. European prehistory occupies 23 pages, and the rest of the world is summarised in the next 19 pages. The main characters of the narrative are indeed the Victorians, whose keen curiosity and scientific minds posed such questions:

> '... in the last two centuries, travellers have observed and described from parts of the world, other than Europe and the Mediterranean, primitive or preliterate folk who now coexist with civilised men. It has been natural to ask how this could be, and what it implied. What was the origin of these savages or barbarians?' (Daniel 1950: 13).

In the 1950s, Glyn Daniel seems to share the 'natural curiosity' of his Victorian predecessors. Judging by the coverage of the various regions of the world in his account, prehistory is pre-eminently a European phenomenon, and the discoveries of the still coexisting 'savages' and the traces of human actions outside the continent are the welcome additional material for explaining *our* past (Babić 2011).

More than half a century later, the task of writing history of archaeology produces different results. The undeniable fact that the discipline originated among the Western European scholars now tends to be situated in a definite intellectual setting and, even when the scope of the research is limited to the particular region, wider implications are discussed (Rowley-Conwy 2007). Global approaches have been tried out, explicitly aiming to demonstrate the embeddedness of the origins of archaeology within the context of the Western European nation-states (Díaz-Andreu 2007). The particularities of the social status of the practitioners have also been investigated, pointing to the groups marginalised or excluded from the profession (Díaz-Andreu & Sørensen 1998). Discussions of the interconnections with other disciplines, principally social anthropology, have demonstrated the significance of archaeology in creating the Western European identity, as opposed to the *Others* (Shanks & Tilley 1997; Gosden 1999; Babić 2008; 2010b; Palavestra 2011;). Some particular segments of the past, notably Classical antiquity, have played the crucial role in distinguishing the *modern, rational, progressive, civilised* world stemming from these sources, from the rest of the world that did not indulge in these benefits (Hingley 1999; 2009; Hamilakis 2007; Babić 2008; Morley 2009). This ultimately led to the conclusion that '*to be a European means to belong to a part of the earth with a definite history of involvement in the Orient almost since the time of Homer*' (Said 1978: 78). This set of stereotypes which is still operating to explain non-Western cultural practices has been described by Edward Said as *the discourse of Orientalism* (Said 1978), setting apart the two opposites and ascribing to them categorised value judgments. The white Western European colonisers, just as the Greeks and Romans before them, were bringing the benefits of progress to the colonised dominions.

There remains another part of Europe. Not all the European nations took part in the colonising enterprises, nor did they all form nation-states. On the contrary, the Balkan lands were dominated by great empires, Austro-Hungarian and Ottoman. The terms *proximate* or *internal colonies* (Donia forthcoming) were defined to denote the political, social, cultural condition of these parts. Not completely remote and utterly different as the Orient, but not quite the same as the Western Europe, the lands on the South Eastern edge have been associated with the image of a crossroad between East and West, 'a bridge between stages of growth' in the words of Maria Todorova (1997: 15, 16). Compared with Said's implied opposition of Orientalism, she identifies the discourse of Balkanism as that of 'imputed ambiguity', according to which the region is perceived as an 'incomplete self' in the eyes of the Western European travelers, administrators, scholars (Todorova 1997: 17). In the course of the nineteenth century, the empires collapsed and their former provinces embarked on a long and complex process of *modernisation*. One of the many tasks faced by the administration of these new states was the establishment of academic life, very much after the models of the German and Austrian universities. The 'founding fathers' of academic departments, who laid down the grounds for further development of many disciplines in their home countries, archaeology among others, were educated in Vienna, Graz and Munich (Babić 2002; 2011; Novaković 2011; in press). Along with their degrees, they brought to the new cultural and political environment the skills and knowledge in which they were trained. These were the knowledges formed in another cultural and political setting, previously developed to meet the needs of different societies. Thus archaeology arrived in the Balkans, charged with an outlook designed to satisfy the curiosity of Victorian gentlemen, filtered through German Romanticism heavily imbued by reverent admiration of the Classical World.

In the case of Serbia, this amalgamation was personified in the figure of Miloje M. Vasić, the first researcher in the country with a degree in archaeology, which he obtained in 1899 in München, under the supervision of Adolf Furtwängler, one of the most esteemed classical scholars of the time (Babić 2002; 2008: 128–32). In 1901, Professor Vasić started his long teaching career of almost five decades at the Belgrade Faculty of Philosophy. Throughout this period, he excavated the settlement Vinča near Belgrade and published the results. His first interpretation was that the site was a Neolithic settlement, the position held by the majority of researchers up to the present day. Shortly afterwards, Vinča became one of the reference points in overviews of the European prehistory (Childe 1929). On the other hand, Professor Vasić slowly drifted away from his initial interpretation and started arguing fervently for interpretations based on the later dates of the settlement on River Danube. By this process, Vinča became exclusively the colony of Ionian Greeks seeking metal mines in their hinterland. Through a very elaborate argument, the founder of academic archaeology in Serbia established stylistic links between the clay figurines from Vinča and Archaic Greek sculpture, by detecting evidence of Balkan contacts in Greek mythology and by tracing Classical heritage in later Serbian folklore (Babić 2008: 129–31). By these means, he offered proof that the land of his people partook in the general development of the European culture, contributing to its most splendid moments. This is what he was trained to do, accompanied by preparation in stylistic and chronological analysis, fieldwork, and other aspects of the archaeological craft, In this way, Furtwängler's student brought into his homeland the value system of his *Alma Mater,* that of late nineteenth century Germany, once described as 'the tyranny of Greece' (Butler 1958). Indeed, it is hard to over-estimate the role of the Pan-Hellenic narrative in the intellectual climate at the time and the importance of this set of ideas about the past for the development of archaeology the German-speaking lands (Morris 1994; Marchand 1996; Shanks 1996). Under this Germanic influence, Professor Vasić transported its very essence into his own research, aiming at the same targets.

Although Professor Vasić firmly held this ground until the end of his life, a new generation of scholars started building chronological charts that followed a broader picture. In 1950, Milutin Garašanin completed his dissertation on Neolithic Vinča. Eight years later, after the retirement of Professor Vasić, he took the professorial post at the Department of Archaeology in Belgrade (Babić & Tomović 1996). In this way, it took several decades to *reintegrate* the most

*Figure 24.1. Vasic at the Vinca excavations of 1912.*

important Neolithic site in Serbia back into the culture-historical framework of European prehistory. At the same time, in Anglo-American archaeology a great upheaval was already under way, and archaeology was about to lose its innocence. But in the small local archaeological community in Serbia, the coming of the *New Archaeology* was eclipsed by the belated ratification of the culture-historical pattern (Babić 2009). However, contrary to what might have been expected, the following decades did not bring a strong, though belated, interest in the processual approach, but diverted into a number of idiosyncratic directions (Palavestra 2011b). Not only the chronological statements of Professor Vasić, but also his very general outlook upon the study of the Balkan prehistoric past have profoundly marked the local practice of archaeology. The long-lasting legacy and the consequences of his work for archaeology in Serbia have recently become the subject of meticulous analysis (cf. Palavestra 2011b, 2012).

The detailed history of prehistoric scholarship in Serbia is yet to come, in a development that mirrors Glyn Daniel's (1950: 10) cautious remark some 60 years later. This short account serves merely to illustrate some points relevant to the current issue of the connection between various European archaeological communities. Firstly, the transfer of knowledge from one academic setting to another is *not* a neutral act. Along with the professional skills and prescribed procedures, the ideas and aims that originated these procedures are transferred too. In the new, different environment they then gain new life and the original intentions may get lost or transformed beyond recognition. In the paradoxical example of Professor Vasić, working hard to bring the Greeks – the fount of *all* European values, into the Central Balkans, he denied that Vinča was, and still is, one of the important reference points of the European Neolithic.

The second point is that the pace of disciplinary changes in various parts of Europe may differ significantly, as a result of internal, local conditions. While Milutin Garašanin was adjusting the prehistory of the Central Balkans to the long established culture-historical order, this same paradigm was already under severe criticism. This brings us to the question: what exactly is the general course of development of archaeology in Europe? What pattern of stages do we usually apply to describe the gradual paradigm of changes taking place in our discipline? What is the sequence of events that we take as the general/global reference when judging the state of the discipline in a particular local setting? How do we account for the differences?

The tide of reconsideration of archaeological theory over the last couple of decades has produced several comprehensive volumes addressing some of these issues (Hodder 1991; Ucko 1995; Preucel & Hodder 1996; Biehl *et al.* 2002). After identifying the differences, some possible explanations have been offered, such as:

> '…the import of theories into East European archaeology has provided more irritation than inspiration. East European theoreticians don't, as a rule, make a career in their homeland if they concern themselves with subjects discussed in Anglo-American circles, which do not provoke interest in their own countries'
> (Minta-Tworzowska 2002: 53).

This statement describes the frustration of a number of colleagues working in Eastern Europe and are concerned with such arcane subjects as, say, identity (cf. Babić 2006; 2009). At the same time, it also echoes the widely held, but rarely explicitly stated opinion that, for reasons not specified, some archaeological communities are *lagging behind*, to the point that they are '*disintegrated*' from the mainstream of the discipline. This also implies that there is a 'natural', inevitable pace of development of archaeological theory, starting with the antiquarian efforts, flowing seamlessly into the achievements of the early academic archaeologists, such as the heroes of Glyn Daniel's account, proceeding over the fully-fledged culture-historical phase to the advanced scientific approach of the processual paradigm, which on realising its positivistic constraints, achieved the present state of the art, very much characterised by the keen and critical interest in its social background and the legacy built into its foundations. The 'newcomers' to the arena are judged by their proficiency to 'catch up' with the established course of development. The 'incomplete self' of Maria Todorova comes to mind.

Beyond doubt, many concerns current in the archaeological literature published in English are far less represented in the texts produced in the other languages of the continent. This is certainly the reflection of the prevailing inclinations of scholars in various parts of Europe. It is worth reminding, however, that: *'Representing the past... is an expression and a source of power. These representations may frame relationships of social inequality, and can be intimately linked to structures of power and wealth'* (Bond and Gilliam 1994: 1). In other words, even when texts dealing with *'subjects discussed in Anglo-American circles'* are written and published in languages other than English (such as: Babić 2010a; 2010b; 2011; Palavestra 2011a), their reception is limited to the local audience. Moreover, such texts are sometimes written specifically to bring the current theoretical discussions into the local archaeological community. However, the dangers of a transfer of ideas are lurking in the background, and an archaeologist in Serbia, working to reconsider the heritage of the discipline in its social context, is not dealing with the *same*social context as his/her Western European colleagues: while the Victorian gentlemen were emulating the Roman imperial examples (cf. Hingley 1999), the Serbian public got their first information about the Roman vestiges through the accounts of an Austro-Hungarian traveller (cf. Babić 2002b).

The identification of the connections between the cultural, intellectual, social, political conditions in Western Europe during the eighteenth and nineteenth centuries and, on the other hand, the basic notions and concerns built into the emerging disciplines researching the past, has enabled the archaeologists to recognise some of the inherent limitations and dead-ends of theoretical concepts, such as cultural groups. However, the processes that brought about the emergence of academic archaeology are not uniform across Europe. The sequence of events leading from culture-historical, to processual and post-processual approaches, each conditioned by particular influences from both scholarly and wider social environment, does not neatly apply to all academic communities. As a heuristic device, it certainly serves the purpose of discerning and evaluating the interpretive value of particular paradigms, their limitations and interconnections. Its teleological reasoning, however, may hamper our more profound understanding of the present *disintegrated* condition of European archaeology. Once more, a useful analogy may be found in our very own toolkit: the idea of unilinear social evolution has been largely abandoned by archaeologists precisely because it presupposes the uniform course of development of human societies. Furthermore, the yardstick according to which various cultures are evaluated is set by the Western European standards, those of progress and modernity (Thomas 2004). The authors working in the post-colonial key have exposed this practice to some radical criticism:

> 'If the West's attempt to understand the otherness of another culture ends up transforming the latter into a variation of itself, and if the same attitude underlies its attempt to understand itself, how do we make sense of its theories about the domains it regards as essential to itself?' (Dhareshwar 2006: 546).

At the same time, even the authors still working to prove the validity of the procedure of classifying human societies into discernible types stress that particular conditions may lead to various outcomes (Yoffee 2005). Likewise, the history of archaeology is not a unilinear process in which all the actors proceed through the same stages, in order to reach the ultimate development. Various local segments of the global archaeological community are geared towards different local needs and demands, conditioned by interplays of global and local factors. In order to understand the differences and to achieve a more fruitful communication among the segments of the global archaeological community, we need to understand the ways of transmission of knowledge and ideas. Before this task, it may be productive to bear in mind that: *'paradoxical and cynical as it may sound, what makes the world "thinkable" as one, in all its relationality, is the symptomatic richness of the term "unevenness"'*(Radhakrishnan 2003: vi). The segments of the global archaeological community have started their quest for knowledge of the past from various conditions and have reached various present forms. It is reasonable to assume that these local practices will continue to respond to various local challenges. The necessary task of situating the global practice of archaeology into its social, political, intellectual environment may be pursued more productively if we take into account that the world of the beginning of the twenty-first century is as diverse as it was in the past. *Integrating* its constituent parts may be possible if we acknowledge and strife to explain it in its '*symptomatic richness of unevenness*'. Archaeologists, by the very virtue of the discipline's ambition to seek explanations in the past, are well equipped to do so by investigating the different histories of their own discipline.

**Acknowledgements**
Many thanks to Aleksandar Palavestra and Predrag Novaković, the invaluable companions in investigating the history of archaeology in the Central Balkans.

# 25. The Celts: More Myths and Inventions

*John Collis*

**Keywords:** Celts, Celtic languages, Celtic Studies, La Tène Culture

In virtually every article I have written on the Ancient Celts in the last twenty years I have denied that I or anyone else who knows anything about the topic has said that the Celts never existed, yet again at this conference it came up, and it has appeared again in recent publications in Britain, Germany and elsewhere, especially in the popular archaeological press (e.g. Meid 2010; Pitts 2011; Schaper 2011, quoting Martin Schönfelder); it is a widespread belief in Spain as well (Manuel Fernández Götz pers. comm.). It originates, I think, from a conference in Cardiff in 1993 where Vincent and Ruth Megaw gave the summing up, with a pre-prepared attack on me which ignored all the other speakers, and indeed what I said in my contribution; they have repeated it at a number of conferences since (e.g. the EAA conference at Zadar), but none of these writers seems capable of providing a reference to where it was said. Personally I have spent many years of my life digging up the Arverni in central France, considered to be Celts both by Roman authors such as Julius Caesar, and by the local author Sidonius Apollinaris who was bishop of Clermont-Ferrand in the fifth century AD and who admits to suffering from 'the scurf of the Celtic tongue'.

What has been said is that no ancient author ever referred to the inhabitants of Britain and Ireland as Celts (James 1999; Collis 2003), and although similarities between the *Galli* and the *Britanni* were noted by several ancient authors, including their languages, often a contrast is made between Celts and Britons. This is something which everyone is agreed about. The problem comes when scholars, especially linguists, insist on imposing modern definitions of the Celts on to the ancient world, for instance that they can be defined as speakers of Celtic languages, or as users of Celtic Art, or as bearers of 'La Tène Culture', whatever that is (the definition varies from one country to another). For historiographical and methodological reasons this is not acceptable and we cannot use art, material culture, genes or language as a proxy for ethnicity. The origin and spread of the term 'Celtic' since the Renaissance is now well documented and should be familiar to anyone who has read the basic literature on the topic (James 1999; Collis 2003; Morse 2005), so one can only request that anyone who wishes to take part in the debate should do that first.

People such as myself who advocate the new approaches to the Celts have been labelled 'Celtosceptics' which has often been read as 'anti-Celtic'. I have tried to demonstrate that the reverse is true and it is the traditionalists who insist on labelling the Celts as illiterate warlike barbarians, and using racial stereotypes (Collis 2010). The person who introduced and popularised the term, Patrick Sims-Williams (1998), and who is now President of the International Celtic Congress, openly admits that he too is a Celtosceptic, and at the ICC conference in Maynooth in July 2011 he explored the significance of the new approaches in fields other than archaeology (Sims-Williams 2012a; 2012b). A paradigm shift is hitting Celtic Studies.

### Paradigm change in Archaeology

In prehistoric archaeology the first half of the twentieth century was dominated by the 'Culture History' paradigm. This approach is already to be found in nascent form in the works of authors such as Hoernes in the late nineteenth century (Karl pers. comm.), but the definition and interpretation was laid down by Gustaf Kossinna (1911) and popularised in the Anglophone community by Gordon Childe (1929). The basic assumption was that a People (or 'Race'), a Language and a 'Culture Group' (or 'Culture') could be equated with one another, and so an origin for all three can be identified from features such as pottery styles, ornaments and burial rites, and that the expansion of these traits over time can document the expansion of a people and language through migration. A major aim of prehistory was thus to set up a chronological framework so that the date of the occurrence of traits in different regions can be compared and areas of origin and of later diffusion differentiated. A key feature of this approach has been the use of distribution maps, though already in the 1950s the simplistic use of such maps by the Kossinna school had come under strong criticism (e.g. by Eggers 1959). It was increasingly recognised that distributions were fundamentally affected not only by ancient processes of deposition (e.g. in hoards, burials, etc.) but also by the processes of discovery.

Another key concept of this paradigm is that of 'continuity', both geographically (it is assumed migrating people will take elements of their culture with them) and chronologically (e.g. the modern Celts in Brittany, Scotland, Ireland and Wales are seen as descendants of the ancient Celts, and to share cultural traits with them – Sims-Williams 2012b). The theoretical basis for this approach lies in the *Stammbaum* or tree model of the development of languages, best documented by the Indo-European group. A feature of the languages is that, though they evolve over time, with changes in vocabulary, sound shifts, different word order and grammatical structure, nonetheless certain features survive allowing family groups to be defined (Romance, Slavic, Celtic, Germanic, etc.), and so allow the evolution to be reconstructed, with 'mother languages' such as Latin which gave rise to the Romance languages, but with local variants and dialects. This contrasted with the preceding biblical paradigm based on the adoption and the diffusion of languages from the Tower of Babel; this biblical paradigm talked of 'original languages' (*linguae matrices*) which were distributed around the world as peoples colonised new areas. Similarities between languages (e.g. between Irish and Latin) were explained as deriving from periods when the two peoples speaking them came into contact and influenced one another rather than envisaging that they had a common origin and ancestry (e.g. Pezron 1703).

In the 1960s, the Culture History paradigm came increasingly under attack especially in Cambridge. For the British Isles various scholars questioned to what extent migrations and new immigrants could be identified from the archaeological record, most notably the seminal paper by Grahame Clark 'The invasion hypothesis' (1966) in which he especially attacked the views of Christopher Hawkes whose scheme for the Iron Age (1959; 1960) envisaged three periods of invasion from the continent into Britain, 'Iron Age A' (Hallstatt), 'Iron Age B' (Early La Tène or 'Marnian') and 'Iron Age C' (Late La Tène or 'Belgic'). In a series of papers, Roy Hodson had already queried the factual basis of Hawke's system and emphasised the indigenous nature of 'The Woodbury Culture' though still accepting limited invasions and the Culture Group approach (Hodson 1960; 1962; 1964). In Cambridge, under the influence of Clark and Eric Higgs, a more economic and environmental approach to archaeology was developed, with strong Scandinavian influence (e.g. the use of pollen, animal bones, seed remains, etc.), but there were also developments in a more culture-based approach pioneered by David Clarke (1968) who, while rejecting the traditional equation of people, language and culture group, nonetheless thought the culture group was a useful archaeological hermeneutic concept, but which needed defining in a different way. Recognising that not all the features of a Culture Group would necessarily be found together, he proposed what he termed a 'polythetic' definition rather than the 'monothetic' approach of Childe and others. These were the academic traditions I encountered as a student in Cambridge in the 1960s. Personally I felt that terms like the Hallstatt and La Tène Cultures hindered rather than helped our understanding of culture (e.g. Collis 1977a; 1977b; 1986), and I reverted to a more anthropological definition of culture as the ideas and traits which could be passed from one individual or community to another and also passed on from one generation to another.

The new paradigm at the time was labelled 'The New Archaeology', but more recently as 'Processual', a term I do not particularly like as it encompasses only some of the theoretical and methodological changes of the late 1960s and 1970s. The new ideas derived especially from Geography and Anthropology, and very different models were put forward to explain the dispersal of new ideas. Thus I put forward an 'overlapping systems' model to explain the introduction and spread of coin use in southern Britain along with the technology of production, following pre-existing social and political links (Collis 1971) rather than a series of invasions of the Belgae from northern France (Allen 1961; Frere 1967:1–26). This allowed us to split apart the three characteristics which were supposed to be introduced by the Belgae at the time of their invasions: cremation burial; wheel-turned pottery; and gold coinage. We now know they are separate phenomena with different chronologies and distributions. The best known model of this type is 'peer polity interaction' developed by Colin Renfrew to explain, for instance, the distribution and development of megalithic tombs along the Atlantic coast, postulating a local origin rather than the *ex oriente lux* model which interpreted the tombs as spreading from the 'higher civilisations' of the Aegean (Renfrew & Cherry 1986).

The mechanisms to explain the diffusion of ideas is now seen more in terms of 'networks', so distribution maps are used to define these networks rather than to define culture groups. The mechanisms fall mainly under the generalised heading of 'socio-economic' rather than 'cultural', for instance through 'trade', mainly in the form of 'gift giving' rather than commercial trade (cf. Mauss 1954; Sahlins 1972), marriage alliances, apprenticeship, etc. Another spin-off of these models is that innovations can occur anywhere in the network rather than having a single origin, and so for instance metalwork such as Gündlingen swords could have an Atlantic origin rather than central European as implied by the Culture History model (Milcent 2008). For the La Tène period the art style could spread from west to east, but other items such as stamped pottery could spread from east to west, and need not be linked with any supposed expansion of the Celts from southern and western Germany (Kimmig 1965). Some scholars have taken these new models to imply that populations were less mobile than under the migration model, but my own assumption was that there was perhaps greater mobility, though mainly in the form of individuals and small groups in reciprocal relationships between communities, and it could be in any direction rather than in one direction only. Contact was thus continuous rather than periodic. This does not exclude mass movements – they are too well documented in the historical record, even if we take a sceptical approach to ancient interpretations; the Romans did not imagine the conflicts with the Cimbri and Teutones in the late second century BC which led to a fundamental reorganisation of the Roman army under Pompey. In some cases, the model of culture change seems to work, for instance, in the invasion of the Anglo-Saxons into Britain in the 5th century AD, though it does not work for northern England and southern Scotland where a Germanic language was introduced but without the distinctive cemeteries. Migration may also be the best explanation for the changes which happened in the first century BC in southern and central Germany and the Czech Republic, with the bearers of the 'Elbe-Germanic Culture' arriving from the lower Elbe, or the 'Przeworsk Group' from southern Poland expanding into central Germany, though as Peter Wells shows in his paper, it is not the simple replacement of one culture by another and we must not assume this explanation but explore it sceptically. These different sorts of models have their equivalents in linguistics in the form of the 'wave' (*Wellen*) model under which new innovations can spread between adjacent dialects and can even cross language boundaries. All we can do with archaeological data is to document them as best we can without preconceptions, explore a variety of interpretations, and then decide which provides the most likely explanation.

## RETHINKING THE CELTS

The concept and definition of the Celts which dominated for most of the twentieth century is derived mainly from British and French scholars, starting in the sixteenth century. While authors such as Tacitus noted similarities in the language and the physical characteristics of the peoples between the Britons and their continental neighbours in *Iberia*, *Gallia* and *Germania*, none referred to them as being Celts. The idea that Gallic tribes such as the Aedui and the Arverni were descended from Greeks or Trojans already appears in authors such as Sidonius Apollinaris, and this idea was to dominate the medieval origin myths – the Trojan Brutus for the Britons, and the Greek Gaythelos and the Egyptian princess Scotta for the Irish and Scots. From the sixteenth century, scholars in Western Europe especially in the Low Countries and France turned to linguistics as a possible means of tracing ancestry, but, with no agreed methodology, numerous different classifications and interpretations were put forward mainly using the similarity of words and vocabulary (van Hal 2013–4).

In Britain, the Scottish scholar George Buchanan belonged to this tradition. In his *Historia Rerum Scoticarum,* published in 1582, he first effectively demolished the medieval Brutus myth, and, to replace it, he suggested that the first settlers arrived from the continent in the fifth century BC, at the time when authors such as Livy suggested the Celts from Gaul were expanding into southern and central Europe (Collis 1999). He considered that there had been a triple invasion of peoples who spoke what he termed 'Gallic' languages: the Picts coming from the Baltic as stated by Bede and that these were related to the Gothuni and Aestiones who according to Tacitus spoke Gaulish or British languages; the Welsh he linked with Caesar's statement about the Belgae from northern Gaul who came to raid and then to settle; and finally he suggested the Irish and the Scots came from Iberia where there were Celts who had, he thought, originated in Gaul. His main evidence was the similarity of place names in Britain, Gaul and Spain, and he systematically listed all the names he could find in the ancient texts ending in –*briga*, –*magus* and –*dunum*, a brilliant piece of work for his time when such a scientific approach was not the norm. He was also one of the few to get the classification of languages right, recognising and differentiating between the 'Gallic' languages (Welsh, Irish, Scots Gaelic and ancient Gallic), a Germanic group (English, German, Flemish), and the Romance languages (Spanish, French and Italian). Though his work was described in the most influential history of Britain, William Camden's *Britannia*, (first published in 1586, but constantly revised and republished) it was not until the eighteenth to nineteenth century that the Celts finally displaced the Trojans and Brutus and theories based on biblical texts, with the story of the Tower of Babel and the descendants of Japheth who colonised Europe (the name of Japheth's son Gomer was linked with the Cimmerians, Cimbri and Cymry e.g. by Camden).

Few Renaissance scholars made the link between the ancient Gallic languages and those still surviving languages which we now call 'Celtic' as there was limited knowledge of them outside the areas where they were spoken in the sixteenth century; Buchanan may have spoken Scots Gaelic and so be the one exception. However, the next two major advances were both made by Celtic speakers, the Breton Abbé Pierre-Yves Pezron (1703) and the Welsh speaking Edward Lhuyd. Pezron thought that Breton was the last survival of the language spoken by Caesar's Celts, and he suggested that it was one of the 'original languages' (*linguae matrices*) spoken at the Tower of Babel. Similarities of words between Greek, Latin, German and Celtic he explained as influences from a period when the Celts had been the dominant people of Europe as they had gradually moved to the west. He recognised the similarity of Breton and Welsh, but makes no mention of Gaelic.

Pezron's work caused considerable excitement in Britain and his work was quickly translated into English (Jones 1705), and Lhuyd planned to visit him but he got no further than the port of Brest where he was arrested by the French authorities and deported. At this time Lhuyd was working on his survey of the origins of the Britons which included an investigation into archaeological monuments and the languages. Due to his early death only his linguistic work was published (1707), but he recognised the links between Breton, Cornish, Welsh, Irish and Scots Gaelic, and with the language spoken in ancient Gaul, evidence of which was gradually being gathered together (e.g. Boxhorn 1654). Importantly he was the first to identify 'sound shifts' by which one consonant could be replaced by another in another language, for instance the prefix meaning 'son of', Mac in Irish and Scots Gaelic, but (M)ap or P in Welsh (e.g. ApSimon, Probert), and this occurs systematically in the two languages giving rise to what Lhuyd termed Brythonic and Goidelic, a fundamental division into 'P' and 'Q' Celtic still commonly referred to up to the modern day. He followed Pezron in seeking a common origin and using his term 'Celtic' for the languages even though he seems aware that it was not a term used for the Ancient Britons. The use of the term 'Celtic' for the language group is thus based on two mistakes, firstly that the Celts could be defined by their language, and secondly that Breton was descended from the language of the Ancient Celts, and that from there it was transferred to Britain. In fact, neither is true, and most linguists now accept that Breton was introduced from Wales and especially Cornwall in late Roman and early post-Roman times, and 'Britannic' might have been a better term. In the ancient world it was the people who gave the name to a language rather than vice versa; Gauls spoke *gallice*, Celts spoke *celtice*, and Britons spoke *britannice* and there is no overall name which groups them together. The relationship between the Britannic languages and ancient Gaelic is more like that between, say, modern English and German; both are Germanic languages but they are cousins. But from these fundamental mistakes in the early eighteenth century flow all our modern usages of the term Celtic, for the language group, for Celtic Art, the Celtic Church, etc. By the late eighteenth century the Celtic origin of the language and peoples of the Atlantic 'fringe' was assumed and contrasted with the 'Gothic' or Germanic English who were descended from the post-Roman Anglo-Saxon immigrants from north west Germany as described by Bede. Their literature was popularised by the Romantic Movement, notably by the epic poems ascribed to Ossian, though in reality mainly by James Macpherson. It influenced poets such as Goethe, composers such as Mendelssohn, and Oscar Wilde was named by his parents after one of the characters in the poems.

In the 1840s and 1850s, there was an upsurge of interest in art styles, notably from the ethnographic collections brought back to Europe by explorers and missionaries. One art style of interest in Britain and Ireland was that of the early Christian manuscripts such as the Book of Kells and the Lindisfarne Gospels which have distinctive features such as 'trumpet scrolls'. As the style seemed to be indigenous, it was labelled as 'Celtic' following the linguistic interpretations. The earliest reference I have found to 'Celtic Art' in the modern sense is in the influential book *The Grammar of Ornament* edited by Owen Jones and published in 1856; it became a major source of designs and motifs from across the world for artists and architects and had a major influence on Victorian art and architecture. The section entitled 'Celtic Art' was written by the Sheffield born John Obadiah Westwood, based on his studies of the manuscripts; he suggested that the major influence on it was Byzantine Art, and that it dated entirely to post-Roman times. The following year John Kemble gave a lecture in Dublin pointing out its prehistoric antecedents like the shields from Battersea, Wandsworth and the River Witham, mainly newly discovered finds. Due to his sudden death a few weeks later, it was not until 1863 that it was published (Kemble *et al.* 1863). Franks who updated the archaeological section of the volume was aware of continental parallels for the art, especially from Switzerland, but the local origin, of what are now the major works of La Tène Art such as the Schwarzenbach bowl, was not recognised by scholars such as Lindenschmit and Reinecke who considered them imports from Italy or southern France. It was not until Joseph Déchelette (1913; 1914) that the continental origin of the art in the fifth century was recognised in the area of northern France, southern and western Germany and Bohemia. Thus Celtic Art was not so-called because it was the art of the continental Celts – that only happened later – but because it was thought the Irish were Celts.

By the late nineteenth century, with the collapse of the biblical chronology and its replacement by one based on Geology and Darwinian evolution, it was assumed that Western Europe had been occupied by pre-Celtic peoples, perhaps speaking the predecessors of Basque or Finnish. It was suggested that the introduction of Indo-European languages meant the arrival of a new race of people and that this might be identifiable in the shape of skulls (craniology). The people buried in the megalithic tombs and long barrows in Britain tend to be 'dolichocephalic' (long headed) in contrast to Beaker burials which were 'brachycephalic' (broad headed) and might indicate the arrival of Indo-European speakers at the beginning of the Bronze Age, and perhaps of the Celts (Morse 1999; 2005). So, for early writers such as Franks and J. Romilly Allen who wrote the first book on Celtic Art (1904), Early Celtic Art was represented by decorated Beakers and the geometric art on bronze objects, while La Tène Art was 'Late Keltic'. With the new chronologies of Déchelette and Reinecke and the developing concept of a 'Hallstatt' and a 'La Tène Culture' a new approach equated the language, the people, the art and the culture group. In this Déchelette largely followed the theories of the professor of Celtic Studies at the Sorbonne, Henri d'Arbois de Jubainville (1903) who, using the texts of Herodotos and Polybius and the evidence of the names of places and especially rivers, had suggested an origin for the Celts east of the Rhine in southern and central Germany, and that they had only expanded into Gaul around the fifth to fourth century BC, paralleling the migrations into Italy and central Europe (Collis 2004a). However Déchelette used the burial rite rather than material culture, assigning crouched inhumation as in Beaker burials to the arrival of the Indo-European speaking Ligurians, extended inhumation to the Celts, and cremation to the Germans and Belgae. Using this he suggested a date around 600 BC for the first Celts in Gaul. Thus by the time Paul Jacobsthal came to write his seminal work *Early Celtic Art* (1944), what had been 'Late Keltic Art' for Franks (in comparison to Beaker decoration) had become 'Early Celtic Art' (compared to the early Christian finds and manuscripts from Ireland).

The seminal work on the Celts in central Europe is Jan Filip's *Keltové ve střední Evropě* (1956), summarised in a more popular overview in 1960. He followed Déchelette in seeing one of the main ethnic indicators of the Celts as the burial rite, extended inhumation, but this he linked with a 'La Tène Culture' with wheel-turned pottery and distinctive ornaments and weapons. These burials were found especially in northern Bohemia, southern Moravia, Slovakia, northern Austria and the Hungarian Plain, but also in southern Poland, in western Romania and in the former Yugoslavia. He dated the arrival of the burial rite (the 'Dux Horizon') to La Tène B in the fourth century, typified by the brooches of Early La Tène construction found in the Duchcov hoard in northern Bohemia. The problem was the presence of La Tène objects in these areas which in the west would be dated to La Tène A in the fifth century; as a student visiting Vienna in 1967, I was told by Richard Pittioni that they also had to be dated to the fourth century as the Celts did not arrive in central Europe until 400 BC, dismissing the new dating put forward in his thesis by Stefan Nebehay (finally published in 1993 when his views had become the norm). Hand-made pottery found on the settlements as late as La Tène D has been interpreted as evidence of the 'survival' of an indigenous Hallstatt population alongside the immigrant Celts, even though hand-made pottery is also found in the 'Celtic heartlands' in Germany and northern France. It was Wolfgang Kimmig (1965) in his review of the Libenice report (Rybová & Soudský 1962) who showed that this 'La Tène A' material such as stamp decorated pottery should be dated to the fifth century in central Europe, the same as in the west. Excavations of settlements such as Radovesice show a continuity of occupation, and the appearance of the extended inhumation burial rite is only a brief part of the history of the settlement, appearing in La Tène B and disappearing in La Tène C1, whereas the associated village was occupied from Late Hallstatt to Late La Tène times (Waldhauser & Arbeitsgruppe 1993); so the burials need not necessarily point to an immigrant population. Clearly new and alternative models are needed to explain the origin and spread of these varied cultural traits.

The traditional explanation of the origin and spread of the Celts is ultimately based on the theories of d'Arbois de Jubainville and Déchelette, and though variations of maps illustrating this have been published by many people such as Pierre-Marie Duval (1977), Ludwig Pauli (1980) and the Megaws (1989),

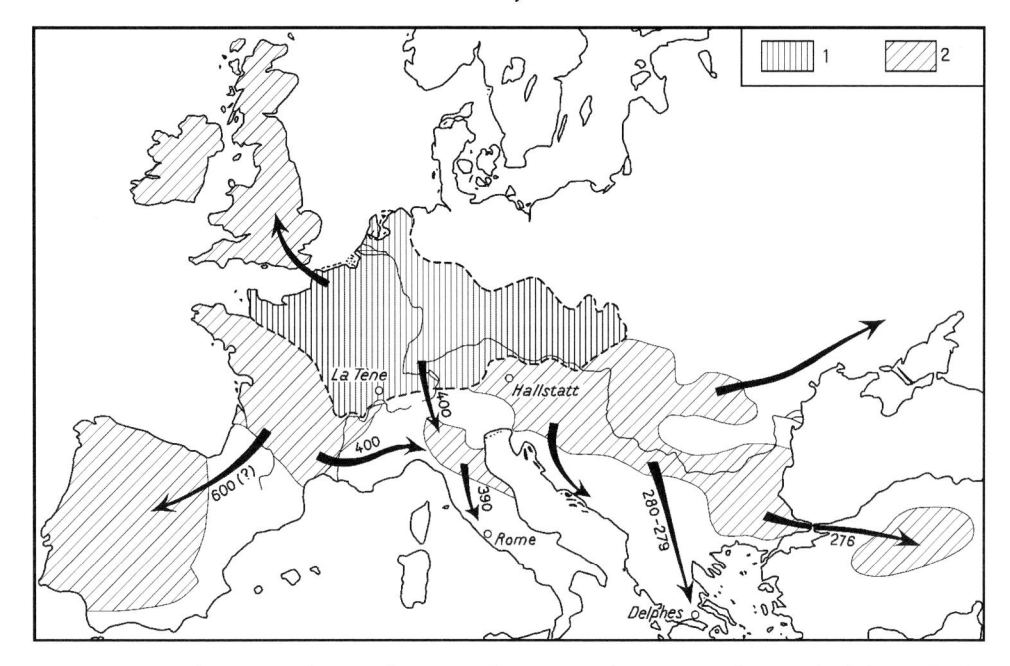

*Figure 25.1. The original map showing the supposed origin and spread of the Celts by André Aymard (1954), based on the ideas of Joseph Déchelette, and the source of many similar maps in the second half of the twentieth century.*

ultimately they all derive from a map (Fig. 25.1) published by the Ancient Historian André Aymard in 1954 (the shape of the area assigned to the Celtiberians in southeast Spain indicates the relationship of these maps). All make a selective and illogical use of historical, linguistic and archaeological data (Fig. 25.2); why, for instance on Pauli's map, do the Celts not cross the Fosse Way in England, and why did it and the accompanying exhibition ignore Ireland (Mac Eoin 1986)? Though the people in southern Germany (the assumed origin of the Celts) may well have been considered as Celts had any ancient authors written about them, the two sources we have (Herodotos and Caesar) are both problematic and vague, and we have better evidence for Celts at an early date in west and central Gaul and Iberia. I have tried to go back to the classical sources to see where they actually refer to the presence of Celts (Fig. 25.3), unclouded by later theories of language and archaeology. Even if we can make a uniform definition of a 'La Tène Culture Group', which I doubt, it would still not correlate either with the language or the people labelled as 'Celts'. Unfortunately the ancient sources are vague and contradictory (where and what was Tylis, for example? – see Emilov 2010), but this map is substantially different from, and better than, the traditional maps which misinterpret or ignore the ancient texts and it demonstrates the need to question the basic factual and theoretical presumptions of the standard works on the Celts.

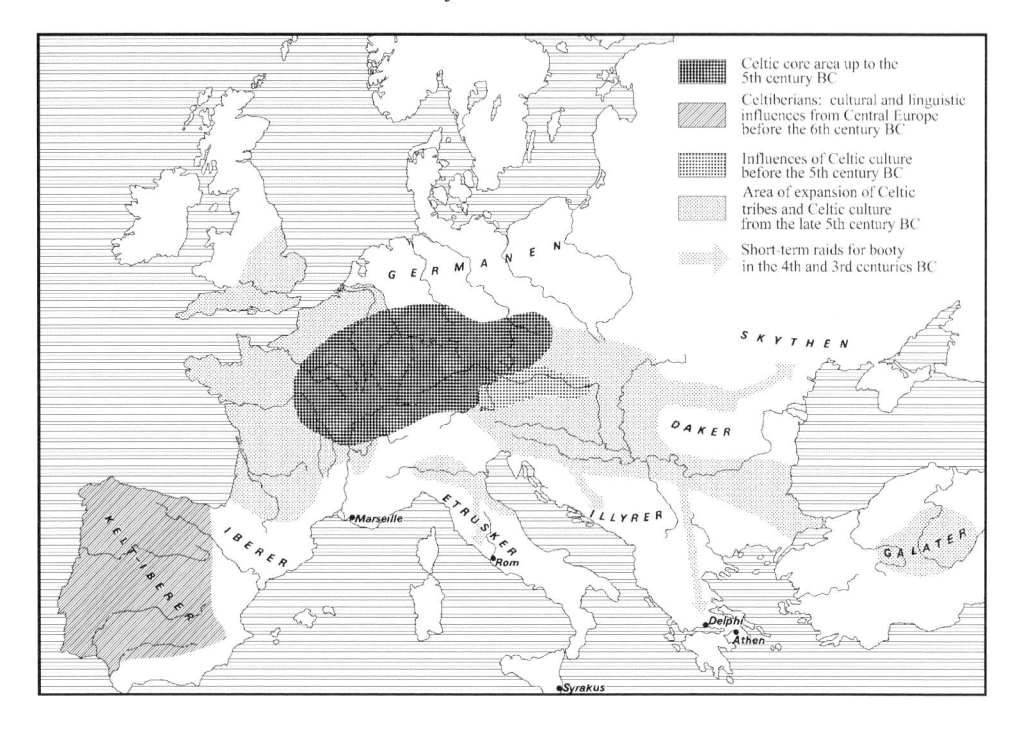

*Figure 25.2. Ludwig Pauli's map used for the exhibition on the Celts in central Europe at Hallein in 1980. The treatment of the Celtiberians is taken straight from Aymard, but it is unclear why Britain and Ireland have largely been ignored.*

### Present problems and disagreements

Though I have suggested above that Celtic Studies is passing through something of a paradigm shift, this does not mean there is agreement on the theoretical and methodological basis on how we can move forward. The disagreements fall under three headings: firstly there are those who simply reject the critique and argue for the old paradigm; secondly there are influential scholars who have not bothered to read the works of others and continue to reiterate or promote ideas that many of us consider to be false; and thirdly scholars who accept most of the critique, but disagree with some elements of it.

In the first category I would place Ruth and Vincent Megaw (1996) who argue that people have multiple identities, and, in the case of the Celts, one identity is evidenced by La Tène Art which indicates a way of seeing the world which is special to those making and using the 'art'. While I would not disagree with this, I would claim that it is confusing to label this as 'Celtic' as the 'art' was not confined to those who spoke Celtic languages for instance in probably Germanic speaking Denmark or Iberian speaking Ensèrune. Nor did it extend to all people who spoke Celtic languages and considered themselves to be Celts, for instance the Celtiberians of the Iberian Peninsula. Though attempts have been made to find elements of La Tène Art in these areas of Spain (e.g. Lenerz-de Wilde 1991), most of this consists of shared elements of 'Orientalising Art', and certainly does

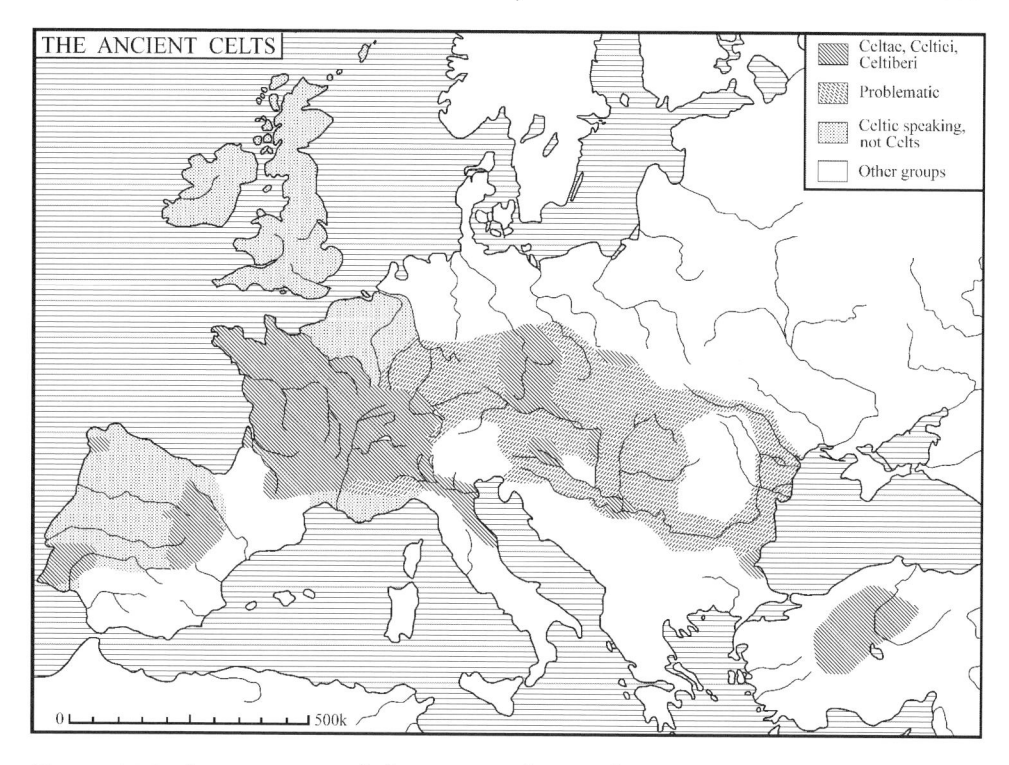

*Figure 25.3. An attempt to define areas where Celts are mentioned in the ancient sources and contrasted with the likely distribution of Celtic languages (the latter partly based on place-names rather than direct evidence). Unlike the two previous maps the location of the Celts is based on the ancient written sources rather than modern (mis-)interpretations of archaeological and linguistic data, but because of the vagueness of the ancient sources, the map should not be taken too literally.*

not conform to what most people would consider to be La Tène Art. The art of the Celtiberians, indeed their whole culture is closer to that of their non-Indo-European Iberian neighbours than to other Celtic speakers. To call all La Tène Art 'Celtic' is both illogical and confusing, and removes potentially interesting questions like how transmission of the art was affected by the language spoken by the users.

In the second category, those who give opinions on defining the Celts without reading the key contributions to the debate or understanding what the debate is about includes a number of recent publications (e.g. McCone 2008; Meid 2010), or misunderstand the argument, e.g. Buchsenschutz 2007: 20 where he suggests I deny the linguistic relationship between ancient and modern languages when what I am pointing out is the mistake made by Pezron in thinking Breton is a survival of the ancient language of the Celts. The most recent publication in this category is *Celtic from the West* edited by Barry Cunliffe and John Koch (2010) which, because of the status of the authors, is likely to be influential on the wider public, though both of them are considerably out of date theoretically and methodologically and make mistakes of logic and fact, indeed are contradicted by other contributors to the volume.

Their basic theory (they call it a new 'paradigm' without understanding the meaning of this concept in the history of science) is that the origin of the Celts and the Celtic languages lies in southeast Iberia where they claim the 'Tartessian' inscriptions are in a Celtic language. As these inscriptions start as early as the eighth to seventh century BC and so, if indeed they are Celtic, it is the earliest evidence of a Celtic language, they claim illogically that this is therefore the origin of the Celtic languages, and Cunliffe goes on to claim (p. 20) that as the ancient Celts were defined by their language (!) it is therefore also for them the origin of the Celts, who spread along the Atlantic coast in the Late Bronze Age and then inland along the rivers into central Europe. As linguists such as Glyn Isaac (in the same volume) suggest the linguistic links of Celtic is rather with the eastern Indo-European languages, then somehow the Indo-Europeans whose language was to evolve into Celtic had to reach Iberia from eastern Europe; Koch suggests a 'group of Indo-Europeans became mariners ... and they sailed west, to the Ocean' (Koch 2010: 192)! However, the present consensus among linguists is that 'Tartessian' is not a Celtic language (Sims-Williams 2012a: 431).

In his attempts to demonstrate an early arrival of the Celts in the west, Cunliffe states that both Ampurias and Narbonne were Celtic towns. In his discussion of the location of the *Pyrene* mentioned by Herodotos as the source of the Danube and in the lands of the Celts, John Hind (1972) states that Ampurias (*Emporion*) is not mentioned in the Massiliot sailing manual, but *Pyrene* is, so this could be an early name for the Greek colony. Cunliffe does not mention Hind's article, but he references Domínguez (2004) as supporting the identification when in fact he states his considerable reservations, and Cunliffe also seems unaware of the other paper, by Fischer (1972), supporting the traditional location in southern Germany where he suggests *Pyrene* may be the Heuneburg. My own thought is that *Pyrene* in fact refers to the mountain range (confusion between names of mountains and a *polis* occur elsewhere in the early Greek literature), and the Ariège or the Garonne may have been confused with the headwaters of the Danube, and, as he does with the Nile, Herodotos may just join up dots to reconstruct the course of the river; this last suggestion would put us in the territory of the Celtic Volcae Tectosages. The truth is these are all guesses and we simply do not know what to make of Herodotos' ambiguous and vague statement. Also Cunliffe misquotes Stephen of Byzantium, that Hecataeus says *Narbo* is a Celtic town, when in fact this statement is assigned to Strabo and Marcian, not Hecataeus (so first century BC rather than sixth century BC), and is almost certainly geographical and administrative rather than ethnic – a town 'in Gaul' not a town 'of the Celts' (Gayraud 1981: 77; Collis 2003: 127; 2010: 37); what little evidence we have suggests *Narbo* was ethnically Iberian and Iberian speaking. However, we now have maps which show Celts living around the Gulf of Lion and in north west Spain (e.g. Cunliffe & Koch 2010: Fig. 1–3) when in fact there is no evidence for them. We simply cannot use, and abuse, the ancient sources in this way. Cunliffe also dismisses the works of Buchanan and Pezron as 'rambling speculations' (p. 15); he has clearly never directly consulted either of them. At the time neither Koch nor Cunliffe had bothered to read my book, though Koch now does admit that it is essential reading (Koch 2009). As Karl (2010) states in his contribution to the volume, looking for the origin of the Celts is a pointless exercise as it is an insoluble question. We are now faced with an influential ill-researched theory which we must waste time and money refuting.

Turning to the third category, these are those who accept much, but not all, of the critique of the Celtosceptics; the most obvious is Raimund Karl, and he and I have been discussing our differences over the last few years in seminars, pubs and publications (Karl 2004; 2006; 2008a; 2011; Collis 2011). There is much on which we agree, but our major disagreement lies in the status we accord the early medieval Welsh and Irish literature. Karl claims that there are basic 'building blocks' which are distinctive of 'Celtic societies' and which can be applied to other Celtic speaking societies such as those of the British Iron Age:

> 'if it looks eastwards like a Celt, separates the household like a Celt, produces like a Celt, and even talks like a Celt, we may very well assume that it actually is a Celt' (Karl 2008b).

None of the features he lists here are ones I would consider uniquely Celtic, or to be found in most Celtic speaking societies. I would argue that the Irish and Welsh sources are so far removed from the ancient Celts in time, space and technology that we can only use them as we would any ethnographic or historical model from other parts of the world to give us ideas of how to interpret our archaeological data. It is basically a matter of how we view 'continuity', and I would suggest that Karl is imposing the linguistic *Stammbaum* model on other aspects of culture where it is not apposite. At Maynooth, Sims-Williams, as a linguist, took a similar attitude to my own, but using other data sets. I have also argued that Celtic speaking societies such as the Celtiberians share more with their neighbours, even non-Indo-European speakers such as the Iberians, than they do with more distant peoples who spoke a related language. The discussion appears among the papers in the proceedings of a conference held in Durham in 2008 (Moore & Armada 2011).

As discussed above, the word 'Celtic' for the language group and its use to define the Ancient Celts are both inappropriate, but I would go further and state that this classification of languages inhibits a detailed understanding of the actual situation in the same way as I suggest that the 'culture group' inhibits archaeologists in their understanding of their data. In a brief exchange of emails with me, John Koch has argued that linguists can 'scientifically' demonstrate the existence of the Celtic language group. Personally I would query this as the original classification starts with the recognition of similarity between the languages which still survived in the eighteenth century, but with a small amount of input from the limited knowledge at that time of the ancient Gallic languages. The next stage was then to define the characteristics that distinguished these languages from other Indo-European languages groups (Slavic, Italic, Germanic, etc.). Newly discovered languages such as Lepontic and Celtiberian could be then compared with the collective characteristics to see if they had enough 'Celtic' characteristics to be assigned to the group. Some pass, others like Lusitanian do not (Wodtko 2010), and in Spain there are several other related languages such as those of the Vettones and the Asturians which are labelled as Hispano-Celtic, but which lack key attributes, or where there is simply not enough data surviving. What if classification could have been based on these ancient languages rather than the much later languages on the fringe of the ancient distribution of Indo-European languages? Would we find a similar problem to that encountered by archaeologists trying to define groupings from analyses of copper-alloy objects or of Bell Beakers where an understanding of the variability of a local geographical group is more informative and produces different and more logical classifications than attempting to deal with the whole of the data set in one analysis (Waterbolk & Butler 1965; Lanting & Van der Waals 1972; discussed in Hodson 1969: 97–98)? But the circular argument and non-scientific nature of the present linguistic classification should be obvious and perhaps using single attributes and using the *Wellen* rather than the *Stammbaum* model might be more informative. Similar problems exist also in the way in which genetic data sets are sometimes analysed, so there are shared methodological questions which transcend the narrow academic disciplines. The concept of a Celtic language group may simply be irrelevant to areas like Spain or central Europe, and it may be a case of the tail of the Celtic 'fringe' wagging the mainland European linguistic dog, and a dead dog at that.

## Conclusions

In this article I have attempted to provide an overall summary of why some of us challenge the traditional interpretations of the Celts, and also consider the problems with the claims that the Celts came from southern Germany or from Spain which are based on a poor knowledge of the historical and archaeological data and outdated theory and methodology. I have primarily discussed what happened in western Europe, but this is because the theory and methodology (whether right or wrong) has from the sixteenth century onwards been mainly developed in western Europe, in France, Britain and Germany, and then applied to central and eastern Europe. It is a theme which has been discussed in a central European context over the last decade, most recently by Sabine Rieckhoff in critiques of the recent exhibition on the Celts in Stuttgart (Rieckhoff 2012a; 2012b) and at the biennial Linz conferences organised by Raimund Karl and Jutta Leskovar (e.g. Karl *et al.* 2012). In her review of the Cambridge conference, Staša Babić admits that the lead in new ideas is still coming mainly from western Europe (Babić 2011), and it is clearly important that modern approaches to ethnicity in archaeology are adopted, given the recent history of the Balkans and the ways in which archaeology has been abused in Europe throughout the twentieth century (Jones 1997). We must prevent our subject being misused for political ends.

The situation in the east may, however, be very different from the west. Problematic though it may be, the historical evidence is richer than it is for Germany, Britain and parts of Spain. Likewise the archaeology in some ways has greater potential; inhumation burials can provide data for DNA and isotope analysis, and in the east they are more common than in Spain and Ireland and in much of France and Britain where the dead have either been cremated or have totally disappeared. A comparison between linguistic, archaeological and anthropological data for the Hungarian Plain, for instance, could be very informative. However, we must not start with the presumption of the Culture-History paradigm idea that we are necessarily dealing with ethnicity and migration to explain the archaeological record. As in our experience in southern Britain, new attitudes may produce better explanations of the archaeological data, though this does not necessarily mean we completely reject the historical interpretations of migrations of large groups of people. I have also suggested that this different way of looking at things is not confined to classification and interpretation but also to the ways in which we construct chronologies – I propose abandoning the Reinecke and Déchelette systems of chronology and nomenclature using type fossils and which tend to emphasise breaks (and so of migrationist interpretations), in favour of one based on seriation and single attributes which can demonstrate more gradual change (Collis 2008; 2009). I have also discussed how changes of paradigm have affected excavation methods and the sorts of site we excavate (Collis 2001; 2004b). Paradigm change potentially affects everything we do as archaeologists.

# 26. Material Culture and Identity. The Problem of Identifying Celts, Germans and Romans in Late Iron Age Europe

*Peter Wells*

**Keywords:** identity, Celts, Germans, Romans, interaction

### Introduction: identity in the Iron Age

In the prehistory of temperate Europe, the Iron Age is unique in offering both a rich database of well documented archaeological material and textual documents written by Greek and Roman commentators that pertain to the peoples north of the Mediterranean basin. Among the named peoples that have attracted the most attention are those known as Celts (or Gauls) and Germans.

### Background: attempts to identify Celts and Germans in the archaeology of Late Iron Age Europe

Serious concern with understanding the peoples of Europe's pre-Roman past began during the Renaissance, and much of the thinking that has dominated the next 500 years had it roots in that period (Moser 1998: 66–106). Two inter-related trends were especially important for the growing interest in the peoples of early Europe. One was the discovery and identification of Roman remains, especially in towns and military bases along the Rhine and Danube frontiers (Kühn 1976: 16). These often included Latin inscriptions on architectural fragments and on coins. The other was the rediscovery in monasteries and churches, and subsequent translation and publication, of Greek and Roman texts that described the native European peoples (Reynolds and Wilson 1974). From these fifteenth and sixteenth century beginnings developed the subsequent efforts to connect the names Celt and German with the archaeological materials of Iron age Europe.

Hecataeus and Herodotos provide the earliest well documented references that associate the name *Keltoi* with a specific geographical context (Freeman 1996; Cunliffe 2011). Hecataeus, whose works survive only in fragments, asserted around the end of the sixth century BC that peoples who lived in southern Gaul were *Keltoi*. Herodotos, writing around the middle of the fifth century BC, said both that the Danube originates in the region inhabited by Celts, and that Celts lived in western Europe. (The peoples the Greeks called *Keltoi* were the same as those the Romans called *Galli* [Niese 1910: 610; Freeman 1996: 12]. In this paper, I shall use just the Greek-derived name Celts.) These statements led early investigators to conclude that both what is now southern France and what is now south western Germany were inhabited by Celts in the fifth century BC.

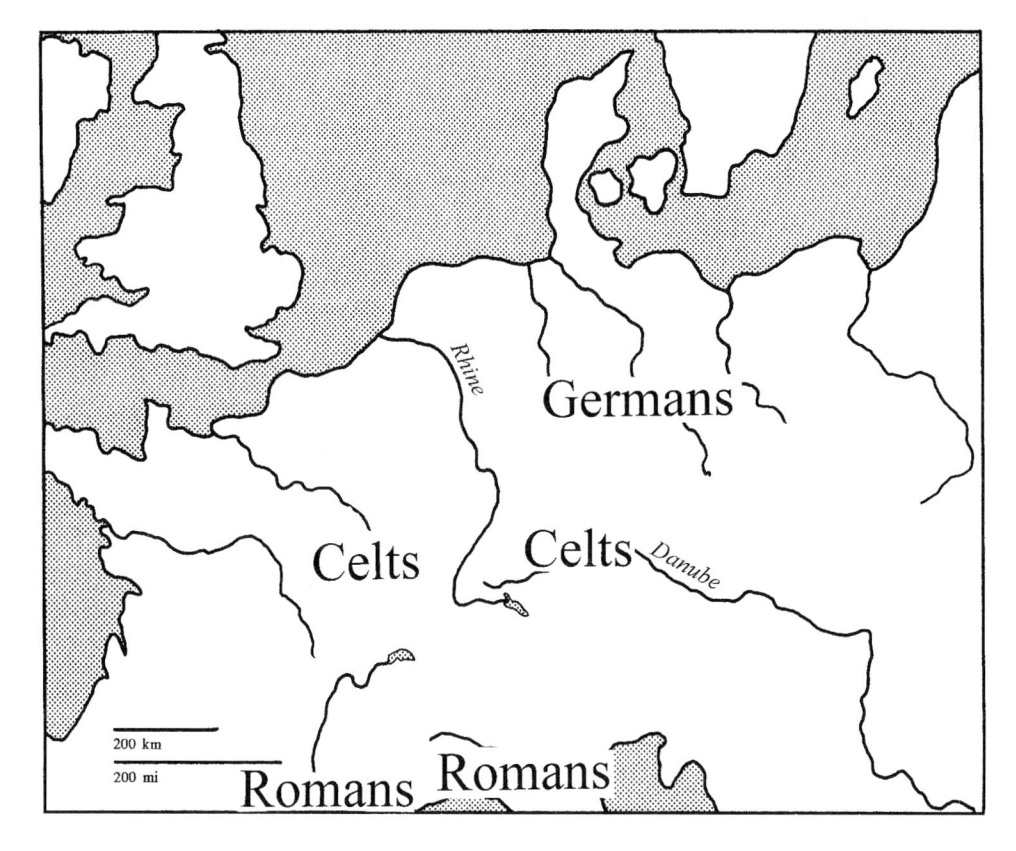

*Figure 26.1. Map illustrating the geographical model of Celts, Germans and Romans in Late Iron Age Europe.*

Subsequent Greek observers based their writings largely on these earlier views (Freeman 1996).

The first well documented naming of the Germans, as *Germani,* is by Julius Caesar in his account of his campaigns in Gaul, 58–51 BC. (Poseidonius may have used the name several decades earlier, but his work does not survive.) Caesar states a number of times in his text that Celts live west of the Rhine, Germans live east of the river. He goes on to note differences between Celts and Germans, characterising Germans as less developed culturally and politically and less like the Romans than the Celts were (Wells 1995).

Since the material culture of the Iron Age peoples of southern Germany, the Czech Republic, Austria, Hungary, and other regions to the east and south was stylistically similar to that of Gaul, especially in the La Tène Period, those lands were thought to have been inhabited by Celts as well (Moscati *et al.* 1991; Fitzpatrick 1996). Caesar's assertions in the middle of the final century BC about Germans living east of the Rhine were understood to refer to the lower Rhine, and the topographical border between the central uplands of Europe and the north European plain was taken as that between Celts to the south and Germans to the north, with the La Tène material culture of the Celts in the south (Dietz 2004) and the Jastorf, Ripdorf, and Seedorf material cultures of the Germans in the north (Hachmann *et al.* 1962; Wells 2011). A result of this geographical model of pre-Roman peoples (Fig. 26.1) was the attributing of 'ethnic' character to particular items of material culture. For example, Early La Tène fibulae decorated with stylised animal heads (Fig. 26.2) were called 'Celtic', as were Late La Tène flat-bowed Nauheim fibulae that are so common in the central upland areas of Europe (Fig. 26.3). The wire fibulae of the variety known as Beltz J, which are common in northern regions, were called 'Germanic' (Fig. 26.4). When Beltz J fibulae are found in southern regions, they have often been understood to indicate the presence of Germans. The flaws in this approach will become evident below.

### CRITIQUE: THREE ASSUMPTIONS ABOUT CLASSICAL WRITERS' PORTRAYALS OF IRON AGE EUROPEANS

The association of the names Celt and German with specific regions, on the basis of the Greek and Roman written sources, makes three fundamental assumptions, all of which we now understand to be unwarranted.

The first is that the Greek and Roman authors portrayed the population geography of temperate Europe in ways that we would accept today. In fact, Hecataeus's locating of the Celts around Massalia in southern Gaul is not very specific, and neither he nor Herodotos indicate anything about how they distinguished Celts from other peoples (Keyser 2011). Nor do they name any other peoples of western or central temperate Europe with whom they compare the Celts. *Keltoi* would thus seem to be so general a term, as far as the early Greek writers were concerned, that it has no useful meaning of identity for us. Recent scholarship on Caesar's representation of the Germans and his designation of the Rhine as their western border has made clear that we cannot accept his assertions about those people at face value (Wells 1995; 2011). It is quite possible that the information that Hecataeus, Herodotos, Caesar, and other writers recorded conformed to what was expected by readers in their societies at the times they were writing, but they do not stand up to our scrutiny today.

The second assumption is that the Greek and Roman writers understood ethnicity in the same way that we do. As Klaus Müller (1972) and Dieter Timpe (1989) have shown, understanding of 'the Other' was quite different in Greek and Roman society from our ideas about different societies today. There were no anthropologists – at least none that we know about – among the ancient Greeks and Romans who attempted to understand societies different from their own. The standard assumption, as it is expressed in the written works that survive, was that *Others* – barbarians – were different from Greeks and Romans in specific ways, and that all barbarians were more or less similar (Ferris 2000). Yet as we know from the archaeological evidence, the communities that inhabited the lands that the ancient writers said were occupied by Celts varied considerably in their material culture and in their cultural practices, both geographically and over time.

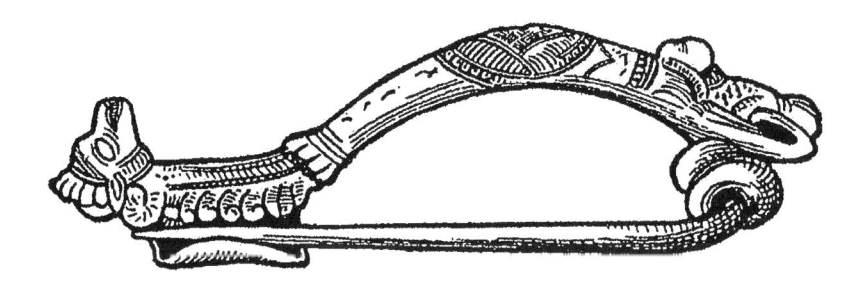

*Figure 26.2. Early La Tène fibula with animal ornament, from Panenský Týnec, Bohemia, Czech Republic. (From Beltz 1911:672 fig. 1).*

The third assumption is that identity is a fixed aspect of an individual's and a group's existence (Timpe 1989). As Eric Wolf (1982) could write of *Europe and the People Without History*, so too Greek and Roman writers believed that other peoples – Celts and Germans – were fixed in their character and identity and did not change – did not have history in the sense that Greece and Rome had history. But today we know that peoples do change their identities in response to changing factors in their cultural and political environments.

### WHAT IS IDENTITY? DEFINITION AND APPROACH

In my book on Iron Age identities (Wells 2001: 22), I defined identity as 'the ever-changing feeling and knowledge people have about their similarity to and difference from others'. Both the dynamic and the relational aspects of identity are important. Identities are not fixed, but always changing with circumstances. And people create their identities to distinguish themselves from others. Without an *Other*, there is no point to an identity.

In their original forms, we encounter the names Celt and German only in the writings of Greeks and Romans; as far as we know, they were never designations used by the peoples of temperate Europe themselves (until much later). The differences that we observe in burial practices and other ritual activity, in designs on pottery and metal ornaments, and in other characteristics apparent in the archaeological evidence make clear that other kinds of distinctions were what mattered to them, not those that are represented in the written sources.

Rather than being inherent and constant, as older models would suggest, identity is constructed by the individual and by the community; it is fluid, and it is dynamic – it changes with the historical circumstances in which the individual and the group find themselves (Jones 1997; Díaz-Andreu et al. 2005). Identity is always contingent – it is fashioned for a particular purpose. In any study of identity, we need to ask – what was the specific identity *for*?

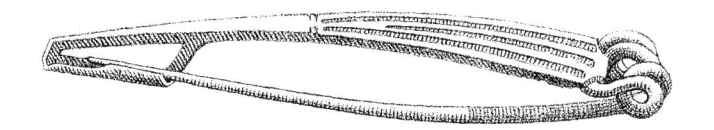

*Figure 26.3. Nauheim-type fibula from Stradonice, Bohemia, Czech Republic. (From Osborne 1881, pl. 3, 8).*

*Figure 26.4. Fibula of the type Beltz J. (From Beltz 1911, 685 fig. 50).*

### THE HISTORICAL CONTEXT AND THE DYNAMICS OF IDENTITY

In order to address the question of identity in Late Iron Age temperate Europe, we need therefore to review briefly what was going on in the the larger context of the continent that is likely to have motivated people and groups to create particular identities. To do this, we can employ both the available written sources and the abundant archaeological evidence. Both sources of information indicate that an increasing amount of interaction was taking place between individuals and communities of temperate Europe and societies in the Mediterranean world. A few examples will serve to make the point.

#### Textual Sources

Greek writers inform us that Celts served as mercenaries in armies in the eastern Mediterranean region during the fourth and third centuries BC (Szabó 1991; Tomaschitz 2002). We are not told where these soldiers came from nor any specific information about who they were, but from the available evidence it is reasonable to conclude that some men from temperate Europe were fighting in the lands of the eastern Mediterranean, thereby becoming familiar with cultural worlds different from their homelands.

Throughout the latter half of the third and the second centuries BC, Rome intensified its economic, political, and military activities in southern Gaul (Dietler 2010). These are documented in written sources of the time, and the archaeological evidence attests to intensifying interaction between the Roman world and the indigenous peoples of Gaul.

|  | HISTORICAL SOURCES | ARCHAEOLOGICAL EVIDENCE | PERIOD |
|---|---|---|---|
| 200 BC | | | |
| | | Earliest imported amphorae at Manching | |
| | | | La Tène C2 |
| | Cimbri, Teutones invade C Europe | *murus Gallicus* built at Manching | |
| 100 BC | | | |
| | | | La Tène D1 |
| | 58-51 BC Caesar in Gaul | Manching decline | |
| | | | La Tène D2 |
| | 15 BC Roman conquest of S Bavaria | | |
| AD 1 | | | |
| | | | La Tène D3 |
| | | Substantial Roman infrastructure in provinces | |
| AD 100 | | | |

*Table 26.1. Chronological chart for Late Iron Age and early Roman Period southern Bavaria.*

Written sources inform us of groups called Cimbri and Teutones who swept southward from northern parts of the continent between 120 and 101 BC, attracting adherents as they moved, invading and plundering lands of central, western, and southern Europe until their defeat by Roman armies. Between 58 and 51 BC, Julius Caesar conducted his military campaigns in Gaul, successfully conquering the entire region and thereby advancing Rome's territory eastward to the Rhine. During the years 16–13 BC, the Emperor Augustus oversaw the strengthening of Rome's military bases on the west bank of the Rhine, and in the year 15 BC, his generals Tiberius and Drusus conquered the lands south of the upper Danube in a single campaign season (Table 26.1).

## Archaeological Evidence

The archaeological material indicates a much more broadly based process of increasing interaction. From the sixth century BC, and especially during the second and first centuries BC, communities in temperate Europe were becoming ever more involved in long-distance interactions. For example, in the sixth and fifth centuries BC, ivory from Africa or Asia was used in the ornament of sword hilts (Meixner *et al.* 1997), silk has been identified in graves in central and western Europe (Good 1995), and a bronze situla from Syria was recovered in a burial at Straubing on the upper Danube (Tappert & Mielke 1998). (For an overview of evidence for such contacts, see Stöllner 2004.)

During the final two centuries BC, a quantitative transformation is apparent in imports from beyond Europe. Transport amphorae from the Roman world become abundant on sites in France (Poux 2004), but also occur in Germany, notably at Manching, in Switzerland at Basel, and at many other sites. Roman bronze vessels, fine ceramics, coins, and writing equipment further attest to the intensifying of interactions between temperate Europe and the Mediterranean basin. All of this archaeological evidence shows that European communities were participating in what Christopher Ehret (2002) has called the 'commercial revolution' that took place during the final millennium BC throughout the Mediterranean, parts of Africa, the Near East, and eastwards to India. Ehret shows that this profound transformation came about as the result of fundamental changes in the nature of commerce, from economies dominated by 'kings' (or other potentates) to trading systems conducted by merchants in their own interests.

## INTERACTION AND IDENTITY

A key element in understanding the creation, expression, and transformation of identities lies in responses to interactions with outsiders. As noted above, identity is relational – it is in relation to something else. In small communities, households could differentiate themselves from others through details in how their pottery was ornamented (Wells 2010), and individuals distinguished themselves from others through details in the decoration of personal ornaments such as fibulae and belt plates (Kilian-Dirlmeier 1972). Communities often distinguished themselves from other communities through cultural practices such as burial rituals (*e.g.* Reim 1995). In the large communities at the *oppida* of the Late Iron Age, most pottery and ornaments were mass-produced and thus did not play the same roles as they did in smaller settings. And burial practices of earlier times were often replaced by very different kinds of ritual disposal of the dead.

The particular identities that individuals and groups choose to express at any given time depend upon the immediate social and political circumstances in which they find themselves. As circumstances change, so do the character of the identity expressed and its means of expression. The individualised pottery vessels, fibulae, belt plates, and other items of everyday material culture that had played significant roles in expressing individual and community identity during

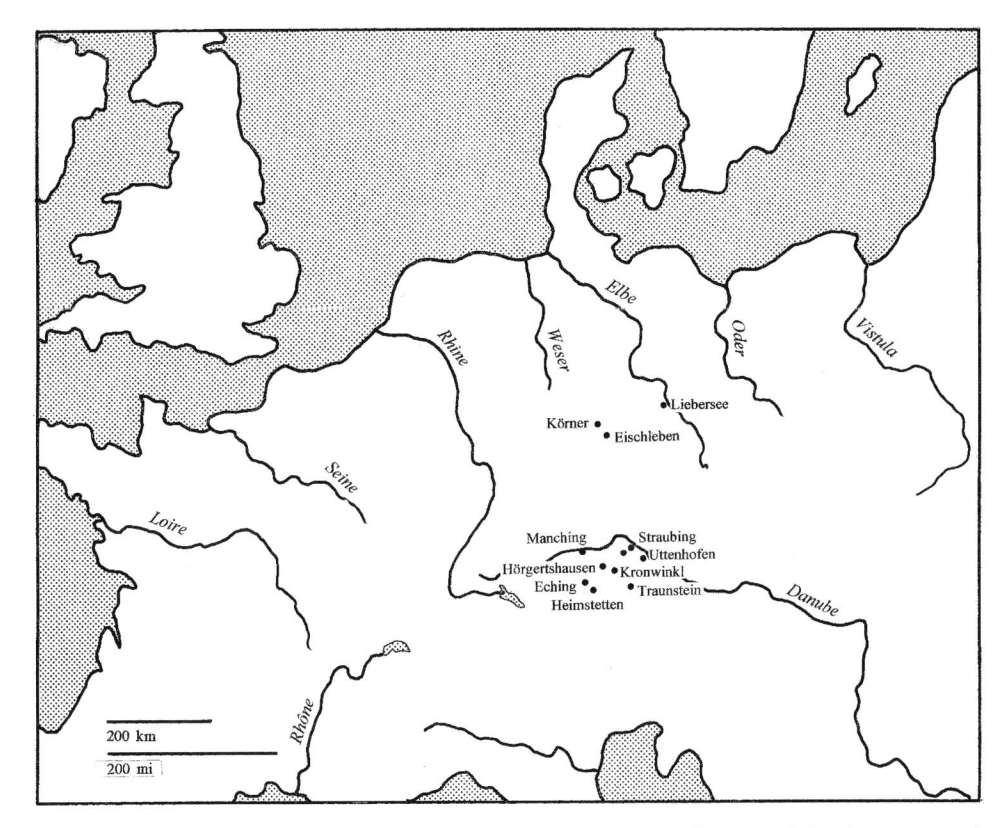

*Figure 26.5. Map showing locations of sites mentioned in the text. (The dot just south west of Straubing represents Sallach.)*

the Bronze and earlier Iron Age became much less important during the second century BC, as political and economic changes led to mass production of objects that had been individually crafted previously.

### MATERIAL CULTURE AND THE COMPLEXITY OF IDENTITY AT THE END OF THE IRON AGE

In order to explore these principles in the patterns of the archaeological material, I turn to brief examination of several sites in the region south of the Danube where Celts are traditionally thought to have been and in the north in Saxony and Thuringia, regions associated with Germans (Fig. 26.5). Some investigators (Rieckhoff 1995) have seen evidence for Germans arriving south of the Danube during the final century BC (Fig. 26.6). Textual sources inform us that the Roman armies of Tiberius and Drusus conquered the territory south of the Danube in 15 BC. Thus from that date on we need to reckon with 'Romans' as another category of people in this region.

Traditional approaches have operated under the assumption that 'Celts', 'Germans' and 'Romans' all had material cultures – including pottery, fibulae, and

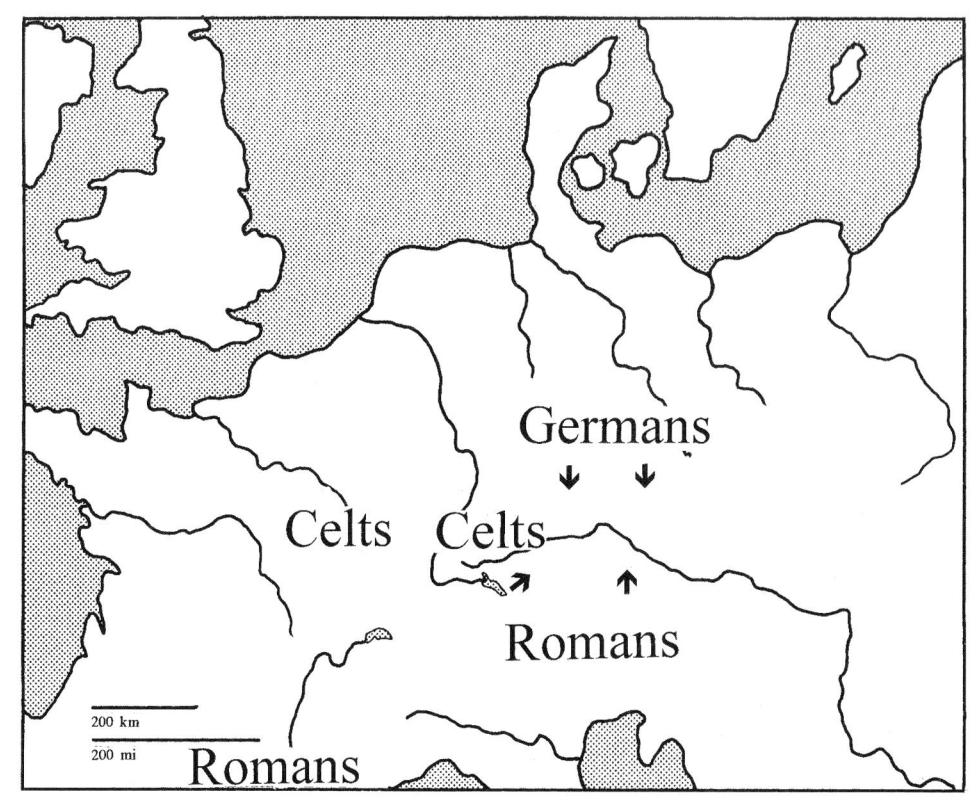

*Figure 26.6. Map showing suggested movements southward by Germans during the Late La Tène Period, and textually documented invasions by Roman armies into southern Bavaria.*

belt hooks – that distinguished them from the other groups (Stöckli 1993; Rieckhoff 1995; 2007; Steidl 2006). In fact, in reality, the situation was much more complex. Since the writings of Stöckli, Rieckhoff, and others, the available material for analysis has expanded vastly, especially from settlement sites that have been discovered and excavated during the past two decades (Hüssen 2000; Hüssen *et al.* 2004; Wells 2005).

## Changes in the Second Century BC: Overview

During the second century BC, fundamental changes took place in all aspects of life among the peoples of temperate Europe, and these bear directly on the subject of identity. *Oppida* were established during the first half of the second century BC as the largest settlements of prehistoric Europe and as centres of manufacturing and both intensive and extensive trade (Sievers 2007). Mass production of goods developed on a scale much larger than at any time before. Pottery, iron tools, fibulae, and other goods were manufacured in series at the *oppida,* representing a reorientation of the economy. Coinage became common, with coins minted at all of the major *oppida* and circulating widely. The practice of burying the dead in substantial flat-grave cemeteries, as had been common during the fourth and third centuries BC, ceased in much of temperate Europe. Other rituals involved with disposing of bodies were developed, and abundant human skeletal remains associated with these rituals have been recovered on many settlement sites (Hahn 1992).

A decline in the highly ornate character of figural representation and decoration accompanied these changes and was replaced by a new emphasis on plain forms that lent themselves to mass production. Personal ornaments such as fibulae and bracelets were much less ornate than those of earlier times. Some of the most common fibulae, such as the Nauheim type, were designed specifically for ease of mass production (Drescher 1955).

## The Wider Cultural Environment and Geographical Interconnections

The changes that took place in temperate Europe during the second century BC were far-reaching and affected all parts of the continent. Some circulation of goods had occurred since Neolithic times, but the scale and intensity of interaction that developed during the second century BC greatly exceeded those earlier (Lang & Salac 2002). Increasing quantities of pottery, personal ornaments, and other materials that were characteristic of the La Tène style of southern temperate Europe were being taken northward, and many objects, among which belt hooks and fibulae are especially evident, from northern regions found their way south.

At the same time that inter-temperate European contacts and trade were increasing, interactions with the expanding Roman world to the south were also intensifying, as shown most clearly by imported ceramic amphorae, bronze vessels, and other such materials.

The 12 sites discussed below exemplify these trends. Nine are located south of the Danube in a region characterised by the La Tène style from the mid-fifth century BC into the Roman Period. The other three are about 200 kilometres to the north in central Germany, in a region characterised during the Late Iron Age by what are known as the Ripdorf and Seedorf styles. As these examples show, these regions, which had been distinguished by distinctive styles of material culture, became much more closely linked during the second and first centuries BC. The exact nature of these connections is not known at present, but probably included movements of individuals and of families, mobility of merchants and craft workers, gift exchange, and marriage alliances.

## Social Contexts of Interaction

Expression of identity through the medium of material culture takes place in the context of social interaction – interaction between individuals within communities, between individuals from different communities, and between communities of individuals. Among the sites presented as examples below, only Manching was an urban settlement. Differentiation in material culture – fibulae, pottery, and other objects – is minimal within the huge assemblages from the site, in accordance with the pattern throughout temperate Europe during the late second and early first centuries BC (Wells 2012). The mass-produced nature of goods largely precluded expression of individual identity through differences in material culture.

Most social interaction in this urban complex took place between individuals of roughly equal status, all of whom identified themselves as members of a common community using the same kinds of pottery and of iron tools, and wearing the same types of fibulae (Gebhard 1991). The community was made up of manufacturers of these and other kinds of objects, farmers who worked the lands surrounding the settlement, and some kind of leaders/administrators who managed the internal affairs of the community and represented it in interactions with other communities. Remains of industrial activities on many parts of the settlement represent the manufacturers; agricultural tools, plant remains, and animal bones attest to the activities of the food producers. The leaders/administrators are not clearly represented by any material evidence yet recovered (on the problem of our lack of understanding of the nature of leadership in the prehistoric Iron Age, see Hill 2007), but we can assume that such a group existed to coordinate the economic and political affairs of a community of this size.

Although elite leaders/administrators have not yet been identified among the material evidence at Manching, such individuals are represented elsewhere. Burial evidence at Kelheim (Krämer 1985), 37 kilometres to the north east, and at Clemency in Luxembourg to the west (Metzler *et al.* 1991) shows that elites had material means through which to express their special statuses. The presence in such burials of Roman bronze vessels associated with the consumption of wine, along with other feasting paraphernalia and sometimes the ceramic amphorae in which wine was transported, shows how the identity of such individuals was represented in the funerary contexts. At Manching, the presence of coin hoards suggests control of wealth by elites but does not tell much about them as a social group.

The urban centre of Manching declined in importance around the middle of the first century BC, after about a century of prominence (recent discussion in Sievers 2010: 31). A very different situation with respect to the expression of identity from that at urban Manching is apparent in the 11 graves at the sites of Hörgertshausen, Kronwinkl, Traunstein and Uttenhofen, all of which post-date the period of Manching's flourishing and represent much smaller communities. Each grave was arranged differently from the others and shows the expression, through distinctive personal ornaments and pottery vessels, of much greater variation regarding individual identity than is suggested by the ornaments and pottery at Manching. The materials in these graves suggest that the individuals, and those burying them, selected from a variety of available objects, including distinctive forms of fibulae, belt hooks, and pottery, as means of expressing different identities in this period of profound change between the decline of the *oppida* and the Roman conquest of the region a few decades later. During this dynamic time, people were able to choose from a wider range of ornaments and pottery than were available to the urban populace of Manching. The character of social interactions in and between the small communities of this post-*oppidum* time was different from that at urban Manching. The pottery and ornaments in these graves were not mass-produced but individually crafted, as was also the case with material culture at the few settlements of this period that have been investigated, such as Regensburg-Harting (Rieckhoff 1995).

As explained below, the materials from the settlements at Straubing and Eching and the burials of the Heimstetten group illustrate complex patterns of continuity of identity expression on the one hand, and selective adoption of new elements of material culture on the other.

The cemeteries at Liebersee, Eischleben, and Körner, located about 200 km to the north, reflect communities of roughly the same size as do the 11 southern Bavarian graves. These communities also were open to greater heterogeneity of expression through material culture. Social interaction in these settings at this time of rapid and far-reaching cultural change was between members of small communities exposed to ever wider ranges of objects, styles, and ideas, and ready to adopt combinations of elements at this time of transition.

**Archaeological Sites**
*Manching*
The *oppidum* at Manching was founded in the first half of the second century BC and thrived as a centre of population, manufacturing, and commerce for several generations. The date of the community's decline is a subject of debate; here I adopt Sievers's date of around the middle of the first century BC for the effective end of Manching (see above). The site was situated on the south bank of the Danube in territory that is commonly associated with the Celts.

The stylistic changes in the material culture noted above can be understood in terms of the larger changes that communities such as that at Manching experienced – joining into the larger 'world system' of commerce that included the Mediterranan basin, Africa, the Near East, and regions further afield. As such communities became increasingly involved in production for commerce with the larger world, the material expression of personal and local identities became less important that it had been in the smaller cultural environments of earlier times.

The settlement at Manching has been labeled 'Celtic' because it is in a landscape that archaeologists have associated with Celts on the basis of the Classical sources, and because the style of some of the objects manufactured there continued to show connections to the classic La Tène style of earlier times. In fact, expression through material culture of identity distinct from that of the peoples to the north of the Danube is lacking, as comparison with sites in Saxony and Thuringia will show (below).

*Graves at Hörgertshausen (5), Kronwinkl (2), Traunstein and Uttenhofen (3)*
A small number of graves have been identified at several sites in southern Bavaria that contain as grave goods fibulae, belt hooks, and pottery that are different from the material culture at Manching (Zanier 2006). These objects are understood to be chronologically later than Manching, which is ordinarily ascribed to the phases La Tène C2 and D1, while these graves are assigned a phase La Tène D2 (Krämer 1962: 304–8; Gebhard 2004). Rainer Christlein (1982) has argued that because the objects in these graves bear resemblance to earlier objects of La Tène style, these graves contained the remains of Celts. Others have suggested that they are graves of Germans on the basis of typological similarities of the metal ornaments to objects in cemeteries north of the Danube, especially in Thuringia (Rieckhoff 1995).

Examination of the objects in these graves reveals that the assemblages, and the burial practices, are not uniform – each grave is significantly different from the others. Both the combinations of objects with which the individuals were buried and the details of the burial rituals (inhumation versus cremation, different structures associated with the graves) indicate that the identity of these individuals, as expressed through material culture, was much more complex than a simple dichtomy of 'Celt' and 'German'.

*Straubing*
Straubing is situated on the south bank of the Danube river, and the site has a long history of occupation starting in the Neolithic. During the Late La Tène Period, several settlements were occupied within what is now the urban area of the modern city (Tappert 2006; 2007). Tappert notes that most of the pottery at the settlements is very similar to that at Manching and other sites in the region. On the other hand, at some of the settlements, Tappert identifies pottery similar to that recovered at sites to the north, in the so-called 'Germanic' lands.

While the community at the *oppidum* at Manching is thought to have declined and the site to have been substantially abandoned well before the Roman conquest in 15 BC, at Straubing, settlement persisted well into the early Roman Period. This situation challenges old ideas about the local character of material culture changing quickly after the Roman conquest to transform into provincial Roman style. In recent years, many more settlements of the immediately pre- and post-conquest period have been discovered (Hüssen *et al.* 2004; Wells 2005), and it is becoming increasingly clear that the old idea that there was a sharp distinction between 'Celts' and 'Romans' after the conquest must be abandoned. Instead, there was considerable and varied blending of identities that is apparent in both material culture (pottery, metal ornaments) and cultural practices (settlement construction, burial).

*Sallach*
Twenty kilometres south west of Straubing at Sallach there are two rectangular enclosures (*Viereckschanzen*) of typical Late La Tène. Müller's (2007) analysis of

the radiocarbon dates from these enclosures indicates that they remained in use well into the Roman Period, probably into the second century AD. Thus, as with the late settlement at Straubing, Sallach points up the complexity of the situation following the Roman conquest and the lack of a clear break between native traditions and the newly arrived administration and culture of the Roman provinces. Rather than clear identities that can be called 'Celtic' and 'Roman', the evidence at these sites shows that we need to think in terms of complex and diverse mixing and blending, as at Straubing.

*Eching*
At Eching just north east of Munich, recent excavations have yielded a settlement with material culture in the fill of four pit houses that bears similarities to both that at Manching and that in the graves noted above (Hüssen 2004). Some of the pottery and metal objects are identified as typical local material (like that at Manching), while some has 'northern' affinities, thus presenting the same kind of heterogeneity apparent in the graves cited above and at the settlements at Straubing.

A Roman villa was built on the southern part of the Late La Tène settlement, but excavation of the site yielded very little typical 'Roman' material, with no fine tableware that often characterises Roman sites. The pottery from the villa was largely of typical Late La Tène character, but it was accompanied by sherds of Roman amphorae dated between 10 BC and 50 AD (a generation or two after the conquest). Fragments of Roman horse-harness equipment were identified among the finds. This mix of Roman architecture, amphorae, and harness gear, together with local pottery, presents a typical complex mixed assemblage of material that would be traditionally attributed to different identities and provides a good example of how complex these developing identities were.

*Heimstetten*
The site of Heimstetten, east of Munich, gives its name to a series of burials, almost all of them of women, that were distributed over much of southern Bavaria (Keller 1984; Volpert 2002; 2006). They date to around the same time as the villa at Eching – 30–50 AD . Burial was by inhumation rather than the introduced Roman practice of cremation, and the relatively abundant grave goods are typical of earlier, local La Tène burials. The burial practice and the character of the jewellery suggests an identity reaching back several generations for themes and motifs in these graves. Like the villa at Eching, the Heimstetten graves illustrate the complexity of identity expressed through material culture – burial practice and object categories are local pre-Roman Iron Age, but some of the graves also contain objects of Roman military dress. The suggestion that the graves are those of wives of auxiliary soldiers in the Roman army begs too many questions and seeks too simplistic an answer to the complex issue of identity here.

*Liebersee*
Liebersee is a recently excavated cemetery in Saxony, north of the Danube in the territory traditionally attributed to Germans (Ender 2002). Some of the graves contain objects characteristic of the region south of the Danube, including both metal ornaments such as fibulae, bracelets, and belt attachments, and also pottery, such as wheel-turned ceramics characteristic of the production at the *oppida* south of the Danube. These objects indicate growing intensity of interaction with that region during the later La Tène Period.

Liebersee provides a counterpart to the graves in southern Bavaria that contain objects thought to represent movement of Germans from the north southward. This newly studied site makes clear that rather than thinking in terms of migrations in one direction (southward) by groups of people bearing objects that display their identities, we need to think in terms of exchange and movement taking place in all directions during this time of intensifying interaction.

*Eischleben*
At the cemetery of Simmel 1 at Eischleben in Thuringia, a number of locally made objects that had been placed in graves were modeled after prototypes from south of the Danube in the region in which the La Tène-style material culture was at home (Grasselt *et al.* 2002).

*Körner*
Objects in the recently investigated cemetery at Körner in Thuringia also exhibit indications of stylistic influences from the south (Grasselt *et al.* 2002). Furthermore, some objects in graves on the site have been identified as actual imports from the La Tène region south of the Danube.

## IDENTITY AT THE END OF THE IRON AGE

This brief review of evidence from several sites teaches us that the notion that we can identify 'Celts' and 'Germans' as distinct peoples on the basis of differences in the archaeological material needs to be revised. In the graves at Hörgertshausen and the several other sites in south eastern Bavaria, at Straubing on the Danube, and at Liebersee, Eischleben, and Körner in the north, we see a mixing of what had once been interpreted as pottery and metal ornaments distinctive of one or the other of those peoples. Instead of clear typological divisions and distinctive burial practices, we find blending of cultural elements (see Bockius & Luczkiewicz 2004: 111–34). Similarly, distinct differences between Late Iron Age indigenous material culture and practice and the material culture and practice of the early provincial Roman communities are not apparent (but see von Schnurbein 2006). The evidence from the Straubing settlements, the Sallach *Viereckschanzen,* the villa at Eching, and the graves of the Heimstetten group, shows in every case that instead of distinctly 'native' and distinctly 'Roman' sites and practices, we consistently find blending of the traditions to form new combinations of elements.

## POTENTIAL MODELS: BLENDING, ENTANGLEMENT, HYBRIDITY

The principal purpose of this paper is to highlight the difficulties of identifying peoples in the archaeological material that correspond to the Celts, Germans and Romans attested by the written sources, not to develop theoretical models for the changes in the material culture of Late Iron Age and early Roman Period Europe. Nonetheless, it is worth considering briefly models that might help to illuminate processes of change during this period, 200 BC – 100 AD.

I have used the term 'blending' to characterise the adoption by communities south of the Danube and in central Germany of common elements of material culture. This term fits the situation of communities of relatively equal status and power engaging in increased interaction with one another, sharing of specific forms of personal ornaments, and fashioning identities that mark them as members of a common though heterogeneous group of Late Iron Age Europeans.

Following the Roman conquest of the lands south of the upper Danube in 15 BC, the concept of 'entanglement' (Thomas 1991) might be appropriate to the situation reflected in the material culture at the settlements of Straubing and Eching. In both instances, the archaeological evidence indicates continuity of local tradition in the manufacture of pottery and metal ornaments on the one hand, along with the introduction of Roman-style material culture on the other. However, at these two sites, there is no clear archaeological evidence to suggest the dominance of Roman political power or of Roman culture. At Eching, the conjunction of Late La Tène pottery with Roman amphorae and horse equipment on the site of a Roman-style villa suggests entanglement in the sense of local communities becoming entangled with the settlement systems, architecture, military equipment and political administration, of the conquering power.

The graves of the mid-first century AD Heimstetten group could be understood in terms of the concept of 'hybridity' (Dietler 2010: 51). If we view each grave as a single cultural expression, then we can understand the assemblages as comprised of ornament types that characterised Late Iron Age material culture, combined in this post-conquest context with elements of Roman military dress. The joining of elements of local and Roman cultural features becomes evident in a wider range of material culture during the succeeding centuries.

## CONCLUSION

I conclude this discussion with three main points.

First, the ethnic categories from Greek and Roman textual sources are not useful to archaeologists for identifying distinct peoples on the basis of the material evidence. In fact, these categories are impediments, because they distract archaeologists from focusing on the processes of identity formation in response to ongoing social and political changes that are reflected in the archaeological evidence.

Second, both the typological and chronological variability in objects (such as fibulae and pottery) and sites (settlements and *Viereckschanzen*) are much wider than the original typological and chronological schemes suggested. Objects crafted in indigenous Iron Age styles continued to be made and used well into the Roman Period, and sites, such as *Viereckschanzen,* continued to be occupied long after the Roman conquest. Zanier (2004) has shown, for example, that the Nauheim type fibula, long regarded as the classic form of the phase La Tène D1, went on in use much longer than believed, well into the Roman Period.

Third, in order to approach the topic of how identity was created and expressed, we need to be much clearer about the kinds of evidence that we use to examine identity. As the examples above demonstrate, using the Greek and Roman sources is problematic, as is relying on purely typological analyses, because of the degree of mixing of materials in the final two centuries BC brought about by the increasing interactions. Instead, we need to focus on the specific archaeological evidence from burials, as potentially indicative of the identity of individuals; and from settlement deposits and cemeteries as reflective of the identity of communities. As the examples above show, there were no standard 'Celtic' or 'German' sets of objects in the final phase of the Iron Age, nor was there a sharp break between indigenous material culture and that introduced by the Roman military and civil institutions. In every case, the archaeological evidence shows a mixing and blending of material cultural traditions and practices, just as we would expect from what we know today about the ways that modern peoples construct and express their identities (Jaarsma & Rohatynakyi 2000). Finally, we need to examine issues of identity in the context of large-scale social and economic changes. Identities are never static, and their construction always takes place in response to changes in the larger cultural environments in which people live.

# 27. Fingerprinting the European Iron Age. Historical, Cultural and Intellectual Perspectives on Identity and Ethnicity

*Cătălin Nicolae Popa and Simon Stoddart*

Identity is a major concern of the present age. It is a field where archaeological research can make a very major contribution, and is indeed often employed in popular and political debate. This topic has been discussed extensively in several volumes (e.g. Kohl and Fawcett 1995; Díaz-Andreu and Champion 1996a; Graves-Brown *et al.* 1996), including some very recent ones (Cifani *et al.* 2012; Ó Ríagáin and Popa 2012a), explaining the social and historical circumstances that led to nationalist approaches to the past, as well as revealing its dangerous political ramifications. The first millennium BC is the period in Europe where some modern European societies situate the origins of their identity, although textual historians tend to under-estimate this deeper past (Ferro 2003).

### Fingerprinting identity in Mediterranean and temperate Europe

In Mediterranean Europe, the transition from the Bronze Age into the Iron Age has been frequently selected as the origin myth for modern political structures of the present. The modern Greek state points to *polis* formation, and more specifically to the *megapolis* formation of Athens, as the foundation of Hellenic culture, conveniently eliminating the intervention of Venetian, Frankish and Ottoman empires that were located between then and now. Archaeology can overturn this modern Hellenisation by revealing prominent material culture from this period through a long walk of discovery usually by field survey (Bintliff 2012: 416–77). The inheritance of the past is more complicated in Italy. Here the rival material legacies of the Romans at a macro-scale, the Latins (sic), Etruscans, Umbrians, Picenes, Venetics, Elymians and Daunians etc at a meso-scale, and the power of place at the community level of Florence and Siena, Perugia and Gubbio, Modena and Bologna, Troina and Centuripe, to name but a few examples, compete for the attention of archaeologists. The Mussolini regime notoriously favoured a Roman inspiration (e.g. Calvesi *et al.* 1992) with some prehistoric additions (Ugolini 1934; Gilkes 2004; Pessina *et al.* 2005); Mussolini's political failure placed this approach in disrepute, and political identity was devolved to the safer supra-community and community identities at the meso-scale defined above (e.g. Mangani 1983; Cristofani 1985; Bergamini Simoni 2001), with the addition of the Celts for the potentially separatist north, often designated *Italia continentale*.

In temperate Europe, the situation was similarly complex since alternative historical realities could be drawn upon by modern political authorities. In France, both Franks and Gauls provided textually recorded identities that could be treated as ancestral to the present (Demoule 1999), but there were considerable ambiguities in the use of Vercingetorix who was defeated by the Romans (Dietler 1994) and could not be considered ancestral to the colonies even if often designated *departements* of France (Ferro 2003). Roman ancestry was tempting as a model, but somewhat scarred by the role of the Napoleons of the two phases of Empire, both brought to an end with Frankish, Germanic or Prussian assistance. In Germany, the anniversary of the defeat of Varus was much celebrated once unification took hold in the mid nineteenth century, and Tacitus's *Germania* was much developed as an ideological strategy in the 1930s and early 1940s. In the United Kingdom, English legitimation was substantially an early Medieval phenomenon vested in King Arthur, Anglo-Saxons and Alfred, an approach deeply seated in historical approaches to landscape (Hoskins 1955), the popular imagination and the national curriculum. Deeper time has been explored as a counter identity by the self-perceived Celts in Wales and Scotland, leading to considerable academic debate (Carr & Stoddart 2002).

These issues appear in this volume within the papers related to the Balkans, where recent events highlight the power of the past in the re-interpretation of the Present. As Babic (this volume) rightly emphasises, most of this area was dominated by other empires, and that this led to a different view of the Past. Furthermore, the region (cf Babic this volume) was a bridge between Temperate and Mediterranean Europe, between East and West. She reads the views of Vasic in Serbia within this framework, as an attempt to re-assert the place of independent Serbia within a European heritage, so much so as to reframe the facts. Other approaches in the volume seek to disentangle the deep seated search for ancient origins of modern peoples. Ghenghea (this volume) shows how many nineteenth and early twentieth century scholars were engaged in this activity. Mihajlović (this volume) critiques the tendency to retroject temporally shallow ethnicities, in this case derived from the Roman world, onto a deeper historical past, an approach that generally has a much wider currency in the European Iron Age (e.g. Peroni *et al.* 1980: 9). A broadly similar perspective is taken by Vranic (this volume), although here the Greek world provided the model for ethnicity, reaching its most controversial form in the Former Yugoslav Republic of Macedonia where rival candidacies for Macedonian authenticity collide (Brown 1994). Stoddart (this volume) reacts against the unitary approach offered by some traditional scholars for the Etruscans, pointing out the essentially fluid nature of Etruscan identity, that, in spite of an apparently greater level of formality, did not have the certainties of identity that urbanism and state formation might suggest. Wells (this volume) especially emphasises that ancient understandings of ethnicity were different from our own, and apparent certainties concealed considerable fluidity that was constrained by changing relations with others. The heartening aspect of research is that while it is easy to criticise the naïve approaches of preceding scholars, there is also evidence that material culture can be employed to elucidate sensitive emic versions of identity.

Modern national identities are built on imagined (*sensu* Anderson 1991) past communities, since 'nations without pasts are a contradiction in terms' (Rowlands 1994: 133). Ancestry offers many potential lines of reconstruction. This past had to be created, or at least selectively routed, in much the same way as the modern political entities themselves. In our modern world, many individuals can trace multiple lines of ancestry back into the past, aided by census returns and gathered incidental records of births, travels and marriages on the internet. Individuals may choose to emphasise one access to the past whilst forgetting others; this activity is substantially flexible, since we are all at a few removes of biological or fictive kin from the notable and notorious, the celebrity figure to enliven our dull bureaucratic lives, unless, of course, we are sensitively pursuing the career of archaeology. This currently *popular* activity was in the first millennium BC, and once again in the nineteenth and early twentieth century, easily manipulated by the charismatic, the literate and powerful, to develop strategies of association and perpetuation, selectively and creatively, out of the many potential sources. Therefore, it often happened that identities associated with past people were drawn up in such a manner so as to correspond with the necessities of modern nations. This phenomenon, which was prevalent in Europe during the nineteenth and early twentieth centuries, but also in the late twentieth and twenty first century in some Eastern European countries and the Caucasus, resulted in the creation of a past populated with ancestors of modern nations rather than people. Over-exaggerating slightly, the sole purpose of these ancestors seemed to have been to *evolve* into the nations that we have today, a result achieved by their apparent descendants tactically selecting the data.

## APPROACHES TO PAST IDENTITY

It is hard to deny that identity is one of the trendiest words in archaeology today. It is also, as so often with theoretical trends, a preoccupation of the modern world. The publication titles that include the term already comprise an endless list. Many of those papers do not actually deal with identity to the level their titles suggest, although it might be invidious to cite them individually here, and it may be argued that the term is often employed simply because it arouses people's attention. A somewhat similar situation was encountered in the 1990s and early 2000 in relation to the words structure, agency and practice, although the popularity of these terms has not entirely faded. Scholars approach all facets of identity (e.g. social, gender, ethnic, religious) in order to understand better and characterise how people and communities in the past situated themselves in the world. Given the huge variety of approaches, there is hardly any consensus about what identity represents, how it is manifested and what it meant to people of the past and present. Through this publication we wished to assemble the wide variety of identity studies in regards to one period, the Iron Age of Europe, so as to offer a general framework of how the topic may be approached.

The theoretical discussion on identity in archaeology is closely linked to anthropological work. Even though there is a large variety in terms of approaches,

326                    *Cătălin Nicolae Popa and Simon Stoddart*

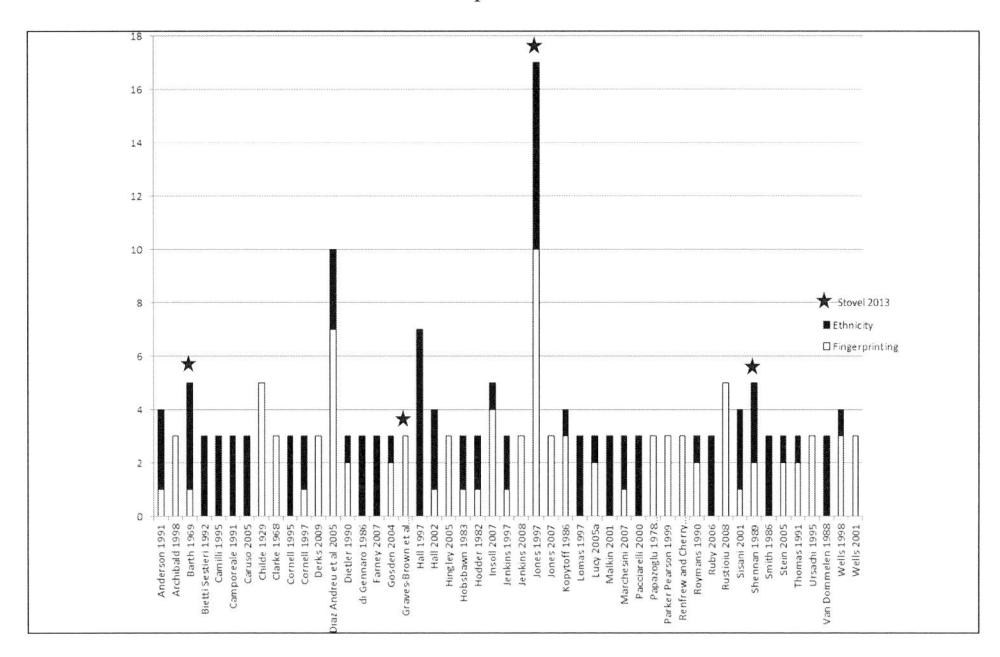

*Figure 27.1. The rates of citation (≥ 3) from contributions to two recent books on Iron Age identity and Ethnicity (Cifani et al. 2012; this volume) and from a recent article on South American pre-columbian ethnicity (Stovel 2013).*

some large general trends can be signalled. A useful comparison is between the frequency of authors cited in the current volume, and those cited in a similar recent volume with a more Mediterranean focus (Cifani *et al.* 2012) (Fig. 27.1), taken further by comparison with the literature on ethnicity a recent author has considered important to cite in analysing the South American archaeological literature on the subject (Stovel 2013). Auto-citation, multiple citation within each contribution and reference in the introductory and or concluding sections of the two volumes were excluded from the analysis. In the two volumes, Sian Jones' 1997 analysis of Ethnicity had the most currency, and was also prominently cited by Stovel (2013). Jones' 1997 book recognises the importance of the concept of ethnicity for study of the Iron Age and was the first make this important statement of integration whilst pointing out wider theoretical issues. In some ways, it is surprising that only this volume had a very widespread citation, suggesting that approaches to identity and ethnicity are either still implicit (scholars know what is meant without stating it) or remain highly diverse in their intellectual origin. Almost all cited sources of a theoretical nature were of English Language, confirming that the driving force of the debate is from the Anglo-Saxon school, although it has to be admitted that the purely English language of the volumes and choice of participants clearly had a major impact on the choice of cited sources. Díaz Andreu and colleagues' edited volume of the wider issues of identity is also popular (and also cited by Stovel 2013), but follows some distance behind in citations. These key general texts which synthesise much anthropological scholarship and then apply it to archaeological research are followed in popularity by the original anthropological texts themselves (notably Barth, also cited by Stovel 2013), some key ancestors (such as Childe), the key analysis of such issues in the Greek world (particularly Hall), some more recent readers' guides to the subject (including Insoll), more specific instances of operationalised identity (such as work on biography by Kopytoff), specific influential regional approaches (such as Rustiou and Wells) and another earlier approach to similar issues by Shennan (also cited by Stovel 2013). A wider range of texts is cited three times between the two volumes, and these include broader theoretical works as well as leading regional texts.

These primary texts give the view that identities are malleable, changing according to circumstances so as to fit people's interests, and are ultimately based substantially on the work of Barth (1969a; b) and its reassessment. In Barth's work, identities are given form through a series of boundaries which are actively maintained but also manipulated by people in order to coincide with their economic or social interest. In this view, identities are constantly 'instrumentalised' which may make them somewhat divorced from the person and arguably reduced to the status of tools. For this reason, this theory has come under attack as being too functionalist and ignoring many of the personal aspects that come into play in the formation and expression of identity (Jones 1997). An 'instrumentalist approach' gained in popularity mainly during the period when many of the archaeological works from the UK and US were following the so-called processualist framework, which stressed the purely scientific nature of archaeological work, with all its implications, such as the importance of functionality, objectivity and generalisations. Nonetheless, this view of identity still remains popular especially given that in the past fifteen years it has provided a considerable point of reference (Barth 2000; Cohen 2000).

The most prominent idea in the last couple of decades is that identity is fluid, personal and embedded to a large degree in everyday practice (Jones 1997; Díaz-Andreu *et al.* 2005). It sustains that there is no general rule in determining how it is formed or manifested, since it is entirely related to context. The few things that can be agreed on are that identity is constructed on a series of significant elements that one shares with the other members of a group and which are not embraced by others. Hence, identity is conceptualised as an interplay of two opposing principles, same-other, with some scholars giving more importance to the former of the two (Shennan 1989b; Graves-Brown 1996; Lucy 2005) and others giving more credit to the latter (Hall 1996). This view rose to popularity in archaeology after the 1990s together with structuration and practice theory on which it is largely based. Many of its ideas can also be seen to stem out of the post-processual critique which shook the discipline in the late 1980s (Hodder 1982a; Shanks and Tilley 1989).

A small variation of the above approach can be debated by employing recent theoretical developments. It involves integrating ideas regarding inter-human interaction and human-object relationships, suggested by Latour (2005), as well as concepts regarding person and individual introduced through the theories of personhood (Strathern 1999; Fowler 2004). In this view, identity is indeed fluid and personal, but it is at the same time entirely relational, meaning that it is based on the relations established with others. People do not define identity through themselves, but through the relationships that they establish with other people. Consequently, speaking about identity makes sense only in the context of these relationships since outside of them it does not exist. In this scenario, material culture plays an important role since many relationships are mediated or indeed defined through objects (cf. Robb 2004). Identity thus becomes open for study by archaeologists, since through the archaeological record we encounter a part of the material remains that were involved in identity-defining relationships. Both objects and individuals have biographies. The task is to place the objects in the relationships that they were part of and reconstruct the network of relations that defined people's identities (see Popa this volume).

## Ethnicity and the Iron Age

Iron Age research on identity is not (only) about studying ethnicity, as many contributions to this volume illustrate. Nevertheless, more widely, a large number of Iron Age scholars seem to be mainly focused on characterising past identities substantially in terms of ethnicity, and for this reason there are numerous publications concerned with Celts, Thracians, Dacians, Germans, Scythians etc. This statement is largely untrue for studies concerned with other periods of European prehistory (i.e. Mesolithic, Neolithic, Bronze Age). In those cases a large array of identities is discussed and their interplay in different contexts is often highlighted. Yet in the case of the Iron Age, and especially the Late Iron Age, this happens much less. Why is this so? Did Europe change so radically in the Iron Age? Probably not! Rather than being based on a real change in terms of peoples identities, it seems far more likely that the reason for focusing on ethnicity has to do with the literary sources of Mediterranean authors, who provided (often cryptic) names of some presupposed populations. These names fuelled the idea that Europe had suddenly become divided into ethnic groups, all of which appeared miraculously nearly at the same time. There are numerous studies which have successfully deconstructed the picture illustrated through the literary sources, showing that it is a purely biased vision, full of gross overgeneralisations, and thus cannot be employed for drawing an ethnic map of the continent (e.g. Edward and Van der Vliet 2003). It is an account from the outside, put together according to the world view of the authors and their readers, mainly from Greece and Italy. Despite such facts being acknowledged by a large majority of today's scholars, there are still numerous volumes focusing on Iron Age ethnic groups which have been defined substantially through ancient texts (e.g. Derks and Roymans 2009; Cunliffe and Koch 2010).

In spite of this valid critique of the encounter with temperate Europe, there is, however, a case to be made, congruent with the presence of the ancient authors, that ethnicity, abstracted as higher order identities, was more prevalent in the presence of political competition. This political competition was provided by the Roman Empire within Europe, by earlier empires in the Mediterranean and the

Near East and can also be detected in the environs of New World, Near Eastern and Asian empires. This atmosphere of political competition housed the ancient writers who recorded the success of this competition. At the same time, higher order identities of more fluid disparate communities can become protective and more coherent, when opposed and threatened by other high order entities, such as aggrandising empires. Communities balanced in a relative equilibrium amongst themselves, such as the Etruscan city states, very probably, created a more coherent higher order identity, only when faced with the advance of the Roman Empire from the south. Less forcefully, the communities centred on Bibracte, in Gaul, or Magdalensberg, in Noricum, may have developed supra community identities even if the term ethnicity is inadvisable with all its modern connotations. Nonetheless, such processes may have occurred during earlier prehistoric periods as well, but, for those times, we lack the textual evidence to point us towards their identification.

The Iron Age is not the only period that has to deal with this kind of problem. The issue of ethnicity also occupies the time of Early Medieval researchers. Once again, because of a large number of writings that employ specific names for different populations, Early Medieval Europe is pictured in numerous archaeological studies as a place inhabited by well-defined groups such as Franks, Bavarians, Alamani, Ostrogoths, Vizigoths, Lombards etc. This approach has similarly come under heavy criticism, arguing that such names refer to constructions of the Late Antique authors or to specific identity types that only have meaning in the context of interaction with the administration of the Roman Empire (Brather 2000; 2004; Geary 2002).

The reasons behind the categorisation of past populations using ethnic terms are undoubtedly much more complex than just believing blindly the antique writings. While indeed the Iron Age is, with some exceptions (e.g. Kossinna 1911; 1926) that took the process back to the Bronze Age, the only period of European prehistory whose people have been divided by some scholars into ethnic groups, archaeologists forced a compartmentalisation on the Neolithic and Bronze Age as well through the use of archaeological cultures. Even though arguments have been given for the existence of such cultures and attempts were made to ground them in the archaeological record, a principal element that stands behind such categorisations, including Iron Age ethnicities, is the practical requirement to organise data. Just like researchers from other disciplines, archaeologists need to organise their data in order to allow for easier comprehension. This leads to simplifications, generalisations and thus the loss of a large amount of information, but it also has the effect of allowing for easier judgments and interpretations, resulting ultimately in more rather than less information (Latour 1999). Cognitive psychologists explain this categorisation of our world, and this includes archaeological data and the past, as a process that is inherent to human brain mechanics; we understand reality by segmenting it into categories each of which is characterised according to a specific set of properties (Boyer and Ramble 2001; Kurzban *et al.* 2001). Therefore, it comes as no surprise that archaeologists divided the past, and implicitly past people, into units that lend themselves to apparently systematic research.

Although the mechanisms behind dividing the Iron Age people and material evidence ethnically are grounded in logical processes, the categories that we have imposed on the past are not driving the research forward. Following Latour, we simplify and categorise our data so as to gain more information in the end. However the use of ethnic constructs for the Iron Age falls outside of this logic since it does not result in more information. The categories that we impose on the Iron Age do not contribute to the creation of knowledge, but rather inhibit it, as they discourage us from asking a wide variety of identity related questions to the archaeological record. Hence, despite the sound logical and cognitive arguments behind a division of the past in ethnic terms, the process fails its purpose.

The issue with using ethnicity is one of methodology not of concept, as it was already well pointed out more than 60 years ago by Eggers (1950; 1959). The problem lies not with the concept of ethnicity itself or with the ancient texts available for the Iron Age, but with the methodology deployed in the study of this period and with the questions that are posed to the archaeological record. If we are interested in obtaining an insight into the identity constructions of Iron Age people as suggested by the material evidence we need not be fixed on one particular type of identity, which may or may not be actually be present in the archaeological record, but rather allow for all possible scenarios to unfold and pick the one(s) that seem(s) most plausible. This implies a substantial reversal in our understanding of the relationship between identity concepts and the material record. We should not construct the material record based on some large (ethnic) identities that we think people shared, but rather reconstruct past identities based on the material record.

Approaching Iron Age identity in this manner has the advantage of making redundant a problem that archaeologists have struggled with for quite some time: the direct link between material culture forms and ethnicity. This is an issue that was entirely constructed by scholars in the process of explaining material culture patterns using *a priori* defined ethnic groups and commenced with Kossinna who desperately tried to trace back the Germans into prehistory (Kossinna 1911; 1926). The problem of ethnically labelling specific material forms disappears if past identity is inferred primarily from the archaeological record itself, instead of simply searching for predefined Germans, Celts or Scythians in the variations of pots. The challenge then becomes to reconstruct identity using the evidence that we have uncovered; in other words we should ask what the variation in pots suggests about their users' identities. This raises the question of whether there is a quantitative rather than qualitative approach to this end. The interface between the quantitative and the qualitative is a key question in the relationship between material culture and identity that has taxed scholars at least since the time of Childe.

Answering the questions above needs to be the primary concern of archaeologists researching past identity. If we are interested in the way Iron Age communities regarded themselves and in processes through which they defined themselves as being different or the same, we have to stop imposing onto them preconceived ethnic labels. Simply giving a name to the population of some particular geographical region does not contribute to our understanding in any manner. Instead we should accept the difficult task of putting together the puzzle that is identity, using the few scattered pieces that are provided to us by the material record.

# Bibliography

Adams, R. L. 2004. An ethnoarchaeological study of feasting in Sulawesi, Indonesia. *Journal of Anthropological Archaeology* 23 (1): 56–78.

Adomnán of Iona, S. 625–704 [1875]. *Life of St Columba*. Dublin: William B. Kelly.

Agre, D. 2011. *The Tumulus of Golyamata Mogila near the Villages of Malomirovo and Zlatinitsa*. Sofia: Avalon.

Alexander, D. 2005. Redcastle, Lunan Bay, Angus: the excavation of an Iron Age timber-lined souterrain and a Pictish barrow cemetery. *Proceedings of the Society of Antiquaries of Scotland* 135: 41–118.

Alexander, J. 1962. Greeks, Italians and the earliest Balkan Iron Age. *Antiquity* 36: 123–30.

Alexander, J. 1964. The pins of the Jugoslav Early Iron Age. *Proceedings of the Prehistoric Society* 30: 159–85.

Alexander, J. 1965. The Spectacle fibulae of southern Europe. *American Journal of Archaeology* 69: 7–23.

Alexander, J. 1972a. The beginnings of urban life in Europe. In Ucko, P., Tringham, R. & Dimbleby, G. W. (eds.), *Man, Settlement and Urbanism*. London: Duckworth, 843–50.

Alexander, J. 1972b. *Jugoslavia before the Roman conquest*. (People and Places). London: Thames and Hudson.

Alexander, J. 1973a. The history of the FibuIa. In Strong, D. E. (ed.), *Archaeological Theory and Practice*. London: Seminar Press, 217–30.

Alexander, J. 1973b. The study of Fibulae (safety pins). In Renfrew, A. C. (ed.), *The Explanation of Culture Change*. London: Duckworth, 185–94.

Alexander, J. 1975. The salt industries of Africa: their significance for European prehistory. In De Brisay, K. & Evans, K. A. (eds.), *Salt: the Study of an Ancient Industry*. Colchester: Colchester Archaeological Group, 81–3.

Alexander, J. 1977. The frontier in Prehistory. In Megaw, J. V. S. (ed.), *Hunters, Gatherers and Farmers beyond Europe*. Leicester: Leicester University Press, 843–50.

Alexander, J. 1979. The archaeological recognition of religion: the examples of Islam in Africa and 'urnfields' in Europe. In Burnham, B. & Kingsbury (eds.), *Space, Hierarchy and Society*. (BAR International Series 59). Oxford: British Archaeological Reports, 215–28.

Alexander, J. 1980a. First-Millennium Europe before the Romans. In Sherratt, A. (ed.), *The Cambridge Encyclopedia of Archaeology*. Cambridge: Cambridge University Press, 222–6.

Alexander, J. 1980b. The spread and development of iron-using in Europe and Africa. In Leakey, R. E. & Ogot, B. A. (eds.), *Proceedings of the 5th Pan-African Congress on Prehistory and Quaternary Studies, Nairobi, 5–10 September 1977*. Nairobi: International Louis Leakey Memorial Institute for African Prehistory, 327–30.

Alexander, J. 1981. The coming of iron-using to Britain. In Haefner, H. (ed.), *Frühes Eisen in Europa. Festschrift W.U. Guyan*. Schamausen: Meili, 57–67.

Alexander, J. 1982. The prehistoric salt trade in Europe. *Nature* 300: 577–8.

Alexander, J. 1983. Some neglected factors in the spread of iron using in Europe. *Offa, Berichte und Mitteilungen zur Urgeschichte, Frühgeschichte und Mittelalterarchäologie* 40: 29–33.

Alexander, J. 1985. The production of salt and salt trading networks of central and western Europe in the first Millennium BC. In Liverani, M., Palmieri, A. & Peroni, R. (eds.), *Studi di Paletnologia in Onore di Salvatore M. Puglisi*. Rome: Università di Roma 'La Sapienza', 563–9.

Alexander, J. & Hopkin, S. 1982. The origins and early development of European fibulae. *Proceedings of the Prehistoric Society* 48: 401–16.

Alexandrescu, D. 1980. La nécropole gete de Zimnicea. *Dacia* 24: 19–126.

Allen, D. F. 1961. The origins of coinage in Britain: a re-appraisal. In Frere, S. S. (ed.), *Problems of the Iron Age in Southern Britain. Papers Given at a CBA Conference Held at the Institute of Archaeology, December 12 to 14, 1958*. (Occasional Paper 11). London: University of London, 97–308.

Allen, J. R. 1904. *Celtic Art in Pagan and Christian Times*. (First edition) London: Methuen and Co.

Almássy, K. 2010. Some new data on the Scythian-Celtic relationship. In Jerem, E., Schönfelder, M. & Wieland, G. (eds.), *Nord-Süd, Ost-West Kontakte während der Eisenzeit in Europa. Akten der Internationalen Tagungen der AG Eisenzeit in Hamburg und Sopron 2002*. Budapest: Archaeolingua, 9–25.

Alt, K., Jud, P., Müller, F., Nicklisch, N., Uerpmann, A. & Vach, W. 2005. Biologische Verwandtschaft und soziale Struktur im latènezeitlichen Gräberfeld von Münsingen-Rain. *Jahrbuch des Römisch-Germanischen Kommission* 52: 157–210.

Amatulli, A. L. & Ciancio, A. 2001. *Monte Sannace: Città dei Peuceti*. Bari: Progedit.

Anderson, A. C. 1884. Notice of the Gold Ornaments found at Lower Largo, and of the Silver Ornaments, etc., found at Norrie's Law, near Largo, recently presented to the Museum by Robert Dundas, Esq., of Arniston. *Proceedings of the Society of Antiquaries of Scotland* 18: 233–47.

Anderson, B. 1991. *Imagined Communities: Reflections on the Origin and Spread of Nationalism*. London: Verso.

Andrieşescu, I. 1912. *Contribuţie la Dacia Înainte de Romani*. Iaşi: Institutul de Arte Grafice N. V. Ştefăniu & Co.

Andriţoiu, I. & Rustoiu, A. 1997. *Sighişoara-Wietenberg. Descoperirile Preistorice şi Aşezarea Dacică*. (Bibliotheca Thracologica 23). Bucureşti: Vavila Edinf.

Anglim, S., Jestice, P., Rice, R. S., Rusch, S. M. & Serrati, J. 2002. *Fighting Techniques of the Ancient World: 3000 BC – AD 500; Equipment, Combat Skills, and Tactics*. London: Greenhill Books.

Archibald, Z. H. 1994. Thracians and Scythians. In Lewis, D., Boardman, J., Hornblower, S. & Oswald, M. (eds.), *Cambridge Ancient History (Second*

Edition). Vol. VI. *The Fifth and the Fourth Centuries BC*. Cambridge: Cambridge University Press, 444–75.

Archibald, Z. H. 1998. *The Odrysian Kingdom of Thrace: Orpheus Unmasked*. Oxford: Clarendon Press.

Archibald, Z. H. 2000. Space, Hierarchy, and Community in Archaic and Classical Macedonia, Thessaly, and Thrace. In Brock, R. & Hodkins, S. (eds.), *Alternatives to Athens: Varieties of Political Organization and Community in Ancient Greece*. Oxford: Oxford University Press, 212–33.

Archibald, Z. H. 2002. Attic Figured pottery from Adjiyska Vodenitsa (Adžijska Vodenica), Vetren, 1989–95. In Bouzek, J., Domaradzka, L. & Archibald, Z. H. (eds.), *Pistiros II: Excavation and Studies*. Prague: Charles University, 131–48.

Archibald, Z. H. 2004. Inland Thrace. In Hansen, M. N. & Nielsen, T. H. (eds.), *An Inventory of Archaic and Classical Poleis: An Investigation Conducted by the Copenhagen Polis Centre for the Danish National Research Foundation*. Oxford: Oxford University Press, 885–99.

Archibald, Z. H. 2010. Macedonia and Thrace. In Roisman, J. & Worthington, J. (eds.), *A Companion to Ancient Macedonia*. Malden: Wiley-Blackwell, 326–41.

Armayor, K. 1978. Did Herodot ever go to the Black Sea? *Harvard Studies in Classical Philology* 82: 45–62.

Armit, I. 1997. Cultural landscapes and identities: a case study in the Scottish Iron Age. In Gwilt, A. & Haselgrove, C. (eds.), *Reconstructing Iron Age Societies*. Oxford: Oxbow Books, 248–53.

Armit, I. 1999. The abandonment of souterrains: evolution, catastrophe or dislocation? *Proceedings of the Society of Antiquaries of Scotland* 129: 577–96.

Armit, I. 2007. Social landscapes and identities in the Irish Iron Age. In Haselgrove, C. & Moore, T. (eds.), *The Later Iron Age in Britain and Beyond*. Oxford: Oxbow Books, 130–9.

Armit, I. 2011. Violence and Society in the deep human past. *British Journal of Criminology* 51 (3): 1–19.

Arnold, B. 2002. A landscape of ancestors: the space and place of death in Iron Age West-Central Europe. In Silverman, H. & Small, D. (eds.), *The Space and Place of Death*. (Archaeological Papers of the American Anthropological Association 11). Arlington: American Anthropological Association, 129–44.

Arnold, B. 2005. Mobile men, sedentary women? Material culture as a marker of regional and supra-regional interaction in Iron Age Europe. In Dobrzańska, H., Megaw, J. V. S. & Poleska, P. (eds.), *Celts on the Margin: Studies in European Cultural Interaction 7th century BC – 1st century AD, Dedicated to Zenon Woźniak*. Kraków: Institute of Archaeology and Ethnology of the Polish Academy of Sciences, 17–26.

Arnold, B. & Wicker, N. (eds.). 2001. *Gender and the Archaeology of Death*. Lanham, MD: AltaMira Press.

Atanassov, G. & Nedelchev, N. 2002. Gonimasedze – zhenata na Sevta i neynata grobnitsa. In Gitcheva, R. & Rabadzhiev, K. (eds.), *ΠΙΤΥΕ. Izsledvaniya v Chest na Prof. Ivan Marazov*. Sofia: Anubis, 550–7.

Avram, A. 1989. Gedanken über den thrakisch-geto-dakischen Adel. *Studii Clasice* 26: 11–26.

Aymard, A. 1954. Les Gaulois. In Aymard, A. & Auboyer, J. (eds.), *Histoire Générale des Civilisations, Vol. II, Rome et Son Empire*. Paris: Presses Universitaires de France, 51–75.

Azzaroli, A. 1972. Il cavallo domestico in Italia dall'età del bronzo agli Etruschi. *Studi Etruschi* 40: 273–306.

Babeş, M. 1985. Date arheologice şi istorice privind partea de nord-est a Daciei în ultimele secole înaintea erei noastre. *Studii şi Cercetări de Istorie Veche şi Arheologie* 36 (3): 183–214.

Babeş, M. 1988. Descoperirile funerare şi semnificaţia lor în contextul culturii geto-dace clasice. *Studii Şi Cercetări de Istorie Veche Şi Arheologie* 39 (1): 3–32.

Babeş, M. 1993. *Die Poieneşti-Lukaševka-Kultur. Ein Beitrag zur Kulturgeschichte im Raum Östlich der Karpaten in den Letzten Jahrhunderten vor Christi Geburt*. Bonn: R. Habelt.

Babeş, M. & Miriţoiu, N. 2011. Practici funerare birituale prelungite în spaţiul carpato-dunărean în secolele V-III a. Chr. *Arheologia Moldovei* 34: 103–49.

Babić, S. 1994. Written sources in the study of the Balkan Iron Age – methodological aspects. *Starinar* 43-4 (1992-3): 125–8.

Babić, S. 2002a. Janus on the Bridge – A Balkan attitude towards ancient Rome. In Hingley, R. (ed.), *Images of Rome Perceptions of Ancient Rome in Europe and the United States of America in the Modern Age*. (Journal of Roman Archaeology, Supplementary Series 44). Portsmouth (Rhode Island): Journal of Roman Archaeology, 167–82.

Babić, S. 2002b. Princely graves of the Central Balkans – critical history of research. *Journal of European Archaeology* 5 (1): 70–88.

Babić, S. 2002c. Still innocent after all these years? – Sketches for a social history of archaeology in Serbia. In Biehl, P. F., Gramsch, A. & Marciniak, A. (eds.), *Archäologien Europas: Geschichte, Methoden und Theorien. Archaeologies of Europe: History, Methods and Theories*. Münster: Waxmann, 309–22.

Babić, S. 2004. *Chiefdom and Polis: Early Iron Age of the Central Balkans and the Greek World*. (in Serbian with an English summary). Belgrade: Serbian Academy of Sciences and Arts, Institute for Balkan Studies.

Babić, S. 2006. Archaeology in Serbia – A Way Forward? In Tasić, N. & Grozdanov, C. (eds.), *Homage to Milutin Garašanin*. Belgrade: Serbian Academy of Sciences and Arts, 655–9.

Babić, S. 2007. "Translation zones" or gateway communities revisited: the case of Trebenište and Sindos. In Galanaki, I., Tomas, H., Galanakis, I. & Laffineur, R. (eds.), *Between the Aegean and Baltic Seas: Prehistory across Borders: Proceedings of the International Conference, Bronze and Early Iron Age Interconnections and Contemporary Developments between the Aegean and the Regions of the Balkan Peninsula, Central and Northern Europe, University of Zagreb, 11–14 April 2005*. (Aegeum 27). Liège: Université de Liège, histoire de l'art et archéologie de la Grèce antique – University of Texas at Austin, Program in Aegean Scripts and Prehistory, 57–61.

Babić, S. 2008a. Arheologija i etnicitet. *Issues in Ethnology and Anthropology* 5 (1): 137–49.
Babić, S. 2008b. *Grci i Drugi (Greeks and Others)*. Beograd: Klio.
Babić, S. 2009. Jezik arheologije II, ili: Kako sam preživela promenu paradigme (The Language of Archaeology II, or: How I survived the paradigm shift). *Etnoantropološki Problemi* 4 (1): 123–32.
Babić, S. 2010a. Arheologija i etnicitet (Archaeology and Ethnicity). *Etnoantropološki Problemi* 5 (1): 137–49.
Babić, S. 2010b. Prošlost kao Drugi Drugi kao prošlost (The Past as the Other The Other as the Past). *Etnoantropološki Problemi* 5 (2): 259–68.
Babić, S. 2011a. Čemu još istorija arheologije? (Why History of Archaeology Matters?). *Etnoantropološki Problemi* 6 (3): 565–77.
Babić, S. 2011b. Fingerprinting the Iron Age – approaches to identity in the European Iron Age. Integrating South-Eastern Europe into the debate. *The European Archaeologist* 36: 45–6.
Babić, S. & Tomović, M. 1996. *Milutin Garašanin Razgovori o Arheologiji*. Beograd: 3T.
Bailey, D. W. 1998. Bulgarian archaeology: ideology, sociopolitics and the exotic. In Meskell, L. (ed.), *Archaeology under Fire: Nationalism, Politics and Heritage in the Eastern Mediterranean and Middle East*. London – New York: Routledge, 87–110.
Bakarić, L., Križ, B. & Šoufek, M. 2006. *Pretpovijesni Jantar i Jtaklo iz Prozora u Lici i Novog Mesta u Dolenjskoj*. Zagreb: Archaeological Museum Zagreb.
Balcer, J. M. 1988. Persia Occupied Thrace (Skudra). *Historia* 37 (1): 1–21.
Banks, M. 1996. *Ethnicity: Anthropological Constructions*. London: Routledge.
Banti, L. 1969. *Il Mondo degli Etruschi*. (Biblioteca di Storia Patria). Roma: Ente per la diffusione e l'educazione storica – Pellicole della fotoincisione Beniamini.
Barker, G. (ed.). 1995. *The Biferno Valley: the Archaeological and Geomorphological Record*. Leicester: Leicester University Press.
Barnes, R. & Eicher, J. B. (eds.). 1997. *Dress and Gender: Making and Meaning*. Oxford: Berg.
Barrett, J. 1994. *Fragments from Antiquity: an Archaeology of Social Life in Britain, 2900–1200 BC*. Oxford: Blackwell.
Barth, F. 1969a. *Ethnic Groups and Boundaries. The Social Organization of Culture Difference (Results of a Symposium Held at the University of Bergen, 23rd to 26th February 1967)*. Bergen/London: Universitetsforlage-Allen & Unwin.
Barth, F. 1969b. Introduction. In Barth, F. (ed.), *Ethnic Groups and Boundaries. The Social Organization of Culture Difference (Results of a Symposium Held at the University of Bergen, 23rd to 26th February 1967)*. Bergen/London: Universitetsforlage-Allen & Unwin, 3–38.
Barth, F. 2000. Boundaries and Connections. In Cohen, A. P. (ed.), *Signifying Identities. Anthropological Perspectives on Boundaries and Contested Values*. London: Routledge, 17–36.
Baudet, L. 1843. Translation. *De Situ Orbis. La Geographie de Pomponius Mela*. (edition bilingue), Paris: Available at:

http://remacle.org/bloodwolf/erudits/mela/livre2.htm#II. [Accessed March 31, 2011].

Bayer, J. 1930. *Excavation Diaries "Blaue Bücher"*. Wien: Unpublished Fundaktenarchiv Prähistorische Abteilung, Naturhistorisches Museum.

Becker, M. J. 2011. Etruscan Infants: Children's cemeteries at Tarquinia, Italy, as indicators of an age of transition. In Lally, M. & Moore, A. (eds.), *(Re)thinking the Little Ancestor; New Perspectives on the Archaeology of Infancy and Childhood*. Oxford: British Archaeological Reports, 24–36.

Beltz, R. 1911. Die Latènefibeln. *Zeitschrift für Ethnologie* 43: 664–817.

Benac, A. 1964. Vorillyrier, Protoillyrier und Urillyrier. In Benac, A. (ed.), *Symposium sur la Délimitation Territoriale et Chronologique des Illyriens à l'Epoque Préhistorique*. Sarajevo: Academie des Sciences et des Arts de Bosnie-Herzegovine, Centre D'Études Balkaniques, 59–94.

Benac, A. 1987a. O etničkim zajednicama starijeg željeznog doba u Jugoslaviji. In Benac, A. (ed.), *Praistorija Jugoslovenskih Zemalja V: Željezno Doba*. Sarajevo: Akademija nauka i umjetnosti Bosne i Hercegovine, Centar za balkanološka ispitivanja, 737–802.

Benac, A. (ed.). 1987b. *Praistorja Jugoslavenskih Zemalja V.* Sarajevo: Akademija nauka i umjetnosti Bosne i Hercegovine.

Berciu, D. 1981. *Buridava Dacică.* Bucureşti: Editura Academiei Republicii Socialiste România.

Berecki, S. 2004. Istoria celţilor din Transilvania. *Buletinul Cercurilor Ştiinţifice Studenţeşti* 10: 85–94.

Berecki, S. 2006. Rite and Ritual of the Celts from Transylvania. In Sîrbu, V. & Vaida, D. L. (eds.), *Thracians and Celts, Proceedings of the International Colloquium from Bistriţa, 18–20 Mai, 2006*. Cluj-Napoca: Editura Mega, 51–76.

Berecki, S. 2008a. The Chronology of the Celtic Discoveries from Transylvania. In Sîrbu, V. & Vaida, D. L. (eds.), *Funerary Practices of the Bronze and Iron Ages in Central and South-Eastern Europe, Proceedings of the 9th International Colloquium of Funerary Archaeology from Bistriţa, May 9th–11th, 2008*. Cluj-Napoca: Editura Mega, 47–65.

Berecki, S. 2008b. *The La Tène Settlement from Moreşti*, (Interferenţe Etnice şi Culturale în Mileniile I a.Chr. – I p.Chr. XIII). Cluj-Napoca: Editura Mega.

Bergamini Simoni, M. 2001. *Todi. Antica Città degli Umbri.* Tod: Editrice Tau.

Bianco Peroni, V. 1970. *Le Spade nell'Italia Continentale. Die Schwerter in Italien* (Prähistorische Bronzefunde IV, 1). München: Beck.

Biehl, P. F., Gramsch, A. & Marciniak, A. (eds.). 2002. *Archäologien Europas: Geschichte, Methoden und Theorien. Archaeologies of Europe: History, Methods and Theories.* Münster: Waxmann.

Binford, L. R. 1962. Archaeology is Anthropology. *American Antiquity* 28: 217–25.

Bintliff, J. L. 2012. *The Complete Archaeology of Greece: from Hunter-gatherers to the 20th century AD.* Chichester, West Sussex – Malden, MA: Wiley-Blackwell.

Bitrakova-Grozdanova, V. 1987. *Spomenici od Helenistickiot Period vo SR Makedonija.* Skopje: Filozofski fakultet.

Bitrakova-Grozdanova, V. 2006. Moenia Aeacia et la Macedonine. In Tasić, N. & Grozdanov, C. (eds.), *Homage to Milutin Garašanin*. Belgrade: Serbian Academy of Sciences and Arts, 587–91.

Boardman, J. 1980. *The Greeks Overseas. Their Early Colonies and Trade*. London: Thames and Hudson.

Boardman, J. 2001. *Greek Gems and Finger Rings: Early Bronze Age to Late Classical* (Second Edition) London: Thames and Hudson.

Bockius, R. & Luczkiewicz, P. 2004. *Kelten und Germanen im 2.-1. Jahrhundert vor Christus: Archäologische Bausteine zu Einer Historischen Frage*. Mainz: Römisch-Germanisches Zentralmseum.

Bojčić, Z., Dizdar, M., Hršak, T. & Leleković, T. 2009. Terenski pregled područja Batine. *Annales Instituti Archaeologici* 5: 125–9.

Bojčić, Z., Dizdar, M., Hršak, T. & Leleković, T. 2011. Rezultati probnih istraživanja nalazišta Batina-Sredno 2010. godine. *Annales Instituti Archaeologici* 7: 13–9.

Bolla, M. 1991. Considerazioni sulla funzione dei vasi in bronzo tardoreppublicani in Italia settentrionale. In Feugère, M. & Rolley, C. (eds.), *La Vaiselle Tardo-Républicaine en Bronze*. Dijon: Université de Bourgogne, 143–53.

Bommas, M. (ed.). 2011. *Cultural Memory and Identity in Ancient Societies*. London: Continuum.

Bond, G. C. & Gilliam, A. 1994. Introduction. In Bond, G. C. & Gilliam, A. (eds.), *Social Construction of the Past. Representation as Power*. London: Routledge, 1–22.

Bondoc, D. 2008. Descoperirile de epocă La Tène de la Padea, jud. Dolj. *Studii și Cercetări de Istorie Veche și Arheologie* 59–60: 137–63.

Bonfante, L. (ed.). 2011. *The Barbarians of Ancient Europe: Realities and Interactions*. Cambridge: Cambridge University Press.

Bonghi Jovino, M. 2000. The Expansion of the Etruscans in Campania. In Torelli, M. (ed.), *The Etruscans*. (Exhibition Catalogue). Milano: Bompiani, 157–67.

Boon, G. C. & Dekówna, M. 1966. Gilt glass beads from Caerleon and elsewhere. *The Bulletin of the Board of Celtic Studies* 22: 104–9.

Boteva, D. 2010. The Ancient Historians on the Celtic Kingdom in South-Eastern Thrace. In Vagalinski, L. (ed.), *Search of Celtic Tylis in Thrace (III C BC). Proceedings of the Interdisciplinary Colloquium Arranged by the National Archaeological Institute and Museum at Sofia and the Welsh Department, Aberystwyth University, Held at the National Archaeological Institute and Museum, Sofia, 8 May 2010*. Sofia: NOUS Publishers Ltd, 33–50.

Bottini, A. 1982. *Principi Guerrieri della Daunia del VII Secolo: le Tombe Principesche di Lavello*. Bari: De Donato.

Bottini, A. 1988. Apulishe-korinthische Helme. In Bottini, A., Egg, M., von Hase, F. W., Pflug, H., Schaaff, U., Schauer, P., Waurick, G. & Heilmeyer, W. D. (eds.), *Antike Helme: Sammlung Lipperheide und Andere Bestände des Antikenmuseums Berlin*. (Römisch-Germanisches Zentralmuseum. Monographien 14). Mainz: Verlag des Römisch-Germanischen Zentralmuseums, 107–36.

Bottini, A. 1991. Da Atene alla Daunia: ceramica ed acculturazione. *Mélanges de l'Ecole Française de Rome* 103 (3): 443–45.

Bottini, A. & Setari, E. 2003. *La Necropoli Italica di Braida di Vaglio in Basilicata: Materiali dallo Scavo del 1994.* Roma: Giorgio Bretschneider.

Bourdieu, P. 1972. *Esquisse d'une Théorie de la Pratique, Précédé de Trois Études d'Ethnologie Kabyle.* Geneva Librairie Droz.

Bourdieu, P. 1976. *Entwurf einer Theorie der Praxis auf der Ethnologischen Grundlage der Kabylischen Gesellschaft.* Frankfurt: Suhrkamp Verlag.

Bourdieu, P. 1977. *Outline of a Theory of Practice.* (Cambridge studies in social anthropology 16). Cambridge: Cambridge University Press.

Bourdieu, P. 1994. *Raisons Pratiques. Sur la Théorie de l'Action.* París: Éditions de Minuit.

Bouzek, J. 1996. Textile industry. In Bouzek, J., Domaradski, M. & Archibald, Z. H. (eds.), *Pistiros I: Excavation and Studies.* Prague: Charles University, 117–63.

Bouzek, J. 2004. *Thracians and Their Neighbours: Their Destiny, Art and Heritage.* (Studia Hercynia 9). Prague: Nakladatelství AMU.

Bouzek, J. & Domaradzka, L. 2009. Thracian Grey Pottery in Bulgaria: Pistiros and Other Sites. In Avram, A., Buzoianu, L., Chera, C., Custurea, G., Dupont, P., Lungu, V. & Nastasi, I. (eds.), *Pontic Grey Wares, International Conference Bucurastt-Constanzza, September 30th–October 3rd 2008.* (Pontica 42, Suplementum 1). Constanza: Muzeul de istorie nationala si arheologie, 199–222.

Bouzek, J., Domaradzki, M. & Archibald, Z. H. (eds.). 1996. *Pistiros I: Excavation and Studies.* Prague: Charles University.

Bouzek, J., Domaradzka, L. & Archibald, Z. H. (eds.). 2002. *Pistiros II: Excavation and Studies.* Prague: Charles University.

Bouzek, J., Domaradzka, L. & Archibald, Z. H. (eds.). 2007. *Pistiros III: Excavation and Studies.* Prague: Charles University.

Bouzek, J. & Ondřejová, I. 2004. Thracian order. *Studia Hercynia* 8: 121–51.

Bouzek, J., Rückl, T. P. & Tsotzev, C. 2007. Trade amphorae. In Bouzek, J., Domaradzka, L. & Archibald, Z. H. (eds.), *Pistiros III: Excavation and Studies.* Prague: Charles University, 133–87.

Boxhorn, M. Z. 1654. *Originum Gallicarum Liber.* (Republished in facsimile, Rodopi, Amsterdam, 1970). Amsterdam: apud Joannem Janssonium.

Boyer, P. & Ramble, C. 2001. Cognitive Templates for Religious Concepts: Cross-cultural Evidence for Recall of Counter-Intuitive Representations. *Cognitive Science* 25: 535–64.

Bozkova, A. & Delev, P. (eds.). 2002. *Koprivlen 1: Rescue Archaeological Investigation along the Gotse Deltsev – Drama Road 1998–1999.* Sofia: Road Executive Agency, Archaeological Institute and Bulgarian Academy of Science.

Bradley, R. 1990. *The Passage of Arms: an Archaeological Analysis of Prehistoric Hoards and Votive Deposits.* Cambridge: Cambridge University Press.

Brady, K., Lelong, O. & Batey, C. E. 2007. A Pictish Burial and Late Norse/Medieval Settlement at Sangobeg, Durness, Sutherland. *Scottish Archaeological Journal.* 29: 51–82.

Brather, S. 2000. Ethnische Identitäten als Konstrukte der frügeschichtlichen Archäeologie. *Germania* 78 (1): 139–77.
Brather, S. 2004. *Ethnische Interpretationen in der Frühgeschichtlichen Archäologie. Geschichte, Grundlagen, Alternativen.* (Eränzungsbände Reallexikon Germanische Altertumskunde 42). Berlin/New York: de Gruyter.
Brather, S. 2008. Bestattungsrituale der Merowingerzeit – Frühmittelalterliche Reihengräber und der Umgang mit dem Tod. In Kümmel, C., Schweizer, B. & Veit, U. (eds.), *Körperinszenierung – Objektsammlung – Monumentalisierung: Totenritual und Grabkult in Frühen Gesellschaften.* Münster: Waxmann Verlag GmbH, 151–77.
Bray, T. 2003. The commensal politics of early states and empires. In Bray, T. (ed.), *The Archaeology and Politics of Food and Feasting in Early States and Empires*. New York (NY): Kluwer Academic, 1–13.
Breeze, D. J., Close-Brooks, J. & Ritchie, J. N. G. 1976. 'Soldiers' burials at Camelon, Stirlingshire, 1922 and 1975. *Britannia* 7: 73–95.
Briquel, D. 1991. *L'Origine Lydienne des Étrusques: Histoire de la Doctrine dans l'Antiquité.* (Collection de l'École Française de Rome, 139). Rome: École Française de Rome.
Brisighelli, F., Capelli, C., Álvarez-Iglesias, V., Onofri, V., Paoli, G., Tofanelli, S., Carracedo, Á., Pascali, V. L. & Salas, A. 2009. The Etruscan timeline: a recent Anatolian connection. *European Journal of Human Genetics* 17: 693–6.
Brown, K. S. 1994. Seeing stars: character and identity in the landscapes of modern Macedonia. *Antiquity* 68 (261): 784–96.
Brown, K. S. 1998. Contests of heritage and the politics of preservation in the Former Yugoslav Republic of Macedonia. In Meskell, L. (ed.), *Archaeology under Fire: Nationalism, Politics and Heritage in the Eastern Mediterranean and Middle East*. London – New York: Routledge, 68–87.
Brück, J. 1999. Ritual and Rationality: some problems of interpretation in European Archaeology. *European Journal of Archaeology* 2: 313–44.
Brücken, G. 2008. Die Archäologischen Untersuchungen auf dem Bleidenberg bei Oberfell an der Mosel, Kreis Mayen-Koblenz. *Berichte zur Archäologie an Mittelrhein und Mosel* 13: 231–316.
Brumfiel, E. 1992. Distinguished Lecture in Archeology: Breaking and entering the ecosystem – Gender, class and faction steal the show. *American Anthropologist* 94 (3): 551–67.
Brumfiel, E. 2006. Methods in feminist and gender archaeology: a feeling for difference – and likeness. In Nelson, S. M. (ed.), *The Handbook of Gender in Archaeology*. Walnut Creek, CA: AltaMira, 31–58.
Brun, P. 1993. La Complexification Sociale en Europe moyenne pendant L'Âge du Fer: Essai de Modelisation. In Daubigney, A. (ed.), *Fonctionnement Social de L'Âge du Fer. Opérateurs et Hypothèses pour la France*. Lons-le-Launier: Centre Jurassien du Patrimoine, 275–89.
Brun, P. 2002. Territoire et Agglomérations chez les Suessiones. In Garcia, D. & Verdin, F. (eds.), *Territoires Celtiques. Espaces Ethniques et Territoires des Agglomérations Protohistoriques d'Europe Occidentale. Actes du XXIVe Colloque*

*International de L'Association Française pour l'Étude de l'Age du Fer, Martigues 2000*. Paris: Editions Errance, 306–14.
Brunaux, J.-L., Méniel, P. & Poplin, F. 1985. *Gournay I: les Fouilles sur le Sanctuaire et l'Oppidum (1975–84)*. Amiens: Revue Archéologique de Picardie Numero Speciale.
Brunšmid, J. 1909. Predmeti iz grobova ranijega latenskoga doba u Bogdanovcima (kotar Vukovar). *Viestnik Hrvatskoga Arheološkoga Društva* NS 10: 231–7.
Brysbaert, A. & Wetters, M. 2010. Practising Identity: a Crafty Ideal? . *Mediterranean Archaeology and Archaeometry* 10 (2): 25–43.
Buchanan, G. 1582. *Rerum Scoticarum Historia*. Edinburgh: Alexander Arbuthnet.
Buchsenschutz, O. 2007. *Les Celtes*. Paris: Armand Colin.
Burghardt, A. F. 1971. A hypothesis about gateway cities. *Annals of the Association of American Geographers* 61: 269–85.
Burke, P. J. & Stets, J. E. 1999. Trust and Commitment through Self-Verification. *Social Psychology Quarterly* 62 (4): 347–66.
Burmeister, S. & Müller-Scheeßel, N. (eds.). 2006. *Soziale Gruppen – Kulturelle Grenzen. Die Interpretation Sozialer Identitäten in der Prähistorischen Archäologie*. Münster: Waxmann Verlag GmbH.
Butler, E. 1958 (1935). *The Tyranny of Greece over Germany. A Study of the Influence Exercised by Greek Art and Poetry over the Great German Writers of the Eighteenth, Nineteenth and Twentieth Centuries*. Boston: Beacon Press.
Butler, J. 1990. *Gender Trouble: Feminism and the Subversion of Identity*. London and New York: Routledge.
Buzdugan, C. 1968. Necropola getică de la Slobozia. *Carpica* 1: 77–94.
Caldarelli, A. 1983. Castellieri nel Carso e nell'Istria: cronologia degli insediamenti tra media età del bronzo e prima età del ferro. In Boiardi, A. & Bartolomeo, G. (eds.), *Preistoria del Caput Adriae. Catalago della Mostra, Trieste, Castello di S. Giusto, 1983*. Udine, 87–112.
Calvesi, M., Guidoni, E. & Lux, S. (eds.). 1992. *E 42 Utopia e Scenario del Regime II. Urbanistica, Architettura, Arte e Decorazione*. Venice: Cataloghi Marsilio.
Camden, W. 1586. *Britannia. Sive Florentissimorum Regnorum Angliae, Scotiae, Hiberniae, et Insularum Adiacentium ex Intima Antiquitate Chorographica Descriptio* London: Radulphus Newbery.
Campbell, L. 2011. *A Study in Culture Contact: the Distribution, Function and Social Meanings of Roman Pottery from Non-Roman Contexts in Lowland Scotland*. Glasgow: Unpublished PhD Thesis University of Glasgow.
Campbell, L. 2012. Modifying Material: social biographies of Roman material culture. In Kyle, A. & Jervis, B. (eds.), *Make Do and Mend: the Archaeologies of Compromise*. (BAR International Series 2408). Oxford: Archaeopress, 13–26.
Campbell, L. in preparation. Culture Contact and the maintenance of cultural identity in northern Britain. In Campbell, L., Hall, N. & Wright, A. D. (eds.), *Roots of Nationhood: the Archaeology and History of Scotland*.

Čangova, I. 1981. Trakiisko seliscte. In Raduncheva, I., Lobenova, A., Gerasimova-Tomova, V. & Jorukova, V. (eds.), *Pernik I: Poseliscten Zsivot na Hulma Krakra ot V hil. pr. n.e. do VI v. na n.e.* Sofia: Bulgarska akademiia na naukite, Arheologicseski institut im muzei, 52–100.

Canuto, M.-A. & Yaeger, J. 2000. Introducing an Archaeology of Communities In Canuto, M.-A. & Yaeger, J. (eds.), *The Archaeology of Communities: a New World Perspective*. London: Routledge, 1–15.

Căpitanu, V. 1986. Raport privind cercetările arheologice de la Răcătău, jud. Bacău. *Materiale şi Cercetări Arheologice* 16: 109–20.

Căpitanu, V. 1992. Noi contribuţii la cunoaşterea civilizaţiei geto-dacice în bazinul Siretului mijlociu. *Carpica* 23 (1): 131–93.

Cappellini, E., Biella, M. C., Chiarelli, B. & Caramelli, D. 2003. Lo studio del DNA antico: il caso della tb 5859 della necropoli dei Monterozzi di Tarquinia. *Studi Etruschi* 69: 263–75.

Cappellini, E., Chiarelli, B., Sineo, L., Casoli, A., Di Gioia, A., Vernesi, C., Biella, M. C. & Caramelli, D. 2004. Biomolecular study of the human remains from tomb 5859 in the Etruscan necropolis of Monterozzi, Tarquinia (Viterbo, Italy). *Journal of Archaeological Science* 31 (5): 603–12.

Carr, G. 2005. Woad, tattooing and identity in later Iron Age and early Roman Britain. *Oxford Journal of Archaeology* 24 (3): 273–92.

Carr, G. 2006. *Creolised Bodies and Hybrid Identities. Examining the Early Roman Period in Essex and Hertfordshire.* (BAR British Series 418). Oxford: British Archaeological Reports.

Carr, G. 2007. Excarnation to cremation: continuity or change? In Haselgrove, C. & Moore, T. (eds.), *The Later Iron Age in Britain and Beyond*. Oxford: Oxbow Books, 444–53.

Carr, G. & Stoddart, S. (eds.). 2002. *Celts from Antiquity.* Cambridge: Antiquity Publications Limited.

Carstens, A. M. 2006. . Cultural contact and cultural change: colonialism and empire. In Bekker-Nielsen, T. (ed.), *Rome and the Black Sea Region. Domination, Romanization, Resistance*. (Black Sea Studies 5). Aarhus: Aarhus University Press, 119–32.

Carter, J. C. 1998. *The Chora of Metaponto: the Necropoleis.* Austin: University of Texas Press – Institute of Classical Archaeology.

Cartledge, P. 2002. *The Greeks: a Portrait of Self and Others.* (Second edition). Oxford: Oxford University Press.

Casan-Franga, I. 1967. Contribuţii cu privire la cunoaşterea ceramicii geto-dacice. Cupele "deliene" getice de pe teritoriul României. *Arheologia Moldovei* 5: 7–35.

Casella, E. C. & Fowler, C. 2004a. *The Archaeology of Plural and Changing Identities: Beyond Identification.* New York: Kluwer Academic/Plenum.

Casella, E. C. & Fowler, C. 2004b. Beyond identification. In Casella, E. C. & Fowler, C. (eds.), *The Archaeology of Plural and Changing Identities: Beyond Identification*. New York: Kluwer Academic/Plenum, 1–8.

Casey, E. S. 1987. *Remembering: A Phenomenological Study.* Bloomington: Indiana University Press.

Casson, S. 1926. *Macedonia, Thrace and Illyria: Their Relations to Greece from the Earliest Times Down to the Time of Philip, Son of Amyntas.* London: Oxford University Press.

Cavruc, V. & Buzea, D. 2005. Vestigiile dacice timpurii de la Olteni. Raport preliminar. *Angustia* 9: 121–53.

Ceka, N. 2005. *The Ilyrians to Albanians.* Tirana: Migieni.

Chaix, R., Austerlitz, F., Khegay, T., Jacquesson, S., Hammer, M. F., Heyer, E. & Quintana-Murci, L. 2004. The Genetic or Mythical Ancestry of Descent Groups: Lessons from the Y Chromosome. *American Journal of Human Genetics* 75: 1113–6.

Chamberlain, A. T. 1997. Commentary: missing stages of life – towards the perception of children in archaeology. In Moore, J. & Scott, E. (eds.), *Invisible People and Processes: Writing Gender and Childhood into European Archaeology.* Leicester: Leicester University Press, 248–50.

Chamberlain, A. T. 2000. Minor concerns: a demographic perspective on children in past societies. In Sofaer Derevenski, J. (ed.), *Children and Material Culture.* London-New York: Routledge, 206–12.

Chapman, J. 1994. Destruction of a common heritage: the archaeology of war in Croatia, Bosnia and Hercegovina. *Antiquity* 68 (258): 120–6.

Chapman, J. 2002. Colourful prehistories: the problem with the Berlin and Kay Colour paradigm. In Jones, A. & MacGregor, G. (eds.), *Colouring the Past. The Significance of Colour in Archaeological Research.* Oxford: Berg, 45–72.

Chaturvedi, V. (ed.). 2000. *Mapping Subaltern Studies and the Postcolonial.* London: Verso.

Chiartano, B. 1994. *La Necropoli dell'Età del Ferro dell'Incoronata e di S. Teodoro: Scavi 1978–1987.* Galatina: Congedo.

Chichikova, M. 1969. Trakiyska mogilna grobnitsa ot s.Kaloyanovo, slivenski ograg (IV v.pr.n.e.). *Izvestiya na Arheologicheskiya Institut* 31: 45–90.

Chichikova, M. 1970. *Sevtopolis.* Sofia: Bulgarski hudozhnik.

Chieco Bianchi Martini, A. M. 1964. Conversano (Bari). Scavi in Via T. Pantaleo. *Notizie degli Scavi* 18: 100–76.

Childe, V. G. 1925. *The Dawn of European Civilisation.* London: Kegan Paul.

Childe, V. G. 1927. *The Dawn of European Civilisation.* London: Kegan Paul.

Childe, V. G. 1929. *The Danube in Prehistory.* Oxford: The Clarendon Press.

Childe, V. G. 1935. Changing Methods and Aims in Prehistory. Presidential address. *Proceedings of the Prehistoric Society* 1: 1–15.

Childe, V. G. 1940. *Prehistoric Communities of the British Isles.* London – Edinburgh: : W. & R. Chambers, Ltd.

Childe, V. G. 1956. *Piecing Together the Past. The Interpretation of Archaeological Data.* London: Routledge and Kegan Paul.

Childe, V. G. 1957. *The Dawn of European Civilisation.* (6th Edition) London: Routledge.

Chochorowski, J. 1985. *Die Vekerzug-Kultur. Charakteristik der Funde.* Warszawa-Krakow: Nakladem Uniwersytetu Jagiellonskiego.

Christaller, W. 1933. *Die Zentralen Orte in Süddeutschland. Eine Ökonomische-*

*Geographische Untersuchung über die Gesetzmässigkeit der Verbreitung und Entwicklung der Siedlungen mit Städtischen Funktionen.* Jena: Karl Zeiss.

Christlein, R. 1982. Zu den jüngsten keltischen Funden Südbayerns. *Bayerische Vorgeschichtsblätter* 47: 275–92.

Ciancio, A. 1997. *Silbion: una Città tra Greci e Indigeni. La Documentazione Archeologica dal Territorio di Gravina in Puglia dall'Ottavo al Quinto Sec.* Bari: Levante editori.

Ciancio, A. 2001. *Guida al Parco Archeologico di Monte Sannace.* Bari: Progedit.

Ciancio, A. 2010. Ruoli e Societa: Il costumo funerario tra VI e IV secolo A.C. In Todisco, L. (ed.) *La Puglia Centrale dall'Età del Bronzo all'Alto Medioevo: Archeologia e Storia – Atti del Convegno di Studi (Bari, 15–16 Giugno 2009).* Roma: Bretschneider, 225–37.

Ciancio, A., Galeandro, F. & Palmentola, P. 2009. Monte Sannace e l'urbanizzazione della Peucezia. In Osanna, M. (ed.), *Verso la Città: Forme Insediative in Lucania e nel Mondo Italico fra IV e III Sec. a.C. Atti delle Giornate di Studio, Venosa, 13–14 Maggio 2006.* Potenza (PZ): Venosa, 285–302.

Cifani, G., Stoddart, S. K. F. & Neil, S. (eds.). 2012. *Landscape, ethnicity and identity in the Archaic Mediterranean area.* Oxford: Oxbow Books.

Cipriani, M. & Longo, F. (eds.). 1996. *I Greci in Occidente. Poseidonia e i Lucani.* Napoli: Electa.

Clark, G. 1966. The Invasion Hypothesis in British Archaeology. *Antiquity* 40 (159): 172–89.

Clarke, D. L. 1968. *Analytical Archaeology.* London: Methuen.

Clarke, D. L. 1987. The Economic Context of Trade and Industry in Barbarian Europe till Roman Times. In Postan, M. M., Miller, E. & Postan, C. (eds.), *The Cambridge Economic History of Europe. Vol.2 Trade and Industry in the Middle Ages*. Cambridge: Cambridge University Press, 263–331.

Cohen, A. P. 1985. *The Symbolic Construction of Community.* London/New York: Ellis Horwood.

Cohen, A. P. 2000. Introduction: Discriminating Relations – Identity, Boundary and Authenticity. In Cohen, A. P. (ed.), *Signifying Identities. Anthropological Perspectives on Boundaries and Contested Values*. London: Routledge, 1–13.

Cohen, M. G. 1995. *The Hellenistic Settlements in Europe, the Islands, and Asia Minor.* Los Angeles and Oxford: University of California Press, Berkeley.

Coles, J. M. 1960. Scottish late Bronze Age metalwork. *Proceedings of the Society of Antiquaries of Scotland* 93: 16–134.

Colivicchi, F. 2004. L'altro vino. Vino, cultura e identità nella Puglia e Basilicata anelleniche. Siris. *Studi e Ricerche della Scuola di Specializzazione in Archeologia di Matera* 5: 23–68.

Collins, R. 2008. Identity in the Frontier: Theory and Multiple Community Interfacing. In Fenwick, C., Wiggins, M. & Wythe, D. (eds.), *TRAC 2007: Proceedings of the Seventeenth Annual Theoretical Roman Archaeology Conference, London 2007.* Oxford: Oxbow Books, 45–52.

Collis, J. R. 1971. Functional and theoretical interpretations of British coinage. *World Archaeology* 3: 71–84.

Collis, J. R. 1977a. An approach to the Iron Age. In Collis, J. R. (ed.) *The Iron Age in Britain: a Review.* Sheffield: Department of Prehistory and Archaeology, 1–7.

Collis, J. R. 1977b. The proper study of Mankind is pots. In Collis, J. R. (ed.) *The Iron Age in Britain: a Review.* Sheffield: Department of Prehistory and Archaeology, 29–31.

Collis, J. R. 1986. Adieu Hallstatt! Adieu La Tène! In Duval, A. & Gomez de Soto, J. (eds.), *Actes du VIIIe Colloque sur les Âges du Fer en France Non-Mediterranéenne, Angoulême, 1984.* (Aquitania, Supplément 1). Bordeaux: Association française pour l'étude de l'âge du fer, 327–30.

Collis, J. R. 1999. George Buchanan and the Celts of Britain. In Black, R., Gillies, W. & Maolalaigh, R. Ó. (eds.), *Celtic Connections, Vol. 1. Proceedings of the Tenth International Congress of Celtic Studies.* East Linton: Tuckwell Press, 91–107.

Collis, J. R. 2001. *Digging up the Past.* Stroud: Sutton Publishing.

Collis, J. R. 2003. *Celts. Origins, Myths and Inventions.* (Second revised edition 2006) Stroud: Tempus.

Collis, J. R. 2004a. D'Amédée Thierry à Joseph Déchelette: hypothèses du XIXe siècle sur l'arrivée des Celtes en Gaule. In Mandy, B. & de Saulce, A. (eds.), *Les Marges de l'Armorique à l'Âge du Fer. Archéologie et Histoire; Culture Matérielle et Sources Écrites. Actes du XXIIIe Colloque de l'Association Française pour l'Etude de l'Age du Fer, Nantes, Mai 1999.* (Revue Archéologique de l'Ouest, Supplément 10). Rennes: Association pour la diffusion des recherches archéologiques dans l'Ouest de la France, 363–8.

Collis, J. R. 2004b. Paradigms and excavation. In Carver, G. (ed.), *Digging in the Dirt: Excavation in a New Millennium.* (BAR International Series 1256). Oxford: J. and E. Hedges Ltd, 32–43.

Collis, J.R. 2007. The polities of Gaul, Britain, and Ireland in the Late Iron Age. In Haselgrove, C. & Moore, T. (eds.), *The Later Iron Age in Britain and Beyond.* Oxford: Oxbow Books, 523–8.

Collis, J. R. 2008. Constructing chronologies: lessons from the Iron Age. In Lehoërff, A. (ed.), *Construire le Temps. Histoire et Méthodes des Chronologies et Calendriers des Derniers Millénaires avant Notre Ère en Europe Occidentale. Actes du XXXe Colloque International de HALMA-IPEL, UMR 8164 (CNRS, Lille 3, MCC) 7–9 Décembre 2006, Lille.* (Collection Bibracte 16). Glux-en-Glenne, Bibracte: Centre archéologique européen, 85–104.

Collis, J. R. 2009. Die Konstruktion von Chronologien. In Karl, R. & Leskovar, J. (eds.), *Interpretierte Eisenzeiten: Fallstudien, Methoden, Theorie. Tagungsbericht der 3. Linzer Gespräche zur Interpretativen Eisenzeitarchäologie.* (Studien zur Kulturgeschichte von Oberösterreich 22). Linz: Oberösterreichisches Landesmuseum, 373–421.

Collis, J. R. 2010a. *Celts. Origins, Myths and Inventions.* Stroud: Tempus.

Collis, J. R. 2010b. Redefining the Celts. In Zimmer, S. (ed.), *Kelten am Rhein. Proceedings of the Thirteenth International Congress of Celtic Studies, 23–27 July 2007 in Bonn; Part 2, Philologie: Sprachen und Literaturen.* (Beihefte der Bonner Jahrbücher 58/2). Mainz: Verlag Philipp von Zabern, 33–43.

Collis, J. R. 2011. 'Reconstructing Iron Age Society' revisited. In Moore, T. & Armada, L. (eds.), *Western Europe in the First millennium BC: Crossing the Divide*. Oxford: Oxford University Press, 223–41.

Condry, J. & Ansell, M. 1978. Excavation of a hut circle at Moss Raploch, Clatteringshaws. *Transactions of the Dumfries & Galloway Natural History and Antiquarian Society* 53: 105–13.

Conovici, N. 1978. Cupele cu decor în relief de la Crăsani și Copuzu. *Studii Și Cercetări de Istorie Veche Și Arheologie* 29. (2): 165–83.

Conovici, N. 1981. Piese ceramice de interes deosebit descoperite la Piscu Crăsani. *Studii Și Cercetări de Istorie Veche Și Arheologie* 32 (4): 571–9.

Cook, M. 1999. Excavation of two cairns, a cist and associated features at Sanaigmhor Warren, Islay, Argyll and Bute. *Proceedings of the Society of Antiquaries of Scotland* 129: 251–79.

Cool, H. E. M. 2004. *The Roman Cemetery at Brougham, Cumbria Excavations 1966–67.* (Britannia Monograph 21). London: Society for the Promotion of Roman Studies.

Cornell, T. J. 1997. Ethnicity as a factor in early Roman history. In Cornell, T. & Lomas, K. (eds.), *Gender and Ethnicity in Ancient Italy*. London: Accordia Research Institute, 9–21.

Côté, J. 2006. Identity Studies: How Close Are We to Developing a Social Science of Identity? – An Appraisal of the Field. *Identity* 6 (1): 3–25.

Čović, B. 1987. Grupa Donja Dolina-Sanski most. In Benac, A. (ed.), *Praistorija Jugoslavenskih Zemalja V, Željezno Doba*. Sarajevo: Posebna izdanja Akademije nauka i umjetnosti Bosne i Hercegovine, Odjeljenje za društvene nauke, 232–91.

Crass, B. 2001. Gender and Mortuary Analysis: What Can Grave Goods Really Tell Us? In Arnold, B. & Wicker, N. (eds.), *Gender and the Archaeology of Death*. Lanham, MD: AltaMira Press, 105–19.

Črešnar, M. 2007. Wooden house construction types in Bronze Age and Early Iron Age Slovenia. In Blečić, M., Črešnar, M., Hänsel, B., Hellmuth, A., Kaiser, E. & Metzner-Nebelsick, C. (eds.), *Scripta Praehistorica in Honorem Biba Teržan*. (Situla 46). Ljubljana: National Museum of Slovenia, 321–39.

Črešnar, M. 2010. New research on the Urnfield period of Eastern Slovenia : a case study of Rogoza near Maribor / Nova spoznanja o pozni bronasti dobi vzhodne Slovenije na primeru naselja Rogoza pri Mariboru. *Arheološki Vestnik* 61: 7–116.

Črešnar, M. 2011. New aspects on the Ha A phase in eastern Slovenia, in Beiträge zur Mittel- und Spätbronzezeit sowie zur Urnenfelderzeit am Rande der Südostalpen. In Gutjahr, C. & Gutjahr, G. (eds.), *Tiefengraber (Internationale Archäologie. Arbeitsgemeinschaft, Symposium, Tagung, Kongress 15.)*. Rahden/Westf: Verlag Marie Leidorf, 63–80.

Črešnar, M. in press. *Rogoza pri Mariboru. Zbirka Arheologija na Avtocestah Slovenije*. Ljubljana: Institute for the Protection of Cultural Heritage of Slovenia.

Crișan, E. 1964. Un craniu trepanat din necropola scitică de la Cristești. *Acta Musei Napocensis* 1: 79–86.

Crişan, I. H. 1969. *Ceramica Daco-Getică. Cu Specială Privire la Transilvania.* Bucureşti: Editura Ştiinţifică.
Crişan, I. H. 1971a. Contribuţii la problema celţilor din Transilvania. *Studii şi Cercetări de Istorie Veche şi Arheologie* 22 (2): 149–64.
Crişan, I. H. 1971b. Necropola celtică de la Apahida. *Acta Musei Napocensis* 8: 37–70.
Crişan, I. H. 1977. *Burebista şi Epoca sa.* Bucureşti: Editura Ştiinţifică şi Enciclopedică.
Crişan, I. H. 1980. Necropola dacică de la Cugir (jud. Alba). *Apulum* 18: 81–7.
Crişan, I. H. 1986. *Spiritualitatea Geto-Dacilor.* Bucureşti: Editura Albatros.
Crişan, V. 2000. *Dacii din Estul Transilvaniei.* Sfântu Gheorghe: Editura Carpaţii Răsăriteni.
Crişan, V. & Ferenczi, S. 1994. Aşezarea dacică de la Mereşti (jud. Harghita). Cercetările arheologice din anii 1986–1993. *Acta Musei Napocensis* 31 (1): 377–432.
Cristescu, C. 2011. *Ceramica Dacică Descoperită în Complexe Închise la Sarmizegetusa Regia (Grădiştea de Munte, jud. Hunedoara).* Cluj-Napoca: Unpublished doctoral thesis.
Cristofani, M. 1965. *La Tomba delle Iscrizioni a Cerveteri.* (Studi e materiali dell'Istituto di etruscologia e antichità italiche dell'Università di Roma 2). Firenze: Sansoni.
Cristofani, M. 1975. Il 'dono' in Etruria arcaica. *Parola del Passato* 30: 132–52.
Cristofani, M. (ed.). 1985. *Civiltà degli Etruschi (Catalogo della mostra).* Milan: Electa.
Cunliffe, B. & Koch, J. T. (eds.). 2010. *Celtic from the West: Alternative Perspectives from Archaeology, Genetics, Language and Literature.* Oxford: Oxbow Books.
Cunliffe, B. W. 2011. In the fabulous Celtic twilight. In Bonfante, L. (ed.), *The Barbarians of Ancient Europe: Realities and Interactions.* Cambridge: Cambridge University Press, 190–210.
Curchin, L. A. 2004. *The Romanization of Central Spain.* New York: Routledge.
Curle, A. O. 1905. Description of the Fortifications on Ruberslaw, Roxburghshire, and Notices of Roman Remains found there. *Proceedings of the Society of Antiquaries of Scotland* 39: 219–32.
Curle, J. 1932. An Inventory of Objects of Roman and Provincial Roman Origin found on sites in Scotland not definitely associated with Roman Constructions. *Proceedings of the Society of Antiquaries of Scotland* 66: 277–397.
d'Agostino, B. & Gastaldi, P. 1998. *Pontecagnano II. La Necropoli del Picentino. 1. Le Tombe della Prima Età del Ferro.* (AION Annali Dipartimento di Studi del Mondo Classico e del Mediterraneo Antico Quaderni 5). Napoli: Istituto Universitario Orientale.
d'Arbois de Jubainville, H. 1903. Conquête par les Gaulois de la région située entre le Rhin et l'Atlantique. *Revue Celtique* 1903: 162.
Daicoviciu, C. 1965. La Dacie et sa conquête par les romains. L'epoque archaïque (la commune primitive). In Daicoviciu, C. & Constantinescu, M. (eds.), *Brève Histoire de la Transylvanie.* (Bibliotheca Historica Romaniae, Monographies 3). Bucarest: Èditions de l'Académie de la République Socialiste de Roumanie, 9–18.

Daicoviciu, H. (ed.). 1981. *Studii Dacice.* Cluj-Napoca: Dacia.

Daicoviciu, H., Ferenczi, I. & Glodariu, I. 1989. *Cetăți și Așezări Dacice în Sud-Vestul Transilvaniei.* București: Ed. Științifică și enciclopedică.

Dana, D. 2008. *Zalmoxis de la Herodot la Mircea Eliade. Istorii despre un Zeu al Pretextului.* Iași: Polirom.

Daniel, G. 1950. *A Hundred Years of Archaeology.* Cambridge (Mass.): Harvard University Press.

Danov, C. M. 1976. *Altthrakien.* Berlin: Walter de Gruyter.

Darwin, C. 1859. *On the Origin of Species by Means of Natural Selection, or the Preservation of Favoured Races in the Struggle for Life.* London: John Murray.

Dautova-Ruševljan, V. & Vujović, M. 2006. *Roman Army in Srem.* Novi Sad: Museum of Vojvodina.

Davidovic, A. 2006. Identität – ein unscharfer Begriff. Identitätskurse in den gegenwartsbezogenen Humanwissenschaften. In Burmeister, S. & Müller-Scheeßel, N. (eds.), *Soziale Gruppen – Kulturelle Grenzen. Die Interpretation Sozialer Identitäten in der Prähistorischen Archäologie.* (Tübinger Archäologische Taschenbücher 5). Münster: Waxmann Verlag GmbH, 39–58.

Davidson, J. 1886. Notice of a Small Cup-shaped Glass Vessel, found in a Stone Cist at the Public School, Airlie, and now presented to the Museum by the School Board of Airlie. *Proceedings of the Society of Antiquaries of Scotland* 20: 136–41.

Davis, M. & Gwilt, A. 2008. Material, style, and identity in the first century AD metalwork, with particular reference to the Seven Sisters Hoard. In Garrow, D., Gosden, C. & Hill, J. D. (eds.), *Rethinking Celtic Art.* Oxford: Oxbow Books, 146–84.

Dawkins, R. 1976. *The Selfish Gene.* Oxford: Oxford University Press.

De Certeau, M. 1984. *The Practice of Everyday Life.* Berkeley, Los Angeles: University of California Press.

De Grossi Mazzorin, J., Riedel, A. & Tagliacozzo, A. 1998. Horse remains in Italy from the Eneolithic to the Roman period. In Anonymous (ed.), *Proceedings of the XIII International Congress of Prehistoric and Protohistoric Sciences, Forlì (Italia) 8–14 September 1996, vol. 6, Tome I.* Forli: ABACO Edizioni, 87–92.

De Juliis, E. M. 1973. Ordona (Foggia) – Scavi nella necropoli. *Notizie degli Scavi di Antichità* 27: 285–399.

De Juliis, E. 1988. *Gli Iapigi: Storia e Civiltà della Puglia Preromana.* Milan: Longanesi.

De Juliis, E. M. (ed.). 2007. *Rutigliano I: La Necropoli di Contrada Purgatorio: Scavo 1978.* Taranto: Scorpione.

De Juliis, E. M. 2010. La Peucezia: Caratteri Generali. In Todisco, L. (ed.), *La Puglia Centrale dall'Età del Bronzo all'Alto Medioevo. Archeologica e Storia. Atti del Convegno di Studi (Bari, 15–16 giugno 2009).* Roma: Giorgio Bretschneider Editore, 151–68.

de Polignac, F. 1995. *Cults, Territory, and the Origins of the Greek City State.* Chicago: University of Chicago Press.

Déchelette, J. 1913. *Manuel d'Archéologie Préhistorique Celtique et Gallo-romaine.*

II *Archéologie Celtique ou Protohistorique. Deuxième Partie. Premier Âge du Fer ou Époque de Hallstatt.* Paris: Auguste Picard.

Déchelette, J. 1914. *Manuel d'Archéologie Préhistorique Celtique et Gallo-romaine. II Archéologie Celtique ou Protohistorique. Troisième Partie. Second Âge du Fer ou Époque de la Tène.* Paris: Auguste Picard.

DeFrance, S. D. 2009. Zooarchaeology in Complex Societies: Political Economy, Status, and Ideology. *Journal of Archaeological Research* 17 (2): 105–68.

DeMarrais, E., Castillo, L. J. & Earle, T. 1996. Ideology, materialisation and power strategies. *Current Anthropology* 37 (1): 15–31.

Demoule, J.-P. 1999. Ethnicity, culture and identity: French archaeologists and historians. *Antiquity* 73: 190–8.

Demoule, J.-P. 1999. *Chronologie et Société dans les Nécropoles Celtiques de la Culture Aisne-Marne, du VIe au IIIe Siècle avant Notre Ère.* (Revue Archélogique de Picardie numéro spécial 15). Amiens: Direction régionale des antiquités historiques de Picardie.

Derks, T. 1998. *Gods, Temples and Ritual Practices. The Transformation of Religious Ideas and Values in Roman Gaul.* Amsterdam: Amsterdam University Press.

Derks, T. 2009. Ethnic identity in the Roman frontier: The epigraphy of Batavi and other Lower Rhine tribes. In Derks, T. & Roymans, N. (eds.), *Ethnic Constructs in Antiquity: the Role of Power and Tradition.* Amsterdam: Amsterdam University Press, 239–82.

Derks, T. & Roymans, N. 2009. *Ethnic Constructs in Antiquity: the Role of Power and Tradition.* Amsterdam: Amsterdam University Press.

Derks, T. & Roymans, N. 2009. Introduction In Derks, T. & Roymans, N. (eds.), *Ethnic Constructs in Antiquity: the Role of Power and Tradition.* Amsterdam: Amsterdam University Press, 1–10.

DeRoche, D. 2012. England: Bronze and Iron Ages. In Gleba, M. & Mannering, U. (eds.), *Textiles and Textile Production in Europe: from Prehistory to AD 400.* Oxbow Books: Oxford, 444–50.

Dhareshwar, V. 2006. Valorizing the Present: Orientalism, Postcoloniality and the Human Sciences. In Moore, H. L. & Sanders, T. (eds.), *Anthropology in Theory. Issues in Epistemology.* Oxford: Blackwell, 546–51.

Díaz-Andreu, M. 2007. *A World History of Nineteenth-Century Archaeology.* Oxford: Oxford University Press.

Díaz-Andreu, M. & Champion, T. (eds.). 1996a. *Nationalism and Archaeology in Europe.* London: UCL Press.

Díaz-Andreu, M. & Champion, T. 1996b. Nationalism and Archaeology in Europe: an introduction. In Díaz-Andreu, M. & Champion, T. (eds.), *Nationalism and Archaeology in Europe.* London: UCL Press, 1–23.

Díaz-Andreu, M. & Lucy, S. 2005. Introduction. In Dìaz-Andreu, M., Lucy, S., Babić, S. & Edwards, D. N. (eds.), *The Archaeology of Identity. Approaches to Gender, Age, Status, Ethnicity and Religion.* London: Routledge, 1–12.

Díaz-Andreu, M., Lucy, S., Babić, S. & Edwards, D. N. (eds.). 2005. *The Archaeology of Identity. Approaches to Gender, Age, Status, Ethnicity and Religion.* London: Routledge.

Díaz-Andreu, M. & Sørensen, M. L. (eds.). 1998. *Excavating Women: History of Women in European Archaeology.* London: Routledge.

Dietler, M. 1990. Driven by Drink: The role of drinking in the political economy and the case of early Iron age France. *Journal of Anthropological Archaeology* 9 (407): 352–406.

Dietler, M. 1994. "Our ancestors the Gauls": archaeology, ethnic nationalism, and the manipulation of Celtic identity in modern Europe. *American Anthropologist* 96: 584–605.

Dietler, M. 1996. Feasts and commensal politics in the political economy. Food, power and status in Prehistoric Europe. In Wiessner, P. & Schiefenhövel, W. (eds.), *Food and the Status Quest: an Interdisciplinary Perspective.* Providence (RI): Berghahn Books, 87–125.

Dietler, M. 1997. The Iron Age in Mediterranean France: Colonial Encounters, Entanglements, and Transformation. *Journal of World Prehistory* 11 (3): 269–358.

Dietler, M. 1999. Consumption, cultural frontiers and identity: anthropological approaches to Greek colonial encounters. In Stazio, A. & Ceccoli, S. (eds.), *Confini e Frontiera nella Grecitá d'Occidente: Atti del Trentasettesimo Convegno di Studi sulla Magna Grecia, Taranto, 3–6 Ottobre, 1997.* Taranto: Istitito per la storia e l'archeologia della Magna Grecia, 475–501.

Dietler, M. 2001. Theorizing the feast: Rituals of consumption, commensal politics and power in African contexts. In Dietler, M. & Hayden, B. (eds.), *Feasts. Archaeological and Ethnographic Perspectives on Food, Politics and Power.* Washington: Smithsonian Institution Press, 65–114.

Dietler, M. 2005. The archaeology of colonization and the colonization of archaeology. Theoretical challenges from an ancient Mediterranean colonial encounter. In Stein, G. J. (ed.), *The Archaeology of Colonial Encounters: Comparative Perspectives.* Santa Fe (NM): School of American Research Press, 33–68.

Dietler, M. 2006a. Alcohol: anthropological/archaeological perspectives. *Annual Review of Anthropology* 35: 229–49.

Dietler, M. 2006b. Culinary encounters: food, identity and colonialism. In Twiss, K. (ed.), *We Are What We Eat: Archaeology, Food and Identity.* (Occasional Paper 34). Carbondale (IL): Center for Archaeological Investigations, University of Southern Illinois Press, 218–42.

Dietler, M. 2010. *Archaeologies of Colonialism: Consumption, Entanglement, and Violence in Ancient Mediterranean France.* Berkeley: University of California Press.

Dietler, M. & Hayden, B. (eds.). 2001. *Feasts: Archaeological and Ethnographic Perspectives on Food, Politics, and Power.* Washington/London: Smithsonian Institution Press.

Dietz, K. 2004. Zur vorrömischen Bevölkerung nach den Schriftquellen. In Hüssen, C.-M., Irlinger, W. & Zanier, W. (eds.), *Spätlatènezeit und Frühe Römische Kaizserzeit zwischen Alpenrand und Donau.* Bonn: Rudolf Habelt, 1–23.

Dilthey, W. 1833. *Einleitung in die Geisteswissenschaften.* Leipzig: Duncker & Humblot.

Dimitrov, D. P. & Ivanov, T. (eds.). 1984. *Sevtopolis, Tom I.* Sofia: Bulgarska akademiia na naukite, Arheologicheski institut im muzei.

Dimitrova, D. & Sirakov, N. 2009. Spasitelni arheologicheski prouchvaniya na mogili v zemlishteto na s.Krushare. *Arheologicheski Otkritiya i Razkopki Prez 2008g* 48: 290–4.

Dimitrova, M. 1989. Obetsi s lavski glavi ot elinisticheskata epoha /po materiali ot Bulgaria. *Arheologia* 31 (3): 1–14.

Dimitrova, S. 2002. Loom Weights and Spindle-Whorls. In Bozkova, A. & Delev, P. (eds.), *Koprivlen 1: Rescue Archaeological Investigation along the Gotse Deltsev – Drama Road 1998–1999*. Sofia: Road Executive Agency, Archaeological Institute and Bulgarian Academy of Science, 173–83.

Dimova, B. 2011. *Gender and Other Elusive Identities in the Funerary Record of Late Iron Age and Early Hellenistic Thrace.* London: Unpublished Master's dissertation, Institute of Archaeology, UCL.

Dizdar, M. 2001. *Latenska Naselja na Vinkovačkom Području.* (Dissertationes et Monographiae 3). Zagreb: Filozofski fakultet.

Dizdar, M. 2010a. Inventory of grave 5, cat. 29. In Radman-Livaja, I. & Ilkić, M. (eds.), *Nalazi Rimske Vojne Opreme u Hrvatskoj = Finds of the Roman Military Equipment in Croatia.* Zagreb: Arheološki Muzej, 244–5.

Dizdar, M. 2010b. Kantharoi of autochtonous-"pannonian" origin from the La Tène culture cemetery in Zvonimirovo, Croatia. In Berecki, S. (ed.), *Iron Age Communities in the Carpathian Basin, Proceedings of the International Colloquiums from Târgu Mureş 9–11 October 2009.* (Bibliotheca Mvsei Marisiensis, Seria Archaeologica 2). Cluj-Napoca: Editura Mega, 297–307.

Dizdar, M. 2011. The La Téne culture in central Croatia. The problem of the eatsern border of the Taurisci in the Podravina region. In Guštin, M. & Jevtić, M. (eds.), *The Eastern Celts, The Communities between the Alps and the Black Sea.* Koper-Beograd: Univerza na Primorskem, Znanstveno-raziskovalno središče, Univerzitetna založba Annales, 99–118.

Dizdar, M. 2012. The Archaeological Background to the Formation of Ethnic Identities. In Migotti, B. (ed.), *The Archaeology of Roman Southern Pannonia, The State of Research and Selected Problems in the Croatian Part of the Roman Province of Pannonia.* (BAR International Series 2393). Oxford: Archaeopress, 117–36.

Dizdar, M. & Potrebica, H. 2003. Latenska kultura na prostoru Požeške kotline. *Opuscula Archaeologica* 26: 111–31.

Dizdar, M. & Radman-Livaja, I. 2004. Finds of Roman Bronze Ware on Celtic Sites in Eastern Slavonia. In Deru, X. & Brulet, R. (eds.), *Actes du XIVème Congrès UISPP, Université de Liège, Belgique, 2–8 Septembre 2001, Section 13, The Roman Age, General Sessions and Posters.* (BAR International Series 1312). Oxford: Archaeopress, 49–53.

Dizdar, M., Šoštarić, R. & Jelinčić, K. 2003. Ranorimski grob iz Iloka kao prilog poznavanju romanizacije zapadnog Srijema. *Prilozi Instituta za Arheologiju* 20: 57–77.

Domăneanţu, C. 2000. *Les Bols Hellénistiques à Décor en Relief.* (Histria 11). Bucureşti: Editura Enciclopedică.

Domaradski, M. 2002. Gray Pottery from Pistiros. In Bouzek, J., Domaradska, L. & Archibald, Z. H. (eds.), *Pistiros II: Excavation and Studies*. Prague: Charles University, 189–207.

Domínguez, A. J. 2004. Spain and France (including Corsica). In Hansen, M. H. & Nielsen, T. H. (eds.), *An Inventory of Archaic and Classical Poleis*. Oxford: Oxford University Press, 157–71.

Donia, R. J. forthcoming. The Proximate Colony. Bosnia-Herzegovina under Austro-Hungarian Rule. In Ruthner, C., Reynolds, D., Reber, U. & Detrez, R. (eds.), *The Political, Social and Cultural Impact of the Austro-Hungarian Occupation of Bosnia-Herzegovina*. New York: Peter Lang – http://www.kakanien.ac.at/beitr/fallstudie/RDonia1.pdf.

Donvito, A. 1992. Un Insediamento Peuceta inedito in Territorio di Gioia. In Girardi, M. (ed.), *Gioia: Una Città nella Storia e Civiltà di Puglia*. Brindisi: Fasano Schena, 23–126.

Dremsizova, T. 1955. Nadgrobni mogili pri selo Yankovo. *Izvestiya na Arheologicheskiya Institut* 19: 61–83.

Dremsizova, T. 1962. Mogilniyat nekropol pri s.Branichevo (Kolarovgradsko). *Izvestiya na Arheologicheskiya Institut* 25: 165–86.

Drennan, R. D. 1996. *Statistics for Archaeologists. A Commonsense Approach.* New York: Plenum Press.

Drescher, H. 1955. Die Herstellung von Fibelspiralen. *Germania* 33: 340–9.

Dular, J. & Tomanič Jevremov, M. 2010. *Ormož, Utrjeno Naselje iz Pozne Bronaste in Starejše Železne dobe/Ormož, Befestigte Siedlung aus der Späten Bronze- und der Älteren Eisenzeit.* (Opera Instituti archaeologici Sloveniae 18). Ljubljana: Scientific Research Centre SASA.

Dunn, J. C. 1974. Some recent investigations of a new fuzzy partitioning algorithm and its application to pattern classification problems. *Journal of Cybernetics* 4: 1–15.

Dunwell, A. 2007. *Cist Burials and an Iron Age Settlement at Dryburn Bridge, Inverwick, East Lothian.* (Scottish Archaeological Interim Report 24). Edinburgh: Society of Antiquaries of Scotland.

Dupoi, V. & Sîrbu, V. 2001. *Pietroasele – Gruiu Dării, Incinta Fortificată I.* Buzău: Editura Alpha.

Dušanić, S. 1967. Bassianae and its territory. *Archaeologia Iugoslavica* 8: 67–83.

Dušanić, S. 1971. The heteroclite metalli on the Roman coins. (in Serbian with an English summary). *Živa Antika* 21: 535–54.

Dušanić, S. 1977a. Aspects of Roman mining in Noricum, Pannonia, Dalmatia, and Moesia Superior. In Temporini, H. & Haase, W. (eds.), *Aufstieg und Niedergang der Römischen Welt. Geschichte und Kultur Roms im Spiegel der Neueren Forschung II. Principat, Sechster Band. Politische Geschichte (Provinzen und Randvölker: Lateinischer Donau-Balkanraum)*. Berlin & New York (NY): Walter de Gruyter, 52–94.

Dušanić, S. 1977b. Two notes on Roman mining in Moesia Superior. (in Serbian with an English summary). *Arheološki Vestnik* 28: 163–79.

Dušanić, S. 2003. Roman mining in Illyricum: historical aspects. In Urso, G. (ed.), *Dall' Adriatico al Danubio, L'Illirico nell'Età Greca e Romana. Atti del Convegno Internazionale Cividale del Friuli 25–27 settembre 2003.* (I convegni della Fondazione Niccolò Canussio 3). Pisa: ETS, 247–70.

Dušek, M. 1978. *Die Thraker im Karpatenbecken.* Amsterdam: B. R. Grüner.

Duval, P. M. 1977. *Les Celtes.* Paris: Gallimard.

Džino, D. 2007. The Celts in Illyricum – whoever they may be: The hybridization and construction of identities in southeastern Europe in the fourth and third centuries BC. *Opuscula Archaeologica* 31: 93–112.

Džino, D. 2008a. Deconstructing 'Illyrians': Zeitgeist, changing perceptions and the identity of peoples from ancient Illyricum. *Croatian Studies Review* 5: 43–55.

Džino, D. 2008b. "The people who are Illyrians and Celts": Strabo and the identities of the 'barbarians' from Illyricum. *Arheološki Vestnik* 59: 415–24.

Džino, D. 2009. The Daesitiates: The identity-construct between contemporary and ancient perceptions. (in Croatian with an English summary). *Godišnjak/Centar za Balkanološka Istraživanja* 38/36: 75–95.

Džino, D. 2010a. *Becoming Slav, Becoming Croat. Identity Transformations in Post-Roman and Early Mediaeval Dalmatia.* Leiden: Brill.

Džino, D. 2010b. *Illyricum in Roman Politics 229 BC–AD 68.* Cambridge: Cambridge University.

Eckardt, H. 2005. The social distribution of Roman artefacts: the case of nail-cleaners and brooches in Britain. *Journal of Roman Studies* 18: 139–60.

Eckardt, H. 2008. Technologies of the body: Iron Age and Roman grooming and display. In Garrow, D., Gosden, C. & Hill, J. D. (eds.), *Rethinking Celtic Art.* Oxford: Oxbow Books, 113–28.

Eckardt, H. & Crummy, N. 2006. 'Roman' or 'native' bodies in Britain: the evidence of late Roman nail-cleaner strap-ends. *Oxford Journal of Archaeology* 25: 83–103.

Eckardt, H. & Crummy, N. 2008. *Styling the Body in Late Iron Age and Roman Britain: A Contextual Approach to Toilet Instruments.* (Monographies Instrumentum 36). Montagnac: Monique Mergoi.

Eckardt, H. & Williams, H. 2003. Objects without a past. In Williams, H. (ed.), *Archaeologies of Remembrance: Death and Memory in Past Societies.* New York & London: Kluwer/Plenum Academic Press, 141–70.

Edward, C. & Van der Vliet, L. 2003. The Romans and Us: Strabo's "Geography" and the Construction of Ethnicity. *Mnemosyne* 56 (3): 257–72.

Eggers, H. J. 1950. Das Problem der ethnischen Deutung in der Frühgeschichte. In Kirchner, H. (ed.), *Ur- und Frühgeschichte als Historische Wissenschaft: Festschrift zum 60 Geburtstag von Ernst Wahle.* Heidelberg: Carl Winter, 49–59.

Eggers, H. J. 1959. *Einführung in die Vorgeschichte.* Munich: Piper Verlag.

Eggl, C. 2003. Ost-West-Beziehungen im Flachgräberlatène Bayerns. *Germania* 81: 513–38.

Egri, M. E. 2007. The use of amphorae for interpreting patterns of consumption. In Croxford, B., Ray, N., Roth, R. & White, N. (eds.), *Proceedings of the 16th Annual Theoretical Roman Archaeology Conference Cambridge 2006*. Oxford: Oxbow Books, 43–58.

Egri, M. E. 2008. *Communal Identity and Provincial Integration in the Lower Danube: an Archaeological Study of Ceramics (late 1st Century BC – early 2nd Century AD)*. Cambridge: Unpublished PhD thesis, University of Cambridge.

Egri, M. E. & Rustoiu, A. 2008. The Social Significance of Conviviality in the Scordiscian Environment. In Sîrbu, V. & Vaida, S. L. (eds.), *Funerary Practices of the Bronze and Iron Ages in Central and South-Eastern Europe, Proceedings of the 9th International Colloquium of Funerary Archaeology, Bistrița, Romania May 9th–11th, 2008*. Cluj-Napoca: Editura Mega, 83–93.

Egri, M. E. & Rustoiu, A. forthcoming. Sacred conviviality in the Lower Danube region. The case of the Sâncrăieni hoard. In Ruscu, L. & Nemeti, S. (eds.), *Banquets of Gods, Banquets of Men. Conviviality in the Ancient World*. Cluj Napoca.

Ehret, C. 2002. *The Civilizations of Africa: A History to 1800*. Charlottesville: University of Virginia Press.

Eibner, A. 2001. Die Donau – Drave – Save – Raum im Speigel gegenseitiger Eiflußnahme und Kommunikation in der frühen Eisenzeit. Zenrtralorte entlang der »Argonautenstraße«. / The Danube – Drava – Sava region in light of the reciprocal exertion of influence and communication in the Early Iron Age. Central Places along the »Route of the Argonauts«. In Lippert, A. (ed.), *Die Drau-, Mur- und Raab-Region im 1. Vorchristlichen Jahrtausend: Akten des Internationalen und Interdisziplinären Symposiums vom 26. bis 29. April 2000 in Bad Radkersburg*. (Universitätsforschungen zur Prähistorischen Archäologie 78). Bonn: Rudolf Habelt, 181–90.

Eicher, J. B. (ed.). 1995. *Dress and Ethnicity*. Oxford: Berg.

Eisner, W. 1991. The consequences of gender bias in mortuary analysis: A case study. In Walde, D. & Willows, N. (eds.), *The Archaeology of Gender: Proceedings of the Twenty-second Annual Chacmool Conference of the Archaeological Association of the University of Calgary*. Calgary: University of Calgary, 252–357.

Emiliozzi, A. (ed.). 1999. *Carri da Guerra e Principi Etruschi. Catalogo della Mostra. Viterbo, Palazzo dei Papi, 24 Maggio 1997 – 31 Gennaio 1998*. Roma: L'Erma di Bretschneider.

Emilov, J. 2010. Ancient texts on the Galatian royal residence of Tylis and the context of La Tène finds in southern Thrace: a reappraisal. In Vagalinski, L. F. (ed.), *In Search of Celtic Tylis in Thrace (III Cent BC). Proceedings of the Interdisciplinary Colloquium Arranged by the National Archaeological Institute and Museum at Sofia and the Welsh Department, Aberystwyth University, Held at the National Archaeological Institute and Museum, Sofia, 8 May 2010*. Sofia: NOUS Publishers Ltd, 67–87.

Ender, W. 2002. Kontinuität von der Bronzezeit bis zu den Slawen: Das Gräberfeld von Liebersee. In Menghin, W. & Planck, D. (eds.), *Menschen, Zeiten, Räume: Archäologie in Deutschland*. Stuttgart: Theiss, 229–31.

Entwistle, J. 2000. *The Fashioned Body.* Cambridge: Polity.
Evans, C., Mackay, D. & Webley, L. 2008. Acknowledgements. The Long Run. In Evans, C., Mackay, D. & Webley, L. (eds.), *Borderlands – The Archaeology of the Addenbrooke's Environs, South Cambridge.* (CAU Landscape Archives: New Archaeologies of the Cambridge Region Series 1). Cambridge – Oxford: Cambridge Archaeological Unit, x-xi.
Evans, J. 1988. Graffiti and the evidence of literacy and pottery use in Roman Britain. *Archaeological Journal* 144: 191–204.
Evans-Pritchard, E. E. 1940. *The Nuer: A Description of the Modes of Livelihood and Political Institutions of a Nilotic People.* Oxford: Oxford University Press.
Everitt, B. S., Landau, S., Leese, M. & Stahl, D. 2011. *Cluster Analysis.* Chichester: Wiley.
Fairclough, N. 1989. *Language and Power.* London: Longman.
Fairhurst, H. 1984. *Excavations at Crosskirk Broch, Caithness.* (Society of Antiquaries of Scotland Monograph Series 3). Edinburgh: Society of Antiquaries of Scotland.
Fehling, D. 1971. *Die Quellenangaben bei Herodot. Studien zur Erzählkunst Herodots.* (Untersuchungen zur antiken Literatur und Geschichte 9). Berlin & New York: de Gruyter.
Fenton, S. 2003. *Ethnicity. Key Concepts.* Oxford: Polity.
Ferencz, I. V. 2011. About the end of the Celtic presence in South-western Transylvania. In Guštin, M. & Jevtić, M. (eds.), *The Eastern Celts. The Communities between the Alps and the Black Sea.* Koper: Univerza na Primoerskem, 171–78.
Ferencz, I. V. & Ciută, M. M. 2005. Considerații pe marginea unor materiale descoperite la Șeușa (com. Ciugud, jud. Alba). *Istros* 12: 239–54.
Ferenczi, Ș. 1965. Cimitirul "scitic" de la Ciumbrud (partea I). *Acta Musei Napocensis* 2: 77–105.
Ferenczi, Ș. 1966. Cimitirul "scitic" de la Ciumbrud (partea II). *Acta Musei Napocensis* 3: 49–73.
Ferenczi, Ș. 1967. Cimitirul "scitic" de la Ciumbrud (partea III). *Acta Musei Napocensis* 4: 19–45.
Ferenczi, Ș. 1969. Cimitirul "scitic" de la Ciumbrud (partea IV). *Acta Musei Napocensis* 6: 47–65.
Ferenczi, Ș. 1971. Cimitirul "scitic" de la Ciumbrud (partea V). *Acta Musei Napocensis* 8: 11–36.
Fernández-Götz, M. 2011a. Niveles sociopolíticos y órganos de gobierno en la Galia de finales de la Protohistoria. *Habis* 42: 7–26.
Fernández-Götz, M. 2011b. Cultos, ferias y asambleas: los santuarios protohistóricos del Rin Medio-Mosela como espacios de agregación. *Palaeohispánica: Revista sobre Lenguas y Culturas de la Hispania Antigua* 11: 127–54.
Fernández-Götz, M. 2014. *Identity and Power: The Transformation of Iron Age Societies in Northeast Gaul* (Amsterdam Archaeological Studies 21) Amsterdam: Amsterdam University Press.

Ferris, I. M. 2000. *Enemies of Rome: Barbarians through Roman Eyes.* Stroud: Sutton.

Ferro, M. 2003. *The Use and Abuse of History, or, How the Past is Taught to Children.* (Revised Edition) London – New York: Routledge.

Fettich, N. 1931. Appendum: Bestand der skythischen Altertümer Ungarns. In Rostovzev, M. (ed.), *Skythien und der Bosporus. Band 2 Wiederentdeckte Kapitel und Verwandtes*. Berlin: F. Steiner, 494–535.

Fichtl, S. 2004. *Les Peuples Gaulois. IIIe–Ier Siècles av. J.-C.* Paris: Errance.

Fichtl, S. 2005. *La Ville Celtique. Les Oppida de 150 av. J.-C. à 15 ap. J.-C.* (Second Edition: corrigée et augmentée) Paris: Errance.

Fichtl, S. 2007. Le IIIe siècles avant notre ère: genèse des entités politiques en Gaule? In Mennessier-Jouannet, C., Adam, A.-M. & Milcent, P.-Y. (eds.), *La Gaule dans Son Contexte Européen aux IVe et IIIe Siècles avant Notre Ère*. Lattes: Édition de l'Association pour le Développement de l'Archéologie en Languedoc-Roussillon, 283–9.

Fichtl, S. 2010. Les places publiques dans les oppida. *L'Archéologue; Archéologie Nouvelle* 108: 36–40.

Fichtl, S., Metzler, J. & Sievers, S. 2000. Le rôle des sanctuaires dans le processus d'urbanisation. In Guichard, V., Sievers, S. & Urban, O. H. (eds.), *Les Processus d'Urbanisation à l'Âge du Fer. Colloque des 8–11 Juin 1998.* (Bibracte 4). Glux-en-Glenne: Centre archéologique européen du Mont Beuvray, 179–86.

Filip, J. 1956. *Keltové ve Střední Evropě.* Prague: Československé Akademie Věd.

Filip, J. 1960. *Keltská Civilizace a Její Dědictví. Celtic Civilisation and Its Heritage.* (Revised edition 1963 – English translation 1962) Prague: Akademia.

Filov, B. 1930. Antichnata grobnitsa pri s.Dalboki, starozagorsko. *Izvestiya na Arheologicheskiya Institut* 6: 45–54.

Filov, B. 1934. *Nadgrobnite Mogili v Duvanlii v Plovdivsko.* Sofia: Darzhavna pechannitsa.

Fischer, F. 1972. Die Kelten bei Herodot: Bermerkingen zu Einigen Geographischen and Ethnographischen Problemen. *Madrider Mitteilungen* 13: 109–24.

Fitzpatrick, A. 1996. 'Celtic' Iron Age Europe: the theoretical basis. In Graves-Brown, P., Jones, S. & Gamble, C. (eds.), *Cultural Identity and Archaeology: the Construction of European Communities*. London- New York: Routledge, 238–55.

Fleischer, F. & Rieckhoff, S. 2002. Bibracte – Eine keltische Stadt. Das gallo-römische Oppidum auf dem Mont Beuvray (Frankreich). In Cain, H.-U. & Rieckhoff, S. (eds.), *Fromm – Fremd – Barbarisch. Die Religion der Kelten*. Mainz: Verlag Philipp von Zabern, 103–18.

Florea, G. 1993. Materiale ceramice descoperite pe terasa a VIII-a de la Grădiştea Muncelului (I). *Ephemeris Napocensis* 3: 95–110.

Florea, G. 1994. Materiale ceramice descoperite pe terasa a VIII-a de la Grădiştea Muncelului (II). *Ephemeris Napocensis* 4: 49–60.

Florea, G. 1998. *Ceramica Pictată Dacică. Artă, Meşteşug şi Societate în Dacia Preromană (sec. I a.Chr. – I p.Chr.).* Cluj Napoca: Presa Universitară Clujeană.

Florea, G. 1998. *Ceramica Pictată. Artă, Meşteşug şi Societate în Dacia Preromană (sec.I a. Chr.-sec.I p.Chr.).* Cluj-Napoca: Presa Universitarã Clujeanã.

Florea, G. 2001. Noi fragmente ceramice cu semne grafice de la Sarmizegetusa Regia. In Crişan, V. (ed.), *Studii de Istorie Antică. Omagiu Profesorului Ioan Glodariu.* (Bibliotheca Musei Napocensis 22). Cluj-Napoca-Deva: Bibliotheca Musei Napocensis, 179–87.

Florea, G. 2004. Dacians and wine (1st century BC – 1st century AD). In Ruscu, L., Ciongradi, C., Ardevan, R., Roman, C. & Găzdac, C. (eds.), *Orbis Antiquus. Studia in Honorem Ioannis Pisonis.* Cluj Napoca: Nereamia Napocae, 517–22.

Florea, G. 2006. The "Public Image" of the Dacian Aristocracy. *Studia Universitatis "Babes-Bolyai".* (Special Issue: Focusing on Iron Age Elites) *Historia* 51 (1): 1–11.

Florea, G. 2011. *Dava et Oppidum. Débuts de la Genèse Urbaine en Europe au Deuxième Âge du Fer.* Cluj-Napoca: Academie Roumaine.

Florea, G. & Pupezã, P. 2008. Les dieux tués. La destruction du chef-lieu du Royaume dace. In Piso, I. (ed.), *Die Römischen Provinzen. Begriff und Gründung.* Cluj-Napoca: Mega Verlag, 281–95.

Florescu, A. & Florescu, M. 2005. *Cetăţile Traco-getice din Secolele VI-III a.Chr. de la Stânceşti (jud. Botoşani).* Târgovişte: Editura Cetatea de Scaun.

Fol, A. 1975. Thraco-Scythica. In Fol, A. & Ognenova-Marinova, L. (eds.), *Frakoskifskie Kul'turnye Sviazi.* (Studia Thracica 1). Sofia: Izdatelstvo na Bulgarskata Akademiya na Naukite, 160–65.

Fol, A. & Marazov, I. 1977. *Thrace and the Thracians.* New York: St. Martin's Press.

Fol, A., Nikolov, B. & Hoddinot, R. F. 1986. *The New Thracian Treasure from Rogozen, Bulgaria.* London: British Museum Publications.

Fol, A. & Spiridonov, T. 1983. *Istoricheska Geografiya na Trakiiskite Plemena do III v.pr.n.e.* Sofia: Izdatelstvo na Bulgarskata Akademiya na Naukite.

Fowler, C. 2004. *The Archaeology of Personhood: an Anthropological Approach.* London: Routledge.

Fowler, E. 1960. The origins and development of the penannular brooch in Europe. *Proceedings of the Prehistoric Society* 26: 149–77.

Fowler, M. J. 1953. The typology of brooches of the Iron Age in Wessex. *Archaeological Journal* 110: 88–105.

Frederiksen, M. W. 1984. *Campania.* London: British School at Rome.

Freeman, P. M. 1996. The earliest Greek sources on the Celts. *Études Celtiques* 32: 11–48.

Freeman, P. W. M. 1993. "Romanisation" and Material Culture. *Journal of Roman Archaeology* 6: 438–45.

Frere, S. S. 1967. *Britannia: A History of Roman Britain.* London: Routledge and Kegan Paul.

Frick, C. (ed.). 1880. *Pomponius Mela. De Chorographia Libri Tres.* Liepzig: Teubner.

Frobenius, L. 1898. *Der Ursprung der Kultur. Bd 1: Der Ursprung der Afrikanischen Kulturen.* Berlin: Borntraeger.

Frobenius, L. 1904. *Geographische Kulturkunde.* Leipzig: Brandstetter.

Frobenius, L. 1923. *Vom Kulturreich des Festlandes. Dokumente zur Kulturphysiognomik.* Berlin: Volksverband der Bücherfreunde.

Gabrovec, S. 1994. *Stična 1, Naselbinska Izkopavanja.* (Katalogi in Monografije 28). Ljubljana: Narodni muzej.

Gaddis, J. L. 2002. *The Landscape of History – How Historians Map the Past.* Oxford: Oxford University Press.

Galaty, M. 2011. Blood of Our Ancestors: Cultural Heritage Management in the Balkans. In Silverman, H. (ed.), *Contested Cultural Heritage; Religion, Nationalism and Exclusion in a Global World.* New York: Springer, 109–29.

Galaty, M., Stocker, S. R. & Watkinson, C. 1999. Beyond Bunkers: Domination, Resistance and Change in Albanian Regional Landscape. *Journal of Mediterranean Archaeology* 12 (2): 197–214.

Galaty, M. & Watkinson, C. (eds.). 2004. *Archaeology under Dictatorship.* New York: Springer.

Gallagher, D. B. & Clarke, A. 1993. Burials of Possible Roman-British Date from Inveresk, East Lothian. *Proceedings of the Society of Antiquaries of Scotland* 123: 315–18.

Galton, F. 1869. *Hereditary Genius: An Inquiry into Its Laws and Consequences.* London: Macmillan.

Galton, F. 1904. Eugenics: Its Definition, Scope and Aims. *American Journal of Sociology* 10: 1–6.

Garašanin, M. 1964. Le problème de la continuité en archeologie (in Serbian with a French summary). In Todorović, J. (ed.), *VI Kongres Arheologa Jugoslavije, Ljubljana, 1963.* Beograd: Société archéologique de Yugoslavie, 9–45.

Garašanin, M. (ed.). 1979. *Sahranjivanje Kod Ilira.* Beograd: Srpska akademija nauka i umetnosti, Balkanološki institut.

Garašanin, M. 1988a. Formation et origines des Illyriens. In Garašanin, M. (ed.), *Les Illyriens et les Albanais: Série de Conférences Tenues du 21 Mai au 4 Juin 1986.* Beograd: Academie Serbe des sciences et des artes, 82–144.

Garašanin, M. (ed.). 1988b. *Iliri i Albanci.* Beograd: Srpska akademija nauka i umetnosti.

Garašanin, M. 1991. Problemes de l'ethnogenèse des peuples paléobalkaniques (Régions centrales et occidentales de la Péninsule). In Benac, A. (ed.), *Tribus Paleobalkaniques entre la Mer Adriatique et la Mer Noire de l'Eneolithique jusqu'a l'Epoque Hellenistique.* Sarajevo & Beograd: Academie des sciences et des artes de Bosne et Herzegovine, Centre d'études balkaniques & Academie Serbe des sciences et des artes, Institut des d'études balkaniques, 9–32.

Garcia Sanjuan, L., P. Garrido Gonzales and F. Lozano Gomez 2008. The Use of Prehistoric Ritual and Funerary Sites in Roman Spain: Discussing Tradition, Memory and Identity in Roman Society. In Fenwick, C., Wiggins, M. & Wythe, D. (eds.), *TRAC 2007: Proceedings of the Seventeenth Annual Theoretical Roman Archaeology Conference, London 2007.* Oxford: Oxbow Books, 1–14.

Gardner, A. 2002. Seeking a material turn: the artefactuality of the Roman Empire. In Carr, G., Swift, E. & Weekes, J. (eds.), *TRAC 2002, Proceedings of the Twelfth Annual Theoretical Roman Archaeology Conference, Canterbury 2002.* Oxford: Oxbow Books, 1–13.

Gardner, A. 2007. *An Archaeology of Identity: Soldiers and Society in Late Roman Britain.* Walnut Creek, California: Left Coast Press.

Garlan, Y. 1985. De l'usage par les historiens du materiel amphorique grec. *Dialogues d'Histoire Ancienne* 11: 238–55.

Garrow, D. 2008. The space and time of Celtic Art: interrograting the 'Technologies of Enchantment' database. In Garrow, D., Gosden, C. & Hill, J. D. (eds.), *Rethinking Celtic Art*. Oxford: Oxbow Books, 15–39.

Gavranović, M. 2011. *Die Spätbronze- und Früheisenzeit in Bosnien.* (Universitätsforschungen zur prähistorischen Archäologie 195). Bonn: Habelt.

Gayraud, M. 1981. *Narbonne Antique des Origines à la Fin du IIIe Siècle.* Paris: Boccard.

Geary, P. J. 2002. *The Myth of Nations: The Medieval Origins of Europe.* Princeton. Oxford: Princeton University Press.

Gebhard, R. 1989. *Der Glasschmuck aus dem Oppidum von Manching.* (Ausgrabungen in Manching Band 11). Stuttgart: Franz Steiner Verlag.

Gebhard, R. 1991. *Die Fibeln aus dem Oppidum von Manching.* (Die Ausgrabungen in Manching 15). Stuttgart: Franz Steiner.

Gebhard, R. 2004. Die spätkeltische Gräbergruppe von Hörgertshausen, Lkr. Freising. In Hüssen, C.-M., Irlinger, W. & Zanier, W. (eds.), *Spätlatènezeit und Frühe Römische Kaizserzeit zwischen Alpenrand und Donau.* Bonn: Rudolf Habelt, 113–22.

Gell, A. 1992. The technology of enchantment and the enchantment of technology. In Coote, J. & Shelton, A. (eds.), *Anthropology, Art and Aesthetics*. Oxford: Clarendon, 40–67.

Gellner, E. 1983. *Nations and Nationalism.* Oxford: Blackwell Publishing.

Georgieva, R. 2007. Pogrebeniya na zheni v Trakiya (ranna zhelyazna epoha). *Spisanie na Bulgarskata Akademija na Naukite* 120 (4): 68–75.

Gerbec, T. in press. *Hotinja vas pri Mariboru. Zbirka Arheologija na Avtocestah Slovenije.* Ljubljana: Institute for the Protection of Cultural Heritage of Slovenia.

Gerritsen, F. & Roymans, N. 2006. Central places and the construction of tribal identities. The case of the Late Iron Age Lower Rhine region. In Haselgrove, C. (ed.), *Celtes et Gaulois, l'Archéologie Face à l'Histoire. 4: Les Mutations de la Fin de l'Âge du Fer. Actes de la Table Ronde de Cambridge, 7–8 juillet 2005.* (Collection Bibracte 12/4). Glux-en-Glenne: Centre archéologique européen, 251–66.

Giannotta, M. T. forthcoming. Apulian Pottery in Messapian contexts. In Carpenter, T. & Robinson, E. G. D. (eds.), *Beyond Magna Graecia. New Developments in South Italian Archaeology: The Contexts of Apulian and Lucanian Pottery.*

Giardino, C. 1998. *I Metalli nel Mondo Antico. Introduzione all'Archeometallurgia.* Roma-Bari: Gius. Laterza & Figli Spa.

Giddens, A. 1984. *The Constitution of Society: Outline of the Theory of Structuration.* Cambridge: Polity Press.

Gilchrist, R. 1999. *Gender and Archaeology: Contesting the Past.* New York: Routledge.

Gilchrist, R. 2004. Archaeology and the Life Course: A Time and Age for Gender. In Meskell, L. & Preucel, R. W. (eds.), *A Companion to Social Archaeology*. Oxford: Blackwell Publishing, 142–60.

Giles, M. 2007. Good fences make good neighbours? exploring the ladder enclosures of late Iron Age East Yorkshire. In Haselgrove, C. & Moore, T. (eds.), *The Later Iron Age in Britain and Beyond*. Oxford: Oxbow Books, 235–49.

Giles, M. 2008. Seeing red: the aesthetics of martial objects in the British and Irish Iron Age. In Garrow, D., Gosden, C. & Hill, J. D. (eds.), *Rethinking Celtic Art*. Oxford: Oxbow Books, 59–77.

Gilkes, O. 2004. The Trojans in Epirus: Archaeology, Myth and Identity in Inter-War Albania. In Galaty, M. & Watkinson, C. (eds.), *Archaeology under Dictatorship*. New York: Springer, 33–54.

Gillespie, S. D. 2001. Personhood, agency, and mortuary ritual: A case study from the Ancient Maya. *Journal of Anthropological Archaeology* 20 (1): 73–112.

Gingell, C. & Lawson, A. J. 1985. Excavations at Potterne, 1984. *Wiltshire Archaeological and Natural History Magazine* 79: 101–8.

Ginoux, N. 2007. *Le Thème Symbolique de "la Paire de Dragons" sur les Fourreaux Celtiques (IVe–IIe siècles av. J.-C.). Etude Iconographique et Typologie,*. Oxford: John and Erica Hedges Ltd.

Given, M. 2004. *The Archaeology of the Colonized*. London: Routledge.

Gleba, M. 2008. *Textile production in Pre-Roman Italy*. (Ancient Textiles Series 4). Oxford: Oxbow Books – Centre for Textile Research.

Gleirscher, P. 2005. Hügelgräber und Herschaftsbereiche im Ostalpenraum/Gomile in območja gospostev v vzhodnoalpskem prostoru. *Arheološki Vestnik* 56: 99–112.

Gleirscher, P. 2006. Urnefelderzeizliche Grabhügel und Siedlungen der älteren Hallstattzeit in der Steiermark. Zum Beginn der Hallstattkultur im Südostalpenraum. *Arheološki Vestnik* 57: 85–95.

Glodariu, I. 1976. *Dacian Trade with the Hellenistic and Roman World*. (BAR international series 8). Oxford: British Archaeological Reports.

Glodariu, I. 1997. Blocuri cu marcaje în construcţiile dacice din Munţii Şureanu. *Ephemeris Napocensis* 7: 65–87.

Glodariu, I. 2001. Viaţa spirituală. In Petrescu-Dâmboviţa, M. & Vulpe, A. (eds.), *Istoria Românilor (I)*. Bucureşti: Ed. Enciclopedică, 779–95.

Glodariu, I. & Iaroslavschi, E. 1979. *Civilizaţia Fierului la Daci (sec. II i.e.n. – I e.n.)*. Cluj-Napoca: Dacia.

Glodariu, I., Iaroslavschi, E., Rusu-Pescaru, A. & Stănescu, F. 1996. *Sarmizegetusa Regia Capitala Daciei Preromane*. Deva: Muzeul Civilizaţiei Dacice şi Romane.

Glodariu, I. & Moga, V. 1994. Tezaurul dacic de la Lupu. *Ephemeris Napocensis* 4: 33–48.

Gocheva, Z. 1981. Herodot. In Velkov, V., Ivanov, V., Gocheva, Z. & Tăpkova-Zaimova, V. (eds.), *Izvori za Istoriyata na Trakiya i Trakite 1*. Sofia: Bulgarskata Akademija na naukite, 193–221.

Goff, B. (ed.). 2005. *Classics and Colonialism*. London: Duckworth.

Good, I. 1995. On the question of silk in pre-Han Eurasia. *Antiquity* 69: 959–68.

Gosden, C. 1999. *Anthropology and Archaeology. A Changing Relationship.* London: Routledge.

Gosden, C. 2004. *Archaeology and Colonialism. Cultural Contact from 5000 BC to the Present.* Cambridge: Cambridge University Press.

Gosden, C. 2005. What do objects want? *Journal of Archaeological Method and Theory* 12 (3): 193–211.

Gosden, C. 2007. The Past and Foreign Countries: Colonial and Post-Colonial Archaeology and Anthropology. In Maskell, L. & Preucel, R. W. (eds.), *A Companion to Social Archaeology.* Malden: Blackwell Publishing, 161–78.

Gosselain, O. P. 1999. In Pots We Trust: The Processing of Clay and Symbols in Sub-Saharan Africa. *Journal of Material Culture* 4 (2): 205–30.

Gostar, N. & Lica, V. 1984. *Societatea Geto-Dacică de la Burebista la Decebal.* București: Junimea.

Graebner, F. 1911. *Methode der Ethnologie.* Heidelberg: Winter.

Graham-Campbell, S. 1991. Nome's Law, Fife: on the nature and dating of the silver hoard. *Proceedings of the Society of Antiquaries of Scotland* 121: 241–59.

Grant, M. 1995. *Greek and Roman Historians: Information and Misinformation.* London and New York (NY): Routledge.

Grasselt, T., Völling, T. & Walter, W. 2002. Nordbayern und Thüringen: Drehscheibe archäologischer Kulturentwicklung in einem Verkehrsraum. In Menghin, W. & Planck, D. (eds.), *Menschen, Zeiten, Räume: Archäologie in Deutschland.* Stuttgart: Theiss, 232–5.

Graves-Brown, P. 1996. All things bright and beautiful? Species, ethnicity and cultural dynamics. In Graves-Brown, P., Jones, S. & Gamble, C. (eds.), *Cultural Identity and Archaeology: the Construction of European Communities.* London-New York: Routledge, 81–95.

Graves-Brown, P., Jones, S. & Gamble, C. (eds.). 1996. *Cultural Identity and Archaeology: the Construction of European Communities.* London-New York: Routledge.

Greiner, C. 2003. *Die Peuketia. Kultur und Kulturkontakte in Mittelapulien vom 8. bis 5. Jh. v.Chr.* Remshalden: Greiner.

Grimson, A. 2010. Culture and identity: two different notions. *Social Identities* 16 (1): 61–77.

Gringmuth-Dallmer, E. 1996. Kulturlandschaftsmuster und Siedlungssysteme. *Siedlungsforschung Archäologie-Geschichte-Geographie* 14: 7–31.

Grünert, H. 2002. *Gustaf Kossinna (1858–1931).* Rahden: Verlag Marie Leidorf.

Guido, M. 1978. *The Glass Beads of the Prehistoric and Roman Periods in Britain and Ireland.* (Reports of the Research Committee of the Society of Antiquaries of London 35). London: Thames and Hudson.

Guštin, M. 2003. Humke starijeg gvozdenog doba sa nalazišta Nova Tabla kod Murske Sobote (Slovenija). In Bojović, N. & Vasić, M. (eds.), *Sahranjivanje u Bronzano i Gvozdeno Doba. Simpozijum Čačak, 4–8. September 2002. Burial customs in the Bronze and Iron Age. Symposium Čačak, 4–8. September 2002.* Čačak: Narodni muzej Čačak, 61–8.

Guštin, M. & Teržan, B. 1976. Malenškova gomila v Novem mestu, Prispevek k poznavanju povezav med jugovzhodnim alpskim svetom, severozahodnim Balkanom in južno Panonijo v starejši železni dobi. *Arheološki Vestnik* 26: 188–202.

Guštin, M. & Tiefengraber, G. 2001. Prazgodovinske najdbe z avtocestnega odseka Murska Sobota – Nova tabla / Vorgeschichtliche Funde aus dem Autobahnabschnitt bei Murska Sobota – Nova tabla *Arheološki Vestnik* 52: 107–16.

Hachmann, R. 1970. *Die Goten und Skandinavien.* (Quellen und Forschungen zur Sprach- und Kultur-Geschichte der germanische Völkern, 34). Berlin: de Gruyter.

Hachmann, R., Kossack, G. & Kuhn, H. (eds.). 1962. *Völker zwischen Germanen und Kelten.* Neumünster: Karl Wachholtz Verlag.

Haggett, P. 1965. *Locational Analysis in Human Geography.* London: Edward Arnold.

Hahn, E. 1992. Die menschlichen Skelettreste. In Maier, F., Geilenbrügge, U., Hahn, E., Köhler, H.-J. & Sievers, S. (eds.), *Ergebnisse der Ausgrabungen 1984–1987 in Manching.* Stuttgart: Franz Steiner, 214–34.

Hakenbeck, S. 2004. Ethnic tensions in Early Medieval Cemeteries in Bavaria. *Archaeological Review from Cambridge* 19 (2): 40–55.

Halkidi, M., Batistakis, Y. & Vazirgiannis, M. 2001. On Clustering Validation Techniques. *Journal of Intelligent Information Systems* 17: 107–45.

Hall, J. M. 1997. *Ethnic Identity in Greek Antiquity.* Cambridge: Cambridge University Press.

Hall, J. M. 2002. *Hellenicity: Between Ethnicity and Culture.* Chicago: University of Chicago Press.

Hall, S. 1996. Introduction: Who needs "Identity"? In Hall, S. & du Gay, P. (eds.), *Questions of Cultural Identity.* London: Sage, 1–17.

Hamilakis, Y. 2007. *The Nation and Its Ruins. Antiquity, Archaeology, and National Imagination in Greece.* Oxford: Oxford University Press.

Handl, J., Knowles, J. & Kell, D. B. 2005. Computational Cluster Validation in Post-genomic Data Analysis. *Bioinformatics* 21: 3201–12.

Haneca, K., Deforce, K., Boone, M. N., Van Loo, D., Dierick, M., Van Acker, J. & Van Den Bulcke, J. 2012. X-Ray sub-micron tomography as a tool for the study of archaeological wood preserved through the corrosion of metal objects. *Archaeometry* 54 (5): 893–905.

Hänsel, B. (ed.). 1995. *Handel, Tausch und Verkehr im Bronze- und Früheisenzeitlichen Südosteuropa.* (Prähistorische Archäologie in Südosteuropa 11 – Südosteuropa-Schriften 17). Berlin: München.

Hansen, K. P. 2003. *Kultur und Kulturwissenschaft.* Tübingen/Basel: A. Francke.

Hansen, K. P. 2009. Kultur und Kollektiv: Eine essayistische Heuristik für Archäologen. In Krauße, D. & Nakoinz, O. (eds.), *Kulturraum und Territorialität: Archäologische Theorien, Methoden, Fallbeispiele. Kolloquium des DFG-SPP 1171 Esslingen 17.-18. Januar 2007. Internationale Archäologie – Arbeitsgemeinschaft, Symposium, Tagung, Kongress 13.* Rahden: Verlag Marie Leidorf, 15–23.

Hansen, M. H. 2006. Emporion, a Study of the use and meaning of the term in Archaic and Classical periods. In Tsetskhladze, G. R. (ed.), *Greek Colonisation: An Account of Greek Colonies and Other Settlements Overseas, Volume One*. Leiden: Bril, 1–39.

Hanson, W. S. 1994. Dealing with Barbarians: The Romanization of Britain. In Vyner, B. (ed.), *Building on the Past: Papers Celebrating 150 Years of the Royal Archaeological Institute*. London: The Royal Archaeological Institute, 149–63.

Harding, D. W. 2004. *The Iron Age in Northern Britain. Celts and Romans, Natives and Invaders.* London: Routledge.

Härke, H. G. H. 1979. *Settlement Types and Patterns in the West Hallstatt Province.* (BAR International Series 57). Oxford: British Archaeological Reports.

Harrison, T. (ed.). 2002. *Greeks and Barbarians.* Edinburgh: Edinburgh University Press.

Hartmann, N. B. 1982. *Iron-working in Southern Etruria in the Ninth and Eighth centuries BC.* Philadelphia: Unpublished PhD, University of Pennsylvania.

Hartmann, N. B. 1985. Society and Technology in the Villanovan Iron Industry. In Stig Sørensen, M. L. & Thomas, R. (eds.), *The Bronze Age – Iron Age Transition in Europe: Aspects of Continuity and Change in European Societies 1200–500.* (BAR International Series S483). Oxford: British Archaeological Reports, 93–9.

Hartog, F. 1980. *Le Miroir d'Hérodote. Essai sur la Représentation de l'Autre.* (Bibliothèque des histoires). Paris: Gallimard.

Hartog, F. 1988. *The Mirror of Herodotus. The Representation of the Other in the Writing of History.* Berkeley: University of California Press.

Haselgrove, C. 1997. Iron Age brooch deposition and chronology. In Gwilt, A. & Haselgrove, C. (eds.), *Reconstructing Iron Age Societies: New Approaches to the British Iron Age*. Oxford: Oxbow Books, 51–72.

Haselgrove, C., Millett, M. & Smith, I. (eds.). 1985. *Archaeology from the Ploughsoil.* Sheffield: John R. Collis.

Hattatt, R. 1985. *Iron Age and Roman Brooches: A Second Selection of Brooches from the Author's Collection.* Oxford: Oxbow Books.

Hattatt, R. 1989. *Ancient Brooches and Other Artefacts: A Fourth Selection of Brooches Together with Some Other Antiquities from the Author's Collection.* Oxford: Oxbow Books.

Hatzopoulos, M. & Loukopoulou, L. 1992. *Recherches sur les Marches Orientales des Téménides (Meletemata 11), vol 1.* Athènes: Diffusion de Boccard.

Hatzopoulos, M. & Loukopoulou, L. 1996. *Recherches sur les Marches Orientales des Téménides (Meletemata 11), vol 2.* Athènes: Diffusion de Boccard.

Hauschild, M. 2010. "Celticised" or "assimilated"? In search of foreign and indigenous people at the time of the Celtic migrations. In Berecki, S. (ed.), *Iron Age Communities in the Carpathian Basin, Proceedings of the International Colloquiums from Târgu Mureş 9–11 October 2009.* (Bibliotheca Mvsei Marisiensis, Seria Archaeologica 2). Cluj-Napoca: Editura Mega, 171–80.

Hawkes, C. F. C. 1959. The ABC of the British Iron Age. *Antiquity* 33: 170–82.

Hawkes, C. F. C. 1961. The ABC of the British Iron Age. In Frere, S. S. (ed.), *Problems of the Iron Age in Southern Britain. Papers Given at a Council of British Archaeology Conference Held at the Institute of Archaeology, December 12 to 14, 1958.* (Occasional Paper 11). London: University of London, 1–16.

Haynes, K. E. & Fotheringham, A. S. 1984. *Gravity and Spatial Interaction Models.* Beverly Hills: Springer.

Haynes, S. 2000. *Etruscan Civilisation. A Cultural History.* London: British Museum Press.

Hays-Gilpin, K. & Whitley, D. S. (eds.). 1998. *Reader in Gender Archaeology.* London: Routledge.

Hedeager, L. 1992. *Iron-age Societies.* Oxford: Blackwell.

Hegel, G. W. 1997 [1830–1831]. *Vorlesungen über die Philosophie der Geschichte.* Stuttgart: Reclam.

Hellebrandt, M. 1988. Szkítakori temető Kesznyéten–Szérűkerten. 1984–85. évi ásatás eredménye. *Herman Ottó Múzeum Évkönyve* 25–26: 107–26.

Hellebrandt, M. 1999. *Celtic Finds from Northern Hungary.* Budapest: Akademiai Kiadó.

Henderson, J. 1982. *X-Ray Flourescence Analysis of Iron Age Glass.* Bradford: Unpublished PhD Thesis University of Bradford.

Henderson, J. 1987. The Iron Age of 'Loughey' and Meare: some inferences from glass analysis. *Antiquaries Journal* 67: 29–42.

Henderson, J. 1989. The Evidence for Regional Production of Iron Age Glass in Britain. In Feugere, M. (ed.), *Le Verre Préromain en Europe Occidental.* Montagnac: Monique Mergoil, 63–72.

Henderson, J. 1995. The scientific analysis of glass beads. In Rasmussen, M., Hansen, U. L. & Näsman, U. (eds.), *Glass Beads: Culture History, Technology, Experiment and Analogy.* Lejre: Historical-Archaeological Experimental Centre, 67–73.

Henderson, J. 2000. *The Science and Archaeology of Materials, an Investigation of Inorganic Materials.* London: Routledge.

Henderson, J. & Warren, S. 1981. X-ray flourescence analysis of Iron Age glass: beads from Meare and Glastonbury Lake Villages. *Archaeometry* 23: 83–94.

Henderson, J. C. 2007. *The Atlantic Iron Age. Settlement and Identity in the First Millennium BC.* London: Routledge.

Herder, J. G. 1990 [1774]. *Auch eine Philosophie der Geschichte zur Bildung der Menschheit.* Stuttgart: Reclam.

Herring, E. 1991. Power relations in Iron Age south east Italy. In Herring, E., Whitehouse, R. & Wilkins, J. B. (eds.), *Papers of the Fourth Conference of Italian Archaeology 2. The Archaeology of Power.* London: Accordia Research Centre, 117–33.

Herring, E. 2000. 'To see ourselves as other see us!' The construction of native identities in southern Italy. In Herring, E. & Lomas, K. (eds.), *The Emergence of State Identities in Italy in the First Millennium BC.* London: Accordia Research Institute, 45–78.

Herring, E. 2007. Identity crises in SE Italy in the 4th c. B.C.: Greek and native perceptions of the threat to their cultural identities. In Roth, R. & Keller, J. (eds.), *Roman by Integration: Dimensions of Group Identity in Material Culture and Text*. Portsmouth (Rhode Island): Journal of Roman Archaeology, 11–26.

Herring, E., Whitehouse, R. D. & Wilkins, J. B. 2000. Wealth, wine and war: some Gravina tombs of the 6th and 5th centuries BC. In Ridgway, D., Serra-Ridgway, F., Pearce, M., Herring, E., Whitehouse, R. D. & Wilkins, J. B. (eds.), *Ancient Italy in Its Mediterranean Setting. Studies in Honour of Ellen Macnamara*. London: Accordia Research Centre, 235–56.

Hildebrand, H. 1876. Sur les commencements de l'âge du fer en Europe. *Compte-rendu de la 7. session/Congrès International d'Anthropologie et d'Archéologie Préhistoriques: Stockholm, 1874*. Stockholm: Norstedt, 599.

Hill, J. D. 1995a. How should we understand Iron Age societies and hillforts? A contextual study from southern Britain. In Hill, J. D. & Cumberpatch, C. G. (eds.), *Different Iron Ages*. Oxford: British Archaeological Reports, 44–66.

Hill, J. D. 1995b. *Ritual and Rubbish: Rethinking the Iron Age of Wessex. A Study on the Formation of a Specific Archaeological Record.* (BAR British Series 242). Oxford: British Archaeological Reports.

Hill, J. D. 1997. "The end of one kind of body and the beginning of another kind of body"? Toilet instruments and "romanisation" in southern England during the first century AD. In Gwilt, A. & Haselgrove, C. (eds.), *Reconstructing Iron Age Societies*. Oxford: Oxbow Books, 96–107.

Hill, J. D. 2007. The dynamics of social change in Later Iron Age Eastern and South Eastern England c.300 BC to AD 43. In Haselgrove, C. & Moore, T. (eds.), *The Later Iron Age in Britain and Beyond*. Oxford: Oxbow Books, 16–40.

Hill, P. H. 1982a. Broxmouth Hill-fort excavations, 1977–78: an interim report. In Harding, D. W. (ed.), *Later Prehistoric Settlement in South-east Scotland*. Edinburgh: Department of Archaeology, University of Edinburgh, 141–88.

Hill, P. H. 1982b. Settlement and Chronology. In Harding, D. W. (ed.), *Later Prehistoric Settlement in South-east Scotland*. Edinburgh: Department of Archaeology, University of Edinburgh, 4–43.

Hill, P. H. 1997. *Whithorn and St Ninian: The Excavation of a Monastic Town; 1984–91*. Stroud: Sutton Publishing.

Hind, J. 1972. Pyrene and the date of the Massiliot sailing manual. *Rivista Storica dell'Antichità* 2: 39–52.

Hingley, R. 1992. Society in Scotland from 700 BC to AD 200. *Proceedings of the Society of Antiquaries of Scotland* 122: 7–53.

Hingley, R. 1996. Ancestors and identity in the later prehistory of Atlantic Scotland: the reuse and reinvention of Neolithic monuments and material culture. *World Archaeology* 28 (2): 231–43.

Hingley, R. 1999. *Roman Officers and English Gentlemen*. London: Routledge.

Hingley, R. 2005. *Globalizing Roman Culture: Unity, Diversity and Empire*. London: Routledge.

Hingley, R. 2009. *The Recovery of Roman Britain 1586–1906*. London: Routledge.

Hirt, A. M. 2010. *Imperial Mines and Quarries in the Roman World: Organizational Aspects 27 BC–AD235.* Oxford: Oxford University Press.

Hirth, K. G. 1978. Interregional trade and the formation of prehistoric gateway communities. *American Antiquity* 43: 35–45.

Hobsbawm, E. & Ranger, T. (eds.). 1983. *The Invention of Tradition.* Cambridge: Cambridge University Press.

Hodder, I. (ed.). 1982a. *Symbolic and Structural Archaeology.* (New Directions in Archaeology).Cambridge: Cambridge University Press.

Hodder, I. 1982b. *Symbols in Action: Ethnoarchaeological Studies of Material Culture.* Cambridge: Cambridge University Press.

Hodder, I. 1990. *The Domestication of Europe: Structure and Contingency in Neolithic Societies.* Oxford: Blackwell.

Hodder, I. (ed.). 1991. *Archaeological Theory in Europe. The Last Three Decades.* London: Routledge.

Hoddinott, R. F. 1981. *The Thracians.* (Ancient Peoples and Places 98). London: Thames and Hudson.

Hodos, T. 2006. *Local Responses to Colonization in the Iron Age Mediterranean.* London: Routledge.

Hodson, F. R. 1960. Reflections on the ABC of the British Iron Age. *Antiquity* 34 (134): 138–40.

Hodson, F. R. 1962. Some pottery from Eastbourne, the 'Marnians' and the pre-Roman Iron Age. *Proceedings of the Prehistoric Society* 28: 140–55.

Hodson, F. R. 1964. Cultural groupings within the British pre-Roman Iron Age. *Proceedings of the Prehistoric Society* 30: 99–110.

Hodson, F. R. 1969. Searching for structure in multivariate archaeological data. *World Archaeology* 1 (1): 90–105.

Hodson, R. F. 1968. *The La Tène cemetery at Münsingen-Rain.* (Acta Bernensia 5). Bern: Verlag Stämpfli & Cie AG.

Hoffiller, V. 1938. *Corpus Vasorum Antiquorum. Yougoslavie. Zagreb – Musée National.* (Corpus Vasorum Antiquorum, Fasc. 2). Beograd: F. Pelikan.

Horedt, K. 1965. Mittellatenezeitliche Siedlungen aus Siebenburgen. *Studien aus Alteuropa* 2: 54–75.

Horedt, K. 1979. *Moreşti, Grabungen in einer vor- und Frühgeschichtlichen Siedlung in Siebenbürgen.* Bukarest: Habelt.

Hornung, S. 2012. Le «Hunnenring » d'Otzenhausen, Lkr. St. Wendel, Sarre. In Schönfelder, M. & Sievers, S. (eds.), *L'Âge du Fer entre la Champagne et la Vallée du Rhin*. Mainz: Römisch-Germanischen Kommission des Deutschen Archäologischen Instituts, 183–216.

Horváth, L. 1979. *A Magyarszerdahelyi Kelta és Római Temető.* (Zalai Gyűjtemények 14). Zalaegerszeg: Zala Megyei Levéltár.

Hoskins, J. 1998. *Biographical Objects. How Things Tell the Stories of People's Lives.* London: Routledge.

Hoskins, J. 2006. Agency, Biography and Objects. In Tilley, C., Keane, W., Kuechler-Fogden, S., Rowlands, M. & Spyer, P. (eds.), *Handbook of Material Culture*. London – Thousand Oaks (CA): Sage Publications, 74–84.

Hoskins, W. C. 1955. *The Making of the English Landscape.* London: Penguin.

Hubert, L. & Arabie, P. 1985. Comparing Partitions. *Journal of the Classification* 2 (193–218).

Hull, M. R. & Hawkes, C. F. C. 1987. *Corpus of Ancient Brooches in Britain: Pre-Roman Bow Brooches.* (BAR British Series 168). Oxford: British Archaeological Reports.

Hunter, F. 1994. Dowalton Loch reconsidered. *Transactions of the Dumfries & Galloway Natural History and Antiquarian Society* 69 (Birrens Centenary Volume): 53–71.

Hunter, F. 1995. Leitchestown (near Deskford). *Discovery and Excavation in Scotland* 1995: 29–30.

Hunter, F. 1996. Recent Roman Iron Age Metalwork finds from Fife and Tayside. *Tayside and Fife Archaeological Journal* 2: 113–25.

Hunter, F. 1997. Iron Age Hoarding in Scotland and Northern England. In Gwiltin, A. & Haselgrove, C. (eds.), *Reconstructing Iron Age Societies.* Oxford: Oxbow Books, 108–33.

Hunter, F. 2001. Roman and native in Scotland: new approaches. *Journal of Roman Archaeology* 14: 289–309.

Hunter, F. 2007. Artefacts, regions, and identities in the northern British Iron Age. In Haselgrove, C. & Moore, T. (eds.), *The Later Iron Age in Britain and Beyond.* Oxford: Oxbow Books, 286–96.

Hunter, F. 2007. *Beyond the Edge of the Empire – Caledonians, Picts and Romans.* Rosmarkie: Groam House Museum.

Hurst, H. & Owen, S. (eds.). 2005. *Ancient Colonizations: Analogy, Similarity and Difference.* London: Gerald Duckworth and Co.

Huskinson, J. 2000. *Experiencing Rome: Culture, Identity and Power in the Roman Empire.* London: Routledge in association with the Open University.

Hüssen, C.-M. 2000. Endlatènezeitliche Fundstellen im oberbayerischen Donauraum. *Bericht der Römisch-Germanischen Kommission* 81: 235–301.

Hüssen, C.-M. 2004. Besiedlungswandel und Kontinuität im oberbayerischen Donauraum und in der Münchner Schotterebene von der Okkupation unter Augustus bis in tiberisch-claudische Zeit. In Hüssen, C.-M., Irlinger, W. & Zanier, W. (eds.), *Spätlatènezeit und Frühe Römische Kaizserzeit zwischen Alpenrand und Donau.* Bonn: Rudolf Habelt, 73–91.

Hüssen, C.-M., Irlinger, W. & Zanier, W. (eds.). 2004. *Spätlatènezeit und Frühe Römische Kaizserzeit zwischen Alpenrand und Donau.* Bonn: Rudolf Habelt.

Hutcheson, N. 2004. *Later Iron Age Norfolk: Metalwork, Landscape and Society.* (BAR British Series 361). Oxford: British Archaeological Reports.

Huxley, J. S. 1956. Evolution, Cultural and Biological. In Thomas, W. L. (ed.), *Current Anthropology: a Supplement to Anthropology Today.* Chicago: University of Chicago Press, 3–25.

Iaia, C. 2005. *Produzioni Toreutiche della Prima Età del Ferro in Italia Centro-Settentrionale. Stili Decorativi, Circolazione, Significato.* (Biblioteca di Studi Etruschi 40). Pisa-Roma: Istituti editoriali e poligrafici internazionali.

Ingemark, D. 2003. *Glass, Alcohol and Power in Roman Iron Age Scotland: A Study of the Roman Vessel Glass from Non-Roman/Native Sites in North Northumberland and Scotland.* Lund: Unpublished PhD Thesis Department of Archaeology and Ancient History University of Lund.

Insoll, T. (ed.). 2007a. *The Archaeology of Identities. A Reader.* London and New York: Routledge.

Insoll, T. 2007b. Introduction: Configuring Identities in Archaeology. In Insoll, T. (ed.), *The Archaeology of Identities. A Reader.* London and New York: Routledge, 1–18.

Iorga, N. 1936. *Istoria Românilor. Vol I. First Part, Strămoșii Înainte de Romani.* București: Editura Știițifică și Enciclopedică.

Irimia, M. 2006. Bols à décor en relief du Sud-Ouest de la Dobroudja. In Conrad, S., Einicke, R., Furtwängler, A. E., Löhr, H. & Slawisch, A. (eds.), *Pontos Euxeinos. Beiträge zur Archäologie und Geschichte des Antiken Schwarzmeer- und Balkanraumes.* Langenweißbach: Beier & Beran, 69–79.

Isaac, B. H. 1986. *The Greek Settlements in Thrace until the Macedonian Conquest.* (Studies of the Dutch Archæological and Historical Society 10). Leiden: E.J. Brill.

Isaac, G. 2010. The origins of the Celtic languages. Language spread from east to west. In Cunliffe, B. & Koch, J. (eds.), *Celtic from the West: Alternative Perspectives from Archaeology, Genetics, Language and Literature.* Oxford: Oxbow Books, 154–67.

Isayev, E. 2007. *Inside Ancient Lucania. Dialogues in History and Archaeology.* (Bulletin of the Institute of Classical Studies Supplement 90). London: Institute of Classical Studies.

Ivantchik, A. I. 1999. Une légende sur l'origine des Skythes (HDT. IV, 5-7) et le problème des sources du Skythicus Logos d'Hérodote. *Revue des Études Grecques* 112 (1): 141–92.

Izzet, V. 2001. Form and Meaning in Etruscan Ritual Space. *Cambridge Archaeological Journal* 11 (2): 185–200.

Izzet, V. 2007. *The Archaeology of Etruscan Society: Identity, Surface and Material Culture in Archaic Etruria.* Cambridge: Cambridge University Press.

Jaarsma, S. R. & Rohatynakyi, M. A. (eds.). 2000. *Ethnographic Artifacts: Challenges to a Reflexive Anthropology.* Honolulu: University of Hawaii.

Jacobsthal, P. 1944. *Early Celtic Art.* Oxford: Clarendon Press.

James, S. 1999. *The Atlantic Celts: Ancient People or Modern Invention?* London: British Museum Press.

Janakieva, S. 2005. Les temoignages des auteurs antiques des "sacrifices" de veuves en Thrace. *Thracia* 16: 151–61.

Jenkins, K. 1995. *On "What is History?".* London: Routledge.

Jenkins, R. 1994. Rethinking ethnicity: Identity, categorization and power. *Ethnic and Racial Studies* 17 (2): 197–223.

Jenkins, R. 1997. *Rethinking Ethnicity. Arguments and Explorations.* London – New Delhi: Sage Publications – Thousand Oaks.

Jenkins, R. 2008. *Social Identity.* London: Routledge.

Jerem, E. 1968. The Late Iron Age Cemetry of Szentlörinc. *Acta Archaeologica Academiae Scientiarum Hungaricae* 20: 159–208.

Jerem, E. 1981. Südliche Beziehungen einiger hallstattzeitlichen Fundtypen Transdanubiens. *Materijali Saveza arheoloških društava Jugoslavije* 19: 201–20.

Jevtić, M. 2007. Sacred groves of the Tribali on Miroč Mountain. *Starinar* 56/2006: 271–90.

Jevtić, M. & Peković, M. 2008. Mihajlov Ponor on Miroč – Tribal cult places. *Starinar* 57/2007: 191–219.

Jiménez, A. 2008. A Critical Approach to the Concept of Resistance: New 'Traditional' Rituals and Objects in Funerary Contexts of Roman Baetica. In Fenwick, C., Wiggins, M. & Wythe, D. (eds.), *TRAC 2007: Proceedings of the Seventeenth Annual Theoretical Roman Archaeology Conference, London 2007*. Oxford: Oxbow Books, 15–30.

Jiménez, A. 2011. Pure hybridism: Late Iron Age sculpture in southern Iberia. *World Archaeology* 43 (1): 101–23.

Johns, C. 1996. The Classification and Interpretation of Romano-British Treasures. *Britannia* 27: 1–16.

Johnson, M. 1999. *Archaeological Theory: an Introduction*. Oxford: Blackwell.

Jones, A. 2003. Technologies of Remembrance: Memory, materiality and identity in Early Bronze Age Scotland. In Williams, H. (ed.), *Archaeologies of Remembrance. Death and Memory in Past Societies*. New York: Kluwer Academic/Plenum Publishers, 65–88.

Jones, A. & MacGregor, G. (eds.). 2002a. *Colouring the Past. The Significance of Colour in Archaeological Research*. Oxford: Berg.

Jones, A. & MacGregor, G. 2002b. Introduction. Wonderful Things – Colour Studies in Archaeology from Munsell to Materiality. In Jones, A. & MacGregor, G. (eds.), *Colouring the Past. The Significance of Colour in Archaeological Research*. Oxford: Berg, 1–21.

Jones, D. 1705. *The Antiquities of Nations; More Particularly of the Celtae or Gauls, Taken to be Originally the Same People as Our Ancient Britains, by Monsieur Pezron, Englished by Mr. Jones*. London: S. Ballard.

Jones, H. L. (ed.). 1924. *Strabo, Geography, Books 6–7*. Cambridge (MA): Harvard University Press.

Jones, O. (ed.). 1856. *The Grammar of Ornament*. London: Day and Son.

Jones, S. 1997. *The Archaeology of Ethnicity. Constructing Identities in the Past and Present*. London: Routledge.

Jones, S. 1999. Historical categories and the praxis of identity: the interpretation of ethnicity in historical archaeology. In Funari, P. P. A., Hall, M. & Jones, S. (eds.), *Historical Archaeology*. London: Routledge, 219–32.

Jones, S. 2007. Discourses of identity in the interpretation of the past. In Insoll, T. (ed.), *The Archaeology of Identities. A Reader*. London and New York: Routledge, 44–58.

Jones, S. & Graves-Brown, P. 1996. Introduction: Archaeology and cultural identity in Europe. In Graves-Brown, P., Jones, S. & Gamble, C. (eds.), *Cultural*

*Identity and Archaeology: the Construction of European Communities.* London: Routledge, 1–21.

Jope, E. M. 2000. *Early Celtic Art in the British Isles.* Oxford: Clarendon Press.

Jovanović, A. 1990. Prilog proučavanju srebrnih emblema iz Tekije. *Glasnik Srpskog Arheološkog Društva* 6: 29–36.

Jovanović, B. 1987. Istočna grupa. In Benac, A. (ed.), *Praistorija Jugoslovenskih zemalja V: željezno doba.* Sarajevo: Akademija nauka i umjetnosti Bosne i Hercegovine, Centar za balkanološka ispitivanja, 815–54.

Jovanović, B. 1992. Celtic settlement of the Balkans. In Tasić, N. (ed.), *Scordisci and the Autochthons: Scordisci and the Native Population in the Middle Danube Region.* Belgrade: Serbian Academy of Sciences and Arts, Institute for Balkan Studies, 19–33.

Jovanović, B. 2005. The Challenge of Plural Identity. *Balcanica* 36: 71–83.

Jovanović, B. & Jovanović, M. 1988. *Gomolava, Naselje Mlađeg Gvozdenog Doba = Late La Tène settlement.* (Gomolava 2). Novi Sad – Beograd: Vojvođanski muzej – Arheološki institut.

Joy, J. 2007. *Reflections on the Iron Age: Biographies of Mirrors.* University of Southampton: Unpublished Doctoral Thesis.

Jundi, S. & Hill, J. D. 1997. Brooches and identity in first century AD Britain: more than meets the eye? In Forcey, C., Hawthorne, J. & Witcher, R. (eds.), *TRAC 97. Proceedings of the Seventh Annual Theoretical Roman Archaeology Conference.* Oxford: Oxbow Books, 125–37.

Jung, M. 2008. Zur Überdeterminiertheit von Grabausstattungen – eine Exemplifikation anhand des späthallstattzeitlichen Grabbefundes von Eberdingen-Hochdorf. In Kümmel, C., Schweizer, B. & Veit, U. (eds.), *Körperinszenierung – Objektsammlung – Monumentalisierung: Totenritual und Grabkult in Frühen Gesellschaften.* Münster: Waxmann Verlag GmbH, 271–86.

Kacarov, G. 1919. Keltite v stara Trakiya i Makedoniya. *Spisanie na Bulgarskata Akademiya na Naukite/Klon Istoriko-Filologichen i Filosofsko-Obshtestven* 18/10: 41–80.

Kacarov, G. 1930. Thrace. In Cook, S. A., Adcock, F. E. & Charlesworth, M. P. (eds.), *Rome and the Mediterranean, 218–133 B.C.* (Cambridge Ancient History 8). Cambridge: Cambridge University Press, 534–60, 781–83.

Kacarov, G. & Dechev, D. 1949. Herodot. In Kacarov, G. & Dechev, D. (eds.), *Izvori za Starata Istoriya i Geografiya na Trakiya i Makedoniya Vol.1.* (2nd edition). Sofia: BAN, 17–37.

Kaczynski, B. 2009. Überlegungen zur Organisation des Münzwesens der Treverer. In Uelsberg, G. & Schmauder, M. (eds.), *Kelten am Rhein. Akten des Dreizehnten Internationalen Keltologiekongresses. Erster Teil: Archäologie. Ethizität und Romanisierung.* (Beihefte Bonner Jahrbücher 58). Mainz: Verlag Philipp von Zabern, 199–204.

Kaenel, G. 1990. *Recherches sur la Période de La Tène en Suisse Occidentale.* Lausanne: Bibliothèque historique vaudoise.

Kaenel, G. 2007. Les mouvements de populations celtiques: aspects historiographiques et confrontations archéologiques. In Mennessier-Jouannet, C.,

Adam, A.-M. & Milcent, P.-Y. (eds.), *La Gaule dans Son Contexte Européen aux IVe et IIIe Siècles avant Notre Ère*. Lattes: Édition de l'Association pour le Développement de l'Archéologie en Languedoc-Roussillon, 385–98.

Kaenel, G. & Müller, F. 1991. The Swiss Plateau. In Moscati, S. (ed.), *The Celts*. New York: Rizzoli, 250–60.

Kaiser, T. 1995. Archaeology and ideology in southeast Europe. In Kohl, P. L. & Fawcett, C. (eds.), *Nationalism, Politics and the Practice of Archaeology*. Cambridge: Cambridge University Press, 99–119.

Kant, I. 1964 [1803]. Über Pedagogik. *Werke in XII Bänden, 12*. Frankfurt am Main: Suhrkamp, 695–761.

Kapuran, A. 2009. *Late Bronze Age and Early Iron Age Architecture in the Južna Morava Basin*. Belgrade: University of Belgrade, Faculty of Philosophy.

Karavanić, S. 2009. *The Urnfield Culture in Continental Croatia*. (BAR International Series 2036). Oxford: Hadrian Books.

Karl, R. 2004. Celtoscepticism: a convenient excuse for ignoring non-archaeological evidence? In Sauer, E. W. (ed.), *Archaeology and History: Breaking down the Borders*. London: Routledge, 185–99.

Karl, R. 2006. *Altkeltische Sozialstrukturen*. Budapest: Archaeolingua Alapitvany.

Karl, R. 2007. Kelten und Germanen. In Mandl, G. & Steffelbauer, I. (eds.), *Krieg in der Antiken Welt*. Essen: Magnus Verlag, 158–94.

Karl, R. 2008a. Feine Unterschiede: Zu Keltengenese und ethnogenetische Prozessen in der Keltiké. *Mitteilungen der Anthropologischen Gesellschaft in Wien* 138: 205–23.

Karl, R. 2008b. Random coincidences? Or: the return of the Celtic to Iron Age Britain. *Proceedings of the Prehistoric Society* 74: 69–78.

Karl, R. 2010. The Celts from everywhere and nowhere: a re-evaluation of the origins of the Celts and the emergence of Celtic Cultures. In Cunliffe, B. & Koch, J. (eds.), *Celtic from the West: Alternative Perspectives from Archaeology, Genetics, Language and Literature*. Oxford: Oxbow Books, 39–64.

Karl, R. 2011. Becoming Welsh: Modelling first millennium BC societies in Wales and the Celtic connection. In Moore, T. & Armada, L. (eds.), *Western Europe in the First Millennium BC: Crossing the Divide*. Oxford: Oxford University Press, 336–57.

Karl, R., Leskovar, J. & Moser, S. (eds.). 2012. *Interpretierte Eisenzeiten: Die Erfundenen Kelten. Mythologie Eines Begriffes und Seine Verwendung in Archäologie, Tourismus und Esoterik. Tagungsbericht der 4. Linzer Gespräche zur Interpretierten Eisenzeitarchäologie*. (Studien zur Kulturgeschichte von Oberösterreich 31).Linz: Oberösterreichisches Landesmuseum.

Kaufman, L. & Rousseeuw, P. J. 2005. *Finding Groups in Data: An Introduction to Cluster Analysis*. New York-Chichester: Wiley.

Kavur, B. 2008. Izgubljeni grob/ Lost grave. *Annales* 18: 397–406.

Kazarov, G. M. 1916. *Beiträge zur Kulturgeschichte der Thraker*. Sarajevo: Kommissionsverlag von J. Studnicka & Co.

Keller, D. 2005. Social and economic aspects of glass recycling. In Bruhn, J., Croxford, B. & Grigoropoulos, D. (eds.), *TRAC 2004: Proceedings of the*

*Fourteenth Annual Theoretical Roman Archaeology Conference which Took Place at the University of Durham 26–27 March 2004*. Oxford: Oxbow Books, 65–78.

Keller, E. 1984. *Die Frükaiserzeitlichen Körpergräber von Heimstetten und die Verwandten Funde aus Südbayern.* Munich: C.H. Beck.

Kemble, J. M., Franks, A. W. & Latham, R. G. 1863. *Horae Ferales. Studies in the Archaeology of the Northern Nations.* London: Lovell Read and Co.

Kemenczei, T. 2000. Zum früheisenzeitlichen Pferdegeschirr in Mitteleuropa. *Acta Archaeologica Academiae Scientiarum Hungaricae* 51: 235–47.

Keppie, L. J. F. 1989. Beyond the Northern Frontier: Roman and Native in Scotland. In Todd, M. (ed.), *Research on Roman Britain 1960–89*. London: Society for the Promotion of Roman Studies, 61–73.

Keppie, L. J. F. 1990. The Romans in Scotland: Future Discoveries. *Glasgow Archaeological Journal* 16: 1–27.

Keppie, L. J. F. 1997. Roman Britain in 1996. 1. Sites explored. 2. Scotland. *Britannia* 28: 412.

Kerman, B. 2001. Luftbildarchäologie in Prekmurje / Aerial Photography in Prekmurje. In Lippert, A. (ed.), *Die Drau-, Mur- und Raab-Region im 1. Vorchristlichen Jahrtausend: Akten des Internationalen und Interdisziplinären Symposiums vom 26. bis 29. April 2000 in Bad Radkersburg*. (Universitätsforschungen zur Prähistorischen Archäologie 78). Bonn: Rudolf Habelt, 57–65.

Kerman, B. 2011. *Kotare-Baza pri Murski Soboti.* (Zbirka Arheologija na avtocestah Slovenije 17). Ljubljana: Institute for the Protection of Cultural Heritage of Slovenia.

Kerman, B. 2011. *Kotare-Krogi pri Murski Soboti.* (Zbirka Arheologija na avtocestah Slovenije 20). Ljubljana: Institute for the Protection of Cultural Heritage of Slovenia.

Keyser, P. T. 2011. Greek geography of the western barbarians. In Bonfante, L. (ed.), *The Barbarians of Ancient Europe: Realities and Interactions*. Cambridge: Cambridge University Press, 37–70.

Kilian, K. 1970. *Früheisenzeitliche Funde aus der Südostnekropole von Sala Consilina (Provinz Salerno).* Heidelberg: Kerle.

Kilian-Dirlmeier, I. 1972. *Die Hallstattzeitlichen Gürtelbleche und Blechgürtel Mitteleuropas.* Munich: C.H. Beck.

Kimes, T. C., Haselgrove, C. & Hodder, I. 1982. A method for the identification of the location of regional cultural boundaries. *Journal of Anthropological Archaeology* 1: 113–31.

Kimmig, W. 1965. Review of A. Rybová and B. Soudský 1962. *Germania* 43: 172–84.

Kimmig, W. 1969. Zum Problem späthallstättischer Adelssitze. In Otto, K.-H. & Hermann, J. (eds.), *Siedlung. Burg und Stadt: Studien zu Ihren Anfängen. Festschrift Paul Grimm*. Berlin: Deutsche Akademie der Wissenschaften, 95–113.

Kissyov, K. 2005. *Thrace and Greece in Ancient Times. Classical Age Tumuli in the Municipality of Kaloyanovo.* Plovdiv: Avtospektar.

Kitov, G. 1994a. Dolinata na tsarete v kazanlashkata kotlovina. *Anali* 1 (2–3): 46–76.

Kitov, G. 1994b. Mogili ot hinterlanda na Sevtopolis. In Draganov, D. (ed.), *Poselishten Zhivot v Drevna Trakiya: III Mezhdunaroden simpozium Kabile*. Yambol: Istoricheski muzei, 85–93.

Kitov, G. 1995. Les tumuli royaux dans "La valée des rois". *Orpheus* 5: 5–21.

Kitov, G. 2003. Dolinata na trakiyskite vladeteli (II). *Arheologia* 44 (2): 28–42.

Kitov, G. 2005. *The Valley of the Thracian Rulers*. Varna: Slavena.

Kitov, G., Dimitrova, D. & Sirakov, N. 2008. Trakiyski mogili v slivensko. *Arheologicheski Otkritiya i Razkopki Prez 2007g* 47: 245–50.

Kitov, G., Shalganov, K. & Kraynov, I. 1980. *Trakite v Loveshki Okrag*. Sofia: Nauchen Ekspeditsionen Klub UNESCO.

Kitov, G. & Theodossiev, N. 1995. New data on Thracian archaeology and religion from the tumuli near the villages of Shipka and Sheynovo in the Kazanluk region (preliminary publication). *Thracia* 11: 317–36.

Klein, J., Lerman, J. C., Damon, P. E. & Ralph, E. K. 1982. Calibration of Radiocarbon dates: tables based on the consensus data of the Workshop on Calibrating the radiocarbon timescale. *Radiocarbon* 24 (2): 103–50.

Knapp, A. B. & van Dommelen, P. 2008. Past practices: rethinking individuals and agents in archaeology. *Cambridge Archaeological Journal* 18 (1): 15–34.

Knopf, T. 2002. *Kontinuität und Diskontinuität in der Archäologie – Quellenkritische-vergleichende Studien.* (Tübinger Schriften zur Ur- und Frühgeschichte 6). Münster/New York: Waxmann.

Koch, J. T. 2009. On Celts calling themselves 'Celts' and related questions. *Studia Celtica* 43: 73–86.

Koch, J. T. 2010. Ancient references to Tartessos. In Cunliffe, B. & Koch, J. (eds.), *Celtic from the West: Alternative Perspectives from Archaeology, Genetics, Language and Literature*. Oxford: Oxbow Books, 185–301.

Kohl, P. L. 1998. Nationalism and Archaeology: on the constructions of nations and the reconstructions of the remote past. *Annual Review of Anthropology* 27: 223–46.

Kohl, P. L. & Fawcett, C. (eds.). 1995. *Nationalism, Politics and the Practice of Archaeology*. Cambridge: Cambridge University Press.

Kopytoff, I. 1986. The Cultural Biography of Things: Commoditization as a Process. In Appadurai, A. (ed.), *The Social Life of Things: Commodities in Cultural Perspective*. Cambridge: Cambridge University Press, 64–91.

Kossak, G. 1959. *Sudbäyern Während der Hallstattzeit*. (Römisch Germanische Forschungen 24). Berlin: De Gruyter.

Kossinna, G. 1911. *Die Herkunft der Germanen. Zur Methode der Siedlungsarchäologie.* (Mannus-Bibliothek 6). Würzburg: Curt Kabitzsch.

Kossinna, G. 1912. Dr. Erich Blume †. *Mannus* 4: 451–57.

Kossinna, G. 1926. *Ursprung und Verbreitung der Germanen in Vor- und Frühgeschichtlicher Zeit.* Berlin: Germanen-Verlag.

Kotova, D. 1998. Trakiyskite zheni. In Delev, P. (ed.), *Yubileen Sbornik v Pamet na akad. D. Dechev.* Sofia: Heron, 66–9.

Kotova, D. 2000a. Témoignages antiques sur les femmes, le mariage et la famille chez les Thraces. *Thracia* 13: 227–39.

Kotova, D. 2000b. Kam sotsialnata istoriya na trakite: polova zryalost i legitimen brak. *Seminarium Thracorum* 4: 71–84.

Kotova, D. 2002. Mezhdu zavisimost i vliyanie: polozhenieto na zhenata v drevna Trakiya. In Boshnakov, D. & Boteva-Boyanova, D. (eds.), *Sbornik v Chest na Prof. Margarita Tacheva*. Sofia: Sofia University, 222–31.

Kotova, D. 2004. Vechnata sapruga. *Seminarium Thracicum* 6: 53–60.

Kotsakis, K. 1998. The past is ours: images of Greek Macedonia. In Meskell, L. (ed.), *Archaeology under Fire: Nationalism, Politics and Heritage in the Eastern Mediterranean and Middle East*. London – New York: Routledge, 44–67.

Kottak, C. P. 2006. *Mirror for Humanity: a Concise Introduction to Cultural Anthropology.* (Fifth Edition) New York: McGraw Hill.

Kovács, Ş. 1915. Station préhistorique de Marosvásárhely; cimetière de l'époque scythe et de la migration des peuples. *Dolgozatok az Erdélyi Nemzeti Múzeum Éremés Régisétárából* 6: 299–315.

Krader, L. 1963. *Peoples of Central Asia.* (Uralic and Altaic series 26). Bloomington: Indiana University Publications.

Krämer, W. 1962. Manching II: Zu den Ausgrabungen in den Jahren 1957 bis 1961. *Germania* 40: 293–316.

Krämer, W. 1985. *Die Grabfunde von Manching und die Latènezeitlichen Flachgräber in Südbayern*. Stuttgart: Franz Steiner Verlag.

Krauße, D. 2004. Frühe Zentralisierungs- und Urbanisierungsprozesse. Zur Genese und Entwicklung frühkeltischer Fürstensitze und ihres territorialen Umlandes. Ein Schwerpunktprogramm der Deutschen Forschungsgemeinschaft. *Archäologisches Nachrichtenblatt* 9: 359–74.

Krauße, D. 2006. *Eisenzeitlicher Kulturwandel und Romanisierung im Mosel-Eifel-Raum* (Römisch-Germanische Forschungen 63). Mainz: Verlag Philipp von Zabern.

Krauße, D. 2008. Etappen der Zentralisierung nördlich der Alpen. Hypothesen, Modelle, Folgerungen. In Krauße, D. (ed.), *Frühe Zentralisierungs- und Urbanisierungsprozesse. Zur Genese und Entwicklung Frühkeltischer Fürstensitze und Ihres Territorialen Umlandes. Koll. DFG-SPP 1171 Blaubeuren Oktober 2006*. Stuttgart: Theiss, 435–50.

Krauße, D. & Nübold, C. 2007. Der Tempelbezirk von Wallendorf. In Uelsberg, G. (ed.), *Krieg und Frieden. Kelten – Römer – Germanen*. Darmstadt: Primus Verlag, 277–81.

Kroeber, A. L. & Kluckhohn, C. 1952. *Culture. A Critical Review of Concepts and Definitions.* Cambridge: Harvard University Press.

Kroeber, A. L. & Parsons, T. 1958. The Concepts of Culture and of Social Systems. *American Sociological Review* 25: 582–3.

Krstić, V. 2005. Slikani kantarosi i skifosi sa lokaliteta Kale – Krševica, kod Bujanovca. *Zbornik Narodnog Muzeja* 43 (1): 191–212.

Kruta, V. 1985. Le port des anneaux de cheville en Champagne et le problem d'une immigration danubienne au IIIe s. avant J.-C. *Études Celtiques* 22: 27–51.

Kruta, V. 2000. *Les Celtes. Histoire et Dictionnaire.* Paris: Robert Laffont.

Kruta, V. & Lička, M. (eds.). 2004. *Celti di Boemia e di Moravia. Exhibition Catalogue, Civico Museo Archeologico – Villa Mirabello, Varese, 28 November 2004 – 25 April 2005.* Paris: Kronos B.Y. Editions.

Kühn, H. 1976. *Geschichte der Vorgeschichtsforschung.* Berlin: Walter de Gruyter.

Kuhn, W. 1955. The Hungarian Method for the assignment problem. *Naval Research Logistic Quarterly* 2: 83–97.

Kull, B. 1997. Tod und Apotheose. Zur Ikonographie in Grab und Kunst der jüngeren Eisenzeit an der unteren Donau und ihrer Bedeutung für die Interpretation von "Prunkgräbern". *Berichte der Römisch-Germanischen Kommission* 78: 197–466.

Kurzban, R., Tooby, J. & Cosmides, L. 2001. Can race be erased? Coalitional computation and social categorization. *Proceedings of the National Academy of Sciences of the United States of America* 98 (26): 15387–92.

Kuzman, P. 2006. Staromakedonski simboli na arheološki predmeti od Samuilova tvrdina vo Ohrid. In Maneva, E. (ed.), *Folia Archaeologica Balkanika In Honoreum Verae Bitrakova Grozdanova.* Skopje: Faculty of Philosophy, Institute of History of Art and Archaeology, 215–44.

Kuzman, P. 2009. Introduction. *Macedonian Archaeological News* 1 (1): http://www.mav.mk/article.php?lang=en&article=1.

La Fontaine, J. S. 1985. Person and individual: some anthropological reflections. In Carrithers, M., Collins, S. & Lukes, S. (eds.), *The Category of the Person: Anthropology, Philosophy, History.* Cambridge: Cambridge University Press, 123–40.

Labate, D. 1987. Ceramica Apula rinvenuta in Turi. In L'Abbate, V. (ed.), *Storia e Cultura in Terra di Bari. Studi e Ricerche.* Conversano: Galatina, 117–23.

Labellarte, M. 1988. Via Giuseppe Martino. In Andreassi, G. & Radina, F. (eds.), *Archeologia di una Città. Bari dalle Origini al X Secolo.* Bari: Edipuglia, 304–39.

Lamut, B. 1988–89. Kronološka slika prazgodovinske naselbine v Ormožu. *Arheološki Vestnik* 39–40: 235–76.

Lamut, B. 2001. Ormož – The Chronological Structure of the Late Bronze and Early Iron Age Settlement. In Lippert, A. (ed.), *Die Drau-, Mur- und Raab-Region im 1. Vorchristlichen Jahrtausend: Akten des Internationalen und Interdisziplinären Symposiums vom 26. bis 29. April 2000 in Bad Radkersburg.* (Universitätsforschungen zur Prähistorischen Archäologie 78). Bonn: Rudolf Habelt, 201–42.

Landes, C. 2003. Lattes étrusque. In Landes, C. (ed.), *Les Etrusques en France. Archéologie et Collections. Catalogue de l'Exposition.* Lattes: Association IMAGO-musée de Lattes, 129–39.

Lang, A. & Salac, V. (eds.). 2002. *Fernkontakte in der Eisenzeit.* Prague: Archäologisches Institut der Akademie der Wissenschaften der Tschechischen Republik.

Lanting, J. N. & Van der Waals, J. D. 1972. British Beakers as seen from the Continent. *Helinium* 12: 20–46.

Laqueur, T. 1990. *Making Sex: Body and Gender from the Greeks to Freud.* Cambridge (MA): Harvard University Press.

Latour, B. 1997. *Nous n'avons Jamais Été Modernes.* Paris: Editions La Découverte.

Latour, B. 1999. *Pandora's Hope: Essays on the Reality of Science Studies.* Cambridge (Mass): Harvard University Press.

Latour, B. 2005. *Reassembling the Social: An Introduction to Actor-Network-Theory.* Oxford: Oxford University Press.

Laurence, R. 2001. Territory, ethnonyms and geography: the construction of identity in Roman Italy. In Laurence, R. & Berry, J. (eds.), *Cultural Identity and the Roman Empire*. London & New York (NY): Routledge, 95–111.

Lazić, M. D. 2009. Who were the Dardani? *Archaica* 2: 54–75.

Lefebvre, H. 1991. *The Production of Space.* Oxford: Oxford University Press.

Legge, T., Sheldon, H., Wouldhusysen, M., Evans, C. & Pickles, J. 2011. Dr John Amyas Alexander (27/01/1922 - 17/08/2010). *Proceedings of the Cambridge Antiquarian Society* 100 (C): 209–13.

Lenerz-de Wilde, M. 1991. *Iberia Celtica. Archäologische Zeugnisse Keltischer Kultur auf der Pyrenäenhalbinsel.* Stuttgart: Steiner Verlag.

Leonhard, G. 1909. Familia. In Wissowa, G. (ed.), *Paulys Realencyclopädie der Classischen Altertumswissenschaft, Zwölfter Halbband, 1980–1984.* Stuttgart: Alfred Druckenmüller Verlag, 6: cols. 1980–85.

Leve, L. 2010. Identity. *Current Anthropology* 52 (4): 513–35.

Lhuyd, E. 1707. *Archaeologia Britannica, Giving Some Account Additional to What Has Been Hitherto Publish'd of the Languages, Histories and Customs of the Original Inhabitants of Great Britain, from Collections and Observations in Travels through Wales, Cornwall, Bas-Bretagne, Ireland and Scotland.* Oxford: Printed at the Theater for the author.

Lilčik, V. 2009. *Korpus na Starite Gradovi i Tvrdine vo Republika Makedonija: Linkestida i Deuriop.* Skopje: Makedonska civilizacija.

Lindner, F. L. 1841. *Skythien und die Skythen des Herodot, und Seine Ausleger: Nebst Beschreibung des Heutigen Zustandes Jener Länder.* Stuttgart: Schweizerbart.

Lippolis, E. & Boschung, D. 1994. *Catalogo del Museo Nazionale Archeologico di Taranto. Vol. III, 1. Taranto. La Necropoli: Aspetti e Problemi della Documentazione Archeologica dal VII al I sec. a.C.* Taranto: La Colomba.

Lippolis, E. & Dell'Aglio, A. 1992. *Catalogo del Museo Nazionale Archeologico di Taranto. Vol. II,1. Ginosa e Laterza, la Documentazione Archeologica dal VII at III sec. a.C., Scavi 1900–1980.* Taranto: La Colomba.

Lo Porto, F. G. 1991. *Timmari. L'Abitato, le Necropoli, la Stipe Votiva.* Roma: Bretschneider.

Lockyear, K. 2004. The Late Iron Age background to Roman Dacia. In Hanson, W. S. & Haynes, I. P. (eds.), *Roman Dacia. The Making of a Provincial Society.* Portsmouth: Rhode Island, 33–74.

Lomas, K. 2000. Cities, states and ethnic identity on southern Italy. In Herring, E. & Lomas, K. (eds.), *The Emergence of State Identities in Italy in the First Millennium BC*. London: Accordia Research centre, 79–90.

Loukopoulou, L. D. 1989. *Contribution a l'Histoire de la Thrace Propontique durant la Periode Archaique.* (Meletemata 9). Athènes: Diffusion de Boccard.

Ložnjak Dizdar, D. 2004. Odnos daljske i bosutskegrupena prostoru hrvatskog Podunavlja početkom starijeg željeznog doba. *Prilozi Instituta za Arheologiju u Zagrebu* 21: 19–36.

Ložnjak Dizdar, D., Mihaljević, M. & Dizdar, M. 2010. Rezultati pokusnog istraživanja prapovijesnog groblja Glavičice i Draganje u Dolini 2009. *Annales Instituti Archaeologici* 6: 41–6.

Ložnjak Dizdar, D., Mihaljević, M. & Dizdar, M. 2011. Dolina 2010. – rezultati probnih istraživanja prapovijesnog groblja Glavičice. *Annales Instituti Archaeologici* 7: 41–4.

Lubšina Tušek, M. 2001. Ptuj in the First Millennium BC. In Lippert, A. (ed.), *Die Drau-, Mur- und Raab-Region im 1. Vorchristlichen Jahrtausend: Akten des Internationalen und Interdisziplinären Symposiums vom 26. bis 29. April 2000 in Bad Radkersburg.* (Universitätsforschungen zur Prähistorischen Archäologie 78). Bonn: Rudolf Habelt, 121.

Lubšina Tušek, M. 2008. Zgornja Hajdina – arheološko najdišče Srednica. *Varstvo Spomenikov* 44: 316–8.

Lucas, J. 2002. Material Culture Patterns and Cultural Change in South-West Britain. In Carruthers, M., van-Driel-Murray, C., Gardner, A., Revell, L. & Swift, A. (eds.), *TRAC 2001: Proceedings of the Eleventh Annual Theoretical Roman Archaeology Conference, Glasgow 2001.* Oxford: Oxbow Books, 51–65.

Lucy, S. 1994. Children on early medieval cemeteries. *Archaeological Review from Cambridge* 13: 21–34.

Lucy, S. 2005. Ethnic and cultural identities. In Dìaz-Andreu, M., Lucy, S., Babić, S. & Edwards, D. N. (eds.), *The Archaeology of Identity. Approaches to Gender, Age, Status, Ethnicity and Religion.* London: Routledge, 86–109.

Lund, H. S. 1992. *Lysimachus: A Study in Early Hellenistic Kingship.* London: Routledge.

Lüning, J. 1972. Zum Kulturbegriff im Neolithikum. *Prähistorische Zeitschrift* 47: 145–73.

Mac Eoin, G. 1986. The Celticity of Celtic Ireland. In Schmidt, K. H. & Ködderitzsch, R. (eds.), *Geschichte und Kultur der Kelten. Vorbereitungskonferenz, 25.–28. Oktober in Bonn.* Heidelberg: Carl Winter Universitäts Verlag, 161–73.

Mac Niocaill, G. 1972. *Ireland before the Vikings.* Dublin: Gill and Macmillan.

Macan, R. W. (ed.). 1895. *Herodotus, The Fourth, Fifth, and Sixth Books. With Introduction, Notes, Appendices, Indices, Maps by R. W. Macan. Vol. I.* London & New York: Macmillan and Co.

Macaulay, G. C. (ed.). 1890. *Herodotus. The History of Herodotus.* (Edited and Translated – Available at: http://www.sacred-texts.com/cla/hh/index.htm [Accessed March 31, 2011]). London and New York: Macmillan.

Macdonald, J. 1897. Note on a cinerary urn, of a type not common in Scotland, lately found near Cramond. *Proceedings of the Society of Antiquaries of Scotland* 31: 244–6.

Macgregor, M. 1976. *Early Celtic Art in North Britain. A Study of the Decorative Metalwork from the Third Century BC to the Third Century AD.* Leicester: Leicester University Press.

Maclagan, C. 1876. Notes on the Sculptured Caves near Dysart, in Fife, illustrated by Drawings of the Sculptures. *Proceedings of the Society of Antiquaries of Scotland* 11: 107–23.

Madsen, J. M. 2000. The Romanization of Greek Elite in Achaia, Asia and Bythinia: Greek Resistance or Regional Discrepancies? *Orbis Terrarum* 8: 87–113.

Magness, J. 2001. A Near Eastern ethnic element among the Etruscan elite? *Etruscan Studies* 8: 79–117.

Majnarić-Pandžić, N. 1970. *Keltsko-latenska Kultura u Slavoniji i Syrmiau.* (Acta Musei Cibalensis 2). Vinkovci: Gradski muzej.

Majnarić-Pandžić, N. 1972–1973. Kasnolatenski keltski grobovi iz Sotina. *Vjesnik Arheološkog Muzeja u Zagrebu* 3rd ser. 6–7: 55–74.

Majnarić-Pandžić, N. 1995. Nekoliko napomena o uvođenju ranolatenskog stla u sjevernu Hrvatsku i Bosnu. *Arheološki Radovi i Rasprave* 12: 31–53.

Majnarić-Pandžić, N. 2003. Ein späthallstattzeitliches Gräberfeld in Vinkovci (Nordkroatien) und das Problem eines neuen Phänomens der Pferdeausstattung in diesem Gebiet. *Germania* 81 (2): 481–511.

Maldonado, A. 2010. *Christianity and Burial in Late Iron Age Scotland.* Glasgow: Unpublished PhD Thesis University of Glasgow.

Malinowski, B. 1931. Culture. *Encyclopedia Social Sciences* 4: 621–46.

Malinowski, B. 2004. Magic, Science and Religion. In Robben, A. C. G. M. (ed.) *Death, Mourning, and Burial: A Cross-Cultural Reader.* Oxford: Blackwell, 19–22.

Malone, C., Stoddart, S. Ceccarelli, L. Cenciaioli, L. Duff, P. McCormick, F. Morales, J.. Armstrong, S Bates, J. Bennett, J. Cameron, J. Cifani, G. Cohen, S. Foley, T. Fulminante, F. Hill, H. Mattacchoni, L. Neil, S. Rosatelli, A. Redhouse, D. and Volhard-Dearman, S. 2014. *Beyond feasting: consumption and life style amongst the invisible Etruscans.* In K. Boyle, R. Rabett and C. Hunt. (eds.), Living in the Landscape. Cambridge: McDonald Institute, 257–266.

Mangani, E. 1983. *Museo Civico di Asciano. I materiali di Poggio Pinci.* Asciano – Siena: Comune di Asciano – Regione Toscana – Soprintendenza ai beni archeologici per la Toscana – Centrooffset – Edizioni Vision – Edizioni Viella.

Mani, L. 1998. *Contentious Traditions. The Debate on Sati in Colonial India.* Berkeley: University of California.

Mann, L. 1933. Some Recent Discoveries, Presidential Address 19 March 1931. *Transactions of the Glasgow Archaeological Society* 8: 138–51.

Manning, W. H. 1981. Native and Roman metalwork in northern Britain: a question of origins and influences. In Kenworthy, J. (ed.), *Early Technology in North Britain*. Edinburgh: Edinburgh University Press, 52–61.

Mano-Zisi, Ð. 1957. *Nalaz iz Tekije.* Beograd: Narodni muzej.

Maráz, B. 1981. A szkítakori őslakósság Latène-kori továbbélése kelet-Magyarországon. *Jannus Pannonius Múzeum Évkönyve* 26: 97–120.

Marazov, I. 1998. *Ancient Gold: The Wealth of the Thracians.* New York: Henry H Abrams.

Marchand, S. L. 2003. *Down from Olympus: Archaeology and Philhellenism in Germany, 1750–1970.* Princeton, N.J.: Princeton University Press.

Marchesini, S. 2007. *Prosopographia Etrusca II, 1: Studia: Gentium Mobilitas.* Roma: L'Erma di Bretschneider.

Marić, Z. 1964. Donja Dolina. *Glasnik Zemaljskog Muzeja* 19: 5–128.

Marin, M. M. 1982. *Ceglie Peuceta I.* Bari: Dedalo.

Marinescu, G. 1984. Die jüngere Hallstattzeit in Nordostsiebenbürgen. *Dacia Nouvelle Série* 28 ((1–2)): 47–83.

Markantonatos, M. J. 1998. Women's roles in Iron Age Basilicata, south Italy: Indigenous women in indigenous and Greek contexts. In Whitehouse, R. D. (ed.), *Gender and Italian Archaeology: Challenging the Stereotypes.* London: Accordia Research Centre, 181–95.

Marshall, Y. & Gosden, C. 1999. The cultural Biography of objects. *World Archaeology* 31 (2): 169–78.

Mattern, S. P. 1999. *Rome and the Enemy: Imperial Strategy in the Principate.* Berkeley, Los Angeles & London: University of California Press.

Mattingly, D. J. 2000. War and peace in Roman North Africa: Observations and models of state-tribe interaction. In Ferguson, R. B., & Whitehead, N. L. (eds.), *War in the Tribal Zone: Expanding States and Indigenous Warfare.* Santa Fe & Oxford: School of American Research Press & James Currey, 31–60.

Mattingly, D. J. 2004. Being Roman: Expressing identity in a provincial setting. *Journal of Roman Archaeology* 17: 5–25.

Mattingly, D. J. 2011. *Imperialism, Power and Identity. Experiencing the Roman Empire.* Princeton: Princeton University Press.

Mauss, M. 1954. *The Gift: Forms and Functions of Exchange in Archaic Societies.* (translated from the French – reprinted, London: Routledge and Kegan Paul, 1966) London: Cohen and West.

McCone, K. R. 2008. *The Celtic Question: Modern Constructs and Ancient Realities. Myles Dillon Memorial Lecture, April 2008.* Dublin: School of Celtic Studies, Dublin Institute for Advanced Studies.

McPherron, A. 1973. Review of: Alexander, J. 1972. Jugoslavia before the Roman conquest. (People and Places). London: Thames and Hudson. *American Anthropologist* 75 (4): 1107–8.

Medeleţ, F. 1995. Über das Salz in Dakien. *Archäologie Österreichs* 6 (2): 53–7.

Medović, P. 1978. *Naselja Starijeg Gvozdenog Doba u Jugoslovenskom Podunavlju.* (Dissertationes et Monographiae 22). Beograd: Savez arheoloških društava Jugoslavije.

Medović, P. 1988. *Kalakača, Naselje Ranog Gvozdenog Doba.* (Posebna izdanja X). Novi Sad: Vojvođanski muzej.

Medović, P. & Medović, I. 2011. *Gradina na Bosutu – Naselje Starijeg Gvozdenog Doba.* Novi Sad: Pokrajinski zavod za zaštitu spomenika kulture.

Megaw, J. V. S. & Megaw, M. R. 1996. Ancient Celts and modern ethnicity. *Antiquity* 70: 175–81.

Megaw, M. R. & Megaw, J. V. S. 1989. *Celtic Art: from Its Beginnings to the Book of Kells.* London: Thames and Hudson.

Meid, W. 2010. *The Celts.* Innsbruck: Institut für Sprachen und Literaturen, Universität.

Meijers, E. 2007. From Central Place to Network Model: Theory and Evidence of a Paradigm Change. *Tijdschrift voor Economische en Sociale Geografie* 98: 245–59.

Meixner, G., Rieder, K. H. & Schaich, M. 1997. Das hallstattzeitliche Grabhügelfeld von Kinding/Ilbling. *Das Archaologische Jahr in Bayern* 1996: 90–3.

Mele, M. 2005a. Hajndl bei Ormož – eine neue Hausform der frühen Hallstattzeit im Südostalpenraum. *Archäologie in Deutschland* 3 (5): 21.

Mele, M. 2005b. Hajndl pri Ormožu – naselbina iz starejše železne dobe / Hajndl bei Ormož – Siedlung aus der älteren Eisenzeit. In Hernja Masten, M. (ed.), *Ormož Skozi Stoletja V.* Ormož, 127–43.

Mele, M. 2009. *Naselbini Hajndl in Ormož v Pozni Bronasti in Zgodnji Železni Dobi.* Ljubljana: Unpublished PhD dissertation, Department of Archaeology, Faculty of Arts, University of Ljubljana.

Melyukova, A. I. 1979. *Skifiya i Frakiiskii Mir.* Moscow: Izdatel'stvo Nauka.

Menghin, W. & Planck, D. (eds.). 2002. *Menschen, Zeiten, Räume: Archäologie in Deutschland.* Stuttgart: Theiss.

Méniel, P. 2008. Les restes d'animaux de l'espace public de l'oppidum du Titelberg. In Castella, D. & Meylan Krause, M.-F. (eds.), *Topographie Sacrée et Rituels. Le Cas d'Aventicum, Capitale des Helvètes. Actes du Colloque International d'Avenches, 2–4 Novembre 2006.* Basel: Archéologie suisse, 167–73.

Meskell, L. 1998. *Archaeology under Fire: Nationalism, Politics and Heritage in the Eastern Mediterranean and Middle East.* London – New York: Routledge.

Meskell, L. 1999. *Archaeologies of Social Life: Age, Sex, Class, Etcetera in Ancient Egypt.* London: Routledge.

Meskell, L. 2000. Writing the body in archaeology. In Rautman, A. E. (ed.), *Reading the Body: Representation and Remains in the Archaeological Record.* Philadelphia: University of Philadelphia Press, 13–21.

Meskell, L. 2001. Archaeologies of identity. In Hodder, I. (ed.), *Archaeological Theory Today.* Cambridge/Malden (MA): Polity/Blackwell, 187–213.

Meskell, L. 2002. The intersections of identity and politics in archaeology. *Annual Review of Anthropology* 31: 279–301.

Meskell, L. 2004. *Object Worlds in Ancient Egypt: Material Biographies Past and Present.* Oxford: Berg.

Meskell, L. 2007. Archaeologies of identity. In Insoll, T. (ed.), *The Archaeology of Identities. A Reader.* London and New York: Routledge, 23–43.

Meskell, L. & Preucel, R. W. 2004. Identities. In Meskell, L. & Preucel, R. W. (eds.), *A Companion to Social Archaeology.* Oxford: Blackwell Publishing, 121–34.

Metzler, J. 1991. Les sanctuaires gaulois en territoire trévire. In Brunaux, J. L. (ed.), *Les Sanctuaires Celtiques et leur Rapport avec le Monde Méditerranéen. Actes du Colloque de Saint-Riquier, Novembre 1990.* Paris: Éditions Errance, 146–55.

Metzler, J. 1995. *Das Treverische Oppidum auf dem Titelberg. Zur Kontinuität Zwischen der Spätkeltischen und der Frührömischen Zeit in Nord-Gallien Band 2.* (Dossiers d'Archeologie du Musée National d'Histoire et d'art 3). Luxembourg: Musée National d'Histoire et d'art.

Metzler, J. 2006. Religion et politique. L'oppidum trévire du Titelberg. In Goudineau, C. (ed.), *Religion et Société en Gaule*. Paris: Errance, 191–202.

Metzler, J. 2008. Du Titelberg à Trèves. De l'oppidum gaulois à la ville romaine. In Castella, D. & Meylan Krause, M.-F. (eds.), *Topographie Sacrée et Rituels. Le Cas d'Aventicum, Capitale des Helvètes. Actes du Colloque International d'Avenches, 2–4 Novembre 2006*. Basel: Archéologie suisse, 155–65.

Metzler, J., Méniel, P. & Gaeng, C. 2006. Oppida et espaces publics. In Haselgrove, C. (ed.), *Celtes et Gaulois, l'Archéologie Face à l'Histoire. 4: Les Mutations de la Fin de l'Âge du Fer. Actes de la Table Ronde de Cambridge, 7–8 Juillet 2005*. (Collection Bibracte 12/4). Glux-en-Glenne: Centre archéologique européen, 201–24.

Metzler, J., Waringo, R., Bis, R. & Metzler-Zens, N. 1991. *Clemency et les Tombes de l'Aristocratie en Gaule Belgique.* (Dossiers d'Archeologie du Musée National d'histoire et d'art 1). Luxembourg: Musée National d'histoire d'art.

Metzner-Nebelsick, C. 1992. Gefäße mit basaraboider Ornamentik aus Frög. In Lippert, A. & Spindler, K. (eds.), *Festschrift zum 50jährigen Bestehen des Instuts für Ur- und Frühgeschichte der Leopold-Franzens-Universität Innsbruck*. (Universitätsforschungen zur Prähistorischen Archäologie 8). Bonn: Rudolf Habelt, 349–83.

Metzner-Nebelsick, C. 2002. *Der «Thrako-Kimmerische» Formenkreis aus der Sicht der Urnenfelder- und Hallstattzeit im Südöstlichen Pannonien.* (Vorgeschichtliche Forschungen Band 23). Rahden/Westf: Verlag Marie Leidorf GmbH.

Mihailov, G. (ed.). 1970. *Inscriptiones Graecae in Bulgaria Repertae, vol. 1.* Sofia: Bulgarian Academy of Sciences.

Mihajlović, D. V. 2010. Ostave i horizonti destrukcije kao pokazatelji probijanja Gornjomezijskog limesa u I i II veku. *Istraživanja* 21: 9–29.

Mihaljević, M. & Dizdar, M. 2007. Late La Tene bronze helmet from the river Sava near Stara Gradiška. *Vjesnik Arheološkog Muzeja u Zagrebu* 3rd ser., 40: 117–46.

Mihaylov, G. 1972. *Trakite.* Sofia: Darzhavno voenno izdatelstvo.

Mihovilić, K. 2001. *Nezakcij Prapovijesni Nalazi 1900–1953: Nesactium Prehistoric Finds 1900–1953.* Pula: Arheološki muzej Istre.

Mikulčik̀, I. 1999. *Antički Gradovi vo Makedonija.* Skopje: Makedonska akademija na naukite i umetnostite.

Milcent, P.-Y. 2001. Le paysage funéraire: Analyse de l'évolution des pratiques funéraires. In Batardy, C., Buchsenschutz, O. & Dumasy, F. (eds.), *Le Berry Antique: Atlas 2000*. (Revue archéologique du centre de la France 21). Tours: Ville de Bourges, 95–9.

Milcent, P.-Y. 2008. À l'Est rien de nouveau. Chronologie des armes de poing du premier âge du Fer médio-atlantique et gènese des standards matériels élitaires hallstattiens et laténiens. In Lehoërff, A. (ed.), *Construire le Temps. Histoire et Méthodes des Chronologies et Calendriers des Derniers Millénaires avant Notre Ère en Europe Occidentale. Actes du XXXe Colloque International de HALMA-IPEL, UMR 8164 (CNRS, Lille 3, MCC) 7–9 décembre 2006, Lille.* (Collection Bibracte 16). Glux-en-Glenne, Bibracte: Centre archéologique européen, 231–50.

Miligan, G. W. & Cooper, M. C. 1986. A study of the comparability of external criteria for hierarchical cluster analysis. *Multivariate Behavioral Research* 21: 41–58.

Miller, D. 2010. *Stuff.* Cambridge: Polity.

Millett, M. 1990. *The Romanization of Britain: an Essay in Archaeological Interpretation.* Cambridge: Cambridge University Press.

Millett, M. 1995. Re-Thinking Religion in Romanization. In Metzler, J., Millett, M., Roymans, N. & Slofstra, J. (eds.), *Integration in the Early Roman West: The Role of Culture and Ideology.* Luxembourg: Musée National d'histoire d'art, 93–100.

Millett, M., Roymans, N. & Slofstra, J. 1995. Integration, Culture and Ideology in the Early Roman West. In Metzler, J., Millett, M., Roymans, N. & Slofstra, J. (eds.), *Integration in the Early Roman West: The Role of Culture and Ideology.* Luxembourg: Musée National d'histoire d'art, 1–6.

Minta-Tworzowska, D. 2002. Between a community of inspiration and the separateness of archaeological traditions. In Biehl, P. F., Gramsch, A. & Marciniak, A. (eds.), *Archäologien Europas: Geschichte, Methoden und Theorien. Archaeologies of Europe: History, Methods and Theories.* (Tübinger Archäologische Taschenbücher 3). Münster: Waxmann, 53–64

Mirdita, Z. 1991. Encore une fois sur le problème d'ethnogènese des Dardaniens, In Benac, A. (ed.), *Tribus Paleobalkaniques entre la Mer Adriatique et la Mer Noire de l'Eneolithique jusqu'a l'Epoque Hellenistique.* Sarajevo & Beograd: Academie des sciences et des artes de Bosne et Herzegovine, Centre d'études balkaniques & Academie Serbe des sciences et des artes, Institut des d'études balkaniques, 101–10.

Mirdita, Z. 2009. O problem etničkog podrijetla Dardanaca. *Vijesnik Arheološkog muzeja u Zagrebu* 42: 357–86.

Mirković, M. 1968. *Rimski Gradovi na Dunavu u Gornjoj Meziji.* Beograd: Arheološko društvo Jugoslavije.

Mirković, M. 1968. *Römische Städte an der Donau in Obermösien.* (in Serbian with a German summary). Beograd: Société archéologique Yougoslavie

Mirković, M. 1971. Sirminum – its history from the I Century AD to 582 AD. *Sirmium* 1: 5-94.

Mitrevski, D. 1997. *Protoistorijske Zajednice vo Makedonija.* Skopje: Republicki zavod za zastita na spomenici na kulturata.

Mlekuž, D. 2004. Listening to the landscapes: Modelling soundscapes in GIS. *Internet archaeology* 16: http://intarch.ac.uk/journal/issue16/mlekuz_index.html.

Mócsy, A. 1957. Zur Geschichte der Peregrinen Gemeinden in Pannonien. *Historia: Zeitschrift für Alte Geschichte* 6 (4): 488-98.

Móscy, A. 1974. *Pannonia and Upper Moesia, a History of the Middle Danube Provinces of the Roman Empire.* London & Boston (MA): Routledge & Kegan Paul.

Momigliano, A. 1971. *Alien Wisdom: The Limits of Hellenization.* Cambridge: Cambridge University Press.

Moore, T. & Armada, L. (eds.). 2011. *Western Europe in the First Millennium BC: Crossing the Divide.* Oxford: Oxford University Press.

Morintz, S. & Şerbănescu, D. 1985. Rezultatele cercetărilor de la Radovanu, punctul "Gorgana a doua" (jud. Călăraşi). I. Aşezarea din epoca bronzului. II. Aşezarea geto-dacică. *Thraco-Dacica* 6: 5–30.

Morley, N. 2009. *Antiquity and Modernity.* Oxford: Wiley-Blackwell.

Morris, I. 1994. Archaeologies of Greece. In Morris, I. (ed.), *Classical Greece: Ancient Histories and Modern Archaeologies*. Cambridge: Cambridge University Press, 8–47.

Morse, M. A. 1999. Craniology and the adoption of the Three-Age System in Britain. *Proceedings of the Prehistoric Society* 65: 1–17.

Morse, M. A. 2005. *How the Celts Came to Britain: Druids, Skulls and the Birth of Archaeology.* Stroud: Tempus Publishing.

Moscati, S., Frey, O.-H., Kruta, V., Raftery, B. & Szabó, M. (eds.). 1991. *The Celts.* London: Thames and Hudson.

Moser, S. 1998. *Ancestral Images: The Iconography of Human Origins.* Stroud: Sutton.

Müller, F. 1989. *Die Frühlatènezeitlichen Scheibenhalsringe.* (Römisch-Germanische Forschungen 46). Mainz: Verlag Philipp von Zabern.

Müller, K. E. 1972. *Geschichte der Antiken Ethnographie und Ethnologischen Theoriebildung, 1.* Wiesbaden: Franz Steiner.

Müller, S. 2007. Beiträge zum spätlatènezeitlichen Siedelwesen am Beispiel der Viereckschanzen von Sallach, Gde. Geiselhöring, Lkr. Straubing-Bogen (Niederbayern). In Prammer, J. & Sandner, R. (eds.), *Siedlungsdynamik und Gesellschaft: Beiträge des Internationalen Kolloquiums zur Keltischen Besiedlungsgeschichte im Bayerischen Donauraum, Österreich und der Tschechischen Republik*. Straubing: Historischer Verein für Straubing und Umgebung, 145–71.

Müller, U. 2009. Netzwerkanalysen in der Historischen Archäologie, Begriffe und Beispiele. In Brather, S., Geuenich, D. & Huth, C. (eds.), *Historia Archaeologia. Festschrift Heiko Steuer.* (Ergänzungsbände zum Reallexikon der Germanischen Altertumskunde 70). Berlin/New York: Walter de Gruyter, 735–54.

Munson, R. V. 2001. *Telling Wonders. Ethnographic and Political Discourse in the Work of Herodotus.* Ann Arbor: University of Michigan.

Murray, R. 2007. *Culduthel Mains Farm, Inverness: Phase 5; Excavation of a Later Prehistoric Settlement: Assessment Report.* Edinburgh: Headland Archaeology Ltd, unpublished report.

Nakoinz, O. 2005. *Studien zur Räumlichen Abgrenzung und Strukturierung der Älteren Hunsrück-Eifel-Kultur* (Universitätsforschung zur Prähistorischen Archäologie 118). Bonn: Habelt.

Nakoinz, O. 2009. Die Methode zur quantitativen Untersuchung kultureller Ähnlichkeiten im Rahmen des Projektes 'Siedlungshierarchien und kulturelle Räume'. In Krauße, D. & Nakoinz, O. (eds.), *Kulturraum und Territorialität: Archäologische Theorien, Methoden, Fallbeispiele. Kolloquium des DFG-SPP 1171 Esslingen 17.-18. Januar 2007. Internationale Archäologie – Arbeitsgemeinschaft, Symposium, Tagung, Kongress 13*. Rahden: Verlag Marie Leidorf, 87–97.

Nakoinz, O. 2010a. *Die Archäologische Kulturgeographie der Ältereisenzeitlichen Zentralorte Südwestdeutschlands: Theorie, Methode und Auswertung.* University of Kiel: Unpublished Habilitationsschrift.

Nakoinz, O. 2010b. Kulturelle Räume der älteren Eisenzeit in Südwestdeutschland. In Krauße, D. & Beilharz, D. (eds.), *'Fürstensitze' und Zentralorte der Frühen Kelten. Abschlußkolloquium des DFG-Schwerpunktprogramms 1171. Teil II.* (Forschungen und Berichte zur Vor- und Frühgeschichte in Baden-Württemberg 120). Stuttgart: Theiss, 317–32.

Nakoinz, O. 2012. Models of Centrality. In Bebermeier, W., Hebenstreit, R., Kaiser, E. & Krause, J. (eds.), *Landscape Archaeology. Proceedings of the International Conference Held in Berlin, 6th – 8th June 2012.* (eTopoi Special Volume 3). Berlin: Excellence Cluster Topoi, 217–23.

Nankov, E. 2008. The fortification of early Hellenistic Thracian city of Seuthopolis: Breaking the mould. *Archaeologica Bulgarica* 12 (3): 15–56.

Nankov, E. 2011. Berenike bids farewell to Seuthes III: the silver-gilt scallop shell pyxis from the Golyama Kosmatka tumulus. *Archaeologia Bulgarica* 15 (3): 1–22.

Nebehay, S. 1993. *Latènegräber in Niederösterreich.* Marburg: Philipps-Universität Marburg.

Nebelsick, L. D. 1994. Der Übergang von der Urnenfelder- zur Hallstattzeit am nördlichen Ostalpenrand und im nördlichen Transdanubien, in Archäologische Untersuchungen von der Bronze- zur Eisenzeit zwischen Nordsee und Kaukasus. *Regensburger Beiträge zur Prähistorischen Archäologie* 1: 307–63.

Necrasov, O. 1982. L'anthropologie de l'aire thrace. Rapport général. In Vulpe, R. (ed.), *Actes du IIe Congrès International de Thracologie (Bucarest, 4–10 septembre 1976), III, Linguistique, Ethnologie (Ethnographie, Folkloristique et Art Populaire), Anthropologie. Volume Sélectif.* Paris – Roma – Montreal – Pelham N.Y: Editrice Nagard, 43–65.

Németi, I. 1982. Das späthalstattzeitliche Gräberfeld von Sanislău. *Dacia* 26: 115–44.

Németi, I. 1988. Necropola Latène de la Pişcolt, jud. Satu Mare. I. *Thraco-Dacica* 9: 49–74.

Németi, I. 1989. Necropola Latène de la Pişcolt, jud. Satu Mare. II. *Thraco-Dacica* 10: 75–114.

Németi, I. 1993. Necropola Latène de la Pişcolt, judeţul Satu Mare (IV). *Thraco Dacica* 14 (1–2): 59–112.

Nestor, I. 1941. Keltische Gräber bei Mediaş. *Dacia* 7–8 (1937–40): 159–82.

Nestor, I. 1970. De la primii locuitori până la daci 3. Epoca fierului. In Oţetea, A. (ed.), *Istoria Poporului Român.* Bucureşti: Editura Ştiinţifică, 32–46.

Neugebauer, J.-W. 1992. *Die Kelten im Osten Österreichs.* St. Pölten: Verlag Niederösterreichisches Pressehaus.

Nickel, C., Thoma, M. & Wigg-Wolf, D. 2008. *Martberg. Heiligtum und Oppidum der Treverer I. Der Kultbezirk. Die Grabungen 1994–2004.* Koblenz: Gesellschaft für Archäologie an Mittelrhein und Mosel.

Nicolucci, G. 1869. *Antropologia dell'Etruria.* (Memoria estratta dal Vol. III degli Atti della Reale Accademia delle Scienze Fisiche e Matematiche). Napoli: Stamperia del Fibreno.

Niculescu, G. A. 2004-2005. Archaeology, nationalism and "The history of the Romanians" (2001). *Dacia* Nouvelle Série 48-49: 99–124.

Niebuhr, B. G. 1828. Untersuchungen über die Geschichte der Skythen, Geten, und Sarmaten. In Niebuhr, B. G. (ed.), *Kleine Historische und Philologische Schriften. Vol I.* Bonn: E.Weber, 352-98.

Niese, B. 1910. Galli. *Paulys Realencyclopädie der Classischen Altertumswissenschaft 13*. Stuttgart: Alfred Druckmüller Verlag, cols. 610-39.

Nikolov, B. 1967. Grobnitsa III ot Moghilanskata mogila vav Vratsa. *Arheologia* 9 (1): 11-8.

Nisard, M. 1883. *Macrobe, Varron, Pomponius Mela (avec la Traduction en Français).* Paris: Librairie de Firmin-Didot.

Nora, P. 1989. Between memory and history: Les lieux de memoire. *Representations* 26: 223-35.

Nortmann, H. 2008-9. Befestigungen der Eisenzeit im Hunsrück-Nahe-Raum. Forschungsstand, Fragen und Hypothesen. *Trierer Zeitschrift* 71/72: 15-25.

Nortmann, H. 2009. Römisches Heiligtum und Theater in Kastel-Staadt. *Jahrbuch Kreis Trier-Saarburg* 2009: 136-44.

Novaković, P. 2011. Archaeology in the new countries of Southeastern Europe: A historical perspective. In Lozny, L. R. (ed.), *Comparative Archaeologies. A Sociological View of the Science of the Past.* New York, Dordrecht, Heidelberg & London: Springer, 339-461.

Novaković, P. 2012. The "German School" and its influence on the national archaeologies of the Western Balkans. In Mason, P., Migotti, B. & Nadbath, B. (eds.), *Bojan Djurić 60th Anniversary Miscellany, Scripta in Honorem Bojan Djurić* (Monografije Centra za Preventivno Arheologijo 1). Ljubljana: Zavod za varstvo kulturne dediščine Slovenije.

Ó Ríagáin, R. & Popa, C. N. (eds.). 2012a. *Archaeology and the (De)Construction of National and Supra-National Polities.* (Archaeological Review from Cambridge 27 (2)).Cambridge: Division of Archaeology.

Ó Ríagáin, R. & Popa, C. N. 2012b. Archaeology and Nationalism in Europe: Two Case Studies from the Northwest and Southeast of Europe. *Archaeological Review from Cambridge* 27 (2): 52-70.

O'Shea, J. 1981. Social configurations and the archaeological study of mortuary practices: a case study. In Chapman, R., Kinnes, I. & Randsborg, K. (eds.), *The Archaeology of Death.* Cambridge: Cambridge University Press, 39-52.

Oișteanu, A. 1998. *Mythos & Logos. Studii și Eseuri de Antropologie Culturală.* București: Nemira.

Oltean, I. A. 2007. *Dacia: Landscape, Colonisation and Romanisation.* London: Routledge.

Oppermann, M. 1984. *Thraker zwischen Karpatenbogen und Ägäis.* Leipzig-Jena-Berlin: Urania-Verlag.

Oppermann, M. 2004. *Die Westpontische Poleis und Ihr Indigenes Umfeld in Vorrömischer Zeit.* (Schriften des Zentrums für Archäologie und Kulturgeschichte des Schwarzmeerraumes 2). Langenweißbach: Beier & Beran.

Orejas, A. 1994. Les populations des zones minieres du Nord-Ouest de la Péninsule Iberique (le Bassin NO du Douro, Leon, Espagne). *Dialogues d'Histoire Ancienne* 20 (1): 245–81.

Orejas, A. & Sánchez-Palencia, F. J. 2002. Mines, territorial organization, and social structure in Roman Iberia: Carthago Nova and the peninsular northwest. *American Journal of Archaeology* 106 (4): 581–99.

Orejas, A. & Sastre, I. 1999. Fiscalite et organization territoriale dans le Nord-Ouest de la Peninsule Iberique: Ciuitates, tributation et ager mensura conprehensus. *Dialogues d'Histoire Ancienne* 25: 159–88.

Orser, C., E 2001. *Race and the Archaeology of Identity.* Salt Lake City: University of Utah Press.

Osborne, W. 1881. Zur Beurtheilung des prähistorischen Fundes auf dem Hradischt bei Stradonic in Böhmen. *Mitteilungen der Anthropologischen Gesellschaft in Wien* 10: 234–60.

Owen, S. 2005. Analogy, archaeology and archaic colonization. In Hurst, H. & Owen, S. (eds.), *Ancient Colonizations: Analogy, Similarity and Difference.* London: Gerald Duckworth and Co, 5–22.

Pahič, S. 1974. Čreta pri Slivnici. *Varstvo spomenikov* 17–19 (1): 98–100, 22–24.

Palavestra, A. 1984. *Princely Tombs during the Early Iron Age in the Central Balkans (in Serbian with an English summary).* (Serbian Academy of Sciences and Arts Institute for Balkan Studies Special Editions). Belgrade: Serbian Academy of Sciences and Arts Institute for Balkan Studies.

Palavestra, A. 1993. *Praistorijski Ćilibar na Centralnom i Zapadnom Balkanu.* (Prehistoric amber in the Central and Western Balkans) (Balkanološki institut, Serbian Academy of Science and Arts 52). Beograd: Serbian Academy of Science and Arts.

Palavestra, A. 2011a. *Kulturni Konteksti Arheologije.* Beograd: Filozofski fakultet.

Palavestra, A. 2011b. U službi kontinuiteta. Etno-arheologija u Srbiji (In the Service of Continuity. Ethno-Archaeology in Serbia). (in Serbian with an English and French summaries). *Etnoantropološki Problemi* 6 (3): 579–94.

Palavestra, A. 2012. Vasić pre Vinče: 1900–1908, (Vasić before Vinča: 1900–1908). *Etno-arheološki Problemi* 7 (3): 649–78.

Pallottino, M. 1947. *Etruscologia.* Milano: Hoepli.

Pallottino, M. 1961. Nuovi studi sul problema delle origini etrusche. Bilancio critico. *Studi Etruschi* 29: 3–30.

Pallottino, M. 1978. *The Etruscans.* (Pelican Books). Harmondsworth: Penguin Books Ltd.

Pandey, G. 2000. Voices from the Edge: The Struggle to Write Subaltern Histories. In Chaturvedi, V. (ed.), *Mapping Subaltern Studies and the Postcolonial.* London: Verso, 281–99.

Papazoglu, F. 1969. *Srednjebalkanska Plemena u Predrimsko Doba. Tribali, Autarijati, Dardanci, Skordisci i Mezi.* Sarajevo: Akademija nauka i umjetnosti Bosne i Hercegovine, Centar za balkanološka ispitivanja.

Papazoglu, F. 1978. *The Central Balkan Tribes in Pre-Roman Times: Triballi, Autariatae, Dardanians, Scordisci and Moesians.* Amsterdam: Adolf M. Hakkert.

Papazoglu, F. 1980. O "helenizaciji" i "romanizaciji". *Glas Srpske Akademije Nauka i Umetnosti* 320 (2): 21–36.

Papazoglu, F. 1988. Ilirska i dardansa krlajevina: poreklo i razvoj, struktura, helenizacija i romanizacija. In Garašanin, M. (ed.), *Iliri i Albanci*. Beograd: Srpska akademija nauka i umetnosti, 145–99.

Párducz, M. 1973. Probleme der Skythenzeit im Karpatenbecken. *Acta Archaeologica Academiae Scientiarum Hungaricae* 25: 27–64.

Pareti, L. 1947. *La Tomba Regolini-Galassi del Museo Gregoriano Etrusco e la Civiltà dell'Italia Centrale nel sec. VII a.C.* Città del Vaticano: Tipografia Poliglotta Vaticana.

Parker Pearson, M. 1999. *The Archaeology of Death and Burial.* Stroud: Sutton.

Pârvan, V. 1926. *Getica. O Protoistorie a Daciei.* București: Cultura Naționala.

Pauli, L. (ed.). 1980. *Die Kelten in Mitteleuropa: Kultur, Kunst, Wirtschaft. Salzburger Landesaustellung 1 Mai – 30 Sept. 1980 im Keltenmuseum Hallein, Österreich.* Salzburg: Amt der Salzburger Landesregierung, Kulturabteilung.

Pearce, J., Millett, M. & Struck, M. (eds.). 2000. *Burial, Society and Context in the Roman World.* Oxford: Oxbow Books.

Pellecchia, M., Negrini, R., Colli, L., Patrini, M., Milanesi, E., Achilli, A., Bertorelle, G., Cavalli-Sforza, L. L., Piazza, A., Torroni, A. & Ajmone-Marsan, P. 2007. The mystery of Etruscan origin: novel clues from Bos taurus mitochondrial DNA. *Proceedings of the Royal Society B: Biological Sciences* 274 (1614): 1175–9.

Pena, J. T. 2007. *Roman Pottery in the Archaeological Record.* Cambridge: Cambridge University Press.

Perkins, P. 2009. DNA and Etruscan identity. In Perkins, P. & Swaddling, J. (eds.), *Etruscan by Definition*. London: British Museum Press, 95–111.

Peroni, R., Carancini, G. L., Bergonzi, G., Lo Schiavo, F. & Von Eles, P. 1980. Per una definizione critica di facies locali: nuovi strumenti metodologici. In Peroni, R. (ed.) *Il Bronzo Finale in Italia*. Bari: De Donato, 9–87.

Pescaru, A. & Ferencz, I. V. (eds.). 2004. *Daco-Geiți: 80 de ani de Cercetări Arheologice Sistematice la Cetățile Dacice din Munții Orăștiei.* Deva: Muzeul Civilizației Dacice și Romane.

Pessina, A., Vella, N. C. & Cappozzo, M. 2005. *Luigi Maria Ugolini: un Archeologo Italiano a Malta.* Sta Venera (Malta): Midsea books – Heritage Malta.

Petre, Z. 2004. *Practica Nemuririi. O Lectură Critică a Izvoarelor Grecești Referitoare la Geți.* Iași: Polirom.

Petrova, E. 1991. Pajonska pleminja i Pajonskoto kralevstvo vo II i I milenium pred n.e. *Macedoniae Acta Archaeologica* 12: 9–130.

Petrović, P. 1995. *Inscriptions de la Mésie Supérieure III/2: Timacum Minus et la Vallée du Timok.* Beograd: Centre d'Études Épigraphiques et Numismatiques.

Petrović, P. & Vasić, M. 1996. The Roman Frontier in Upper Moesia: Archaeological Investigations in the Iron Gate Area. In Petrović, P. (ed.), *Roman Limes on the Middle and Lower Danube*. (Cahiers des Portes de Fer. Monographies 2). Belgrade: Archaeological Institute, 15–26.

Peyre, C. 2000. Documents sur l'organisation publique de l'espace dans la cité gauloise. Le site de Villeneuve-Saint-Germain et la Bilingue de Verceil. In Verger, S. (ed.), *Rites et Espaces en Pays Celte et Méditerranéen. Étude Comparée à Partir du Sanctuaire d'Acy-Romance (Ardennes, Frances)*. Rome: École française de Rome, 155–206.

Pezron, P. Y. 1703. *Antiquité de la Nation et de la Langue de Celtes autrement Appellez Gaulois.* Paris: Prosper Marchand.

Piana Agostinetti, P. & Priuli, S. 1985. Il tesoro di Arcisate. *Archeologia Classica* 37: 182–237.

Piggott, S. 1966. A scheme for the Scottish Iron Age. In Rivet, A. L. F. (ed.), *The Iron Age in Northern Britain*. Edinburgh: University Press, 1–15.

Piso, I. 2008. Les débuts de la province de Dacie. In Piso, I. (ed.), *Die Römischen Provinzen. Begriff und Gründung*. Cluj Napoca: Mega Verlag, 297–331.

Pitts, M. 2011. Why did people give up hunting and gathering? *British Archaeology* 117: 21.

Pontrandolfo Greco, A. 1982. *I Lucani: Etnografia e Archeologia di una Regione Antica.* Milano: Longanesi.

Pontrandolfo Greco, A., Rouveret, A. & Cipriani, M. 2004. *The Painted Tombs of Paestum.* Salerno: Pandemos.

Pop, H. (ed.). 2008. *Dacian Studies in Memoriam Dr. Mircea Rusu.* Cluj-Napoca: Mega.

Popa, C. I. 2008. A possible Dacian burial in the vicinity of the Piatra Craivii fortress. *Apulum* 45: 357–65.

Popa, C. N. 2010. A New Framework for approaching Dacian Identity. In Berecki, S. (ed.), *Iron Age Communities in the Carpathian Basin*. (Bibliotheca Musei Marisiensis. Seria Archaeologica). Cluj-Napoca: Mega, 395–423.

Popa, C. N. 2012. Till Death do us Part. A Statistical Approach to Identifying Burial Similarity and Grouping. The Case of the Late La Tène Graves from the Eastern Carpathian Basin. In Berecki, S. (ed.), *Iron Age Rites and Rituals in the Carpathian Basin*. (Bibliotheca Mvsei Marisiensis, Seria Archaeologica). Târgu Mureș: Mega, 401–12.

Popa, C. N. 2013. The trowel as chisel. Shaping modern Romanian identity through the Iron Age. In Ginn, V., Enlander, R. & Crozier, R. (eds.), *Exploring Prehistoric Identity. Our construct or theirs?* Oxford: Oxbow Books, 164-174.

Popa, C.N. 2014. *Uncovering Group Identity in the Late Iron Age of South-East Europe.* Cambridge: Unpublished PhD thesis, University of Cambridge

Popescu, C. 2006. Sigillate orientale descoperite pe teritoriul României (sec. I p.Chr.). *www.simpara.ro/ara7*.

Popescu, D. 1943. Sciţii în Transilvania. Starea cercetărilor arheologice. *Transilvania* 74 (3–4): 1–20.

Popescu, D. 1958. Le trésor dace de Sâncrăeni. *Dacia* 2: 157–206.

Popescu, M. C. 2011. Lamps discovered in pre-Roman Dacia (2nd century BC – 1st century AD). Notes on the adoption of an innovation. *Caiete Asociaţia Arhitectură. Restaurare. Arheologie* (2): 5–21.

Popov, H. 2002. *Urbanizaciia v Vtreshnite Raioni na Trakiia i Iliriia: Prez VI – I Vek Predi Christa.* Sofia: NOUS Publishers Ltd.

Popović, I. & Borić-Brešković, B. 1994. *Ostava iz Bara.* Beograd: Narodni muzej.

Popović, P. 1987. *Novac Skordiska: Novac i Vovčani Promet na Centralnom Balkanu od IV do I Veka pre n. e.* Beograd: Arheološki institut, Matica srpska.

Popović, P. 1992. The Scordisci from the fall of Macedonia to the Roman conquest. In Tasić, N. (ed.), *Scordisci and the Autochthons: Scordisci and the Native Population in the Middle Danube Region*. Belgrade: Serbian Academy of Sciences and Arts, Institute for Balkan Studies, 35–52.

Popović, P. 1994. The territories of Scordisci. *Starinar* 43–4/1992–3: 14–21.

Popović, P. 1996. Early La Tène Between Pannonia and the Balkans. *Starinar* 47: 105–25.

Popović, P. 2005. Kale-Krševica: Investigations 2001–2004 Interim Report. *Ybornik Narodnog Muzeja* 18 (1): 141–73.

Popović, P. 2006. Central Balkans between the Greek and Celtic World: Case study Kale-Krševica. In Tasić, N. & Gvozdanov, C. (eds.), *Homage to Milutin Garašanin*. Belgrade: Serbian Academy of Sciences and Arts & Macedonian Academy of Sciences and Arts, 523–36.

Popović, P. 2007. Krševica et les contacts entre l'Egée et les centre des Balkans. *Histria Antiqua* 15: 125–36.

Popović, P. & Vranić, I. 2008. The Textile industry at Krševica (Southeastern Serbia) in the fourth-third centuries B.C. *Starinar* n.s. 41: 309–19.

Potrebica, H. 2002. Istraživanje nekropole pod tumulima iz starijega željeznog doba na nalazištu Gradci kod sela Kaptol (sezona 2001.). *Opuscula Archaeologica* 26: 331–9.

Potrebica, H. 2008. Contacts between Greece and Pannonia in the Early Iron Age with Special Concern to the Area of Thessalonica. In Biehl, P. & Rassamakin, Y. (eds.), *Import and Imitation in Archaeology*. (Schriften des Zentrums für Archäologie und Kulturgeschichte des Schwartzmeerraumes 11). Langenweissbach: Beier & Beran, 187–212.

Potrebica, H. 2012. Kaptol – a centre on the periphery of the Hallstatt world. In Tappert, C., Later, C., Fries-Knoblach, J., Ramsl, P. C., Trebsche, P., Stefanie Wefers & Wiethold, J. (eds.), *Wege und Transport*. (Beiträge zur Ur- und Frühgeschichte Mitteleuropas 6). Langenweissbach: Beier & Beran, 235–45.

Potter, D. S. 1999. *Literary Texts and the Roman Historian.* London and New York (NY): Routledge.

Poux, M. 2004. *L'âge du Vin. Rites de Boisson, Festins et Libations en Gaule Indépendente.* (Protohistoire européene 8). Montagnac: Éditions Monique Mergoil.

Poux, M. 2006. Religion et société. Le sanctuaire arverne de Corent. In Goudineau, C. (ed.), *Religion et Société en Gaule*. Paris: Errance, 116–34.

Poux, M. (ed.). 2011. *Corent. Voyage au Coeur d'une Ville Gauloise*. Paris: Errance.

Preda, C. 1986. *Geto-dacii din Bazinul Oltului Inferior. Dava de la Sprâncenata*. București: Editura Academiei Republicii Socialiste România.

Prendi, F. 1982. Die Bronzezeit und der Beginn der Eisenzeit in Albanien. *Prähistorische Archäologie in Südösteuropa* 1: 203–33.

Preucel, R. W. & Hodder, I. 1996. *Contemporary Archaeology in Theory*. Oxford: Blackwell.

Price, J. 1997. The Roman glass. In Hill, P. H. (ed.), *Whithorn and St Ninian: The Excavation of a Monastic Town; 1984–91*. Stroud: Sutton Publishing, 294.

Pritchett, W. K. 1993. *The Liar School of Herodotos*. Amsterdam: J.C. Gieben.

Protase, D. 1971. *Riturile Funerare la Daci și Daco-Romani*. București Editura Academiei Republicii Socialiste România.

Proudfoot, E. 1996. Excavations at the long cist cemetery on the Hallow Hill, St Andrews, Fife, 1975–7. *Proceedings of the Society of Antiquaries of Scotland* 126: 387–454.

Purcell, N. 2005. Colonization and Mediterranean history. In Hurst, H. R. & Owen, S. (eds.), *Ancient Colonizations: Analogy, Similarity and Difference*. London: Duckworth, 115–39.

Pydyn, A. 1999. *Exchange and Cultural interactions. A Study of Long-distance Trade and Cross-cultural Contacts in the Late Bronze Age and Early Iron Age in Central and Eastern Europe*. (BAR International Reports 813). Oxford: Archaeopress.

Rackham, H. (ed.). 1961. *Pliny Natural History (with an English Translation in Ten Volumes). Vol. II*. Cambridge, Massachusetts: Harvard University Press.

Radhakrishnan, R. 2003. *Theory in an Uneven World*. Oxford: Blackwell Publishers.

Rallo, A. (ed.). 1989. *Le Donne in Etruria*. Roma: L'Erma di Bretschneider.

Ramsl, P. C. 2002a. *Das Eisenzeitliche Gräberfeld von Pottenbrunn*. (Fundberichte aus Österreich, Materialhefte A 11). Wien: Bundesdenkmalamt.

Ramsl, P. C. 2002b. Die keltischen Gräberfelder von Pottenbrunn und Mannersdorf am Leithagebirge. Zwei Drehscheiben zwischen West und Ost. *Archäologie Österreichs* 13 (2): 6–23.

Ramsl, P. C. 2003. Migrationsphänomene(?!) in der Frühlatènezeit. *Mitteilungen der Anthropologischen Gesellschaft in Wien* 133: 101–09.

Ramsl, P. C. 2011. *Das Latènezeitlichen Gräberfeld von Mannersdorf am Leithagebirge, Flur Reinthal Süd, Niederösterreich*. (Mitteilungen der Prähistorischen Kommission 74). Wien: Verlag der Österreichischen Akademie der Wissenschaften.

Rathje, W. L. 1974. The garbage project. *Archaeology* 27: 236–41.

Ratimorská, P. 1981. Keltské pohrebisko v Chotine I. *Západné Slovensko* 8: 15–88.

Rawlinson, G. (ed.). 1933. *History of Herodotus. Vol. I*. London & Toronto: J. M. Dent & Sons LTD., E. P. Dutton & Co. Inc.

Redfield, R., Linton, R. & Herskovits, M. J. 1936. Memorandum for the study of acculturation. *American Anthropologist* 38: 149–52.

Redhouse, D. I. & Stoddart, S. K. F. 2011. Mapping Etruscan State formation. In Terrenato, N. & Haggis, D. (eds.), *State Formation in Italy and Greece. Questioning the Neoevolutionist Paradigm.* Oxford: Oxbow Books, 161–78.

Rehbein, B. 2006. *Die Soziologie Pierre Bourdieus.* Konstanz: UVK Verlagsgesellschaft mbH.

Reim, H. 1995. Zum Abschluss der archäologischen Ausgrabungen in der keltischen Nekropole im "Lindele" in Rottenburg a. N., Kreis Tübingen. *Archäologische Ausgrabungen in Baden-Württemberg* 1995: 90–6.

Renfrew, A. C. 1969. Trade and culture process in European prehistory. *Current Anthropology* 10: 151–69.

Renfrew, A. C. & Cherry, J. F. (eds.). 1986. *Peer Polity Interaction and Sociocultural Change.* Cambridge: Cambridge University Press.

Rev. Canon Roberts (ed.). 1912. *Titus Livius, History of Rome.* New York (NY): E. P. Dutton and Co.

Revell, L. 2009. *Roman Imperialism and Local Identities.* Cambridge: Cambridge University Press.

Reynolds, L. D. & Wilson, N. G. 1974. *Scribes and Scholars: A Guide to the Transmission of Greek and Latin Literature.* (Second) Oxford: Clarendon Press.

Riccardi, A. 1989. Le necropoli peucezie dei VI e V a.C. Tipologia funeraria e composizione dei corredi. In Ciancio, A. (ed.), *Archeologia e Territorio. L'Area Peuceta. Atti del Seminario di Studi, Gioia del Colle, Museo Archeologico Nazionale 12–14 Novembre 1987.* Gioia del Colle: Nuovo Servizio, 69–89.

Riccardi, A. 2003. *Gli Antichi Peucezi a Bitonto: Documenti ed Immagini dalla Necropoli di Via Traiana. S Spirito.* Bari: Edipuglia.

Riccardi, A. 2008. *Donne e Guerrieri da Ruvo e Bitonto: e Scoperte del III Millennio.* Bari: Edipuglia.

Rieckhoff, S. 1995. *Süddeutschland im Spannungsfeld von Kelten, Germanen und Römern. Studien zur Chronologie der Spätlatènezeit im Südlichen Mitteleuropa.* (Trierer Beiheft 19). Trier: Rheinisches Landesmuseum.

Rieckhoff, S. 2007. Wo sind sie geblieben? – Zur archäologischen Evidenz der Kelten in Süddeutschland im 1. Jahrhundert v. Chr. In Birkhan, H. (ed.), *Kelten-Einfälle an der Donau.* Vienna: Österreichische Akademie der Wissenschaften, 409–40.

Rieckhoff, S. 2012a. Das Ende der Kelten. Kelten – Römer – Germanen. *Antike Welt. Zeitschrift für Archäologie und Kulturgeschichte* 5/2012: 10–7.

Rieckhoff, S. 2012b. Spurensuche; Kelten oder was man darunter versteht. In Röber, R., Jansen, M., Rau, S., von Nicolai, C. & Frech, I. (eds.), *Die Welt der Kelten. Zentrum der Macht; Kostbarkeiten der Kunst.* Ostfildern: Jan Thorbecke Verlag, 26–36.

Rieckhoff, S. & Sommer, U. (eds.). 2007. *Auf der Suche nach Identitäten: Volk-Stamm-Kultur-Ethnos. Internationale Tagung der Universität Leipzig vom 8.-9- Dezember 2000.* Oxford: Archaeopress.

Riva, C. 2010. *The Urbanisation of Etruria: Funerary Practices and Social Change, 700–600 BC.* Cambridge: Cambridge University Press.

Riva, C. & Stoddart, S. K. F. 1996. Ritual landscapes in archaic Etruria. In Wilkins, J. B. (ed.), *Approaches to the Study of Ritual. Italy and the Mediterranean.* London: Accordia, 91–109.

Riva, C. & Vella, N. (eds.). 2006. *Debating Orientalization: Multidisciplinary Approaches to Change in the Ancient Mediterranean.* London: Equinox Press.

Roach-Higgins, M. E. & Eicher, J. B. 1995a. Dress and identity. In Roach-Higgins, M. E., Eicher, J. B. & Johnson, K. K. P. (eds.), *Dress and Identity.* New York: Fairchild Publications, 7–18.

Roach-Higgins, M. E. & Eicher, J. B. (eds.). 1995b. *Dress and Identity.* New York: Fairchild Publications.

Robb, J. E. 2004. The extended artefact and the monumental economy: a methodology for material agency. In DeMarrais, E., Gosden, C. & Renfrew, C. (eds.), *Rethinking Materiality: The Engagement of Mind with the Material World.* (McDonald Institute Monographs). Cambridge: McDonald Institute for Archaeological Research, 131–9.

Robb, J. E., Bigazzi, R., Lazzarini, L., Scarsini, C. & Sonego, F. 2001. Social 'status' and biological 'status': a comparison of grave goods and skeletal indicators from Pontecagnano. *American Journal of Physical Anthropology* 115 (3): 213–22.

Robben, A. C. G. M. 2004. Death and Anthropology: An Introduction. In Robben, A. C. G. M. (ed.), *Death, Mourning, and Burial: A Cross-Cultural Reader.* Oxford: Blackwell, 1–16.

Robertson, A. S. 1970. Roman Finds from Non-Roman Sites in Scotland: More Roman 'Drift' in Caledonia. *Britannia* 1: 198–226.

Röder, B. 2002. Statisten in der Welt der Erwachsenen: Kinder auf archäologischen Lebensbildern. In Alt, K. W. & A, K.-G. (eds.), *Kinderwelten: Anthropologie, Geschichte, Kulturvergleich.* Köln: Böhlau, 95–105.

Roisman, J. & Worthington, J. (eds.). 2010. *A Companion to Ancient Macedonia.* Malden: Wiley-Blackwell.

Roska, M. 1915. Kelta sírok és egyéb emlékek Balzáról. *Dolgozatok az Erdélyi Nemzeti Múzeum Érem- és Régiségtárából* 6: 18–48.

Roska, M. 1937. Der Bestand der skythischen Altertümer Siebenbürgens. *Eurasia Septentrionalis Antiqua* 11: 167–203.

Roska, M. 1942. *Erdély régészeti repertóriuma = Thesaurus antiquitatum Transsilvanicarum.* Kolozsvár: Erdélyi Tudományos Intézet.

Roska, M. 1944. A kelták Erdélyben. *Közlemények az Erdélyi Nemzeti Múzeum Érem- és Régiségtárából* 4: 53–80.

Rossi, L. & van der Wielen-van Ommeren, F. 1983. *Canosa II.* Bari: Dedalo.

Rossi, S. 2005. Uso alimentare o ritualità alimentare? Il caso dei mortai in ceramica di tipo etrusco padano in Veneto: analisi tipocronologica, aspetti tecnologici e ipotesi su funzione e uso. In Attema, P., Nijboer, B. & Zifferero, A. (eds.), *Papers in Italian Archaeology VI. Communities and Settlements from the Neolithic to the Early Medieval period. Proceedings of the 6th Conference on Italian archaeology (Groningen, April 2003) Volume I.* Oxford: Archaeopress, 426–34.

Rotroff, S. I. 1982. *Hellenistic Pottery. Athenian and Imported Mouldmade Bowls.* (The Athenian Agora 22). Princeton (New Jersey): American School of Classical Studies at Athens.

Rousseeuw, P. J. 1987. Silhouettes: A graphical aid to the interpretation and validation of cluster analysis. *Journal of Computational and Applied Mathematics* 20: 53–65.

Rowlands, M. 1994. The politics of identity in archaeology. In Bond, G. C. & Gilliam, A. (eds.), *Social Construction of the Past: Representation as Power.* London: Routledge, 129–43.

Rowlands, M. 2002a. Heritage and Cultural Property Introduction. In Buchli, V. (ed.), *The Material Culture Reader.* Oxford: Berg, 105–15.

Rowlands, M. 2002b. The Power of Origins: Question of Cultural Rights. In Buchli, V. (ed.), *The Material Culture Reader.* Oxford: Berg, 115–35.

Rowlands, M. 2007. The politics of identity in archaeology. In Insoll, T. (ed.), *The Archaeology of Identities. A Reader.* London and New York: Routledge, 59–71.

Rowley-Conwy, P. 2007. *From Genesis to Prehistory. The Archaeological Three Age System and its Contested Reception in Denmark, Britain and Ireland.* Oxford: Oxford University Press.

Roymans, N. 1990. *Tribal Societies in Northern Gaul. An Anthropological Perspective.* (Cingula 12). Amsterdam: Universiteit van Amsterdam.

Roymans, N. 1996. The Sword or the Plough. Regional dynamics in the Romanisation of Belgic Gaul and the Rhineland area. In Roymans, N. (ed.), *From the Sword to the Plough: Three Studies on the Earliest Romanisation of Northern Gaul.* Amsterdam: Amsterdam University press, 9–126.

Roymans, N. 2004. *Ethnic Identity and Imperial Power: The Batavians in the Early Roman Empire.* Amsterdam: Amsterdam University Press.

Ruby, P. 1995. *Le Crépuscule des Marges: le Premier Âge du Fer à Sala Consilina.* (Bibliothèque des Écoles françaises d'Athènes et de Rome 290; Collection du Centre Jean Bérard 12). Rome: École française de Rome.

Russell, I. 2006a. Freud und Volkan: Psychoanalysis, group identities and archaeology. *Antiquity* 80 (307): 185–95.

Russell, I. (ed.). 2006b. *Images, Representation and Heritage; Moving beyond Modern Approach to Archaeology.* New York: Springer.

Russo Tagliente, A. 1995. *Armento: Archeologia di un Centro Indigeno.* Roma: Istituto Poligrafico e Zecca dello Stato, Libreria dello Stato.

Russo Tagliente, A. & Berlingò, A. 1992. Chiaromonte (Potenza) – La necropoli arcaica in località Sotto La Croce: Scavi 1973. *Notizie degli Scavi di Antichità* 3 (9): 233–407.

Rustoiu, A. 1997. *Fibulele din Dacia Preromană (sec. II Î.e.n. – I E.n.).* București: Institutul Român de Tracologie, Ministerul Educației Naționale.

Rustoiu, A. 2002a. Habitat und Gesellschaft im 4.-2. Jh. v. Chr. In Cosma, C. & Gudea, A. (eds.), *Habitat und Gesellschaft im Westen und Nordwesten Rumäniens vom Ende des 2. Jahrt. V. Chr. zum Anfang des 1. Jhrt. N. Chr.* Cluj-Napoca: Napoca star, 49–90.

Rustoiu, A. 2002b. Locuirile dacice. In Vasiliev, V., Rustoiu, A. & Balaguri, A. (eds.), *Solotvino-"Cetate" (Ucraina Transcarpatică). Așezările din Epoca Bronzului, a doua Vârstă a Fierului și din Evul Mediu Timpuriu [summary: Solotvino-"Cetate" (Transcarpathian Ukraine). The Settlements of the Bronze Age, the Second Iron Age and Early Medieval Times].* (Bibliotheca Thracologica 33). Cluj-Napoca: Napoca star, 46–90.

Rustoiu, A. 2002c. *Metalurgie și Magie. În Legătură cu Unele Tehnici și Instrumente Metalurgice din Dacia Preromană, in Ateliere și Tehnici Meșteșugărești. Contribuții Arheologice.* Cluj Napoca: Accent.

Rustoiu, A. 2002d. *Războinici și Artizani de Prestigiu în Dacia Preromană.* Cluj Napoca: Nereamia Napocae.

Rustoiu, A. 2004–2005. Celtic-indigenous connections in Oltenia during the middle La Tène. Observations concerning a Celtic grave from Telești. *Ephemeris Napocensis* 14–15: 53–71.

Rustoiu, A. 2005a. Dacia și Italia în sec. I a.Chr. Comerțul cu vase de bronz în perioada republicană târzie (studiu preliminar). In Cosma, C. & Rustoiu, A. (eds.), *Comerț și Civilizație. Transilvania în Contextul Schimburilor Comerciale și Culturale în Antichitate.* Cluj Napoca: Editura Mega, 53–117.

Rustoiu, A. 2005b. Die in die 4.-3. Jh. v. Chr. Beziehungsweise ins 2. Jh. v. Chr.-1. Jh. n. Chr. datierten befestigten dakischen Siedlungen aus Maramureș. In Nemeth, E., Rustoiu, A. & Pop, H. (eds.), *Limes Dacicus Occidentalis. Die Befestigungen im Westen Dakiens vor und nach der Römischen Eroberung.* Cluj-Napoca: Editura Mega, 10–24.

Rustoiu, A. 2005c. The Padea-Panagjurski Kolonii Group in south-western Transylvania (Romania). In Dobrzańska, H., Megaw, J. V. S. & Poleska, P. (eds.), *Celts on the margin: Studies in European Cultural Interaction 7th century BC – 1st century AD, Dedicated to Zenon Woźniak.* Kraków: Institute of Archaeology and Ethnology of the Polish Academy of Sciences, 109–19.

Rustoiu, A. 2006. A journey to Mediterranean. Peregrinations of a Celtic warrior from Transylvania. Studia Universitatis "Babeș-Bolyai". *Historia* 51 (1): 42–85.

Rustoiu, A. 2008. *Războinici și Societate în Aria Celtică Transilvăneană. Studii pe Marginea Mormântului cu Coif de la Ciumești.* (Interferențe Etnice și Culturale în Mileniile I a.Chr. – I p.Chr. XIII). Cluj-Napoca: Editura Mega.

Rustoiu, A. 2009. Masters of metals in the Carpathian Basin (workshops, production centres and funerary manifestations in the early and middle La Tène). *Ephemeris Napocensis* 19: 7–21.

Rustoiu, A. 2011. The Celts from Transylvania and eastern Banat and their southern neighbours. Cultural exchanges and individual mobility. In Guštin, M. & Jevtić, M. (eds.), *The Eastern Celts. The Communities between the Alps and the Black Sea.* Koper-Beograd: Univerza na Primorskem, 163–70.

Rustoiu, A. & Berecki, S. 2012. Thracian' Warriors in Transylvania at the Beginning of the Late Iron Age. The Grave with Chalcidian Helmet from Ocna Sibiului. In Berecki, S. (ed.), *Iron Age Rites and Rituals in the Carpathian Basin, Proceedings of the International Colloquium from Târgu Mureș, 7–9 October 2011.* (Bibliotheca Mvsei Marisiensis 5). Târgu Mureș: Editura Mega, 161–81.

Rustoiu, A. & Comşa, A. 2004. The Padea-Panagjurski Kolonii Group in south-western Transylvania. Archaeological, historical and paleo-anthropological remarks. In Pescaru, A. & Ferencz, I. V. (eds.), *Daco-Geiţi: 80 de Ani de Cercetări Arheologice Sistematice la Cetăţile Dacice din Munţii Orăştiei.* (Acta Musei Devensis). Deva: Muzeul Civilizaţiei Dacice şi Romane, 267–76.

Rustoiu, A., Comşa, A. & Lisovschi-Cheleşanu, C. 1993. Practici funerare în aşezarea Dacică de la Sighişoara-Wietenberg (observaţii preliminare). *Ephemeris Napocensis* 3: 81–95.

Rustoiu, A. & Gheorghiu, G. 2009. An iron variant of the Jezerine-type brooches from Pre-Roman Dacia. *Instrumentum* 30: 30–1.

Rustoiu, A. & Gheorghiu, G. 2010. 'General' and 'particular' in the dressing fashion and metalwork of Pre-Roman Dacia (an iron variant of the Jezerine-type brooches from Piatra-Craivii – Alba County). In Cândea, I. (ed.), *The Thracians and Their Neighbours in Antiquity. Studia in Honorem Valerii Sîrbu.* Brăila: Muzeul Brăilei- Editura Istros, 447–57.

Rustoiu, A. & Megaw, J. V. S. 2011. A foreign flowering in Transylvania: the Vegetal style armring from Fântânele-Dealul Popii, jud. Bistriţa-Năsăud, grave 62. In Măgureanu, D., Măndescu, D. & Matei, S. (eds.), *Archaeology: Making of and Practice. Studies in Honour of Mircea Babeş at his 70th Anniversary.* Piteşti: Editura Ordessos, 217–37.

Rybová, A. & Soudský, B. 1962. *Libenice: Keltská Svatně ve Středních Čechách.* Prague: Československé Akademie Věd.

Sabath, G. (ed.). 1999. *Ammianus Marcellinus. Histoire (Livres XXIX–XXXI).* Paris: Belles Lettres.

Sahlins, M. D. 1972. *Stone Age Economics.* Chicago: Aldine.

Said, E. W. 1978. *Orientalism.* New York: Pantheon.

Sanders, T. 2001. Save our skins: structural adjustment, morality and the occult in Tanzania. In Moore, H. L. & Sanders, T. (eds.), *Magical Interpretations, Material Realities: Modernity, Witchcraft and the Occult in Postcolonial Africa.* London: Routledge, 160–83.

Šašel-Kos, M. 2005. *Appian and Illiricum.* Ljubljana: Nardni muzej Slovenije.

Saunders, B. A. C. & Van Brakel, J. 1988. Re-evaluating basic colour terms. *Cultural Dynamics,* 1 (3): 359–78.

Šavel, I. 2001. The Region of Pomurje in the Iron Age. In Lippert, A. (ed.), *Die Drau-, Mur- und Raab-Region im 1. Vorchristlichen Jahrtausend: Akten des Internationalen und Interdisziplinären Symposiums vom 26. bis 29. April 2000 in Bad Radkersburg.* (Universitätsforschungen zur Prähistorischen Archäologie 78). Bonn: Rudolf Habelt, 67–75.

Šavel, I. & Sankovič, S. 2010. *Za Raščico pri Krogu.* Ljubljana: Institute for the Protection of Cultural Heritage of Slovenia.

Šavel, I. & Sankovič, S. 2011. *Pri Muri pri Lendavi.* (Zbirka Arheologija na avtocestah Slovenije 23). Ljubljana: Institute for the Protection of Cultural Heritage of Slovenia.

Scarfì, B. M. 1961. Gioia del Colle. Scavi nella zona di Monte Sannace. Le tombe rinvenute nel 1956. *Monumenti Antichi* 45: 144–33.

Scarre, C. & Healy, F. (eds.). 1993. *Trade and Exchange in Prehistoric Europe: Proceedings of a Conference Held at the University of Bristol, April 1992.* (Oxbow monograph 33). Oxford: Oxbow Books.

Schaper, M. 2011. Editorial. Die Kelten. *Geoepoche* 47: 3.

Schiffer, M. B. 1972. Archaeological Context and Systemic Context. *American Antiquity* 37 (2): 156–65.

Schiffer, M. B. 1975. Archaeology as behavioral science. *American Anthropologist* 77: 836–48.

Schnapp, A. 1996. *The Discovery of the Past.* London: British Museum.

Schortman, E. & Urban, P. A. 1998. Culture Contact Structure and Process. In Cusick, J. G. (ed.), *Studies in Culture Contact: Interaction, Culture Change and Archaeology.* Carbondale: Southern Illinois University Press, 102–25.

Schwartz, S. J. 2001. The Evolution of Eriksonian and, Neo-Eriksonian Identity Theory and Research: A Review and Integration. *Identity* 1 (1): 7–58.

Schwartz, S. J. & Montgomery, M. J. 2002. Similarities or differences in identity development? The impact of acculturation and gender on identity process and outcome. *Journal of Youth and Adolescence* 31 (5): 359–72.

Schweitzer, A. 2007 [1923]. *Kulturphilosophie.* München: C.H. Beck.

Serritella, A. 1995. *Pontecagnano II: 3. Le Nuove Aree di Necropoli del IV e III sec. a.C.* Napoli: Istituto universitario orientale Dipartimento di studi del mondo classico e del Mediterraneo antico.

Shankar, S. 2006. Metaconsumptive Practices and the Circulation of Objectifications. *Journal of Material Culture* 11: 293–317.

Shanks, M. 1996. *Classical Archaeology of Greece – Experiences of the Discipline.* London: Routledge.

Shanks, M. & Tilley, C. 1989. Archaeology into the 1990s. *Norwegian Archaeological Review* 22: 1-54.

Shanks, M. & Tilley, C. 1997. *Social Theory and Archaeology.* Albuquerque: University of New Mexico Press.

Shennan, S. (ed.). 1989a. *Archaeological Approaches to Cultural Identity.* London: Unwin Hyman.

Shennan, S. 1989b. Introduction: archaeological approaches to cultural identity. In Shennan, S. (ed.), *Archaeological Approaches to Cultural Identity.* London: Unwin Hyman, 1–32.

Sherlock, S. J. & Welch, M. G. 1992. *An Anglo-Saxon Cemetery at Norton, Cleveland.* (CBA Research Report 82). London: Council for British Archaeology.

Shinnie, P. L. 2004. John Alexander – A Memoir. *Azania: Archaeological Research in Africa* 39 (1): 3–6.

Shukriu, E. 1996. *Dardania Paraurbane: Studime Arkeologjike të Kosovës.* Peje: Dukagjini.

Sievers, S. 2003. *Manching – Die Keltenstadt.* Stuttgart: Konrad Theiss Verlag.

Sievers, S. 2007. *Manching: Die Keltenstadt.* (Second edition) Stuttgart: Theiss.

Sievers, S. 2010. Vom Fürstensitz zum Oppidum. In Krauße, D. & Beilharz, D. (eds.), *"Fürstensitze" und Zentralorte der Frühen Kelten, vol. 1.* Stuttgart: Konrad Theiss Verlag, 31-4.

Silverman, H. (ed.). 2011. *Contested Cultural Heritage; Religion, Nationalism and Exclusion in a Global World.* New York: Springer.

Šimek, M. 1998. Ein Grabhügel mit Pferdebestattung bei Jalžabet, Kroatien. In Hänsel, B. & Machnik, J. (eds.), *Das Karpatenbecken und die Osteuropäische Steppe.* (Prähistorische Archäologie in Südosteuropa Band 12). München: Südosteuropa-Gesellschaft und Verlag Marie Leidorf, 493–510.

Šimek, M. 2001. Weitere Aspekte vom Grabhügel II in Jalžabet bei Varaždin. In Lippert, A. (ed.), *Die Drau-, Mur- und Raab Region im 1. Vorschristlichen Jahrtausend. Akten des Internationalen und Interdisziplinären Symposiums vom 26. bis 29. April 2000 in Bad Radkersburg.* (Universitätforschungen zur Prähistorischen Archäologie 78). Bonn: In Kommission bei Rudolf Habelt, 311–8.

Šimek, M. 2004. Grupa Matijanec-Kaptol. In Balen-Letunić, D. (ed.), *Ratnici na Razmeđu Istoka i Zapada, Starije Željezno Doba u Kontinentalnoj Hrvatskoj.* Zagreb: Arheološki muzej u Zagrebu, 79–129.

Šimić, J. 1984. Stariji nalazi bosutske grupe iz Vukovara. *Izdanja HAD-a sv* 9: 107–15.

Simmel, G. 1890. *Über Sociale Differenzierung.* Leipzig: Duncker & Humblot.

Simpson, D. D. A. 1969. Excavations at Kaimes Hillfort, Midlothian, 1964–1968. *Glasgow Archaeological Journal* 1: 7–28.

Sims-Williams, P. 1998. Celtomania and Celtoscepticism. *Cambrian Medieval Celtic Studies* 36: 1–35.

Sims-Williams, P. 2012a. Bronze- and Iron-Age Celtic-speakers: what we don't know, what we can't know, and what could we know? Language, genetics and archaeology in the twenty-first century. *Antiquaries Journal* 92: 427–49.

Sims-Williams, P. 2012b. Celtic civilisation: continuity or coincidence? *Cambrian Medieval Celtic Studies* 64: 1–44.

Sindbæk, S. M. 2007. Networks and Nodal Points: The Emergence of Towns in Early Viking Age Scandinavia. *Antiquity* 81: 119–32.

Sîrbu, V. 1983. Nouvelles considérations générales concernant l'importation des amphores grecques sur le territoire de la Roumanie (les VI–I siècles av.n.e.). *Pontica* 16: 43–67.

Sîrbu, V. 1986. Rituels et pratiques funéraires des gèto-daces IIe siècle av. notre ère – Ier siècle de notre ère. *Dacia* 30 (1–2): 91–108.

Sîrbu, V. 1993. *Credinţe şi Practici Funerare, Religioase şi Magice în Lumea Geto-Dacilor: (Pornind de la Descoperirile Arheologice din Câmpia Brăilei).* Galaţi: Porto-Franco.

Sîrbu, V. 1996. *Dava Getică de la Grădiştea, jud. Brăila I.* Brăila: Editura Istros.

Sîrbu, V. 2003. Funerary Practices in the Iron Age between the Carpathians and the Danube. In Bojović, N., Vasić, M. & Vasić, R. (eds.), *Sahranjivanje u Bronzano i Gvozdeno Doba.* Čačak: Narodni muzej Čačak, 139–70.

Sîrbu, V. 2008. Ritual Inhumations and "Deposits" of Children among the Geto-Dacians. In Murphy, E. M. (ed.) *Deviant Burial in the Archaeological Record.* (Studies in funerary archaeology). Oxford: Oxbow Books, 71–90.

Sîrbu, V., Cavruc, V. & Buzea, D. 2006. A 4th–3rd centuries BC Dacian community in south-eastern Transylvania: the findings from Olteni, Covasna

Sîrbu, V., Cavruc, V. & Buzea, D. 2008a. A Dacian necropolis from 4th–3rd Centuries B.C. found in Olteni (South-Eastern Transylvania). In Sîrbu, V. & Vaida, D. L. (eds.), *Funerary Practices of the Bronze and Iron Ages in Central and South-Eastern Europe. International Colloquium – Bistriţa, May 9–11, 2008*. Cluj-Napoca: Editura Mega, 191–228.

County. In Sîrbu, V. & Vaida, D. L. (eds.), *Thracians and Celts. Proceedings of the International Colloquium from Bistriţa, 18–20 May 2006*. Cluj-Napoca: Editura Mega, 229–51.

Sîrbu, V., Cavruc, V. & Buzea, D. 2008b. O comunitate dacică din sec. IV–III a. Chr. la Olteni, jud. Covasna. *Angvstia* 12: 109–48.

Sîrbu, V. & Florea, G. 1997. *Imaginar şi Imagine în Dacia Preroman*. Brăila: Editura Istros.

Sîrbu, V., Luca, S. A. & Roman, C. 2007. Tombs of Dacian Warriors (2nd–1st C. BC) found in Hunedoara–Grădina Castelului (Hunedoara County). *Acta Terrae Septemcastrensis* 7 (1): 155–77.

Sîrbu, V., Luca, S. A., Roman, C., Purece, S., Diaconescu, D. & Cerişor, N. 2007. *Vestigiile Dacice de la Hunedoara/The Dacian Vestiges in Hunedoara*. (Bibliotheca Brukenthal 12). Sibiu: Editura ALTIP – Alba Iulia.

Sîrbu, V., Matei, S. & Dupoi, V. 2005. *Incinta Dacică Fortificată Pietroasa Mică-Gruiu Dării II*. Buzău: Editura Alpha.

Sirbu, V. & Stefan, M. 2010. Images of gendered identities. North-Thracian case 5th–3rd Century BC. *Istros* 16: 235–65.

Sivik, L. 1997. Colour systems for cognitive research. In &, C. L. H. & Maffi, L. (eds.), *Color Categories in Thought and Language*. Cambridge: Cambridge University Press, 163–93.

Škoberne, Ž. 1999. *Budinjak, Kneževski tumul*. Zagreb: Muzej grada Zagreba.

Školjev-Dončo, A., Nikolovski-Katin, S. & Stefou, C. 2010. *Macedonia in Ancient Times*. Skopje: Makedonska Iskra.

Small, A. 2000. The use of javelins in central and south Italy in the 4th century BC. In Ridgway, D., Serra Ridgway, F. R., Pearce, M., Herring, E., Whitehouse, R. D. & Wilkins, J. B. (eds.), *Ancient Italy in Its Mediterranean Setting. Studies in Honour of Ellen Macnamara*. London: Accordia Research Institute, University of London, 221–34.

Smith, J. 1919. Excavation of the forts of Castlehill, Aitnock, and Coalhill, Ayrshire. *Proceedings of the Society of Antiquaries of Scotland* 53: 123–34.

Snodgrass, A. M. 1964. *Early Greek Armour and Weapons: from the End of the Bronze Age to 600 B.C.* Edinburgh: University Press.

Snow, C. P. 1960. *The Two Cultures*. Cambridge: University Press.

Sofaer, J. 2007. Introduction: Materiality and Identity. In Sofaer, J. (ed.), *Material Identities*. Oxford: Blackwell, 1–10.

Sokefeld, M. 1999. Debating self, identity, and culture in anthropology. *Current Anthropology* 40 (4): 417–48.

Sokol, V. 2001. Neue Latènfunde aus der Umgebung von Zagreb (Croatia). *Instrumentum* 16: 16.

Sokolovska, V. 1986. *Isar – Marvinci i Povardarje vo Antičko Vreme*. Skopje: Muzej na Makedonija.

Sokolovska, V. 1992. Ranoanticka siva keramika vo Makedonija. *Macedoniae acta Archaeolodica* 13: 141–8.

Sommer, C. S. (ed.). 2006. *Archäologie in Bayern: Fenster zur Vergangenheit.* Regensburg: Verlag Friedrich Pustet.

Sommer, U. & Gramsch, A. 2011. German archaeology in context: an introduction to history and present of Central European archaeology. In Gramsch, A. & Sommer, U. (eds.), *A History of Central European Archaeology. Theory, Methods, and Politics*. (Series Minor 30). Budapest: Archaeolingua, 7–40.

Sørensen, M. L. 2000. *Gender Archaeology.* Cambridge: Polity Press.

Sørensen, M. L. 2004. Stating Identities: The Use of Objects in Rich Bronze Age Graves. In Cherry, J., Scarre, C. & Shennan, S. (eds.), *Explaining Social Change: Studies in Honour of Colin Renfrew.* Cambridge: McDonald Institute, 167–76.

Şovan, O. L. & Ignat, M. 2005. *Aşezarea Getică Fortificată de la Cotu – Copălău, jud Botoşani.* Târgovişte: Editura Cetatea de Scaun.

Spânu, D. 2002a. Studien zum Silberschatzfund des 1. Jahrhunderts v. Chr. von Lupu, Rumänien. *Prähistorische Zeitschrift* 77: 84–136.

Spânu, D. 2002b. Un mormânt de epocă târzie de la Dubova. *Studii şi Cercetări de Istorie Veche şi Arheologie* 52–53: 83–132.

Spengler, O. 1918/1922. *Der Untergang des Abendlandes. Umrisse einer Morphologie der Weltgeschichte.* Wien/München: Verlag Braumüller/C. H. Beck.

Spindler, K. 1991. *Die Frühen Kelten.* Stuttgart: Reclam.

Srejović, D. 1973. Karagač and the problem of the ethnogenesis of the Dardanians. *Balcanica* 4: 39–82.

Srejović, D. 1979. Un essai de délimitation ethnique et territoriale des tribus paléobakaniques, basé sur la manière d'enterrer. (in Serbian with a French summary). In Garašanin, M. (ed.), *Rites d'Inhumation chez les Illyriens, Recuil des Travaux Préséntes au Colloque de l'Academie Serbe des Scienses et des Arts et de l'Institut d'Etudes Balkaniques de l'Academie Serbe, Zlatibor, 10–12 mai 1976.* Beograd: Academie Serbe des sciences et des arts, Institut d'études balkaniques, 79–87.

Srejović, D. 1991. Triballic graves in Ljuljaci. (in Serbian with an English summary). *Starinar* 40–1/1989–90: 141–53.

Stahl, A. B. 2010. Material Histories. In Hicks, D. & Beaudry, M. C. (eds.), *The Oxford Handbook of Material Culture Studies.* Oxford: Oxford University Press, 160–72.

Stalsberg, A., Arnold, B. & Wicker, N. 2001. Visible women made invisible: interpreting Varangian women in Old Russia. In Arnold, B. & Wicker, N. (eds.), *Gender and the Archaeology of Death.* Lanham, MD: AltaMira Press, 65–81.

Stary, P. F. 1981. *Zur Eisenzeitlichen Bewaffung und Kampesweise in Mittelitalien (ca. 9. bis 6. Jh. v. Chr.).* (Marburger Studien Zur vor- und Frühgeschichte Band 3). Mainz am Rhein: Verlag Philipp von Zabern.

Steger, F. 2004. Medizinische Streitkultur im 16. Jahrhundert. Zu einer kulturellen Kontextualisierung von Georgius Agricola "Bermannus sive de re metallica Dialogus" (1528). In Steger, F. (ed.), *Krankheit: Kulturtransfer Medizinischen*

*Wissens von der Spätantike bis in die Frühe Neuzeit*. (Beihefte zum Archiv für Kulturgeschichte 55). Köln: Böhlau, 201–18.

Stegmann-Rajtár, S. 1992. Spätbronze- und früheisenzeitliche Fundgruppen des mittleren Donaugebietes. *Bericht der Römisch-Germanischen Kommission 73*: 29–179.

Steidl, B. 2006. Von den Kelten zu den Germanen. In Sommer, C. S. (ed.), *Archäologie in Bayern: Fenster zur Vergangenheit*. Regensburg: Verlag Friedrich Pustet, 224.

Stein, G. J. 2005. Introduction: The Comparative Archaeology of Colonial Encounters. In Stein, G. J. (ed.), *The Archaeology of Colonial Encounters: Comparative Perspectives*. Santa Fe (NM): School of American Research Press, 1–29.

Stenger, G. 1994. 'Fréret, Maffei et l'origine des anciens peuples de l'Italie (à propos d'une lettre inédite de Fréret)'. In Volpilhac-Auger, C. & Grell, C. (eds.), *Nicolas Freret, Légende et Vérité, Colloque des 18 et 19 Octobre 1991, Clermont-Ferrand* Oxford: Voltaire Foundation, 131–51.

Stets, J. E. & Burke, P. J. 2000. Identity Theory and Social Identity Theory. *Social Psychology Quarterly* 63 (3): 224–37.

Stevens, S. S. 1946. On the Theory of Scales of Measurement. *Science* 103 (2684): 677–80.

Stöckli, W. E. 1993. Römer, Kelten und Germanen: Probleme von Kontinuität und Diskontinuität zur Zeit von Caesar und Augustus zwischen Hochrhein und Rheinmündung. *Bonner Jahrbücher* 193: 121–40.

Stoddart, S. K. F. 2007–8 (2009). The Etruscan Body. *Accordia Research Papers* 11: 137–52.

Stoddart, S. K. F. 2009. *Historical Dictionary of the Etruscans*. (Historical Dictionaries of Ancient Civilizations 24). Lanham, MD: Scarecrow Press.

Stoddart, S. K. F. 2010. Boundaries of the State in Time and Space: Transitions and Tipping Points. *Social Evolution & History* 9 (2 (September)): 28–52.

Stoddart, S. K. F. and Redhouse, D. 2014. The Umbrians. In Aberson, M., Biella, M. C., Wullschleger, M., Di Fazio, M. (eds.), *Entre Archéologie et Histoire: Dialogues sur Divers Peuples de l'Italie Préromaine*. Geneva: Université de Genève – Faculté des Lettres – Département des Sciences de l'Antiquité, 107–124

Stoddart, S. K. F., Baroni, M., Ceccarelli, L., Cifani, G., Clackson, J., Ferrara, F., della Giovampaola, I., Fulminante, F., Licence, T., Malone, C., Mattacchioni, L., Mullen, A., Nomi, F., Pettinelli, E., Redhouse, D. & Whitehead, N. 2012. Opening the Frontier: the Gubbio – Perugia frontier in the course of history. *Papers of the British School at Rome* 80: 257–94.

Stoddart, S. K. F. & Neil, S. 2012. Situating ethnicity. In Cifani, G., Stoddart, S. K. F. & Neil, S. (eds.), *Landscape, Ethnicity and Identity in the Archaic Mediterranean Area*. Oxford: Oxbow Books, 287–93.

Stojić, M. 1986a. *Die Eisenzeit im Becken der Velika Morava*. (in Serbian with a German summary). Beograd: Philosophische Fakultät & Landemuseum Svetoyarevo.

Stojić, M. 1986b. *Gvozdeno Doba u Basenu Velike Morave.* Beograd: Filizofski fakultet, Centar za arheološka istraživanja.

Stojić, M. 1990. Early Iron Age in the Pomoravlje (Morava Valley). In Jevtović, J. (ed.), *Masters of Silver: the Iron Age in Serbia.* Belgrade, Novi Sad & Priština: National Museum, Belgrade, Museum of Vojvodina & Museum of Kosovo, 89–100.

Stojić, M. 2009. New finds from Rutevac and deliberation on purpose, origin place of production and ethnic attribution of Mramorac type belt. *Starinar* 58/2008: 87–94.

Stöllner, T. 1998. Grab 102 vom Dürrnberg bei Hallein. Bemerkungen zu den Dürrnberger Kriegergräbern der Frühlatènezeit. *Germania* 76 (1): 67–176.

Stöllner, T. 2004. 'Verborgene Güter' – Rohstoffe und Spezereien als Fernhandelsgut in der Späthallstatt- und Frühlatènezeit, In Guggisberg, M. A. (ed.), *Die Hydria von Grächwil: Zur Funktion und Rezeption Mediterraner Importe in Mitteleuropa im 6. und 5. Jahrhundert v. Chr.* Bern: Bernisches Historisches Museum, 137–58.

Stopponi, S. 2011. Campo della Fiera at Orvieto: new discoveries. *Journal of Roman Archaeology* S81: 16–44.

Stovel, E. M. 2013. Concepts of ethnicity and culture in Andean Archaeology. *Latin American Antiquity* 24 (1): 3–20.

Stoyanova, D. 2011. Vault and dome in Thracian funerary architecture. In Nikolov, V., Bacvarov, K., Popov, H., (eds.), *Interdisziplinäre Forshungen zum Kulturerbe auf der Balkanhalbinsel.* Sofia: Nice AN, 2011, 335–55.

Strathern, M. 1988. *The Gender of the Gift. Problems with Women and Problems with Society in Melanesia.* Berkeley: The University of California Press.

Strathern, M. 1999. *Property, Substance and Effect: Anthropological Essays on Persons and Things.* London: Athlone.

Straub, J. 1998. Personale und kollektive Identität. In Assmann, A. & Friese, H. (eds.), *Identitäten.* Frankfurt am Main: Suhrkamp, 73–104.

Strmčnik Gulič, M., Ravnik, M. & Kajzer Cafnik, M. 2008. Hotinja vas. *Varstvo Spomenikov* 44: 72–3.

Strmčnik-Gulič, M. & Teržan, B. 2004. O gomili halštatskega veljaka iz Pivole pod Poštelo. *Časopis za Zgodovino in Narodopisje* n.v. 40: 217–38.

Strobel, K. 1996. *Die Galater. Geschichte und Eigenart der Keltichen Staatenbildung auf dem Boden des Hellenistischen Kleinasien.* Berlin: Akademie Verlag.

Stronk, J. P. 1995. *The Ten Thousand in Thrace. An Archaeological and Historical Commentary on Xenophon's Anabasis, Books VI.iii-vi–VII.* (Amsterdam Classical Monographs 2). Amsterdam: J.C. Gieben.

Suciu, L. 2000. Organizarea şi amenajarea spaţiului în locuinţele aşezării civile de la Grădiştea de Munte. *Revista Bistriţei* 14: 36–47.

Suciu, L. 2001. Indicii pentru reconstituirea vieţii cotidiene în aşezările dacice. Aspecte ale alimentaţiei. *Studii de Istorie Antică. Omagiu Profesorului Ioan Glodariu.* Cluj Napoca: Muzeul Naţional de Istorie a Transilvaniei, 159–77.

Swaddling, J. & Perkins, P. (eds.). 2009. *Etruscan by Definition: the Culture, Regional and Personal Identity of the Etruscans: Papers in Honour of Sybille Haynes.* London: British Museum.

Swan, V. G. 1992. Legio VI and its men: African legionaries in Britain. *Journal of Roman Pottery Studies* 5: 1–33.
Swan, V. G. 1999. The Twentieth Legion and the history of the Antonine Wall reconsidered. *Proceedings of the Society of Antiquaries of Scotland* 129: 399–480.
Swan, V. G. 2008. Builders, suppliers and supplies in the Tyne-Solway region and beyond, In V P. T. Bidwell (ed.), Understanding Hadrian's Wall: papers from a conference held at South Shields, November 3rd–5th 2006. *Arbeia Journal* 9: 1–35.
Szabó, M. 1991. Mercenary activity. In Moscati, S., Frey, O.-H., Kruta, V., Raftery, B. & Szabó, M. (eds.), *The Celts*. London: Thames and Hudson, 333–6.
Szabó, M. 1994. Kelta harcosok Delphoi előtt és után. Adalékok az ókori kelták történetének egyik kritikus periódusához. *Antik Tanulmányok* 38: 37–56.
Szabó, M. & Petres, E. F. 1992. *Decorated Weapons of the La Tene Iron Age in the Carpathian Basin.* (Inventaria Praehistorica Hungariae 5). Budapest: Magyar Nemzeti Múzeum.
Tainter, J. 1988. *The Collapse of Complex Societies.* Cambridge: Cambridge University Press.
Tappert, C. 2006. *Die Gefässkeramik der Latènezeitlichen Siedlung Straubing-Bajuwarenstrasse.* Kallmünz: Michael Lassleben.
Tappert, C. 2007. Die eisenzeitliche Besiedlungsentwicklung im Stadtgebiet von Straubing (Niederbayern). In Prammer, J. & Sandner, R. (eds.), *Siedlungsdynamik und Gesellschaft: Beiträge des Internationalen Kolloquiums zur Keltischen Besiedlungsgeschichte im Bayerischen Donauraum, Österreich und der Tschechischen Republik*. Straubing: Historischer Verein für Straubing und Umgebung, 173–205.
Tappert, C. & Mielke, D. P. 1998. Eine kleine syrische Bronzesitula aus frühkeltischer Zeit. *Jahresbericht des Historischen Vereins für Straubing und Umgebung* 99: 15–31.
Tasić, N. 1971. Bosutska grupa-nova kultura starijeg gvozdenog doba na području Vojvodine i uže Srbije. *Materijali Saveza Arheoloških Društava Jugoslavije* 7: 61–83.
Tasić, N. 1980. Neki problemi kulturne i etničke pripadnosti bosutskog i basarabi stila. *Balcanica* 11: 7–17.
Tasić, N. 1995. *Eneolithic Cultures of Central and Western Balkans.* Belgrade: Institute for Balkan Studies, Serbian Academy of Science and Arts.
Tasić, N. 1998a. Gvozdeno doba. In Tasić, N. (ed.), *Arheološko Blago Kosova i Metohije od Neolita do Ranog Srednjeg Veka*. Beograd: Srpska akademija nauka i umetnosti, Muzej u Prištini, 148–225.
Tasić, N. 1998b. The Iron Age. In Tasić, N. (ed.) *The Archaeological Treasures of Kosovo and Metohija: from the Neolithic to the Early Middle Ages*. Belgrade: Gallery of Serbian Academy of Sciences and Arts, 152–225.
Taylor, T. F. 1985. Palmettes on the cuirass from Dalboki. *Oxford Journal of Archaeology* 4 (3): 293–304.

Taylor, T. F. 2001. Thracians, Scythians, and Dacians, 800 BC–AD 300. In Cunliffe, B. W. (ed.), *The Oxford Ilustrated History of Prehistoric Europe*. Oxford: Oxford University Press, 373–410.

Taylor, T. F. 2011. The Brno Effect: From Culture to Mind. *Journal of World Prehistory* 24: 213–25.

Teleagă, E. 2008. *Griechische Importe in den Nekropolen an der Unteren Donau. 6. Jh. – Anfang des 3. Jh. v. Chr.* (Marburger Studien zur Vor- und Frühgeschichte Bd. 23). Rahden/Westf: Verlag Marie Leidorf.

Teodor, S. 1988. Elemente celtice pe teritoriul est-carpatic al Romaniei. *Arheologia Moldovei* 12: 33–51.

Teržan, B. 1977. Certoška fibula. *Arheološki Vestnik* 27: 317–443.

Teržan, B. 1990. *Starejša Železna Doba na Slovenskem Štajerskem = The early Iron Age in Slovenian Styria.* (Catalogi et monographiae 25). Ljubljana: Narodni muzej.

Teržan, B. 1995a. Handel und sociale Oberschichten in früheisenzeitlichen SüdostEuropa. In Hänsel, B. (ed.), *Handel, Tausch und Verkehr im Bronze- und Früheisenzeitlichen Südosteuropa*. Berlin: München, 81–159.

Teržan, B. 1995b. Stand und Aufgaben der Forschungen zur Urnenfelderzeit in Jugoslawien. In Erbach, M. (ed.), *Beiträge zur Urnenfelderzeit Nördlich und Südlich der Alpen. Ergebnisse eines Kolloquiums*. (Monographien des Römisch-Germanischen Zentralmuseums 35). Bonn: Rudolf Habelt, 323–72.

Teržan, B. 1998. Auswirkungen des skytisch geprägten Kulturkreis aif die hallstattzeitlichen Kulturgruppen Pannoniens und des Ostalpenraumes. In Hänsel, B. & Machnik, J. (eds.), *Das Karpatenbecken und die Osteuropäische Steppe: Nomadenbewegungen und Kulturaustausch in den Vorchristlichen Metallzeiten (4000–500 v.Chr.)*. (Prähistorische Archäologie in Südosteuropa 12). München: Südosteuropa-Gesellschaft und Verlag Marie Leidorf, 511–60.

Teržan, B. 1999. An Outline of the Urnfield Culture Period in Slovenia/Oris obdobja kulture žarnih grobišč na Slovenskem. *Arheološki Vestnik* 50: 97–143.

Teržan, B. 2001. Die spätbronze- und früheisenzeitliche Besiedlung im nordöstlichen Slowenien. Ein Überblick. In Lippert, A. (ed.), *Die Drau-, Mur- und Raab-Region im 1. Vorchristlichen Jahrtausend: Akten des Internationalen und Interdisziplinären Symposiums vom 26. bis 29. April 2000 in Bad Radkersburg*. Bonn: Rudolf Habelt, 125–35.

Teržan, B., Črešnar, M. & Mušič, B. 2007. Pivola – gomilno grobišče. *Varstvo Spomenikov* 43: 159–60.

Theodossiev, N. 2000a. The Dead with Golden Faces. II. Other Evidence and Connections. *Oxford Journal of Archaeology* 19 (2): 175–209.

Theodossiev, N. 2000b. *North-Western Thrace from the Fifth to First Centuries BC*. (British Archaeological Reports International Series 859). Oxford: Archaeopress.

Theodossiev, N. 2011. Ancient Thrace during the First Millennium BC. In Tsetskhladze, G. R. (ed.), *The Black Sea, Greece, Anatolia and Europe in the First Millennium BC. Dedicated to Jan Bouzek*. (Colloquia Antiqua 1). Leuven-Paris-Walpole: Peeters, 1–60.

Thoma, M. 2000. Der gallo-römische Kultbezirk auf dem Martberg bei Pommern an der Mosel, Kr. Cochem-Zell. In Haffner, A. & von Schnurbein, S.

(eds.), *Kelten, Germanen, Römer im Mittelgebirgsraum zwischen Luxemburg und Thüringen*. Bonn: Habelt, 447–83.

Thomas, J. S. 1996. *Time, Culture and Identity: An Interpretative Archaeology.* London: Routledge.

Thomas, J. S. 2004. *Archaeology and Modernity.* London: Routledge.

Thomas, N. J. 1991. *Entangled Objects. Exchange, Material Culture and Colonialism in the Pacific.* Cambridge (MA): Harvard University Press.

Thomas, N. J. 1992. The Cultural Dynamics of Peripheral Exchange. In Humphrey, C. & Hugh-Jones, S. (eds.), *Barter, Exchange and Value: An Anthropological Approach.* Cambridge: Cambridge University Press, 21–41.

Thomsen, C. J. 1836. *Ledetraad til Nordisk Oldkyndighed.* København: Det kongelige nordiske oldskriftselskab.

Tiefengraber, G. 2001. Vorberichte über die Ausgrabungen 1999 und 2000 in Murska Sobota/Nova tabla. In Lippert, A. (ed.), *Die Drau-, Mur- und Raab-Region im 1. Vorchristlichen Jahrtausend: Akten des Internationalen und Interdisziplinären Symposiums vom 26. bis 29. April 2000 in Bad Radkersburg.* (Universitätsforschungen zur Prähistorischen Archäologie 78). Bonn: Rudolf Habelt, 77–101.

Tiefengraber, G. 2005. *Untersuchungen zur Urnenfelder- und Hallstattzeit im Grazer Becken* Bonn: Rudolf Habelt.

Tilley, C. 2006. Objectification. In Tilley, C., Keane, W., Kuechler-Fogden, S., Rowlands, M. & Spyer, P. (eds.), *Handbook of Material Culture.* London – Thousand Oaks (CA): Sage Publications, 60–73.

Tilley, C. Y. & Bennett, W. 2001. An archaeology of supernatural places: the case of West Penwith. *Journal of the Royal Anthropological Institute* 7: 335–62.

Timpe, D. 1989. Entdeckungsgeschichte: die Römer und der Norden. *Reallexikon der Germanischen Altertumskunde* 7: 337–47.

Titz, P. 2002. Transport amphorae from Pistiros: Introduction. In Bouzek, J., Domaradzka, L. & Archibald, Z. H. (eds.), *Pistiros II: Excavation and Studies.* Prague: Charles University, 33–5.

Tocilescu, G. 1880. *Dacia Înainte de Romani. Cercetări Asupra Poporeloru Carii au Locuitu Tierile Române de a Stâng'a Dunării, mai Înainte de Concuista Acestoru Tieri de Cotra Imperatoriulu Traianu.* Bucureşti: Tipografia Academiei Române.

Todorova, M. 1997. *Imagining the Balkans.* Oxford: Oxford University Press.

Todorova, M. 2009. *Imagining the Balkans.* (Updated edition). Oxford: Oxford University Press.

Tomanič Jevremov, M. 2001. The »Urbanization« of Ormož and the Cemeteries. In Lippert, A. (ed.), *Die Drau-, Mur- und Raab-Region im 1. Vorchristlichen Jahrtausend: Akten des Internationalen und Interdisziplinären Symposiums vom 26. bis 29. April 2000 in Bad Radkersburg.* (Universitätsforschungen zur Prähistorischen Archäologie 78). Bonn: Rudolf Habelt, 191–205.

Tomanič Jevremov, M. 2005. Novo odkrite prazgodovinske naselbine v okolici Ormoža v letih 1990–1996 / Die neuentdeckten prähistorischen Siedlungen in der Umgebung vo Ormož in den Jahren 1990–1996. In Hernja Masten, M., Korpič, N., Kresnik, Z., Toš, M. & Vidic, K. (eds.), *Ormož Skozi Stoletja V.* Ormož: Skupščina občine, 73–96.

Tomaschek, W. 1893. Die alten Thraker. Eine ethnologische Untersuchung. I. Übersicht der Stämme. *Sitzungsberichte der Kaiserlichen Akademie der Wissenschaften* 128 (IV): 1–130.

Tomaschitz, K. 2002. *Die Wanderungen der Kelten in der Antiken Literarischen Überlieferung.* Vienna: Österreichische Akademie der Wissenschaften.

Tomedi, G. 2001. Die Drau als Verkehrsweg während der frühen Eisenzeit am Beispiel Frög / The Drava as the traffic route during the Early Iron Age: the example of Frög. In Lippert, A. (ed.), *Die Drau-, Mur- und Raab-Region im 1. Vorchristlichen Jahrtausend: Akten des Internationalen und Interdisziplinären Symposiums vom 26. bis 29. April 2000 in Bad Radkersburg.* (Universitätsforschungen zur Prähistorischen Archäologie 78). Bonn: Rudolf Habelt, 289–96.

Tomičić, Ž. & Dizdar, M. 2005. Grobovi latenske kulture s Velikog polja u Zvonimirovu – rezultati istraživanja 1993–1995. *Prilozi Instituta za Arheologiju u Zagrebu* 22: 59–125.

Tonkova, M. 1997. Traditions and Aegean influences on the jewellery of Thracia in Early Hellenistic times (sic). *Archaeologia Bulgarica* 1 (2): 18–31.

Tonkova, M. 2002. Aristokratichni ukrasi ot 5v.pr.Hr. v Trakiya. In Gitcheva, R. & Rabadzhiev, K. (eds.), *ΠΙΤΥΕ. Izsledvaniya v Chest na Prof. Ivan Marazov.* Sofia: Anubis, 494–505.

Tonkova, M. 2007. Jewellery Fashion of the Western Pontic Colonies in the Hellenistic Times. In Stefanovich, M. & Angelova, C. (eds.), *PRAE In Honorem Henrieta Todorova.* Sofia: Archaeological Institute with Museum, 279–94.

Torbov, N. 2005. *Moghilanskata Mogila vav Vratsa.* Vratsa: Mayobo.

Torelli, M. 1975. *Elogia Tarquiniensia.* Firenze: Sansoni.

Trachsel, M. 2004. *Untersuchungen zur Relativen und Absoluten Chronologie der Hallstattzeit.* (Universitätsforschungen zur prähistorischen Archäologie 104). Bonn: R. Habelt.

Trigger, B. G. 1984. Alternative Archaeologies: Nationalist, Colonialist, Imperialist. *Man* 19 (3): 355–70.

Trigger, B. G. 1995. Romanticism, nationalism and archaeology. In Kohl, P. L. & Fawcett, C. (eds.), *Nationalism, Politics and the Practice of Archaeology.* Cambridge: Cambridge University Press, 263–79.

Trigger, B. G. 1996. Alternative Archaeologies: Nationalist, Colonialist, Imperialist. In Preucel, R. & Hodder, I. (eds.), *Contemporary Archaeology in Theory.* Malden: Blackwell Publishing, 615–31.

Trigger, B. G. 2003. *Understanding Early Civilizations: a Comparative Study.* Cambridge: Cambridge University Press.

Trigger, B. G. 2006. *A History of Archaeological Thought.* Cambridge: Cambridge University Press.

Trohani, G. 2006. *Locuirea Getică din Partea de Nord a Popinei Borduşani (com. Borduşani, jud. Ialomiţa).* Târgovişte: Editura Cetatea de Scaun.

Trunk, M. 2007. Anmerkungen zum römischen Theater von Belginum. In Cordie, R. (ed.), *Belginum. 50 Jahre Ausgrabungen und Forschungen*. Mainz: Verlag Philipp von Zabern, 321–32.

Tsetskhladze, G. R. 1998a. Greek Colonisation of the Black Sea Area: Stages, Models, and Native Population. In Tsetskhladze, G. R. (ed.), *The Greek Colonisation of the Black Sea Area: Historical Interpretation of Archaeology*. (Historia Einzelschrift 121). Stuttgart: Franz Steiner, 9–68.

Tsetskhladze, G. R. 1998b. Who built the Scythian and Thracian royal and elite tombs. *Oxford Journal of Archaeology* 17 (1): 55–92.

Tsetskhladze, G. R. 2000. Pistiros in the system of Pontic Emporia (Greek Trading and Craft Settlements in the Hinterland of the Northern and Eastern Black Sea and Elsewhere). In Domaradzki, M., Domaradzka, L., Bouzek, J. & Rostropowicz, J. (eds.), *Pistiros et Thasos: Structures Économiques dans la Péninsule Balkanique aux VIIe – IIe Siècles avant J.-C*. Opole: Zuk Vogar, 233–46.

Turcu, M. 1976. Les bols à reliefs des collections du Musée d'Histoire du Municipe de Bucarest. *Dacia* 20: 199–204.

Turcu, M. 1979. *Geto-dacii din Câmpia Munteniei*. București: Editura Științifică și Enciclopedică.

Turner, J. C., Hogg, M. A., Oakes, P. J., Reicher, S. D. & Wetherell, M. S. 1987. *Rediscovering the Social Group: A Self-Categorization Theory*. New York: Basil Blackwell.

Tylor, E. B. 2010 [1871]. *Primitive Culture*. Cambridge: Cambridge University Press.

Tzochev, C. 2009. Notes on the Thasian amphora stamps chronology. *Archaeologica Bulgarica* 14 (1): 55–72.

Ucko, P. J. 1995. *Theory in Archaeology*. London and New York: Routledge.

Ugolini, L. M. 1934. *Malta. Origini della Civiltà Mediterranea*. Roma: La Libreria dello Stato.

Ursachi, V. 1995. *Zargidava. Cetatea Dacică de la Brad*. (Bibliotheca Thracologica 10). Bucuresti: SC Cardo Trading SRL.

Ursachi, V., Istina, L. E. & Plantos, C. 2003. Răcătău de Jos, com. Horgești, jud. Bacău. Punct: Movila lui Cerbu In Anonymous (ed.), *Cronica Cercetărilor Arheologice din România. Campania 2002*. www.cimec.ro/Arheologie/cronicaCA2003/cd/index.htm

Vaida, L. D. 2003. Cimitirul celtic de la Fântânele (punctul "La Gâța") – informare privind cercetările arheologice. *Arhiva Someșană* 2: 11–8.

Vaida, L. D. 2009. Preliminary considerations regarding the Celtic cemetery from Fântânele (the point – La Gâța). In Sîrbu, V. & Vaida, D. L. (eds.), *Funerary Practices of the Bronze and Iron Ages in Central and South-Eastern Europe, Proceedings of the 9th International Colloquium of Funerary Archaeology from Bistrița, May 9th-11th, 2008*. Cluj-Napoca: Editura Mega, 237–46.

Van der Sleen, W. G. N. 1973. *A Handbook on Beads*. Librarie Halbart: Liege.

van Dommelen, P. A. R. 1998. Punic Resistance: Colonialism and Cultural Identities in Roman Identities. In Lawrence, R. & Berry, J. (eds.), *Cultural Identity in the Roman Empire*. London: Routledge, 25–48.

van Dommelen, P. A. R. 2007. Beyond Resistance: Roman Power and Local Traditions in Punic Sardinia. In van Dommelen, P. A. R. & Terrenato, N. (eds.), *Articulating Local Cultures, Power and Identity under the Expanding Roman Republic*. Portsmouth (Rhode Island): Journal of Roman Archaeology, 55–70.

van Dommelen, P. A. R. & Rowlands, M. 2011. Material concerns and colonial encounters. In Maran, J. & Stockhammer, P. (eds.), *Materiality and Practice. Transformative Capacities of Intercultural Encounters*. Oxford: Oxbow Books, 20–31.

Van Dyke, R. M. 2007. Memory, place and the memorilization of landscape. In David, B. & Thomas, J. (eds.), *Handbook of Landscape Archaeology*. (Word Archaeological Congress Research Handbooks in Archaeology). Wallnut Creek (CA): Left Coast Press, 277–84.

Van Hal, T. 2013–4. From Alauda to Zythus: collecting and interpreting Old-Gaulish words in Early Modern Europe. *Keltische Forschungen* 6: 225–283.

Vasić, R. 1973. *Kulturne Grupe Starijeg Gvozdenog Doba u Jugoslaviji = The Early Iron Age Cultural Groups in Yugoslavia*. (Posebna izdanja Arheološki institut 12). Beograd: Arheološki institut.

Vasić, R. 1977. *The Chronology of the Early Iron Age in Serbia*. (BAR Supplementary Series 31). Oxford: Archaeopress.

Vasić, R. 1982. O početku gvozdenog doba u Srbiji. *Starinar* 32: 1–7.

Vasić, R. 1987a. Bosutska grupa. In Benac, A. (ed.), *Praistorija Jugoslavenskih Zemalja V, Željezno Doba*. Sarajevo: Posebna izdanja Akademije nauka i umjetnosti Bosne i Hercegovine, Odjeljenje za društvene nauke, 536–54.

Vasić, R. 1987b. Centralnobalkanska regija. In Benac, A. (ed.), *Praistorija Jugoslovenskih Zemalja V: Zeljezno Doba*. Sarajevo: Akademija nauka i umjetnosti Bosne i Hercegovine, Centar za balkanološka ispitivanja, 571–724.

Vasić, R. 1987c. Oblast istočnog Kosova, Južne Srbije i istočne Makedonije. In Benac, A. (ed.), *Praistorija Jugoslavenskih Zemalja V: Zeljezno Doba,*. Sarajevo: Akademija nauka i umjetnosti Bosne i Hercegovine, Centar za balkanološka ispitivanja, 673–89.

Vasić, R. 1990. The early Iron Age in southern Serbia and Kosovo. In Jevtović, J. (ed.), *Masters of Silver: the Iron Age in Serbia*. Belgrade, Novi Sad & Priština: National Museum, Belgrade, Museum of Vojvodina & Museum of Kosovo, 119–23.

Vasić, R. 1995. Srebrni nakit IV veka pre n. e. na teritoriji srednjeg Podunavlja. In Popović, I., Cvjetićanin, T. & Borić-Brešković, B. (eds.), *Radionice i Kovnice Srebra: Akta Naučnog Skupa Održanog od 15. do 18. Novembra 1994 Godine u Narodnom Muzeju u Beogradu*. Beograd: Narodni muzej, 83–91.

Vasić, R. 2001. Gold and Silver in Iron Age Serbia. *Archaeologia Bulgarica* 5 (3): 23–8.

Vasić, R. 2005. Srebrni nalaz iz Nikinaca. *Starinar* 55: 67–73.

Vasiliev, V. 1976. Necropola de la Băiţa şi problema tracizării enclavei scitice din Transilvania. *Marisia* 6: 49–87.

Vasiliev, V. 1980. *Sciţii Agatârşi pe Teritoriul României*. Cluj-Napoca: Editura Dacia.

Vasiliev, V. 1999. Date noi despre necropola de incineraţie de la sfârşitul primei vârste a fierului, descoperită la Uioara de Sus (judeţul Alba). *Thraco-Dacica* 20 (1–2): 181–8.

Vasiliev, V. 2004. À propos de quelques aspects concernant le groupe scythique de l'aire Intracarpatique de la Transylvanie. In Chochorowskiego, J. (ed.), *Kimmerowie, Scytowie, Sarmaci. Księga Poświęcona Pamięci, Profesora Tadeusza Sulimirskiego*. Kraków: Księg. Akademicka, 465–71.

Vasiliev, V. & Zrinyi, A. 1974. Necropola scitică de la Ozd. *File de Istorie* 3: 89–137.

Vassileva, M. 2010. *Representations of Status: Women's Visibility in the Archaeological Record of Phrygia and Thrace*. The Hague: Unpublished conference paper from 16th Annual Meeting of the European Association of Archaeologists.

Veit, U. 1984. Gustaf Kossinna und V. Gordon Childe. Ansätze zu einer theoretischen Grundlegung der Vorgeschichte. *Saeculum* 35: 236–64.

Veit, U. 2008. Zur Einführung. In Kümmel, C., Schweizer, B. & Veit, U. (eds.), *Körperinszenierung – Objektsammlung – Monumentalisierung: Totenritual und Grabkult in Frühen Gesellschaften*. (Tübinger ArchäologischeTaschenbücher 6). Münster: Waxmann Verlag GmbH, 17–30.

Venedikov, I. 1966. Novootkrito trakiysko mogilno pogrebenie vav Vratsa. *Arheologia* 8 (1): 7–15.

Venedikov, I. 1977. La condition de la femme en Thrace antique. *Thracia* 4: 163–75.

Verger, S. (ed.). 2000. *Rites et Espaces en Pays Celte et Méditerranéen. Étude Comparée à Partir du Sanctuaire d'Acy-Romance (Ardennes, France)*. Rome: École française de Rome.

Verger, S. 2009. Société, politique et religion en Gaule avant la conquête. Éléments pour une étude anthropologique. *Pallas* 80: 61–82.

Vernesi, C., Caramelli, D., Dupanloup, I., Bertorelle, G., Lari, M., Cappellini, E., Moggi-Cecchi, J., Chiarelli, B., Castrì, L., Casoli, A., Mallegni, F., Lalueza-Fox, C. & Barbujani, G. 2004. The Etruscans: A Population-Genetic Study. *American Journal of Human Genetics* 74 (4): 694–704.

Vidović, J. 1990. Nekropola tumula kraj sela Dvorišća kod Turčišća u Međimurju. *Izdanja HAD-a sv* 14: 77–88.

Vidović, J. 2003. Pogrebni ritus u grobnim humkama Međimurja. *Izdanja HAD-a sv* 21: 57–78.

Vinski, Z. & Vinski-Gasparini, K. 1962. O utjecajima istočno-alpske halštatske kulture i balkanske ilirske kulture na slavonsko-sremsko Podunavlje. *Arheološki Radovi i Rasprave* 2: 263–93.

Vinski-Gasparini, K. 1961. Iskopavanje kneževskog tumula kod Martijanca u Podravini. *Vjesnik Arheološkog Muzeja u Zagrebu, 3rd ser* 2: 39–66.

Vinski-Gasparini, K. 1973. *Kultura Polja sa Žarama u Sjevernoj Hrvatskoj*. (Monografije 1). Zadar: Filozofski fakultet u Zadru.

Vinski-Gasparini, K. 1983. Kultura polja sa žarama sa svojim grupama, U. In Benac, A. (ed.), *Praistorija Jugoslavenskih Zemalja IV, Brončano Doba*. Sarajevo: Posebna izdanja Akademije nauka i umjetnosti Bosne i Hercegovine, Odjeljenje za društvene nauke, 547–646.

Vinski-Gasparini, K. 1987. Grupa Martijanec-Kaptol. In Benac, A. (ed.), *Praistorija Jugoslavenskih Zemalja V, Željezno Doba*. Sarajevo: Posebna izdanja

Akademije nauka i umjetnosti Bosne i Hercegovine, Odjeljenje za društvene nauke, 182–231.

Viollier, D. 1912. Le cimetière gallo-helvéte d´Andelfingen (Zürich). *Anzeiger der Schweizer Altertumskunde* N.F. 14: 16–57.

Volpert, H.-P. 2002. Neue Körpergräber der Heimstettener Gruppe. *Das Archäologische Jahr in Bayern* 2001: 79–82.

Volpert, H.-P. 2006. Die "Heimstettener Gruppe". In Sommer, C. S. (ed.), *Archäologie in Bayern: Fenster zur Vergangenheit*. Regensburg: Verlag Friedrich Pustet, 196.

von Schnurbein, S. 2006. Germanen und Römer im Vorfeld des obergermanischen Limes. *Bericht der Römisch-Germanischen Kommission* 87: 19–40.

Vranić, I. 2009. Theoretical and methodological problems of the interpretation of the pottery material from the site Kale in Krševica. (in Serbian with an English summary). *Recueil du Musée National (Archéologie)* 19 (1): 163–204.

Vranić, I. 2011a. "Early classical settlements" and the Iron Age of the Central Balkans: Issues of ethnic identity. Ethno-archaeology in Serbia. (in Serbian with an English and French summaries). *Issues in Ethnology and Anthropology* n.s. 6 (3): 659–78.

Vranić, I. 2011b. "Ranoantička naselja" i gvozdeno doba centralnog Balkana: pitanja etničkog identiteta. *Issues in Ethnology and Anthropology* 6 (3): 659–79.

Vulpe, A. 1967. *Necropola Hallstattiană de la Ferigile Monografie Archeologică*. București: Academiei Republicii Socialiste România.

Vulpe, A. 1976. La nécropole tumulaire gète de Popești. *Thraco-Dacica* 1: 193–215.

Vulpe, A. 1983. Pe marginea a trei cărți noi despre traci Și sciți. *Istros* 2–3: 115–44.

Vulpe, A. 1988. Istoria și civilizația Daciei în sec. IX–IV î.e.n. In Dumitrescu, V. & Vulpe, A. (eds.), *Dacia Înainte de Dromihete*. București: Editura Științifică și Enciclopedică, 85–113.

Vulpe, A. 1989. Cu privire la agatirși. *Symposia Thracologica* 7: 62–70.

Vulpe, A. 1990. *Die Kurzschwerter, Dolche und Streitmesser der Hallstattzeit in Rumänien*. (Prähistorische Bronzefunde 6, 9). München: C.H.Beck.

Vulpe, A. 2003. Problema scitică în România. In Ștefănescu, Ș., Constantiniu, F. & Rusu, D. (eds.), *Identitate Națională și Spirit European. Academicianul Dan Berindei la 80 de Ani*. București: Editura Enciclopedică, 113–34.

Vulpe, A. 2004. Die Agathyrsen. Eine zusammenfassende Darstellung. In Chochorowskiego, J. (ed.), *Kimmerowie, Scytowie, Sarmaci. Księga Poświęcona Pamięci, Profesora Tadeusza Sulimirskiego*. Kraków: Księg. Akademicka, 473–82.

Vulpe, A. 2010. Sfârșitul primei epoci a fierului Și formarea civilizației celei de-a doua epoci a fierului (Hallstattul Târziu: 650–450 Și începuturile Latène-ului: 450–300 a.Chr.). In Petrescu-Dîmbovița, M. & Vulpe, A. (eds.), *Istoria Românilor. Moștenirea Timpurilor Îndepărtate. Vol. I.* (Second edition). București: Editura Enciclopedică, 478–515.

Vulpe, A. 2012. Herodot and the Scythian problem in Romania. *Dacia* N.S. 61: 47–75.

Vulpe, A. & Gheorghiță, M. 1976. Bols à reliefs de Popești. *Dacia* 20: 167–98.

Vulpe, A. & Popescu, E. 1976. Une contribution archéologique à l'étude de la religion des géto-daces. *Thraco-Dacica* 1: 217–26.

Vulpe, R. 1970. Un secol de cercetări asupra epocii fierului în România. *Historica* 1: 9–29.

Vulpe, R. & Teodor, S. 2003. *Piroboridava. Aşezarea Geto-dacică de la Poiana.* (Bibliotheca Thracologica 39). Bucureşti: Vavila Edinf.

Wahida, G. & Wahida, S. 2004a. John Amays Alexander A Short Biography. *Azania: Archaeological Research in Africa* 39 (1): 7–10.

Wahida, G. and S. Wahida 2004b. John Alexander: Fieldwork and Bibliography. *Azania: Archaeological Research in Africa* 39 (1): 337–341.

Wahle, E. 1941. *Zur Ethnischen Deutung Frühgeschichtlicher Kulturprovinzen. Grenzen der Frühgeschichtlichen Erkenntnis I.* (Heidelberger Akademie der Wissenschaften Sitzungsberichte1940–1 2). Heidelberg: Winter Universitatsverlag.

Waldhauser, J. & Arbeitsgruppe 1993. *Die Hallstatt-und Latènezeitliche Siedlung mit Gräberfeld bei Radovesice in Böhmen* (two volumes). Prague: Regionalni muzeum knihovna.

Walker, L. 1984. The deposition of human remains. In Cunliffe, B. (ed.), *Danebury: An Iron Age Hillfort in Hampshire, vol. 2*. London: Council for British Archaeology, 442–63.

Wallace, C. 2006. Long-lived Samian? *Britannia* 37: 259–72.

Wason, P. K. 1994. *The Archaeology of Rank*. Cambridge: Cambridge University Press.

Waterbolk, H. T. & Butler, J. J. 1965. Comments on the use of metallurgical analysis in prehistoric studies. *Helinium* 5 (3): 231–51.

Watkins, T. 1980. Excavation of an Iron Age Open Settlement at Dalladies, Kincardinshire. *Proceedings of the Society of Antiquaries of Scotland* 110: 122–64.

Webber, C. 2001. *The Thracians 700 BC–AD 46*. Oxford: Osprey Publishing.

Webster, J. 2001. Creolizing the Roman Provinces. *American Journal of Archaeology* 105: 209–27.

Weekes, J. 2008. Classification and Analysis of Archaeological Contexts for the Reconstruction of Early Romano-British Cremation Funerals. *Britannia* 39 (1): 145–60.

Weiss-Krejci, E. 2001. Restless corpses: 'secondary' burial in the Babenberg and Habsburg dynasties. *Antiquity* 75 (290): 769–80.

Weiss-Krejci, E. 2004. Mortuary representations of the noble house. A cross-cultural comparison between collective tombs of the ancient Maya and dynastic Europe. *Journal of Social Archaeology* 4 (3): 368–404.

Wellington, I. 2002. Considering Continuity of Deposition on Votive Sites in Northeastern France from 200 BC to AD 100. In Carruthers, M., van-Driel-Murray, C., Gardner, A., Revell, L. & Swift, A. (eds.), *TRAC 2001: Proceedings of the Eleventh Annual Theoretical Roman Archaeology Conference, Glasgow 2001*. Oxford: Oxbow Books, 1–12.

Wells, P. S. 1995. Identities, material culture, and change: "Celts" and "Germans" in Late Iron-Age Europe. *Journal of European Archaeology* 3: 169–85.

Wells, P. S. 1998. Identity and material culture in the later prehistory of Central Europe. *Journal of Archaeological Research* 6 (3): 239–98.

Wells, P. S. 1999. *The Barbarians Speak: How the Conquered Peoples Shaped Roman Europe.* Princeton: Princeton University Press.

Wells, P. S. 2001. *Beyond Celts, Germans and Scythians: Archaeology and Identity in Iron Age Europe.* London: Duckworth.

Wells, P. S. 2005. Creating an Imperial frontier: archaeology of the formation of Rome's Danube borderland. *Journal of Archaeological Research* 15 (1): 49–88.

Wells, P. S. 2006. Objects, meanings and ritual in the emergence of the oppida. In Haselgrove, C. (ed.), *Celtes et Gaulois, l'Archéologie Face à l'Histoire. 4: Les Mutations de la Fin de l'Âge du Fer. Actes de la Table Ronde de Cambridge, 7–8 Juillet 2005*. (Collection Bibracte 12/4). Glux-en-Glenne: Centre archéologique européen, 139–53.

Wells, P. S. 2010. Early Bronze Age pottery at Hascherkeller in Bavaria: visuality, ecological psychology, and the practice of deposition in Bronze Age A2/B1. *Archäologisches Korrespondenzblatt* 40: 191–205.

Wells, P. S. 2011. The ancient Germans. In Bonfante, L. (ed.), *The Barbarians of Ancient Europe: Realities and Interactions*. Cambridge: Cambridge University Press, 211–32.

Wells, P. S. 2012. *How Ancient Europeans Saw the World: Vision, Patterns, and the Shaping of the Mind in Prehistoric Times.* Princeton: Princeton University Press.

Wenskus, R. 1961. *Stammesbildung und Verfassung. Das Werden der Frühmittelalterlichen Gentes.* Cologne/Graz: Böhlau.

Wenskus, R. 1984. Ding. *Reallexikon der Germanischen Altertumskunde* 5: 444–55.

West, S. 1985. Herodotus' Epigraphical Interests. *Classical Quarterly* 79: 278–305.

West, S. 2002. Scythians. In Bakker, E. J., De Jong, I. J. F. & Van Wees, H. (eds.), *Brill's Companion to Herodotus*. Leiden: Brill, 437–56.

Westwood, J. O. 1856. Celtic Ornament. In Jones, O. (ed.), *The Grammar of Ornament*. London: Day and Son, 89–97.

Wheatley, D. 1995. Cumulative viewshed analysis: a GIS-based method for investigating intervisibility, and its archaeological application. In Lock, G. & Stancic, Z. (eds.), *Archaeology and Geographical Information Systems: a European Perspective*. London: Taylor and Francis, 171–85.

Wheatley, D. & Gillings, M. 2000. Vision, perception and GIS: developing enriched approaches to the study of archaeological visibility. In Lock, G. (ed.), *Beyond the Map*. Amsterdam: IOS Press, 1–27.

Whimster, R. 1981. *Iron Age Burial Practice in Britain: a Discussion and Gazetteer of the Evidence c. 700 – AD 43.* (BAR British Series 90). Oxford: British Archaeological Reports.

Whittaker, D. 2009. Ethnic discourses on the frontiers of Roman Africa. In Derks, T. & Roymans, N. (eds.), *Ethnic Constructs in Antiquity: The Role of Power and Tradition*. Amsterdam: Amsterdam University Press, 189–206.

Wieland, G. (ed.). 1999. *Keltische Viereckschanzen. Einem Rätsel auf der Spur.* Stuttgart: Theiss.

Wilkes, J. J. 1992. *The Illyrians.* Oxford: Blackwell.

Wilkes, J. J. & Fischer-Hansen, T. 2004. The Adriatic. In Hansen, M. N. & Nielsen, T. H. (eds.), *An Inventory of Archaic and Classical Poleis: An*

*Investigation Conducted by The Copenhagen Polis Centre for the Danish National Research Foundation*. Oxford: Oxford University Press, 321–37.

Wilkins, J. B. 1990. Nation and language in Ancient Italy: problems of linguistic evidence. *Accordia Research Papers* 1: 53–72.

Wilkins, J. B. 1991. Power and idea networks: theoretical notes on urbanisation in the early Mediterranean and Italy. In Herring, E., Whitehouse, R. & Wilkins, J. B. (eds.), *Papers of the Fourth Conference of Italian Archaeology 1. The Archaeology of Power, Part 1*. London: Accordia, 221–30.

Williams, D. & Ogden, J. 1994. *Greek Gold: Jewellery of the Classical World*. London: British Museum.

Williams, H. 2003. Objects without a past? The use of Roman objects in early Anglo-Saxon graves. In Williams, H. (ed.), *Archaeologies of Remembrance: Death and Memory in Past Societies*. New York: Kluwer/Plenum, 141–7.

Willis, S. 1997. Samian: Beyond Dating. In Meadows, K., Lemke, C. & Heron, J. (eds.), *TRAC 96: Proceedings of the Sixth Annual Theoretical Roman Archaeology Conference: Hosted by the Research School of Archaeology & Archaeological Science, the University of Sheffield, March 30th & 31st 1996*. Oxford: Oxbow Books, 38–54.

Willis, S. 1999. Without and Within: aspects of culture and community in the Iron Age of north-eastern England. In Bevan, B. (ed.), *Northern Exposure: Interpretative Devolution and the Iron Ages in Britain*. Leicester: School of Archaeological Studies, 81–111.

Wilson, D. 1851. *The Archaeology and Prehistoric Annals of Scotland*. Edinburgh: Sutherland and Knox.

Wilson, D. 1854. Discovery of Bronze Vessels at Cockburnspath, Berwickshire. *Proceedings of the Society of Antiquaries of Scotland* 1: 43–4.

Wodtko, D. 2010. Ancillary Study: the problem of Lusitanian. In Cunliffe, B. & Koch, J. (eds.), *Celtic from the West: Alternative Perspectives from Archaeology, Genetics, Language and Literature*. Oxford: Oxbow Books, 335–68.

Wolf, E. R. 1982. *Europe and the People without History*. Berkeley: University of California Press.

Woodward, S. 2005. Looking good: feeling right-aesthetics of the self. In Küchler, S. & Miller, D. (eds.), *Clothing as Material Culture*. Oxford: Berg, 21–39.

Woolf, A. 1998. Romancing the Celts: A Segmentary Approach to Acculturation. In Lawrence, R. & Berry, J. (eds.), *Cultural Identity in the Roman Empire*. London: Routledge, 111–24.

Woolf, G. 1993. Rethinking the Oppida. *Oxford Journal of Archaeology* 12 (2): 321–36.

Woolf, G. 1998. *Becoming Roman: the Origins of Provincial Civilization in Gaul*. Cambridge: Cambridge University Press.

Woolf, G. 2003. The Social Significance of Trade in Late Iron Age Europe. In Scarre, C. & Healy, F. (eds.), *Trade and Exchange in Prehistoric Europe. Proceedings of a Conference Held at the University of Bristol, April 1992*. Oxford: Oxbow Books, 211–8.

Worrell, S. 2007. Detecting the Later Iron Age: a view from the Portable Antiquities Scheme. In Haselgrove, C. & Moore, T. (eds.), *The Later Iron Age in Britain and Beyond*. Oxford: Oxbow Books, 371–88.

Woźniak, Z. 1974. *Wschodnie Pogranicze Kultury Lateńskiej*. Wrocław: Zakład Narodowy im. Ossolińskich.

Xenopol, A. D. 1888. *Istoria Românilor. Dacia Anteromană, Dacia Romană Şi Năvălirile Barbare. 513 înainte de Hr.-1290. Vol. I.* Iaşi: Tipo Litografia H. Goldner.

Yoffee, N. 2005. *Myths of the Archaic State. Evolution of the Earliest Cities, States and Civilisations*. Cambridge: Cambridge University Press.

Yonge, C. D. 1862. *The Roman History of Ammianus Marcellinus (During the Reign of the Emperors Constantius, Julian, Jovianus, Valentinian, and Valens)*. London: H.G. Bohn.

Yordanov, K. 1990. Politicheski otnosheniya mezhdu traki i skiti. *Vekove* 19 (5): 5–12.

Yordanov, K. 2003. Achaemenido-Thracica: Attempts at Political and Administrative Control (ca. 515–466 BC). *Thracia* 15 (In honorem annorum LXX Alexandri Fol): 39–54.

Yordanov, Y. 2000. Plastic anthropological reconstruction of the head by the skull of the Thracian princess of Vratsa (IV century BC). *Acta Morphologica et Anthropologica* 5: 121–8.

Young, D. 2006. The colour of things. In Tilley, C., Keane, W., Kuechler-Fogden, S., Rowlands, M. & Spyer, P. (eds.), *Handbook of Material Culture*. London- Thousand Oaks (CA): Sage Publications, 173–85.

Zahrnt, M. 1997. Die Perser in Thrakien. *Actes. 2e Symposium International des Études Thraciennes. Thrace Ancienne*. Komotini: Musée Archéologique de Komotini, 91–9.

Zanier, W. 2004. Ende der Nauheimer Fibeln in früher römischer Kaiserzeit? *Archäologisches Korrespondenzblatt* 34: 65–80.

Zanier, W. 2006. Ausklang – Die Zeit von ca. 50 v. Chr. bis um Christi Geburt. In Sommer, C. S. (ed.), *Archäologie in Bayern: Fenster zur Vergangenheit*. Regensburg: Verlag Friedrich Pustet, 190–93.

Zeeb-Lanz, A. 2008. *Der Donnersberg. Eine Bedeutende Spätkeltische Stadtanlage*. (Archäologische Denkmäler in der Pfalz 2). Speyer: Direktion Landesarchäologie Speyer.

Zipf, G. 2004. *Studien zu den Anfängen Figürlicher Darstellungen im Endbronze- und Früheisenzeitlichen Frankreich und Italien*. Berlin: Unpublished PhD Thesis, Fachbereich Geschichts- und Kulturwissenschaften, Freie Universität.

Zirra, V. 1967. *Un Cimitir Celtic în Nord-vestul României*. Baia Mare: Muzeul Regional Maramures.

Zirra, V. 1975a. Influence des géto-daces et de leurs voisins sur l'habitat celtique de Transylvanie. *Alba Regia* 14: 47–64.

Zirra, V. 1975b. Aspects of the Relations between Dacians and Celts in Transylvania. In Constantinescu, M., Pascu, Ş. & Diaconu, P. (eds.), *Relations between the Autochthonous Population and the Migratory Populations on the Territory of Romania: a Collection of Studies*. Bucureşti: Editura Academiei

Republicii Socialiste România, 25–34.

Zirra, V. 1976. La nécropole La Tène d'Apahida. *Dacia* n. s. 20: 129–65.

Zirra, V. 1980. Locuiri din a doua vârstă a fierului în nord-vestul României (Aşezarea contemporană cimitirului La Tène de la Ciumeşti şi habitatul indigen de la Berea, jud. Satu Mare). *Satu Mare. Studii şi Comunicări* 4: 39–84.

Zirra, V. V. 1997. Contribuţii la cronologia relativă a cimitirului de la Pişcolt, Analiză combinatorie şi stratigrafie orizontală. *Studii şi Cercetări de Istorie Veche şi Arheologie* 48 (2): 87–137.

Zotović, R. 2003. Romanization of the population of the eastern part of the province of Dalmatia. *Balcanica* 34: 19–38.

# Index

Achaemenid empire 44, 157, 159
Adria 276
Adriatic 60, 123, 132, 168, 255, 277–8
Adzijska Vodenica (Vetren) (Pistiros) 166–7
Aedui 143, 295
Aegean 44, 50, 75, 157–9, 163, 168, 284, 294
Aestiones 295
Afghanistan 109
Africa 1, 312, 317
Agathyrsi 76–7, 79–81, 83–7, 147
Age 249, 258
Agriculture 22, 145, 264
    Cycle 221
    Labour 78, 264
    Land 63
    Tools 264, 316
Airlie School (Angus) 219
Aitnock dun (North Ayrshire) 221
Alamani 329
Albania 4, 162, 164, 166–9, 249
Alexander the Great 159, 165, 170–1
Alexander, John 1–2
Alfred, King 324
Alpine (area) 6, 60, 68, 132, 137, 203
Amantia 168
Ambarri 142
Amber 123, 132, 256
Ambigatus 142
Amphorae
    Greek, 59, 163
    Roman 49–52, 60–1, 312, 315–6, 319
Ampurias (Emporion) 302
ancestor(s) 21, 99, 108, 164, 166, 168–9, 270, 273, 325, 327
ancient author(s) 6, 36, 87, 90, 99, 101, 104, 142, 266–7, 269, 278, 291, 299, 328
Antigoneia 168
Apahida 14
Apulia(n) (Puglia) 250, 255–6, 263
    Red figure 256

Acquarossa 275
Armit, Ian 248
Armour *see* weaponry
Arthur, King 324
Asia 312, 329
Asia Minor 33, 52, 54, 104, 157
Assemblies 175–6, 178, 180, 182, 185
Athens 323
Asturians 304
Attic red-figure 162, 256
Augustus, Emperor 311
Aulerci 143
Austria(n) 23–4, 77, 202–8, 285, 298, 307
Austro-Hungarian
    Empire 285, 289
    Excavations 167
Autariatae 101
Arverni 143, 186, 292, 295
Avile Tite 270
Aymard, Andre 299–300

Babić, Staša 4, 6, 324
Bačka 126–7
Baden-Württemberg 197
Balkans 17, 58, 91–2, 98, 99–101, 104–5, 107, 123, 127, 130–1, 135, 161–2, 165–9, 172, 203, 266, 286, 304, 324
    central 5, 97, 101, 162, 172, 288
    northern 145, 147, 155
    western 60, 92
Baranja 126
Barbarian (savage) 49, 62, 90, 105, 160, 165, 172, 284, 292, 308
Bare hoard 93–5
Barth, Frederik 327
Basilicata 244, 249–51, 253, 264
Basel 312
Batina 123–4, 127–8
Bavaria, Bavarians 144, 203, 311, 314, 317–20, 329
Bede, Venerable 295–6
Bellovesus 142

Benac, Alojz 98–100
Bibracte 179–80, 182, 185, 329
Biferno Valley 250
Bila Cerkva 153–5
Biological Anthropology 38, 78, 256, 261, 262, 263
Bituriges 143
Blackburn Mill 220
Black Sea 48, 50, 52, 56, 59, 157–9
Bleidenberg 179–80
Blending (of material culture) 318–22
Blera 273
Bohemia 144, 297–8, 309–10
Boljetin 93–4
Bologna 324
Book of Kells 297
Bordușani 52
Bosnia 128, 132
Bosut Group 126–7, 135
Bourdieu, Pierre 200, 214, 222
Brad (by Siter River) 52, 56, 72, 117, 120
Braida di Vaglio 250
Bronze Age 75, 97–8, 100, 126, 323, 328–9, 219, 277, 313
   Beginning 297
   Early 100
   Middle 132
   Urnfield 18, 20, 23–6, 29, 124, 126, 127, 128, 130, 131,
   Late(r) 123–4, 127, 161, 225, 302
   Final 268
   End 100, 241, 244
Bronzework(ing) 14, 43, 45, 54, 56, 58, 60–1, 75, 78, 94, 117, 121, 130, 132, 137, 139, 151, 176, 179, 219, 220, 221, 246–50, 258, 262, 264, 271, 277, 297, 312, 315, 316
   Casting 14, 130, 246
   Moulds 52, 130
Brooch *see* Dress
Broxmouth hillfort 221
Brutus (Trojan) 295
Buchanan, George 295, 302
Budinjak 124, 126, 128
Bulgaria 4, 33–61, 162, 164, 166–7, 168–9, 171

burial practice (graves) 4, 6, 12–4, 18, 22, 24, 26–8, 34–44. 46–7, 52, 56, 58, 59, 76, 78, 86, 108–22, 126–8, 130–2, 135, 137, 139, 144–55, 158, 163, 200–208, 217, 219, 223, 249, 254–65, 270, 276–7, 292, 298, 309, 312, 316–22.
   Barrow/Tumulus burials 18, 19, 21, 22, 24–32, 28, 33, 44–5, 52, 56, 59, 62, 116, 111, 115, 116, 117, 118–9, 121–2, 126, 128–31, 134–6, 139, 150
   Beaker 297–8
   Bi-ritual 12, 81, 42, 78, 81
   Cart 147
   *Cassa* 255, 256, 258
   Cenotaph 109, 114, 115, 116,
   Chambered tombs 38, 43, 255, 258
   Cremation 12, 13, 18, 24, 26, 27, 42, 79, 81, 86, 108, 111, 114, 115, 116, 118, 119, 121, 122, 126–8, 130, 132, 135, 147, 150, 155, 217, 219, 293, 298, 305, 318, 319
   Crouched 12, 13, 217, 255, 298
   *Enchytrimoi* 255, 258
   Flat cemeteries 18, 22, 24, 26, 27, 28, 29, 78, 111, 113, 114, 115, 116, 119, 121, 126, 135, 141, 147, 315
   *Fossa* (trench) 255, 256, 258
   Horse 39, 135, 147
   Inhumation 12, 13, 42, 44, 78, 79, 81, 85, 86, 108, 111, 113, 114, 116, 118, 120, 121, 127, 128, 132, 135, 147, 150, 204, 217, 225, 255, 298, 305, 318, 319
   Inurned 12, 13, 22, 24, 27, 150
   Long Barrow 297
   Ring-ditch 21, 22, 24, 27, 28
   Sarcophagus 256, 258, 272
   Urnfield 18
   *See* Ritual, Funerary
Burebista 48–9, 62
Butler, Judith 214
Byllis 168

Caesar 176, 182, 206, 291, 295, 299, 307–08, 311
Cairnhill (Aberdeenshire) 219

Cairnholly 220
Camden, William 295
Camelon 217
Campania 244, 249, 250, 251, 252, 253, 266
Campo della Fiera (Orvieto) 279
Capua 276
Carnutes 142
Carpathian(s) (mountains) n 5, 48, 52, 54, 56, 58–60, 62, 72, 83, 110, 112, 115–16, 127, 135, 147, 152–3, 155–7
Carpathian Basin 11, 13–17, 76, 110, 142–6, 153, 155–6, 203
Cassius Dio 75
Cetățeni 52
Celtic
   area 13
   Art 291, 296–8
   communities 11, 137, 147, 150, 153
   groups 13, 76, 144, 147, 150, 152–3, 155
   identity 5, 136
   language 291, 296, 300–4
Celtiberians 299–301, 303
Celticisation 135–7
Celts 3–4, 11–5, 17, 79, 83, 89, 104–5, 108, 136, 142, 159–60, 291–2, 294–304, 306–10, 313, 317–8, 320–1, 323–4, 328, 330
Centuripe 323
Cemeteries *see* Burial practices
Central Balkan tribes 91, 97, 101–2
Ceramics
   Apulian 250, 256,
   Askos 43
   Beaker 52, 54, 56, 58, 60–1, 153, 217
   Bell Beaker 304
   Campanian 250, 252
   Chytra(i) 257, 258
   Craters 54, 56, 256–7, 262
   Daunian 277
   Hellenistic 14, 15, 54, 162–3
   *Kantharoi* 54–8, 136–7, 257
   *Lopades* 257–8
   Mould 52–3
   Roman 56, 215, 217, 220
Cerveteri (Caere) 271, 272, 275

Chalcolithic *see* Eneolithic
Chernozem *see* Kaloyanovo-Chernozem
Childe, Gordon 172, 187, 212, 292, 293, 330
Chotin 152
Christaller, Walter 198–9
Christlein, Rainer 318
Cimbri 294–5, 311
Cimmerians 83, 295
Cingetorix *see* Vercingetorix
Ciumbrud 76–8, 81, 84–8, 147
Ciumeşti 13, 143, 153
Civitas/civitates 105, 177, 180, 182, 183
Clarke, David 1, 188, 192, 293
Clark, Grahame 293
Classical
   Architecture 170
   Civilisation 158–60, 165, 167, 285, 286
   Period 158–9
Claudius 66
Clemency 316
Colonia Ulpia Traiana Augusta Dacica *See* Sarmizegetusa
cluster analysis/clustering 111, 115, 122, 193–6
coins/coinage 58, 66, 94, 95, 104, 106, 163, 176, 178, 179, 182, 215, 275, 293, 306, 312, 314, 315
colonisation 11, 16, 143, 145, 147, 150, 153, 155–6, 168
Collis, John 4, 6, 187
Colour 81, 223, 228, 231–7
convivial practice(s) and material culture 5, 39, 43–4, 46, 48, 49, 50, 52, 54, 56, 58, 59, 60, 61–2, 72, 110, 175, 184, 256, 257, 259–60, 264, 271, 316
Corent 182–3, 186
Cosmetic instruments 139, 256, 225
Costume *See* Dress
Côté, James 254
Cotu-Copălău 153
Cramond 217
Cremation *see* burial practice
Creolisation 143
Cristofani, Mauro 270

Croatia 4, 6, 23, 123–41, 266, 276–8
Crosskirk (Caithness) 219
Cuisine 152
   *See* convivial practices
Culbin Sands (Morayshire) 231
Culduthel Farm (Inverness) 231
culture-history 161, 292–4, 305
Cunliffe, Barry 301–03
Czech Republic 294, 307, 309, 310

Dacia 49–50, 54, 58, 59, 72, 74, 82–3
Dacian
   communities 13, 59
   religion 49, 64
   kingdom 64, 68, 75
Dacians 5, 13, 14, 48–9, 62, 70, 81, 95, 108, 328
Daco-Moesian 169
Dalladies souterrain (Aberdeenshire) 221
Dalj (Group) 123–4, 126–8, 135
Daniel, Glyn 284, 287–8
Danebury 118
Danube river 48, 50, 58, 60, 62, 83, 86, 93, 94, 95, 104–5, 107, 115, 123, 126–8, 130, 135, 137–8, 144–5, 147, 150–3, 203, 286, 302, 306, 311–3, 315, 317, 318, 320, 321
D'Arbois de Jubainville, Henri 297, 298
Dardanian 102–04, 106, 162, 168
Dardanians 16, 99, 101–04, 106, 168–9
Darwin, Charles (Darwinian evolution) 187, 297
Daunia(n) 244, 249–51, 276, 278
Daunians 255, 323
Dawkins, Richard 191
Decebalus 64, 68, 70
Deceneus 48
Dechelette, Joseph 297–9, 305
Delphi 104, 204
Demoule, Jean-Paul 187
Deskford 220
Diana, Goddess 179
Díaz-Andreu, Margarita 326
Dietler, Michael 259
Donja Dolina (Group) 128, 132
Dolina 124, 128

Domitian 94, 95
Donnersberg 179
Dornach 144
Dowalton Loch 220
Dress (clothing, costume and personal ornaments) 6, 28, 35, 44, 61, 84, 113, 114, 116, 117, 128, 130, 131, 132, 135, 137, 144, 145, 206–8, 220, 223, 224–6, 234, 237–8, 312, 315, 316, 319, 321
   Ankle-ring 114
   Bead 14, 28, 40, 42, 43, 113, 117, 132, 217, 223–38, 256,
   Belt (hook/plate) 45, 95, 117, 262, 264, 308, 312, 314, 315, 316, 318, 320
   Bracelet 14, 15, 24, 27, 28, 94, 95, 135, 205, 206, 217, 220, 223, 225, 315, 320
   Earring 37, 40, 42, 43, 117, 135
   Fibula(e) (Brooch) 1, 13, 14, 28, 39, 43, 78, 113, 116, 117, 176, 178, 206, 217, 221, 223, 225, 227, 247, 256, 262, 298, 308, 312–6, 318, 320, 322
      Beltz J fibula 308, 310
      Crossbow brooch 220
      Early La Tène 132, 135, 151, 308, 309
      Jezerine 117
      La Tène 187
      Nauheim fibula 178, 308, 310, 315, 322
   Necklace 40–4, 113, 116–7, 120, 145, 206
   Pendant 43, 113, 130, 179, 256
      Amphora-shaped 43
      Axe-shaped 93–5
      Bucket 113, 117
   Pins 1, 132
   Ring (finger) 39, 41, 42, 44, 45, 46, 179, 206, 225, 237
   Torc 223, 225
Drinking *see* convivial practices
Drusus 311, 313
Duchcov hoard 298
Dun Mor Vaul (Tiree) 219
Duval, Pierre-Marie 298

Duvanlii 37, 40–1, 43–4, 46
Dvorišće 128
Džino, Danijel 105

Eching 317, 319–21
Eggers, Hans Jürgen 330
Egri, Mariana 5, 110
Egypt(ian) 284, 295
Eicher, Joanne 226
Eischleben 317, 320
Ehret, Christopher 312
Elymians 323
Emic 102, 324
Eneolithic 97, 98, 100
Entanglement (cultural) 270, 276–7, 321
Entwistle, Joanne 226
Environment
Erickstanebrae 220
Este 278
ethnic group 3, 87, 98, 100, 141, 158–9, 182, 214–5, 328–30
ethnicity 3–5, 14, 89–91, 95–6, 97–101, 104–5, 107, 108, 136, 161–5, 168–72, 175–6, 200, 212, 214–5, 223–4, 254, 266, 268–9, 275–6, 278–9, 291, 304–5, 308, 324, 326, 328–30
ethnogenesis/ethno-genesis 82, 84, 98, 100, 104, 162, 164, 168
Etruria 4, 249, 268–9, 273, 275, 278
Etruscan
  identity 6, 267–9, 275–6
  centre(s) 248
  ethnicity 276, 279
  language 267, 273
Etruscans 6, 266–8, 270–1, 273–9, 323–4, 329
Eurasia 80
Europe
  central 4, 6, 13, 17, 33, 77, 123–4, 127, 130–1, 135, 137, 150, 152, 156, 160, 169, 200, 247, 249, 294–5, 298, 300, 302, 304
  eastern 160, 288, 302, 304, 325
  northern 123, 269
  south east 3–5, 81, 108, 123, 128, 157–8, 160–1, 283
  southern 311, 315

  temperate 72, 176, 185, 306, 308–10, 312, 314–6, 323, 328
  western 4, 6, 142, 284–5, 289, 295, 297, 304, 306, 312
Evans-Pritchard, Edward 214
Exchange 19, 47, 52, 59, 63, 128, 132, 138, 178, 198, 244, 263, 270, 315, 320

Fan 266, 277
Fântânele 12–14, 76, 150–2
Feasting see convivial practices
Filip, Jan 298
Florence 323
Forteviot 217
Fortification 23, 54, 56, 79, 120, 137, 138, 144, 146, 153, 155, 156, 162, 166, 179, 182, 185, 255
Frankish, Franks 297, 323–4, 329
Franks, Augustus 297–8
Fregellae 177
Frobenius, Leo 187–8
Furtwängler, Adolf 286

G. Valerius Crescus 95
Gallo-Roman 177–9, 182, 213
Garašanin, Milutin 98–100, 286, 288
Gaul (Gaulish) 61, 142, 176, 180–2, 295–6, 298, 299, 302, 306, 307, 308, 310, 311, 329
Gauls/Galli 182, 296, 306, 324
Gaythelos 295
gender 14, 19, 33–8, 40–2, 44, 46, 92, 111, 117, 175, 192, 212, 214, 223–4, 226, 254, 260–3, 270, 325
Genealogy 270–1, 273, 276
  Modern 325
  Tarχna 271–2
  Tute 271–2
  Spurinna 271, 273
Genetics (DNA) 84, 106–7, 267–8, 273–6, 304–5
Gens 99
Germans/Germani/Germanic 16, 178, 183, 267, 286, 292, 294, 295, 296, 298, 300, 303, 306–09, 313–4, 318, 320–1, 324, 328, 330

Germany 6, 22, 61, 188–99, 286, 291, 294, 296, 297, 298, 299, 302, 304, 306, 307, 312, 315, 321, 324
Gift 16, 25, 52, 270, 294, 315
Glasinac Group 128, 132, 135
Glastonbury Lake Village 231
Glass 6, 14, 15, 28, 75, 132, 139, 217, 220, 223–238, 256
Goethe, Johann Wolfgang 296
Gold 40, 43–6, 64, 78, 80, 94, 95, 135, 155, 159, 166, 179, 203, 220, 236, 293
Gomer 295
Goričan 130
Gothuni 295
Gournay-sur-Aronde 177, 183, 185
Graebner 188
Grădiştea-Brăila 52
Grădiştea de Munte *see* Sarmizegetusa Regia
*graffiti* 68, 70
Graves see burial practices
Graz 286
Great Hungarian Plain 13, 144–5, 147, 150, 152–3, 156, 298, 305
Greece 52, 87, 157, 163, 168, 169, 286, 309, 328
    Classical 159, 165
    Hellenistic 165
Greeks 80, 90, 99, 105, 136, 158, 160, 167, 285, 286, 288, 295, 306, 308, 309,
Greek colonies/colonisation/colonists 50, 52, 59, 157–8, 160, 244, 257, 261, 264, 302
Guido, Peggy 225–34, 237
Gubbio 323

Habakuk plateau/group 24, 26–31
*habitus* 200, 214, 222
Hadrian 65
Hall, Jonathan 327
Hallow Hill cemetery (Fife) 217, 219
Hallstatt (culture/period) 2, 22, 23, 76, 78, 79, 81, 86–8, 123–4, 126–8, 130, 131, 132, 134, 135, 136, 137, 180, 195, 196, 293, 297, 298

Hallstatt, Eastern (region) 133
Halstatt, Western (region) 61
*Hallstattisation* 126
Hansen, Klaus 188–91, 198
Hanson, William 211
Hapsburg 273–4
Hawkes, Christopher 293
Hecataeus 302, 306, 308
Hegel, Georg 188
Heimstetten 317, 319, 321
Heirloom 41, 44
Hellebrandt, Magdolna 147
Hellenistic Architecture 64
Hellenistic Culture 16, 43, 48, 94–5, 159, 165
Hellenistic Period 103, 158, 159, 160
'Hellenisation' 5, 159, 161,163–5,168–70, 254, 256, 260, 264, 323
Helvetii 182
Henderson, Julian 227
Hercynian forest 142
Herder, Johann 187
Herodotus/Herodotos 33, 36–8, 78–84, 87,106, 244, 251, 297, 299, 302, 306, 308

Heritage 89, 135–6, 141, 164, 166, 167, 168, 170, 172, 286, 289, 324
Herskovits, Melville 191
Heuneburg 196, 302
Hide (animal skin) 225, 226
Higgs, Eric 293
High Torrs (Dumfries and Galloway) 217
Hildebrand, Hans 188
Hind, John 302
Historic Environment Records (HER) 228

History 5, 36, 49, 82, 83, 84, 101, 136, 142, 166, 167, 201, 270, 295, 302, 304, 309
    of archaeology 90, 188, 284–5, 287, 290
    ancient 97
Histri 52, 99
Hobsbawn, Eric 188
Hodson, Roy 5, 293
Hoernes, Moritz 292
Hörgertshausen 316, 318, 320

Horse gear 14, 41, 78, 81, 116, 117, 128, 130, 134, 135, 138, 158, 220, 241, 319, 321
Hoxha, Enver 167
Hunedoara-Grădina Castelului 113, 118
Hungarians 85
Hungary 14, 147, 298, 203, 307
  See Great Hungarian Plain
Hunsrück-Eifel-Kultur 195–6, 198
Hunting 204, 205, 241, 250
Huxley, Julian 191
Hybridity 4, 6, 62, 74, 90, 92, 152, 167, 170, 171, 211, 212, 213, 215, 222, 270, 278, 321
hybridisation 143, 156, 165, 168, 170–171

Iapygians 255
identity(ies)
  community 110, 248, 267–8, 275–6, 278, 312, 323, 329
  cultural 141, 170, 211–3, 216. 219–20, 247
  ethnic 33, 77, 79, 97, 175–6, 182, 215, 222, 251, 230
  elite 120, 131, 250, 270, 274
  group 19, 31–2, 43, 46, 49, 61, 78, 110–1, 117, 120, 143–4, 153, 156, 161, 164, 183, 212–3, 224, 248, 254, 260, 272, 283
  local 141, 171, 266, 277–8, 317
  regional 35, 42, 46, 236, 247
  social 75, 149, 175, 213, 249, 273
  status 19, 35, 92, 95–6, 223
  warrior 33, 38, 241, 243–4, 247, 250–3, 261–2
Ideology 13, 48–9, 68, 74, 139, 141, 142, 143, 156, 213–6, 219–20, 257, 260–1, 270, 277, 324,
  National Socialist 187
Ilok 126, 139, 140
Illyrian 11, 60, 91, 132, 158, 162,164–5, 168–9
Illyrians 83, 98–100, 158–9, 167–9
Indian 225, 273
Incoronata 248–9

Indo-European(s) 99–100, 161, 292, 297–8, 302–4
Indutiomarus 182
Influences (cultural) 3, 11, 12, 13, 14, 17, 83, 84, 85, 94, 98, 100, 105, 106, 123, 127, 128, 131–3, 135, 139, 141, 144, 152, 155, 158–60, 161, 163, 169, 180, 213, 215, 217, 222, 248, 257, 264, 273, 293, 296, 320
Insoll, Tim 224
Interaction 19, 60, 99, 111, 119, 120, 123, 131, 141, 143, 144, 147, 152, 156, 158–60, 175, 184, 188–90, 194, 196, 198, 200, 211, 213, 214, 216, 237, 252, 254, 260, 263, 268, 293, 310, 312, 315–7, 320, 321, 322, 327, 329
Inveresk 217
Irish literature 303
  See language
Ironwork(ing) 2, 26, 30, 63, 66, 70, 71, 72, 74, 75, 78, 117, 126, 130, 151, 176, 203, 244, 246, 247, 248, 250, 261, 262, 264, 314, 316
Iron Age 1, 3–6, 11, 47, 84, 86, 88, 91, 92, 93, 97, 99–101, 103, 107, 120, 123, 126, 136, 137, 141, 160, 161, 165, 168, 169, 172, 175, 179, 184, 186, 200, 203, 211, 213, 214, 216, 217, 219, 220, 222, 223, 225, 226, 227, 228, 231, 232, 236, 237, 238, 241, 243, 244, 248, 249, 250, 252, 253, 269, 277, 293, 303, 306, 307, 309, 316, 319, 322, 323–6, 328–30
  Early 13–14, 18–9, 20, 21–6, 31–2, 61, 77, 79, 86, 98, 99, 104, 123, 124, 126, 127, 128–132, 145–6, 150, 153, 155, 156, 196–8, 247, 277, 313
  Late 12, 16, 33, 35, 38, 39, 42, 43, 46, 61, 63–4, 72, 74, 77, 108, 123, 124, 127, 136, 137, 155, 162, 164–6, 167, 170, 171, 176, 180, 260, 263, 264, 307, 310, 311, 312, 313, 315, 320, 321, 322, 328
Isaac, Glyn 302
Isayev, Elena 247
Italic 50, 52, 56, 58, 135, 247, 255, 256, 261
  See Language
Ivory 203, 312

Izzet, Vedia 266-7, 270

Jacobsthal, Paul 298
Jalžabet 130, 131, 134
Japheth 295
Jastorf 195-6, 308
Jones, Andrew 234
Jones, Owen 297
Jones, Sian 326

Kale-Krševica 163
Kaloyanovo-Chernozem 42, 44-6
Kant, Immanuel 187
Kaptol 23, 124, 128-32
   Group 128, 131-2, 137
Karl, Raimund 303-4
Kastel-Staadt 179-80
Kelheim 316
*Keltoi*
   See Celts
Kemble, John 297
Kimmig, Wolfgang 298
Kleinklein 23, 24, 28, 131
Koch, John 301-3
Kopytoff, Igor 327
Körner 317, 320
Kos Barrow 28-31
Kosd 203
Kosovo 162, 164, 168, 169
Kossina, Gustaf 3,187-8, 292, 330
Kotare near Murska Sobota 21
Kotare – Krogi 22
Kroeber, Alfred 191
Kronwinkl 316, 318

Lake Balaton 135
(Late) Urnfield
   Culture 124, 126-8, 130
   period 18, 20, 23-6, 29
Lamberton Moor 220
landscape(s) 4-5, 18-9, 21, 25-6, 29-32, 63-4, 66, 68, 74, 131, 182, 268-9, 275, 371, 324
Language
   Breton 295-6, 301

Celtiberian 303
Celtic 291, 296, 300-4
Cornish 296
English 295, 296, 326
Etruscan 267, 273
Gaelic 295
Germanic 300, 303
Greek 38, 68, 70, 158, 296
Hispano-Celtic 304
Irish 292, 295-7
Italic 184, 303
Latin 64, 70, 95, 273, 292, 296, 306
Lepontic 303
Lusitanian 304
Oscan 241
Romance 292, 295
Philology 86, 87, 78
Slavic 292, 303
*Stammbaum* (Tree model of languages) 292, 303, 304
Tower of Babel 292, 295, 296
*Wellen* model 294
Welsh 295, 296
La Tène 2, 13, 14, 15, 17, 76, 104, 105, 108, 110, 112, 116, 120, 132, 135, 136, 137, 141, 144, 146-53, 155, 176, 178, 179, 180, 182, 184, 187, 203-5, 207, 291, 293, 294, 297-301, 307-9, 314, 315, 317-22
Latènisation 135
Latins 184, 323
Latour, Bruno 109, 266, 327, 330
Lattes 278
Lavello 249
Legio VII Claudia 95
Legionary camp 93
Lhuyd, Edward 295, 296
Lijeva Bara see Vucovar
Liebersee 317, 320
Liburnians 99
Lindisfarne Gospels 297
Lineage 31, 46, 99
Linton, Ralph 191
Literacy 267, 270-1, 274
   Inscriptions 41, 46, 49, 70, 75, 178, 302
   Etruscan 270-2, 278

Greek 38, 158
Latin 95, 306
North Italic 184
Livy (Titius Livius) 142, 269, 295
Leskovar, Jutta 304
Lombards 329
Loom weights *see* Weaving
Loot (Plunder) 83, 91, 94, 95, 311
Lucania 241
*Lucanianisation* 244
Lucy, Sam 224
Lüning, Jens 188

Macedonia(n) 5, 16, 102–5, 157, 159, 162, 164–5, 168, 170–1, 324
Macedonia (Former Yugoslav Republic of) 4, 162, 168–71, 324
MacGregor, Gavin 234
Macpherson, James 296
Mains of Throsk (Stirlingshire) 220
Malkata Mogila 40–1, 43–4
Mali Bilač 124, 137
Malinowski, Bronislaw 191
Manching 182, 185, 312, 315-9
Mannersdorf 202–3, 205–6
Maramureş 144, 153, 155
Marriage 91, 94, 158, 160, 178, 206, 274, 294, 315, 325
Martberg 178–80, 184
Martijanec 130
Massalia 308
material culture 1–2, 3–6, 11–2, 19, 28, 70, 80–1, 86, 90–6, 98–101, 104, 106–7, 109–110, 116, 123, 131, 135–7, 139, 141, 143, 152, 153, 156, 157, 158, 161, 162, 163, 164, 165, 172, 187–8, 191–3, 196, 200, 201, 204, 205, 208, 211, 214–7, 219, 222, 264, 266, 271–2, 274, 275, 278, 291, 298, 307–8, 312, 313–4, 315–6, 317–20, 321–2, 323, 324, 328, 330
materiality 19, 236, 237
Maynooth (ICC conference) 292, 303
Meare Lake Village in Somerset 231
Mela 36
Mediterranean 4, 33, 40, 50, 52, 54, 56, 59–62, 70, 72, 123, 131, 156, 161, 165–6, 168, 172, 176, 206, 247, 263, 278, 284, 306, 310, 312, 323–4, 326, 328
Megaw, Ruth 291, 298, 300
Megaw, Vincent 291, 298, 300
Mendelssohn, Felix 296
Mercenaries 143, 171, 206, 310
Merchant 50, 52, 75, 312, 315
Messapian 255
Metaponto 257, 261
Migration 97, 98, 100, 104, 119, 123, 142–4, 169, 188, 227, 292–4, 298, 305, 320
*See* Mobility
*See* Colonisation
Mihovilić, Kristina 277
Miller, Danny 224–5
Mining 103–4
Mirebeau 183
Mirror 39–40, 43–44, 78, 225, 270
Mobility 5, 14–16, 143, 145, 206, 273–4, 294, 315
*See* Colonisation
Modena 323
Modernity 162, 164, 168, 284, 289
Moesi 101, 106–07
Mogilanska Mogila 38
Mokronog Group 137
Moesia(n) 5, 93, 103, 106–7, 169
Moldova 16, 112, 115, 116, 119, 120, 121
Moravia 144, 203, 298
Moreşti 15–6, 153
Mosel(lle) River 176, 186
Moss Raploch 220
Muhi – Kocsmadomb 147–50, 152
Müller, Klaus 308, 318
Müller-Scheeßel, Niels 200
Munich 286, 319
Münsingen-Rain 14, 205
Muntenia 16, 52, 54, 59, 112, 115–6, 118, 119, 120, 121
Murlo 275
Mussolini, Benito 323

Napoleone, Buonaparte 324
Narbonne 302 Narrative(s) 19, 21, 29, 34,

36, 37, 38, 49, 54, 97, 99–101, 103, 105, 107, 161, 163, 165–9, 172, 188, 216, 283–4, 286
Nationalism 77–8, 164–9
   Romanian 5, 84
   Yugoslav 169
National Socialism 187
Near East 268, 284, 312, 317, 329
Nebehay, Stefan 298
Németi, Ioan 147
Nesactium 6, 266, 276–8
New Archaeology 287, 293
   Processual Archaeology 287–9, 293, 327

Nile river 302
Norries' Law (Fife) 220
Norman 273
Nova Tabla 22
Nyrség 147

Ocnița 72
Odrysian kingdom 157, 159, 166–7
Olteni 13, 146, 154–5
Oltenia 83, 85, 113, 114, 115, 116, 118, 119, 120, 121
Olt River 120
*oppidum* (a) 63, 176–86, 312, 314–8, 320
Orientalising 271
Ornaments, personal see Dress
Osijek 124
Ostrogoths 329
Ottoman Empire 285, 323
(The) Other 6, 19, 36, 87, 90, 101, 110, 136, 166, 172, 269, 285, 289, 308, 309, 312, 314, 316–7, 328
   See Barbarian
Otzenhausen 179–80

Paeonia(n) 158, 165
Paestum (Paestan) 177, 241, 248, 251–2
*Pagi* 180, 182, 183
Palaeobalkan peoples 161
Pallottino, Massimo 267
Panenský Týnec 309
Pannonia

(southern) Pannonia(n)/ 11, 50, 123, 135–7, 139, 141
(southern) Pannonian plain 5, 18, 24, 32, 123
Pannonians 99
Papazoglu, Fanula 91, 97, 101, 165
Parsons, Talcott 191
*Paterae* 95, 217, 220, 221
Pauli, Ludwig 298–300
Perkins, Philip 267, 273
Perugia 275, 323
Petrie, Flinders 284
Peucetia 6, 254–8, 260–5
Pezron, Pierre-Yves 295–6, 301, 302
*Phialae* 43, 262
Philip the Second of Macedon 159, 170, 171
Philip the Fifth of Macedon 16
Phoenician 247, 267
Piatra Craivii 117
Picene 267, 323
Picts 219, 295
*Pincenses* 106
Pișcolt 13–4, 76, 149–50, 152
Pistiros see Adzijska Vodenica
Pittioni, Richard 298
Pitt Rivers, General 284
Pliny (the Elder) 80, 106, 266
Poiana (by Siret River) 52, 56, 117, 120
Poienești–Lukaševka culture 15
Poland 203, 294, 298
Polybius 297
Pompey 294
Pontecagnano 244, 248–9
Pontic 50, 76, 87, 130, 156
   region/area 54, 81, 145, 147, 155–6
Popești 52–3, 56, 117
Portable Antiquities Scheme (PAS) 228
Poseidonius 307
Poštela 24–32
Post-processual Archaeology 164, 289, 327
Potterne, Wiltshire 225
Pottenbrunn 202-05
Pottery See Ceramic
Prehistorian 93

Prehistory 5, 34, 37, 83, 89, 96, 118, 97–100, 136, 161–3, 165, 169, 188, 225, 228, 237, 284, 286–8, 292, 297, 306, 314, 316, 324, 328–30
Processual Archaeology
  See New Archaeology
Priest(ess) 48–9, 58, 61, 108
Pri Muri 21
Protohistory 5, 101, 136, 161
Ptolemy 106
Prussia 324

Răcătău (by Siret River) 52, 56, 117, 120
Radovesice 298
Rakičan – Pri Starem križu 22
Ranger, Terence 188
Rapin, André 203
Razor 225
Redfield, Robert 191
Regensburg-Harting 317
Reinecke, Paul 297, 305
Religion 2, 36, 37, 49, 90, 170, 175–6, 183–4, 213, 216, 224
  Dacian 49, 64
Renaissance 291, 295, 306
Renfrew, Colin 293
Rhine river 145, 176, 186, 195, 297, 306, 307, 308, 311
Ribemont-sur-Ancre 183
Ritual 6, 12, 13, 14, 16, 19, 49, 58, 59, 61, 63, 66, 72, 75, 150, 152, 155–6, 158, 182–4, 202, 212, 214–7, 220–2, 225, 241, 256–7, 258–9, 274–5, 278, 309
  Funerary/mortuary 12, 13, 14, 21, 79, 86, 109–111, 115–7, 120–2, 126, 128, 132. 135, 152, 155–6, 217, 249, 254–6, 260–2, 312, 315, 318
Rieckhoff, Sabine 304, 314
Ripdorf 308, 315
Riva, Corinna 270
Roach-Higgins, Mary Ellen 226
Robb, John 248
Roman (s) 48–9, 70, 89–92, 95, 102, 103, 104, 105, 109, 136, 139, 142, 211, 237, 285, 294, 306–8, 313, 318–9, 321, 323–4

Administration 92, 103
Allies 139
Border(s) (Limes) 62, 96
Conquest (invasion) 50, 68, 72, 99, 102, 110, 123, 139, 179, 227, 231, 241, 316, 318, 321–2
Culture 89–90, 92–3, 139, 141, 167, 215, 219, 321
Empire 64, 81, 90, 91, 104–5, 211, 213, 289, 328–9
Law 202
Material culture 6, 92, 94–6, 211, 214–7, 219–20, 222, 227–8, 231, 306, 312, 316, 319, 321
Military 50, 75, 94–5, 102, 211, 213, 217, 221, 294, 311, 313–4, 319, 321
Period 22, 92, 103, 105–6, 178–9, 182, 227, 263, 268, 294, 311, 315, 318, 319, 321–2
Power (influence, jurisdiction, occupation, rule) 52, 62, 65. 96, 98, 99, 105–7, 139, 141, 211, 216–7, 321
Province 5, 91, 93, 102, 319
Republic 104
Romanitas 91
Sanctuary 177–9
Villa 319
World 60, 103, 310–1, 315, 324
Romania 4, 5, 12–14, 49, 63–4, 72, 76–7, 83–6, 108, 110, 120, 150, 153, 298
Romanisation 90–93, 139, 141, 164–165, 211–13, 215, 255
Romanticism 166–7, 169, 286, 296
Rome 168, 177, 211, 213, 216–7, 219, 269, 276, 279, 309, 310, 311
Romilly Allen, John 297
Rotary quern 221
Ruberslaw 220
Ruby, Pascal 246
Ruše 124
Rustoiu, Aurel 5, 16, 117, 119, 327
Rutigliano 256–9, 262–3

Said, Edward 285
Saint Sulpice 205–6

Sala Consilina 244, 248
Sallach 313, 318–320
Salt 2, 145
Saltaleone/i 78
Sanctuaries 61, 66, 138, 175–6, 178–80, 182–6, 220, 279
Sanislău 13, 150
Sanislău-Nir group 146–7, 150
Sarmizegetusa
    Regia 56, 63–6, 68, 70, 72, 74, 78
    Colonia Ulpia Traiana Augusta Dacica 75
Sâncrăieni 57–8, 61
Šarengrad 126
Sava River 50, 60, 104–5, 128, 131, 135, 138
Saxony 313, 317, 320
Schliemann, Heinrich 284
Schweitzer, Albert 191
Scordisci 104–06, 137–9
Scordiscian 58, 61, 105–6
Scorilo (Dacian king) 68, 70
Scotland 217–8, 220, 225, 228, 231–4, 236–7, 292, 294, 324
Scots 295
Scotta 295
Scythian
    debate 77–8, 82, 87
    group 77, 81, 85–6
    population 11, 13
Scythians 76, 79–85, 87, 158–9, 328, 330
Seedorf 308, 315
Senones 143
Serbia(n) 4, 6, 89, 93, 97–8, 100, 127, 162–3, 168–9, 283, 286–7, 289, 324
Segovesus 142
Sesvete 138
Settlement(s) 11–12, 15, 18–19, 21–6, 28–9, 31–2, 52, 54, 56, 63–6, 68, 70, 72, 75, 78–9, 81, 88, 112–4, 116, 120, 124, 128, 130, 137, 138, 141, 143, 144, 146, 153–5, 156, 157, 159, 160, 161–2, 164–8, 170–1, 176, 179–80, 186, 199, 223–5, 244, 248, 253, 255, 267, 269, 277, 286, 298, 314–5, 316–9, 320–2

Seuthopolis 40, 166–7
Shennan, Steven 327
Sickle 264
Sidonius Apollinaris 291, 295
Siena 324
Silk 312
Simmel, Georg 190
Sims-Williams, Patrick 292, 303
Singidunum (Belgrade) 93
Siret River 50, 56, 72
Situla 43, 56, 58, 61, 132, 277, 312
Skopje 170–1
Slavonia 104, 126–7, 135, 137
Slobozia 155
Slovakia 144, 147, 152, 298
Small, Alistair 261
Snow, Charles P 191
Social Anthropology 3, 214, 260, 267, 269, 276, 285, 293, 305, 308, 325–7
social status 35, 41–2, 44, 46, 59, 61–3, 70, 108, 117–8, 120, 132, 137, 139, 198, 202, 204, 206, 223, 241, 249, 254–6, 258–61, 264, 273, 285, 316, 321
Solotvino 153–5
Sotin 123–7, 137
Spain 291, 295, 299–300, 302, 304, 305
Spengler, Oswald 191
Spiritual 11, 13, 16, 98–100, 131
Srednjica 24
Stable isotopes 144, 305
Stâncești 153
Statistics 40, 108–122, 111, 231–4, 252, 258–9, 263, 270
    relational database 33, 228
Statue(tte) 170, 220, 221, 270
Steger, Florian 191
Stelloch 220
Stephen of Byzantium 302
Stöckli, Werner 314
Stoneyburn Clava-cairn 219
Stoneyfield (Inverness) 217
Stovel, Emily 326
Strabo 36, 48–9, 62, 64, 175, 302
Stradonice 310
Straubing 312–3, 317–321

Strigil 260-2, 264
Structured deposition 211, 214-7, 219-22
Süttő 131
Sv. Petar Ludbreški 130
Switzerland 14, 61, 203, 207, 297, 312
Symbol(ic) 41, 54, 61, 68, 70, 75, 109, 132, 155-6, 167, 176, 180, 183, 191, 203, 214-6, 234, 236, 241, 257, 259, 262-4
Symposium *See* Convivial practices
Syrmia 104, 127, 135, 137
Syria 312

Tacitus 183-4, 294, 295, 324
Tappert, Claudia 318
Taranto 257
Tarquinia 248, 273-4
Tartessian 302
Taurisci 137-9
Taylor, Tim 187
Tay River 320
Tekija hoard 93-5
Teutones 294, 311
Textile(s) *See* Weaving
Theory 3-5, 19-21, 34-5, 97-101, 109-110, 163-5, 175-6, 187-92, 200-3, 212-6, 224-6, 254-5, 266-8, 283-90, 292-4, 309, 321
Thomsen, Christian 188
Thrace 5, 33, 36-9, 41, 46, 86, 104-5, 157-60, 165, 166, 171
Thracian
  ethnicity 164
  elite 41, 166
  princess 38
  tribes 157-8
  women 36-7
Thracians 36, 76, 79-81, 83, 87, 99, 158-60, 167, 328
Thuringia 313
Tiberius 177, 311, 313
Tiber River 267
Timachi 107
Timpe, Dieter 308
Tinosu 52
Titelberg 6, 176-8, 180, 182, 184, 186

Tisza river 49, 86, 146, 147, 153
Todorova, Maria 166, 285, 288
Trade 19, 33, 52, 75, 95, 128, 137, 138, 198, 227, 263, 278, 294, 314, 315
Trajan 64, 75
Transylvania 5, 11-7, 50, 52, 54, 56, 58-62, 63, 68, 70, 72, 76-77, 79, 81, 83, 85-8, 110, 112-3, 115-6, 119-21, 144-5, 147, 150, 152-3, 155-6. 157
Traunstein 316, 318
Treveran 176, 179-82
Treveri 176-7, 180, 182, 184, 186
Triballi 101, 106-07, 169
Tribe(s) 48, 91, 97-104, 142, 143, 157-9, 161, 175, 184, 295
Tricornenses 106
Trinidad 225
Troina 323
Trojans 295
Tuscania 270, 273
Tweezer 225
Tylor, Edward 187, 191
Typenspektren 193-4, 196, 198

Umbrians 323
Uttenhofen 316, 318

Vác 14, 148, 152
Van der Sleen, Wicher 227
Vardar River 157-8
Vasić, Miloje M. 286-8, 324
Veii 248
Velika Gorica-Dobova 124, 132-3, 135
Vekerzug 13, 146-7, 150
Venetian 323
Venetics 323
Vercingetorix 182, 324
Vettones 304
Victorian 284, 286, 289, 297
Vienna 203, 286, 298
*Viereckschanzen* (rectangular enclosures) 179, 318, 320, 322
Villeneuve-Saint-Germain 182
Villeperrot 204
Viminacium (Kostolac) 93

Vinča 286–8
Vinkovci 135
Vizigoths 329
Volterra 270
Vukovar 126–7
Vulci 248, 272

Wahle, Ernst 188
Wallendorf 179–80, 184
warfare 241, 247, 250, 261–2
   hoplite 248, 261
weaponry and armour
   armour 134, 242, 256, 261–2
   breast-plate 132, 261
   shields 46, 116, 203, 204, 297
   arrow(head) 44, 45, 78, 204
   dagger 76, 78,
   greave 132, 261
   helmets 12, 116, 132, 138, 261
   lance 203
   *sauroter(es)* 242, 251, 252
   spear(head) 6, 27, 44, 45, 46, 114, 130, 132, 134, 176, 179, 204, 241–253, 261–2, 264, 270
   Swords 110, 114, 121, 132, 140, 145, 179, 203, 204, 243, 247, 248, 251, 270, 312
      Gundlingen 294
      *Machairai* 278
Weaving (cloth) 225, 262

Loom-weights 27, 28, 125, 162, 249, 256, 260, 262–3
Spindle-whorls 27, 262–3
Textiles 74, 206, 225, 263
Walker, Lucy 118
Wells, Peter S. 63, 96, 294
Welsh Literature 303
Western (cultural) 159–60, 165–7, 224–5, 234, 260, 284, 285, 289, 324
Westwood, John Obadiah 297
Whithorn Monastic town 219
Wilde, Oscar 296
Woodward, Sophie 225
Wolf, Eric 309
Writing *See* Literacy

Xenophon 36, 250

Yorkshire 225
Yugoslavia 97–9, 165, 168–70, 298

Zadar 291
Zanier, Werner 322
Zvonimirevo 124, 137